PRAISE FOR *AMERICA:*
THE LAST BEST HOPE

"A necessary book for our time."
　—COMMENTARY

"[Bennett] has a strong sense of narrative, a flair for anecdote, and a lively style. And the American story really is a remarkable one, filled with its share of brilliant leaders and tragic mistakes. Bennett brings that story to life."
　—ALAN WOLFE, WASHINGTON POST

"The importance of *America: The Last Best Hope* probably exceeds anything Dr. Bennett has ever written, and it is more elegantly crafted and eminently readable than any comprehensive work of history I've read in a very long time. It's silly to compare great works of history to great novels, but this book truly is a page-turner."
　—AMERICAN COMPASS

"The role of history is to inform, inspire, and sometimes provoke us, which is why Bill Bennett's wonderfully readable book is so important. He puts our nation's triumphs, along with its lapses, into the context of a narrative about the progress of freedom."
　—WALTER ISAACSON, AUTHOR OF *STEVE JOBS* AND *LEONARDO DA VINCI*

"A great piece of work."
　—MICHAEL BESCHLOSS, AUTHOR OF *PRESIDENTS OF WAR*

"Bennett has a gift for choosing the pithy, revealing anecdote and for providing fresh character sketches and critical analyses of the leading figures. This is an American history that adults will find refreshing and enlightening and that younger readers will find a darn good read."
　—US NEWS & WORLD REPORT

"This lively book acknowledges mistakes and shortcomings, yet patriotically asserts that the American experiment in democracy is still a success story."

—SCHOOL LIBRARY JOURNAL

"Will stand as perhaps the most important addition to American scholarship at this, the start of a new century.... An exciting and enjoyable history of what makes America the greatest nation on earth."

—BRIAN KENNEDY, PRESIDENT OF THE AMERICAN STRATEGY GROUP

AMERICA:
THE
LAST
BEST
HOPE

AMERICA: THE LAST BEST HOPE

WILLIAM J. BENNETT

NELSON
BOOKS

An Imprint of Thomas Nelson

Published in Nashville, Tennessee, by Nelson Books, an imprint of Thomas Nelson. Nelson Books and Thomas Nelson are registered trademarks of HarperCollins Christian Publishing, Inc.

Thomas Nelson titles may be purchased in bulk for educational, business, fund-raising, or sales promotional use. For information, please email SpecialMarkets@ ThomasNelson.com.

Scripture quotations marked KJV are from the King James Version. Public domain.

Scripture quotations marked NKJV are from the New King James Version®. © 1982 by Thomas Nelson. Used by permission. All rights reserved.

Any internet addresses, phone numbers, or company or product information printed in this book are offered as a resource and are not intended in any way to be or to imply an endorsement by Thomas Nelson, nor does Thomas Nelson vouch for the existence, content, or services of these sites, phone numbers, companies, or products beyond the life of this book.

ISBN 978-1-4002-1284-2 (HC)
ISBN 978-1-4002-1287-3 (eBook)

Library of Congress Control Number: 2019947995

Printed in the United States of America
19 20 21 22 23 LSC 10 9 8 7 6 5 4 3 2 1

To the American soldier, whose fidelity,
patriotism, and valor have made this
land the last best hope on earth.

CONTENTS

CONTENTS

INTRODUCTION

Those of us around in 1976 remember the Bicentennial that marked the two hundredth anniversary of the Declaration of Independence. It was a grand, joyous celebration of the country's birthday and founding principles, a year of parades, flags, tricornered hats, fifes, drums, tall ships, and fireworks.

It came at a somewhat uneasy time. The country had been through the Vietnam War, Watergate, race riots, high inflation, and an oil crisis. The Bicentennial helped pull Americans together. It helped us remember our great history, achievements, and finest aspirations. It made us proud and grateful to be Americans.

Nearly a half century has passed. As of this writing, we are four years away from the 250th anniversary of the Boston Tea Party. A little more than five years away from the 250th anniversary of those first shots heard 'round the world at Lexington and Concord. And somewhat more than six years away from the Semiquincentennial of the Declaration of Independence.

What kind of birthday celebration will it be?

Abraham Lincoln once warned that the further we get from the miracle of the American Revolution, the less likely we are to appreciate it. "This state of feeling [patriotic pride] must fade, is fading, has faded, with the circumstances that produced it," he said. The scenes of the revolution, like everything else, "must fade upon the memory of the world, and grow more and more dim by the lapse of time."[1]

Our freedom will crumble, Lincoln said, unless we make efforts to sustain it, to "furnish all the materials for our future support and defence."[2] Those materials, Lincoln believed, included "general intelligence, sound morality, and in particular, a reverence for the constitution and laws." And, of course, an appreciation of our past.

Since 1976, we've reached a time when, I fear, patriotic pride isn't always as strong as it used to be, or as strong as Lincoln would like. Television reports and political websites are often full of cynicism. Many express doubts about American motives on the world stage. Some Americans seem ready to believe the worst about our leaders and our country, as well as their fellow Americans. The country is divided. The eminent historian Allen Guelzo even believes we are the most divided since one of the most epic events in this book, the Civil War.[3]

We've experienced an awful lot of running down of this country. Our national anthem asks, "O say does that Star-Spangled Banner yet wave o'er the land of the free and the home of the brave?" It's a good question. Are we teaching our children to proudly hail that banner? Do we still laud our country as the land of the free and home of the brave?

One can imagine the commentaries from elites in the media and academia as 2026 approaches. The Boston Tea Party patriots who disguised themselves as Mohawk Indians were appropriating a culture they ravaged. That shot heard 'round the world was all about power and empire. The Founders were rich, white men greedy for their own liberty but intent on oppressing or enslaving everyone else.

When Thomas Nelson suggested that I edit the three volumes of my American history—*America: The Last Best Hope* volumes one and two, and *A Century Turns*—into a single, updated volume, I was delighted. It has given me a chance to think about those promises and principles of

1776, fulfilled and unfulfilled. As the United States reaches the quarter-millennium mark, I hope this book will help us stand up for those principles, cherish them, and be grateful for them. I also hope—and this is a hope that I've nurtured for many years—that this one-volume history might find its way into schools as well as homes, into the hands and before the eyes of young people. After all, national test scores tell us that history is our students' worst subject. They fair worse, perform worse, in American history than even math and reading.

I offer this book for many reasons. The first and most important is the need for hope. When President Lincoln wrote to Congress in December 1862, shortly after he issued the preliminary Emancipation Proclamation, he wrote, "We shall nobly save, or meanly lose, the last best hope of earth."[4] For nearly a century before that message—and easily for a century afterward—Americans would not have doubted that this country was indeed that last, best hope. Democrat, Republican, Federalist, Antifederalist . . . it hardly mattered. An abiding sense of American greatness, of American purpose, of American exceptionalism has long characterized many of our leaders and tens of millions of the rest of us as well.

I believe America still represents the world's best hope. But I also believe we have to make explicit efforts to nourish that hope and to keep our grasp of it from—in Lincoln's great word—fading. It is my humble wish that those who read this book will find reason to reclaim some hope when the national discourse seems full of division and distrust.

The second reason I wrote this book is to give Americans an opportunity to enjoy the story of their country, to take pleasure and pride in what we have done and become. Many books about America not only fail to counter cynicism and hopelessness but also don't encourage anything positive in their place. They do not engage, entertain, educate, or encourage. History textbooks are often the worst in this regard. National tests repeatedly show that many high school (and college) students know little about their country's past. Dull histories drive young people away—from serious study, from reading history as adults, and from a reasoned, thoughtful, and heartfelt embrace of their country. Dumbed-down history, civics, and—worst of all—social studies textbooks may be one cause of voter and citizen apathy. An encouraging countertrend is the huge popularity of a few histories and biographies. David McCullough's *1776* and Ron Chernow's *Grant* come to mind. The success of these books is much deserved: they give pleasure, they educate, and they entertain. But few such books have attempted to tell the *whole* American story. I hope this will be one.

The third reason I wrote this book is to give thanks and to remind my fellow citizens of their obligation of gratitude to those who made it possible for us to lead free and happy lives. To Lincoln and the Founders before him, and to many historical figures afterward, much is due. Obscurity and oblivion are not what they deserve.

Americans can be grateful that time and again, our ancestors and our contemporaries have chosen wisely and have by their demeanors defined us as a people. Over and over again we have shown the almost uniquely American capacity for self-renewal. And over and over again in our story, intelligence and leadership have counted in the nick of time. Think of those Americans at Philadelphia in 1787 who devised the most miraculous political document in history just as the young nation seemed to be falling apart.

Or Americans coming together to rebuild this nation after the long and devastating Civil War.

Or Americans standing fast against totalitarianism during the Cold War.

At the same time, it is regrettable but true that any number of American choices were not wise. For example, we failed to eliminate slavery when this nation was founded. For too long we failed to uphold our stated principles in the face of Jim Crow segregation laws.

We can be grateful that leaders like Frederick Douglass and Dr. Martin Luther King Jr. rose to prod our consciences and to force us to look into the mirror of our own souls, however belatedly. We needed them to help us right those wrongs. It is important to note that when such leaders stepped forward, they acknowledged a debt of gratitude: both Frederick Douglass and Dr. King appealed to the ideals of America's Founding Fathers. They reminded Americans that this country, in order to be true to itself, had to attend to the business of establishing justice and respecting the inalienable right to life, liberty, and the pursuit of happiness. To deny some people these universal rights because of the color of their skin, these reformers pointed out, was to deny the essence of what America was to the world. Those who would deny fundamental rights were, as Lincoln said, "blowing out the moral lights around us" and dishonoring our Fathers.[5] We need to remember the Fathers and the lights that showed them the way.

The fourth reason I wrote this book is to tell the truth, get the facts out, correct the record, and put forward a reasoned, balanced presentation of the American story. In this work, I will not try to cover up great wrongs. Injustices need sunlight—always, as Justice Brandeis said, the best disinfectant.[6] I will try to paint America as Oliver Cromwell asked to be painted: warts and all. But I will not follow the fashion of some today who see America as nothing *but* warts: "warts, that's all."

We must remember that America is still a great success story. When we criticize—as criticize we must—we should play the part of what James Madison called a "loving critic." Former Democratic Senator Daniel Patrick Moynihan put it best: "Am I embarrassed to speak for a less than perfect democracy? Not one bit. Find me a better one. Do I suppose there are societies that are free of sin? No, I don't. Do I think ours is on balance incomparably the most hopeful set of human relations the world has? Yes, I do. Have we done obscene things? Yes, we have. How did our people learn about them? They learned about them on television and in the newspapers."[7]

The fifth reason I wrote this book is to encourage a new patriotism—a new reflective, reasoned form of patriotism. Ronald Reagan was especially proud of the new patriotism he had helped to spark during his two terms. It was something even his opponent Fritz Mondale was gracious enough to praise him for. But Reagan recognized that this spirit would not last unless it was an *informed* patriotism. Interestingly, the Old Man who dreamed dreams—and lived to see those dreams become reality—looked backward in his Farewell Address to the American people. It was something he rarely did:

> [T]here is a great tradition of warnings in Presidential farewells, and I've got one that's been on my mind for some time. But oddly enough it starts with one of the things I'm proudest of in the past 8 years: the resurgence of national pride that I called the new patriotism. This national feeling is good, but it won't count for much and it won't last unless it's grounded in thoughtfulness and knowledge.
>
> An informed patriotism is what we want. And are we doing a good enough job teaching our children what America is and what she represents in the long history of the world? Those of us who are over thirty-five or so years of age grew up in a different America. We were taught, very directly, what it means to be an American. And we absorbed, almost in the air, a love of country and an appreciation of its institutions. If you didn't get these things from your family you got them from the neighborhood, from the father down the street who fought in Korea or the family who lost someone at Anzio. Or you could get a sense of patriotism from school. And if all else failed you could get a sense of patriotism from the popular culture. The movies celebrated democratic values and implicitly reinforced the idea that America was special. TV was like that, too, through the mid-sixties.
>
> But now, we're about to enter the nineties, and some things have changed. Younger parents aren't sure that an unambivalent appreciation of America is the right thing to teach modern children. And as for those who create the popular culture, well-grounded patriotism is no longer the style. Our spirit is back, but we haven't reinstitutionalized it.

We've got to do a better job of getting across that America is freedom—freedom of speech, freedom of religion, freedom of enterprise. And freedom is special and rare. It's fragile; it needs [protection].

So we've got to teach history based not on what's in fashion but what's important—why the Pilgrims came here, who Jimmy Doolittle was, and what those thirty seconds over Tokyo meant. You know, four years ago on the fortieth anniversary of D-Day, I read a letter from a young woman writing to her late father, who'd fought on Omaha Beach. Her name was Lisa Zanatta Henn, and she said, "We will always remember, we will never forget what the boys of Normandy did." Well, let's help her keep her word.

If we forget what we did, we won't know who we are. I'm warning of an eradication of the American memory that could result, ultimately, in an erosion of the American spirit. Let's start with some basics: more attention to American history and a greater emphasis on civic ritual.[8]

Finally, I write this story to kindle romance, to encourage Americans to fall in love with this country, again or for the first time. Not unreflectively, not blindly, but with eyes wide open.

The great writer, adventurer, and map enthusiast Bernard DeVoto once had good reason to write to his friend Catherine Drinker Bowen, the wonderful historian whose works *Miracle at Philadelphia* and *Yankee from Olympus* made history come to life to a wide audience. She was losing heart, getting discouraged in her history-writing craft. Were her stories of America important? Was her celebration of her country and its achievements right? Where was the romance? DeVoto wrote this to her:

> If the mad, impossible voyage of Columbus or Cartier or La Salle or Coronado or John Ledyard is not romantic, if the stars did not dance in the sky when the Constitutional Convention met, if Atlantis has any landscape stranger or the other side of the moon any lights or colors or shapes more unearthly than the customary homespun of Lincoln or

the morning coat of Jackson, well, I don't know what romance is. Ours is a story mad with the impossible, it is by chaos out of dream, it began as dream and it has continued as dream down to the last headline you read in a newspaper. . . . The simplest truth you can ever write about our history will be charged and surcharged with romanticism.[9]

The dream of which DeVoto writes is, of course, the American dream, and as he reminds us, despite obstacles, setbacks, stupidities, and atrocities, there is an unparalleled and *documented* record of this dream being real. America was, is, and—we pray—will continue to be where, more than anyplace else, dreams actually do come true. And let us hope that dream and its reality, to recall Lincoln once more, never fades.

ONE

THE GREATEST REVOLUTION

(1765–1783)

I. STAMPING OUT UNFAIR TAXES

Deborah Franklin had just begun to enjoy her new home on Philadelphia's Market Street. She missed her husband, who was in London as an agent for the colony's assembly. Her fear of sailing had prevented her from going to England to be with him. Fearing water, she by no means feared fire. In late September 1765, when some Philadelphians spread the rumor that Benjamin Franklin had consented to the hated Stamp Tax, a mob gathered to set fire to the Franklin home. Franklin's business partner, David Hall, had warned him in a letter. "The spirit of the people is so violently against anyone they think has the least concern with the Stamp Law," he wrote, telling his friend they had "imbibed the notion that you had a hand in framing it, which has occasioned you many enemies."[1]

Deborah reacted like a lioness to the threat of having her house torched. She sent her daughter to New Jersey but summoned her cousin and his friends to help defend the home. "Fetch a gun or two," she said defiantly.[2] Her wits and resolve saved the home.

Franklin had been in London as a colonial agent since 1759, and although he corresponded regularly with friends in Pennsylvania and other colonies, it took at least six weeks for a letter to go from America to England. Franklin was woefully behind on recent developments. While he sternly opposed the new tax, Franklin did not know just how hostile the colonists were toward it. When it passed in Parliament with neither representation nor consent, George Grenville, the British chancellor of the exchequer, sought to make the pill more palatable by having *Americans* do the tax collecting.[3] Franklin went along with the idea and nominated his friend John Hughes for the job in Pennsylvania.[4] Misreading the political pulse at home, neither man realized that the act was so hated that Hughes's appointment would destroy his political career.[5] It would not take long for everyone on both sides of the Atlantic to judge America's true feelings about the Stamp Act.

The tax was intended to raise revenue in the colonies to cover the huge debts Britain had incurred during the French and Indian War. Grenville believed that taxing the colonies for the expense of their defense was only right and just. After all, the costs of maintaining military defense and civilian administration in the colonies had jumped from £70,000 in 1748 to £350,000 in 1764.[6] Under his Stamp Act, colonists would pay a tax on almost anything written or printed. This would include licenses, contracts, commissions, mortgages, wills, deeds, newspapers, advertisements, calendars, and almanacs—even dice and playing cards.[7]

Passed in February 1765, the act was to go into effect in America on November 1. Details of the act began to appear in colonial newspapers—as yet untaxed—in May. Ominously, those accused of violating the act would not be tried in their own communities by juries of their peers, but taken to far-off Halifax, Nova Scotia, and tried before special Admiralty courts.[8] The reaction was immediate—and hostile.

The Virginia House of Burgesses was sitting in Williamsburg when word came. As young member Patrick Henry took his seat for the first time on 20 May 1765, older, more seasoned members waited for the fiery orator to respond. They did not have to wait long. On May 29, Colonel George Washington was almost surely in his accustomed place.[9] Young Thomas Jefferson, not yet a member of the Burgesses but already a leading graduate of the College of William and Mary, stood in the assembly's doorway. Everyone listened intently as the new member from Louisa County rose to speak.

Henry introduced a series of five resolutions. He had hastily jotted them down on a blank page of an old law book.[10] The resolutions supported the idea that only the people's elected representatives could lawfully tax them. The resolutions were mildly phrased and offered little more than what John Locke, the philosopher of England's Glorious Revolution of 1688, had written—to general approval. But it was his speech, not his resolutions, that caused a stir. Henry's words stunned the crowded, hushed legislative hall.

"Caesar had his Brutus, Charles the First his Cromwell," he said, citing the two most famous cases of rulers whose actions had led to their own deaths, "and George the Third . . ." Members were shocked that a British colonist would name the ruling sovereign in such company. "Treason!" roared the Speaker. "*Treason!*" echoed some other members. But the famous courtroom advocate neatly avoided their charge by concluding cleverly: ". . . and George the Third may profit from their example." He then added cockily: "If *this* be treason, make the most of it!"[11] Jefferson would later say that Henry spoke as the Greek poet Homer wrote.[12]

The Burgesses quickly adopted the Virginia Resolves, denouncing the Stamp Act as unconstitutional. They knew their rights as Englishmen. They had studied the Magna Carta and the Petition of Right from the English civil war of the previous century.

Resistance flared up throughout the colonies. In Charleston, South Carolina, Christopher Gadsden led protests. There, a mob tore up the homes of two "stampmen."[13] Gadsden said, "There ought to be no New England man, no New Yorkers known on this continent, but all of us Americans."[14] Annapolis, Maryland, was a scene of destruction as a crowd pulled down a warehouse owned by a tax collector.[15] In New York City, the royal governor's coach was attacked. Rhode Island stamp protesters hanged tax collectors in effigy. In Newport, their signs accused one collector of being an infamous *Jacobite*—a charge that meant he was a supporter of the deposed Stuart monarch James II, a Catholic.[16]

Following the lead of Massachusetts's brilliant James Otis, nine colonies agreed to send delegates to a *congress* in New York in October 1765. Virginia, whose royal governor had dismissed the House of Burgesses, could send no delegates. New Hampshire, Georgia, and South Carolina were also unrepresented, but Nova Scotia sent delegates.[17] The Stamp Act Congress met and issued a Declaration of Rights on October 19. Despite their professions of loyalty to the king and to his royal family, the delegates took a firm line *against* the claims of the Grenville government. They approved Patrick Henry's resolution that only the colonial legislatures had the right to tax colonists. Three of the key resolutions passed by the delegates were:

> 1st. That His Majesty's subjects in these colonies owe the same allegiance to the crown of Great Britain that is owing from his subjects born within the realm, and all due subordination to that august body, the Parliament of Great Britain.
>
> 2nd. That His Majesty's liege subjects in these colonies are entitled to all the inherent rights and privileges of his natural born subjects within the kingdom of Great Britain.
>
> 3rd. That it is inseparably essential to the freedom of a people, and the undoubted rights of Englishmen, that no taxes should be imposed on them, but with their own consent, given personally, or by their representatives.[18]

In the face of such united opposition, the Stamp Tax simply could not be collected. By autumn of 1765, no Americans could be found to serve as stampmen. They all had been co-opted or scared away.[19] The crisis had made thousands of Americans acutely aware of their rights. As John Adams wrote, the people were "more attentive to their liberties, more inquisitive about them, and more determined to defend them."[20] They were still loyal to the king, however. Even at the height of the crisis, children would dance around Boston's Liberty Tree with a flag that read, "King, Pitt, and Liberty." Thus, colonists showed their continued allegiance to the Crown, while openly favoring the return to power of William Pitt, the respected wartime prime minister.[21] Groups such as the Sons of Liberty, organized in Massachusetts, were not willing to break with all royal authority. By adopting that name, colonists showed themselves aware of having been "born free," and willing to stand up for their rights as Americans *and as Englishmen.*[22]

Reflecting on the Stamp Act crisis that December, Adams would say 1765 was "the most remarkable year of my life. The enormous engine fabricated by the British Parliament for battering down all the rights and liberties of America . . . has raised through the whole continent a spirit that will be recorded to our honor with all future generations."[23]

Prior to this, America was governed at only the cost of paper and ink; Americans were "led by a thread," as Franklin said.[24] Afterward, the stubbornness and stupidity of the British Crown and Parliament made America increasingly *ungovernable.*[25] John Adams later wrote that "the child independence was born" during the colonists' legal challenge to the unconstitutional Writs of Assistance. But we might say that was premature. The resistance to the Stamp Tax was continent-wide. It was then that Americans from Maine to Georgia first came together to resist British tyranny.[26]

When, in the spring of 1766, Parliament repealed the Stamp Act, the colonies exploded with joy. There were bonfires and fireworks— *illuminations* in the language of the day. Americans credited the king with this turnabout (even though his dismissal of Grenville hinged on totally different issues). In New York City, the people put up a statue of King George III mounted on a horse. It was happily paid for by public subscription.[27] They did not protest, either, when Parliament passed the Declaratory Act that reasserted its right to legislate for Americans on all matters whatsoever.

For a brief season, Americans seemed content to live under what they readily acknowledged was the freest government on earth. They were overjoyed when their friend William Pitt returned to power as the king's first minister in 1766. But their celebrations proved to be premature. Pitt was ailing, and the dominant personality in his government was Charles Townshend. Townshend understood that Americans objected only to "internal taxes" like the Stamp Tax. Internal taxes were levied on items produced and sold *within* the colonies. So he decided to lay "external" duties on items imported to America, such as glass, paint, lead, paper, and tea. The Townshend Acts went into effect 1 January 1767.[28] They were supposed to raise as much as £400,000 a year to contribute to the cost of administering the colonies.

Parliament had also passed the Quartering Act of 1766 that required colonists to provide British soldiers—*redcoats* as they were soon called—with barracks, bedding, fuel, candles, and even beer, cider, and rum.[29] Americans saw that the great increase in the number of British troops in the colonies—greater than they had seen in wartime—was not being directed to the frontier, where they might have been expected to defend against such dangers as Pontiac had posed. Instead, the redcoats were seen in growing numbers in major colonial cities—especially Boston.

Americans began to suspect that the redcoats were being sent to control *them*. This suspicion grew when the royal authorities began to issue "Writs of Assistance" to customs officials. These writs were generalized search warrants. They did not have to specify a specific good to be searched for. They allowed the customs officers to *break into* ships, warehouses, even private homes! The heavy import taxes had encouraged smuggling by colonial merchants; the writs were an attempt to stop their tax evasion. Anytime any royal official merely suspected smuggled goods, he had the power to search.[30] What's more, Admiralty courts and Boards of Customs commissioners had the power to try those who sought to evade the king's duties.[31] Americans soon saw that their cherished right to trial by jury was in jeopardy.

John Dickinson spoke for many Americans when he wrote a series of articles in 1767–68, *Letters from a Farmer in Pennsylvania*. Dickinson attacked the "excesses and outrages" of the British ministry. He urged his fellow colonists to resist. But he was careful to assert his loyalty to the king and to channel the opposition into "constitutional methods of seeking redress," such as continued petitions to the government and even resuming the costly *nonimportation* policy that had proved so successful against the Stamp Tax.[32] Dickinson, who had been an opponent of Franklin in Philadelphia politics, completely *rejected* the use of force "as much out of the way."[33]

For now, colonists were inclined to follow Dickinson's lead. But some leaders, such as Washington, were beginning to think that force might be necessary for Americans to preserve their freedom.[34] As early as 1769, Washington was telling his neighbor George Mason that America must arm to resist British tyranny.[35] In saying this, Washington had many reasons, some high-minded; some less so. He was particularly upset about the financial drain he was suffering because of the duties levied on his expensive tastes. But luxury and concern for liberty are not mutually exclusive, and Washington was fully in the tradition of John Locke, who had laid down the philosophical basis for the English constitution. Locke had specified the resort to force—"The appeal to heaven," as he called it—as the final *but legitimate* course of action when a ruler refused to listen to reason.

Boston soon became the center of unrest. In June 1768, the royal governor disbanded the Massachusetts Assembly. Almost at the same time, the sailing sloop called *Liberty*—owned by the rich and popular merchant John Hancock—was seized by customs officials. They charged Hancock with smuggling Madeira wine and imposed a fine. A city mob soon spilled into the town's narrow streets and chased the customs officials.

They escaped with their lives, but their houses were trashed.[36] Sam Adams made sure that colonists up and down the eastern seaboard were fully informed of the Boston outrages. Adams was able to make excellent use of the efficient colonial postal system that Benjamin Franklin had established. Franklin's efforts had cut the time for a letter to travel up and down the coast from six weeks to three.[37]*

By 1770, tensions were rising between the people of Boston and the British troops whom they saw as occupiers. In March, following a winter of sporadic incidents, a mob of boys and young men began to taunt British soldiers, calling them *lobsters* and pelting them with trash, oyster shells, and snowballs. With their backs to the royal Customs House, and feeling hemmed in, the frightened soldiers opened fire on the mob. Crispus Attucks, a free black man and a whaler, was one of the first to fall. In all, five colonists were killed in what instantly became known as "the Boston Massacre."[38]

Realizing the explosive situation he had on hand, Governor Thomas Hutchinson had the Customs House guards arrested on a charge of murder and ordered the rest of the British garrison to return to Castle William, a fort in the harbor.[39] Quickly, the colonists had taken up the cry of murder. Boston's Paul Revere, a silversmith, soon engraved a powerful—but *exaggerated*—depiction of the killings. In Revere's rendering, the number of fallen is greater and the redcoats fire a volley on the order of their officer. The truth was much more complicated than that.

Surprisingly, or perhaps not so surprisingly, young John Adams, Samuel's cousin, and *his* cousin Josiah Quincy, took responsibility for the legal defense of the accused British soldiers. Determined to prove that British soldiers could be fairly tried in an American courtroom, John Adams demonstrated that most of the soldiers fired in self-defense, that no order to fire on the crowd had ever been given, and that the unruly

---

* For example, Franklin published in his and other newspapers the names of those with letters in the post office. This sped up delivery.

colonials had provoked the soldiers. Adams argued persuasively that hanging the redcoats for murder would disgrace Massachusetts's name in history. It would be worse than the blot of the Salem witch trials and the hanging of the Quakers.[40] John Adams made a name for himself when the jury found all but two of the accused not guilty and convicted those two of lesser charges. Their punishment, an odd one, was the branding of their thumbs.

Cousin Sam, however, was not dismayed. For the next five years, he and the Sons of Liberty organized mass demonstrations on the anniversary of the Boston Massacre.[41]

II. A TOTAL SEPARATION

After a decade of political upheaval in London and in the colonies, a new ministry was finally installed in Parliament. King George found in Lord North a man after his own mind. In an attempt to reconcile with the colonies, the North administration persuaded Parliament to repeal all of the objectionable Townshend duties *except* the tax on tea.[42]

While they attempted to bring the colonists to order, Parliament was determined *not* to recognize Americans' rights to rule themselves in a union of equals under the same crown. In the spring of 1772, Rhode Islanders had a chance to take out their resentments of British high-handedness. The HMS ("His Majesty's Ship") *Gaspée* had been particularly active as a customs ship in the Narragansett Bay, roughly handling fishermen and small boats. The officers of the *Gaspée* applied the laws strictly in a region that previously had seen little or no enforcement. When the ship ran aground chasing smugglers, boatloads of Patriots rowed out, surrounded the ship, and forced the crew ashore. Then they gleefully burned to the waterline this symbol of British misrule.[43]

The entire conduct of the royal authorities in America smacked of a lordly disdain for the colonists. All Americans became aware of how they were looked down upon by the English. *Yankee* was a well-known term of contempt for all Americans. For a time, Americans lived in the hope that it was only certain British *ministers* who were responsible for tormenting them. They held on to the belief that the king and the British people were in sympathy with them. But Franklin knew better. As early as 1769, he was writing that the British people were "in full cry against America."[44]

Despite Samuel Adams's continual agitation, the period of 1771–73 saw a lessening of tensions between colonial subjects and the mother country. Then, without explanation, Lord North committed "a fatal blunder." He passed through Parliament a Tea Act that would have allowed the nearly bankrupt East India Company to claim a monopoly on tea in the colonies.[45]

Americans instantly recognized that if Britain could monopolize the importation of this important staple, there was no place they might stop. They could strangle American commerce and industry. Once again, resistance to British taxation was *continental*. It flamed up from Maine and Georgia. In Charleston, ship owners were allowed to unload their tea, but it was kept under guard in a warehouse. Philadelphia and New York refused to allow the tea to be off-loaded at all. Everyone waited for Boston's reaction.

On 16 December 1773, under cover of darkness, some two thousand Boston men went down to Griffin's Wharf. There, a smaller party of thirty men disguised as Mohawk Indians boarded three vessels and dumped their cargoes of tea into the harbor. "Boston harbor a tea-pot tonight!" cried one of the supporters. Samuel Adams had planned the whole raid with great care.[46] The damage to property was extensive. In today's terms, the losses to the East India Company would be valued at $1 million.[47] A British admiral, who had watched the entire episode from a house near the wharf, called out good-naturedly to the "Mohawks": "Well, boys, you have had a fine pleasant evening for your Indian caper, haven't you? But mind, you have got to pay the fiddler yet."[48]

By now, John Adams had cast his lot with his cousin, Sam, and the Patriots. He wrote in his diary: "This destruction of the tea is so bold, so daring, so firm, intrepid and inflexible, and it must have so important consequences . . . that I cannot but consider it as an epoch in history."[49]

Indeed, Boston would be made to pay the fiddler. Outraged by this act of colonial defiance, King George III appeared the following spring in person before Parliament, demanding harsh reprisal. "We must master them or totally leave them alone," he said.[50] Lord North was in full accord with his royal master. He was determined to show the colonies who was boss.

Parliament's answer in 1774 to floating tea was the speedy passage of five *coercive* acts. Patriots in America quickly dubbed them the "Intolerable Acts."[51] The first of these closed the Port of Boston and removed the Customs House. Another act changed Massachusetts's revered charter, stripping colonists of the right to elect members of the Upper House of their assembly. The Quartering Act allowed royal officials to place soldiers in colonists' homes at the colonists' expense. Still another act provided that royal officers indicted for murder while suppressing riots should be tried in London rather than where the offense occurred. This act, despite John Adams's proof that British soldiers could get a fair trial in America, was a calculated insult. Finally, Parliament passed the Quebec Act. The new law extended the southern border of Quebec to the Ohio River, thus effectively closing off the Ohio Country to American expansion.

George Washington reacted sharply to Parliament's Intolerable Acts. The North ministry was setting up "the most despotic system of tyranny that was ever practiced in a free government," he charged.[52] He rallied to the plight of his Massachusetts countrymen: "The cause of Boston . . . is the cause of America," he said.[53]

Unwilling to take the Intolerable Acts lying down, Patriot leaders in the colonies elected delegates to attend the first Continental Congress in Philadelphia in the fall of 1774. As they assembled, Philadelphia merchants were determined not to get burned again. If there was to be a renewal of the nonimportation, nonexport pledges that had proved so successful at the time of the Stamp Act crisis, Philadelphia's men of commerce demanded that this time the entire continent must take part. They had lost precious business when Baltimore merchants failed to support previous embargoes. This time, it must be all or nothing.

In this way, a continental *union* was being forged. The first Continental Congress quickly adopted the radical "Suffolk Resolves" that rider Paul Revere had brought to them from Massachusetts. Those resolves, drafted by the Patriot leader Dr. Joseph Warren, declared the Intolerable Acts null and void. Congress urged Massachusetts to form a free government and, ominously, advised Massachusetts's citizens to arm themselves.[54] When Congress adjourned in October 1774, delegates pledged to reassemble the following May if Parliament failed to repeal the Intolerable Acts.

In England, when the brilliant Edmund Burke rose in the House of Commons on 22 March 1775 to plead for *conciliation*, the eloquent Irishman warned that America could never be subdued by force. He urged Britons to change their course, to adopt mild measures for dealing with the colonies. For more than a century, American high school students were required to memorize portions of Burke's magnificent speech. "Great empires and little minds," he cried, "go ill together." Burke went unheeded. Thus did the British Parliament arrogantly and stupidly throw away the lifeline that alone could have tied them to their empire in America.

Burke's eloquence found an answer in Virginia the very next day, 23 March 1775. Patrick Henry appealed to his fellow Virginians to take up arms and stand with imperiled Boston. "I know not what course others may take," Henry cried, "but as for me, *give me liberty or give me death!*"

III. "THE SHOT HEARD 'ROUND THE WORLD"

In Boston, the British general Thomas Gage had been named royal governor. He was determined not to let colonists arm. On the night of 18 April 1775, he ordered his troops to seize the militia's military stores at Concord and to arrest Patriot leaders Samuel Adams and John Hancock.

Hoping to catch the colonists unaware, Gage's troops moved out of their barracks by night, by boat. But there was a spy under Gage's roof. The general's American wife, Margaret, got word to Dr. Warren who passed it on to Paul Revere.[55]

Revere had arranged a signal—two lanterns—to be placed in the tower of Old North Church to let the Patriots know the regulars were moving out. Revere himself was rowed past HMS *Somerset,* a British warship. The low-hanging moon behind Boston's buildings cast a shadow that concealed Revere's movements.[56] Once mounted on horseback, Revere and William Dawes managed to evade British patrols and brought the warning to Lexington. There at the home of Reverend Jonas Clarke, where the Patriot leaders were sleeping, Revere was challenged by Sergeant William Munroe. Munroe shushed him for making too much noise. "Noise!" Revere shouted. "You'll have noise enough before long. The regulars are coming out!" (Revere would only have confused colonists if he had yelled, "The British are coming," since Massachusetts people still thought of themselves as British.)[57]

At five o'clock the next morning, the Minutemen (so called because they could be ready for military duty in a minute) were drawn up on the village green in Lexington as the British regulars came marching up. Captain Jonas Parker ordered the Minutemen to stand their ground. "Don't fire unless fired upon," he said, "but if they mean to have a war, let it begin here!"[58] British Major of Marines John Pitcairn ordered the Americans to lay down their arms. "You damned rebels, disperse!" he cried.[59] The Americans were beginning to disperse when a shot rang out. In a flash, there were competing volleys that left eight Americans dead in the spring sunlight. Three British soldiers were wounded.[60] In vain, Major Pitcairn had tried to stop his men from shooting.

The British column marched on to Concord, where another force of colonials met them. There the British destroyed militia stores and turned back toward Boston, mission accomplished. The road back became a highway of death, with Minutemen firing from behind walls and trees. Many of the regulars, who had been marching for more than twenty-four hours carrying heavy packs on their backs, fell out, exhausted. By the time they got back to Boston, they had 73 dead, 174 wounded, and 26 missing. The Americans suffered 49 dead, 39 wounded, and 5 taken prisoner.[61] These were little more than skirmishes as the world measures warfare, but the American farmers had indeed "fired the shot heard 'round the world.'"*

Less than a month later, the second Continental Congress assembled in Philadelphia. One of its first acts was to authorize a Continental Army. This army pledged its loyalty to Congress, and not to the individual colonies, as was the practice in the militia.[62] John Adams and other Massachusetts men worried that Boston might be abandoned by other colonies. To prevent this from ever happening, Adams nominated Colonel George Washington of Virginia to command all American forces, with the rank of general. Congress knew it needed a leader it could trust. The delegates recalled Oliver Cromwell, who had fought King Charles I in the name of Parliament only to wind up using the force he had been given to purge Parliament itself.[63] George Washington not only had more military

---

* In 1836, New Englander Ralph Waldo Emerson would immortalize the "embattled farmers" of the Revolution with his poem "Concord Hymn":

> By the rude bridge that arched the flood,
> Their flag to April's breeze unfurled,
> Here once the embattled farmers stood,
> And fired the shot heard round the world,
>
> The foe long since in silence slept,
> Alike the Conqueror silent sleeps,
> And Time the ruined bridge has swept
> Down the dark stream which seaward creeps.
>
> On this bank green, by this soft stream,
> We set to-day a votive stone,
> That memory may their deed redeem,
> When like our sires our sons are gone.
>
> Spirit! who made those freemen dare
> To die, or leave their children free,
> Bid time and nature gently spare
> The shaft we raise to them and Thee.

experience than any other colonist, he had been a reliable member of the House of Burgesses since 1759. Washington, resplendent in his full dress military uniform, humbly accepted Congress's call and left immediately for embattled Boston. Congress also named as postmaster general Benjamin Franklin, recently returned from London.[64]

En route to Boston, Washington received word of a battle that was no skirmish. Stung by his earlier losses to ragtag colonials, General Gage was determined to overawe the rebels by a show of military force in clear view of all of Boston. He ordered General William Howe to take Bunker Hill.* On 17 June 1775, Howe led his disciplined regulars up the slope, vowing never to order them to go where he was unwilling to lead. When they neared the American lines, they were cut down by a fierce musket volley. "Don't fire until you see the whites of their eyes," was the order given all along the line of determined American defenders.

In his blood-spattered white silk breeches, General Howe rallied his men and finally drove the Americans off the hill. British losses, including Major Pitcairn, were tremendous—nearly 1,000 out of 2,000 in action.[65] American losses were far fewer—about 440 out of 3,200 defenders. Among the Patriot dead, though, was the revered Dr. Joseph Warren. Although the Americans were driven back, they had inflicted major casualties on the most professional and well-trained army in the world, an impossible accomplishment that imbued them with a swelling sense of confidence and pride.

When Washington arrived a week later to take command of American forces surrounding Boston, he had another advantage. He had amassed considerable artillery. These cannon had been captured from the British at Fort Ticonderoga in upper New York. Colonel Ethan Allen, supported by his Vermont "Green Mountain Boys" and ably aided by the courageous Benedict Arnold, had taken the defenders by surprise. Allen demanded surrender from the startled British commander "in the name of the great

---

* A historical misnomer, the battle was actually fought on nearby Breed's Hill.

Jehovah and the Continental Congress." A young Boston bookseller—the energetic, three-hundred-pound Henry Knox—was put in charge of the cannon, dragging them across mountains and valleys to the aid of Boston Patriots. His patriotism and zeal impressed General Washington.[66] With the addition of the captured artillery, Washington was able to force the evacuation of the British from Boston. This was another great boost to American morale.* And it helped establish the Continental Army as an effective force.

Congress sent General Richard Montgomery and Benedict Arnold to take on the British in Canada in the summer of 1775. Montgomery succeeded in taking Montreal but was stopped in Quebec City at year's end, where he lost his life. The ragged American force soon bogged down and was driven out. Arnold was wounded, but he won praise for bringing order to the retreat.

Against this background, Washington's actions in camp have special significance. In November 1775, he learned that New England soldiers were preparing their annual celebration of Pope's Day, during which effigies of the pope were burned to the amusement of their Protestant neighbors. New England had been celebrating this holiday for more than a century. Washington issued an order sternly forbidding this "ridiculous and childish" display. He explained that the aid of French Catholics in Canada and across the sea was important to the American cause. He also wanted help from Catholics throughout the colonies. Washington's firmness ended a New England tradition and marked a major step forward in religious tolerance and national unity.

Events were moving quickly. Thomas Paine, whom Franklin had met in London and given letters of recommendation just two years previously, came out with the most influential pamphlet of all: *Common Sense*. Published in January 1776, and selling for a mere eighteen pence,

---

* Evacuation Day, 17 March 1776, is commemorated in Boston to this day. And it does not hurt that Beantown revelers can mix their celebrations with St. Patrick's Day festivities!

Common Sense sold more than 150,000 copies. Americans had heard the case for their rights put with great legal expertise and scholarship from men such as John Adams and John Dickinson, but Paine had a flair for colorful writing, and he surely had the common touch. As a recent immigrant from England, his fierce writing against this king—*and against all kings*—struck a responsive chord. As soon as it came off the presses, New Hampshire delegate Josiah Bartlett noted, *Common Sense* was "greedily bought up and read by all ranks of people."[67] John Adams was probably more influential than any other American in moving Congress, but it was Paine who moved the people.[68] Of all the arguments Paine made, his charges against the king were most devastating. He attacked the pretended "FATHER OF HIS PEOPLE [who] can unfeelingly hear of their slaughter, and composedly sleep with their blood upon his soul."[69]

Paine knew the religious beliefs of his readers. He used the Bible to hammer home his points: "[T]he children of Israel in their request for a king urged this plea, 'that he may judge us, and go out before us and fight our battles.' But in countries where he is neither a judge nor a general, as in England, a man would be puzzled to know what *is* his business."[70] This was amazingly bold. Paine might have been making a personal appeal with this powerful and emotional plea: "O! ye that love mankind! Ye that dare oppose not only the tyranny, but the tyrant, stand forth! Every spot of the old world is overrun with oppression. Freedom hath been haunted round the globe. Asia, and Africa, have long expelled her. Europe regards her like a stranger, and England hath given her warning to depart. [America] receive the fugitive, and prepare in time an asylum for mankind."[71]*

The Americans, recalling how grasping Parliament had been for their taxes, were shocked to see Lord North's ministry hiring German and Scottish mercenaries to make war on the colonies (although the *need* to do so betrayed the war's deep unpopularity in Britain). News that the king would send twelve thousand *Hessian* troops (hired from the German state

---

* What better example of "American exceptionalism" can we find?

of Hesse) reached America in May.[72] Every American coffin seemed to bring death, as well, to the idea of reconciliation with England.

In addition to their increasing bitterness caused by British warfare against their colonies, Americans were facing the practical problem that no European state would support them while they were still formally members of the British Empire. They were still rebels. And there was a danger to the French, the Dutch, and the Spanish that the Americans might make peace with the mother country and leave them to fight a vengeful England by themselves. Independence would help Americans gain European recognition and practical help.

Finally, on 7 June 1776, Virginia's Richard Henry Lee introduced before Congress his motion "that these United Colonies are, and of right ought to be, Free and Independent States."[73] Congress then named a committee to draft a declaration of causes for independence: John Adams (Massachusetts), Benjamin Franklin (Pennsylvania), Thomas Jefferson (Virginia), Robert Livingston (New York), and Roger Sherman (Connecticut). Adams was keenly aware that there were four Northerners and only one Southerner on the drafting committee. During the debate in Congress, one reluctant member (probably Pennsylvania's John Dickinson) argued that the colonies were not yet "ripe" for Independence. He was answered by a Scottish-born member from New Jersey. The colonies were not only ripe, he said with his rich burr, but "in danger-r-r of becoming r-r-rotten for the want of it!" The Reverend John Witherspoon, who was also president of the college we know today as Princeton, spoke for the majority of delegates. The motion for Independence soon carried.[74]

Once again, Adams made a fateful decision. He was desperate to have Virginia's support. He knew that Virginia led the South. And with Virginia's help, Massachusetts would never have to stand alone. Again, he opted for a Virginian to take the lead for the sake of national unity. He nominated Jefferson to draft the Declaration of Independence. Later, Adams would recall the reasons why he did so:

1. That [Jefferson] was a Virginian and I a Massachusettensian. 2. That he was a southern Man and I a northern one. 3. That I had become so obnoxious for my early and constant Zeal in promoting [Independence] that any [draft] of mine would undergo more severe Scrutiny and Criticism in Congress than one of his composition. 4thly and lastly that would be reason enough if there were no other, I had a great Opinion of the Elegance of his pen and none at all of my own. . . . He accordingly took the Minutes and in a day or two produced to me his [draft].[75]

In this passage—wordy, stuffy, but brutally honest—we see the best of John Adams. He was acutely conscious of his own role, undeniably ambitious to make his mark, but he constantly put his country first. Seldom could such a world-changing event be described in such spare terms—"In a day or two produced to me his draft."

And what a draft! Jefferson's "peculiar felicity of expression" (another Adams phrase) gave America a founding document that surpasses any other in the world for beauty, logic, and inspirational power. About the *philosophy* of the Declaration of Independence, there was no debate in Congress. It was what the Founders believed. Jefferson's immortal words were conventional wisdom of the time.[76] And the words of the Declaration became the greatest, most consequential statement of political philosophy of all time:

We hold these truths to be self-evident, that all men are created equal, that they are endowed by their Creator with certain unalienable Rights, that among these are Life, Liberty and the pursuit of Happiness—That to secure these rights, governments are instituted among Men, deriving their just powers from the consent of the governed. . . .[77]

This is America's political creed in a nutshell. Yes, they meant *all* men, regardless of race, religion, sex, or riches. They imposed no religious test for adherence to these ideals except belief in a creator God who *endows* us with our inalienable rights. They defined the purpose of all government. And they laid down the requirement that governments must rule by consent if they were to rule with justice at all. We will return to the philosophy of this Declaration in future chapters. Suffice for now, the Founders did not immediately free the slaves, give votes to their wives, or invite the Indian tribes to sign the Declaration with them. But we must realize that *all* the greatest advocates for human equality in America—Abraham Lincoln and Frederick Douglass, Elizabeth Cady Stanton and the Suffragettes, Martin Luther King Jr.—pointed to this passage in the Declaration to give force to their demands for justice.

The philosophical sentiment was near universal, but the practical matter of voting for independence was less so. The final tally was close. Congress had to wait for uninstructed delegates to return to Philadelphia. Caesar Rodney, suffering from asthma and cancer, rode eighty miles from his Delaware home to the sweltering capital on the night of 1 July 1776 in order to break a tie in his state's delegation and carry the motion for independence.

The men who signed the Declaration knew this was no casual debating society resolution. They acknowledged this as they pledged "our lives, our fortunes and our sacred honor" to support independence. When John Hancock summoned the delegates to sign the parchment "fair" copy of the Declaration, he wrote his own signature in large, bold strokes so that King George (legend has it) could read his name without his glasses.

He urged them to make it unanimous. "There must be no pulling different ways," he said. "We must all hang together." To that, Franklin, ever the wit, reportedly responded: "Yes, we must indeed all hang together, or most assuredly, we shall all hang separately."[78] Though none of the signers was hanged, seventeen served in the military, and five were captured by the British during the war. Richard Stockton, a New Jersey signer, never recovered from slow torture during captivity and died in 1781.[79]

IV. A CONTINENTAL WAR

While Congress made its fateful move, General Washington was facing the danger of entrapment by the British army in New York. It was there that he had the Declaration of Independence read to his troops. There, the famous statue of George III was pulled down and its lead melted into bullets. Washington had been widely acclaimed when the British withdrew from Boston in March, but a string of defeats followed. Boston was to be his last victory for almost a year. Washington knew that no one who did not control the sea could hold waterborne Manhattan Island. Congress did not want to abandon the new nation's second largest city to the enemy.

Colonel John Glover's Marblehead men from Massachusetts were sailors and fishermen, more at home on the water than on dry land.[80] The night of 29 August 1776, their seagoing ways would prove vital to the Patriot cause.

The Continental Army had initially held firm under murderous British fire on Long Island, but the redcoats marched through the night, in perfect military order, to take the Americans by surprise.[81] Hessian soldiers took no prisoners. They stabbed the surrendering Americans with their bayonets, the blades of which were seventeen inches long.

Washington knew he had to withdraw from Brooklyn on Long Island and escape with his army to Manhattan. Five British warships were prepared to sail up the East River to block Washington's retreat, but the wind "miraculously" shifted and the British squadron was unable to come upriver.[82] Then, when Washington ordered Glover's Marblehead men to man the boats, he evacuated the bulk of the army from Brooklyn. Only a portion of the army was able to escape under the cover of darkness the night of August 29, but then a thick fog rolled in to hide the action as the remainder of the army entered the boats. One Connecticut officer claimed he made eleven crossings of the East River that night.[83] Author David McCullough called that covering fog incredible—an unlikely turn of fate. Believers in Providence called it the Hand of God.[84]*

Washington felt the disappointment personally when his men ran before the advancing Hessians and Scots Highlanders. In anguish, he threw his hat to the ground and cried out: "Are *these* the men with whom I am to defend America?"[85] But he could also point with pride at troops who stood their ground and did their duty, as when 250 Marylanders attacked General Cornwallis's forces to cover the army's retreat, risking death or capture. "Good God, what brave fellows I must lose this day," Washington said. He then gave Maryland troops the name by which the state is known to this day—The Old Line.

The city could not be held. In September, as Washington withdrew to Harlem Heights, the city of New York caught fire. No one knows how it started. Loyalists—called Tories—who supported the Crown naturally blamed the rebels. Angered, British General William Howe seized a young American officer whom he accused of spying for Washington. Nathan Hale of Connecticut was about twenty-four. Howe gave him no trial. Hale was in civilian clothes, so he was treated as a spy. Shocking Americans, Howe denied the young man's last request for a pastor, or even a Bible. As Howe prepared to hang him, the fearless Patriot recited words from the popular play *Cato:*

> How beautiful is death, when earned by virtue!
> Who would not be that youth? What pity is it
> That we can die but once to serve our country.[86]

The quote has come down to us, in paraphrase, as "I regret I have but one life to give for my country." The Revolution had its first martyr.

Benjamin Franklin agreed to go to France in the fall of 1776 to plead

---

* When the British Expeditionary Force was similarly evacuated from Dunkirk in 1940, thus saving England and the cause of freedom from the Nazi menace, Winston Churchill called it "a miracle of deliverance."

the American cause. Franklin embarked on a ship named *Reprisal*. It was a very rough crossing, with many seasick. It was also dangerous as Franklin was the most recognizable of all the rebels and the British still held mastery of the seas. Even when he disembarked in France, he found himself on a country road where a gang of thieves had only recently murdered a party of twelve travelers. Happily, Franklin entered Paris safely in December 1776.[87]

Throughout that fall, General Howe and his lieutenant, Lord Cornwallis, pushed Washington south through New Jersey. The military position was helped when Benedict Arnold delayed a British thrust down from Canada, and Patriots defending Charleston, South Carolina, repelled a British assault. Although Washington had kept his army together and with it the Revolution, retreat was still dispiriting. Throughout New Jersey, farmers were tacking red ribbons to their doors to show sympathy with the king. By December 1776, with enlistments running out for many militia forces, Washington's Continental Army was dwindling.

At Christmastime, most armies went into winter quarters. Washington had retreated across the Delaware River into Pennsylvania, chopping down bridges and taking boats with him. Washington knew that as soon as the river froze solid, Lord Cornwallis's superior numbers could cross over on the ice. Washington was running out of money and supplies. He appealed to Pennsylvania's master of finance, Robert Morris, to raise hard cash to pay bonuses to his soldiers. Only when they had been paid did some of his ragged, starving soldiers agree to extend their enlistments into the new year.

So, on Christmas night, in foul weather, General Washington prepared a sudden assault on Trenton, New Jersey. Once again, Washington relied on Colonel John Glover's seasoned Marblehead, Massachusetts troops. They were all excellent sailors and boat handlers. They had already saved the Continental Army by ferrying it from Brooklyn to Manhattan. Now, Glover's men carried the entire army—with horses and cannon—across the ice-choked Delaware. The little band of ragged men took the Hessian defenders by surprise. In a short, sharp action, Washington's men killed the Hessian commander, Colonel Johann Rall, and took nearly a thousand prisoners. Only two Americans were wounded, one of them Lieutenant James Monroe, the future president. Captain Alexander Hamilton's cannon, whose touch holes had been kept dry on the boat trip over, were used to devastating effect. Another in the boats that night was young John Marshall, the future chief justice of the United States. America in 1776 could have fielded an army of 280,000 men, but that Christmas night, just 2,400 held the fate of a continent in their hands.[88]

Washington's attack had been a great success. He quickly put into practice the "policy of humanity" that John Adams and others in Congress had urged upon him. Instead of bayoneting the surrendering Hessians—as the Hessians had done to Americans who gave up on Long Island—Washington treated them with compassion. As a result of this enlightened policy, thousands of Hessian Germans would later settle in the backcountry of Pennsylvania and Virginia.

American Patriots rejoiced with the retaking of Trenton and were overjoyed when, just two weeks later, Washington followed up his victory with another successful attack on Princeton. In this battle, Washington galloped directly into the smoke of British cannon fire. One of his young aides, Colonel John Fitzgerald, covered his eyes with his hat, certain the commander in chief would be killed. Washington came riding out of the smoke, eyes ablaze with victory. "Thank God your Excellency is safe," Fitzgerald cried out, offering his hand. Washington grasped it with enthusiasm, perhaps realizing how close to death he had come. "It's a fine fox chase, my boys," Washington cried, as his men sent the British defenders of Princeton into headlong retreat.[89]

Independence did not bring French help immediately, at least not openly. But one man was to be a harbinger of things to come. In July 1777, a tall, nineteen-year-old French aristocrat named Marie Joseph Paul Yves Roch Gilbert du Motier, better known to history as the Marquis de Lafayette, arrived in Philadelphia. Congress was embarrassed when the eager young nobleman—who had already seen plenty of military action—showed up to present his credentials from the American minister in Paris, Silas Deane. They had no money to pay him, members explained, and Deane had exceeded his authority in promising commissions. Lafayette could not return home. He had defied King Louis XVI in sailing to America. Instead, he offered to serve *without pay* as a volunteer in the ranks.[90] By August, he was riding by Washington's side as a major general—at age twenty! Lafayette would soon see action in September 1777, at the Battle of Brandywine in Pennsylvania. There, he was wounded as he gallantly led American troops. Although Washington's forces fought bravely, they lost and the road to Philadelphia lay open to the British.

Washington was hundreds of miles away when America's greatest military victory was achieved. Americans waited expectantly as Patriot forces faced British General John Burgoyne at Saratoga, New York, in October 1777. Burgoyne, "Gentleman Johnny" to London society, was a member of Parliament, a playwright, and flamboyant figure. He had bet parliamentary leader Charles James Fox a substantial wager that he would come home from America victorious by Christmas Day 1777. His task was to come down from Canada and link up with General Howe, leading a British force north from New York. But Howe was headed for Philadelphia—trying to catch Washington. Burgoyne let it be known his Indian soldiers had permission to scalp any British deserters. Initially crowned with success, Burgoyne had retaken Fort Ticonderoga and had burned the fine Albany home of American General Philip Schuyler.[91]

But Burgoyne's army moved too slowly—burdened by a huge baggage train—and he was trapped by the Americans. The sound of turkey gobble calls—Americans signaling each other before the attack—spooked the British troops. Gunfire erupted, and Dan Morgan's riflemen, who, according to legend, could drop a redcoat a mile away, quickly cut down Burgoyne's men.[92]

Surrendering his entire force of more than six thousand at Saratoga on 17 October 1777, Burgoyne was amazed by the merciful response he received from General Schuyler. "Is it to *me*, who have done you so much injury, that you show so much kindness?"[93]

Gentleman Johnny had lost his big wager. Fox, who predicted his friend would return a prisoner on parole, had won.[94] Saratoga was America's greatest victory to this point. American General Horatio Gates was quick to claim the victor's laurels, but as before, much of the credit for victory goes to General Benedict Arnold. Although seriously wounded, Arnold had nonetheless rallied American soldiers for action. The French foreign minister, Charles Gravier, the Comte de Vergennes, would see in Saratoga evidence of the Americans' ability to outlast the English.

General Washington's position was not improved as he moved into winter quarters at Valley Forge. With General Howe's British forces firmly in control of Philadelphia, Washington could only watch and wait. This was the worst winter of the war. Once again, he desperately appealed to Congress for aid. He wrote that you could trace his men's tracks by the bloody footprints in the snow. When he said his men were naked and starving, that was not an exaggeration. Some Continental soldiers had to borrow pants just to go out to stand watch.[95]

Fortunately, another foreign addition to America's army arrived on the scene at this moment. A Prussian officer, Baron von Steuben, had met Benjamin Franklin in Paris and was recommended to Congress. Von Steuben, who spoke no English, was a colorful figure who had inflated his credentials—an eighteenth-century résumé-padder. Still, he knew the art of drill, and he knew the importance of discipline and training to turn a rabble into a fighting force. Von Steuben began whipping the ragged, dispirited men of Valley Forge into shape. He comically employed an interpreter to translate his French and German curses into English the men could understand. (Every drill instructor in the American military since is a spiritual descendant of the outlandish Prussian.)

V. THE FRENCH ALLIANCE AND A TRAITOR

"These are the times that try men's souls," Thomas Paine wrote before Washington crossed the Delaware in December 1776. Now, a year later, things were little better. New York and Philadelphia were occupied by the British. Washington and his starving, freezing army watched warily from winter quarters outside Philadelphia at Valley Forge. In the spring of 1778, however, came news that changed everything. Benjamin Franklin had succeeded in securing the French Alliance. After years of secret aid, France now would openly recognize the United States and take her side in the war with England. The Dutch and Spaniards would also now begin to help. This meant, among other things, that Britain would have to bring ships back to its home waters to guard against French raids and would also have to reinforce the garrison at Gibraltar in case of Spanish attack.

Meanwhile, the American frontier was ablaze. In the Wyoming Valley of Pennsylvania, Sir John Butler and his Indian allies struck on 4 July 1778, killing hundreds. Farmers were burned at the stake, thrown on beds of burning coals, and held down with pitchforks as their horrified families watched.[96] Virginia sent native son George Rogers Clark to re-establish her claims to the old Northwest Territory across the Ohio River. British Colonel Henry Hamilton, known as "Hair Buyer" because he paid Indians to bring in American scalps, holed up at a fort at Vincennes (in present-day Indiana). According to legend, Clark marched his small force of 130 Americans and French for days through chest-deep waters in midwinter to get at his enemy.[97] Surrounding "Hair Buyer" and marching his men back and forth outside the British encampment, Clark gave the illusion of thousands. Most of Henry Hamilton's Indians took flight. Then, when Clark captured five Indians with scalps on their belts, he had them tomahawked to death in front of the British fort. Henry Hamilton immediately surrendered. He would later describe the big Virginian, speaking "with rapture of his late achievements while he washed the blood from his hands."[98] With this victory and his success at Kaskaskia (near present-day East Saint Louis, Illinois), George Rogers Clark laid the basis for America's claim to the entire Northwest Territory (Ohio, Indiana, Michigan, Illinois, Wisconsin, and part of Minnesota).*

The news from France lifted American spirits, but several months later came news that shocked American patriots everywhere. General Benedict Arnold, the hero of many battles, felt he had been unjustly treated by Congress. As lesser men like Horatio Gates received promotions and credit that rightly belonged to Arnold, he became embittered. His young wife, Peggy Shippen, came from a rich Tory family. When Washington named Arnold as military commander of Philadelphia, Arnold clashed with the radical political leader, Joseph Reed. Because Arnold refused to hang five hundred Tories and seize their property, as Reed demanded, the Pennsylvanian spread rumors that Arnold was disloyal.[99] It became a self-fulfilling prophecy.

Arnold pleaded with Washington to make him commander of the American fortress at West Point, New York. Overlooking the Hudson River, sixty miles north of New York City, West Point was essential to preventing the British from cutting the United States in two. Arnold began to conspire with Sir Henry Clinton, General Howe's replacement in Manhattan. For £10,000, Arnold promised he would turn over West Point to the British. Arnold even plotted with Clinton's dashing young aide-de-camp, Major John André, how they might capture General Washington and turn him over to the British, but they soon dropped the idea as impractical.[100]

To capture or kill Washington had long been a British war aim.[101] Arnold and André met at a farmstead now known as Treason House. Sending the young man back to Clinton, Arnold persuaded André to change into civilian clothes. André carried papers in his boot that incriminated both Arnold

---

* George Rogers Clark richly deserves his title: Conqueror of the Northwest. His exploits would significantly add to America's territory—an area twice the size of Great Britain and larger than France. And his record would spur on his younger brother, William Clark of the Lewis and Clark Expedition, to match his deeds.

and himself. When André was taken prisoner, Arnold escaped to a British warship anchored in the Hudson—the aptly named HMS *Vulture*.[102]

Washington had been meeting in Hartford, Connecticut, with General Jean Baptiste Donatien de Vimeur, comte de Rochambeau, the commander of the newly arrived army of five thousand French regulars. When he arrived at West Point on 25 September 1780, a seemingly insane Peggy Shippen Arnold confronted General Washington. Only partially clothed, she ranted that the general wanted to kill her baby. Washington, Henry Knox, Lafayette, Alexander Hamilton, and the other American officers felt pity for the beautiful young woman, who had seemingly been driven to madness by her husband's treachery. It was all an act. When Washington chivalrously allowed Peggy to rejoin her treasonous husband, it became clear that she had been plotting with Arnold from the outset. She would have richly merited hanging for treason.

Instead, that sad fate befell the talented, brave, young Major André. Court-martialed and sentenced to die, André did not plead for his life but asked only to be shot as an officer and gentleman. Washington's officers recommended granting this plea. Stout-hearted Nathanael Greene, who had presided at the trial, dissented. André was either a spy or an innocent man, Greene reasoned. If innocent, he should be released, but if a spy, then the penalty for spying was death by hanging.[103] Perhaps remembering young Nathan Hale, Washington sternly sided with General Greene. With Americans weeping openly, Major John André, resplendent in his scarlet uniform, was hanged on 2 October 1780.[104]

Arnold escaped but died in poverty and disgrace in London twenty years later.[105] Benedict Arnold's name has ever after been a synonym for betrayal.

VI. "THE WORLD TURNED UPSIDE DOWN"

The British had shifted their major combat operations to the American South in 1780. Following the loss of Charleston, South Carolina, on 12

May 1780, Congress placed General Horatio Gates, the victor of Saratoga, in command of the Southern army. They rejected Washington's recommendation of General Nathanael Greene. (Gates still had support in Congress, despite the failure of a move two years prior to remove Washington and put Gates in his place.) Soon, however, Gates proved his unfitness to command.

In a battle at Camden, South Carolina, on 16 August 1780, General Cornwallis's troops scattered the Virginia and North Carolina militiamen. The rout was shameful, the worst American defeat of the war.[106] General Gates managed to arrive in Charlotte, North Carolina, sixty miles away, well *ahead* of his fleeing army. Alexander Hamilton expressed the views of most Americans when he asked: "Was there ever such an instance of a general running away . . . from his whole army?"[107] Behind him, Gates left the mortally wounded Baron de Kalb, another of the brave foreigners who had come to fight for America. By October, Congress agreed with Washington. Gates was out; Greene was in.

Lord Cornwallis had the help of Colonel Banastre Tarleton, a twenty-six-year-old dashing cavalry officer who specialized in raiding the coasts. Tarleton came within minutes of capturing Virginia's governor, Thomas Jefferson, as well as leaders of the Old Dominion's legislature, in June of 1781. Fortunately, Jefferson, Patrick Henry, and other Virginia Patriot leaders were warned in time. Jack Jouett rode all night, fifty miles through dense woodlands along Indian trails, to carry the warning to Jefferson's home at Monticello. Captain Jouett is justly known as "the Paul Revere of the South."*

The South experienced the full rigors of war—actually civil war—as Loyalists clashed with Patriot forces for two years. Francis Marion, renowned as the "Swamp Fox," harassed the British and Tory forces in South Carolina.

---

* Hearken good people: awhile abide
  And hear of stout Jack Jouett's ride;
  How he rushed his steed, nor stopped nor stayed
  Till he warned the people of Tarleton's raid.
  —*Charlottesville Daily Progress,* 1909

General Marion's fearless raids saved South Carolina from being overrun by the British.[108] Neglected by a distracted Congress, Marion's contribution to the war effort was generously recognized by Virginia's "Lighthorse Harry" Lee.[109]* Cornwallis found he could win battles and take towns, but he could not get supplies or information from the people.

Nathanael Greene was the son of a Rhode Island farmer, a Quaker. His appointment to head the Southern army was very popular with the soldiers.

General Greene encouraged Patriots in the South to operate independently. They won a signal victory over British Major Patrick Ferguson and his American Loyalists at Kings Mountain, South Carolina, in October 1780. The intrepid Ferguson made a point of listening to his American Loyalists and not treating them with disdain, as so many regular British officers did. Major Ferguson had brought his troop to this high point, saying he could defend it against "God almighty and all the rebels out of hell." When Ferguson fell, at the head of his forces, he had taken seven rifle balls, and his hat and clothing were shot through.[110] Ferguson's defeated forces cried for "Quarter!"—a plea for mercy. But the Patriot soldiers answered back, "Tarleton's Quarter!" as they killed the desperate Tories. Tarleton had slaughtered surrendering Patriots at the Battle of Waxhaws the previous May.[111]

General Daniel Morgan, affectionately called the "Old Wagoner" by his men because he had been a wagon driver in the French and Indian War, won another great victory at Cowpens, South Carolina, on 17 January 1781. There, Morgan decisively defeated Tarleton's British regulars and sent Tarleton himself scurrying back to Cornwallis.[112]

Greene fought Cornwallis's force at Guilford Court House, near Greensboro, North Carolina, on 15 March 1781. Greene was defeated in the fierce battle, but his forces maintained order and so mauled Cornwallis's army that the British had no choice but to regroup and fall

---

* South Carolinians long remembered General Lighthorse Harry Lee's enthusiasm for their hero, the Swamp Fox. They later rallied around General Lee's even more famous son— General Robert E. Lee.

back for supplies. Greene had won no major battles, but he had forced Cornwallis to exhaust himself and his army, marching more than five hundred miles through the Virginia and North Carolina countryside.[113]

Greene's success is shown by Cornwallis's letter to Sir Henry Clinton in New York: "I am quite tired of marching about the country. . . . If we mean an offensive war in America, we must abandon New York and bring our whole force into Virginia."[114] The wearing down of the British forces in the South is what led them to Yorktown. Nathanael Greene, Dan Morgan, and the guerilla leaders Swamp Fox Francis Marion and Thomas Sumter achieved this result.

General Washington, with the help of Rochambeau and seven thousand French soldiers, was preparing to lay siege to the British in New York City in the summer of 1781. Then stunning news came. On August 14, Washington received a message informing him that French Admiral Francois Joseph Paul, the comte de Grasse, was bringing twenty-eight warships to the Chesapeake Bay.[115] Leaving a portion of his army behind to deceive General Clinton, Washington and Rochambeau quickly departed for Virginia. His swift, bold move, taking the bulk of his forces away from their positions around British-occupied New York City and striking out for the South, may have been his greatest achievement of the war.[116]

Local command of the sea—critical to American success—was established thanks to the French. On September 5, Admiral de Grasse defeated a smaller British squadron in the Battle of the Capes.[117] The battle was fought between Virginia's Cape Henry and Cape Charles, and it prevented Cornwallis's force from being evacuated by sea—or even resupplied.

By 26 September 1781, Washington's combined American-French force of seventeen thousand—including Rochambeau's regulars, Lafayette's and Anthony Wayne's Virginians, and reinforcements from de Grasse—had Cornwallis's seven thousand British troops trapped on the York Peninsula, a spit of land that juts into the Chesapeake Bay.[118]

Lafayette had assured Washington that Cornwallis could not escape. When he and Washington met again, the enthusiastic young Frenchman grabbed Washington and smothered him with kisses. Washington, who had begun to look upon Lafayette as a son, did not object.[119] He quickly ordered a siege. Following the tactics taught by the great French military engineer Sébastien Le Prestre de Vauban, the allied force soon began to squeeze the life out of the encircled British. Lord Cornwallis used the Yorktown home of Virginia's Governor Thomas Nelson as his headquarters—and the governor urged Washington to cannonade his own house.[120]

Within weeks, Cornwallis's men were reduced to eating their horses. Their attempts at answering the daily battering from Washington's artillery were feeble. Once, when a British cannonball landed in the American trenches, Colonel Alexander Hamilton jumped back and took shelter behind the ample Henry Knox. The normally genial Knox scolded Hamilton, warning him "not to make a breastwork of me again!"[121]

Finally, on 19 October 1781, Lord Cornwallis bowed to the inevitable and surrendered unconditionally. As his men marched out to lay down their weapons, they were surrounded by French hussars; Cornwallis was nowhere to be seen.[122] Claiming illness, he had sent his second-in-command, General Charles O'Hara, to offer his sword. First, the embarrassed O'Hara tried to give it to General Rochambeau, who nodded in the direction of General Washington. But Washington, standing on ceremony, indicated that only *his* second-in-command, General Benjamin Lincoln, could properly take the surrender.[123]

The common redcoat soldiers wept in frustration and smashed their muskets. British drummer boys bashed in their drumheads.[124] They were all headed for a prisoner-of-war camp. The British band played "The World Turned Upside Down." Indeed, it was.

VII. A DANGEROUS PEACE

Washington returned to New York to keep General Clinton hemmed in. As long as the British controlled the seas, however, he had little hope of starving the British out. King George III, who had cried out, "Oh, God, it's all over!" when he received the news of Yorktown, faced the defeat in Parliament of Lord North's government in March 1782. The new British government determined to make peace.

Congress dispatched John Jay, the head of its committee on foreign affairs, to join Benjamin Franklin, Henry Laurens, and John Adams for peace talks in Paris. While the negotiations dragged on and on, Congress was sinking further into debt, and its inability to pay the army was creating a very dangerous situation. Washington knew this. In May 1782, he received a shocking letter from Colonel Lewis Nicola, an Irish immigrant and former commander of Fort Mifflin. Nicola, citing the rising disorder in the army and the country, urged Washington to *use* the army to set himself up as a king. Washington's response was short and sharp:

> No occurrence in the course of the war has given me more painful sensations than your information of there being such ideas existing in the army. . . . I must view with abhorrence and reprehend with severity [an idea that was] big with the greatest mischiefs that can befall my country.[125]

Always aware, painfully aware, of the impression he was making, Washington demanded to know what in his conduct could ever have given rise to such a notion. In forcefully putting down Nicola's suggestion, Washington drove a stake through the heart of monarchy in America: if he would not be king, *nobody* could be king. And that was the end of kingship in America *forever*. America has had forty-five presidents—including some liars, "lemons," and losers—but we have never had a tyrant. For that we can thank George Washington.

An unpaid army that is unable to disband but not fully engaged against the enemy is a very dangerous instrument. Early in the next year, 1783, there were more rumblings of discontent. Anonymous pamphlets began to circulate in the camp around Newburgh, New York, urging the army to march on Congress to enforce its legitimate demands *at the point of a bayonet.* Washington summoned his officers to a meeting for March 15. He planned his address carefully. Appearing before a large, sullen gathering, Washington made a dramatic entrance. He urgently pleaded with his men to understand the slowness of deliberative bodies, to have patience. Do not, he pleaded, "open the flood gates of civil discord, and deluge our rising empire in blood."[126]

The officers' response to this powerful appeal was an angry silence. They remained unconvinced. They had heard all that before. Their families were hungry, and the Congress was doing nothing to honor its promises to those who had bled and died for independence.

Then Washington remembered a letter he'd received from a congressman. He rummaged through his pockets for an embarrassing few seconds. Opening the envelope, he realized he could not read the small handwriting. Slowly, deliberately, he went through his pockets again, this time bringing out his spectacles. Few of the officers present had ever seen their fifty-one-year-old commander in chief wearing eyeglasses. "Gentlemen," said Washington as he carefully put them on, "you will permit me to put on my spectacles, for I have not only grown gray but almost blind in the service of my country."[127] His soft words turned away wrath. Many of the battle-hardened veterans wept openly. The movement toward a military coup d'état collapsed at that moment.

When word came of the final ratification of the Treaty of Paris, a treaty in which American independence was fully recognized, the British agreed to evacuate New York and Charleston. In November 1783, the redcoats boarded their ships and sailed away from Manhattan. Washington invited his officers to dine with him at Fraunces Tavern, near Wall Street, in what is now the city's financial district. There, on 4 December 1783, another emotional scene occurred. Washington was no marble man, as his grim visage on the dollar bill would suggest. At the conclusion of the evening, when he invited his officers to come and take him by the hand, all of those present, including Washington, dissolved in tears.

"With a heart full of love and gratitude, I now take leave of you," he told the assembled officers. "I most devoutly wish that your latter days will be as prosperous and happy as your former ones have been glorious and honorable."[128]

It remained for Washington to return to Congress—the source of all his authority—to close out his service in the war. Meeting in Annapolis, Maryland, Congress was eager to welcome him back. At noon, on 23 December 1783, Washington appeared in the Senate Chamber of the Old Maryland State House. The chamber was packed with members, visiting dignitaries, and ladies. Washington rose to congratulate Congress on the successful achievement of independence and peace. When he came to that part of his text that contained a tribute to his fellow officers, his hands shook, and he struggled to maintain his composure. Then he closed with these words: "And of presenting myself before them [Congress] to surrender into their hands the trust committed to me and to claim the indulgence of retiring from the service of my country."[129]

King George III had said if Washington voluntarily gave up power, then he truly *would* be the greatest man on earth. Cromwell hadn't done it. Napoleon would not do it. But Washington did it.

How great a general was Washington? Winners *always* seem like great generals. He lost more battles than any general in modern history, indeed. But he won some very big ones.

Washington had many superior qualities—bravery, self-control, administrative skill, strategic sense, tactical boldness—and an ability to learn from his mistakes. But most of all, he had *judgment*. He refused to burn American towns and refused to take hostages or shoot collaborators. He kept the army under firm control. He *always* subordinated himself and his restive army to the authority of Congress. So despite short-comings and defeats, he was greater than any other American general of the Revolution.

Congress's official response was delivered by its president, Thomas Mifflin. In an earlier day, Mifflin had conspired to replace Washington with Horatio Gates. Fortunately for Mifflin and for us, his text was prepared for him by Thomas Jefferson:

> You have conducted the great military contest with wisdom and fortitude, invariably regarding the rights of the civil power, through all the disasters and changes. . . . You have persevered until these United States have been enabled, under a just Providence, to close the war in freedom, safety and independence. . . . And for you, we address to Him our earnest prayers that a life so beloved may be fostered with all His care.[130]

Freedom, safety, independence, and peace. By 1783, that was already George Washington's legacy to his country. Soon, he would give more.

TWO

REFLECTION AND CHOICE: FRAMING THE CONSTITUTION

(1783–1789)

I. A CRITICAL PERIOD

The Articles of Confederation, under which the federal government operated during the nation's early war-filled years, was designed primarily to help win independence. The states, under the Articles, retained a great deal of independence. Congress had the power to wage war, conduct foreign affairs, borrow money, deal with the Indians, and settle disputes among the states.[1] But, in order to raise an army or cover its bills, Congress could only *requisition* men and money from the state governments. If the states failed to meet their obligations to the Union, Congress could not compel them. For major issues, it took nine states to render a decision. The Articles instituted neither an executive branch nor a judiciary.

Despite these drawbacks, the Congress under the Articles of Confederation did boast some remarkable accomplishments. After independence and peace, its greatest achievement was the Northwest

Ordinance of 1787. From the old Northwest Territory would be carved a huge region—the modern states of Ohio, Indiana, Michigan, Illinois, Wisconsin, and part of Minnesota. It was the culmination of a series of land measures that began as early as 1780.[2] Under that wise, far-seeing measure, slavery was forever banned in those lands.[3] Settlers in the territories could establish free governments and write constitutions, and once they had achieved sixty thousand inhabitants, they could apply for admission to the Union as new states. Each new state would be admitted on an equal basis with all previous states.[4]

This was the first time in the history of the world that the principle of equality was so recognized. American territories would not be colonies, held in perpetual subordination to the "mother" country. We had learned from the failure of the British Empire.

A critically important feature of the Northwest Ordinance was its treatment of religion. The first article stated: "No person, demeaning himself in a peaceable and orderly manner shall ever be molested on account of his mode of worship, or religious sentiments, in the said territory." This enlightened principle was little short of revolutionary for its time. No other government had ever laid out such a principle for administering newly acquired territories.[5]

Despite these advances for civil and religious liberty, the *financial* situation of the new United States was spinning out of control. Some states tried to solve debt problems by printing paper money and forcing the near-worthless currency on creditors. The Union also showed signs of coming unglued over foreign affairs. The Articles of Confederation made it difficult for Congress to ratify treaties.

Strains on the Union grew. Most alarming of all was an armed uprising in Massachusetts. Revolutionary War veteran Captain Daniel Shays led an "army" of desperate farmers who tried to close down the courts to prevent foreclosures and imprisonment for debt. When Shays's ragged forces tried to seize a federal arsenal, they were repulsed with cannon fire.[6] The state organized the militia with funding from major merchants and soon put down Shays's Rebellion. Those captured rebels who were sentenced to death, however, were soon pardoned.[7]

Shays's Rebellion alarmed most of the responsible leaders of the Revolution. George Washington was especially upset. "I feel . . . infinitely more than I can express . . . for the disorders that have arisen. Good God! Who besides a Tory could have foreseen, or a Briton predicted them!"[8] Franklin, recently returned from France, was one of the mildest. He said, "Having dreaded giving too much power to our governors, now we are faced with the danger of too little obedience in the subjects."[9]

To Thomas Jefferson, faraway in France, too much was being made of Shays's Rebellion. Jefferson wrote to Madison and famously put the case for periodic uprisings:

> I hold it that a little rebellion now and then is a good thing, and as necessary in the political world as storms in the physical. Unsuccessful rebellions, indeed, generally establish the encroachments on the rights of the people which have produced them. An observation of this truth should render honest republican governors so mild in their punishment of rebellions as not to discourage them too much. It is a medicine necessary for the sound health of government.[10]

His friend did not agree. Once again, this may have been an example of the distortions of distance. Paris was far from the disorders in Massachusetts. Madison was alarmed that the "seditious party have become formidable . . . and have opened a communication with the [British] viceroy of Canada."[11]

Madison had already begun his active cooperation with Alexander Hamilton the previous September at the Annapolis Convention. That meeting of delegates from a mere five states had accomplished one thing only: it called for a general convention for the following May in Philadelphia. In Hamilton's words, delegates were being summoned "to render the Constitution of the Federal Government adequate to the exigencies of the Union."[12] This was a bold move.

Madison thought such boldness was necessary. He warned of monarchists' maneuvers to capitalize on the discontent. "All the real friends of the Revolution" needed to come together "to perpetuate the Union and redeem the honor of the Republican name," he wrote.[13] Washington, too, worried that supporters of an American king would take advantage of the rising disorders. He could hardly believe what he was hearing: "Even respectable [citizens] speak of [monarchy] without horror."[14] Madison knew he had one important supporter for his and Hamilton's project—the *most* important one. George Washington prodded the younger man on. He wrote Madison in November 1786:

> No morn ever dawned more favorably than ours did; and no day was ever more clouded than the present! Wisdom and good examples are necessary to rescue the political machine from the impending storm.[15]

II. "THE GREAT LITTLE MADISON"

James Madison, small and slight, usually wore black. He was no match in oratory for the powerful Patrick Henry or other strong speakers. Yet, if knowledge is power, Madison was a Titan. He had spent his days in the spring and summer of 1786 "boning up" on the history of every previous experiment with *republican* government. He knew the strengths and weaknesses of all those states in which the people governed. In his extensive reading, Madison had help from his friend Jefferson. The American minister in Paris had sent to Montpelier, Madison's country home, a "literary cargo" of books on history, politics, and economics.[16]

Madison's immediate concern in the upcoming convention in Philadelphia was whether General George Washington would attend. Washington fully supported Madison and Hamilton's efforts, but he hesitated about whether he could go. Washington's reasons for holding back were weighty. He had dramatically surrendered his commission in Annapolis less than four years before. For that selfless act, he was revered throughout the world.[17] Would plunging back into politics now sully his reputation? Also, he had told his friends in the Society of the Cincinnati—an honorary group of officers from the Continental Army—that he could *not* attend their meeting in Philadelphia.* Would his attendance at the federal convention in the same city at the same time now constitute a breach of his word to his dearest wartime friends? Then there was the very real danger that the convention would fail.[18] In fact, Benjamin Franklin had warned of that possibility. In a letter to Thomas Jefferson in Paris, Franklin wrote:

> I hope Good from their Meeting [in Philadelphia]. Indeed, if it does not do good, it must do Harm, as it will show that we have not Wisdom enough among us to govern ourselves; and will strengthen the opinion of some Political writers that popular Governments cannot long support themselves.[19]

Finally, Washington bowed to the urgent pleas of army colleague Henry Knox, Virginia governor Edmund Randolph, Madison, and Hamilton, and agreed to attend.[20] He was greeted upon his arrival in Philadelphia by pealing church bells, booming cannon, cheering crowds, and a mounted troop of Pennsylvania cavalry. He went straight to the grand home of Robert Morris, where he would lodge throughout the summer. Morris, who had served as financial secretary under the Confederation, repeatedly saving the Patriot cause, was Philadelphia's richest merchant. As soon as he had settled in, Washington headed for Benjamin Franklin's home on Market Street. There, under his famous mulberry tree, the old sage was greeting arriving delegates. Franklin was president (in today's terms, governor) of Pennsylvania and the official

---

* Thomas Jefferson was among the critics of the Society of the Cincinnati who saw it as a budding aristocracy that threatened to bring hereditary privilege into the new republic. Washington took Jefferson's criticisms seriously and tried to reform the bylaws of the Society.

host of the convention. Washington had not seen Franklin since 1775, but they had been friends since Franklin supplied Braddock's army in 1755.

By agreeing to attend, Washington and Franklin lent their enormous prestige to the project of Madison and Hamilton. Washington and Franklin also, interestingly, were two of the Founders who lacked a formal education. Many of the others among the fifty-five who framed the Constitution had received college educations at such institutions as Princeton (9), Yale (4), William & Mary (4), Harvard (3), Columbia (2), University of Pennsylvania (2), and such British institutions as Oxford (1) and St. Andrews (1).

When the delegates assembled, tardily, on May 25, they unanimously elected General Washington president of the convention. They met in the old Pennsylvania State House, now known as Independence Hall. Their first decision—to conduct all their discussions secretly—was probably essential to completing their business, but it was not uncontroversial. When Jefferson learned of it, he wrote immediately to John Adams, who was serving as the American minister in London. Jefferson strongly disapproved, but the reputations of Washington and Franklin and many of the other delegates allayed the suspicions of most Americans.

James Madison's first decision at the Constitutional Convention would echo down the centuries. He took up his seat near the presiding officer—Washington—and began taking copious notes of the proceedings.[21] He would later say that he was absent from the sessions for only a few minutes at a time, so that only the briefest of comments by a delegate would have gone unrecorded. Each evening, following the day's meeting, Madison would painstakingly write out his record from the shorthand notes he had taken that day. Thus we have the best record of the convention's proceedings from the man who was the main engine of the meeting.

Madison had crafted a plan of government based on his extensive studies. With typical tact, he asked Governor Randolph of Virginia to introduce the plan. Soon, it became known as the Virginia Plan. It was a breathtaking proposal because it went far beyond the Confederation Congress's instructions to the convention. Congress approved the

Philadelphia meeting "for the sole and express purpose of revising the Articles of Confederation."[22] The Virginia Plan—which called for a two-chamber national legislature based on population—was a bold departure. It represented the entering bid of the large states.*

Soon, William Paterson of New Jersey responded with his state's plan, the key element of which was equal representation of the states in a one-house legislature, just as it was under the Confederation Congress. The New Jersey Plan became the small states' response to the Virginia Plan. Both plans contained many specific details, which Pennsylvania's James Wilson—a key ally of Madison—compared and contrasted for the delegates. The Scottish-born Wilson had a powerful, organized mind and was a strong proponent of a federal union:

Virginia Plan proposes two branches in the legislature.

Jersey, a single legislative body.

Virginia, the legislative powers derived from the people.

Jersey, from the states.

Virginia, a single executive.

Jersey, more than one.

Virginia, a majority of the legislature can act.

Jersey, a small minority can control.

Virginia, the legislature can legislate on all national concerns.

Jersey, only on limited objects.

Virginia, the legislature can negative all state laws.

Jersey, giving power to the executive to compel obedience by force.

Virginia, to remove the executive by impeachment.

Jersey, on application of a majority of states.

Virginia, for the establishment of inferior judiciary tribunals.

Jersey, no provision.[23]

---

* "Large," in this sense, meant greater in population, not necessarily in territory. Georgia, which was the second largest state after Virginia, was a decidedly small state in the Constitutional Convention because of its sparse population.

As temperatures outside the convention hall rose, tempers inside the crowded chamber rose too. Delaware's Gunning Bedford—described as "fluent, fat, and angry"—arose to challenge the Virginia Plan. The large states "insist . . . they will never hurt or injure the lesser states. *I do not, gentlemen, trust you!*" Then Bedford shocked the delegates with this response to the threat of the large states to form a federal union *without* the small states: "The small states will find some foreign ally of more honor and good faith who will take them by the hand and do them justice!"[24]

The delegates knew this was no idle threat. Spain had been secretly dealing with settlers in the western territories. There was talk of disunion in the Mississippi Valley. British ministers had contemptuously told John Adams, the ambassador in London, that they would rather deal with *thirteen* state governments than with him.[25] And no one could be quite sure what part France or Holland might take if the Union fell apart.

Alexander Hamilton stunned many delegates when he arose to attack *both* plans. Both plans, he charged, gave too much power to the people. He thought the people were "turbulent and changing" and they "seldom judge or determine right."[26] Hamilton urged a purely *national* government, with states having no more authority than counties do in relation to the states. Hamilton argued for giving propertied men a larger share of authority and influence in the new government.[27]

Did Hamilton really believe this? Or was he skillfully laying out a case for a centralized government dominated by wealth that would make Madison's Virginia Plan look moderate by comparison?

With tensions building, the revered Benjamin Franklin made one of his rare speeches to the convention. He recalled that when the Continental Congress sat in days of great danger, they had asked God's help in prayer. "Have we forgotten our powerful Friend? Or do we imagine we no longer need its assistance?" Franklin said he had lived a long time—he was the oldest delegate—"And the longer I live the more convincing proofs I see of this truth, *that God governs in the affairs of men.* And if a sparrow cannot fall to the ground without his notice, is it probable than an empire can rise without his aid?" Franklin concluded, quoting the Bible: "Except the Lord build the house, they labor in vain that build it."[28] We know that the delegates did *not* follow Franklin's suggestion to begin their sessions with prayer—they had no funds to hire a clergyman! But they didn't break up, either, and that answered Franklin's fervent prayer.

To answer Gunning Bedford's furious assault, "the great little Madison" (his wife's charming description of him) responded with invincible logic: "If the large states possess the avarice and ambition with which they are charged, will the small ones in their neighborhood be more secure when all control of a general government is withdrawn?"[29] Who would really suffer more from *disunion*, he asked mildly.

Unless the deadlock could be broken, the convention would fail. George Washington had seen this danger before. It had nearly caused the Continental Army to collapse. Washington called this assertion of a veto power by the states the "monster sovereignty."[30]

Connecticut's Roger Sherman arose to break the deadlock. Sherman was a small, spare man, who dressed plainly and wore his hair straight back. Unadorned and simply spoken, Sherman had risen from humble beginnings to become a respected figure in his little state. Sherman—Madison called him "Mr. Sharman" in his notes—offered what became the Great Compromise: the national legislature would be comprised of *two* houses—a House of Representatives based on population and a Senate based on the principle of equality of the states. Madison bitterly regretted this compromise. He thought it violated the essential principle of republican government—the equality of citizens. Franklin, too, opposed it. Only when they saw it as the only way to save the Union did they accept it. This was a greater source of dissension than any other issue before the convention, Madison would later write.[31]

Now, curiously, once they found themselves protected by a federal Senate, many of the small state delegates began to support a *stronger* federal government. Other issues remained to be resolved. The executive would be single—a president. He would be elected not by the legislature,

but by an electoral college specially chosen every four years for that purpose. The president would have a veto over legislation, but two-thirds of
Congress could override his veto. He could negotiate treaties, but two-
thirds of the Senate had to ratify. The president would serve a term of
four years, but he would be eligible for reelection indefinitely.* A president
who abused his powers could be impeached by a majority of the House of
Representatives but could only be removed from office following trial and
conviction by two-thirds of the Senate. The president would be the commander in chief of the armed forces, but he would have to ask Congress
for a declaration of war. And Congress always held the "power of the
purse" to hold him in check.

Once it had been determined that the House of Representatives
would represent the people directly, the delegates required that all bills
for taxation must originate in the House. Nor could monies be appropriated unless they also originated in the House. The federal judiciary
would try "real cases and controversies" arising out of the Constitution
and laws. Although the Constitution does not say so, judicial review of
federal and state laws was *presumed* when the Framers asserted that "this
Constitution and all laws and treaties made pursuant thereto shall be *the
supreme law of the land.*" This supremacy clause assured ours would be a
federal union, that the states would no longer have power over the Union.

Most discussion of the Constitution and religion today focuses naturally on the First Amendment, but the original Constitution contained
a powerful provision that receives less attention. Article VI, Section 3
states: "No religious Test shall ever be required as a Qualification to any
Office or public Trust under the United States." This was a revolutionary
breakthrough for religious liberty, one of the most advanced statements
in the world—then or even now.

Maryland's John Carroll, a Catholic, had noted that "the American

---

* This was changed by the Twenty-Second Amendment in 1951, which limited the president
to two terms.

army swarmed with Roman Catholic soldiers." How could the new government justify denying them full civil rights? Similarly, Jewish Americans had participated in the struggle for independence, notably Haym Solomon, who had arranged loans for the Continental Congress and helped save Washington's army from starvation. By banning religious tests for office, the Constitution assured that religion would never be a bar to any able American serving the new republic.

But what about *slavery*? "Persons held to service or labor." That is the awkward phrase the Constitution uses to describe slaves. After the fight over large state / small state representation, the treatment of slavery became the greatest source of conflict. Very early, a clash occurred over this "peculiar institution."* The Founders' reticence in dealing with this explosive topic came from their belief, as Madison pointed out, that it was "wrong to admit in the Constitution the idea that there could be property in men."[32] At the time of the Constitutional Convention, slavery existed in nearly all of the states—and had existed since they were founded. Massachusetts had abolished slavery and four states—New Hampshire, Rhode Island, Connecticut, and Pennsylvania—were in the process of doing so. Emancipation was advancing in New York and New Jersey. The Founders believed that slavery was on the path to extinction.[33] Ninety percent of slaves lived in the South.[34]

The Founders were born into a society that permitted slavery. Connecticut's Roger Sherman called the slave trade "iniquitous." New York's Gouverneur Morris, a brilliant orator and a representative of great wealth, stood stoutly on his wooden leg and denounced slavery in the harshest terms. This "nefarious institution" was "the curse of heaven in the states where it prevailed," he said, ignoring the fact that his own New York still permitted slavery.[35] He compared the slave states with the free regions. Slavery is characterized by misery and poverty, but the free

---

    * *Peculiar* in these times did not mean "odd" or "strange" as it does to us today. It meant "characteristic of" or "unique to."

regions (actually, states with relatively few slaves) were characterized by "rich and noble cultivation."[36]

This was brave talk from a man who was a close friend to George Washington. Sitting silently in the chair, Washington was America's most prominent slaveholder. But Morris was hardly alone in his disdain for slavery. Washington's good friend and neighbor, George Mason, was also a slaveholder. Still, Mason expressed the enlightened prevailing opinion of the Upper South: "Slavery discourages arts and manufactures. The poor despise labor when performed by slaves. Slavery prevents whites from immigrating and produces the most pernicious effects on manners." Those were the practical reasons. Mason went further: "Every master of slaves is born a petty tyrant. They bring the judgment of heaven on a country!" Mason passionately called for the general government to *prevent* the increase of slavery.[37]

High-minded as they were, these noble arguments ran into a stone wall of resistance. "Interest alone is the governing principle of nations," South Carolina's John Rutledge answered coolly.[38] Morris, Mason, and Madison did not move him with their moral case against slavery. Just as bluntly, Rutledge said that *any* attempt to interfere with slavery in the states would result in the South's refusing to ratify the Constitution.[39] Once again, the threat of disunion loomed.

Faced with this impasse, the Founders carefully crafted a Constitution that avoided even mentioning *slavery*, Africans, or the slave trade. It dealt with slavery by talking *around* the subject. First, it based representation in the House of Representatives on a *three-fifths* formula carried over from the Articles of Confederation. The Constitution required a census to count the whole number of free persons, to exempt "Indians not taxed," and to count "three-fifths of all other Persons." Second, they compromised on abolishing the African slave trade by permitting Congress to outlaw it, but only twenty years after ratification of the Constitution. Third, the Constitution required states to return to their states of origin all "persons held to service or labor" in another state. In effect, this was a fugitive slave clause.

Volumes have been written about these *compromises* with the existence

of slavery. Some have claimed that by compromising with this hated institution, the Founders surrendered all moral claims to being defenders of
liberty and human rights. Foreigners laughed when England's Samuel
Johnson asked: "How is it that we hear the loudest *yelps* for liberty among
the drivers of Negroes?" Some even argue that they voided the philosophy
of the Declaration that "all men are created equal."[40]

It is clear that all but a tiny few of the delegates to the Constitutional
Convention morally *disapproved* of slavery. It is equally clear that not a
word of the Constitution would have to be changed if the states continued
to emancipate the slaves on their own.

Even some of the compromises with slavery can be seen in this light.
For example, the Three-Fifths Compromise was a mere mathematical
formula, advanced by Northern delegates, and was never intended as a
statement that the Founders thought slaves to be less than fully human.
After all, they referred to slaves as *persons*. Who, after all, wanted slaves
counted fully for purposes of representation? *Slaveholders*. This would artificially increase their representation in the House of Representatives and as
well in the electoral college. Also, and this cannot be stressed enough, the
Three-Fifths Compromise provided an *incentive* for states to continue the
emancipation process. When a state freed its slaves, it would get *increased*
representation in the House of Representatives. And, because each state's
electoral vote was based on its number of representatives, the state that
abolished slavery would also be *rewarded* in the selection of the president.

Madison, we know, was deeply downcast over the failure of the delegates
to outlaw the African slave trade immediately. He thought it "dishonorable
to the American character."[41] Yet the choice was not between ending or not
ending the slave trade. If the Founders had not accepted a twenty-year delay
in banning the trade, South Carolina and Georgia would have stayed out
of the Union and there would have been *no ban at all* on this "execrable
traffic." The virtue of this compromise was that it clearly and unequivocally
spelled the end of the slave trade in the not-too-distant future.

The fugitive slave clause was a bitter pill Northern delegates had to swallow. They did so only because they sincerely believed the Constitution would not have been ratified without it.

Benjamin Franklin was dissatisfied with the slavery compromises. He wasn't big on equal representation of the states either. But in the closing hours of the convention, he used his famous wit to try to soothe raw nerves. He quoted the highborn French lady who said: "I don't know how it is, sister, that I meet with nobody but myself that's always in the right."[42] He shared with his fellow delegates a British writer's description of the "only" difference between the Anglican and Roman Catholic churches: "The Church of Rome is infallible and the Church of England is never in the wrong."[43] Franklin went on to make the serious point that the older he grew, the more he doubted his own judgment and the more regard he had for the opinions of others.

That was a powerful statement coming from Franklin. Considered the greatest sage of the age, if even *he* could so humbly put aside his strongly held views, how could other delegates stubbornly persist in opposition? Yet some of them did just that. Two powerful Virginians, George Mason and Edmund Randolph, would refuse to sign. So would Maryland's Luther Martin, whose long-winded, rambling, sometimes boozy speeches against federal power had bored so many.[44] Massachusetts's Elbridge Gerry was the only Northern delegate who refused to sign. Most of these *nonsigners* argued that the Constitution created a federal government that was *too* powerful.

George Washington's influence is harder to find. He spoke very rarely. Once, when a delegate suggested limiting the standing army to five thousand, Washington dryly observed that it would be a good idea *provided that we could also require that no enemy would ever invade with more than five thousand troops.* Just before adjournment, he descended from the chair to encourage delegates to amend a provision for representation in the House of Representatives. By changing the formula from 40,000:1 to 30,000:1, he argued, the House would be closer to the people it represented. The change—toward a more *democratic* House—was adopted unanimously.

Washington may have had the least formal education of any member of the convention, yet still he was held in awe. Once, when he sternly rebuked members for leaving notes of the secret discussions where they could be picked up, the greatest men on the continent sat shamefaced like errant schoolboys.[45] Another incident showed Washington's famous reserve. When delegates were talking about it, Gouverneur Morris disagreed with them. He was sure he could approach his good friend quite familiarly, he said. Alexander Hamilton bet Morris a dinner he would not put his hand on the general's shoulder and greet him. When Morris said: "My dear general, how happy I am to see you look so well," Washington stepped back and froze Morris with a disapproving stare.[46] Happily, Washington did not hold a grudge, and within days he was seen laughing at the merry Morris's witticisms.

It was Morris who shared Washington's confidence in the constitutional project. He noted that Washington told him it was all too likely the people would reject *any* new Constitution. "If to please the people, we offer what we ourselves disapprove, how can we afterwards defend our work? Let us raise a standard to which the wise and honest can repair. The event is in the hand of God."[47]

At the last session, Franklin remarked that he had long watched the carving on the back of the presiding officer's chair. Was it, he asked himself, a rising or a setting sun? With the signing of the Constitution, Franklin said, he was now sure. "I have the happiness to know that it is a rising and not a setting sun."[48]

When a lady asked him what kind of government he and his fellow delegates had given them, Franklin replied: "A republic, if you can keep it."

III. THE STRUGGLE FOR RATIFICATION

When the delegates left Philadelphia in September 1787, prospects for ratification of the new Constitution were by no means bright. Yes, they had not broken up in bitter disagreement. But of fifty-five who convened in May, only thirty-nine were willing to put their names to the final draft, which was polished and refined by the expert penmanship of Gouverneur Morris. It must have taken courage for some of those who refused to then face the stern, disapproving stare of George Washington.[49] They knew they could be committing political suicide by their failure to support the Constitution.

Madison knew that key battleground states would be Massachusetts, New York, and his home state of Virginia. Rhode Island—"Rogue Island," as some of the delegates called it—had refused to send representatives. The old Confederation Congress, then meeting in New York, helped immeasurably by accepting the draft of the Constitution and affirming its call for "nine necessary states" before it could take effect. Had they stuck to the Articles' *unanimity* requirement, Rhode Island, or any one recalcitrant state, could have doomed the entire project.

Even so, "the nine necessary states" to ratify would be hard to find. Madison hurried to New York and began to work for ratification with Alexander Hamilton and John Jay. Their joint efforts—a series of essays published in pamphlet form—became known as *The Federalist Papers*, and the two parties that formed in favor of and in opposition to the new Constitution quickly adopted the names of *Federalist* and *Antifederalist*. The Antifederalists were formidable. In Massachusetts, they included (at least at the start) Sam Adams and John Hancock, and in New York, the powerful Livingstons and the Clintons. In Virginia, Patrick Henry led the opposition. He had memorably refused to attend the Philadelphia convention ("I smelt a rat"). In addition, the Lees and George Mason spoke against ratification.

Hamilton began *The Federalist Papers* with an essay by "Publius," a name taken up by his fellow writers. They wrote anonymously, and it has taken extensive efforts by later scholars to determine which man wrote which essay. The essays—written at a feverish pace while the debates raged in the states—had a certain "slap-dash" quality to them.[50] Even so,

The Federalist Papers has become a treasure of political theory and the most reliable source of information about the *intentions* of the Founders. George Washington praised the work and even paid to have it reprinted in Richmond. He wrote to Hamilton:

> That work will merit the Notice of Posterity; because in it are candidly and ably discussed the principles of freedom and the topics of government, which will always be interesting to mankind.[51]

Madison, who may have lacked Jefferson's winged prose, nonetheless laid out in compelling terms the case for the new government. As he had done with Gunning Bedford's furious attacks, he turned the arguments of the Antifederalists on their head. First, he argued, "If men were angels, no government would be necessary." Then he continued, laying out the best case for a system of checks and balances: "Ambition must be made to counteract ambition." He showed how the Constitution enabled each branch—executive, legislative, and judicial—to perform its assigned function, while resisting power grabs by other branches. To critics who said that no republic—a government of the people—could exist over so vast a territory, Madison pointed out that previous failed attempts at republican government failed *because they were not extensive enough*! Here, in *Federalist* No. 10, he boldly argued that free people inevitably formed "factions." These factions corresponded to their economic, religious, and social interests. In a far-flung republic—like the expanding United States—no one faction, no one *coalition* of factions, could form that would oppress those in the minority. The larger the number of contending groups, therefore, the more likely freedom would be to prevail.

If Madison was especially concerned to make the case for *the preservation of liberty,* Hamilton argued passionately for "energy in the executive." Government under the Articles was dying away because it could not enforce its obligations—neither enforcing treaties with foreign powers nor raising and equipping an army and a navy at home. Hamilton wanted a government that could defend the country, promote a strong economy, and create a stable future for investment. When writing of the judiciary in *Federalist* No. 78, Hamilton stated his belief that the courts would always be "the least dangerous branch" because judges possessed "neither the sword (executive) nor the purse (legislative)."

The Federalist Papers remains today the best source for explaining the ideas and principles that Americans held in the 1780s and which, to a great extent, Americans still hold. Although Hamilton is often seen as an antidemocratic figure, aligning himself with the rich and wellborn, he could write as memorably of natural law and human rights as any of the Founders:

> The sacred rights of mankind are not to be rummaged for among old parchments or musty records. They are written, as with a sunbeam, in the whole volume of human nature, by the hand of the Divinity itself and can never be erased or obscured by mortal power.[52]

In Massachusetts, Sam Adams was persuaded to drop his opposition when Boston merchants pledged to build new ships if the state would only ratify the Constitution. The shipwrights, caulkers, and chandlers—always Sam Adams's most loyal backers—pressed the old Patriot to come over to the Federalist side.[53] They needed the work! Sam Adams brought John Hancock around.

Massachusetts ratified by a close vote of 187–168 in February 1788. Maryland heard another interminable harangue from Luther Martin—and voted overwhelmingly to ratify in April 1788.[54]

Madison hastened back to Virginia in time to be elected to the state's ratifying convention. His election was by no means assured. Only after he met with the leader of Virginia's Baptists and gave him assurances that the new Congress would take up the pressing issue of a Bill of Rights did Elder John Leland give Madison his endorsement. Leland wanted the new federal government to provide protections for religious liberty.[55]

Madison would not be alone in arguing the case for the new Constitution in Richmond. He would be supported by George Wythe (Jefferson's law professor at William & Mary) and by young John Marshall. Also, curiously, the state's governor, Edmund Randolph, one of the famous nonsigners in Philadelphia, now urged ratification.

Patrick Henry charged that the new Constitution "squints toward monarchy"[56] and condemned it. He charged a power grab. He even took issue with Gouverneur Morris's eloquent opening lines of the Constitution's Preamble, "We the People":

> I have the highest veneration for those Gentlemen—but, Sir, give me leave to demand, what right had they to say, We, the People. My political curiosity, exclusive of my anxious solicitude for the public welfare, leads me to ask, who authorised them to speak the language of, We, the People, instead of We, the States? States are the characteristics, and the soul of a confederation. If the States be not the agents of this compact, it must be one great consolidated National Government of the people of all the States.

Debate continued for weeks through a sweltering June in Richmond. Madison patiently, quietly answered Henry's objections. He rebutted point-by-point Henry's impassioned but ill-organized attack on the Constitution. Sometimes the gallery could hardly hear Madison's soft, almost inaudible voice. But the delegates listened intently. Yes, a Bill of Rights might be added, as Antifederalists demanded, but only *as amendments and only after the Constitution had been ratified.*

Finally, Henry rose dramatically at the end to say, "I see the awful immensity of the dangers [of the new Constitution].... I *feel* it." Then, as a summer storm shook the convention hall with violent thunder and lightning, Henry argued that heaven itself was watching the delegates' actions. Despite Henry's own flashes of eloquence and rhetorical thundering, the delegates voted with Madison—but barely: 89–79.[57]

Virginia was not the ninth "necessary state." New Hampshire's ratification had beaten the Old Dominion by mere days. But without Virginia's ratification, George Washington would have been *ineligible* to serve as the new government's first president. Jefferson and Madison and all other distinguished Virginians would have been disqualified too.

The debate shifted to New York. Even though the Constitution could go into effect with only ten states, New York State, by staying out, would cut the Union in half. When New York Antifederalists maneuvered to keep the state out of the new Union, Hamilton and Jay threatened *to take New York City out of the state!*[58] In the end, New York ratified by the heart-stopping close vote of 30–27.

Ratification was celebrated by a huge victory parade down Broadway in Manhattan. Thirty seamen and ten horses pulled a twenty-seven-foot model ship named *Hamilton*. Workers, artisans, and craftsmen joined merchants in celebration. The teamsters—called *cartmen*—carried a banner with this poem:

> Behold the federal ship of fame;
> The *Hamilton* we call her name;
> To every craft she gives employ;
> Sure cartmen have their share of joy.[59]

It was the first of many more tumultuous parades down Broadway under the new government. Later, they would add "ticker tape" to celebrate peace, victory, and—sweetest of all—liberty.

THREE

THE NEW REPUBLIC

(1789–1801)

I. "THE SACRED FIRE OF LIBERTY"

George Washington stood on the north portico of Mount Vernon, over-looking the majestic Potomac River, on 14 April 1789. There he received word that the electoral college had met and *unanimously* chosen him to be the new republic's first president.

There was no cheering there. Washington knew that the new government was nearly bankrupt. The old government of the Articles of Confederation had expired, quietly and peacefully but deeply in debt. Like many planters, even the wealthy Washington was "cash poor." He had to borrow money to travel the 250 miles between Mount Vernon and New York City for the inauguration.[1] Washington was concerned that people might think he had gone back on his solemn promise to retire, assuaging concerns that he aimed to assume the mantle of king. He had given that promise to Congress in Annapolis, just before Christmas 1783. Now he was back—though under different circumstances and in a different capacity.

He need not have worried.

Jubilant crowds greeted his coach in every village and town on his way to the temporary capital in New York City. They shouted themselves hoarse in praise. But Washington was wise. He knew that the popular acclaim might not last. Such an emotional outpouring, he thought, might easily turn "into equally extravagant (though I will fondly hope unmerited) censures."[2]

Perhaps like the reluctant Moses, Washington often expressed doubts about his abilities to measure up to his appointed tasks. It was just what he had done in 1775 when the Continental Congress unanimously made him commander in chief of the army. Washington also knew that others might come to doubt his abilities. Good graces in politics are more like winds than mountains. Hadn't he seen some of those who cheered him in Congress conspire only a few years later to replace him? So it would be with those raucous citizens who hailed the conquering hero now.

The great Revolutionary leader had been the model for the presidency. He had presided with dignity, patience, and strength for five long, sultry months while delegates to the Constitutional Convention measured the constitutional fabric to his frame like so many tailors. Despite the delegates' heated arguments and occasional long-winded speeches, Washington had been an attentive student in the greatest graduate seminar in political science, history, and economics ever conducted on this continent. Not as bookish or brilliant as many, Washington could weigh each speaker's words against his own rich experience as farmer, surveyor, legislator, military commander, and diplomat. Only Franklin could rival Washington's breadth of experience. Although he had never been to Europe, or even to Canada, George Washington had traveled more extensively throughout America than all but a few men of his day. If Washington was not prepared, then no one was. That was precisely what many of the world's most powerful thought; they did not believe *any* people were capable of self-government, least of all the Americans.

Washington arrived in the festive city and proceeded to Federal Hall, in Lower Manhattan, for the inaugural ceremonies. The building had been redesigned for the occasion by Major Pierre L'Enfant. Washington had known the talented French émigré since he arrived at Valley Forge as a member of Baron von Steuben's staff.

On 30 April 1789, before the assembled crowds, George Washington took the presidential oath from Chancellor Robert Livingston. (Yes, Livingston, the *Antifederalist*, now apparently reconciled to the new government.) Dressed in a homespun American-made brown suit with eagles on the buttons, he placed his hand on the Bible and recited the oath, adding, significantly, four words repeated by every president since—as a matter of tradition if not sincere belief: "So help me God." Then he kissed the Bible. In his brief inaugural address to members of Congress, he claimed that heaven itself seemed to have ordained that the republican model of government—indeed, "the sacred fire of liberty" itself—had been placed in the hands of the American people. It was, he said, an *experiment*.[3] There were no proud boasts, no rah-rah claims of sure success. As an experiment, it might fail.

The odds were certainly not in the Founders' favor. Washington had listened carefully to the debates of the Constitutional Convention—as most of the members of the new government had. He heard, as they all did, the long and detailed descriptions offered by James Madison and other delegates of the failure of republican governments of the past. The track record was less than reassuring. Every effort would have to be made to see the experiment did not fail; if eternal *vigilance* was required to guard against tyranny, then eternal *diligence* was required to secure the success of the new nation.

Washington proceeded with dispatch to organize the executive branch of government. He chose Alexander Hamilton, just thirty-five years old, as his secretary of the Treasury. Hamilton had already served Washington as an aide-de-camp in the army. Washington knew his mercurial temper. He was a serious man with a habit of speaking his mind—bluntly. But the president also knew his young friend was brilliant and tireless. Add to that pair of highly desirable qualities Hamilton's undying realism, and he was perfect for the bill.

For secretary of state, Washington chose a fellow Virginian, Thomas

Jefferson, forty-seven, still serving as ambassador in France. Jefferson would be uncharacteristically tardy in joining the new administration. As attorney general, Washington selected the charismatic but indecisive Edmund Randolph, just a year Hamilton's senior. This was a generous act on Washington's part, since Randolph had dithered about signing the Constitution, declined, but then lined up behind Madison at the Virginia ratifying convention. Rounding out the president's cabinet—although it was not yet called that—was the redoubtable Henry Knox, thirty-nine, now secretary of war. The former bookseller from Boston had served Washington faithfully throughout the war as chief of artillery.

An astute and natural manager, Washington had carefully balanced geographical sections and political points of view in selecting the heads of the executive departments. These were young men of the Revolution— their average age, including Washington himself at fifty-seven, was only forty-two years old. Other leading figures in the new government would be John Adams, fifty-four, the vice president; James Madison, thirty-eight, newly elected to the House of Representatives; and John Jay, forty-four, soon to become the nation's first chief justice.

The First Congress was to be a very productive one; some even called it a second constitutional convention. But it got off to a rocky start. Meeting in temporary quarters in New York City, the House and Senate had to flesh out the new government. There were executive departments to be organized, a judiciary to be created, treaties to be considered, and pressing financial business.

And the difficulties didn't end with policy and procedure. Recently returned from five years as America's ambassador to the Court of Saint James's in London, John Adams stumbled in his new role as presiding officer of the Senate. He had faithfully and ably represented his country's cause abroad but had also lost touch with many in the new Congress. In a routine discussion of titles for the new president, Adams weighed in, *disastrously*. He monopolized the debate for a full month, with long and pedantic speeches. Completely missing the tenor of the times,

Adams suggested the chief executive should be called "His Highness, the President of the United States and Protector of Their Liberties."

Senators were put off by the *royalist* tone of Adams's suggestion. Had he spent too much time in a foreign court filled with the bowing and scraping lackeys of the king?

Fortunately, the House of Representatives voted that the chief executive would be called, simply, "Mr. President," and the Senate concurred. John Adams, the bold Patriot of '76, was seriously misunderstood and deeply wounded by this affair. He never wished to give hereditary titles to officers of the new republic; he simply thought a *dignified* title would be some compensation for the times away from family and farm and for the many criticisms public officers had to endure. The incident was politically sticky enough that it caused George Washington to pull away from his vice president. Adams would not be included in discussions of Washington's official family, a slight that greatly hurt the sensitive Adams.*

Arguments about titles for public officials may seem silly to us today, but in a world still dominated by monarchies, they were serious matters. Creating a new republic required new ways of behaving. America, the Founders believed, had to leave behind all the trappings of monarchy *and* an aristocratic social system.

President Washington received many official greetings from voluntary associations and religious groups upon taking office. His formal response to one of these—the Hebrew Congregation in Newport, Rhode Island—made a significant contribution to the new American etiquette and religious freedom. In 1790, he wrote:

It is now no more that toleration is spoken of as if it were by the indulgence of one class of people that another enjoyed the exercise of their inherent natural rights, for, happily, the Government of the United States,

---

* Washington's appointed department heads were not yet called the cabinet, but Washington as general had always referred to his aides as his *military* family.

which gives to bigotry no sanction, to persecution no assistance, requires only that they who live under its protection should demean themselves as good citizens in giving it on all occasions their effectual support.

As Claremont professor Harry Jaffa has pointed out, this was the first time in human history that any ruler addressed the Jews as *equals*.[4] President Washington closed his letter with these gentle words, taken from Scripture: "May the Children of the Stock of Abraham, who dwell in this land, continue to merit and enjoy the good will of the other inhabitants; while every one shall sit in safety under his own vine and fig tree, and there shall be none to make him afraid."[5]

II. MADISON'S BILL OF RIGHTS

When Congress turned to constitutional matters, they took up the question of amendments—what was to become known as a Bill of Rights. During the battle for ratification, promises were made to Antifederalists that the federal Congress would be open to suggestions for amendment. Madison, who had originally argued that a Bill of Rights was *unnecessary* because the new government had no power to violate the rights of citizens, now honored his commitment to his Virginia neighbors. As a leading member of the new House of Representatives, Madison became the author of the Bill of Rights. Only ten of the twelve amendments that passed Congress were ratified by the states, but they became justly famous as Americans' charter of freedom.[*]

To read the first ten amendments, we can read the history of the colonial struggle against British despotism. Freedom of speech, press, and religion were guaranteed by the First Amendment, as well as the right to

---

[*] Another amendment that required members of Congress to face the voters before receiving a pay increase they had voted for—surely a constitutional "little engine that could"—was also passed by the First Congress in 1789. It was ratified as Amendment XXVII only in 1992. It shows that good ideas have a long shelf life.

assemble and to petition for "redress of grievances." These rights form the core of a free society, and they had been violated in one way or another by British misrule. The Second Amendment—still controversial in our day—meant what it said. Americans remembered that General Howe's redcoats marched out of Boston to seize the militia's gunpowder and weapons. An armed people remained a free people because they are the last redoubt against a hostile government's tyrannical advances. And, just as importantly, an armed people could resist the demands of militarists to *regiment* society. Americans would be free without ever resorting to the sort of goose-stepping mindlessness of Prussian (not to mention Soviet or North Korean) dictatorial states. The Third Amendment prevented government from stationing, or "quartering," troops in private homes in peacetime—a major abuse of the British in Boston.

The next *five* amendments, all relating to judicial procedures, each corresponded to very real British acts of tyranny, many of which are detailed in the Declaration of Independence. Those notorious "Writs of Assistance" were general warrants that allowed British colonial officials to rummage through Americans' homes, farms, and shops, looking for incriminating evidence. The Fourth Amendment banned them, specifying no "unreasonable searches or seizures." The Fifth protected Americans from having to testify against themselves or from being tried twice for the same offense. The Sixth Amendment called for a speedy public trial, with the right of the accused to confront witnesses, compel witnesses for the defense to testify, and to have the assistance of counsel. The Seventh Amendment guaranteed the right of trial by jury, while the Eighth outlawed "cruel and unusual punishment."

The final two amendments were the capstones—the bookends to the preamble's acknowledgment that the powers of government were delegated by the people. The Ninth Amendment recognized that rights enumerated in the Constitution were not the *only* rights the people enjoyed, and the Tenth assured that any powers *not* granted to the federal government or prohibited to the states were retained by the states or by the people.

Madison's careful drafting and skilled floor management of the Bill of Rights through Congress gives him just title to two great tributes—Father of the Constitution and Father of the Bill of Rights. The Founders deeply admired classical heroes. But no figure of antiquity—no Greek like Pericles or Solon, no Roman like Cicero or Cincinnatus—can claim an equal standing with Madison as lawgiver and champion of liberty. Madison told his fellow members of Congress, who exercised powers he had carefully crafted for them, why a Bill of Rights was necessary: "If we can make the Constitution better in the opinion of those who are opposed to it, without weakening its frame, or abridging its usefulness in the judgment of those who are attached to it, we act the part of wise and liberal men to make such alterations as shall produce the effect."[6]

Madison hoped the Bill of Rights would bring the Antifederalists around, especially those still holding out against ratification in North Carolina and Rhode Island.[7] In this, he was strongly supported by Jefferson, who generally supported the new Constitution yet embodied so many of the Antifederalist concerns. While still in Paris, Jefferson spoke for many when he wrote to Madison: "A bill of rights is what the people are entitled to against every government on earth . . . and what no just government should refuse."[8]

Madison's rhetoric does not soar as Jefferson's does, but he keeps pace in the dignity, reason, and *force* of his arguments. In keeping his promises to Elder John Leland and the Virginia Baptists, and to a host of political allies and opponents, Madison's inspired draftsmanship helped dispel much of the lingering suspicion that had attended the work of the Philadelphia Convention.

III. "A HOST IN HIMSELF": HAMILTON'S NEW SYSTEM

When Hamilton wrote in *The Federalist* of the urgent need for "energy in the executive," he may not have had himself in mind. Yet Hamilton's incredible outpouring of energy, creativity, and purpose still stuns us. He knew that the new government would be judged in no small measure on how it managed the new republic's economy.

With the Constitution ratified, Hamilton quickly responded to Congress's call for a *Report on the Public Credit*. It was Hamilton's chance to exhibit his genius as well as to tutor men twice his age in the realities of modern finance. In this, Hamilton was as justified as Madison had been in making good the pledges made in the heated state contests. The new secretary of the Treasury, barely thirty-five, would call for two key moves by the new administration—*funding* the debt and *assuming* the debts of the states. "The only plan that can preserve the currency is one that will make it to the immediate interest of the monied men to cooperate with the government in its support," said Hamilton with his characteristic forthrightness.[9] *Funding* meant that the federal government would honor the obligations incurred under the Articles of Confederation—a sum of about $55 million. On the surface, this was an obvious move. Had the new government repudiated the debts of its predecessor, investors would have scattered like dry leaves before a gust of wind. The tricky question was *how* the debt should be funded. Should the federal government pay the holders of government bonds the full face value? Many of these bonds were originally issued to Patriots and their families in the first flush days of revolutionary enthusiasm. The Patriots had pledged their lives, their *fortunes*, and their sacred honor to the American cause. Over the years, however, the Confederation Congress had authorized worthless paper money (giving rise to the dread phrase "not worth a Continental [dollar]"). Seeing little chance their bonds would ever be redeemed, thousands of hard-pressed soldiers, farmers, and small merchants had sold their bonds for a fraction of their face value. Purchasers of these discounted bonds were highly unpopular, seen as trafficking in human misery. To fund the debt meant paying these "speculators" at par. Thus, a one-hundred-dollar bond would be redeemed at one hundred dollars face value.

Assumption meant that the federal government would pay off some $25 million in war debts incurred by the states. This would help bind the states to the new government. (It might be an incentive, as well, for Rhode Island to ratify the Constitution.) It would be an act of justice, since the war had been fought for the Union, not for any single state or group of states. The costs of the war were not equally distributed throughout the country, just as the battles were not evenly spread out over the extensive territory.

Madison was quick to respond to Hamilton's program—negatively. Madison thought it would be a travesty not to recognize the original holders of bonds—especially war widows and veterans—and to give, in effect, a windfall profit to the entire class of speculators in discounted bonds. He also pointed out that some of the states had met their obligations to creditors in a timely fashion, while other states had avoided prompt payments. (That these solvent states tended to be in the South was early evidence of a sectional split in Congress.) Thomas Jefferson joined Madison in criticizing Hamilton's plan.

In the end, President Washington sided with Hamilton, whose financial system soon bore fruit. The new republic thrived. The government's credit was "as good as gold." Small, swift cutters of Hamilton's Revenue Marine (today known as the Coast Guard) began immediately to enforce customs laws, helping to generate large import duties for the new government. The economic boom greatly increased revenues for the federal government, allowing it to strengthen its credit and meet its new obligations.

Meanwhile, President Washington began a series of presidential tours of the country. In the summer of 1790, he visited New England, traveling by carriage. Americans accustomed to presidential travel in the age of Air Force One can hardly imagine that the president of the United States would actually journey without guards, without a Secret Service, being jostled along deeply rutted and dusty roads in a single coach. Jefferson expressed concern for Washington's safety—not because of outlaws or Indian raids, but because of the incredibly bad roads.[10] Tiring and uncomfortable as it was, Washington knew that such visits helped the American people to feel the presence of their new government. Despite grousing by some that these trips seemed like royal *progresses*, Washington knew they served to unify the republic. In his first such trip to Connecticut and Massachusetts, he had carefully *avoided* going through Rhode Island, which had still not ratified the Constitution. Shortly after, little Rhody came in and was rewarded with a presidential visit to Newport.

On his southern tour in April 1791, President Washington would be completely out of contact with the government literally for weeks on end. Innkeepers would be stunned to see pulling up to their establishments "the greatest man in the world."[11] Washington endured the heat and dirt, but he positively beamed in the company of "fair compatriots," always enjoying the company of beautiful and intelligent women. In ever-fashionable Charleston, South Carolina, he reached the high point of his presidential tour. As he delighted in recording, he was flattered by "four hundred ladies, the number and appearance of which exceeded anything of the kind I had ever seen."[12]

When Washington fell ill, the country shuddered. In New York, he suffered through surgery without anesthesia to remove a carbuncle deeply imbedded in his thigh. While he recovered, the city fathers spread straw on the streets to quiet the clop-clop of horses and let the weary executive get his rest.

New York's leaders had more thought for Washington than did all too many of his colleagues. Hamilton reacted to increasing opposition to his program from Jefferson and Madison and their many allies in Congress. He appealed to Washington to dismiss Jefferson, saying that the divisions in his official family "must destroy the energy of the government."[13]

Not to be outdone, Jefferson and Madison took to calling themselves and their supporters *Republicans*.* They were uneasy with the idea of a powerful federal government that, like a monarchy, might seize more

---

* Mr. Jefferson's Republicans are not to be confused with the Republican Party of today. Today's Republicans were not founded until 1854. The Jeffersonians were called first Republicans, then *Democratic*-Republicans, and finally, from Andrew Jackson's time onward, simply the Democrats.

and more power. Hamilton's followers came to be known as *Federalists*. They favored a strong central government as the best defense against anarchy and the surest way to hold the country together. The Founders had rejected the idea of *party* differences in the American government, but differing ideas about how to govern gradually increased and took on a permanent cast—Federalists versus Republicans.

At the close of his first term, Washington wanted to leave public office, to return to Mount Vernon. More frequently now, he would speak of having only a few years left of his life. He often said the time could not be far off when he would, in the words of the Bible, "sleep with my fathers." With Madison's help, he even prepared a Farewell Address to the nation for 1792. And he tried, without notable success, to keep *both* of his brilliant aides in his cabinet. Washington wrote to Jefferson: "I have a great, a sincere esteem and regard for you both, and ardently wish that some line could be marked out by which both of you could walk."[14]

Hamilton's advantage over Jefferson cannot be traced only to Washington's support for his program. Hamilton headed up the Treasury. At this point, it was the *largest* of the federal departments, with nearly five hundred full-time employees. The other departments had only twenty-two![15] Congress and the courts were in session for only a few months, while Hamilton and his subordinates labored ceaselessly.[16] *Energy in the executive, indeed.*

Hamilton went out of his way to deflect criticism of his department. He insisted on keeping the Treasury clean and above corruption. His instructions to captains in the Revenue Marine—read by Coast Guard commanders to this day—show a keen appreciation for how to deal with Americans. Commanders should "always keep in mind that their Countrymen are Freemen. . . . They will therefore refrain with the most guarded circumspection from whatever has the semblance of haughtiness, rudeness or insult."[17]

As President Washington prepared for his southern tour in April 1791, he asked his cabinet to meet in his absence. Jefferson invited Henry

Knox, John Adams, and Hamilton to join him for dinner. It was a friendly affair as after-dinner conversation turned to the British constitution.

Adams said, "Purge that constitution of its corruption . . . and it would be the most perfect constitution ever devised by the wit of man."[18]

To Jefferson, this was a shocking statement, coming as it did from "the Colossus of Independence." But what Hamilton said next was truly breathtaking: "Purge [the British constitution] of its corruption . . . and it would become an *impracticable* government: as it stands at present, with all its supposed defects, it is the most perfect government which ever existed."[19]

For Jefferson, such sentiments would be scandalous if expressed by *any* American. But coming from one man who stood "a heartbeat away" from the presidency and another who had just pushed through Congress his bill to create a national bank, the ideas were enough to make his head spin. All the Patriot leaders had denounced the corruption of the monarch during the Revolution. The king used the vast wealth brought into Crown revenues from India to bribe members of Parliament to support his policies. For twenty years, the eloquent Edmund Burke impeached Warren Hastings of the East India Company and decried the corruption of the rich young "nabobs" who had fattened themselves on the riches of India.*

Could Jefferson really be exaggerating the dangers of monarchy in America if this is what the highest officials of the government said in their unguarded moments?

How could Britain have *any* admirers in this government after all she had done? Didn't these men believe what Jefferson had written in the Declaration? Those who governed under this same British constitution that Adams and Hamilton claimed to admire had, in fact, incited savage attacks on their countrymen and had "a design to reduce them under absolute Despotism."

This may have been the most important dinner party in American

---

* In this context, Burke's *impeachment* of Hastings was a lengthy, public denunciation of his conduct and character.

history. From this fateful encounter, we might date the beginning of America's two-party system. Jefferson certainly saw the significance of the evening in terms of the attitudes of Adams and Hamilton toward England. He wanted no part of their stated admiration for the British constitution.

IV. A TURBULENT SECOND TERM

During Washington's first term, Americans busied themselves in establishing their new government and enjoying "the blessings of liberty." All sides agreed that Washington's continued service was "indispensable." Though opposed to many of Washington's policies, Jefferson nonetheless told him he must serve a second term: "North and South will hang together if they have you to hang on," he told his chief.

Washington heeded his friend's words. In 1792, the president was reelected by a unanimous vote in the electoral college—the first and only American president to be twice elected unanimously. The harmony at home was contrasted by the shocking discord across the Atlantic. Hardly had Washington been inaugurated for a second term in March 1793, when news reached America that King Louis XVI had been tried, convicted of treason, and put to death in Paris by the new and frighteningly efficient instrument of execution, the *guillotine*. With its monarch beheaded, France proclaimed itself a republic and promptly declared war on Britain.

Although they shuddered at the fate of King Louis XVI—fondly remembered for his timely help during the Revolution—many Americans nonetheless welcomed the news of the French republic. But the revolution in France presented the Washington administration with a dilemma. Should the new American republic ally itself with the new French republic?

France was then at war with Britain. As of April 1793, the United States was officially neutral. President Washington knew that the United States could not afford to become entangled in war between the great powers of Europe. He issued the nation's first Proclamation of Neutrality.

Thomas Jefferson supported the proclamation even though he admired the French cause. He knew the United States was not prepared for war. And from his avid reading of newspapers, he had a keen sense of popular opinion. As he wrote Gouverneur Morris in Paris, "No country perhaps was ever so thoroughly against war as ours."[20] Madison did not agree. He thought we were dishonoring our Treaty of 1778 with France and that the president did not have constitutional authority to proclaim neutrality. After all, if the Constitution gave to Congress, not the executive, the power to declare war, was it not logical to infer that the power to declare *no war* also resided there?[21] Thanks to Washington's steady hand, the government steered a middle course between impassioned partisans of Britain and France.

If President Washington hoped for a more serene second term, he was to be sadly disappointed. Little did he think, when he laid down his soldier's sword at Annapolis in 1783, that he would have to take it up again. Yet in 1794, that is what President Washington did. In western Pennsylvania, resistance to Secretary Hamilton's new taxes flared up. Farmers there needed to be able to convert corn and other grains into whiskey. This was because they lacked the means to preserve their crops for the long term. Hamilton's Excise Act of 1791—which placed a levy on liquor—hit them hard.

When resistance broke into open rebellion, the government was alarmed. Rebels overcame small numbers of federal troops, closed down courts, and vowed to march on Pittsburgh.[22] Hamilton urged Washington to act. The authority of the new government was in jeopardy. Washington personally led twelve thousand heavily armed militiamen from four states—Pennsylvania, Virginia, Maryland, and New Jersey—across the Alleghenies. He wore the full uniform of a lieutenant general.

Attorney General William Bradford wrote that "the Presdt. means to convince these people & the World of the moderation & the firmness of the Gov."[23] Hamilton was all for overwhelming force. "Wherever the Government appears in arms it ought to appear like a *Hercules*," for it was dangerous for the authority of the United States to seem weak and irresolute. The Whiskey Rebellion was quickly put down. The more radical leaders of the rebellion immediately fled, others faded away, and two were brought back to Philadelphia for trial for treason. Convicted, they were soon pardoned by the gracious and understanding Washington.[24]

Washington blamed the rebellion on local "Democratic clubs," voluntary associations generally loyal to Jefferson's Republicans. The president's vigorous action—and his merciful treatment of the defeated rebels—seemed exactly the right combination. The American people broadly supported him.[25] Some were still unconvinced that such a show of force was necessary. Thomas Jefferson—who had been fairly casual about Shays's Rebellion of 1786 from the distance of his Paris salon—wrote that "an insurrection was announced and proclaimed and armed against, but could never be found."[26]

The importance of the Whiskey Rebellion cannot be minimized. Washington knew he was walking "on untrodden ground." So many of his actions as president would become precedents for later leaders. This action showed the president willing to brook no unruly defiance of federal law. The place to change federal law was at the ballot box. Washington's spirited action in that beautiful autumn in the Pennsylvania mountains would form the basis for action by Presidents Jackson and Lincoln (as well as Presidents Eisenhower and Kennedy).*

In 1794, Washington dispatched Chief Justice John Jay to London to negotiate a treaty with England. Americans were incensed that the British had refused to evacuate their forts in the Northwest, and that the British navy frequently impressed our seamen and seized American ships trading with France. Washington knew that the United States was unprepared for war and instructed Jay to smooth things over.

The resulting treaty won some concessions and kept the peace, but

---

* In the movie *Gods and Generals*, produced by Ted Turner, Robert Duval plays the part of Robert E. Lee. Lee says he never thought he would live to see the day when an American president would "invade" an American state. In real life, Lee was the step-grandson-in-law of George Washington. He surely would have known of President Washington's autumn campaign against rebels in the Pennsylvania mountains—and his use of Maryland and Virginia troops to do it!

the public outcry was terrifying. Virginia's Republican congressman, John Randolph, went so far as to raise a toast of "Damn George Washington!"[27]

Republican newspapers poured out torrents of abuse, not sparing the president. He wanted to be king, many of them claimed. Washington was deeply wounded by these irresponsible charges. As he had said during the Whiskey Rebellion, Washington only did his duty as he knew it—one of the reasons he led the troops himself, accepting responsibility for the action. "By God, I had rather be on my farm than be made emperor of the world!" he said.[28]

In the wake of this menacing and bruising fight, George Washington prepared to step down as president. He asked Hamilton to help him craft his final message to the American people.* It has come down to us as Washington's Farewell Address, even though it was published in a Philadelphia newspaper and never delivered as a speech.

Washington reminded Americans of those qualities necessary to maintain free government:

> Of all the dispositions and habits which lead to political prosperity, Religion and morality are indispensable supports. In vain would that man claim the tribute of Patriotism, who should labor to subvert these great Pillars of human happiness, these firmest props of the duties of Men and citizens.[29]

The heart of the address was his warning against twin evils—the spirit of party and "permanent" alliances with foreign states. Washington had just seen how the contention of political parties and the intrigues of foreign agents threatened the very unity of the country. Although the

---

* The brilliant Hamilton might normally have been considered the likeliest successor to Washington as president. But Hamilton had effectively eliminated himself when he admitted to congressional investigators that he had paid blackmail to hush up an adulterous affair with Maria Reynolds. Hamilton's forthright confession is a model for political men—if rarely followed.

address could have been written with reference to the battle over Jay's treaty, it has taken on a timeless quality that contains wise counsel for us even today.

As the election of 1796 approached, Republicans and Federalists prepared to fight for the top prizes in government. Federalists had little choice but to line up behind Vice President John Adams. The Republican choice was obvious. Thomas Jefferson had left the Washington administration in 1793, but he had kept in regular contact with James Madison, James Monroe, and other Republican leaders.

Adams received seventy-one electoral votes to Jefferson's sixty-eight. The Federalists had failed to deliver the votes necessary to elect Thomas Pinckney vice president; therefore, under the Constitution as it was then written, Jefferson won the office. Since the Founders had not anticipated the creation of parties, they did not foresee the top two offices being held by men from different parties. It would prove an awkward arrangement for the next four years.

V. WAR, PEACE, AND HONEST JOHN ADAMS

When, on 4 March 1797, George Washington attended the inauguration of his successor, he created yet another precedent. John Adams reflected on the scene in a letter to his beloved wife, Abigail: "It was made more affecting to me by the presence of the General, whose countenance was as serene and unclouded as the day. He seemed to me to enjoy a triumph over me. Methought I heard him say, 'Ay! I am fairly out, and you fairly in. See which of us will be happiest.' When the ceremony was over, he came and made me a visit, and cordially congratulated me, and wished my administration might be happy, successful and honorable."[30]

As the new president left the hall where he had been sworn in, Vice President Jefferson waited for now *former* president Washington to precede him. Washington, with a firm gesture of command, indicated to Jefferson to go out before him. Washington was now a private citizen and was unwilling to hold on to any of the honors of office. Even in this, Washington was setting the standard for the government of a free people. Once again, the "greatest man in the world" was surrendering power and assuring a peaceful and orderly succession. President Adams was keenly aware of the *importance* of this first transition, but, as usual, his bluff exterior masked a tender heart. His acute sense of participating in an historic moment was all mixed up with his *personal* feelings. He could not resist telling Abigail about the reaction of the crowds at his inaugural.

> [T]here has been more weeping than there has ever been at the representation of any tragedy. But whether it was from grief or joy, whether from the loss of their beloved President, or from the accession of an unbeloved one, or from the pleasure of exchanging Presidents without tumult, or from the novelty of the thing, or from the sublimity of it arising out of the multitude present, or whatever other cause, I know not.[31]*

Adams's first task was to try to keep peace with the French. No greater contrast could be imagined than that between revolutionary France and the new American republic. During Washington's second term, France had lived under Maximilian Robespierre's Reign of Terror. The guillotine had claimed 16,600 victims nationwide in less than a year (1793–94).[32] As many as half a million languished in the prisons of the Revolution. Although the Terror would largely end with the death of Robespierre "the Incorruptible," the politics of France would be "poisoned" for centuries to come.[33]

Even trying to deal with such a government was hazardous. Hoping for a stable balance in foreign affairs, President Adams sent a delegation to negotiate a new treaty with France, just as President Washington had done with Jay's treaty with England. Adams was worried about the

---

* Pulitzer Prize–winning author David McCullough says his biography of John Adams was helped immeasurably by transcripts of the letters of John and Abigail Adams. The microfiche record of this remarkable couple's letters to each other is five miles long!

threat of a "quasi-war" at sea because French frigates had begun to seize American ships—just as the British were doing.

The slippery French foreign minister Talleyrand refused even to see the American diplomats. He demanded a huge personal bribe just to talk to them. And he claimed France should be paid the staggering sum of $10 million to compensate France's honor for an insulting speech by President Adams. Talleyrand sent three agents to sound out the Americans and see if they would pay. One member of the American delegation, John Marshall, was a brave Revolutionary War veteran. He was a Virginian who had crossed the Delaware River with Washington in 1776, and he was having none of this French nonsense. Marshall labeled the three French agents "Messers X, Y, and Z" in his secret dispatches home. And he soon turned on his heels and set sail for America.

When word of the "XYZ Affair" reached America in April 1798, the country exploded in anti-French rage. "Millions for Defense, but not One Cent for Tribute" became the Federalists' rallying cry.[34] Once again, Jefferson's Republicans—known as "Gallomen" to their opponents—were deeply embarrassed by French conduct.

President Adams basked in his newfound popularity. In 1798, Congress readily agreed to his proposal to rebuild the navy. (The modern navy dates from Adams's administration.) Soon, Captain Thomas Truxton, commanding the powerful new USS *Constellation*, thrilled Americans with his daring capture of the French frigate *L'Insurgente* on 5 February 1799. Off the Caribbean island of Nevis, Captain Truxton's guns killed twenty-nine French sailors and wounded seventy-one, with the loss of only two dead and two wounded. The following year, his well-trained crew battled another French warship in the great Age of Fighting Sail. *La Vengeance* barely escaped sinking by *Constellation's* deadly accurate fire. As Americans celebrated their independence from *both* great powers on the Fourth of July, they said they'd finally found in Captain Truxton an "envoy" whom the French would *have* to receive.[35]

John Adams might have been reelected handily in 1800 had he not been goaded into a disastrous misstep. Stung by truly vicious press criticism and harassed in Congress by one of Jefferson's allies, Swiss immigrant Albert Gallatin, Adams agreed to two of the most ill-advised bills in American history—the Alien and Sedition Acts. The Alien Act lengthened from five to fourteen years the time necessary for an immigrant to become a naturalized U.S. citizen.[36] The Sedition Act was passed to permit prosecution of any person who published "false and defamatory" statements against the leaders of the government.

Neither Adams nor Hamilton *wanted* these bills. Hamilton realized they could be counterproductive. "Let us not establish a tyranny," he warned. "Energy is a very different thing than violence."[37] But the ultra-Federalists in Congress pressed hard. They were certain that an invasion by France was imminent. Adams resisted panic—with humor: "There is no more prospect of seeing a French army *here* than there is in Heaven."[38] Nor were these Federalist leaders the only ones to oppose the extremely unwise measures. Running as a Federalist for election to Congress from Virginia, John Marshall said he "certainly would have opposed them" and that he thought they were only "calculated to create unnecessary discontents and jealousies."[39] Adams might have *vetoed* the Alien and Sedition Acts, but that would have opened a fatal division between him and the Federalist majority in Congress that was hell-bent on passing them. Soon, the Federalists would have cause to regret their haste. The Irish and the Germans were two large groups—especially numerous in critical Pennsylvania—who were *alienated* by this unwise legislation.

Jefferson and Madison responded to this challenge with their now famous "Virginia and Kentucky Resolutions." In 1798, the resolutions' authorship was unknown, but many of the ideas contained within them had been visible in the two men's response to Hamilton's national bank proposal of 1791. Madison's Virginia Resolutions were the more restrained, more tightly reasoned of the two state responses. Jefferson's Kentucky Resolutions, longer and bolder, attracted wide attention. The Jeffersonian style was recognizable:

> In questions of power, then, let no more be heard of confidence in man, but bind him down from mischief by the chains of the Constitution. That this commonwealth [Kentucky] does therefore call on its co-States for an expression of their sentiments on the acts concerning aliens, and for the punishment of certain crimes [sedition] . . . plainly declaring whether these acts are or are not authorized by the federal compact [Constitution].[40]

Jefferson scholar Merrill Peterson provides the linkages and underscores their importance: "The secession movement was a remarkable testament to the compact theory of government which Jefferson, more than anyone, had fixed upon the American mind."[41] If the American Union was a compact of the states, then might not any individual state *leave* the Union as it wished? Jefferson declined to spell that out. And, most importantly, he recognized that the American people would not permit *armed* resistance. Shays's Rebellion and the Whiskey Rebellion had taught him that. "Keep away from all use of force and [the American people] will bear down the evil propensities of the government by *election and petition*," he concluded.[42]

Nevertheless, it is possible to argue that Mr. Jefferson planted the seeds of secession with his anonymous Kentucky Resolutions. Jefferson comes perilously close to this. But Madison holds him back, by the coattails. The ever-practical Madison *always* keeps Jefferson from going over the brink. (Madison would later *denounce* nullification.)

What Jefferson and Madison really sought was a *change in behavior* by Congress by this form of pressure from the state legislatures—or by electoral change.[43] If resistance to unconstitutional legislation was to be by election and petition, then what was called for was an organized appeal to voters. This was a major shift in party politics. Not only had Jefferson and Madison helped form a political party, their Virginia and Kentucky Resolutions offered, in effect, the first party platform and initiated a national political campaign.

The Undeclared Naval War with France (1798–1800) came closer and closer to declared war as former president Washington was called out of retirement to head up an army to meet a French invasion. Over President Adams's objections, Washington insisted on making Hamilton inspector general of the army. Many feared that Hamilton would create a power base for himself in the new army—much as Napoleon Bonaparte had done in France. American sailors, on a high state of alert, sang out their feelings in a sea chanty:

> Now let each jolly tar [sailor], with one heart and one voice
> Drink a can of good grog [rum] to the man of our choice;
> Under John [Adams], the State pilot, and George's
> [Washington] command,
> There's a fig for the French and that sly Tallyrand.[44]

Despite Hamilton's agitation for war with France, despite the support given the idea by Federalists in Congress, President John Adams decided to make one last try for peace with France.

Surprisingly, the French were in a receptive mood. Napoleon, now clearly in charge, wanted no war with America. The Federalists exploded in rage—against their own president. They wanted to seize New Orleans and the Floridas. They wanted to further discredit the pro-French Jeffersonians. Adams's stubbornness, his *independent* streak, would be their undoing, they were sure.

After eight long months of negotiation, the French bluntly refused to pay $20 million in damages to the United States for shipping seized during the Quasi-War. But the two sides found room for agreement. The French let America out of her obligations under the Treaty of Alliance of 1778. In effect, we got a divorce from France for $20 million in alimony.[45]

The news of the Convention of 1800 between the United States and France came too late to affect the presidential election. History will always wonder what would have happened if voters had learned of Adams's diplomatic success before marking their ballots for president. One thing is sure: had Adams given in to Hamilton's war cry, there is no chance the French would have sold Louisiana to the United States three years later.[46] While Jefferson is rightly regarded as the father of the Louisiana Purchase, Adams was at least its godfather.[47]

Adams knew he was courting political disaster by sending his diplomatic mission to France: "I will defend my missions to France as long as I have an eye to direct my hand, or a finger to hold my pen," he said. "They were the most disinterested and meritorious actions of my life. I reflect on them with so much satisfaction that I desire no other inscription over my gravestone than: Here lies John Adams, who took upon himself the responsibility of peace with France in the year 1800."[48]

Americans were stunned by the news many received just before Christmas in 1799. George Washington had died at Mount Vernon after an illness that lasted barely thirty-six hours.

The Father of the Country gone!

And they felt like orphans for his passing. None more than Hamilton. "He was an *aegis* [protector] very essential to me," he later wrote. Stricken members of Congress gathered in Philadelphia's German Lutheran Church at a memorial service to hear Virginian Henry "Light-Horse Harry" Lee eulogize Washington as "first in war, first in peace, and first in the hearts of his countrymen."*

VI. THE REVOLUTION OF 1800

The campaign of 1800 was the first true presidential campaign in American history. Republicans fought Federalists in every state. Few elections since would match this one in the scurrilous attacks made on both candidates. The partisan newspapers called Adams "senile" and denounced him for his pride, vanity, and pigheadedness. This was mild,

---

* These words would long be remembered by Americans. One who knew them "by heart" was Henry Lee's son, Robert E. Lee.

however, compared to the all-out assault on Thomas Jefferson. The soft-spoken, philosophical Virginian was accused of atheism and of seeking to bring the bloodiest of French revolutionary violence to America's peaceful shores. "Mad Tom," "Jacobin," "apostle of the racetrack and cock-pit" were but some of the gibes of the Federalist press.[49] (The racetrack charge was particularly ridiculous since Mr. Jefferson *never* frequented them, but the Federalist icon, George Washington, clearly did!)

Jefferson was constantly compared, unfavorably, with Washington. The death in late 1799 of the nation's first president had plunged the country into deepest mourning. Logic is usually the first casualty in political campaigns. If Jefferson was, in truth, such a notorious radical, how loyal could Washington have been in choosing him as his first secretary of state?

Nothing, however, that the Republicans could say about the Federalists could compare with what the Federalists said about each other. In this most extraordinary of presidential campaigns, the Federalist Party literally fell apart. Personal rancor was its undoing. Without the unifying figure of Washington to hold them together, Federalists tore into one another.

In May of 1800, Adams had flown into a rage in a discussion with his secretary of war, James McHenry. He had learned that members of his cabinet were regularly reporting to Hamilton. He called Hamilton "the greatest intriguer in the world—a man devoid of every moral principle—a Bastard and as much a foreigner as Gallatin. Mr. Jefferson is an infinitely better man . . . you are subservient to Hamilton, who ruled Washington, and would still rule if he could."[50] Stunned, McHenry had little choice but to resign—and give a blow-by-blow description of Adams's tirade to Hamilton.

Alexander Hamilton, stung by the old man's denunciation, struck back. He wrote to Adams demanding an explanation. Receiving none, he produced a fifty-four-page pamphlet originally intended only for party leaders. The *Letter from Alexander Hamilton, Concerning the Public Conduct and Characters of John Adams, Esq., President of the United States*, of course, could not *stay* private. It was one of the most unbelievable documents in American history.

In the midst of a hotly contested presidential campaign, one in which President Adams was a strong candidate, Hamilton, the acknowledged leader of the Federalist Party, attacked his own team! Hamilton denounced Adams for his "great intrinsic defects of character," his "disgusting egotism," and his "ungovernable temper."[51] Hamilton did not quite call Adams insane, but he charged, "It is a fact that he is often liable to paroxisms of anger which deprive him of self-command and produce very outrageous behavior."[52] Still, at the end of the tirade, Hamilton incredibly called for Adams's reelection!

No one has ever recorded Jefferson or Madison in a similar rant. Perhaps Jefferson got it all out of his system by means of letters, some of them unguarded and unwise. We also know that poor John Adams was suffering great heartache at this time. His son, Charles, was descending into the depths of alcoholism and insanity that would eventually claim his life. Abigail had written to her husband: "I am wounded to the soul by the consideration of what is to become of him. What will be his fate embitters every moment of my life."[53] Parents can suffer no greater pain.

The Hamilton pamphlet had done its damage. John Adams received sixty-five electoral votes and Charles Cotesworth Pinckney received sixty-four. The Federalists were narrowly defeated. That much was clear. But who had won?

Thomas Jefferson received seventy-three electoral votes, but so had his running mate from New York, Aaron Burr! The Republicans' party discipline had proven too disciplined. This tie in the electoral college meant that the House of Representatives would have to resolve the election. Worse, under the Constitution as then written, the election would be decided *not* by the House of Representatives just elected, but by the "lame duck"* House that had been elected in 1798.** That House had a *Federalist* majority.

---

* Formally, a "lame duck" officeholder is one who is retiring or who has been defeated but who is still serving out his term. More recently, a lame duck is any politician the media is tired of.

** The terms of the House of Representatives, the Senate, the president, and vice president were changed by Amendment XX in 1933 to shorten the length of time between election and taking office.

Some of these Federalists saw an opportunity to confound their opponents by elevating Aaron Burr to the presidency. They reasoned that the ambitious Burr would be indebted to them for letting him enter the newly completed president's house in the new city of Washington. They thought they could deal with Burr far more readily than with Jefferson.

When the House convened for the first time in the nation's new capitol, it began balloting to select the new president. When the House is called upon to elect the president, it does so *by state*. That means that small states have an equal say with large states in the choice of the president. And when a state had only *one* representative, that congressman wielded great power.

The prospect of Burr's election as president shocked most Americans. Burr cagily resisted a clear, forthright statement of what everyone in America knew: that the Republican Party had intended Jefferson for president and Burr for vice president, and that is what its voters thought they were getting. Burr waited, in silence.[54]

Hamilton became alarmed after thirty-five ballots failed to produce a winner. There had even been talk of how the Federalist John Marshall might become president if the House could not resolve its deadlock. Virginia's governor James Monroe, Jefferson's loyal friend, threatened the use of state troops if the defeated Federalists should steal the election.

In a feverish set of letters, Hamilton pleaded with Federalists to resolve the election in favor of his archrival Jefferson. "For heaven's sake, let not the Federal Party be responsible for the elevation of this man [Burr]," he wrote to one friend. To Gouverneur Morris, "[Burr] could be bound by no agreement—will listen to no monitor but his own ambition." To the thought that Burr might bargain for the office, Hamilton scoffed: "He will laugh in his sleeve when he makes them and he will break them the first moment it may serve his purpose."[55]

Hamilton had a point. Aaron Burr was the grandson of the great colonial preacher and writer Jonathan Edwards. But no one had ever found much holiness in Burr's career as womanizer, or as a man whose greatest skill seemed to be eluding creditors.[56] He was charming and intelligent, to be sure. But it is no accident we do not study the writings of Aaron Burr. He was all maneuver, all action, all ambition—little else than a gamesman. And the Republicans knew this when they selected him.

Finally, on the thirty-sixth ballot, Delaware's Federalist congressman, James A. Bayard, broke the deadlock by *casting a blank ballot*. He had previously agreed with several others in his party to do the same thing. This resolved the issue in Jefferson's favor.[57] It was 17 February 1801, just fifteen days before the scheduled inauguration.

Thomas Jefferson walked from his rooming house to the new Capitol, where he took the oath as president on 4 March 1801.

"We are all republicans: we are all federalists," he said in his inaugural address. "We have called by different names brethren of the same principle."[58] Jefferson extended the olive branch to his political opponents. He also took advantage of the general disgust many Americans felt at the dangerous wheeling and dealing of the lame-duck Federalists in Congress.[59]

Jefferson was no great orator; his voice was almost inaudible in public addresses. But his words on this occasion—in which our country was spared a civil war—bear study two hundred years later.

> All, too, will bear in mind this sacred principle, that though the will of the majority is in all cases to prevail, that will, to be rightful must be reasonable; that the minority possess their equal rights, which equal laws must protect, and to violate which would be oppression.

Here, he laid down the philosophical basis for free government, even as he took part in history's first peaceful transfer of political power from one ruling party to another. He went on to give a moving appeal for civil concord:

> Let us then, as fellow-citizens, unite with one heart and one mind. Let us restore to social intercourse that harmony and affection without which liberty and even life itself are but dreary things.

And let us reflect that having banished from our land that religious intolerance under which mankind so long bled and suffered, we have yet gained little if we countenance a political intolerance as despotic, as wicked, and capable of as bitter and bloody persecutions.[60]

The next two hundred years would see examples of such religious and political persecution. America would suffer from them, as well. We would have Jefferson's words to encourage us to redouble our efforts for "harmony and affection" in public life.

John Adams had left the Executive Mansion that morning. Not having been invited to witness his successor's inauguration, he took the early coach home to Braintree, Massachusetts. Before departing, he had left a benediction for the new house: "I pray Heaven to bestow the best of blessings on this house, and on all that shall hereafter inhabit it. May none but honest and wise men ever rule under this roof."

FOUR

THE JEFFERSONIANS

(1801–1829)

I. "AN EMPIRE FOR LIBERTY"

Thomas Jefferson was fifty-seven years old when he entered the President's House. His public career had included service as a Virginia legislator and a member of Congress, a highly successful term as America's minister to France (following a conspicuously unsuccessful term as Virginia's wartime governor), the first secretary of state, the second vice president, and now the third president of the United States. The author of the Declaration of Independence and of Virginia's Statute for Religious Freedom, Jefferson was described as a man who could "calculate an eclipse, survey an estate, tie an artery, plan an edifice, try a cause, break a horse, dance a minuet, and play the violin."[1]*

Not all of Jefferson's successors were so impressed. Young Theodore

---

* Small wonder that President Kennedy would welcome forty-nine Nobel Prize winners
    to a 1962 White House dinner with these words: "I think this is the most extraordinary
    collection of talent, of human knowledge, that has ever been gathered at the White
    House—with the possible exception of when Thomas Jefferson dined alone."

Roosevelt described Jefferson as "perhaps the most incapable Executive that ever filled the presidential chair . . . utterly unable to grapple with the slightest danger . . . it would be difficult to imagine a man less fit to guide the state."[2]

Impressions of Jefferson were no less divided during his lifetime. He began his presidential term determined to make a sharp change from the previous administrations. In part because he was a poor public speaker, in part because he wanted to do nothing that looked like delivering a king's "speech from the throne," Jefferson in 1801 began the practice of sending written messages to Congress on the state of the Union. That tradition lasted until 1913, when the polished orator Woodrow Wilson resumed the practice of delivering the address in person.

Jefferson dispensed with the levies that had been the Washingtons' preferred method of entertaining. These were stiffly formal affairs. Instead, the widower invited members of Congress regularly to small dinners in the President's House. In these small groups, the new president was able to exercise firm leadership. Political men were eager to dine with the man they knew as "Mr. Jefferson."

Jefferson often provided guidance by means of letters. One of the first of these letters has had great influence on church-state relations in America. He had received a letter of congratulations on his election from the Danbury Baptist Association on 30 December 1801. He responded with astonishing speed. On 1 January 1802, President Jefferson wrote a letter that has become one of the most famous he ever wrote. It has also been one of his most misunderstood public acts.

Jefferson thanked the Connecticut Baptists and took the opportunity to explain *why* he had declined to proclaim days of fasting and thanksgiving. Expressing his "strict constructionist" constitutional beliefs, he explained that the president is only empowered to execute the laws that Congress passes. The people have wisely approved the First Amendment to the Constitution, he wrote. Since the amendment specifically *prohibits* Congress from passing any law "respecting the establishment of religion or restricting the free exercise thereof," he believed he had no constitutional authority to proclaim days of fasting and thanksgiving.

Jefferson then used the phrase that has been associated with him ever since. He wrote there is "a wall of separation between Church & State."[3] This letter needs to be seen in the context of the still-bubbling controversy over Jefferson's election in 1800. Federalists and their supporters in many New England pulpits had denounced Jefferson as an atheist and "infidel." Yale University President Timothy Dwight, a Congregationalist minister, had warned that if the Jeffersonian Republicans were elected, "we might see the Bible cast into a bonfire." Worse, children would be taught to chant "mockeries against God."[4] Presbyterian pastor John Mitchell Mason assured his congregation that electing Jefferson would be "a crime never to be forgiven . . . a sin against God."[5] The Federalist *Gazette of the United States* had summed up the election as a choice between "God and a Religious President [Adams]" and "Jefferson—AND NO GOD!"[6]

Jefferson spoke out against such unreasoning hysteria and blatant abuse of religious authority for partisan politicking. "I have sworn upon the altar of God eternal hostility against every form of tyranny over the mind of man," penned Jefferson in a letter to Dr. Benjamin Rush.[7] He assured Rush he would *oppose* any attempt to establish one particular form of Christianity in America.[8] This stance made Jefferson highly popular among minority religious groups. In time, it would soon lead to the *disestablishment* of the Congregational Church in New England.

As the elections of 1802 approached, the Federalist Party of Adams, Hamilton, and Jay grew more desperate. Jefferson had not pulled down church altars, nor seized Bibles, nor had he set up a guillotine on the National Mall. One Federalist leader, Fisher Ames, cried out, "Our country is too big for union, too sordid for patriotism, too democratic for liberty."[9] Even the energetic Alexander Hamilton seemed to despair. "Every day proves to me more and more that this American world was not made for me," he wrote.[10] Facing political disaster in the upcoming congressional elections, Federalists became even more strident than they had been in 1800. They seized upon a scandalous article written by James T. Callender. Callender charged that President Jefferson had fathered children by one of his Monticello slaves, Sally Hemings.

Jefferson had tried to help Callender with money and jobs, but he should have broken off all contact when the alcoholic Scottish refugee publicized Hamilton's adulterous affair with Maria Reynolds. Instead, Jefferson's help began to look like hush money. When Callender turned on him, Jefferson had no one to blame but himself. "The serpent you cherished and warmed," wrote Abigail Adams to Jefferson, "bit the hand that nourished him."[11] It was a deserved rebuke.*

Callender's revenge on Jefferson did him little good. He was found the next year facedown in the James River in Virginia. He had gotten drunk and drowned.[12] Nor did the scandal raise the Federalists' fortunes. In the midterm elections of 1802, Republicans triumphed. They won 102 seats in the House of Representatives to a mere 39 for the Federalists.

Jefferson faced a lingering foreign crisis early in his administration. For more than twenty years, he had been urging military action against Arab corsairs on the Barbary coast. These were fast, cheap warships that preyed upon merchant shipping along the northern shore of Africa. Various Arab rulers there would regularly declare war against European countries and then begin seizing their ships and men. The captured crews would be held for ransom or sold in the market as slaves. "Christians are cheap today!" was the auctioneer's cry.[13]

---

* Jefferson's alleged liaison with Sally Hemings surfaced again in 1998, when it was claimed that DNA evidence now confirmed he was the father of some or all of her children. The Jefferson-Hemings Scholars Commission, however, considered the new findings and disagreed: "After a careful review of all of the evidence, the commission agrees unanimously that the allegation is by no means proven." The Scholars Commission does not deny that Sally Hemming's children were sired by a Jefferson, they simply maintain that it cannot be proven they were fathered by *Thomas* Jefferson. Most likely, according to Pulitzer Prize winning journalist Virginia Dabney, the real father of Sally Hemming's children was Jefferson's nephew, Peter Carr (Adair, Douglass, *The Jefferson Scandals*, Dodd, Mead, and Company, New York: 1981).

This practice had been going on for centuries. As many as a million and a quarter Europeans had been enslaved by Muslims operating out of North Africa.[14] When he served as America's minister to France in the mid-1780s, Jefferson had once confronted an Arab diplomat, demanding to know by what right his country attacked Americans in the Mediterranean:

> The Ambassador answered us that it was founded on the Laws of the Prophet, that it was written in their Koran, that all nations who should not have answered their authority were sinners, that it was their right and duty to make war upon them wherever they could be found, and to make slaves of all they could take as prisoners.[15]

Confronted by such obstinacy, Jefferson appealed to John Adams, who was then America's minister to England. But Adams was unwilling to fight. Jefferson resolved from those early days to fight the Muslim hostage takers. "We ought to begin a naval power, if we mean to carry on our own commerce. Can we begin it on a more honourable occasion or with a weaker foe?" he wrote to James Madison in 1784.[16] The kidnapping and ransoming of American merchantmen continued for nearly twenty years.

The Washington and Adams administrations had gone along with the European practice of paying off the Barbary rulers. It was a protection racket, pure and simple. Adams believed paying tribute was cheaper than war. "We ought not to fight them at all unless we determine to fight them forever," he said.[17] Paying off the Barbary rulers was not cheap. When Jefferson came into office, the United States had already paid out nearly $2 million. This was nearly one-fifth of the federal government's yearly income![18]

The Bashaw of Tripoli declared war on the United States in 1801. Jefferson was determined to fight rather than pay tribute. Jefferson sent Commodore Edward Preble in command of the USS *Constitution* to strengthen America's naval forces in the Mediterranean Sea. Preble stirred American hearts with his spirited reply to an arrogant British naval captain who had challenged him to identify himself when shrouded in fog: "This is His Britannic Majesty's ship *Donnegal*, 84 guns," the captain hailed, demanding Preble put over a boat and prepare to be searched.

"This is the United States ship *Constitution*, Edward Preble, an American commodore, who will be *damned* before he sends his boat on board of any vessel. Strike your matches, boys!" Faced with this threat of cannon fire, the Royal Navy captain backed down.[19] Before Preble could arrive, however, the USS *Philadelphia* went aground off Tripoli harbor. The Bashaw took the crew captive.

Young Navy Lieutenant Stephen Decatur knew that he must not allow the Bashaw to convert the *Philadelphia* to his own use. He stole into the harbor by night and set the ship ablaze.[20] America's consul in Tunis, William Eaton, followed this daring exploit. He gathered a motley crew of U.S. Marines, sailors, and Greek and Arab mercenaries and their camels. Eaton marched his men five hundred miles across the Libyan desert to take the coastal town of Derna. Three U.S. warships, in a coordinated attack, bombarded the town.[21] From this stunning victory, the Marine hymn takes the line "to the shores of Tripoli," and their officers still wear Mameluke swords shaped like Arab scimitars.[22] Stephen Decatur added to his reputation by offering this famous toast: "Our Country: In her intercourse with foreign nations, may she always be in the right; but our country right or wrong!"[23]

By 1805, the pirates had had enough. Jefferson's willingness to use force had triumphed in America's first war on terror in the Middle East.[24]

Another foreign danger loomed in Jefferson's first term. By means of a secret treaty, France's conqueror Napoleon Bonaparte had gained control of the vast expanse of North America known as Louisiana. France had given this tract over to Spain forty years before. Now she reclaimed it. Jefferson knew that New Orleans was vital. "There is on the globe one spot, the possessor of which is our natural and habitual enemy," he wrote. "It is New Orleans, through which the produce of three eighths of our territory must pass to market."[25] In 1803, Spain was weak. But France was the greatest military power in the world. Despite his long friendship with France, Jefferson sensed danger. "The day that France takes possession of New Orleans, we must marry ourselves to the British fleet and nation."[26] Jefferson knew that only the powerful British fleet could prevent Napoleon from bringing tens of thousands of soldiers to control the Mississippi.

Napoleon might have sent those troops, too, had it not been for the Haitian revolt. Inspired by the French Revolution, Toussaint L'Ouverture led a slave uprising on Haiti. A French army sent to put down the rebellion bogged down, with thousands dying of the dreaded yellow fever. Napoleon was planning to renew his war with England. But without an army, without superior naval power, Napoleon knew the British might seize Louisiana at the outbreak of war. Then he would have nothing. Better to sell it to the Americans.[27]

Still, America's minister in Paris was stunned when Napoleon offered to sell *all of Louisiana*—which was then a vast territory, much larger than the present-day state that bears its name. Robert Livingston had only been empowered to buy the city of New Orleans—and maybe small portions of Florida. Jefferson sent his good friend James Monroe to aid in the negotiations.

The French told the American that the Louisiana territory would be useless to them without New Orleans. Livingston found it hard to live in Paris under Napoleon's dictatorship. He was relieved when he was able to deal with Napoleon's finance minister, Francois Barbé-Marbois, instead of the bribe-taking Talleyrand. Barbé-Marbois was known for his honesty—and for his pro-American spirit.[28] Initially, Barbé-Marbois demanded $25 million, but he soon lowered the price to $15 million.[29]

At home in America, no one knew what Napoleon had in mind. Federalists in Congress attacked the Monroe mission. They wanted President Jefferson to threaten war over New Orleans. Some even wanted Alexander Hamilton to lead an army to capture the Crescent City.[30] Hamilton said there was "not the remotest chance" Napoleon would sell the territory for money.[31]

Publicly, Jefferson talked peace. He let it be known that he was restraining the western governors from taking matters into their own hands. Privately, he let his loyal secretary of state, James Madison, talk tough to the French minister. Americans disliked the secrecy with which Napoleon had reclaimed Louisiana, Madison told Louis André Pichon. More to the point, Madison warned Pichon that "France cannot long preserve Louisiana against the United States."[32]

Few people in Napoleon's Paris knew what was happening. But his brothers—Joseph and Lucien—opposed the deal. The British had bribed both heavily. They confronted their brother while he was in the bathtub. "There will be no debate," Napoleon yelled. The sale of Louisiana would be arranged by a treaty with the Americans. And that treaty would be "negotiated, ratified and executed *by me alone.*" With that, the first consul of France threw himself back in the tub and soaked his brothers with perfumed water.[33] As a virtual dictator, Napoleon knew he did not have to consult his "rubber stamp" legislature.

The Americans, fortunately, did *not* get soaked. When Monroe joined Livingston, he agreed that the offer was simply too good to pass up. Seizing the opportunity, they inked the treaty before Napoleon changed his mind. Monroe had dared to *exceed* his instructions because he knew Jefferson's mind. Monroe was Jefferson's intimate friend and neighbor and Livingston was not.

Thomas Jefferson had the pleasure of announcing the Louisiana Purchase in the President's House on 4 July 1803.[34] The nation had *more than doubled its size.* "It is something larger than the whole U.S.," Jefferson wrote, "probably containing 500 millions of acres, the U.S. containing 434 millions."[35] He couldn't resist adding that the purchase would make the new United States *sixteen and a half times larger* than Great Britain and Ireland.[36] This vast territory had been acquired for $12 million—or about three cents an acre![37]

Some embittered Federalists feared that what they called "a Virginia dynasty" of Jefferson, Madison, and Monroe could never be beaten. They began to plot secession.[38] But the son of the Federalists' last president, John Quincy Adams, understood it best. The Louisiana Purchase would be "next in historical importance to the Declaration of Independence and the adoption of the Constitution," he said.[39]

II. LEWIS AND CLARK:
"THE CORPS OF DISCOVERY"

Thomas Jefferson had been planning an expedition to the Pacific for at least ten years. Statesmen had been seeking a Northwest Passage to the Orient for centuries. Jefferson thought there might be an all-water route across the continent. As early as 1792, Jefferson had persuaded the American Philosophical Society in Philadelphia to sponsor a party to explore the upper reaches of the Missouri River and sail down the Columbia River to the sea. That effort got no farther west than Kentucky.[40]

Now, President Jefferson chose a young man who was his neighbor, his personal secretary, and whom he treated like a son—Captain Meriwether Lewis. Lewis was the son of a deceased Revolutionary War soldier. He had not been formally educated, but he was bright and eager to learn. From youth, he had been an avid hunter and explorer. Service in the army added to his preparation.

Jefferson planned the expedition at Monticello, teaching Lewis himself, then sending him on to Philadelphia for further training. There, Captain Lewis was taught basic medical care by Dr. Benjamin Rush. Rush was Jefferson's close friend, a signer of the Declaration of Independence, and probably America's leading physician. Rush also supplied Lewis with *fifty dozen* of his famous pills. These were purgatives. Comprised of calomel, mercury, and chlorine, they were known as "Rush's Thunderclappers."[41] Jefferson's Philadelphia friends also taught Lewis such essentials as celestial navigation and how to preserve animal and plant specimens for transport back to Monticello.[42]

Lewis's choice of a partner was an inspired one. William Clark was a tall, powerfully built outdoorsman. Four years older than Lewis, he was the younger brother of General George Rogers Clark, "the conqueror of the Northwest." The general was a close friend of President Jefferson. Lewis then did something *very* unusual: he agreed to share command with Clark. Both would be captains. There is hardly an example before or since of such an arrangement working, but here it served brilliantly.[43] Fittingly, they have been known to history as Lewis and Clark.

Lewis outfitted what Jefferson called "the Corps of Discovery," beginning with fifteen Kentucky rifles issued from the federal arsenal at Harpers Ferry. He bought a large boat and stocked it with trading goods for dealing with the Indians. A key item was a brass medallion with Jefferson's profile on it—a token of respect from the Great Chief to the Indian leaders. Jefferson gave Lewis a letter of credit that enabled him to obtain other supplies at government expense—perhaps the original American credit card.[44]

The Lewis and Clark Expedition comprised thirty-three individuals. In addition to the captains, there were sergeants and privates—subject to strict military discipline. Then there was the famous French trapper Toussaint Charbonneau; his Shoshone Indian wife, Sacagawea; their infant son (nicknamed "Pomp" by Lewis); and York, the corps' only black man. York was a slave of William Clark. And Lewis also took Seaman, his large Newfoundland dog.

Lewis and Clark set out from St. Louis in their fifty-five-foot keelboat in May 1804. They sailed up the Missouri River to Mandan, near present-day Bismarck, North Dakota.[45] Pressing on to the "Stony Mountains"—now the Rockies—they made contact with Shoshone tribesmen. Sacagawea was overcome with joy to see her long-lost brother as a chief. This helped greatly to resupply the corps with horses and helpers. Crossing the Bitterroot Mountains in September 1805, Lewis later reported, "We suffered all Cold, Hunger, and Fatigue could impart" during the eleven-day trek.[46]

Add to cold the bitter disappointment Lewis and Clark felt at realizing there was no easy all-water route to the Pacific. The dream of centuries died on that trail.

President Jefferson had instructed the captains to take special care to make a favorable impression on the powerful Sioux nation.[47] This proved harder to do when several Sioux warriors seized the boat's lines and demanded "presents." Lewis trained the boat's cannon on the warriors and had his men ready to fire on them when a chief, Black Buffalo, intervened to keep the peace. Black Buffalo then invited the corps to attend the first "scalp dance" ever witnessed by travelers from the East. With some care, Lewis turned down the chief's offer of a young woman to share his bed.[48]

After nearly two years of grueling marches and boat voyages, the Corps of Discovery descended the Columbia River to the Pacific. Clark captured the excitement of the corps in this typical journal entry: "Ocian in view! O! the joy." They built Fort Clatsop on the Pacific shore and wintered there in 1805–06. They had hoped to find an American sailing ship to take them home. The local Indians' use of phrases like "son-of-a-pitch" told them that American sailors had been in the region.[49] When no ship appeared, Lewis and Clark decided to make the arduous return journey overland.

Once, when a critical decision had to be made, the captains put the measure up for a vote. It was the first *referendum* held by Americans in which voters included an Indian, a black man, and a woman. Sometimes, the clash of cultures produced humorous results. When an Indian chieftain expressed shock at the one hundred lashes Lewis had meted out to an enlisted man who had fallen asleep on watch, Lewis asked him how *he* would make an example of a disobedient warrior. He would *kill* him, the chief said, but he would never beat him. Lewis and Clark were equipped with many small gifts to give the Indians along the way, including tobacco and whiskey.[50] Once, a small tribal group asked the captains a hard question. If President Jefferson really was their great *father*, why would a father want them to lose their reason by getting them drunk? It remains an excellent question.

Jefferson and the country were delighted with Lewis and Clark's discoveries. The president praised their "undaunted courage" upon their return to St. Louis in September 1806. Their success remains heroic in the annals of discovery. Only one man—Sergeant Charles Floyd—died on the journey. Except for a brief clash over horse stealing, the Corps of Discovery maintained good relations with the Indians. Jefferson had instructed them to tell the Indians we wanted their commerce, not their lands. It would soon become apparent we wanted their commerce *and* their lands.*

III. PLOTS, TRIALS, AND TREASON

Stunning events were happening in the East as Lewis and Clark braved the wilds of Montana and Idaho. Vice President Aaron Burr was widely distrusted by the Jeffersonians. They suspected him of trying to slip past the party's presidential nominee by backroom dealings with the Federalists. Burr knew he would not be renominated for the job in 1804, so he decided to run for governor of New York. Backing Burr were certain "High" Federalists who had given up hope of returning to power on the national stage. Men like Timothy Pickering of Massachusetts and Roger Griswold of Connecticut believed the only chance for cultured gentlemen like themselves to continue in office would be for New England to join New York in a Northern Confederacy. They needed Burr as governor to accomplish this.[51]

Federalists like Pickering and Griswold hated Jefferson. Jefferson's brilliant diplomatic stroke in the Louisiana Purchase convinced such

---

* Lewis's subsequent career was marked by tragedy. Appointed governor of Louisiana, he became depressed, took to drink, and eventually took his own life. William Clark served for more than thirty years as a respected Indian agent—"The red-haired chief." But he dishonored himself by brutally refusing brave York's request to be freed from slavery. York had trudged every step of the way to the Pacific and back, the first son of Africa to do so.

men—correctly, as it turned out—that the Federalist Party would never win another national election. They could foresee new states being admitted from the vast expanse that would be carved out of the Louisiana Territory. These new states, they were sure, would support Jefferson's Republicans. Facing such a dismal prospect, these New England Yankees thought it was better to secede from the Union.

Alexander Hamilton was still respected by most Federalists. And Hamilton would have no part of secession. To Massachusetts Federalist Theodore Sedgwick, he wrote that secession would do no good because the real problem was *democracy* itself. And that "poison" was spreading through every state.[52]* Hamilton continued his bitterly anti-Burr campaign, denouncing the man as an unprincipled adventurer. Burr was defeated by Morgan Lewis, another Republican, but one who had the lion's share of Federalist backing. Burr naturally blamed Hamilton—and demanded satisfaction. In those times, that meant a duel.

Though dueling was illegal in New York and increasingly looked down upon throughout the North, Hamilton felt he could not refuse Burr's challenge without appearing cowardly. It could not have been an easy decision; Hamilton's eldest son, Phillip, had been killed in a duel just two and a half years earlier.[53] He said he would reserve his fire. He was resolved to "live innocent" rather than "die guilty" of shedding another man's blood.[54] Knowing he was very likely to die, Hamilton wrote to his wife the night before he met Burr. She had charitably forgiven him for his affair with Maria Reynolds. Now, hoping to console her, he wrote: "Remember, my Eliza, you are a Christian."

Hamilton and Burr were each rowed separately over to the New Jersey

---

* Hamilton's reference to democracy as a "poison" spreading through all the states would not have been as shocking to the Founders' generation as it is to us. They tended to view democracy as direct rule, sometimes leading to mob action, such as Shay's Rebellion and the Whiskey Rebellion. Many of them equated democracy with the Paris mobs that cheered as heads fell from the guillotine. Hamilton clearly supported what we today know as democracy: regular elections, freedom of the press, and majority rule. He demonstrated this by backing Jefferson, clearly the people's choice, in the 1801 presidential decision.

side because dueling was not yet illegal in that state. There, on an out-cropping in Weehauken, the two men faced each other on the morning of 11 July 1804. True to his word, Hamilton held fire. Burr leveled his pistol and shot Hamilton, his bullet passing through his enemy's liver, diaphragm, and lodging in his spine. Hamilton knew the wound was mortal. Carried back to New York City by boat, he warned his friends to be careful of a still-loaded pistol. Friends fetched the Episcopal Bishop of New York, Benjamin Moore, to give the dying man communion. At first, the bishop hesitated, so strong was his revulsion at dueling. But when Hamilton pleaded, forgave Burr, and confessed his faith in Christ, Bishop Moore relented.[55]

Hamilton died after thirty hours of pain. His death was widely mourned. Even the Republican press took up the cry. He was the only one of the Founders to die a violent death. Now, he seemed a martyr to national unity. New York City hung out the crepe for Hamilton's funeral. Ships in the harbor boomed out a final salute. While dueling itself may not have been illegal in New Jersey, Burr was nonetheless indicted for murder in that state and pursued throughout New York—the fugitive vice president.

Fearing for his life, Burr fled to Philadelphia, where he found himself at a reasonable enough distance from his troubles to court a lady friend.[56] From there he traveled to South Carolina and then Virginia, where his reception was much warmer. Hamilton had never been popular in the South, and dueling was considered the ultimate way to preserve a gentle-man's honor.[57]

Jeffersonian Republicans faced the 1804 elections that fall with con-fidence. They replaced Burr with the aged George Clinton, New York's longtime governor. Jefferson carried *every* state except Connecticut and Delaware. In Congress, the Republicans had an overwhelming majority—116–25 in the House, 27–7 in the Senate.[58]

In firm control of the two elective branches of the federal govern-ment, Republicans now prepared to bring the judiciary to heel. For years, Jefferson and his party had denounced the "midnight judges" appointed in the last days of the outgoing Adams administration. Foremost of these was Chief Justice John Marshall. Jefferson's Republican Party was even more outraged when Marshall gave his famous opinion in the case of *Marbury v. Madison* (1803).

In this landmark opinion, the chief justice led the Supreme Court in ruling *against* Federalist William Marbury. He could *not* force Secretary of State Madison to sign a commission so he could have the federal office to which the outgoing President Adams had appointed him. This part of the ruling seemed like a surrender by the Federalist Marshall to the powerful Jeffersonians.

But Marshall ruled that the reason Marbury could not have his commission was that a portion of the Judiciary Act of 1789 that gave the Supreme Court the power to issue such writs was *unconstitutional*. It was the first time the Supreme Court had exercised the power of judicial review. It was a bold stroke by Marshall. In *seeming* to give in to Jefferson and Madison on a minor point, he had assumed a great and powerful weapon to use against his fellow Virginians. Jefferson responded that "the doctrines of that case were given extra-judicially and against law, and . . . their reverse will be the rule of action with the Executive."[59]

No sooner had Burr left the vice presidential chair than he began to conspire with the British minister in Washington. Burr was plotting to take the western states and the Louisiana territory *out* of the Union. He appealed for half a million dollars from the British to help him assemble a force to attack Spanish colonies.[60] In this plot, Burr involved his old friend, General James Wilkinson. Wilkinson was the military governor of the Louisiana Territory. More than that, he had been an agent of a foreign government for twenty years—*Agent 13* in the pay of the king of Spain.[61*]

Burr swept through the West, hailed as a hero. Dueling presented no problems for these rough-and-ready frontiersmen. Nor would they be put

---

* Shockingly, General Wilkinson was then the most senior officer in the U.S. military, a position equivalent to chairman of the Joint Chiefs of Staff!

off by a plan to attack the Spaniards. Obviously, Burr would not have told such new friends as General Andrew Jackson that he was plotting with the hated British to destroy the Union.[62] He wisely denied any secessionist intent, as his conspiracy stirred throughout 1805 and 1806. But then, in December 1806, the plot unraveled. General Wilkinson betrayed his fellow plotter and wrote to President Jefferson, informing him of "a deep, dark, wicked, and widespread conspiracy" by Burr to destroy the Union.[63] Jefferson immediately ordered the arrest of his former vice president, and Burr was hauled back to Richmond for trial. The charge would be treason. The penalty: death by hanging.

Chief Justice John Marshall presided over the trial. His final instruction to the jury construed treason *very narrowly*. In order to prove a charge of treason, the accused must not only have *conspired*, but there must also be two witnesses to some *overt* act.[64] As a result of this charge to the jury, Burr was "not proved to be guilty."[65]

Burr escaped with his neck, but not his reputation. He sailed to Europe, where he continued his plotting. He sought money from Napoleon and from Napoleon's enemies, the British—*anyone* who might pay him to betray his country. He found no takers. Aaron Burr was a spent force.

Today, we can be grateful for Marshall's courage. Aaron Burr was surely guilty. But it would have been very dangerous to hang a former vice president of the United States on anything less than overwhelming evidence. As it happened, Burr was politically dead, and that was enough.

The summer of 1805 saw an epic sea battle beyond the eastern horizon that was to influence America's development throughout the nineteenth century. English Admiral Horatio Nelson chased a combined French-Spanish fleet across the Atlantic and back. At a time when nothing on land moved faster than a horse, the sailing ships manned by Nelson's sailors were the most complex man-made machines on earth.* French

---

* Some of Nelson's ships' could top twelve knots (or more than thirteen miles per hour). This was faster, over time, than teams of horses could run. And Nelson's ships—famously—could direct accurate cannon broadsides three times in less than five minutes—a lethal rate of fire.

Admiral Pierre de Villeneuve was skilled and brave, but he had no chance against Nelson's fleet, and he knew it. The Royal Navy was disciplined. Press gangs made sure that the best sailors were dragged into service, including many unfortunate Americans. On the morning of 21 October 1805, Nelson sighted the French-Spanish fleet off Spain's Cape Trafalgar and hoisted his famous signal: "England expects that every man will do his duty." Though fewer in numbers than the combined French-Spanish fleet, Nelson had superior firepower. English crews could fire more rapidly, more accurately. "Nelson's touch" destroyed the combined fleet and ended Napoleon's hopes of invading England. Nelson died heroically, shot down by a French sniper on the quarterdeck of HMS *Victory*. Nelson's victory at Trafalgar established England's naval supremacy *for a full century*.

And that meant England alone would have the power to threaten America's westward expansion.

IV. "A SPLENDID MISERY": JEFFERSON'S LAST YEARS

Thomas Jefferson had described the presidency as "a splendid misery" when he saw the toll it took on George Washington's health and happiness. That was in 1797. Ten years later, he would experience this misery for himself.

Early in June 1807, HMS *Leopard* attacked the USS *Chesapeake* barely ten miles outside the Chesapeake Bay.[66] The attack came because the American warship had refused to be boarded by Royal Navy press gangs. The British had for years resorted to impressment to man their ships. They would simply board American merchant ships and grab any man whom they thought was an English sailor. This time, they humiliated America by seizing crewmen right out from under the flag of the United States. Jefferson might have had a unanimous declaration of war had he called Congress into session at that moment.

Jefferson was desperate to avoid war. To do so, he resorted to two disastrous alternatives. First, he built more small, cheap gunboats. He wanted to avoid "the ruinous folly of a navy."[67] Next, he tried to pressure Britain by threatening a cutoff of trade. For years, he and Madison had hoped to pressure England by an *embargo* on their manufactured goods. They believed that mobs of unemployed English workers would march on London demanding action to save their jobs.[68] Soon, Jefferson prevailed upon the Republican majority in Congress to pass his embargo. Not only were Federalists almost unanimously opposed to it, even some of Jefferson's Republicans saw it as folly. Virginia Congressman John Randolph mocked Secretary of State Madison. He said Madison had pathetically thrown a sheaf of paper at Britain's *eight hundred warships.*[69]

Only one shining moment relieved the gloom of Jefferson's second term. In his annual Message to Congress in 1806, President Jefferson "congratulated" his fellow citizens on the approach of the year 1808, when they could legislate against the slave trade. In a compromise, the Constitution had permitted the outlawing of the importation of "such persons" as the states saw fit to receive. But Congress had to wait twenty years from the adoption of the Constitution to act. Now, Jefferson urged Congress to act *early* by passing a law to go into effect on 1 January 1808. He wanted to make sure no slave ships would even depart from the Gold Coast of Africa if they could not arrive here before the cutoff date. Jefferson's words were significant. He wanted "to withdraw the citizens of the United States from all further participation in those violations of human rights which have been so long continued on the unoffending inhabitants of Africa, and which the morality, the reputation, and the best interests of our country have long been eager to proscribe."[70] The great English evangelical, William Wilberforce, had been pleading for just such a measure in the British Parliament for a generation; his efforts would be crowned with success in March 1807. Jefferson wanted the United States similarly to reject this inhuman trafficking in human lives. His eloquent statement was the strongest *official* condemnation of slavery to be penned by a president before the election of Abraham Lincoln.*

Despite the economic downturn caused by the embargo, Jefferson was happy to see his chosen successor elected easily in 1808. Despite the unpopularity of Jefferson's embargo, James Madison trounced the unfortunate Federalist Charles Cotesworth Pinckney by 122 electoral votes to 47. Madison swept every region except New England and Delaware. After signing the repeal of the failed embargo, Jefferson rode simply to his successor's inauguration. He had no guard of honor. He hitched his own horse to the hitching post and joined the throng at the ceremony.

"Never did a prisoner, released from his chains, feel such relief as I shall on shaking off the shackles of power," he wrote to a friend.[71] We sense that he meant it.

V. "MR. MADISON'S WAR"

Very early in his presidency, James Madison lost control of events. One of the greatest of the Founders, he was not as well suited for governing what he had helped gather.

Madison eagerly sought peace with England. When he negotiated a treaty with the British minister in Washington, it seemed the English would withdraw their Orders in Council that had punished neutral shipping. Unfortunately, this chance to avert war was lost when Britain's foreign minister turned thumbs down on the treaty.[72]

In 1810, Republicans in Congress responded, incredibly, to the renewed threat by *slashing* appropriations for the army and navy.[73] Although Thomas Jefferson had approved the creation of West Point in

---

* Jefferson's increasing indebtedness, and the hardening attitudes of his Virginia neighbors against manumission of slaves, would shackle the master of Monticello to the hated institution of slavery. But this should not blind us to many of his official words and deeds registered against it.

1802, it remained a Republican belief that a standing army and navy were dangerous and too expensive. They preferred to rely on militia forces and on the woefully inadequate fleet of little gunboats.

The northwest frontier grew restive. An astonishing leader arose among the Indians. Tecumseh was a powerful orator with an even more powerful message: "Where today are the Pequot? Where are the Narragansett, the Mohican, the Pokanoket, and many other once powerful tribes of our people? They have vanished before the avarice and oppression of the white man, as snow before a summer sun."[74]

Tecumseh traveled throughout the territory urging the tribes to form a confederation to resist the Americans' steady pressure. With his brother, known as the Prophet, Tecumseh sternly told the Indians to give up the white man's ways—and especially to avoid alcohol. Tecumseh had seen how other chiefs had been plied with whiskey during negotiations and had signed away some forty-eight million acres since the 1790s.[75] Carried away by this powerful rhetoric, the Prophet refused to be held back by Tecumseh. Instead, he attacked the American militia at a place called Tippecanoe, in modern-day Indiana.*

The Americans, led by General William Henry Harrison, fought off the attackers and claimed the victory on 11 November 1811 that would make him president thirty years later. All recognized Harrison's cool courage in fending off what was rare for the Indians, a night attack.[76]

Americans on the frontier naturally blamed the British for stirring up the Indians. The elections of 1810 had brought to Congress a powerful new group of young Republicans known as "the War Hawks."[77] These War Hawks installed Henry Clay of Kentucky as Speaker of the House. South Carolina's John C. Calhoun joined the group that would shape America's destiny for the next forty years. Older Republicans like Virginia Congressman John Randolph ridiculed the war fever of the new

---

* "Tippecanoe" would come to symbolize a heroic victory that secured the old Northwest Territory against a grave and growing threat.

members. He believed that men who had never smelled salt water cared little for "Free Trade and Sailor's Rights."[78] Randolph compared his new colleagues to the whippoorwill that calls "but one monotonous tone— Canada! Canada! Canada!"[79] It was true that the frontiersman wanted to take Canada and remove the British threat once and for all. In retirement, Thomas Jefferson even encouraged them, saying the conquest of Canada would be "a mere matter of marching."

The British government in London withdrew the despised Orders in Council on 16 June 1812. But the U.S. Congress did not know that and declared war just two days later. Then, in utter defiance of anything resembling sense, Congress adjourned without increasing the navy.[80] Soon, Americans were stunned by the surrender of General William Hull at Detroit. The British commander in Canada, General Isaac Brock, had threatened Hull with an Indian massacre if he resisted.[81] Then, in Chicago, there occurred another of the horrors that so inflamed the people of the American frontier. A Canadian writer tells the story of what happened when six hundred Pottawatomie Indians overwhelmed the Illinois militia:

> At the wagon train, the soldiers' wives, armed with their husbands' swords, fight as fiercely as the men. Two are hacked to pieces: a Mrs. Corbin, wife of a private, who has vowed never to be taken prisoner, and . . . Cicely [a black woman, and a slave] who is cut down with her infant son. Within the wagons, where the younger children [of the soldiers] are huddled, there is greater horror. One young Indian slips in and slaughters twelve single-handed, slicing their heads from their bodies in a fury of bloodlust.[82]

Black Bird, a Pottawatomie chieftain, does not keep his word to spare survivors in return for a ransom of one hundred dollars each:

> Sergeant Thomas Burns of the militia is killed almost immediately by the squaws. His is a more fortunate fate than that of five of his comrades

who are tortured to death that night, their cries breaking the silence over the great lake and sending shivers through the survivors.[83]

Mrs. John Simmons survives the massacre in the wagons. Her husband died in a desperate charge. It is worth recounting her heroic and tragic story in full:

> Believing that the Indians delight in tormenting prisoners who show any emotion, this remarkable woman resolves to preserve the life of her six-month-old child by suppressing all outward manifestations of grief, even when she is led past a row of small, mutilated corpses which includes that of her two-year-old boy, David. Faced with this grisly spectacle, she neither blinks an eye nor sheds a tear, nor will she during the long months of her captivity.
>
> Her Indian [captors] set out for Green Bay on the western shore of Lake Michigan. Mrs. Simmons, carrying her baby, trudges the entire distance working as a servant in the evenings, gathering wood and building fires. When the village is at last reached, she is insulted, kicked, and abused. The following day, she is forced to run the gauntlet between a double line of men and women wielding sticks and clubs. Wrapping her infant in a blanket and shielding it in her arms, she races down the long line, emerging bruised and bleeding but with her child unharmed.
>
> She is given over to an Indian "mother," who feeds her, bathes her wounds, allows her to rest. She needs such sustenance, for a worse ordeal faces her—a long tribal [trek] back around the lake. Somehow, Mrs. Simmons, lightly clad, suffering from cold, fatigue, and malnutrition, manages to carry her child for the entire six hundred miles and survive. She has walked with the Indians from Green Bay back to Chicago, then around the entire eastern shore of the lake to Michilimackinac. But a second even more terrible trek faces her—a three-hundred-mile journey through the snow to Detroit, where the

Indians intend to ransom her. Ragged and starving, she exists on roots and acorns found beneath the snows. Her child, now a year old, has grown much heavier. Her own strength is waning. Only the prospect of release sustains her. . . .

[E]ven after her release, her ordeal is not over. The route to her home is long and hard. By March of 1813 she reaches Fort Meigs on the Maumee [in Ohio]. Here she manages to secure passage on a government wagon [that deposits her] in mid-April, four miles from her father's farm [near Piqua, Ohio].

Mother and child walk the remaining distance to find that the family, which has . . . given her up for dead, has taken refuge in a block-house against Indian marauders. Here, safe at last, she breaks down and for several months cannot contain her tears. In August, she has further reason to weep. Her sister and brother-in-law, working in a nearby flax field, are surprised by Indians, shot, tomahawked, and scalped in front of their four horrified children. Such . . . is the legacy of Tippecanoe and all that proceeded it.[84]

This extended passage helps us understand the intense hostility so many American settlers felt toward the Indians—and toward British officers like Isaac Brock in Canada whom they charged with using the Indians as a terror weapon against them.

Not only are Americans horrified by the terror on the burning frontier, they are deeply disappointed that Canada would be no easy conquest. Far from being "a mere matter of marching," Americans find that Canadians are determined to resist forcible incorporation into the Yankee republic.

Americans are shocked to find they are *not* welcomed by the vastly outnumbered Canadians. As in the Revolutionary War, the French in Canada remain loyal to the British Crown. Even American settlers here, who had been lured north by the promise of cheap land, proved unwilling to help their invading fellow countrymen.

"Mr. Madison's War," as the War of 1812 was called throughout New England, proved to be highly unpopular. It is always trouble for a president when a war is identified with him—and not with the country's enemy. A number of state governments there refused to supply militia troops for the war effort.[85] Some Federalists who bitterly opposed the war were even accused of putting lights on the shore to signal British warships blockading their country. This charge of "blue light Federalist" would be hurled at them for a generation.

By 1814, America was exposed to invasion on three fronts at once: Niagara–Lake Champlain in the north, New Orleans in the south, and in the Chesapeake Bay.[86] On 11 September 1814, a British fleet on Lake Champlain tried to establish control of the area. They were met by Americans under Captain Thomas McDonough in his flagship, the USS *Saratoga*. McDonough wound his badly battered ship around while still at anchor and forced the surrender of HMS *Confiance* and three other British vessels. British Captain George Downie was killed when one of his big guns was hit by one of McDonough's cannonballs.*

McDonough's great victory caused the British general, Sir George Prevost, to retreat. Thus, McDonough's ship *Saratoga* accomplished what the Battle of Saratoga had accomplished for the Americans in 1777. Britain's northern invasion of the United States was turned back.

Americans in the Chesapeake Bay region were not so fortunate. A powerful British fleet raided Maryland's coastal towns and landed a large force of veteran British soldiers.**

Led by General Robert Ross, British regulars met little opposition as they marched toward Washington, D.C. Winning victories at Bladensburg

---

* The British gun, with the indentation made by McDonough's cannonball clearly visible, is on display to this day at the U.S. Naval Academy in Annapolis. It is in front of McDonough Hall.

** The little town of St. Michael's on Maryland's eastern shore staged what was perhaps the first blackout in history during the 1814 British assault. Residents hung lanterns in trees outside of the town and doused their candles. The British fleet shelled the stand of trees, leaving the town unharmed.

and Upper Marlboro, Maryland, the British force entered Washington on 24 August 1814. American Commodore Joshua Barney with only 400 sailors and 120 Marines bravely held the British off for two hours. But the bulk of American militia forces commanded by the grossly incompetent General William Winder broke and ran. They were put to flight by the new Congreve rockets the British employed. These rockets couldn't be aimed accurately. Few hit their targets. But despite the harmlessness of most of them, they made a lot of noise and scared the horses—and the militia.[87]

James Madison was doing his best to organize the resistance to the triumphant British forces. He rode out to the front, where he hastily penciled a note to his heroic wife, Dolley, warning her to flee the city. She and Paul Jennings, a fifteen-year-old black youth, cut the famous Gilbert Stuart portrait of George Washington hanging in the White House from its frame so it could be carried off to safety. The government evacuated the capital before the advancing redcoats. Fortunately, Secretary of State James Monroe had ordered Stephen Pleasanton, a clerk, to save such historic documents as George Washington's commission, the Declaration of Independence, and the Constitution.[88] Secured in a canvas sack, they were spirited away in a carriage.

British Marines entered the Executive Mansion unopposed. After eating the dinner that had been prepared for the Madisons, General Ross ordered his men to torch the President's House. The new Capitol building, too, was burned, as well as the Library of Congress.

Dr. William Thornton, a brave local physician, saved the U.S. Patent Office by appealing to the British not to burn the hundreds of inventors' models. That would be as barbarous, he warned them, as the Turks' burning of the great Alexandria Library in Egypt.[89]

Confident they could continue to rout the poorly led Americans, General Ross and Admiral Cockburn sailed up the Chesapeake to Baltimore. General Ross jauntily told a Maryland farmer in whose house he had breakfasted that he would not return for dinner. "I'll have supper tonight in Baltimore, or in hell."[90] He may have gotten his wish. Shortly afterward, two American sharpshooters fired on the advancing British column. One of them hit General Ross, mortally wounding him on 12 September 1814.[91]

Admiral Cockburn continued on toward Baltimore. First, he would have to get past the stout Fort McHenry. Again, he used the fearsome Congreve rockets. But the defenders of Baltimore were made of sterner stuff. The fort held.

During the nights of September 13–14, a young lawyer named Francis Scott Key boarded a British warship. Key was determined to obtain the release of an elderly American doctor who had been caught taking British stragglers prisoner. Key persuaded the British that Dr. Beanes had actually treated his prisoners very humanely. The Americans could not be released, however, while the bombardment of Fort McHenry was in progress. Throughout the night, old Dr. Beanes asked Key if "our flag was still there." Thus was born the inspiration for Francis Scott Key's poem, "The Defense of Fort M'Henry." The poem, later to become our national anthem as "The Star-Spangled Banner," lifted American spirits even as Baltimore was spared.[92]

The British invasion force then withdrew to the island of Jamaica to prepare their next assault on America. This time their target would be New Orleans. In the Southwest, Americans had already faced another Indian uprising. Upper Creeks, known as "Red Sticks," had overwhelmed Fort Mims on 30 August 1813. The fort was located forty miles from present-day Mobile, Alabama. There, the Red Sticks under Chief Red Eagle had massacred nearly 250 settlers. "The children were seized by the legs, and killed by batting their heads against the stockading. The women were scalped, and those who were pregnant were opened while they were still alive and the embryo infants were let out of the womb."[93] Red Eagle tried to stop these atrocities but could not.

The news of the Fort Mims massacre electrified Tennessee. General Andrew Jackson was on a sickbed, recuperating from wounds he received in a barroom fight with Thomas Hart Benton and Jesse Benton. Despite the loss of blood and the bullet still lodged in his shoulder, the pale, gaunt Jackson got up to lead militia troops against the Creeks. When some of his men panicked and tried to escape duty, Jackson had six of them executed "to encourage the others" and quickly proceeded to defeat the Creeks.[94] Jackson's tall, lean, ramrod-straight stance and his hard, unyielding discipline quickly gained him the nickname "Old Hickory." The Indians who felt his wrath called him "Sharp Knife."

The Upper Creeks had been inspired by Tecumseh's brave resistance. When Jackson killed nine hundred Creeks at the Battle of Horseshoe Bend, 27 March 1814, he broke the back of the uprising. He ordered the Creeks to meet him at Fort Jackson (present-day Wetumpka, Alabama), where he forced them to cede some twenty-three million acres to the United States. Nearly three-fifths of Alabama and one-fifth of Georgia were obtained by the hard treaty Jackson demanded. "Until this is done, your nation cannot expect happiness or mine security," Jackson told the assembled Creeks on 10 July 1814.[95]

As President Madison's diplomatic representatives met their British counterparts for peace talks in Ghent, Belgium, the American position was weak, indeed. The British demanded large parts of Maine, which they then occupied, and the creation of a large Indian buffer state along the Ohio River. America's John Quincy Adams already had thirty years of experience in diplomacy. And Henry Clay had thirty years of experience playing poker. Both men's skills were to prove indispensable.[96]

VI. THE BATTLE OF NEW ORLEANS

The leader of the British invasion force was the brave young general, Sir Edward Pakenham. General Pakenham was the brother-in-law of the Duke of Wellington, England's greatest soldier. Among Sir Edward's 7,500 redcoats were many veterans of Wellington's successful campaigns against Napoleon's troops. The British intended to take the city of New

Orleans and as much of Louisiana as possible. These would be valuable bargaining chips in the peace negotiations in Ghent. Pakenham was to encourage the people of Louisiana to secede from the United States and join either the Spanish empire or attach themselves to the British.[97] Some Americans worried that Louisiana, purchased a decade earlier and admitted as a state only in 1812, might be lured away.

As General Jackson prepared to meet the British invaders, he imposed strict martial law on the lively city. This was a very unpopular move. He also had to deal with the famed Baratarian pirates—led by Jean Lafitte. Seemingly loyal to no side but their own, Lafitte's pirates had turned down a British offer because it was too small. Jackson needed every man he could find to defend the besieged city. Although he had denounced Lafitte and his men as "hellish banditti," Jackson gave in to the pleas of Edward Livingston and other leaders of New Orleans and accepted Lafitte's help.

As the British advanced toward New Orleans, they were undetected until 23 December 1814, when they came to the plantation of Major Gabriel Villaré. He had been sitting on his front porch, smoking a cigar and talking to his brother. Suddenly, redcoats came crashing through the dense woods and seized both brothers. Villaré jumped out an open window. "Catch him or kill him!" yelled the British colonel. Villaré was too fast for them. He jumped over a picket fence and ran into the underbrush. Legend has it he had to kill a favorite dog, "with tears in his eyes," to keep it from giving him away.[98]

Villaré's timely warning enabled Jackson to fortify his position in front of the Crescent City. Jackson had his men arrange themselves in front of the Rodriguez Canal, which ran perpendicular to the Mississippi River. With the river on his right and an impassable cypress wood on his left, Jackson's defensive position was a commanding one. He led an extraordinary group of some five thousand men. He had volunteers from New Orleans, including Creole aristocrats, tradesmen, and manual workers. He had Tennessee and Kentucky militia. Free Negroes formed a key element of his force. Also included were Spanish, French, Portuguese, Italians, and Indians. And, of course, he had the pirates.[99] It was just the kind of "rabble" the British had been taught to despise. They called the Americans "dirty shirts."[100] But high manners and neatly laundered tunics would not save the day.

On Christmas Day 1814, a number of fugitive slaves entered the British lines in front of New Orleans. They would gladly work if they could only achieve their freedom. One of these poor men addressed a British officer in perfect French. He implored them to remove a horrible spiked collar. It had been fastened around his neck as punishment for his attempts at escape. Freeing him from this torture, a British officer sneered at the Americans' claims. "This [is an] ingenious symbol of a land of liberty," he said. Still, the British were no liberators for the oppressed slaves of Louisiana. Their agents posted notices throughout the bayou country: YOUR SLAVES SHALL BE PRESERVED TO YOU. They appealed to the formerly French plantation owners to forsake their new American identity.[101]

When the British commenced their attack on the morning of 8 January 1815, General Pakenham ordered a rocket fired off. Jackson's calm courage inspired his men. "Don't mind those rockets," he said, "they are mere toys to amuse children."[102] Pakenham's invaders included the famed Ninety-Third Highland Regiment, the fierce, kilted Scots. Jackson's men took dead aim on the advancing redcoats and mowed them down. Described as "more a massacre than a battle," the redcoats could not overcome the murderously accurate rifle and artillery fire that Jackson poured into them.[103] General Pakenham himself was shot to death, along with several subordinate general officers. The British toll was devastating. In just minutes, they lost 291 dead, 1,262 wounded, and 484 captured or missing. The American toll, incredibly, was just 13 dead, 39 wounded, and 19 missing in action.[104]

It was a bitter blow to British pride. Who could believe the American "dirty shirts" could inflict such a defeat on His Majesty's best troops? When a Tennessee militiaman demanded the surrender of a wounded invader, the redcoat officer turned around and saw a wild-eyed, unshaven, unwashed American. He was appalled: "What a disgrace for a British officer to have to surrender to a chimney sweep!"[105]

One revealing incident suggests why the Americans were so formidable. Immediately after the battle, three dead British soldiers' bodies were taken out of a ditch. Several members of a New Orleans militia company were disputing among themselves about which one had killed the colonel. "If he isn't hit above the eyebrows," said a merchant named Withers, "it wasn't my shot." Sure enough, the colonel's body revealed Withers's shot—a testament to the deadly *withering* fire of the American line.[106]

Jackson did not pursue the retreating British. Nor did he relax his strict military discipline over his men and the now-saved city. Soon, however, the British withdrew, never to return. Jackson told the leading Catholic cleric in the city, Abbé Guillaume Dubourg, that the victory was the result of the "signal interposition of heaven."[107] Few Americans would disagree. The Abbé agreed and asked Jackson to join him in a *Te Deum*, a Mass of celebration in the cathedral.

Within weeks, news of the great victory came to Washington, D.C. Still depressed over the burning of the capital the previous August, Washingtonians now went wild with joy. "Incredible Victory!" read the headlines. Editors with a more literary bent quoted Shakespeare's *Henry VI*: "Advance our waving colors on the walls / Rescued is Orleans from the English wolves."[108]

Within days of Jackson's great victory the capital had further reason to rejoice. The Treaty of Ghent had been signed on Christmas Eve 1814. The news had taken almost six weeks to cross the Atlantic. Had there been a cable, the Battle of New Orleans might never have been fought. If Americans had known what this treaty would look like *before* they had gone to war, few would ever have approved the course. The Treaty of Ghent gave America no gains. The British had yielded not one inch on impressment. But neither had they insisted on territorial concessions.

It settled nothing, and yet it settled everything.

For, with the victory of New Orleans, Americans could be proud of themselves once more. They had taken on the greatest power in the world and survived with their independence intact. Even if they had not conquered Canada, they now had what Theodore Roosevelt would call "a hostage" for Britain's good behavior. They had a great naval tradition, a beloved new hero in Old Hickory, and a renewed sense of patriotism as evidenced by "The Star-Spangled Banner." To this day, America has never enjoyed so stunning and spectacular a military triumph as Jackson gained at New Orleans. And the War of 1812 helped to form a new American consciousness. This American identity was fused in the crucible of battle.[109]

VII. THE MISSOURI COMPROMISE

Efforts to make states out of the vast lands conveyed in the Louisiana Purchase were bound to bring conflict. Louisiana had been admitted as a slave state in 1812. But slavery had already existed there under the French and the Spanish.

The Missouri Territory was different.

Northerners were concerned to see that slavery was not withering away, as so many of the Founders' generation thought it would. Instead, it seemed to be expanding. Alabama and Mississippi had been admitted as slave states, but they were in the Deep South. There, the strength of slavery seemed to be increasing. The cotton gin had been invented in 1793 by Eli Whitney of Connecticut. This device helped make cotton much more profitable. And cotton was the basis of slave agriculture. But with Missouri, slavery seemed to be pressing dangerously north and west.

Northern members of Congress managed to hold out for concessions. Missouri would be admitted as a slave state even as Maine, formerly a region of Massachusetts, was admitted as a free state. The *southern* boundary line of Missouri at 36°30' north latitude would be the dividing line. No slavery would be allowed *north* of that line. Both sides seemed satisfied.

Henry Clay of Kentucky was the moving force in crafting this legislative solution to a seemingly insoluble problem. His efforts to preserve the Union earned him the admiration of thousands and the title "the Great Compromiser."*

But Thomas Jefferson was troubled. In retirement at Monticello, the former president wrote that "this momentous question, like a fire bell in the night, awakened and filled me with terror. I considered it the knell of the union."[110] Jefferson presciently saw that "a geographical line, coinciding with a marked principle, moral and political, once conceived and held up to the angry passions of men, will never be obliterated; and every new irritation will mark it deeper and deeper."[111] Here, Jefferson forecast with astonishing precision the history of his country over the next forty years. At this point, Jefferson had changed his position on the expansion of slavery. He previously had *opposed* slavery's extension (and had fallen just one vote short of establishing that as national policy when he proposed it to the Confederation Congress in 1784). Now, perhaps influenced by Madison's writings in *Federalist* No. 10, Jefferson thought it might be easier to eradicate slavery if it were more *diluted* throughout the Union. Jefferson admitted his own paradox. "We have a wolf by the ears, and we can neither hold him, nor safely let him go."[112]

VIII. THE MONROE DOCTRINE

James Monroe, elected in 1816 to be the fifth president, tried to ease some of the political tensions that marked the early republic. The years of his presidency are sometimes called the "Era of Good Feelings," with Monroe embarking on a goodwill tour of the country to promote unity. As he neared the end of his second term, President Monroe began to cast about

---

* The Missouri Compromise preserved the peace of the Union for forty years. It can be argued that the *repeal* of the Missouri Compromise in the 1850s led directly to civil war.

for a way to make his mark on history. When the British foreign secretary, George Canning, proposed a joint Anglo-American declaration on Latin America, Monroe was keenly interested. Relations had warmed with Britain since the end of the War of 1812. This would be a way to advance ties. Jefferson and Madison, both now retired, commended the idea of declaring the Western Hemisphere "off-limits" to further colonization by the powers of Europe. Canning wanted to preserve Britain's strong commercial ties with the newly independent Latin American republics. America wanted to limit Russia's advance in the Pacific Northwest.[113]

It was Secretary of State Adams, however, who gave Monroe his great opening. Adams proposed that President Monroe issue the declaration *on his own*. "It would be more candid as well as more dignified to avow our principles explicitly to France and Russia than to come in as a cock-boat in the wake of a British man-of-war," Adams told Monroe's cabinet.[114]

And so it was decided that the document that bears his name would be announced in the president's annual Message to Congress in December 1823. President Monroe's message came to be known as the Monroe Doctrine. He offered it as the policy of the United States that the Western Hemisphere would not be open to further colonization by the Great Powers of Europe. The United States would not try to seize colonial possessions—a point welcomed by the British who still ruled Canada—but they would not permit any European nation to retake colonies that had already become independent—or that might *become* independent in the future.

The Monroe Doctrine has been a pillar of American foreign policy ever since. Surprisingly, the British did not react negatively to having been "left at the altar." The British *chargé* in Washington wrote home to London commending "the explicit and manly tone" of the declaration.[115] The truth, of course, was that it was the "oaken walls" of the British fleet that protected Latin America's independence at this point and not the "parchment picket fence" of Mr. Monroe's declaration. Still, this bold move showed that America intended to stand on her own two feet in the community of nations.

IX. "IS IT THE FOURTH?":
ADAMS AND JEFFERSON DIE

Thomas Jefferson had not rested in retirement. He maintained an active correspondence with hundreds of friends and political allies. He developed new strains of plants, reportedly saying, "I am an old man, but a *young* gardener." And he received hordes of visitors at Monticello.

In one of his famous letters, he wrote this advice to the son of a good friend, the young Thomas Jefferson Smith. It was to be shown to the lad when he was old enough to appreciate it:

> Few words will be necessary, with good dispositions on your part. Adore God. Reverence and cherish your parents. Love your neighbor as yourself, and your country more than yourself. Be just. Be true. Murmur not at the ways of Providence. So shall the life into which you have entered be the portal to one of eternal and ineffable bliss. And if to the dead it is permitted to care for the things of this world, every action of your life will be under my regard. Farewell.[116]

One of the most illustrious of his visitors was the aged Marquis de Lafayette. Three hundred people gathered at the entrance to Jefferson's mountaintop home when the aged French hero's coach arrived. "Ah, Jefferson!" cried the sixty-seven-year-old general. "Ah, Lafayette!" replied the declining eighty-one-year-old statesman. Both men broke into tears.[117] The next night, 5 November 1824, Jefferson hosted Lafayette at a grand dinner in the Dome Room of the not-yet-completed Rotunda of the University of Virginia. Among those in attendance were former presidents James Madison and James Monroe.[118] Both of these Jefferson friends and intimates were involved in the project of his old age, the university.*

---

* If Thomas Jefferson had done nothing else, he would still have gained distinction as an architect. In 1976, the American Institute of Architects selected Jefferson's designs for the University of Virginia—his "Academical Village"—as the greatest achievement of American architecture in two hundred years.

Jefferson and Madison had engaged in "a great collaboration" for nearly fifty years. Now, both retired to their farms in the rolling Piedmont country, they worked together to establish the University of Virginia. American history affords no better example of a friendship so true, so intimate, so filled with productive labors for their country. "To myself you have been a pillar of support through life. Take care of me when dead, and be assured that I shall leave you with my last affections," Jefferson wrote to the Great Little Madison in the last year of his life.[119]

There now occurred during John Quincy Adams's single term an event that even today astonishes. President Adams's father, John, had been reconciled to Thomas Jefferson in 1811 after nearly a decade of sullen silence between the two giants of the Revolution. Dr. Benjamin Rush brought about the end of their estrangement. It was one of Rush's innumerable services to America. "I have always loved Thomas Jefferson!" said Adams to two of Jefferson's young Virginia neighbors. They immediately resumed writing one another.[120] Although they would be no closer than Braintree, Massachusetts, is to Charlottesville, Virginia, they conducted a long, affectionate correspondence for the rest of their lives.

As the fiftieth anniversary of the Declaration of Independence approached, the country began to turn its eyes once again to these two revolutionary leaders. When the mayor of Washington, D.C., invited Mr. Jefferson to a celebration in the capital, the author of the Declaration had to decline. He was eighty-three years old and in failing health. But he sent a letter, in which he said: "All eyes are opened or opening to the rights of man. The general spread of the light of science has already laid open to every view that the mass of mankind has not been born with saddles on their backs, nor a favored few booted and spurred ready to ride them legitimately by the grace of God. . . . Let the annual return to this day forever refresh our recollection of these rights, and an undiminished devotion to them."[121]

John Adams, at ninety, could no longer wield his pen. But he gave a visiting delegation on June 30 an eloquent answer to their request for a Fourth of July message. "Independence Forever!" the old patriot said.

As Jefferson lay dying at Monticello, he asked, "Is it the Fourth?" It was. Five hundred miles north, John Adams, unaware that Jefferson had died earlier that day, said, "Thomas Jefferson still survives." He then slipped away. His death was followed by a violent thunderstorm; it was called "the artillery of Heaven."[122] The simultaneous passing of the two heroes of the Revolution touched Americans as nothing had since New Orleans. Many saw the hand of Providence in the event. Many still do.

FIVE

JACKSON AND DEMOCRACY

(1829–1849)

I. FROM CAUCUS TO RAUCOUS: THE ELECTION OF 1828

John Quincy Adams knew that he was cold, austere, respected, but never much liked. Unlike his great father, he lacked any trace of humor. Even his most innocent diversions from the crushing burdens of office came back to haunt him. When he purchased a billiard table with his own money, he was loudly attacked for installing "gaming tables and gambling furniture" in the President's House.[1] He was an awkward and uninspiring speaker. So was Jefferson, but John Quincy Adams lacked the Virginian's "peculiar felicity of expression."

Once, when called upon in Baltimore to celebrate the defense of the city in the War of 1812, President Adams was asked to propose a toast. "Ebony and Topaz," the scholarly president cried out, explaining it was British General Robert Ross's posthumous coat of arms, "and to the Republican militiamen who gave it." His hearers were stunned. You had to know about British heraldry and that Ross had been killed by American sharpshooters. The toast was so pedantic, so muddled, that he might as well have spoken in the classical Greek in which he was so accomplished. The president was hooted at throughout the country. "Ebony and Topaz" became a rallying cry for the Jacksonians nationwide to show how out of touch with the rising democratic spirit of the age John Quincy Adams was.[2] It did not help that Adams spent much of his term in a blue funk, exuding the impression of a loser.

When Adams laid out his program in a Message to Congress, it bore strong resemblance to the "American System" advocated by Henry Clay. Adams supported tariffs and a national bank. He proposed a national university, a naval academy, further explorations on the model of Lewis and Clark, and an extensive system of roads, canals, and harbors. He knew such an ambitious program would meet with resistance from taxpayers, but he urged members of Congress not to let the world see that America's government was "palsied by the will of our constituents." British states-man Edmund Burke might have been proud of that statement, but it was political suicide for Adams to say it.

Andrew Jackson was about as different from John Quincy Adams as a man could be. Strong men feared Jackson. A story from his past shows why. When he was a judge in Tennessee in the 1790s, he sent a succession of bailiffs, sheriffs, and deputies to apprehend a huge, strong man who, in a drunken rage, had cut off his own child's ears. When all of these came back empty-handed, Judge Jackson himself went to seize the accused. Asked why he meekly surrendered to Jackson after resisting an entire posse, the man said: "Why, when he came up, I looked him in the eye, and I saw shoot. And there wasn't shoot in nary other eye in the crowd."[3] Stories like this made Jackson a legend in his own time.

Jackson and his followers sincerely believed he represented the true Jeffersonian philosophy. To Jackson, Adams's frosty manner concealed a man of aristocratic pretensions. Was John Quincy Adams not, after all, the son of Jefferson's defeated rival?

The Jacksonians immediately seized upon Adams's *elitist* disdain for the common man. If the will of the people was not to govern in a *demo-cratic* republic, whose will would rule?[4]

With the collapse of the Federalists after 1816, Jeffersonian Republicans dominated national politics. The Adams and Clay faction of this Jeffersonian party was known as National Republicans. Their leaders knew they were saddled with an unattractive candidate. They knew he lacked the fundamental skills of politics. So they did what today we would call "driving up the opponent's negatives." They began a vicious campaign of character assassination directed at Jackson.

Without authorization from President Adams, to be sure, they nonetheless accused Andrew Jackson of adultery. He had married his beloved Rachel, they charged, *before* she was divorced from her first husband, Lewis Robards. The accusation was true, but more complicated. Robards, an abusive and vindictive man, had filed for divorce before the Virginia legislature, *but had failed to complete the divorce proceedings.* Impetuous Andrew had married Rachel before seeing the documents that would prove she was finally free. When, in 1793, the couple learned that Robards had belatedly gone through with the process, they quickly *remarried.* The vast majority of people in Tennessee gave no more thought to the matter. Such irregularities were not uncommon on the frontier where communications were slow and law and custom more flexible.

What was less flexible was Jackson's temper when someone was foolish enough to impugn Rachel's honor. The fierce Jackson was fire-flash quick to call him to account—usually by pistol duel. People feared Jackson with good cause. He participated in more than a dozen recorded duels, many of them over his wife's besmirched name. Until his dying day, he bore in his chest a bullet from Charles Dickinson. He had met Dickinson, who had taken Rachel's "sacred name" in his "polluted mouth," for a duel on what frontiersmen called "the field of honor" in 1806.[5] Dickinson, a crack shot, had fired first at Jackson. Due to an ill-fitting suit on which the vest buttons were too far to the left, Jackson was hit two inches to the *right* of his heart. Jackson took deadly aim and killed the dashing young man. "I should have hit him if he had shot me through the brain," Jackson reportedly said.[6]

Not content with smearing Jackson's darling wife, opponents charged his mother had been a common prostitute. In an overt appeal to racism, they said his father was a mulatto, a man of mixed black and white racial background.

When it seemed the campaign of 1828 could not get uglier, it did with the "Coffin Handbill," a classic example of a *negative* ad. No obscure references to topaz and ebony here, this poster was as crude as it was effective. It depicted six black coffins with the names of the Tennessee militiamen whom General Jackson had ordered shot for desertion. The purpose of the Coffin Handbill was to tarnish the reputation of the Hero of New Orleans and show him up as a cruel and barbarous tyrant. It little mattered that even the revered Washington had had to execute mutinous soldiers in the Revolution. Or that *failure* to instill military discipline had opened up the nation's capital to the torches of British invaders in the same war Jackson was fighting.

Jackson's backers were hardly innocent in this first campaign of the new mass democracy. They charged President Adams with having pimped for the tsar when he was U.S. ambassador to Russia. There was no truth whatsoever to the malicious lie that Adams had provided an *American* girl to "the Autocrat of all the Russias," but the story fit in with Americans' rising suspicions of all haughty aristocrats.

Isn't this what the critics of democracy throughout the ages had warned of? Wasn't it *inevitable* that popular government would descend into the gutter? All this talk of pimps and prostitutes was just what the friends of aristocracy found so distasteful in democracy. Here, in the first truly mass contest in American history, the standards for decency and just plain truthfulness could hardly have been lower.

The vicious mudslinging barely slowed the Jackson juggernaut. Jackson swept most of the nation. Adams's support was confined to New England, New Jersey, and the old Federalist strongholds in New York,

Maryland, and Delaware. With 178 electoral votes to 83, Jackson had also triumphed in the newly important *popular* vote. Carrying more than 56 percent of the people's votes, Jackson rode in on a tide of democracy. This was the first election in history in which more than one million votes were cast. Although women generally did not vote and very few black males were enfranchised, the election of 1828 is nonetheless important because it began an ongoing process of an ever-expanding electorate.* With 1,155,340 votes cast in a population of thirteen million, American democracy in 1828 offered a broader franchise than any nation in history had ever enjoyed.[7]

Following the vindication Jackson must have felt on election day, tragedy struck at the Hermitage, his Nashville home. Just before Christmas 1828, Rachel Jackson suffered a massive heart attack and died suddenly. The grief-stricken Andrew Jackson knew his wife was a deeply religious woman. He believed the shame and stress of seeing her name dragged through the mud had killed her. He would never forgive his political enemies for this. At times, his vengeance would be self-defeating, but his enemies had good reason to fear his wrath.

"Jackson and Reform" had been the campaign cry of the Democrats. What the reform would be had been left purposely vague. One thing it meant to Jackson was "rotation in office." He intended to remove long-time officeholders from the federal payroll. "To the victor belong the spoils," one politico cried. The general's opponents denounced this as a "spoils system," but Jackson thought it was basic good government. No one was entitled by birth or family connection to hold a paid position. Too many had seen their federal jobs as lifetime appointments. In the end it was more sound and fury than substance; the president replaced only about 10–20 percent of federal appointees during his two terms. Many of these were replacements for vacancies.[8]

---

* Some women *did* vote in early America, though it may not have been more than 1 percent. Women who voted were those who met the property qualification in their own right. Thus, they would most likely have been older women and widows.

As Jackson approached the Federal City by steamboat and by coach, there was a growing sense of excitement. President Adams, deeply hurt by Americans' rejection, noted that the general had failed even to call upon him after he arrived in Washington. Adams was stung by this incivility. He denied having anything to do with the scurrilous attacks on the Jacksons. He resolved to depart the President's House and break the tradition of attending his successor's inauguration. This decision was taken for the same reason his father had sullenly departed the city in 1801: no one had bothered to invite him to the ceremony. Even so, both Adamses looked like sore losers to their countrymen and to history.

Wearing a black mourning suit with a "weeper" wrapped around his tall hat, General Jackson stood erect and commanding as he approached the inaugural stand on 4 March 1829.* A huge crowd had come from all parts of the country to see the "Gin'ral" take the oath. Senator Daniel Webster marveled at the sight of fifteen to twenty thousand citizens who jostled one another for a better view: "Persons have come five hundred miles to General Jackson and they really seem to think that the country is rescued from some dreadful danger!"[9] Before letting Chief Justice John Marshall administer the oath, the general gave a sweeping and stately bow to the assembled multitude. *Democracy!*

All were impressed with Jackson's natural dignity. Although his sketchy education and his irregular spelling brought him contempt from Adams's Harvard friends, Jackson was well versed in the Bible. For his countrymen, this was enough. Following the inauguration at the Capitol, a huge mob arrived by cart and carriage, by horse and on foot at the White House.

There had been no planning for such a throng as that which invaded

---

* Although Queen Victoria would be seen as a model of devotion for wearing widow's weeds for forty years after the loss of her beloved Albert, Andrew Jackson set an earlier standard for the grieving spouse. Jackson wore funeral black from the day of Rachel's death in 1828 until his own in 1845. It was doubtless a sincere expression of his grief, but it was also a rebuke to the opponents he believed had hounded his beloved Rachel into her grave.

the Executive Mansion that inauguration day. President Jackson was nearly crushed as the crowd pressed in on him. Rough frontiersmen stood on elegant chairs wearing muddy boots, trying to see the Hero. The president had to be rescued by a "flying wedge" of friends as butlers carried buckets of liquor punch out onto the lawn. People jumped out of windows, breaking glass and tearing at curtains. To Washington's "cliff dwellers," the somewhat stuffy social elite, the scene looked like the Paris mob invading Versailles. One Unitarian minister, horrified by the scene, preached the next Sunday on Luke 19:41: Jesus "saw the city and wept over it."[10] Nothing like it had ever been seen before, and nothing since.

Criticism of the vulgarity of the mob cannot alter one fact: no one could imagine such a multitude even *wanting* to rub elbows with the frosty Adams. It was doubtless the most incredible inauguration party in our history. And Jackson, even more than Jefferson, was determined to be "the people's president."

II. THE PEGGY EATON AFFAIR

One of the undistinguished choices Jackson made was to have great significance. Former Tennessee senator John Eaton was named to be secretary of war. He had no particular experience or aptitude for the post. This came not to matter at all. Eaton had become involved with the daughter of the tavern keeper where he roomed. The lively and pretty Peggy O'Neale was the widow of a U.S. Navy lieutenant who either died or committed suicide when his accounts came up short. Gossiping Washington socialites believed that Peggy had been the senator's mistress for years. To put an end to it all, Jackson urged his new secretary of war to speedily marry the comely widow and "make an honest woman" of her. But the hasty marriage didn't solve the problem. Cabinet wives, led by the wife of Vice President John C. Calhoun, refused to receive Mrs. Eaton. Even Jackson's own niece refused to have anything to do with the unfortunate Peggy. All of social Washington, it seemed, had come down with a case of "Eaton malaria."[11]

Whether President Jackson thought Peggy Eaton was wronged as his precious Rachel had been wronged is not clear. He did believe that the rumors were being circulated by "the minions of Mr. Clay." By attacking the Eatons, Clay was really trying to get at the president, Jackson believed.[12]

Jackson himself had a "past" to live down. And not just the untimely marriage to Rachel, the duels, the brawls, and the executions. As a young *blood* on the frontier, the high-spirited Jackson had been a definite rowdy. Card playing, horse racing, drinking, and crude jokes had marked the earliest years of this war orphan. One elderly North Carolina woman expressed her astonishment:

> What! Jackson up for President? Jackson? Andrew Jackson? The Jackson that used to live here in Salisbury? Why, when he was here, he was such a rake that my husband would not bring him into the house. It is true, he might have taken him out to the stable to weigh horses for a race, and might drink a glass of whiskey with him there. Well, if Andrew Jackson can be President, anybody can![13]

Once he even cruelly invited the town prostitute and her wayward daughters to a society ball in Salisbury, North Carolina. But ever since the day the thirteen-year-old Andrew had warded off the saber blow of a brutal British officer with his bare hand, no one doubted his courage.

It took courage to claim that Mrs. Eaton was "as chaste as a virgin," but President Jackson's steel blue eyes flashed as he told his cabinet she would be received socially. As secretary of state, Martin Van Buren had an advantage over all his colleagues. He was a widower. He could pay a respectful call on the embattled Peggy and not have to worry about the disapproval of the society ladies. When Henry Clay heard about Jackson's staunch defense of Mrs. Eaton, he sarcastically replied: "Age cannot wither nor time stale her infinite virginity!"[14]* Surely, Jackson learned of Clay's cruel gibe. It could only have confirmed in his mind Clay's involvement in the assault on the mourned Rachel.

There was, of course, another side to all this. Peggy O'Neale Eaton bore one of the most distinctive of *Irish* names. By sticking up for the shunned Peggy, the president was making a strong statement for inclusion in the new *democratic* America. The Irish were only now beginning to flood the cities of the East. They would become one of the most loyal of the groups devoted to Andrew Jackson.

Vice President John C. Calhoun was the great loser in this affair. He had made clear his opposition to President John Quincy Adams for the first four years he served in the vice presidency. Calhoun's support for Jackson in the 1828 contest helped line up the planters of the South for the Hero. He certainly could have looked to the aged Jackson to return the favor in 1832. It was not farfetched for Calhoun to think *he* might be the next president of the United States.

But now Jackson blamed Calhoun's wife, Floride, for stirring up the cabinet wives against Peggy Eaton. From this point on, Jackson would show a clear preference for Martin Van Buren. Not for nothing was the clever New Yorker known as "the Magician." Peggy Eaton would prove worthy of Old Hickory's friendship. Once, when she attended a dinner at the Hermitage, Mrs. Eaton saw Jackson out in the garden, stretched out over Rachel's grave. "This great old hater was also a grand old lover," she said tenderly.[15]

Jackson would also learn that Calhoun had secretly sought to have him censured for his Florida exploits when the South Carolinian had served in the Monroe cabinet. Only Adams had defended the daring general behind those closed doors. While this belated truth did not bring Jackson to look more kindly on his defeated rival, it did sour his relations with his vice president.

---

* Clay was at least as clever as he was cruel. His jest was a turn on a phrase from Shakespeare's *Antony and Cleopatra*: "Age cannot wither her, nor custom stale/Her infinite *variety*" (Act II, Scene 2).

III. JOHN C. CALHOUN: THE CAST-IRON MAN

Upon assuming office, President Jackson immediately installed the able Martin Van Buren as secretary of state. The rest of his cabinet he filled with mediocre men whose only distinction seemed to be unbending loyalty to Jackson. This would matter little, since over time Jackson would take his advice from an informal group of advisers known as "the Kitchen Cabinet." The press gave this group of Jackson's intimates this name because they supposedly slipped into his White House study by way of the kitchen.[16] John C. Calhoun of South Carolina was anything but mediocre. Born in 1782 in the upcountry region of the Palmetto State, he attended Yale University, an unusual choice for a Southerner in those times. At six feet two inches, rangy, with a shock of dark hair and dark, penetrating eyes, Calhoun had no trouble attracting attention at Yale. Because he felt the views of his Connecticut neighbors uncongenial, Calhoun burrowed ever deeper into his books. He became an excellent student, soon selected for academic honors and membership in Phi Beta Kappa.[17]

After graduating from Yale and studying law in Connecticut, Calhoun returned to South Carolina. There he was both drawn to and repelled by his state's great seaport, Charleston. He compared it with the dour, serious ways of the upcountry: "It was Cavalier from the start; we were Puritan."* Charleston's merchant princes welcomed to their beautiful city French Huguenots, Irish Catholics, German Lutherans, and Sephardic Jews, creating a lively, cultured ambience. George Washington considered the comely women of Charleston the high point of his entire southern tour of 1791. Charlestonians were confident, capable, and proud. "Here, sir, the Ashley and Cooper Rivers join to form the Atlantic Ocean," they would tell visitors with a merry twinkle in their eyes.

---

* The reference was to the English civil war of two centuries earlier. There, royalist Cavaliers sported long hair, feathered hats, elegant manners, and a fondness for high living. The serious, sober, pious Puritans fought for Parliament against the king in defense of their rights.

Calhoun was put off by the city's worldly ways. At Yale he had been accused of Sabbath-breaking because he took long walks instead of attending church, but here in Charleston, Sunday was given over to social visits and horse racing.[18] He thought the city corrupt and "inattentive to every call of religion."[19]

George Washington was not the only Southerner, however, to be captivated by Charleston's charms. John C. Calhoun soon courted and married the lovely Floride Calhoun. She was from the Charleston branch of his extended family. They would remain devoted to one another throughout their lives. And she would bring him wealth and social prominence.

Very soon, Calhoun entered Congress. He quickly joined the "War Hawks" in the House of Representatives who were banging the war drums, ready to fight England in 1812. Calhoun suddenly rose to the top rank and was called "the young Hercules" of the prowar party.[20]

Calhoun in Congress was respected more than he was loved. Kentucky's Henry Clay, also an avid War Hawk, described him thus: "[T] all, careworn, with furrowed brow, haggard and intensely gazing, looking as if he were dissecting the last abstraction which sprung from the metaphysician's brain, and muttering to himself, in half-uttered tones, 'This is indeed a real crisis.'"[21]

Women in Washington followed politics avidly. They flocked to the House and Senate galleries to watch the members contend on the floor below. Harriet Martineau was an acute Englishwoman who reported on political economy for the *Washington Globe*. She offered this penetrating portrait of South Carolina's Calhoun:

> Mr. Calhoun, the cast-iron man, who looks as if he had never been born and never could be extinguished, would come in sometimes to keep our understanding upon a painful stretch for a short while, and leave us to take to pieces his close, rapid, theoretical, illustrated talk, and see what we could make of it.[22]

Calhoun was twice Andrew Jackson's running mate, in 1824 and 1828. When the House chose Adams in 1824, the Senate selected Calhoun as vice president.* When Jackson was finally elected president in 1828, Calhoun succeeded in winning his second term in the position.

In his youth, Calhoun had been a disciple of Thomas Jefferson's natural rights philosophy. As he aged, however, his views changed profoundly. Boldly, bluntly, he *denied* Jefferson's Declaration of Independence. "Taking the proposition literally," Calhoun stated, "there is not a word of truth in it. It begins with 'all men are born,' which is utterly untrue. Men are not born. Infants are born. They grow to be men.... They are not born free. While infants, they are incapable of freedom."[23] Actually, Jefferson had said nothing about *born*. He said, of course, all men are *created*. And Calhoun's unimaginative logic-chopping would have gotten him short shrift at the Second Continental Congress.

The change in Calhoun's political stance came about as he recognized the need to defend slavery—the "peculiar institution." Unlike Jefferson, Washington, Franklin, and virtually every one of the Founders, Calhoun did not view slavery as wrong. It guaranteed equality for whites and was a "positive good" for blacks, he argued.[24]

Calhoun thought he had no choice. He saw the Northern states expanding in population and wealth. He saw the immigrants flooding into Northern cities. He feared a future in which more and more *free* states would be admitted to the Union until such time as they comprised *three-fourths* of all the states. Then, they would simply pass a constitutional amendment to emancipate the slaves. That was why he insisted that the territories remain open to slavery. South Carolina's slaves outnumbered her white citizens. Once free, black South Carolinians would first be made citizens, then voters, and finally masters. This was the fear that stalked John C. Calhoun's days and haunted his dreams.

---

* This provision of the Constitution is still in force. If the House of Representatives had chosen George W. Bush as president in 2000, the Senate would have chosen Dick Cheney as vice president.

IV. "OUR FEDERAL UNION:
IT *MUST* BE PRESERVED!"

South Carolina was in turmoil in 1828 over what it called the Tariff of Abominations. The Constitution did not permit the federal government to tax exports. South Carolinians and other planter aristocrats would never have signed the document if it had. But tariffs—taxes on *imports*—could prove onerous for an agriculture-based economy. They had to import many of their machines and nearly all their luxuries.

As planters and slaveholders, they expected Jackson to side with them against the Tariff of Abominations that Congress approved in 1828. That same year, Vice President Calhoun not-so-anonymously penned his famous Exposition and Protest. He argued that when a state's rights were violated by the federal government, the state had a right to *nullify* the offending federal law and prevent its enforcement within the borders of the state. If that failed, Calhoun clearly implied, the state had a right to leave the Union. Thus, *secession*, the logical end result of *nullification*, began seriously to be argued by slaveholders. The South was, to be sure, not the only section that had argued for secession. High Federalists had toyed with it in New England during the War of 1812. Westerners had from time to time threatened it. But this was the first time *disunion* was incorporated into a serious political philosophy.

Calhoun's ideas were publicly defended by South Carolina's senior U.S. senator, Robert Y. Hayne. In January 1830, Hayne spoke at length on his "compact theory" of the Union. Under this theory, the Union was a league, or compact, of the states. They formed it; if it ever threatens their rights, they can dissolve it. Hayne's conclusions were carefully and closely reasoned and would have been persuasive—if the Union were a mere league or compact.

Massachusetts Senator Daniel Webster arose to dispute Hayne's interpretation of the Constitution. Vice President Calhoun presided over the Senate, adding to the drama of the clash. The "Godlike Daniel"—as his admirers called him—proceeded to shred the case made by Hayne. "I go for the Union as it is," he cried, flinging his words as a challenge to Calhoun. "It is, Sir, the people's Constitution, the people's government, made for the people, made by the people, and answerable to the people."[25]

The Senate galleries were packed to hear Webster's reply to Hayne. Webster thrilled his listeners with his emotional but reasoned defense of the Union. The conclusion of his two-day, six-hour address was so stirring that generations of American schoolchildren learned it by heart:

> When my eyes shall be turned to behold for the last time the sun in heaven, may I not see him shining on the broken and dishonored fragments of a once glorious Union; on States dissevered, discordant, belligerent; on a land rent with civil feuds, or drenched, it may be, in fraternal blood! Let their last feeble and lingering glance rather behold the gorgeous ensign of the republic, now known and honored throughout the earth, still full high advanced, its arms and trophies streaming in their original luster, not a stripe erased or polluted, not a single star obscured, bearing for its motto, no such miserable interrogatory as "What is all this worth?" nor those other words of delusion and folly, "Liberty first and Union afterwards"; but everywhere, spread all over in characters of living light, blazing on all its ample folds, as they float over the sea and over the land, and in every wind under the whole heavens, that other sentiment, dear to every true American heart—Liberty *and* Union, now and forever, one and inseparable![26]

Imagine the excitement of the people in the gallery as they heard Webster speak. Nicholas Trist was one of those who witnessed this drama. Grandson-in-law of Thomas Jefferson and an advisor to President Jackson, Trist wrote to James Madison that Webster's devastating reply to Hayne was like "the mammoth deliberately treading the canebrake."[27]

Attention soon focused on the Jefferson Day banquet—13 April 1830—at Washington's Indian Queen Hotel. Toasts and speeches by the leading Democrats praised the Sage of Monticello's commitment to states' rights. They implied he would favor nullification. Out of courtesy, President Jackson was asked to deliver a toast. No "Ebony and Topaz" on this occasion, Jackson looked directly at John C. Calhoun and vowed: "Our federal Union. It *must* be preserved!"

There was stunned silence. Little Van Buren stood on a chair to see the clash of wills. Pale and shaken, Calhoun raised his glass, even spilling some of his wine. Then he said: "The Union, next to our liberty, the most dear."[28]

President Jackson regarded himself as a sincere Jeffersonian. He believed in states' rights. But he was firmly opposed to nullification. Jackson could rely on the great prestige of James Madison, the Father of the Constitution and Jefferson's intimate friend of half a century. Former president Madison spoke out from his retirement home, Montpelier.

The *people*, not the states, had created the Union, Madison argued. The people had created the Union *and* the states. Still vigorous in his eightieth year, Madison denounced Calhoun's doctrine of nullification in October 1830. The result of nullification must be "a final rupture and dissolution of the Union." Such an event "must be shuddered at by every friend to his country, to liberty, to the happiness of man," Madison wrote.[29]

Madison enjoyed enormous prestige as the last survivor of the Constitutional Convention and as Jefferson's political lieutenant, successor, and heir. He utterly rejected the "nullies'" (Jackson's name for them) propositions. If they did not yield to reason, he wrote, "the explanation will lie between an impenetrable stupidity and an incurable prejudice."[30]

As the crisis over nullification intensified, Calhoun cast his lot with South Carolina. When Jackson chose Van Buren as his running mate and was reelected in 1832, Calhoun knew he would never be president. He even resigned as vice president. South Carolina immediately sent him to represent her in the Senate (a seat he held until his death in 1850). Congress passed a new Tariff of 1832 designed to mollify South Carolina by removing some but not all of the offending portions of the Tariff of Abominations.

Urged on by Calhoun, South Carolina convened a Nullification Convention. South Carolina planters believed the tariff was responsible for their economic depression. They even spoke of it as a "forty bale" tariff. They charged the tariff with costing them forty of every one hundred bales of cotton they produced.[31] On 24 November 1832, this convention passed an Ordinance of Nullification. This ordinance said the Tariff of 1832 was "null and void" and would not be obeyed in South Carolina after 1 February 1833. Even more ominously, the ordinance declared that if Jackson attempted to use force, the state would secede from the Union.[32] Some "nullies" even struck medals bearing the inscription: "John C. Calhoun, First President of the Southern Confederacy."[33]

Jackson responded quickly with his own Proclamation to the People of South Carolina on 10 December 1832. The Union, he said, was not the creature of the states. The Union was older than the states. He declared, "Perpetuity is stamped upon the Constitution by blood."[34*] "Those who told you," he wrote to the people of his native state, "that you might peacefully prevent . . . execution [of the laws] deceived you. . . . Their object is disunion. But be not deceived by names. Disunion by armed force is treason. Are you really ready to incur its guilt?"[35]

Jackson did not rule out compromise. He called for a *lowering* of the tariff to more acceptable levels. And he sought support from Unionists within South Carolina and other Southern states. He was not disappointed. Virginia, Georgia, and Alabama gave him support.[36] Leading South Carolina *opponents* of nullification took heart. "What have we to fear, we are right and God and Old Hickory are with us," they exulted.[37]

South Carolina had reason to fear. In many low-country districts, slaves outnumbered freemen three and four to one.[38] The Denmark Vesey plan for a slave rebellion had been nipped in the bud in 1822, but white Carolinians read with horror the story of Nat Turner's 1831 rebellion in

---

* On this point, even Ronald Reagan got it wrong. He told the crowds at his First Inaugural: "All of us need to be reminded that the Federal Government did not create the States; the States created the Federal Government."

Virginia. Turner was a slave, a spellbinding preacher who believed he had a God-given mission to raise a band of slaves to slaughter remote farm families. He killed nearly a hundred whites before the militia subdued him and his small force. The retribution that was carried out chilled everyone's blood. South Carolinians had also rushed to beat Jefferson's 1808 deadline for cutting off the African slave trade. They hastily imported forty thousand slaves from the "Gold Coast" of Africa. Many of these, still speaking the *Gullah* dialect the planters could not understand, added to the South Carolinians' fears of being surrounded on their farms.[39]

With a 1 January 1831 editorial, a new paper appeared in America that would herald the birth of a powerful movement. Editor William Lloyd Garrison cast away the tact and moderation of the past. Inaugurating his journal, the *Liberator,* Garrison stated, "I do not wish to think, or speak, or write, with moderation. . . . I am in earnest—I will not equivocate—*I will not excuse—I will not retreat a single inch*—and *I WILL BE HEARD.*" To Southerners, Garrison and his little newspaper seemed as reckless as a man smoking in a powder magazine. From the safe distance of Massachusetts, Garrison could demand immediate *abolition* of slavery. The planters of South Carolina felt they would be not only economically ruined but perhaps even exterminated were they to relax their grip on their slaves. But Garrison was heard.

South Carolinians led the entire South in these days in taking care not to refer to slavery directly. They talked *around* the subject, using such terms as "our peculiar institution" and "our domestic policy." Southern slaveholders did not want Congress even to debate slavery. They feared that any open discussion of the topic would provide the "spark" that would ignite a full-scale revolt. They suppressed abolitionist newspapers as "incendiary." Even one of their favorite holidays—the Fourth of July—came to be a time of unbearable tension as planters feared their slaves would hear the inspiring words of Thomas Jefferson's Declaration of Independence and realize that their Creator intended that they, too, should be free.[40]

If the nullies carried out their plans, the Hero let it be known he would lead ten thousand volunteers into South Carolina to "crush and hang" all traitors.[41] He vowed to hold Fort Sumter, in Charleston harbor, "to the last extremity."[42]* He rammed a Force Bill through Congress, a measure that authorized him to coerce South Carolina into compliance with law.

Although the immediate cause of the controversy was the tariff, everyone knew that at the bottom of it all lay slavery. Calhoun acknowledged this. "I consider the Tariff but the occasion rather than the real cause of the present unhappy state of things." The states must be allowed to guard their "domestick institutions" or be forced to rebel, he said.[43]

Into this explosive mix stepped Kentucky Senator Henry Clay. Although recently defeated by Jackson for the presidency, Clay labored mightily to put together the Compromise Tariff of 1833. The bill met many of the demands of the nullifiers. This bill passed Congress and went to the president's desk on the same day that the Force Bill arrived there. This combination of firmness and flexibility proved successful.[44] Senator Calhoun's mind doubtless was concentrated on Jackson's threat to hang him "as high as Haman."** Calhoun accepted the Compromise Tariff and the crisis eased.

President Jackson had been born in South Carolina. He was himself a planter, a slaveholder. He had sympathy for the South Carolina planters. But on disunion, he would not budge. He was not called Old Hickory for nothing.

"Nullification is dead," Jackson pronounced, but he knew the long-term clash was not resolved. "The next pretext will be the Negro or slavery question," he accurately predicted.[45] Henry Clay here earned the title "the Great Compromiser." His unselfish and timely action helped save the Union. But it was the fearless Old Hickory who had "shoot" in his eyes. Even on his deathbed in 1845, Jackson admitted that he regretted only two things: that none of his racehorses had ever beaten the famed Haynie's Maria—and that he had *not* hanged John C. Calhoun.[46]

---

* Here, this Democratic president would set the bar for the first Republican president. Could Lincoln in 1861 surrender what Jackson had vowed never to give up?

** "So they hanged Haman on the gallows that he had prepared for Mordecai. Then the king's wrath subsided" (Esther 7:10).

V. THE TRAGEDY OF INDIAN REMOVAL

During the same years that the nullification crisis was coming to a head, President Jackson had to contend with the question of Indian removal. "Sharp Knife" Jackson had gained much of his reputation and his immense popularity as an Indian fighter. Americans on the frontier looked to him for protection from the depredations of warlike tribes.

The greatest of the Indian warriors, Tecumseh, had planned a war of extermination against the settlers. Tecumseh rallied his powerful confederation with strong words. "Let the white race perish!" he said to his people. "They seize your land; they corrupt your women; they trample on the bones of your dead! Back—aye, back to the great water whose accursed waves brought them to our shores! Burn their dwellings—destroy their stock—slay their wives and children, that the very breed may perish! War now! War always! War on the living! War on the dead!"[47]

Congress had resolved to deal with the problem of Indians by *removing* them west of the Mississippi River. Ideally, they were to receive money and western lands to compensate them for their losses in the East. This policy was begun under President Monroe but had slowed during the administration of the humane John Quincy Adams.[48] When Jackson became president, Americans looked to him to speed up the removal of the Indians. Georgia, Alabama, and Mississippi were particularly impatient. They asserted that *state* laws would apply to all persons living within their borders.[49] This was a fundamental Jeffersonian principle, they argued.

But this abstract principle would have ominous consequences for the Indian tribes. It meant they would be at the mercy of hostile state legislatures—in which they would have no genuine representation. More outrageous, it meant they would not be able to claim the protection of treaties they had duly signed with the *federal* government.

Facing the mounting danger of nullification in South Carolina, Jackson could not afford to antagonize other Deep South states over the Indian question. Besides, Jackson *agreed* with the people of Georgia, Alabama, and Mississippi. His commitment to ending the bloody raids on the frontier was a major factor in his election as president. Jackson did not lose a single state in which Indian warfare was still a public concern.

Georgia tried to prevent whites from working with the Indians. Georgia's law might have been a wise one if it prevented whites from plying the Indians with liquor and defrauding them of their lands. But the state's law applied even to Christian missionaries. Vermonter Rev. Samuel Worcester brought suit in federal court. He wanted to continue his work among the Cherokee. Chief Justice John Marshall spoke for the majority of the U.S. Supreme Court when he ruled in the missionary's favor in the case of *Worcester v. Georgia* (1832): "The Cherokee nation, then, is a distinct community occupying its own territory in which the laws of Georgia can have no force. The whole intercourse between the United States and this nation is, by our constitution and laws, vested in the government of the United States."*

Marshall thus found that Georgia's action was *unconstitutional*. Old Hickory is supposed to have responded: "John Marshall has made his decision. Now let him enforce it."[50] It sounds so much like Jackson. But it is more likely Jackson adopted a wait-and-see attitude toward the Court's ruling.[51] He disagreed that tribes were independent nations. He sincerely believed that unscrupulous chieftains had exploited their own people.[52] Although he never sought to extend democracy to the Indian tribes, he was unwilling to consider them as privileged corporations exempt from the laws of the states.

In the spring of 1832, the Illinois frontier erupted in the Black Hawk War. Chief Black Hawk had been a British ally during the War of 1812. His Sac and Fox tribe had been resettled west of the Mississippi, but they were starving. They returned to their old homes when hostile Sioux forced them back into Illinois. The state's governor called out

---

* The issue remains with us. In 2003, Arnold Schwarzenegger campaigned for the governor of California, pledging to make casinos located on Indian tribal lands pay *state* taxes.

the militia—including company commander Abraham Lincoln. Black Hawk's vastly outnumbered Sac and Fox tribe chased Major Stillman's half-drunk volunteers twenty-five miles in what became known as "Stillman's Run."[53] Encouraged by this unexpected win, Black Hawk terrorized the frontier, burning farms and taking scalps. When a large force of 1,300 troops finally overtook Black Hawk's small force in August, the Indians tried to surrender. No quarter was given as the militiamen proceeded to massacre the remnant of the Sac and Fox tribe, including women and children. Black Hawk escaped to Wisconsin, where the Winnebagos turned him over to the army.[54] Here, at least, he received chivalrous treatment from West Pointer Jefferson Davis.[55] The courtly Davis would permit no humiliation of his Indian captive and, in fact, treated him with typical Southern courtesy.

President Jackson met with Black Hawk. He sternly told the chief: "You behaved very badly in raising the tomahawk against the white people, and killing men, women and children upon the frontier." Jackson sent Black Hawk on a tour of eastern cities. This was done not so much to humiliate the captive foe as to impress him with the overwhelming power of America. "You will see that our young men are as numerous as the leaves in the woods," Jackson told him.[56] While visiting the population centers of the East, Black Hawk was introduced at hotel dinners. Audiences applauded as the defeated warrior politely nodded and smiled.[57]

No case of Indian removal was more tragic than the fate that befell the Cherokee nation. The great Indian leader, Sequoia, developed a written language for the Cherokee. His people read the weekly *Cherokee Phoenix* in their own language, printed Bibles and other books, accepted Christian missionaries, organized a legislature, and settled into stable farming communities. None of this high civilization saved them from the depredations of their neighbors, however. When gold was discovered on Cherokee lands, President Jackson *removed* the federal troops that John Quincy Adams had sent into Georgia to protect them.[58] More than one-quarter of the Cherokee died on the long, heartbreaking "Trail of

Tears" that they were forced to take to the Indian Territory, modern-day Oklahoma. Although the worst of the outrages against the Cherokee occurred in 1838, under the administration of President Martin Van Buren, Jackson ruthlessly pursued the removal policy and therefore bears the responsibility for it.[59] In this instance, too, Jackson had shoot in his eye, and the result is an indelible stain on America's reputation.

In Andrew Jackson's mind, his policy was the only humane one that could be pursued. From vast experience, he believed that the Indians could not survive if they remained within the eastern states. Hundreds of thousands of immigrants flooded into America in the 1830s, creating enormous pressure for more land. Immigrants and native-born citizens voted. Indians did not. Jacksonian democracy had proclaimed that the people shall rule. The American people, with few exceptions, not only supported but *demanded* Indian removal.[60]

Some of Jackson's Senate opponents, notably Kentucky's Henry Clay and New Jersey's Theodore Frelinghuysen, spoke out eloquently against Indian removal. Frelinghuysen was a devoutly religious man. His ancestor had founded the Dutch Reformed Church in America. Clay's opposition was perhaps even more remarkable since his Kentucky constituents had no sympathy for the Indians.[61]

Maverick Davy Crockett's lonely stand against Jackson's policy of removal finished his political career. The colorful Crockett, an Indian fighter and frontiersman, was defeated for reelection to Congress. He had opposed Indian removal on principle, and on that principle his neighbors voted him out. "I'm going to Texas," he bluntly told his Tennessee constituents, "and you can go to hell."

Jackson is often portrayed as a semiliterate backwoodsman. That is certainly how his opponents saw him. And his Indian policy is cited as an example of ignorance and bigotry. Yet Jackson had the support of millions of Americans who agreed with his policy. The Indians were regarded as *terrorists*—pure and simple. Terrorists were those who killed innocent men, women, and children. Jefferson was very pro-Indian, defending them to European philosophers who called them degenerate. President Jefferson gave Lewis and Clark orders to pursue a humane policy toward the Indians that they labored dutifully to carry out. Yet even the enlightened Jefferson in the Declaration of Independence as much as calls the Indians terrorists: "[The King] has excited domestic insurrections amongst us, and has endeavoured to bring on the inhabitants of our frontiers, the merciless Indian Savages, whose known rule of warfare is an undistinguished destruction of all ages, sexes and conditions."

The problem was that too many Americans made no distinctions; none between the ferocity of a Tecumseh and a peaceful Cherokee leader like Sequoia. Some Indians, certainly, behaved like terrorists. But Jackson's cruel policy made no allowances for the highly civilized tribes. And even the warlike Tecumseh was honored when he spared American prisoners taken in Canada during the War of 1812.

America in 1831 and 1832 was a field of dreams for a young French nobleman. Alexis de Tocqueville toured the United States, ostensibly to report on prison conditions. His *Democracy in America*, published in 1835 when he was just thirty, is an enduring classic of what he called "political science." Tocqueville believed in the inevitability of democracy's spreading throughout Europe, and he saw America as the world's leading democratic society. Tocqueville wrote about *everything* he observed, and he observed much. He wrote, for example, of the effect of the advance of settlement on the Indian tribes: "The approach of the whites was often felt at two hundred leagues from the frontier.* Thus their influence is exerted on tribes whose names they hardly know, and who suffer the evils of usurpation long before recognizing its authors."[62]

Tocqueville happened to see one episode of Indian removal that was less *impersonal*, less benign than the inexorable process he described above. It is worth quoting in full:

---

* A *league* as a traditional measure of distance was three miles long. Thus, the impact of settlement was felt by Indians as much as *six hundred miles* away.

At the end of the year 1831, I found myself on the left bank of the Mississippi, at a place named Memphis by the Europeans. While I was at this place, a numerous troop of Choctaws came. . . . [T]he savages were leaving their country and sought to cross to the right bank of the Mississippi, where they flattered themselves they would find the refuge that the American government promised them. It was then in the heart of winter, and the cold ravaged that year with an unaccustomed violence; snow had hardened on the ground, and the river carried enormous pieces of ice. The Indians brought along their families with them; they dragged behind them the wounded, the ill, infants who had just been born, and the old who were going to die. They had neither tents nor carts, but only some provisions and arms. I saw them embark to cross the great river, and this solemn spectacle will never leave my memory. One heard neither tears nor complaints among this assembled crowd; they were silent. Their misfortunes were old, and they felt them to be irreparable. All the Indians had already entered the vessels that were to carry them; their dogs still remained on the shore; when the animals finally saw that they were going away forever, together they let out frightful howls, and dashing at once into the icy waters of the Mississippi, they followed their masters swimming.[63]

VI. FROM JACKSON TO "TIPPECANOE AND TYLER, TOO!"

Andrew Jackson had a lifelong hostility to what he regarded as aristocratic privilege. He believed passionately in *democracy* as he understood it. Therefore, when Senator Henry Clay in 1832 pushed through Congress a bill to recharter the Second Bank of the United States, the stage was set for a great contest. Jackson shared the prejudice of most frontiersmen against large and powerful central banks. Jackson hated the Bank of the United States for issuing what he regarded as unreliable paper currency—"Rag money."* When the bill arrived at his desk, Jackson vigorously vetoed the recharter. He called the bank a "Monster." In his view, it helped the rich get richer at the expense of farmers, laborers, and other "humble members of society."

Senator Henry Clay, running for president as a Whig in 1832, used the bank issue to attack Jackson and the Democrats. But the voters sided with Jackson, who won in a landslide victory. Jackson succeeded in destroying the Bank of the United States and forced the Democratic Party to support him, even when the economy began to slide into recession.

The year 1837 brought a financial panic and severe economic depression. By that time, Jackson had finished his second term and retired to his beloved Hermitage in Tennessee. The roof fell in on his chosen successor, Martin Van Buren, who had served as Jackson's second vice president and was elected president in 1836.

Van Buren had labored all his life to succeed in the game of politics. But when the Panic of 1837 struck shortly after his inauguration, the new president seemed incapable of rallying the country behind him as his mentor Andrew Jackson had done. To a very real extent, the depression was the result of Jackson's war on the bank. He and Van Buren had succeeded in ruining it, but they failed to create any effective and responsive institution to replace it.

Van Buren acted decisively in the Canadian crisis of 1837, however. When prodemocracy rebels tried to overthrow the aristocratic British colonial government in Ontario, many Americans saw this as the natural outgrowth of the Spirit of '76. In Quebec province there was even a *Fils de la Liberte* (Sons of Liberty) group organized in open imitation of the American Patriots.[64] Canadian Loyalists pursuing rebels stormed across the Niagara River and sank an American vessel on the U.S. side of the border. Van Buren resisted demands for war with Britain. He was

---

* It's hard to know what Old Hickory would think of the fact that his stern image is one of the most familiar to Americans more than 180 years after his term. His face adorns the paper twenty-dollar bill, the one most often issued by automatic teller machines.

willing to lose popularity by jailing Canadian rebels, even while protesting to the combative British foreign minister, Henry John Temple, Lord Palmerston, about intrusions onto American soil.[65] When the rebels returned to Canada, many of them were hanged.

Texans, too, had rebellion in mind. They had captured many American hearts with their bold insurrection against Mexican authority. Soon after achieving independence from Spain, Mexico had fallen under military dictatorship. In 1836, General Lopez de Santa Anna abolished the Mexican constitution with its guarantees of "states' rights" to provinces like Texas. The Americans—many from Kentucky and Tennessee—who had flooded into Texas when Mexico ruled, revolted against the despotic Santa Anna. Frontier heroes Davy Crockett and Jim Bowie were among 183 defenders who held out against Santa Anna's overwhelming force at the Alamo in San Antonio. When Colonel William Travis drew his famous "line in the sand" with his sword, none of the defenders chose to leave the embattled old mission. On March 6, Santa Anna's Mexicans finally stormed the Alamo; cruelly, he ordered every one of the defenders killed.

The bravery of the fighters for Texas independence inspired General Sam Houston's army of volunteers. "Remember the Alamo!" was their battle cry. Houston was a devoted friend of Andrew Jackson and was cut from the same cloth. Houston overwhelmed the Mexicans on April 21 at the Battle of San Jacinto and took Santa Anna prisoner. Texas's independence was achieved. Sam Houston became president of the "Lone Star Republic."[66] The Texans appealed for admission to the Union.

Van Buren could not afford to be so decisive about Texas. Northerners were deeply suspicious of annexation attempts, viewing them as a bid by slaveholders to increase their power. Southern Democrats clamored for annexation. Calhoun even threatened to break up the Union if Texas was not admitted as a slave state.[67] Jackson knew that New England whaling interests might be more agreeable to Texas's annexation if California's rich coast could be added to the United States. Somewhat uncharacteristically, Jackson advised *patience*. Resistance to Texas's "reannexation" did not disappear overnight, however. In 1838, John Quincy Adams spoke *for three weeks* on the House floor and defeated a move to annex Texas.[68]

With the approaching election of 1840, the opposing Whigs determined to do to Van Buren what Democrats had done to Adams in 1828. They nominated the aged hero of the War of 1812, William Henry Harrison. "Old Tippecanoe" took no public positions. The Whigs did not issue a party platform. Their campaign featured fierce attacks on Van Buren as a pampered aristocrat. "Van, Van, the Used-Up Man!" They lampooned the New Yorker's elegant dress and manners and his taste for fine wines. Old Tippecanoe was born in a log cabin, Whigs claimed, and preferred hard cider. The old general's running mate was an anti-Jackson Democrat from Virginia, John Tyler. The ticket was immortalized as "Tippecanoe and Tyler, Too!" The campaign slogan was not as mindless as it seemed. It reminded voters that Whigs, too, had played their part in ending the threat of Indian attacks on the frontier. "Keep the ball rolling" was the Whig cry, and, for once, this party of educated and refined men achieved real popular appeal. Harrison buried Van Buren by 234 electoral votes to 60. The popular vote was closer—1,275,016 to 1,129,102. This popular vote total—*nearly two and a half million*—reflected the enormous expansion of the electorate under Jackson.

Harrison at sixty-eight years was the oldest man elected president prior to Ronald Reagan. He wrote his own inaugural address, filled with classical allusions. Whig leaders drafted Senator Daniel Webster to edit it down. Webster joked that he had killed "seventeen Roman proconsuls as dead as smelts, every one of them." Even so, Harrison's speech was the longest ever delivered. Speaking in a cold and driving rain, the aged general soon came down with pneumonia. He died after just a month in office, on 4 April 1841. Vice President John Tyler moved with dispatch to claim the title deeds of office. He would not be "acting President," he informed Harrison's cabinet, but would function fully as the chief executive.* When he vetoed a bill for internal improvements, however, he seemed to Whig leaders no better than the strong-willed Jackson. Very shortly, President Tyler became a man without a party. Secretary of State Daniel Webster was the only Whig to stay in the Tyler cabinet— and that was only because he was negotiating a vitally important treaty with England. The Webster-Ashburton Treaty of 1842 resolved nearly all remaining disputes between England and America and formed the basis of an Anglo-American "special relationship" that exists to this day.

VII. REANNEXING TEXAS AND REOCCUPYING OREGON

In 1844, Democrats nominated James K. Polk for president. A former Speaker of the U.S. House of Representatives and governor of Tennessee, Polk was a faithful Jackson supporter. Running on a platform that called for "Reannexation of Texas and Reoccupation of Oregon," he won a narrow victory over the Whigs' nominee, Henry Clay.

President Tyler took Polk's election as evidence of popular support for "Manifest Destiny" and quickly proposed admitting Texas to the Union by joint resolution. The reason Democrats spoke of the reannexation of Texas is because they maintained Texas had been part of the original Louisiana Purchase and that John Quincy Adams had failed when he negotiated the Transcontinental Treaty with Spain in 1819. (The fact that the treaty was approved by President Monroe and ratified by a majority of Democratic-Republicans in the Senate did not seem to deter these eager expansionists.) Similarly, reoccupation of Oregon was intended to assert America's claim to all of the Pacific Northwest. Expansionists aggressively called for extending the border to 54°40' north latitude. This

---

* Tyler's bold assertion set an important precedent for presidential succession and was formally agreed to when Congress passed and the states ratified Amendment XXV on presidential disability in 1967.

meant they wanted all of the Oregon Territory up to the southern border of Russian Alaska. The claim to Oregon rested on the 1792 voyage of American Captain Robert Gray in his ship USS *Columbia*. Gray had anchored off Cape Disappointment, unable to enter the mouth of the raging river he named *Columbia*. Lewis and Clark had wintered near this site on their famous expedition.

Democrats hoped that adding Oregon to their list of territorial ambitions would persuade Northerners to look more kindly on the admission of Texas.[69] Texas's annexation was rushed through Congress in the last days of the Tyler administration because Southerners feared that England might make a favorable treaty with the Republic of Texas that would call for emancipation of the slaves.

The British Hudson's Bay Company had been the power and the law in the Pacific Northwest for a generation. The company's influence was based on fur trapping and trading. When "Oregon Fever" struck the Midwest in 1842, thousands of Americans packed up and took their Conestoga wagons along the Oregon Trail. The rich farmland of the Willamette Valley beckoned. If the land was a *pull*, the rising agitation over slavery in the territories was surely a *push*. American missionaries—both Protestant and Catholic—had led the way.[70] In Massachusetts, Henry David Thoreau spoke for many when he wrote:

> I must walk toward Oregon, and not toward Europe.*
> And that way the nation is moving,
> And I may say that mankind progress from east to west.

The trail had been blazed by twenty years of "Mountainy Men." Most of these rough trappers were Americans who lived beyond the settled frontiers and knew the land intimately.

---

* It is perhaps not too unpoetic to point out that walking eastward would have required Thoreau to walk on water.

Jim Clyman's life illustrated the Mountain Man restlessness. Clyman saw George Washington in Fauquier County, Virginia, where he was born in 1792. He "lit out for the territories" early. By the time he died, Chester Alan Arthur was president. Clyman died in 1881 on his Napa, California, ranch. His life had spanned the continent.[71] There were other Mountain Men whose lives were no less remarkable:

> The mountain man's eye had the Indian's alertness, forever watching for the movement of boughs or grasses, for the passage of wildlife downwind, something unexplained floating in a stream, dust stirring in a calm, or the configuration of mere scratches on a cottonwood. His ear would never again hear church bells or the noises of a farm but, like the Indian's, was tuned to catch any sound in a country where every sound was provisionally a death warning. He dressed like an Indian, in blankets, robes, buckskins, and moccasins, and it was sometimes his humor to grease his hair and stripe his face with vermilion. He lived like an Indian in bark huts or skin lodges, and married a succession of squaws. . . . He had a call on brutality as instant as the Indian's and rather more relentless. The Indians who had proved themselves his friends were his friends just so long as they seemed to be; all others were to be shot and scalped at sight. It was the Indian law, no violence to be left unavenged.[72]

However hard these Mountain Men were, Americans could not have crossed the Rockies or settled the fertile valleys of California and Oregon without them. They were the guides who led the wagon trains west. They were the hunters who staved off starvation when the wagons were hit by blizzards in the mountain passes. When they failed—as they did with the doomed Donner party—the results would be catastrophic. In 1846, these inexperienced pioneers were trapped on the eastern slope of the Sierra Nevada Mountains. Of the eighty-seven members of the party, only forty-six survived the cold, hunger, and even horrors of cannibalism. But thousands more got through.

Another amazing westward trek was made by the Mormons. Led by the visionary and strong-willed Brigham Young, thousands of Mormons journeyed to the Great Salt Lake in 1847. Mormons were fleeing persecution in Missouri and Illinois, where the man they regarded as their prophet, Joseph Smith, had been murdered by a mob. The Mormon practice of polygamy deeply offended their neighbors, as did the economic muscle they wielded through communal buying and selling. This tactic seemed a direct threat to the economic individualism of single-family farm homesteads that was seen as central to the American way. Brigham Young was determined to find a remote region in which to build his "Deseret."[73]

In just a few years, the thousands of Americans who went to Oregon created new realities on the ground. By 1845, the bottoming out of the fur trade prompted the Hudson's Bay Company to abandon their trading post at Fort Vancouver, north of the Columbia River. Withdrawing to the outpost of Victoria on Vancouver Island, the British presence in the Pacific Northwest was melting away like snows receding up the side of the mountain.

"Fifty-Four Forty or Fight!" became the rallying cry of Democrats bent on westward expansion. It meant Americans wanted all the territory in the Pacific Northwest up to 54°40' north latitude. Democratic editor John O'Sullivan saw heavenly approval for this policy. In his *New York Morning News*, he wrote it is "our *manifest destiny* to overspread and to possess the whole of the continent which Providence has given us for the development of the great experiment of liberty and federated self-government" (emphasis added).[74] Some expansionists even bragged openly of extending American rule from sea to sea and from pole to pole.

Not all Americans were willing to fight for Oregon. *Niles' Weekly Register*, a Whig paper, poured cold water on all such wild talk. War with Britain over Oregon, the editor said, "would be one of the most reckless and insane exhibitions that the civilized world has ever witnessed."[75] President Polk did not want war with Britain. But he did not shrink from the possibility of war. "[T]he only way to treat John Bull [Great Britain] was to look him straight in the eye. . . . I considered a bold & firm course on our part the pacific one."[76]

Events proved "Young Hickory" correct. Britain was unwilling to fight a war over a remote territory whose fur trade was increasingly trapped out. We didn't get Fifty-Four Forty. We didn't get the fight, either. Americans were fortunate in this, for by the time Britain agreed to compromise at the line of 49° north latitude, the United States was already headed for war with Mexico. Missouri's Senator Thomas Hart Benton laughed at Polk: "Why not march up to 'Fifty-four Forty' as courageously as we march upon the Rio Grande? Because Great Britain is powerful and Mexico is weak."[77] Polk could take ridicule and resentment. He had pocketed the first of the great Pacific coast harbors. He now turned his attention to Mexico to secure the other two.

VIII. "THE HALLS OF MONTEZUMA"

President Polk had instructed his envoy, John Slidell, to offer the Mexicans $4.5 million to settle claims for damages from the incessant Mexican civil wars if Mexico would recognize the Rio Grande as Texas's southern border. Slidell was also empowered to offer a further $5 million if the Mexicans would sell their province of New Mexico.[78] Slidell was even instructed to offer up to $25 million if California were thrown into the bargain. "Money would be no object," Secretary of State James Buchanan wrote to the American ambassador in Mexico City.[79]

Mexicans found the very offer insulting. They refused to receive Slidell. Another military uprising (*golpe*)—an increasingly familiar phenomenon in Latin America—ousted the moderate Herrera government and installed the militantly anti-American General Mariano Paredes in power. Paredes vowed to stand up to the pushy *Yanquis*.[80] By New Year's Day 1846, Paredes was eager for war with America.[81]

President Polk also feared rumored British attempts to buy California. The British Admiralty was said to covet the fine harbor of San Francisco Bay.[82] Polk reasserted the principles of the Monroe Doctrine. This hemisphere would be off-limits to European colonization. He said nothing about American expansion.

Polk ordered General Zachary Taylor to take an army into the disputed territory between the Nueces and Rio Grande Rivers. General Pedro de Ampudia warned Taylor that he was intruding on Mexican land and ordered him to leave. Taylor ignored Ampudia's warning, instead building an American fort.[83] On 25 April 1846, a Mexican force ambushed an American patrol, killing eleven. Polk had resolved to go to war even before this clash. Now, he told Congress, Mexico had "shed American blood on American soil." Congress soon gave him his declaration of war by a lopsided vote of 174–14 in the House and 40–2 in the Senate.[84]

Mexico was hardly blameless in all this. Contemptuous of the *Yanquis*, Mexicans remembered the American failure to conquer Canada and the humiliating British capture of Washington, D.C., in the War of 1812. A Mexican officer bragged that his cavalry could take care of American infantry by *lassoing* them. Mexico was not alone in holding America in low regard. London's *Britannia* sneered that the United States "as an aggressive power is one of the weakest in the world . . . fit for nothing but to fight Indians."[85]

Although the war was very popular in the Mississippi Valley, and in the South, New England once again broadly opposed the war. The Whig Party questioned the war but made sure to vote to supply the troops. Whigs remembered how Federalists had been tainted with disloyalty during the War of 1812.[86] Literary figures like James Russell Lowell saw only the designs of the Slave Power in the rush to war:

> They just want this Californy
> So's to lug new slave-states in
> To abuse ye, an' to scorn ye,
> An' to plunder ye like sin.[87]

Massachusetts's legislature denounced the war as an effort to strengthen the Slave Power. And his strong opposition led Henry David Thoreau to spend a night in jail for refusing to pay war taxes. Thoreau's *Essay on Civil Disobedience* became a classic of American literature.[88] Theodore Parker, a Unitarian minister, said that if the "war be right then Christianity is wrong, a falsehood, a lie." Abolitionist Garrison's *Liberator* expressed open support for the Mexican people: "Every lover of Freedom and humanity throughout the world must wish them the most triumphant success."

Garrison went even further. His *Liberator* proclaimed: "Accursed be the American Union, as a stupendous republican imposture! Accursed be it, as the most frightful despotism, with regard to three millions of the people, ever exercised over any portion of the human family! NO UNION WITH SLAVEHOLDERS!"[89]

To men of Garrison's mind, O'Sullivan's concept of Manifest Destiny was the foulest hypocrisy. And Garrison's new, young ally would give them more reason to resist the Slave Power. A brilliant runaway slave in 1845 published the sensational autobiography, *Narrative of the Life of Frederick Douglass*. Now, thousands of Americans could read of the horrors of life under the lash in the compelling words of a polished writer and orator. Douglass appeared on the scene just in time to put flesh and blood onto the abstract idealism of Garrison and the abolitionists.

The campaign in Mexico, despite some early setbacks, proceeded swiftly. General Zachary Taylor, known as "Old Rough and Ready," gained a reputation for victory. President Polk feared his growing popularity, though, and was determined not to make another Whig a military hero. Polk ordered General Winfield Scott to take Mexico City. Scott fought a brilliant campaign, ably assisted by the first *amphibious* landing staged by the U.S. Navy.*

---

* A greater awareness of the importance of sea power led President Polk to break from Jeffersonian tradition and found the U.S. Naval Academy at Annapolis (1845).

Army Captain Robert E. Lee moved around the main Mexican force to bring victory. Two of his subordinates who also won laurels in this operation were Lieutenants George B. McClellan and Ulysses S. Grant.[90]* U.S. Marines marched from Vera Cruz and earned their famous "blood stripe"—the crimson stripe that runs down their trouser leg—at the Battle of Chapultepec. They suffered heavy casualties in this action, but they reached the Halls of Montezuma in Mexico City.

The American assault on Mexico City took place over the bitter resistance of two amazing groups of fighters. The young cadets of the Mexican Military Academy, aged just thirteen to nineteen, fought with astonishing bravery against the grimly advancing *Gringos*.** These brave youngsters are known in Mexican history as *los Niños* (the boys). Many of them paid with their lives for every mile the Americans moved.[91] The other fighters were the *San Patricios* (Saint Patricks). These were mostly deserters—many of them Irish—from the American army. They fought valiantly against their former comrades. Twenty-nine captured *Patricios* were made to stand in wagons, condemned as traitors, in the broiling September sun. With nooses around their necks, they were forced to witness the final *Yanqui* attack on Mexico City. When the Stars and Stripes were raised on the heights above the city, the *Patricios* actually cheered their old flag! Then the wagons jolted forward, ending a sad but compelling little chapter in the history of American warfare.[92]

U.S. battle deaths in the Mexican War were not heavy by ancient or even modern standards. Killed in combat were 1,733, or 2 percent of 78,718 troops committed. But the greatest toll was taken by disease. Add to combat deaths the figure of 11,550 noncombat deaths, or 14 percent.

---

* Both Lee and Grant thought that the war against Mexico was unjust, but both nonetheless distinguished themselves in their military capacities.

** *Gringo*—Mexican slang for an American—was long thought to have come from the song American troops sang as they marched through Mexico's parched, dusty valleys: "Green grow the lilacs." More likely, *Gringo* is a corruption of *griego*—to speak Spanish like a Greek.

This means fully 16 percent of those engaged died.[93] This was all too typical of warfare in the days before modern medicine.

In the Southwest, Americans moved swiftly to take New Mexico and move on to California. General Steven Kearny led a force that included the extraordinary Mormon Brigade in an easy conquest. Mormon leader Brigham Young made a crucial decision to *support* the United States in its war against Mexico. He sent hundreds of young recruits to aid the American forces in the Southwest. The army pay these clean-living young men tithed to the Mormon Church helped the embattled colony to survive.

California's short-lived "Bear Flag Republic" was almost a comical affair. Meeting little resistance from the Mexican natives, Captain John Charles Frémont took action to detach the province from the mother country. But Frémont's reputation as "The Pathfinder" was largely the result of skillful public relations and family connections. (His father-in-law was the powerful Senator Thomas Hart Benton.) General Kearny generally found Frémont a nuisance. Despite Frémont's court-martial and his threats of a duel (his opponent proposed shotguns no less), a semblance of order was restored, and California was soon incorporated into the Union.[94]

Meanwhile, Polk had to deal with opposition. His war aims were widely misunderstood, even in his own cabinet. When his secretary of state, the fussy James Buchanan, wrote to American diplomats, informing them that the United States had no territorial ambitions in California, Polk overruled him. The humorless president ordered Buchanan to remove such a self-denying statement.[95]

Many Whigs called him "the mendacious Polk," rudely suggesting that the president was a *liar*. Congressman Abraham Lincoln of Illinois was more respectful but no less pointed. Waiting until hostilities ended in September 1847, Lincoln offered his "Spot Resolution" in December. Lincoln's resolution asked President Polk to point out precisely the *spot* on which American blood had been shed on American soil. Lincoln could not deny American blood had been shed, but he wanted Polk to prove that it had been shed on *American* soil. Polk ignored him.

Less easy to ignore was the measure introduced by Pennsylvania Democratic Congressman David Wilmot. "Neither slavery nor involuntary servitude shall ever exist" in any territory we might take from Mexico, Wilmot's amendment read. This Wilmot Proviso passed the House in 1846, but the Senate failed to act on it. Wilmot introduced it again in 1847 and this time the Senate *rejected* it.[96] Senator John C. Calhoun had rightly feared that a war with Mexico would lead to just such antislavery agitation.

The war continued to drive Americans apart. When a resolution to praise the veterans of the war was offered in the House of Representatives on 21 February 1848, Old Man Eloquent rose to *oppose* it! John Quincy Adams was voted down overwhelmingly. When the House clerk read a tribute to the soldiers, Adams struggled to his feet to object. He soon collapsed, felled by a stroke. He was carried off to the Speaker's office, where he died two days later.[97] Among those chosen by the House for the funeral committee was a one-termer from the prairies—Congressman Abraham Lincoln.

James Knox Polk received few thanks for adding vast territories to the American republic. He is the American Bismarck. Just as "the Iron Chancellor" is credited with creating the greater German empire in the 1860s and 1870s, James Knox Polk had three great objects in mind: the harbors of San Diego, San Francisco, and Puget Sound. Like Bismarck, Polk was willing to go to war to achieve his objects. But unlike Bismarck, Polk could rely on the sweep of thousands of settlers to achieve most of his goals without fighting. While the Mexicans in Mexico bravely resisted American invaders, the huge Southwest was seized almost bloodlessly.

Polk treated his envoy in Mexico City, Nicholas Trist, with shocking ingratitude. But he had the good sense to submit Trist's Treaty of Guadalupe-Hidalgo (1848) to the Senate. In doing so, he wisely rejected the demands of some ultra-nationalists here and some young reformers in Mexico that the entire country be incorporated into the United States.*

Mexico gave up California, Arizona, and New Mexico and recognized the Rio Grande as the southern border of the United States. America agreed to pay Mexico $15 million. The treaty was quickly ratified. The territory of what was called the Mexican Cession comprised 525,000 square miles. Of course, the Louisiana Purchase had brought 828,000 square miles of rich, well-watered lands into the American Union. Still, the great Southwest was a region of incomparable mineral wealth and natural beauty.

Did the $15 million payment represent an uneasy conscience on Polk's part? Or was it an astonishing act of compassion? One thing is clear: such an act is almost unimaginable by any other great power at the conclusion of a successful war with a weaker neighbor.

Polk kept his promise to serve only one term. Rigid and suspicious but brave and determined, he left the White House in March 1849 and died just three months later at the age of fifty-four. His labors had worn him out. "His administration has been a curse to the country," said William Lloyd Garrison, who found no reason to deplore the former president's death.[98]

Americans, reflecting on the contribution these vast territories have made to the national life, and the hope and aspiration of many immigrants drawn to them, may think otherwise.

---

* The war also saved West Point. Although founded under Jefferson's administration in 1803, the military academy was viewed as an *unrepublican* institution by Jefferson's political heirs. The outstanding performance of so many well-trained West Point officers in the Mexican War, however, ended congressional attempts to close it down.

SIX

THE RISING STORM

(1849–1861)

I. CALIFORNIA AND THE COMPROMISE OF 1850

Grim, determined James Knox Polk had achieved his major territorial goals. He succeeded in expanding U.S. power to the Pacific. Polk single-mindedly pursued the goal of adding San Diego harbor and San Francisco Bay to the American Union. It was this presidential decisiveness—far more than the enthusiasm of newspapermen for Manifest Destiny—that accounted for the stunning expansion of U.S. power and influence in the late 1840s.[1] But Polk found he could not do all this without creating military heroes for his great political rivals—the Whigs. The Whig Party had led the opposition to the Mexican War. Now, ironically, the Whigs nominated General Zachary Taylor, a Louisiana slaveholder who had earned the nickname "Old Rough and Ready" in the war, as their presidential candidate in 1848.

Unfortunately for Jackson's political heirs, the issue of slavery was splitting the Democratic Party. A new faction, the Free-Soil Party, was comprised of many ex-Democrats who were willing to tolerate slavery in the South but were *unwilling* to see it expand into the territories won from Mexico. The Free-Soilers nominated Martin Van Buren for president. Northern Democrats, who were willing to let slavery expand across the hot and sparsely populated Southwest to keep peace with their Southern slaveholding allies, nominated Lewis Cass. With the Democratic Party split, Taylor and the Whigs won the White House.

Zachary Taylor had not so much as cast a ballot for president in over forty years of army service.[2] As president, though, he would not be able to avoid the issues much longer. Events in California would astonish the world—and put pressure on Washington to keep pace. The peace had not even been signed with Mexico before gold was discovered at Sutter's Mill on the south fork of the American River, near Coloma, California. Word spread throughout the United States, speeded by means of the newly developed telegraph. The California Gold Rush began almost immediately. Tens of thousands of Americans from all regions, and others from around the world, struck out for the gold fields of the Sacramento Valley.

They came overland and by sea. As far away as China, California became known as *Gum Shan*—the Mountain of Gold.[3] Many of them entered by way of the *Golden Gate*. With a typical pitchman's flourish, U.S. Army Major John Charles Frémont, the Pathfinder, had named this entrance to San Francisco Bay.[4] These "Forty-Niners" (1849) swelled the territory's population. As much as $30,000 to $50,000 in gold was being taken out of the mines *each day*! West Pointer William Tecumseh Sherman, serving with the army in California, thought the gold would be more than sufficient to pay for the entire Mexican War.[5]

Soon California would be pressing for statehood. And, to Taylor's chagrin, a decision about slavery in the territories could not be avoided. It was a decision that would split the nation.

California's fate would be decided in Washington, where the slavery issue dominated. Southerners feared that if California entered the Union as a free state, anti-slavery forces would control the Senate and, eventually, outlaw slavery. "If the South is to be saved," wrote an ailing

John C. Calhoun, "now is the time."[6] The South must be assured that it would continue to have equal representation in the national government *or it would have to consider secession.* New York Senator William H. Seward matched Calhoun's militancy. Seward, a Whig, said that Congress surely had the right under the Constitution to limit the expansion of slavery. Even so, he argued provocatively, there was a "higher law" than the Constitution—natural law.[7] Not only could slavery's expansion be limited, Seward said, but in time it could be abolished.[8]

Henry Clay of Kentucky arose on the Senate floor, thundering that "I know no South, no North, no East, no West, to which I owe any allegiance. . . . My allegiance is to the American Union and to my state."

Clay offered a bundle of legislative proposals that covered many aspects of the dispute over slavery in the territories. Whether it was *great* or not, it was aptly called a compromise. First, California was to be admitted as a free state. Second, New Mexico would be organized as a territory with no restrictions on slavery. Third, the slave trade in the District of Columbia would be abolished. But fourth, Congress would pledge no further interference with the owning of slaves in the nation's capital. Fifth, Congress would refrain from using its great power under the Commerce Clause of the Constitution to regulate the slave trade *among* the states. Sixth and finally, Congress would pass a new, more stringent Fugitive Slave Act.[9] Southerners claimed that as many as thirty thousand slaves had run away from their masters. This *fugitive slave* problem, they claimed, had cost Southerners as much as $15 million.[10]

We must be guided by the wisdom of George Washington in his Farewell Address, Clay argued.[11] When someone suggested that this latest effort would prevent his ever becoming president, Clay memorably responded: "Sir, I had rather be *right* than be President!"[12]

All eyes now looked to Daniel Webster to respond to Calhoun and Clay. Would he help Clay to pass this controversial compromise? Or would he speak for the North and *reject* it? The "Godlike Daniel" rose by his desk, his voice filling the crowded chamber: "I wish to speak today not as a Massachusetts man, nor as a Northern man, but as an American, and a member of the Senate of the United States. . . . I speak today for the preservation of the Union. 'Hear me for my cause!'"[13]*

Speaking for more than three hours on 7 March 1850, Webster endorsed Clay's compromise, giving it essential backing at a critical moment. Webster still had confidence that the preservation of the Union would in the end bring an expansion of liberty. He still hoped to see slavery wither away in the West.

John C. Calhoun sat in his seat, glowering, almost unable to speak. When Webster warned the Senate that *dissolution of the Union* could never be achieved peaceably, Calhoun cried out: "No sir! The Union *can* be broken."[14] Calhoun and his followers insisted that California's admission be delayed until she was organized as a territory—as almost all other states had been admitted. Calhoun hoped to use that time to settle California's rich central valley with slave agriculture. A slaveholding California would have given Calhoun's "peculiar institution" a window on the Pacific.

President Zachary Taylor presented an obstacle to the passage of Clay's Compromise of 1850. Old Rough and Ready saw no reason to make all these concessions to the South on California. But that summer, Taylor was struck with "cholera morbus" after enduring hours of Fourth of July oratory. Consuming large quantities of ice milk and cucumbers, in the stifling heat of a Washington summer, he quickly took to his sickbed in the White House.[15] There, the doctors invaded the sick room, and he was dead within the week.

The new president, Millard Fillmore of New York, was an anti-Seward Whig. He was more malleable than Taylor and quickly signaled his willingness to sign the Compromise of 1850. When Henry Clay was unable to get the legislation passed, Senator Stephen A. Douglas of Illinois took up the task. He broke the bill into smaller pieces and drove them through the Senate.

---

* From Brutus's speech in Shakespeare's *Julius Caesar*, act 3, scene 2.

No one was especially happy with the result. Slaveholding Southerners feared the admission of California as a free state portended the end of slavery. Many Northerners despised the new Fugitive Slave Act, which brought the long arm of slavery into Northern communities that had previously thought themselves "free." A unique system of escape for runaway slaves had been organized by former slaves with the help of sympathetic whites. The Underground Railroad was funded and supported largely by Quakers. It was neither underground nor really a railroad, but it nonetheless carried hundreds of fugitive slaves to freedom in the North or even in Canada. Former slave Harriet Tubman served as "conductor" on this railroad, and she reentered the South scores of times to help her brothers and sisters escape. Braving the hangman's noose if captured, Miss Tubman humorously said she never ran her railroad off the tracks. Now, the Fugitive Slave Act required the citizens of free states to cooperate in handing escaped slaves over to their masters.

Despite the unpopularity of the Compromise of 1850, many Americans breathed a sigh of relief when it became law. They hoped it might finally resolve the slavery issue once and for all.

John Calhoun died in early 1850 before final passage of the compromise. Henry Clay and Daniel Webster would also soon pass away. A rising generation, represented by men like Stephen A. Douglas of Illinois, Jefferson Davis of Mississippi, William H. Seward of New York, and Charles Sumner of Massachusetts, now moved to center stage in the Senate. Douglas earned the nickname "the Little Giant" when he took up and passed Clay's compromise as individual bills. Douglas, too, hoped to end the growing controversy over slavery.

Calhoun's loss was deeply mourned by the people of the South. Even his frequent foe, Missouri's Thomas Hart Benton, said of him, "He is not dead, sir—he is not dead. There may be no vitality in his body, but there is in his doctrines."[16]

Those doctrines! Calhoun was important because he dared to contradict Jefferson directly. Men were *not* born equal, he said, but *unequal.* He dared to say that slavery was *not* a necessary evil but a positive good. He recognized that the "peculiar institution" could never be defended if men thought it was fundamentally wrong. For all the intellectual force of his ideas on the rights of political minorities within a genuinely federal government, it is also true that no man's *doctrines* did more to put his country on the road to civil war than did those of John C. Calhoun.

At the end of the war, poet Walt Whitman reported a dispute between two battle-weary, wounded Union veterans. One said he had seen Calhoun's monument while marching through South Carolina. The other soldier disagreed, "*I* have seen Calhoun's monument. That you saw is not the real monument. It is the desolated, ruined South; nearly the whole generation of young men between seventeen and thirty used up: the rich impoverished; the plantations covered with weeds; the slaves unloosed and become the masters; and the name of Southerner blackened with every shame—all that is Calhoun's *real* monument."[17]

The second great generation of national leaders had passed from the scene. But the agitation over the meaning of slavery in a nation dedicated to freedom had not slackened. In fact, it had hardly begun.

II. RAILROADS AND REFORM

In a single generation, Americans had seen canals and steamboats revolutionize transport. Railroads revolutionized it yet again. Just as the nation's territory had expanded to the Pacific, the means for tying the country together physically were found in the railways.

Technical questions abounded: What should be the means of propulsion? Horses? Sails? Steam? *Steam*, emphatically, steam.

How should rails be constructed? Of steel? Of wood? Steel.

These decisions were not made by the government but by rigorous experimentation by inventors, investors, and industrialists. The free enterprise system was proving to be the most creative and productive force in the world.

Americans understood that their national life was being transformed by the railroad, and what Indians called the Iron Horse had profound implications for the spread of free institutions across the continent. When the Baltimore & Ohio Railroad (B&O) drove the first spike on 4 July 1828, Maryland leaders asked Charles Carroll, the oldest living signer of the Declaration of Independence, to preside over the ceremony.[18] South Carolina followed soon thereafter, building her first railroad in the critical year of 1833.[19] *DeBow's Register*, a Southern newspaper, boasted of the phenomenal growth of U.S. railroads. In just over a decade, the United States had created the world's *largest* railroad system. With 3,688 miles of track, America led Britain (2,069), Germany (1,997), and France (552).[20]

The development of American railroads was not uniform throughout the country, however. The rise of "King Cotton" in the South meant that transportation would be at the service of the slave-based plantation economy. In the North and West, rails often *led* the way in the development of the economy. Southern entrepreneurs were not encouraged to invest in railroads as they were in the North.[21] Most railroads ran east and west, especially those that carried the waves of new immigrants. Because so few immigrants wanted to go to the South—or were welcomed *in* the South—this east-west development of the rail lines further served to isolate and alienate the South from the rest of the country.*

The first decades of development had shown that steam locomotives required single tracks, and the idea of competition over a single line of track would not work.[22] Soon, the railroads came to rely on long, single cars called saloons with an aisle running down the center.[23] First-class tickets provided more comfortable travel, but they also reinforced social

---

* It should be noted that in this decade, the western states were increasingly tied to the East and Northeast by railroad connections. The fact that western states were free states also became critically important to the rising idea that the South meant only those states that held slaves—and everything else was North.

divisions. This was an idea that ran counter to Jacksonian democracy. Many Americans came to have concerns about the rise of monopoly in the railroad industry. Vast fortunes were made in railroads. Some Americans worried about a class system based on wealth. They feared that the great disparities in wealth that characterized Europe would undermine the Jeffersonian ideal of yeoman farmers, independent and free.

Even in the North, however, racial prejudice dictated that segregation would prevail. "Jim Crow" cars were put on behind other passenger cars to accommodate black passengers.[24*] Frederick Douglass created a national stir when he *refused* to leave his seat in a first-class railroad car in Massachusetts. Douglass challenged the enraged white conductor to give him "one good reason" why he should leave his seat. "Because you are black!" the conductor shouted as he summoned several muscular stevedores to eject the famous abolitionist. "Snake out the damned n——!" the conductor yelled. Douglass, who had fought and floored a vicious "slave breaker" on Maryland's Eastern Shore, grabbed his seat tightly. By the time he was finally put off on the station platform, he had the seat he had paid for still held in his powerful grip. He had wrenched it from its mount. "They should at least have let me travel half way," Douglass later told an English audience. "After all, I'm only *half* a Negro!"[25] The "half a Negro" gibe referred to the fact that Frederick's father had been a white slaveholder on Maryland's Eastern Shore.

By the end of the 1850s, railroad construction had more than tripled. A government grant of twenty-two million acres of public lands provided a huge incentive for industry growth; though the rail system could not have been built as quickly or as efficiently by other means, this system was open to criticism for bringing corruption into state legislatures and

---

* "Jim Crow" was a character created by a white entertainer, "Daddy" Dan Rice, in 1832. Rice blackened his face with burnt cork and shucked and jived in a crude caricature of a black man. Jim Crow became synonymous with a Negro and lived a long and less-than-honorable life in American culture (http://xroads.virginia.edu/~HYPER/JACOBS/hj-jcrow.htm).

Congress.[26] Despite these political challenges and the severe but temporary depression of 1857, America had clearly become a nation on wheels. In the North, some 22,385 miles of track connected the major cities and provided railheads for an agricultural revolution that was keeping pace with rapid industrialization. The vast territory of the South was less well served. Even here, however, the 8,783 miles of track exceeded most other nations in the world.[27]

Paralleling the railroads came the development of Samuel F. B. Morse's telegraph. After he tapped out his famous message—"What hath God wrought?"—in 1844, Morse would see his invention quickly spread. By 1850, telegraph lines stretched from Maine to Florida and soon spanned the continent.[28] Morse also developed for his invention the Morse Code, a system of dots and dashes memorized for a century by Boy Scouts and military recruits; it was essential to communication.* At the same time, Cyrus McCormick's reaper did for wheat what Eli Whitney's cotton gin had done for cotton half a century before.[29]

The rush of immigrants into America's coastal cities and the spread of public education in the Northern states prompted the yearnings for reform. Emerson said that the young men of these days had been born "with knives in their brains."[30] Labor unions began to demand better conditions for urban workers. Southern writers were quick to point to the unhealthy conditions these "wage slaves" labored under. (Nonetheless, no Northern manufacturers ever sought a national Fugitive *Employees* Act. This truth was doubtless attributable in part to the tide of cheap labor from immigration.)

The 1850s saw such city-based labor federations as the National Typographic Union (1852), the United Hatters (1856), and the Iron Moulders' Union (1859).[31] Some of the German immigrants—radical refugees from the failed European Revolution of 1848—brought Marxist

---

* Morse was a virulent anti-Catholic. He shared this dubious distinction of inventive genius and religious bigotry with Henry Ford (except, in Ford's case, the objects of his contempt were Jews).

socialism in their steamer trunks.[32] By contrast, English writer Charles Dickens marveled at the clean and bright factories where Massachusetts's famous "Lowell Girls" worked.[33] Still, the model textile plants where these young women were employed were hardly representative of the rising new industrialism. The Democratic Party—known in these years simply as the Democracy—reached out to labor and to immigrants.

Women's rights groups began their long march toward freedom with the Seneca Falls, New York, convention in 1848. Elizabeth Cady Stanton and Lucretia Mott led the way in demanding votes (suffrage) for women.[34] This movement soon expressed itself in other ways too. The dignified Mrs. Stanton—daughter of a distinguished judge and wife of a New York senator—shocked many when she discarded the familiar floor-length hooped skirt and adopted the newly fashionable "bloomers." This practical attire featured a short skirt and leggings. The respectable Mrs. Stanton and her fellow *suffragettes* faced the ridicule expressed in this doggerel verse:

> Heigh! ho! Carrion crow,
> Mrs. Stanton's all the go;
> Twenty tailors take the stitches.
> Mrs. Stanton wears the britches.[35]

Undeterred, women took the lead in such important social reform movements as Temperance (abstinence from alcoholic beverages), prison reform, and improvements in the treatment of the insane. "Cold Water Armies" formed to discourage drunkenness and saloons and to offer "the pledge" to young men. "Lips that touch liquor shall never touch mine," promised legions of virtuous young women.

Many hardworking, hard-drinking laborers not surprisingly took a dim view of these efforts from socially prominent "do-gooders." (Even in our own time, we've seen this superior and disdainful attitude of many reformers who look down their noses at hard hats and others who smoke and polish off a few beers after work.) As in England and Europe, the saloon often fulfilled an important social need for immigrants crammed into dark and unsanitary tenements. Party organizers often found in these taverns a ready audience for political recruitment.

Nor was the spirit of reform confined to dry land. Commodore Uriah Philips Levy finally succeeded in 1850 in banning *flogging* in the U.S. Navy. He had campaigned for decades against the inhuman practice. Now, neither black nor white American sailors could be beaten as a form of discipline. Although he may not have intended it as an abolition measure, the contrast with the treatment of slaves in the cotton fields could not have been more striking.*

Nativism—a political and social movement to restrict the flood of immigration—flared in the 1850s to challenge the two-party system. In a number of Northern states—including Massachusetts and New York—a new group virtually eclipsed the Whig Party. Calling themselves the American Party, movement leaders organized secretly to take over legislatures and prevent immigrants' voting. They answered all questions from outsiders: "I know nothing"; hence the name of derision history gives them—"Know-Nothings." In Baltimore, groups like the "Plug Uglies" used violence to prevent immigrants from voting.[36]

Much of this Nativism took on an anti-Catholic tone, with legislatures investigating Catholic parochial schools and convents. Requests for Catholic public school students to be allowed to read from their own *Douay* version of the Bible led to riots in Philadelphia. When Nativists elected a mayor in New York City, the legendary Catholic Archbishop John Hughes requested a meeting. If any of his houses of worship were attacked, he mildly informed His Honor, Catholics would "turn New York into a second Moscow." *Dagger John's* warning produced the desired

---

* Levy (pronounced *LEV-ee*) was the first Jewish commodore in the U.S. Navy. He was also a leader in historic preservation. He purchased Thomas Jefferson's Monticello in 1836, thus saving this architectural jewel. Marc Leepson, author of *Saving Monticello*, says this was the first instance of historic preservation in America.

effect: New York remained at peace.* It surely didn't help the abolitionist cause with Democrats that most Nativists were ardently antislavery.

The 1850s also gave America a literary treasure trove. Henry Wadsworth Longfellow published his immortal works—*The Golden Legend*, *Hiawatha*, and *The Courtship of Miles Standish*. Nathaniel Hawthorne wrote *The Scarlet Letter* and *The House of the Seven Gables*. Herman Melville penned *White Jacket* and *Moby Dick*. Henry David Thoreau wrote *Walden*, and Walt Whitman produced *Leaves of Grass*.[37] Of all these masterpieces, however, the work that reached more Americans and more readers throughout the world than the rest combined was Harriet Beecher Stowe's *Uncle Tom's Cabin*, written in 1852.

This book hit America like an earthquake. Written at the moment when the Fugitive Slave Act lacerated consciences throughout the North, Stowe's book created unforgettable characters—like poor Eliza, the young slave woman. Carrying her infant at her breast, she raced across the frozen Ohio River. Stowe took care to depict Southern slave owners with charity. She showed them trapped in a system they did not devise. The worst villain of the book was the vicious Simon Legree, a transplanted Yankee. Even so, many Southerners reacted with hurt and rage. The book was banned in many Southern communities.

"Uncle Tom" has become a term of abuse in our own time, referring to a black man who is obsequious toward whites. But Stowe's Uncle Tom was a messianic figure with whom millions of Americans—especially the evangelicals of the North—identified deeply. In England, Queen Victoria wept over the book. Her prime minister, Lord Palmerston, read it. For generations thereafter, Americans repeated the legend that when

---

* "A second Moscow" referred to Tsar Alexander's decision to burn the city to the ground rather than let Napoleon occupy it. Dagger John's nickname referred to his pointed homilies that went straight to the heart—not to any likelihood that he would actually use a dagger (An archbishop nicknamed 'Dagger John,' Anthony D. Andreassi, March 15, 2018, *America: The Jesuit Review*, April 20, 2018 Issue, https://www.americamagazine.org/arts-culture/2018/03/15/archbishop-nicknamed-dagger-john).

Abraham Lincoln met Mrs. Stowe, he said, "So you are the little woman who wrote the book that started this great war."[38] *Uncle Tom's Cabin* has been translated into dozens of languages and has sold millions of copies. Since its first publication, it has never been out of print.

Frederick Douglass did not need to read *Uncle Tom's Cabin* to know the evils of slavery. As an escaped slave, he was asked to address an Independence Day crowd in Rochester, New York, in 1852. Douglass took care to *praise* the Founders. The signers of the Declaration, he said, "were brave men. They were great men, too—great enough to give fame to a great age . . . for the good they did, and the principles they contended for, I will unite with you to honor their memory."[39]

With penetrating insight, Douglass told his audience that Virginia had passed seventy-two laws mandating the death penalty for infractions committed by a black man, compared to only two such laws that similarly punished a white man. What was this, he asked, but an official *concession* by Virginia that the black man was fully human, fully moral, fully capable of choosing between good and evil? Does anyone think it necessary to pass death penalty laws for their cattle and horses? Who could answer Douglass's piercing logic? Douglass defied anyone to say that the Constitution was a proslavery document. Instead, he believed it could be interpreted freely as an *antislavery* charter. Finally, he asked, "What to the Slave is the Fourth of July?"[40]

How thoroughly unlike William Lloyd Garrison. The outspoken white leader of American abolitionists publicly burned a copy of the Constitution. Polar opposite of John C. Calhoun on the question of slavery, Garrison nonetheless shared with the Southern senator a vitriolic loathing of cherished American institutions. He denounced the Constitution in the *Liberator* and damned it as "a covenant with death and hell."

Not only did Frederick Douglass break the chains by which white slaveholders bound him, but he also had the courage to declare his independence from William Lloyd Garrison. Instead of calling for secession of the North from the South, Douglass stood for union. Douglass disputed the Garrisonian view that an abolitionist could never vote and could never even participate in the sinful American political system. Where Garrison condemned Washington and Jefferson to hell for the sin of owning slaves, Douglass spoke of the Founders with respect. Jesus Christ himself, Douglass pointedly reminded Garrison, ate with sinners and tax collectors.[41] Douglass made his break public with these bold words: "I would unite with anybody to do right; and with nobody to do wrong. And as the Union, under the Constitution, requires me to do nothing which is wrong, and gives me many facilities for doing good, I cannot go with the American Anti-Slavery Society in its doctrine of disunion."[42]

Harriet Stowe recognized Douglass's superior abilities. Once, when lecturing in Britain, Douglass said that *he* had as much right to sell Thomas Auld, his former owner, as Auld had a right to sell him. Then, with a sparkle of wit, Douglass offered *to sell Auld to any and all comers!* The crowd whooped in delight.

III. "BLEEDING KANSAS"

The election of 1852 represented the Whig Party's last stand. The anti-Jackson party nominated General Winfield Scott, hero of the War of 1812 and the Mexican War, for president. He lost to the Democrats' nominee, former U.S. senator Franklin Pierce of New Hampshire.

The most influential Democrat of this time, however, may well have been Senator Stephen Douglas of Illinois, who had won national fame by pushing the Compromise of 1850 through the Senate. Ambitious for the White House, the Little Giant led Senate Democrats to support his Kansas-Nebraska Bill of 1854. Under Douglas's bill, the Missouri Compromise that had preserved sectional peace for thirty years would be repealed. It made the spread of slavery possible, at least in theory, anywhere in the western territories if local citizens voted for it.

Douglas advanced his Kansas-Nebraska bill under the flag of *Popular Sovereignty.* Under this banner, Democrats argued that the "sacred principle" of democracy was that the people of any territory could decide whether or not to permit slavery. Douglas famously took a neutral position on the extension of slavery itself. "I don't care," he often said, "whether slavery is voted up or down."

Douglas used his powerful position as chairman of the Senate Territories Committee to advance his bill. The law galvanized antislavery sentiment throughout the country. It meant that slavery could spread to the Pacific if local settlers voted for it. Denounced as "squatter sovereignty," Douglas's solution to the slavery issue offended not only abolitionists and Free Soil supporters, but also those Southern "fire-eaters" who considered *any* limitation on slavery to be intolerable.*

Who could answer Douglas? He seemed to be rolling over all opposition. His natural opponents, the Whigs, were themselves splitting over the slavery issue.

Abraham Lincoln at this point was a successful lawyer in Springfield, Illinois, and a former one-term Whig congressman. As the Whig Party disintegrated, men like him were left without a political home. Lincoln hesitated before joining the new political party that was formed in Ripon, Wisconsin, in 1854. *New York Tribune* editor Horace Greeley urged the new alliance of anti-Nebraska groups, giving it the name *Republican.* Choosing this name was a good public relations move. Jefferson's Democratic-Republicans had long since dropped *Republican* from their name. Here, Greeley's friends could claim roots for their new party that went back to the Founder's vision (even if, in truth, these new Republicans were probably closer to the nationalism, financial conservatism, and antislavery beliefs of Hamilton than they were to Mr. Jefferson's agrarian

---

* "Fire-eaters" were Southern proslavery speakers who liked their rhetoric, their arguments, and their threats of disunion hot. They contrasted with "barn burners"—Northern antislavery men who were willing to burn down their own barns to get rid of the rats—in this case, the institution of slavery.

roots). It was not entirely clear what direction the Republicans would take. Would they align with the anti-immigrant Know-Nothings? In a number of states, just such an unholy alliance did occur.[43] Lincoln was having none of it. In a letter to Joshua Speed, a friend of his youth, he wrote:

I am not a Know-Nothing. That is certain. How could I be? How can any one who abhors the oppression of Negroes, be in favor of degrading classes of white people? Our progress in degeneracy appears to me to be pretty rapid. As a nation, we began by declaring that "all men are created equal." We now practically read it "all men are created equal, except Negroes." When the Know-Nothings get control, it will read "all men are created equal, except Negroes, and foreigners, and Catholics." When it comes to this I should prefer emigrating to some country where they make no pretence of loving liberty—to Russia, for instance, where despotism can be taken pure, and without the base alloy of hypocrisy [sic].[44]

Soon, as we shall see, Lincoln's dedication to liberty and the equality of man would prompt him to take up the challenge laid down by Stephen Douglas. Douglas's Kansas-Nebraska Act was signed by President Pierce, but it did not bring an end to conflict over slavery. In fact, it inflamed it. "Border Ruffians" from Missouri swept across the border and brought violence to the prairie. Antislavery elements throughout the North urged their followers to strengthen the Free Soil factions in Kansas.

Abolitionist preacher Henry Ward Beecher (Harriett Beecher Stowe's brother) encouraged resistance by force. Crates full of "Beecher's Bibles"— rifles, actually—turned up in the territory that newspaperman Horace Greeley had labeled "Bleeding Kansas."

Following a Border Ruffian raid on Lawrence, Kansas, in May 1856, Massachusetts's Charles Sumner delivered a stinging speech on the Senate floor titled "The Crime Against Kansas." Sumner grievously insulted

Andrew Butler, an elderly South Carolina senator. His rude and personal attack suggested the old man was drooling. South Carolina, Sumner cried, had sent to the Senate "a Don Quixote who had chosen a mistress who, though polluted in the sight of the world, is chaste in his sight—I mean the harlot, Slavery."[45]

This talk of drooling and prostitutes was too much. Talk of sexual connection between white Southerners and slaves was always explosive.* Butler's nephew, South Carolina Congressman Preston Brooks, did not bother to challenge Sumner to a duel. The Yankee would never "give satisfaction," he felt sure. Instead, Brooks strode into the Senate chamber and, finding the Massachusetts lawmaker alone, caned Sumner brutally, nearly killing him. The violence of the slavery issue could not be confined to Bleeding Kansas. Now, it had invaded the Senate floor. "The only men who don't have a revolver and a knife," said South Carolina Senator James Hammond, "are those who have two revolvers!"[46]

Following the raid on Lawrence, Kansas, New England abolitionist John Brown determined to claim "an eye for an eye." He and his sons and several followers staged their own attack on Pottawotamie, Kansas. There, on 23 May 1856, they hacked to death several proslavery men— even as the men's terrified wives pleaded for their lives.

Stunned by all this violence, the Democracy in 1856 turned against President Pierce and chose instead James Buchanan. An elderly bachelor, Buchanan had the good fortune to be out of Congress and serving as ambassador to England during the rancorous debates over the Compromise of 1850 and the Kansas-Nebraska Act. Also known as a doughface, Buchanan's diplomatic skills would enable him, it was hoped, to resolve the deepening divisions at home.

The new Republican Party was determined to field a candidate.

---

* It was explosive because it might be true. Southerner Mary Chesnut would admit as much in her famous Civil War diary. Or, it might be false, in which case it was seen as defamatory. Even in our own time, the revelation of Strom Thurmond's natural daughter by a family maid shows the issue remains one of the most sensitive and controversial.

John Charles Frémont, the famous "Pathfinder," was a young, dynamic choice. The slogan: "Free Soil, Free Labor, Free Speech, Free Men, and Frémont." The first Republican Party platform condemned both slavery *and* polygamy as "relics of barbarism." Republicans championed the cause of freedom, striving to defend the Founders' vision. They opposed Calhoun's ideas and the Democrats' "don't care" indifference to the survival of freedom in an expanded republic.

Hopes for a calm resolution of issues in reasoned debate were in vain. The election of 1856 was another very ugly one. It was further complicated when the Know-Nothings nominated former president Millard Fillmore.

Frémont was attacked because he had been born out of wedlock, the son of a French Catholic. He had married Senator Thomas Hart Benton's intelligent and vivacious daughter, Jessie—a decided plus—but the ceremony had been performed by a Catholic priest. This was an affront to the Nativists. Buchanan, on the other hand, had no wife at all. Some Republican papers depicted him as a spinster—*in a dress!*

Southern politicians regularly called the new party the "Black Republicans." This was to distinguish them from the *Jeffersonian* Republican Party and to taint them with the black flag of anarchy. But most of all, it was to associate the Republicans with black people. Increasingly, Southern leaders followed the earlier tack of the High Federalists and current path of the Garrisonians and threatened disunion: "The election of Frémont would be the end of the Union, and ought to be," growled fire-eater Robert Toombs of Georgia.[47]

In the end, Buchanan was elected with 45.3 percent of the popular vote. He carried the entire South, his own Pennsylvania, and Illinois. Frémont, with 33.1 percent of the vote, swept the Upper North. It was a truly impressive showing for the candidate of a new national party. Fillmore won 21.6 percent of the vote, carrying only Maryland. It was the last gasp of the Know-Nothings.

IV. DRED SCOTT

President-elect James Buchanan and many other national Democrats hoped that the U.S. Supreme Court would resolve the divisive issue of extending slavery into the territories for them. Buchanan wrote privately— and quite improperly—to friends on the Supreme Court, urging a broad ruling. He thus tried to influence the outcome of the Court's decision. When he mounted the inaugural stands on 4 March 1857, Buchanan was seen whispering animatedly with Chief Justice Roger B. Taney. Could they have been discussing the momentous case then before Taney's court?[48] The case of *Dred Scott v. John F. A. Sandford* had been wending its way through federal courts for nearly a decade. The case was brought by Dred Scott, a slave, who sued to seek his own freedom and that of his family because his master had taken the Scotts to the free state of Illinois.

After his whispered discussion with Taney, Buchanan delivered his inaugural address, telling the assembled crowd the ruling was coming: "[I]n common with all good citizens, I shall cheerfully submit" to the Supreme Court's ruling, "whatever it may be."[49] This was a singularly *dishonest* comment, since it now appears that he knew very well what the ruling would be. Buchanan went on to express the hope that mere "geographical" parties would rapidly become extinct. Of course, he meant the Republicans. That is surely *one* way to dispense with your opponents. Thomas Jefferson, who actually embraced *his* opponents in his inaugural address and pronounced their dissent legitimate, would have marveled to see what had become of the Democratic Party he and Madison had founded.

Two days later, the eighty-year-old Taney read his fifty-page opinion in a Supreme Court chamber jammed with spectators.[50*] The ruling

---

* Taney is pronounced TAW-nee in his home state of Maryland. The famous Coast Guard cutter named for him when he served as Jackson's Treasury secretary is pronounced TAY-nee.

was truly breathtaking. First, Taney found that Dred Scott was not an American citizen and could never become so because of his race. Taney might have stopped his reading there. Case dismissed. Despite the patent absurdity of the claim, if Scott were not a U.S. citizen, he could not sue in a U.S. court. But Taney was determined to plow ahead. He next ruled the Missouri Compromise *unconstitutional*, saying Congress had no power to interfere with Sandford's "property" without due process, as spelled out in the Fifth Amendment. Of course, Congress is *granted* authority under Article IV, Section 3 to make "all needful regulations in territories."[51] In effect, Taney was ruling the ancient and revered Northwest Ordinance of 1787 unconstitutional too. That act of Congress under the Articles of Confederation had famously banned slavery north of the Ohio River.

Finally, Taney offered the outrageous *obiter dictum* that, as a black man, Scott was "so inferior [that he] had no rights which the white man is bound to respect."[52]* His opinion—which rested on an obviously false reading of the history of the American founding—adopted Calhoun's doctrines. Under Taney's ruling, America would be a slave nation and free states would be mere local exceptions to the general rule.[53] Now, Frederick Douglass mourned, every black man in America would have to sleep with a pistol by his pillow.

If the Supreme Court's *Dred Scott* opinion had been meekly accepted, America would truly have ended her experiment in ordered liberty. She would have "lost the bubble" in 1857.

Southerners welcomed Taney's opinion. Following the doctrines of John C. Calhoun, many in the South began to clamor for territorial expansion, not for greater human liberty at all. Instead, they wanted more land to be brought under cultivation by more slaves. Senator Jefferson Davis, a Mississippi Democrat, demanded annexation of Cuba and her half million slaves.[54] Davis's colleague, Albert Gallatin Brown, spoke for

---

* *Obiter dictum*—something said by way of passing. In law, it is a superfluous comment not necessary to decide the case at hand.

this contingent when he declared on the Senate floor: "I want Cuba and sooner or later we must have it. I want Tamalpais, Potosi, and one or two other Mexican States; and I want them for the same reason—for the planting and spreading of slavery."[55]

But as much as Southerners appreciated the *Dred Scott* ruling, Northerners condemned it. No ruling more inimical to the Founders' vision had ever been handed down. But it was an overreach—and a grave misstep for the defenders of slavery. In a stroke, Taney the Marylander shocked millions of Northerners into a belated recognition of freedom's peril. Horace Greeley spoke of it with sneering contempt. The *Dred Scott* opinion, he wrote in the *New York Tribune*, was entitled to "just so much moral weight as would be the judgment of a majority of those congregated in any Washington barroom." To the *Chicago Tribune*, Taney had set back the "current of progressive ideas and Christian humanity."[56]

Far from settling the slavery question, Taney's *Dred Scott* ruling inflamed opposition to the extension of slavery. It served as the greatest recruitment tool for the new Republican Party.

Following his single term in Congress, Abraham Lincoln had returned to the circuit as a lawyer. He now made a comfortable living, especially as an advocate for the rising force of railroads. He continued, however, to maintain his interest in politics. Now fully committed to the new Republican Party, Lincoln used temperate language to challenge the opinion. But challenge the *Dred Scott* ruling he did.

> While the opinion of the Court . . . expressly declare[s] that the Constitution of the United States neither permits Congress nor a Territorial legislature to exclude slavery from any United States territory, the [majority justices] all omit to declare whether or not the same Constitution permits a state . . . to exclude it.[57]

A shudder must have gone through Lincoln's hearers. Despite the careful, lawyerly language, Lincoln raised the most frightening specter imaginable—that the United States would cease to have any free states at all. If slaves were nothing but "property," if Congress and the territories could not deprive slaveholders of the full use of that "property," how logically could free states prevent slavery from flooding the Union from Maine to California? Under the misrule of *Dred Scott*, the question was, *How indeed?*

V. LINCOLN MEETS DOUGLAS

To New England abolitionists, *any* concession to Southern slaveholders was unthinkable. But to Lincoln, the peace of the Union required Northerners to make some allowances.

Unlike the abolitionists, he went out of his way to recognize the humanity of his opponents—Northern and Southern alike. In a speech in Peoria, Illinois, in 1854, Lincoln pointedly said, "Only a small percentage [of the people] are natural tyrants. That percentage is no larger in the slave states than in the free. The great majority, south as well as north, have human sympathies." But granting this, Lincoln powerfully argued that these very human sympathies "manifest in many ways their sense of the wrong of slavery and their consciousness that, after all, there is humanity in the Negro." He showed how Southerners had joined Northerners to impose the death penalty on African slave traders in 1820. "But you never thought of hanging men for catching and selling wild horses, wild buffaloes or wild bears."[58] Lincoln's mild manner combined with his powerful use of *logic* made him a star of the new Illinois Republican Party.

Meanwhile, the powerful Stephen A. Douglas would have to win reelection to the Senate or fade from prominence. "A steam engine in britches," the energetic Douglas determined to win.[59] His task was complicated by his open feud with his fellow Democrat, President Buchanan. First, they clashed over patronage. But soon they fought over Bleeding Kansas. Senator Douglas thought the proslavery constitution, written by a rump legislature in Lecompton, Kansas, was a fraudulent expression of the people's will. He was right. President Buchanan, however, endorsed the Lecompton Constitution. Horace Greeley was so impressed with Douglas's stance that he publicly urged Illinois Republicans to back the Little Giant.[60]

Lincoln knew this would destroy the Republicans—in Illinois and nationally. Ignoring the meddling of a faraway New York editor like Greeley, Lincoln challenged Douglas to a series of debates around the state. Douglas could have stiff-armed the tall and gangly Lincoln. The one-term former congressman had gained a fine reputation in Illinois courtrooms and a good income as a lawyer for the railroads, but he could not match Douglas's international fame. Still, despite his underdog status, Lincoln had his reasons for throwing down the gauntlet, just as Douglas had his for accepting. He wanted—perhaps even *needed*—to show the Illinois legislature that he still commanded a great following among the voters; it was, after all, the legislature that would select the United States senator.*

Douglas had great confidence in his own booming voice, his quick wit, his slashing debating style. He had sharpened his skills in the United States Senate for five years, sitting next to men like Webster, Clay, and Calhoun.

But beyond demonstrating that his rhetorical mastery merited a return trip to the Senate, there were serious ideological issues at stake. Douglas accepted Lincoln's challenge in part because he was eager to show that *his* argument for Popular Sovereignty was superior to Lincoln's case for limiting the extension of slavery. "Let the people decide" had a powerful appeal. Lincoln's case for the Founders' vision of liberty and the equality of man could be made to sound woefully impractical, Douglas felt sure.

Douglas traveled around the state in high style. He had his own private railroad car, well-stocked with whiskey and refreshments. It was provided to him by George B. McClellan. McClellan was a West Pointer who had

---

* From 1789 until the passage of the Seventeenth Amendment in 1914, U.S. senators were chosen by their state legislatures.

risen to become president of the Illinois Central Railroad.[61] Douglas's arrival in each town was hailed by a booming cannon and brass bands. Lincoln rode in the public cars and brought no contingent of campaign aides with him. Even so, some young women greeted him with a banner: "Westward thy Star of Empire takes its way / Thy girls *Link-on* to Lincoln / Their Mothers were for Clay."[62]

Douglas immediately attacked Lincoln's "House Divided" speech. Earlier that summer (1858), Lincoln had electrified the state's Republican convention with this speech, in which he said that a house divided against itself—half free and half slave—could not stand. Lincoln was a dangerous radical, Douglas maintained. And he was for mixing the races. Slavery, he argued, was perfectly acceptable *if the people of each state desired it.*

Lincoln once again used logic to deflate his opponent. "Although volume upon volume has been written to prove slavery a very good thing, we never hear of the man who wishes to take the good of it *by being a slave himself.*"[63]

Douglas could not resist playing on racial prejudice. "Those of you," he told one crowd, who believe the Negro is your equal and ought to be on equality with you socially, politically, and legally, have a right to entertain those opinions, and of course will vote for Mr. Lincoln."[64*] He accused Lincoln of seeking to promote marriage between whites and blacks.

Lincoln responded by saying that because he did not want a black woman for a *slave* that did not mean he had to take her for a *wife.* He already *had* a wife, he said, and as to the black woman, he could "just leave her alone." Then Lincoln showed from the Census of 1850 that the vast majority of mixed-race persons lived in the South. Clearly, slavery and not freedom produced such results.

Once again, Lincoln used *logic* to trip up his debate opponent. While he did not favor complete social equality between blacks and whites, he said:

---

* Douglas meant they should vote for candidates for the state legislature pledged to Lincoln.

[T]here is no reason in the world why the Negro is not entitled to all the natural rights enumerated in the Declaration of Independence, the right to life, liberty, and the pursuit of happiness. I hold that he is as much entitled to these as the white man. I agree with Judge Douglas he is not my equal in many respects—certainly not in color, perhaps not in moral or intellectual endowment. But in the right to eat the bread, without leave of anybody else, which his own hand earns, he is my equal, and the equal of Judge Douglas, and the equal of every other man.

Douglas attempted to show himself humane with a crude analogy. In the struggle between the crocodile and the Negro, he said, he favored the Negro. But in the struggle between the white man and the Negro, he favored the white. Thus, he tried to dehumanize the black man and place him outside the community of concern for which the white majority had responsibility. Under Douglas's definition of Popular Sovereignty, it was always the white majority that would make decisions about black men's freedom. And he thought that was just. Lincoln responded that for a man to rule himself was freedom. But for a man to rule another man *without his consent* was tyranny.

Lincoln succeeded in pressing Douglas on slavery in the territories *after* Taney's *Dred Scott* decision. What was left of Douglas's Popular Sovereignty, Lincoln wanted to know. How could the people of a territory vote slavery *down* if Taney said every American had a right to carry his "property" with him?

In response, Douglas introduced his so-called Freeport Doctrine. Named for the Illinois town where they met, the Freeport Doctrine said slavery could not exist without "friendly legislation" to support it. Anti-slavery voters could simply refuse to pass such laws and slavery would effectively be kept out of a territory, Douglas claimed. Thus, he said, Popular Sovereignty was entirely consistent with Taney's ruling.

Like the seasoned lawyer he was, Lincoln had skillfully maneuvered

Douglas into making a concession that would prove fatal—not only to Douglas but also to his Democratic Party. Southern fire-eaters were outraged. Douglas would *never* get their support for president, they cried. But unless Douglas had devised *some* barrier to the spread of slavery in the territories, how could he ever claim election as a Northern man? Lincoln would later exploit Douglas's fatal misstep. He knew it was absurd to contend that "a thing may be lawfully driven away from where it has a lawful right to be."[65] *Checkmate.*

Lincoln's performance in the debates marked him as a leader. Lincoln was also a powerful wrestler, and wrestlers know how to use their opponents' strength against them. Lincoln used Douglas's worldwide fame to catapult himself into national prominence, though the positive results seemed slow in coming. Douglas, for instance, went on to win reelection by the Illinois legislature, despite Lincoln's impressive showing. Lincoln admitted he felt like the little boy who stubbed his toe in the dark: he was too big to cry, but it hurt too much to laugh. Yet he would later recognize that his famous sparring match was "a stumble, not a fall."

The Lincoln-Douglas debates were the most important since the ratification of the Constitution. Lincoln showed a mastery of law, philosophy, and history that raised him not only above Douglas but above every other statesman of the age. After these debates, there would be no more Republicans flirting with Douglas the Democrat. The future of the Republican Party was now bound up with the future of freedom in America. "The fight must go on," Lincoln said after the votes were counted. "The cause of civil liberty must not be surrendered at the end of *one*, or even, one *hundred* defeats."[66]

VI. JOHN BROWN AND HARPERS FERRY

Extreme abolitionists like John Brown were in no way willing to merely place slavery on the path of *ultimate* extinction. They demanded action and they demanded it *now*. Brown moved freely among the leaders of the abolition cause. He began to share, but not completely, his plans for a dramatic strike against slavery. A group of financial backers known as the Secret Six helped Brown rent a Maryland farmhouse across the Potomac River from the federal arsenal at Harpers Ferry, Virginia.* Brown assembled a small force of twenty-one impressionable young men—including his own sons and some former slaves. He planned to raise the banner of liberation in that strategic town and call on slaves to join in a bold bid for freedom.

Brown was an unlikely choice to organize a revolution—or anything else. Father of twenty, he had failed as farmer, as a merchant, and in every other line of work. Still, he was charismatic. Tall, straight as a ramrod, bedecked with blazing eyes and a bushy beard, Brown seemed the picture of an Old Testament prophet to many. Others saw in him the demon of *unreasoning* fanaticism. No one would ever meet John Brown and think of Lincoln's appeal to "mind, all-conquering mind." Brown had escaped capture for his murders of proslavery men in Kansas. This only emboldened him to greater exploits. He tried to enlist Frederick Douglass in his plot, but Frederick recoiled from his friend. He was "shocked" at the plot and thought it would immediately be stamped out.[67] Embittered, Brown determined to go ahead without Douglass's aid.

When he finally struck on 16 October 1859, John Brown seized the federal arsenal at Harpers Ferry and took several Virginians as hostages. The news alarmed the entire nation.

Colonel Robert E. Lee was home on leave in Virginia when the news of Harpers Ferry came. He immediately reported to the White House, taking Lieutenant J. E. B. Stuart with him.[68]

There, President Buchanan authorized Lee to take a detachment of U.S. Marines to Harpers Ferry to capture Brown and his cohorts. Lee raced to retake the federal arsenal. He sent Stuart under a white flag of truce to demand the immediate surrender of Brown and his fellow

---

* Harpers Ferry today is part of West Virginia.

insurrectionists. From inside the arsenal, Lee and his Marines could hear cries coming from some of the hostages. They feared they would die in an assault on the building. One of the hostages, Lewis W. Washington, yelled out, "Never mind about us, *fire!*" Lee knew the voice well. It was the grandnephew of George Washington. Smiling amid the tension, Lee told his Marines, "The old revolutionary blood does tell!"[69]

As soon as Brown rejected the lieutenant's demand, J. E. B. Stuart touched his hat. He gave the signal to Lee and the Marines to storm the place. Instantly, the Marines charged forward, battering the heavy oaken doors in, using their bayonets instead of bullets to spare the hostages.[70] Within minutes, Brown and his remaining men were captured. Two of Brown's sons were among the dead. The raid had ended barely thirty-six hours after it had begun.

Brown's venture was a complete and bloody failure. Frederick Douglass had predicted that. But Brown was soon able to change the impression. When he was brought to trial, he rejected with scorn his lawyers' attempt to plead not guilty by reason of insanity. Brown impressed all who saw him with his calm composure, his ready willingness to die for the cause of abolition. Even Virginia's proslavery governor, Henry A. Wise, who visited the abolitionist in prison, marveled at Brown's steadfastness.[71]

Brown was charged with "treason" against Virginia and tried in a state court. This was further evidence of President Buchanan's dough-face policies, since Brown's target was the *federal* arsenal. The verdict was a foregone conclusion. Sentenced to be hanged, Brown addressed the court:

> I believe to have interfered as I have done . . . in behalf of His despised poor, was not wrong, but right. Now, if it be deemed necessary that I should forfeit my life for the furtherance of the ends of justice, and mingle my blood further with the blood of my children, and with the blood of millions in this slave country whose rights are disregarded by wicked, cruel, and unjust enactments, I submit: so let it be done.

Brown's pose as Christian martyr was almost perfect. Northern writers generally praised him. Emerson said the "gallows would be glorious like the cross."[72] Henry David Thoreau told the citizens of Concord, Massachusetts: "No man in America has ever stood up so persistently and effectively for the dignity of human nature."[73]

Unknown to the general public was the letter Brown received from Mahala Doyle. She reminded Brown how he had invaded her Kansas home three years earlier and taken her husband and sons out to butcher them. "My son John Doyle whose life I begged of you is now grown up and is very desirous to be at Charlestown on the day of your execution," the unforgiving widow wrote.[74]

John Brown was hanged on 2 December 1859 in Charlestown, Virginia. On his way to the gallows, he handed this message to one of the officials: "I, John Brown, am now quite certain that the crimes of this guilty land will never be purged away but with Blood."[75]

In the crowd that assembled at Charlestown that day, a professor from the Virginia Military Institute, Thomas J. Jackson, noted Brown's "unflinching firmness." Soon, Professor Jackson—*Stonewall* Jackson—would be giving lessons in unflinching firmness. Standing nearby, fire-eater Edmund Ruffin actually admired Brown's courage. But young John Wilkes Booth, already a famous actor, had only contempt for the old man. Abolitionists were "the *only* traitors in the land," Booth said.[76]

VII. THE ELECTION OF 1860

The Republican Party was eager to avoid the brand of John Brown's dangerous radicalism. Although Democrats in Congress struggled to implicate the "Black Republicans," none of their charges could be proved. A congressional investigation of John Brown's activities yielded no evidence of Republican support. The fury that was unleashed in the wake of John Brown's raid was enough, however, to convince Frederick Douglass he had better *accept* the longstanding offer of a British speaking tour. Frederick's friends feared he might be kidnapped and dragged southward in chains to face an enraged all-white jury on charges he conspired with Brown. For such an offense, Douglass could have been hanged. Hurriedly, Douglass departed for England through Canada.

As for Abraham Lincoln, he had always stood *against* just such extremism as John Brown represented. Reverence for law must be the "political religion" of this country, Lincoln had said in his address to the Young Men's Lyceum in Springfield as long ago as 1838. "Old John Brown is hanged," Lincoln now told his fellow Republicans. "We cannot object." Lincoln acknowledged Brown's courage and his moral opposition to slavery, but he thought the raid demonstrated Brown's insanity.[77] Then he reminded his listeners that just as Brown had been hanged for treason, so would they have to treat *other* traitors if they tried to rebel against the lawful government.

Lincoln moved boldly in February 1860 to give an address in New York City. Many Republicans assumed that New York Senator William H. Seward would be the party's 1860 presidential nominee. By speaking at the Cooper Union, Lincoln offered a challenge to Seward in his very backyard.

His speech thrilled New Yorkers. He carefully outlined the Founders' views on slavery and aligned the Republicans *with those views*. He presented the Republican cause as prudent, moderate, but *firm*. To Southerners, he was patient, almost pleading. Lincoln concluded with a ringing affirmation of freedom in these words:

> All they ask, we could readily grant, if we thought slavery right; all we ask, they could as readily grant, if they thought it wrong. Their thinking it right, and our thinking it wrong, is the precise fact upon which depends the whole controversy. Thinking it right, as they do, they are not to blame for desiring its full recognition, as being right; but, thinking it wrong, as we do, can we yield to them? Can we cast our

votes with their view, and against our own? In view of our moral, social, and political responsibilities, can we do this?

Wrong as we think slavery is, we can yet afford to let it alone where it is, because that much is due to the necessity arising from its actual presence in the nation; but can we, while our votes will prevent it, allow it to spread into the National Territories, and to overrun us here in these Free States? If our sense of duty forbids this, then let us stand by our duty, fearlessly and effectively. . . .

Let us have faith that right makes might, and in that faith, let us to the end dare to do our duty as we understand it.[78]

William Seward lacked this fluency of expression. His previous speech on the "irrepressible conflict" between slavery and freedom had hung the title of *radical* around his neck. He frightened people. When Lincoln said essentially the same thing in his "House Divided" speech, he took care to take his text from the Bible.* It was much harder to label him dangerous—as Stephen Douglas had learned.

When the Republican Party convention met in Chicago in May, the leading candidates were William H. Seward of New York; Salmon P. Chase, an ex-Democrat, of Ohio; and Simon P. Cameron of Pennsylvania. Lincoln's campaign manager, Judge David Davis, had shrewdly worked to make Lincoln everyone's *second* choice. Judge Davis made sure to fill the visitors' galleries at the Wigwam with Illinois "leather lungs." These were burly young men hired to shout their lungs out for Lincoln. Judge Davis took pains to show all the delegates that Lincoln could carry the states of the lower North.

Lincoln was concerned by reports that Judge Davis was wheeling and dealing to get him the nomination. "I authorize no bargains and will be bound by none," Lincoln telegraphed Davis.[79] Davis reportedly replied when he read the note: "Lincoln ain't here and don't know what we have

---

* "And if a house is divided against itself, that house cannot stand" (Mark 3:25).

to meet."[80] When Seward was blocked, Lincoln was nominated on the third ballot. In Springfield, cannons were fired in celebration. All seemed exultant except Lincoln.

Democrats were deeply divided. Mississippi Senator Jefferson Davis had demanded a federal slave code for the territories. There would be no states' rights for the North. If the federal government protected slavery in the territories—as Davis and his supporters argued—then these territories were overwhelmingly likely to vote to become slave *states*. This, Senator Stephen Douglas and many Northern Democrats could not accept.

When the Democratic Party's nominating convention gathered in Charleston, South Carolina, disunion was already in the air. Unable to agree on a nominee for president—their rules required two-thirds to nominate—the Democrats suffered a walkout by cotton-state delegates. They agreed dispiritedly to reconvene in Baltimore. Baltimore was only slightly less vehement on the slavery issue than Charleston had been.

It was there that the fatal split finally occurred. When the convention refused to approve a platform calling for a federal slave code for the territories, another walkout occurred. The Southern delegates reconvened in Richmond, Virginia, to nominate Vice President John C. Breckinridge. This faction actually wanted to reopen the African slave trade. Senator Stephen A. Douglas had finally achieved his long-sought prize, the nomination for president of the national Democratic Party. But by the time he won it, the prize was hardly worth having.

A small faction of Old Line Whigs and former Know-Nothings assembled as the Constitutional Union Party and nominated Kentucky's John C. Bell and Massachusetts's distinguished Edward Everett. Now, the national election would be a four-way split.

Many Democrats understood that their party's split could only elect Lincoln. Stephen Douglas defied tradition and took to the rails to campaign with vigor. He wore himself out with speeches from train platforms in the North and the South, denouncing secession and calling for national unity. Lincoln did not even appear on the ballot in ten Southern states. His supporters carried rails in honor of his title, the rail-splitter. Republicans gloried in the fact that Lincoln had worked with his hands.

By this time, Lincoln was a wealthy and successful lawyer. This did not detract from the appeal of his hardscrabble youth. Actually, this was a great part of the Republicans' appeal. You, too, by hard work and honesty can become rich, Republicans told workers. His young supporters marched in all the Northern cities in a quasi-military company of "Wide Awakes."* Soon, all of America would be on the march.

When the votes were tallied in November, Lincoln swept the populous Northern states. He won 1,866,452 votes in a four-way contest (more than Buchanan four years earlier). He gained 180 electoral votes (152 were required to win). Douglas came in second in popular votes (1,375,157), but because most of those votes were cast in the North, he won only 12 electoral votes. Breckinridge swept the South with 847,953 votes and 72 electoral votes. Bell prevailed only in the Border States, winning 590,631 votes and 39 electoral votes.

It was the most important election in American history. Immediately, preparations began in the South for secession. The legislature in South Carolina called for a secession convention to meet in Charleston in December. There was no time to lose, secessionists told reluctant fellow Southerners. Once Lincoln had entered the White House, they reasoned, it would be harder to break free.

President Buchanan was in thrall to his Southern cabinet members. Secretary of War John Floyd made no effort to prevent the seizure of federal forts and arsenals throughout the South. Buchanan frittered. When South Carolina voted for secession, Buchanan was paralyzed. Fire-eater Robert Barnwell confronted him, demanding he turn over Fort Sumter. Buchanan waved his hands in impotent frustration: "You are pressing me too importunately, Mr. Barnwell; you don't give me time to consider;

---

* Wide Awakes, a paramilitary group of young men, were so called because of their torchlit parades at nightfall. They supported the Republican Party but were widely suspected of voter intimidation and anti-Catholicism.

you don't give me time to say my prayers. I always say my prayers when required to act upon any State affair."[81]

Loyal Unionists prayed for "just one hour of Andrew Jackson" instead of the invertebrate Buchanan.

Seven states had seceded by the time Lincoln prepared to take the oath. Lincoln had been informed of an assassination threat against his life during his journey to Washington. Refusing to cancel his speech on Washington's Birthday at Philadelphia's Independence Hall, he told the anxious crowd he would give his life for

> that sentiment in the Declaration of Independence which gave liberty, not alone to the people of this country, but, I hope, to the world, for all future time. It was that which gave promise that in due time the weight would be lifted from the shoulders of all men. This is a sentiment embodied in the Declaration of Independence. Now, my friends, can this country be saved upon that basis? If it can, I will consider myself one of the happiest men in the world, if I can help to save it. If it cannot be saved upon that principle, it will be truly awful. But if this country cannot be saved without giving up that principle, I was about to say I would rather be assassinated on this spot than surrender it.[82]

It was an *uncharacteristically* emotional moment for Lincoln. Against his better judgment, he was persuaded to change his plans and pass through secessionist Baltimore—where the plot was said to be thickening—in the middle of the night. When he arrived safely in Washington, he faced international ridicule. It was said he had come through Baltimore disguised as a Scotchman. Cartoonists lampooned him.

Washington was little better. Rumors of treasonous plots swirled through the muddy streets of the capital. Old General Winfield Scott, a Virginian and a staunch Unionist, pledged to defend the city's streets. There would be no violence, no armed disruption of the peaceful transfer of government. For the inauguration on 4 March 1861, Scott stationed sharpshooters on all the federal buildings. Breathing defiance of the rebels, Scott said he would stuff them into his artillery pieces positioned at the Capitol and "manure the Virginia hills" with their bodies.[83]

President Buchanan and the president-elect came onto the inaugural stands arm in arm.[84] Lincoln approached the podium to be sworn in as the sixteenth president of the United States. None other than Chief Justice Roger B. Taney would administer the oath. Senator Stephen A. Douglas, his defeated rival, held Lincoln's tall, black hat.[85]

His inaugural address was the most eloquent yet delivered in Washington City. He offered an olive branch to the states that had passed secession ordinances even as he denied the right of any state to secede. In a passage sometimes overlooked, he laid out his view of Fort Sumter. The federal installation in Charleston harbor was surrounded by a Confederate "ring of fire." "The power confided to me will be used to hold, occupy, and possess the property and places belonging to the government and to collect the duties and imposts," Lincoln said, trying not to provoke. He spoke to his dissatisfied fellow countrymen: "You have not oath registered in heaven to destroy the government, while I shall have the most solemn one to 'preserve, protect, and defend it.'"* He appealed to reason, to friendship, and to those "mystic chords of memory stretching from every battlefield and patriot grave to every living heart and hearthstone."

The future of freedom hung on those words. Not just American freedom, but *world* freedom was at stake. If a dissatisfied minority could break up the government whenever it lost an election, popular government was indeed impossible. If the failure to gain sufficient ballots led dissenters to resort to bullets, this grand experiment in ordered freedom would fail.

The next four years would be the years of freedom's fiery trial. Before Abraham Lincoln looked out on another inaugural assembly, the sacred

---

* It sounds as if he had not yet taken the oath of office. He hadn't. At this time in our history, presidents delivered their inaugural addresses *before* taking the oath.

fire of liberty was nearly extinguished. The American republic would come close to death and would be reborn. The new president knew what was at stake. He believed our sacred Union was "the last, best hope of Earth." To save this precious experiment in ordered liberty, Lincoln in this inaugural address appealed to sweet reason and to "the better angels of our nature."[86]

SEVEN

FREEDOM'S FIERY TRIAL

(1860–1863)

I. SECESSION WINTER (1860–61)

"South Carolina is too small for a republic and too large for an insane asylum," responded James L. Petigru to fire-eater Robert Barnwell Rhett, during Christmas week 1860.[1] Following Lincoln's election, Petigru was one of a small number of Charleston Unionists who found themselves outgunned and outvoted that fateful winter. South Carolina's secession convention voted to take the state out of the Union on 20 December 1860.

The mood was festive in Charleston. Fireworks greeted the Ordinance of Secession, and revelers placed blue cockades on the bust of John C. Calhoun. Bands played France's revolutionary anthem, the *Marseillaise*.[2] Convention delegates drew up a declaration in which they gave their reasons for leaving the Union. The delegates condemned the Northern people for "denouncing as sinful the institution of Slavery."[3] They condemned abolition societies in the North. Governor William H. Gist ordered a state militia officer to carry the news to other Southern states. The officer chosen was named—jesting aside—States Rights Gist.[4]

Many fire-eaters in the South not only expected Lincoln's election, they *welcomed* it. They intended to use the election of an antislavery president to shock their fellow Southerners into seceding from the old Union. It did not matter to them that Lincoln and the Republicans had repeatedly assured them there would be no interference with the institution of slavery *in the South*. The Republican platform of 1860 was decidedly less radical than that of 1856. There was now no talk of slavery as "a relic of barbarism." Lincoln was widely viewed in the North as much more moderate than John Charles Frémont, the party's first presidential nominee, had been.

Lincoln was still in Springfield, dealing with the endless demands of office-seekers. He felt, he said, like a man renting rooms at one end of his house while the other end is on fire. Still, he had to form a cabinet and staff a new administration. "We must run the machine as it is," he wrote.[5]

While Lincoln struggled to balance all factions of the very factious new Republican Party, secessionists moved quickly to take more states out of the Union before Lincoln took the oath of office on 4 March 1861.

To these extreme advocates of slavery, it did not matter that Lincoln and the Republicans were bound not to interfere with slavery in the states where it *already* existed. It did not matter that he even pledged to enforce the Fugitive Slave Act. He would enforce it because the Constitution commanded it (although, as he wrote his friend Joshua Speed, it would "crucify our feelings"). It did not matter that Lincoln's moderation had earned him the contempt of all-out abolitionists like William Garrison and Wendell Phillips. Phillips sneeringly dismissed Lincoln as "that slavehound from Illinois."[6] None of this mattered as the South was dragooned and Calhouned into secession. What mattered was that Lincoln had said "if slavery is not wrong, then nothing is wrong."

When seven states had seceded, they sent delegates to Montgomery, Alabama, in February 1861 to write a constitution for their new government. The Confederate States of America, as they would call their new nation, would have a president eligible for a single six-year term. He would have a line-item veto.* Members of the cabinet could sit in the Confederate Congress, thus opening the way for the development over time of a cabinet government like that in Britain.

The most important aspects of the Confederate constitution were, however, less obvious. For a movement that claimed states' rights, their constitution allowed *no state* the right to emancipate slaves. *No state* could even be admitted to the Confederacy from the old Union unless it agreed to maintain slavery always. And, a stunning development: the drafters of this constitution debated and emphatically *rejected* a passage that would have recognized a right of a state to secede from this Confederacy.[7]

When the delegates moved to choose a president and vice president, they shunned fire-eaters like Robert Barnwell Rhett of South Carolina and Robert Toombs of Georgia. The able Toombs might have fared better had he never gone to Montgomery. His friend Alexander Stephens reported that he was drinking heavily there. "He was *tighter* than I ever saw him, too tight for his character and reputation."[8] Delegates instead chose the sober Mississippian Jefferson Davis. Davis, a West Pointer, hero of the Mexican War, and former secretary of war and U.S. senator, seemed admirably qualified. As Davis's vice president, the secessionists chose none other than Lincoln's old friend, Alexander Hamilton Stephens of Georgia. A slight, short man, Stephens was chosen precisely because he was no fire-eater. His very moderation would appeal to many other Southerners who were still not sure about secession.[9] Once Georgia acted, however, little Aleck Stephens threw in his lot wholeheartedly with the Confederacy.

He expressed his beliefs in another speech a month after his election. Stephens's Cornerstone Speech emphasized that the Founders were *wrong*

---

* Some wags have said the line-item veto, long sought by President Reagan, was the only thing in the Confederate constitution worth fighting for. That was before Bill Clinton showed everyone how the line-item veto could be used creatively to bid *up* federal spending. President Clinton threatened to veto public works bills favored by congressmen unless they voted *for* his social spending bills.

when they asserted all men are created equal. Just as Lincoln had chosen to base his famous "House Divided" speech on the words of Jesus, now Stephens also cited Scripture.*

> Our new [Confederate] government is founded upon exactly the opposite idea [to the idea of equality in the Declaration]; its foundations are laid, its cornerstone rests upon the great truth that the negro is not equal to the white man. That slavery—subordination to the superior race, is his natural and normal condition. This, our new Government, is the first, in the history of the world, based upon this great physical and moral truth.[10]

No one in the South contradicted Vice President Stephens when he delivered this Cornerstone Speech. It was a clear defense of the Confederates' reasons for secession and going to war.

Mindful of the need for European intervention on behalf of the Confederacy, President Jefferson Davis avoided any direct mention of slavery in his inaugural address, which he delivered in Montgomery on 18 February 1861. That is because slavery was widely condemned in Europe. Instead, he stressed the right of self-determination for the states. "Thus the sovereign States, here represented, proceeded to form this Confederacy, and it is by abuse of language that their act has been denominated a revolution," said Davis. "They formed a new alliance, but within each State its government has remained, and the rights of person and property have not been disturbed."[11]

Two important things stand out. First, Jefferson Davis specifically and explicitly rejected the idea that the Confederacy is based on the natural right of revolution. This makes tactical if not philosophical sense: had he cited the right of revolution, he would have justified the right of his

---

* "The stone which the builders rejected has become the chief cornerstone" (Psalm 118:22). The *cornerstone*, as listeners to a thousand Christian sermons knew, was Jesus himself.

slaves to revolt against *him*. His namesake Thomas Jefferson had explicitly invoked Americans' natural right to revolution in the Declaration of Independence. Jefferson Davis was having none of it.

Second, he speaks *in code* about property rights. For slaveholders who regarded their slaves as *chattels* and who followed Chief Justice Roger B. Taney's reasoning in the *Dred Scott* ruling, this language was confirmation that slavery would exist as long as the right to property existed—that is, forever.

II. FORT SUMTER: THE CIRCLE OF FIRE

One of President Lincoln's first acts was to sign a commission for Lee's promotion to full colonel.[12] Lee accepted this, giving hope to General Scott that Lee might stay with the Union in any clash. The aged, infirm Scott was a Virginian, yes, but he was also the hero of many battles. For him, the Union was his life. But Lee's friend Jefferson Davis now led the Confederacy and his Mexican War comrade, Pierre Gustave Toutant Beauregard, was ringing Fort Sumter with a "circle of fire."[13]

Soon, Lee was invited to meet with Francis P. Blair Sr., a powerful member of Washington's political establishment. Blair had been a member of President Jackson's "Kitchen Cabinet," and he now wanted to sound out Lee's plans.[14] Blair told Lee he had been authorized by President Lincoln to offer him command of all Union forces—a vast army of seventy-five to one hundred thousand—a greater force than had ever been seen on the continent.

Lee heard Blair out, but refused in his famously courteous manner. "Though opposed to secession and deprecating war," he said, "I could take no part in an invasion of the Southern States." General Scott was heartbroken. Lee was his favorite. Scott and most others thought Lee the ablest man in the U.S. Army. Deeply moved, Scott told Lee, "You have made the greatest mistake of your life; but I feared it would be so."[15] It was, as Lee's illustrious biographer Douglas Southall Freeman wrote, "the answer he was born to make." Lee would spend a long, wakeful night in prayer. He stayed at Arlington House, his stately home overlooking the city of Washington. There, he penned his letter of resignation to Secretary of War Simon P. Cameron.

The die was cast.

Meanwhile, on the third of March in Charleston, General Beauregard had taken command of the forces surrounding Fort Sumter on behalf of the Confederate States. He tactfully but forcefully rearranged the guns and repaired the slapdash breastworks that had been thrown up by South Carolina state militiamen more eager than able. Beauregard knew his task well; he had been trained for it at West Point. There, his instructor was Robert Anderson. Anderson was so highly impressed with the young Beauregard that he had held the Louisiana cadet back in order to train incoming plebes in artillery.[16] Like Lee, Beauregard had been a West Point superintendent. But Beauregard had resigned when Louisiana seceded.[17]

Major Robert Anderson now faced his pupil across the water. Anderson, a military professional from a slaveholding Kentucky family, commanded the federal garrison at Fort Sumter. With a small force and dwindling supplies, Anderson continued to fly the flag of the United States and to resist Confederate demands that he surrender.

Meanwhile, Abraham Lincoln was receiving contradictory advice on whether Fort Sumter should or even *could* be held. Secretary of State William H. Seward was telling Southerners Lincoln would withdraw from the fort. But Senator Ben Wade of Ohio—*Bluff Ben Wade* as he was known—lived up to his name. If you surrender Fort Sumter, he told Lincoln, "Jeff Davis will have you as a prisoner of war in less than thirty days."[18] It was little wonder that Charles Francis Adams, the son and grandson of presidents, confided to his diary that Lincoln was "not equal to the hour."[19] But Seward, Wade, Adams—everyone, actually— misjudged Lincoln.

Lincoln ordered a naval flotilla to resupply Fort Sumter. He sent word to South Carolina's new governor that the federal installation would be provisioned but the garrison would not be strengthened. War, if it came, would be the Confederates' decision.[20]

Too late, Robert Toombs awoke to the South's danger. "The firing upon that fort will inaugurate a civil war greater than any the world has yet seen. . . . [It] is suicide, murder." He warned President Davis that attacking Fort Sumter would be like striking a hornets' nest. Legions would swarm from that hornets' nest and "sting us to death."[21] The timing couldn't have been worse. Toombs's ardor had cooled, just as President Davis's heated up.

Davis disregarded Toombs's words. He ordered Beauregard to open fire on Fort Sumter if any relief squadron approached. When a delegation of Southerners delivered an ultimatum to Major Anderson to surrender Fort Sumter, he politely refused. Escorting them back to their boat, the major said, "If we never meet in this world again, God grant that we may meet in the next."[22]

Before dawn on the morning of 12 April 1861, General Beauregard signaled for his batteries to open fire on the fort out in the middle of the harbor. Edmund Ruffin of Virginia, his long, white hair flowing down over his shoulders, was given the honor of firing the first shot. Ruffin, a transplanted New Yorker, thirsted for action. "The shedding of blood," he wrote, "will . . . change many voters from the hesitating states, [and make them] zealous for immediate secession."[23] The aged fire-eater was quick to pull the lanyard and plunge his country into war.

Beauregard's batteries lit up the predawn darkness in Charleston harbor. Major Anderson had only a token force of brave federal troops, but he held out as long as he could. Finally, after thirty hours of furious bombardment, and with flames creeping toward his powder magazines, Anderson was forced to surrender. The still incomplete Fort Sumter— built from sturdy New Hampshire granite—was turned over to the triumphant Confederate forces. Anderson and his men were treated with all the "honors of war," but all over the North, men rushed to enlist.

III. "A PEOPLE'S CONTEST":
THE CIVIL WAR BEGINS

The attack on Fort Sumter electrified the North. Senator Stephen Douglas spoke for the Northern Democratic Party in pledging his full support to the new administration in putting down the rebellion. President Lincoln issued a proclamation calling for seventy-five thousand volunteers to put down "combinations too powerful to resist" to ensure that federal law would be enforced. It would be four long years before the flag of the United States would fly once again over Sumter's broken battlements. After Sumter's fall, Lincoln called Congress into a special Fourth of July session. The outbreak of hostilities ended Virginia's hesitation. The Old Dominion's secession convention voted to leave the Union. Delegates now forgotten voted to break their ties with the American Republic that Virginia's greatest sons—Washington, Jefferson, Madison, Marshall, Mason, and Henry—had risked their lives to bring forth. They voted, too, to invite the Confederate government to relocate to Richmond.

With Virginia's secession and Maryland on the verge, Washington, D.C., might have been encircled. Lincoln could see Confederate batteries from his Executive Mansion windows. As Massachusetts and New York troops hurried south to relieve the capital, they encountered a secessionist mob in Baltimore. A riot broke out as some of the civilians heaved paving stones at the federal troops. Massachusetts soldiers fired on the crowd, killing twelve of the civilians and suffering four dead. It was April 19, the eighty-sixth anniversary of Lexington and Concord. That was a fight for liberty. Not all Americans agreed during the Revolution on the meaning of liberty. Some, especially the Tories, fought *against* independence. Especially in the South, this struggle turned bloody and bitter. Now, because Americans could not agree on the meaning of liberty, they were once again killing each other.

Lincoln told skittish Maryland Unionists he would not bring more troops through bleeding Baltimore, but he could not promise to avoid the

Old Line State altogether. He told Maryland's governor the troops were not birds who could fly into Washington, nor were they moles to burrow underground. Wisely, though, he ordered General Ben Butler to ferry his forces by water to Annapolis and bring them into Washington by rail. Butler was a political general, one of many promoted not for any military ability but to cement the loyalties of political factions. A Massachusetts Democrat, Butler only the year before had been scheming to make Senator Jefferson Davis his party's presidential candidate!

Lincoln would take no chances with strategic Maryland. He authorized the temporary imprisonment of pro-secession state legislators and the suppression of disloyal newspapers in the state. He also suspended the writ of habeas corpus. That meant more arrests could follow, without recourse to the courts. Lincoln's suspension of habeas corpus was the first such action on so broad a scale. Still, the Constitution specifically allows for such a suspension in time of rebellion. ("The privilege of the Writ of Habeas Corpus shall not be suspended, unless when in Cases of Rebellion or Invasion the public Safety may require it," Article I, Section 9.) His quick and effective actions in Maryland are debated to this day. The Old Line State's official song, "Maryland, My Maryland," which speaks of spurning the "Northern scum," still contains these anti-Lincoln lyrics:

> The despot's heel is on thy shore, Maryland!
> His torch is at thy temple door, Maryland!
> Avenge the patriotic gore
> That flecked the streets of Baltimore,
> And be the battle queen of yore,
> Maryland! My Maryland!*

The despot referred to in the first stanza is President Lincoln.

---

* "Maryland, My Maryland" was adopted as the state song in 1939 (Chapter 451, Acts of 1939; Code State Government Article, sec. 13–307).

Surely rebellion was afoot. If a vote of the white citizens of Maryland had been taken, the state would very likely have seceded. Western Maryland was loyal to the Union, just as mountainous western Virginia was. But crowded Baltimore and Maryland's Eastern Shore were "secesh." Lincoln was determined to save Maryland and the nation's capital for the Union.

He had little choice. Secession was in the air. Disloyalty, real and suspected, was everywhere. The situation was critical. The Confederate secretary of war boasted that the rebel flag would "float over the old Capitol dome before the first of May."[24]

Many high-ranking military officers—but no enlisted men—"Went with their states." The superintendent of the U.S. Naval Academy in Annapolis, Maryland, sensed the spirit of his neighbors. Captain Franklin Buchanan joined the Southern forces.*

Even many in the North were willing to let the Union be sundered. *New York Tribune* editor Horace Greeley wrote of the seceding states: "Wayward sisters, depart in peace." Many abolitionists—but *not* Frederick Douglass—similarly saw secession as a means to rid the United States of slaveholding states.[25]

As he reported in his first Message to Congress, Lincoln acted to preserve the Union. That was the first duty of the president. The chief executive also has a constitutional duty to "take care that the laws be faithfully executed" (Article II, Section 3). Pointing out that the laws were being flouted in all the seceding states, Lincoln asked, "Are all the laws *but one* to go unexecuted and the Government itself go to pieces lest that one be violated?"[26] Despite arguments at the time (and those that continue to this day) that Lincoln was acting as a *dictator,* the president reminded Congress that it *shared* responsibility for saving the Union and that it had the ultimate power to remove him from office if Congress found he had violated his oath of office. His Fourth of July message spoke powerfully of the stakes involved in the war:

---

* Despite this, the superintendent's spacious thirty-seven-room mansion at the Naval Academy is called *Buchanan House*—named for Franklin Buchanan, the academy's first "supe."

This is essentially a People's contest. On the side of the Union, it is a struggle for maintaining in the world that form and substance of government whose leading object is to elevate the condition of men—to lift artificial weights from all shoulders—to clear the paths of laudable pursuit for all—to afford all an unfettered start and a fair chance in the race of life. . . . I am most happy to believe that the plain people understand and appreciate this . . . [for] not one common soldier or common sailor is known to have deserted his flag. . . . It is now for [Americans] to demonstrate to the world that those who can fairly carry an election can also suppress a rebellion—that ballots are the rightful and peaceful successors of bullets; and that when ballots have fairly and constitutionally decided, there can be no successful appeal back to bullets.[27]

Lincoln hoped that pro-Union sentiment in other border states would assert itself. There was plenty of evidence that secession was not being accepted across the South. In East Tennessee, a mountainous region where few farmers held slaves, men like Andrew Johnson and William G. Brownlow fought *against* the rebellion. Johnson was a staunch Jackson Democrat. Brownlow, a former Whig newspaper editor, vowed to fight "the Secession leaders till Hell freezes over—*and then fight them on the ice!*"[28] Johnson and Brownlow had no aristocratic pretensions. They were feisty commoners and proud of it.

In Virginia, the western counties that had voted *against* secession refused to follow Richmond's lead. With the help of federal troops under General George B. McClellan, they withdrew from the state of Virginia. (In time, West Virginia would be admitted as a separate state of the Union.)

Lincoln treated Kentucky with kid gloves. Unwilling to challenge for the time being Kentucky's dubious claim of "neutrality," Lincoln hoped through patience and mild measures to retain its loyalty. Kentucky was not only Lincoln's birthplace, it was also the birthplace of Jefferson Davis and the home state of John Bell, a minor party candidate for president in 1860. His critics laughed at the president's caution: "Lincoln would like to have God on his side, but he *must* have Kentucky."[29] That was very nearly true, for without Kentucky, the entire heartland of the Union—states like Ohio, Indiana, and Illinois—would have been exposed to Confederate attack.

Early in the war, the Union suffered military disaster when General Irwin McDowell—prodded by Lincoln and an impatient Congress—marched out to meet a Confederate force near Manassas Junction, a day's march from Washington. The fickle Greeley now joined the general cry of "On to Richmond!" Green federal troops broke and ran in panic before the victorious rebels. "Skedaddled" was the humiliating description of the federal rout. General Beauregard added the victor's laurels at Manassas to his win at Fort Sumter. (But in so doing, the "Napoleon in gray" earned the jealous mistrust of his chief, President Davis.) At this battle, General Thomas Jonathan Jackson commanded his line of Virginians, ignoring cannon and rifle fire. "There stands Jackson, *like a stone wall*," cried General Bernard Bee.*

Meanwhile, Lincoln found himself facing a different sort of trouble in 1861. His wife, Mary Todd Lincoln, embarrassed Lincoln greatly by overspending a $20,000 congressional appropriation for refurbishing the badly dilapidated Executive Mansion. It had seemed important—like the plan to go ahead with the construction of the half-completed Capitol dome—to underscore the continuity of the Union and its institutions. But while a distracted president cast about for a winning general with a winning plan, "the first lady of the land" went on a shopping spree in New York and Philadelphia.

She innocently wanted to make the Executive Mansion a showplace (the better to answer her catty critics among the capital's pro-Southern society matrons). But Mrs. Lincoln's sense of style exceeded her sense

---

* Whether General Bee was *admiring* Jackson's brave stand or *annoyed* that Jackson was not moving up to support him—as Civil War writer Shelby Foote suggests may have been the case—will never be known. General Bee was killed by a federal bullet moments after giving Jackson his immortal nickname.

of propriety. Merchants saw in her an easy mark. When a Philadelphia decorator demanded payment for some $7,000 worth of elegant Parisian wallpaper, Mrs. Lincoln's extravagance was exposed. Lincoln was infuriated. How could Mary so thoughtlessly overspend on "*flubdubs* for this damned old house," he demanded to know. Lincoln was acutely aware that some Union soldiers were going without blankets.[30] Mortified, the president said he would pay the difference out of his own salary of $25,000 a year.* Congress, belatedly, would quietly decide to cover for Mrs. Lincoln's spendthrift ways, but the damage done to her reputation was irreparable.

IV. 1862: "YEAR OF JUBILEE"

When Lincoln had to replace General McDowell following the embarrassing Union defeat at Manassas, General Scott recommended the brilliant young George Brinton McClellan. It was a natural choice. McClellan had been the star of his West Point class of 1846. Following exemplary service in the Mexican War, he was sent by the army as an observer of the Anglo-French effort in the Crimean War. When he left the army, McClellan rose quickly to become president of the Illinois Central Railroad.

The charismatic thirty-four-year-old wore a neat mustache and French-style goatee to conceal his boyish features. In uniform, he wore a French hat, a *kepi*, and was happy to accept the nickname "the young Napoleon" that journalists had given him.**

Son of a socially prominent Philadelphia family, the dashing "Little

---

* President Lincoln's salary would be worth approximately $760,000 today. Presidents today receive $400,000 a year ("$1 in 1860 → $30.45 in 2019," CPI Inflation Calculator, https://www.officialdata.org/us/inflation/1860?amount=1).

** Despite the Emperor Napoleon's defeat at Waterloo, French military thinking, engineering, and fashion continued to dominate in the United States. Both Northern and Southern armies fielded colorful *Zouave* regiments outfitted in French North American uniforms. Their baggy, red pantaloons were soon discarded, however, when they proved to have a fatal attraction for sharpshooters on the battlefield.

Mac" cut an impressive figure in the saddle. (He had, in fact, designed the saddle used throughout the U.S. Army.) And McClellan was a Democrat. Following Senator Stephen A. Douglas's untimely death from cirrhosis, McClellan was probably the country's most prominent pro-Union Democrat.

McClellan's politics meant trouble for him in Congress. Increasingly, *radical* Republicans sought a hard war. When McClellan gathered up the broken elements of the army following Manassas, he was grudgingly accepted on Capitol Hill. McClellan loved his men, and they returned his affection. He trained them and equipped them with the best uniforms, boots, and weaponry. He made sure that food and medical care were always the best for his army. He held regular, impressive military parades. He excelled in the ceremonial and celebratory side of military life. His men called out "Little Mac" wherever he went and cheered him lustily. He succeeded in restoring the morale of his men, grandly renaming the federal force the Army of the Potomac. An organizational genius, McClellan built the greatest fighting force ever seen on this continent. He did everything with his army—except fight.

Determined not to push McClellan as he had pushed McDowell, Lincoln nonetheless offered Little Mac some fatherly advice. "You must act," he wrote his commanding general when Congress and the press began to complain of McClellan's too-frequent reports of "all quiet on the Potomac." But action was not soon coming. As the first year of the war ended, McClellan came down with typhoid fever. Lincoln was discouraged. Turning to the Union quartermaster, Montgomery Meigs, Lincoln opened his heart: "General, what shall I do? The people are impatient; [Secretary] Chase has no money and tells me he can raise no more; the General of the Army has typhoid fever. The bottom is out of the tub. What shall I do?"[31] Lincoln's new secretary of war, Edwin M. Stanton, resolved to put an end to McClellan's inactivity. No more elegant staff dinners of "champagne and oysters," Stanton said.[32]

The power was truly going to McClellan's head—all the more after he forced the aged General Scott out of office and claimed his title of general in chief. He even treated the president with contempt. Privately, he referred to Lincoln as "the original gorilla" and "a well-meaning baboon." Once, he even returned home from a wedding celebration and left the president and Secretary Seward sitting in his front parlor. After an hour, a servant told the president his general had retired for the night! Lincoln bore this rudeness with patient humility: "Never mind, I will hold McClellan's horse if he will only bring us success."[33]

And what of that success?

McClellan finally decided on a bold move in which he would transport a huge portion of the Army of the Potomac to the Virginia Peninsula, near the city of Norfolk, to attack the Confederate capital at Richmond. McClellan's force of more than one hundred thousand men, twenty-five thousand horses and mules, and some three hundred artillery pieces was transported by four hundred ships. This entire force was assembled by General Montgomery Meigs, the Union's brilliant, determined, loyal quartermaster.[34] In the spring of 1862, Meigs's logistical miracle was the largest amphibious assault in history.

And the success?

When Lincoln visited McClellan and the Army of the Potomac on the Virginia Peninsula, the headstrong general proceeded to lecture the president on the need to avoid "an abolition war." The army, he told Lincoln menacingly, would not support any action on emancipation of the slaves. Clearly, he intruded on civilian authority. In February, he boasted he would be in Richmond "in ten days."[35] A month later, he was no closer to the rebel capital. Always, always, McClellan complained that he had too few troops and inflated the enemy's strength. Relying on *unreliable* reports from private detective Allan Pinkerton, McClellan's estimate actually *tripled* the size of the Confederate army he faced. He put its numbers at 200,000. In truth, it was McClellan's Army of the Potomac that vastly outnumbered the defending rebels.[36] McClellan had every Napoleonic quality save two: speed and the willingness to fight.

So much for success.

In frustration, Lincoln finally said, "If General McClellan does not want to use the army, I would like to *borrow* it."[37]

McClellan lost his nerve on the peninsula. He began sending hysterical telegrams to the War Department, blaming Secretary Stanton, blaming everyone in Washington for his army's failure to take Richmond. Lincoln, who had *never* favored McClellan's waterborne invasion but who had indulged his high-strung young general, telegraphed him: "I give you all I can, and act on the presumption that you will do the best you can with what you have, while you continue, ungenerously I think, to assume that I could give you more if I would."[38]

The truth about McClellan was emerging. Lincoln grimly concluded that the Army of the Potomac may have a grand title, but in reality "it is only McClellan's bodyguard."[39]

The peninsula campaign was as inconclusive as it was preposterous. Richmond was never taken, McClellan spent his energies blaming everyone else for the failure, and—most troublesome for the Union— wounded Confederate General Joseph Johnston was replaced by the more capable Robert E. Lee.

Lincoln was finally forced to remove McClellan from command. Typical of Union luck in those months, his replacement proved no better. General John Pope had all the soldierly bearing but proved to be a blowhard. On assuming command, he told the Army of the Potomac he had just come from the West, "where we have always seen the backs of our enemies." He reported to Lincoln from his "headquarters in the saddle," leading the president memorably to observe it might be "a better place for his *hind*quarters."[40] When Pope led the army into a second humiliating defeat at Manassas, Lincoln had no choice but to restore McClellan.

It wasn't all bad news and embarrassment, however. While McClellan and the star-crossed Army of the Potomac were busy bolstering Confederate morale in the East, the Union enjoyed several important victories in the West. General Ulysses S. Grant demanded and got *unconditional surrender* from the defenders of Fort Donelson on the Cumberland River between Kentucky and Tennessee—thereby becoming an instant hero throughout the North and earning him the nickname "Unconditional Surrender Grant."

The war on the water was roiling. A naval blockade was a key part of the North's war plan. The aim was to choke the South's economy—especially its cotton trade with Europe—by sealing off its ports. Union control of the seas, as well of the Mississippi River, would be vital. At the war's outset, Southern blockade runners had little trouble slipping in and out of Southern ports. Lincoln ordered a shipbuilding program to rapidly expand the small Union navy.

The Confederacy got busy building ships as well. In the Chesapeake Bay, the Confederate navy launched a new warship, the CSS *Virginia*, formerly the USS *Merrimack*. This ironclad, propeller-driven vessel rammed and sank two of the blockading Union wooden warships. The *Merrimack* was skippered by Captain Franklin Buchanan, the former superintendent of the U.S. Naval Academy at Annapolis. Buchanan later reported to Stephen R. Mallory, the able Confederate secretary of the navy, that the *Cumberland* "commenced sinking, gallantly fighting her guns as long as they were above water. She went down with her colors flying."[41] He had trained those midshipmen well. Next, Captain Buchanan trained the *Merrimack*'s guns on the USS *Congress*—where his own brother was serving.[42]

The USS *Congress* and the USS *Cumberland* were lost. The *Merrimack* next ran the USS *Minnesota* aground, its direct cannon fire bouncing off the sloping armor-plating of the *Merrimack*. The Union blockade—in fact the entire U.S. Navy—was in the gravest danger. The worst day in the U.S. Navy's history prior to Pearl Harbor was 8 March 1862.[43] But on March 9 an improbable little craft chugged into action against the Southern monster.

The USS *Monitor* looked like "a cheesebox on a raft." She was also an ironclad. She rode low in the water and had but a single turret with two powerful Dahlgren guns to face the *Merrimack*'s ten guns. For three hours, the *Monitor* and the *Merrimack* were locked in a deadly embrace off Hampton Roads, Virginia. When both damaged vessels broke off the action, it appeared to be a tie. But, because the Confederates had a greater need of a naval breakthrough, *Monitor*'s action represented a Union victory. The Union fleet—and hence, the strategically indispensable blockade of the South—was saved. Control of the sea, a critical advantage to the Union, was maintained.[44]

The world took notice. Even the *London Times*, normally so contemptuous of the Yankees, said the British fleet could not be risked against such a warship as the USS *Monitor*.[45] This stunning example of "Yankee ingenuity" had actually been designed by Swedish immigrant John Ericsson. An engineering genius, the irascible Ericsson would live to see his designs incorporated into every modern navy in the world.

The navy also provided the Union's first great victory in 1862, when a fleet under Flag Officer David Glasgow Farragut sailed past menacing shore batteries and seized the greatest Confederate port—New Orleans. Farragut, a Southerner, had rejected pleas from other Southerners in the fleet that he join the Confederates. "You fellows will catch the *devil* before you get through with this business," the sixty-year-old salty sailor told them.[46] When the irrepressible General Ben Butler came ashore with his fifteen thousand bluecoats, he established firm control of the Crescent City.

High-spirited Southern ladies showed their contempt for Butler and his troops by throwing slops and chamber pots on them as they passed beneath the elegant balconied windows in the city's fabled French Quarter. Butler earned international condemnation with his notorious "woman's order." He said that any woman who insulted U.S. forces would be treated as "a woman of the town plying her trade"—by which he meant a prostitute. Butler's order earned him the nickname "The Beast," but it stopped outrages against the uniform of the United States.

In New Orleans Butler continued his controversial "contraband" policy. Since Southerners boasted that slave labor enabled them to keep more white men in the front lines for combat, Butler seized slaves as "contraband of war." Previously, the term *contraband* had been applied only to war materiel, not to human beings. But if Southerners were going to claim that slaves were mere *chattels*, then Ben Butler was only too happy to oblige them. Slaves caught on as well. Soon, thousands of slaves were liberating themselves, coming into Union army lines crying, "Contraband!"

By the summer of 1862, the "friction of war" that Lincoln spoke of was bringing the slavery issue more sharply into focus. Lincoln was disappointed that congressmen from the loyal slave states would not embrace his *compensated* emancipation plan.*

If they did not respond to the government's generous offer, he warned them in an Executive Mansion meeting, they were likely to lose all in "the friction of war." How could the Union continue to fight with one hand tied behind its back, Frederick Douglass demanded to know. How was it that the "[c]olored men were good enough to fight under Washington, [but] they are not good enough to fight under McClellan?" Douglass asked pointedly.[47]

President Lincoln invited a delegation of free men of color to the Executive Mansion on 14 August 1862. It was the first official meeting between a president and black Americans. But Lincoln was inviting the gentlemen *in* only in order to invite them *out*. He told his visitors that irreducible white prejudice had condemned black people to suffer injustice throughout the United States. Nowhere, he said, was the black man regarded as the equal of the white. He deplored white prejudice but said he was powerless to change it. "But for your race among us there could not be war," he told them. Therefore, it was better that the two races should part. He encouraged his listeners to consider his plan for colonization of black Americans in Central America. They would have the full support of his administration, he assured them.[48]

Frederick Douglass spoke for nearly all black Americans when he

---

* These loyal states that maintained slavery were Delaware, Maryland, Kentucky, and Missouri.

denounced Lincoln's colonization bid. He charged that Lincoln's address to the free men of color "showed all his inconsistencies, his pride of race, his contempt for Negroes and his canting hypocrisy."[49] "We live here—have lived here—have a right to live here, *and mean to live here*," Douglass wrote.[50]

Douglass threw himself into the fight *against* the "bugbear of colonization" with a fury. Passionately, he lashed out at those who continued to deny the human rights of black Americans. "We are *Americans* by birth and education, and have a preference for *American* institutions as against those of any other country."[51] It's an astonishing statement! Black Americans were regularly denied education in the land of their birth, forced, even in the North, to attend *segregated* schools. As for American institutions, the highest Court in the land had declared black people non-citizens, bearing *no rights* that the white man was bound to respect. Nonetheless, Frederick Douglass demanded justice: "That we should wish to remain here is natural to us and creditable to you." With unassailable logic, Douglass pierced the heart of the case for colonization: "The argument that makes it necessary for the black man to go away when he is free equally makes it necessary for him to be a slave while he remains here."[52]

When Lincoln had first raised the question of colonization for emancipated slaves, it was to have been completely voluntary—and under the benevolent protection of the U.S. Navy. Colonization in Africa or Central America for black Americans had been the position espoused by such "enlightened" Americans as James Monroe and Henry Clay. None of them had consulted black men's feelings on the subject. No one asked Frederick Douglass, either, but the outspoken Douglass would not go quietly. In fact, he wouldn't go at all. Lincoln may well have been persuaded by the force of Frederick Douglass's passionate opposition to colonization.

Next, Lincoln turned to white Americans. He answered Horace Greeley's shrill editorial, "The Prayer of Twenty Million," that had demanded immediate emancipation. (This is the same Greeley who, just a year before, had been eager to let the Southern states "depart in peace.")

My paramount object in this struggle is to save the Union, and it is not either to save or to destroy slavery. If I could save the Union without freeing any slave I would do it, and if I could save it by freeing all the slaves I would do it; and if I could save it by freeing some and leaving others alone I would also do that. What I do about slavery and the colored race I do because I believe it helps to save the Union; and what I forbear, I forbear because I do not believe it would help to save the Union.[53]

This letter is often cited by critics who think Lincoln an insincere friend of freedom and a man of callous indifference to the plight of black Americans. But we must remember that this was the Lincoln who said a house divided could not stand, that it would become all slave or all free. It was the Lincoln who firmly believed that slavery confined to the Southern states would be put on the "path to ultimate extinction." It was the same Lincoln who had advised the Republicans to hold fast against the extension of slavery into the Territories "as with a chain of steel." And it was this very Lincoln who, even as he wrote this famous letter to Greeley, had a draft of the Emancipation Proclamation in his desk drawer. He waited only for a Union victory to issue it.

The trouble was that in any conflict there are too many competing visions, agendas, hopes, and opinions to easily appease or reconcile. In these trying years, Lincoln was barely afloat in the middle, trying to coordinate the mess to the best advantage of the Union.

As if the domestic issues were not enough, Lincoln continued to suffer frustration in his relations with his reluctant general in chief. "If by magic" he could reinforce McClellan with 100,000 men, Lincoln told Senator Browning, "[the general] would be in ecstasy over it, thank [me] for it and tell [me] he would go to Richmond tomorrow, but when tomorrow came [McClellan] would telegraph that he had certain information that the enemy had *400,000* men and that he could not advance without reinforcements."[54] Besides, Lincoln noted in exasperation, every time he did send reinforcements, only a fraction of the number actually arrived. It was, he noted, "like shoveling fleas."

In September, General Robert E. Lee boldly took his Army of Northern Virginia into Maryland. He was joined by Stonewall Jackson, who had spent the spring making fools of Union Generals McDowell, Frémont, and Banks. Nathaniel Banks, another political general, had been a Democratic speaker of the House of Representatives. Banks not only was routed but left behind so many supplies for the hungry Confederates that they cheerfully nicknamed him "Commissary Banks." Jackson's "Valley Campaign," in the Shenandoah in the spring of 1862, was so daring and brilliant that military colleges the world over study it to this day.

With their bands playing "Maryland, My Maryland," the rebels spread panic through Northern cities. Lee hoped to influence the fall elections for Congress and to gain British and French recognition of the Confederacy by winning a signal victory in the North. But Lee reckoned without one "accident" of history. A copy of Lee's "General Order No. 191" to his subordinate commanders, wrapped around three cigars, was picked up by a Union soldier. Immediately, General McClellan knew Lee's plans.

Near the town of Sharpsburg, Maryland, on the banks of Antietam Creek, ragged, hungry, but determined Confederates met a superior Union army. All day on 17 September 1862, the two armies clashed.*

McClellan fed his men into the meat grinder of Southern fire piece-meal, never committing enough to win the battle, never risking enough to lose. Typical of the day was this eyewitness account left by a young Georgia soldier of Lee's army:

> Five bullets struck down the 34th New York's color bearer. "You could hear laughing, cursing, yelling and the groans of the wounded and dying, while the awful roar of musketry was appalling," Sergeant William Andrews of the 1st Georgia recalled. "Where the line stood

---

* Confederate records call this battle Sharpsburg; the Union forces styled it Antietam.

the ground was covered in blue, and I believe I could have walked on them without putting my feet on the ground."[55]

The First Minnesota Volunteers reported how "hot" the rebel artillery made it for them. A young Virginia artilleryman was helping to make it hot for the Minnesotans that bloody day. He was seventeen-year-old Private Robert E. Lee Jr., whose father was in command of the Army of Northern Virginia.[56]

Another survivor of the Battle of Antietam was Colonel John Brown Gordon of the Sixth Alabama. He had been hit five times at the Sunken Road. When his wife was ushered into his sickroom, he yelled out, "Here's your handsome husband; been to an Irish wedding!" He recovered from the bullet in his face, and with his wife's skillful nursing, even his shattered arm was saved.[57]

America had never experienced anything like this. Matthew Brady, the famous New York photographer, sent his assistant Alexander Gardner to record the horror at Sharpsburg. Brady displayed the photos of the battle's carnage to a stunned society audience as "The Dead of Antietam." "There is one side of the picture that has escaped the photographer's skill," wrote a *New York Times* reporter: "It is the background of widows and orphans. . . . Homes have been made desolate, and the light of life in thousands of hearts has been quenched forever. All of this desolation imagination must paint—broken hearts cannot be photographed."[58]

Although McClellan had fresh troops in reserve at Antietam, he never committed them to the battle. Instead, both armies fought to a bloody stalemate. Lee was forced to retreat. McClellan claimed it as a great victory. In anguish, Lincoln pressed McClellan to pursue Lee and destroy the Army of Northern Virginia. McClellan held back.

The Union casualties of Antietam were reckoned at 2,108 dead, 9,540 wounded, and 753 missing—one-quarter of all those engaged.[59] Confederate losses were fewer, but Lee could afford them less. Because he was operating on Northern soil, there would never be a full account of

Lee's "butcher's bill." Estimates suggest the Confederates suffered 1,546 dead, 7,752 wounded, and 1,018 missing.[60] Combined losses are counted as 22,719, making the Battle of Antietam the bloodiest single day in American history.

The North rejoiced as a battered Southern army withdrew. Lincoln accepted this bloodiest day in American history as a sign from the Almighty. He issued his Preliminary Emancipation Proclamation. Unless they rejoined the Union by 1 January 1863, Lincoln warned the seceded states, *all* their slaves would be freed. Reaction in the North initially was *not* favorable. The Republicans lost some key state races and several seats in Congress. Even abolitionists did not welcome this preliminary Emancipation Proclamation. What if the rebellious states *did* return to the Union? Then the slaves would remain in bondage. Lincoln was taking an enormous risk.

McClellan continued to stall. He complained that his *horses* were tired. Finally, Lincoln's patience snapped. Confederate horses weren't tired. He telegraphed the Young Napoleon: "Will you pardon me for asking what the horses of your army have done since the battle of Antietam that fatigues *anything*?"[61] The powerful Frank Blair tried to intercede with the president, to prevent the blow he knew was coming. He had tried long enough to "bore with an auger too dull to take hold," Lincoln told Blair. "I said I would remove him if he let Lee's army get away from him, and I must do so. He's got the 'slows,' Mr. Blair."[62]

When Senator Ben Wade earlier that summer had demanded McClellan's ouster, Lincoln replied, "Whom shall I replace him with?" *Anybody,* replied Bluff Ben, exasperated. "Anybody will do for *you*, Wade, but I must have *somebody*," Lincoln responded wearily.[63] Now the lack of *somebody* came home to haunt Lincoln's deliberations. He decided to name General Ambrose Burnside, one of Little Mac's closest subordinates, to succeed McClellan. He sent one of McClellan's good friends, General Catharinus Buckingham, through a blinding snowstorm with orders for McClellan to turn over his command.

This was a moment of grave danger for the republic. Freedom hung in the balance. There had been ugly talk at McClellan's headquarters of turning the Army of the Potomac *against* the politicians of Washington. McClellan made little secret of his opposition to emancipation. And he was still adored by his troops, who cheered him at every opportunity. If McClellan could not fight like Napoleon, might he have Napoleon's skill for political intrigue—and for a coup d'état?

Fortunately, McClellan's relations with the Democratic Party were excellent. He saw his future not as a military dictator, but as the standard bearer for the opposition party. This he was to become. And the country was spared the specter of the army's turning its guns on civilian authority.

Lincoln knew his place in history would be determined by forces beyond his control. He said he had made a "covenant with his Maker." If Lee was driven out of Maryland, he would hit slavery, and hit it hard. "The moment came when I felt that slavery must die that the nation might live," Lincoln said, when he hearkened to "the groaning of the children of Israel whom the Egyptians keep in bondage."[64*] The American people also seemed to sense a change had come over him. Up to this time, Lincoln was popularly known as "Old Abe" or "Uncle Abe." Following his issuance of the Preliminary Emancipation Proclamation, however, the common people began to refer to their president as "Father Abraham."[65]

As the year 1862 closed, General Burnside took the Army of the Potomac deep into Virginia. At Fredericksburg on December 13, Burnside proved to all what he had modestly said of himself: that although he was a competent corps commander, he was *not* capable of commanding an entire army. Ordering one futile frontal assault after another against the terrible stone wall, Burnside saw his men mowed down like wheat before a scythe. Burnside had to be restrained from leading a suicidal charge himself. Viewing the carnage from Marye's Heights above the battlefield, General Lee said, "It is well that war is so terrible, lest we should grow

---

* Exodus 6:5.

too fond of it."[66] That night, soldiers marveled at seeing the aurora borealis, a rare occurrence at such southerly latitudes. It was as if the heavens themselves were draped in iridescent waves of purple mourning crepe.

In the Executive Mansion, Lincoln was nearly in despair. Not only had this terrible year seen the death of his beloved son, Willy, it had closed out with the loss of some 12,600 young men killed and wounded at Fredericksburg. "We are on the brink of destruction," Lincoln told his friend, Illinois Senator Orville Browning. "It appears to me the Almighty is against us."[67]

Rebel editors taunted Lincoln as the winter gloom deepened:

> The days are growing shorter,
> The sun has crossed the line,
> And the people are all asking
> Will Abraham resign?[68]

V. EMANCIPATION: "FOREVER FREE"

Abraham would not resign; instead, he would *sign*. On 1 January 1863, Secretary of State William H. Seward and his son, Frederick, came early to the Executive Mansion with a copy of the engrossed Emancipation Proclamation, ready for the president's signature.* Quickly reading it over, Lincoln noted an error in the text. It had to be sent back to the State Department for correction.[69] Lincoln could not afford to have a single syllable wrong. He knew this proclamation would be picked apart by a hostile judiciary. No one was more hostile to emancipation than was Chief Justice Roger B. Taney.

The president then proceeded to receive hundreds of visitors at the annual New Year's Day reception. He shook their hands vigorously. Only

---

* To *engross* is to prepare a "fair copy" of a state document for a high official's signature.

at 2 p.m. were the doors closed, and Lincoln could turn once again to the corrected text of the Emancipation Proclamation.[70]

"I never, in my life, felt more certain that I was doing right than I do in signing this paper," Lincoln told the handful of witnesses.[71] He then took up a pen, but his right hand began to tremble. He had difficulty holding it. At first, he had a superstitious feeling: was this a sign that he had made a fatal error?[72] Then he recalled that he had been shaking hands for three hours and that that was not a way to improve one's penmanship.

Lincoln was concerned because he knew his signature would be examined. "They will say, 'he had some compunctions,'" he explained to the witnesses.[73] Flexing his arm, he set about resolutely to sign the historic document. He wrote out his full name—*Abraham Lincoln*—then looked up, smiling, and said, "That will do."[74]

Some modern scholars have disparaged the proclamation. Historian Richard Hofstadter spoke to several generations when he sneered that the proclamation had "all the moral grandeur of a bill of lading."[75] But could Hofstadter be serious about any document that so eloquently concludes:

> And upon this act, sincerely believed to be an act of justice, warranted by the Constitution, upon military necessity, I invoke the considerate judgment of mankind, and the gracious favor of Almighty God.[76]

What more could we ask of Lincoln? Today, the proclamation is rarely displayed. When it is, the text, which those State Department clerks labored so diligently on a holiday to correct, is faded and indistinct. But the signature of Abraham Lincoln stands forth bold and bright and clear.

When Lincoln declared the slaves in rebel hands "shall be, then, thenceforward, and forever free," he had carefully *exempted* from his proclamation the vast territories then under Union control. These included not only the four loyal border states—Missouri, Kentucky, Maryland, and Delaware—but also the occupied areas of Tennessee, Louisiana, Florida, Virginia, and North Carolina. The *London Spectator* sneered that the only *principle* in the proclamation was that a man may not own another *unless* he is loyal to Lincoln's government.[77] But the *Spectator* then (and cynical Lincoln critics ever since) misunderstood the basis of Lincoln's action. Because he was a *constitutional* leader and not a despot, Lincoln could only free the slaves as a war measure to suppress rebellion. The confiscation of enemy property during wartime is recognized as legitimate under the rules of war.

Thus, it is not true to say he freed the slaves where he had no power and left in bondage those over whom he exercised control. Lincoln had no constitutional authority to free the slaves in the loyal border states. And he knew he could not emancipate slaves in those areas where Union arms had quelled the rebellion. The practical effect of the Emancipation Proclamation was that the Union army became an army of liberation. Wherever it moved, thousands of slaves swarmed into its ranks, because the soldiers of the United States carried *freedom* in their haversacks.

Jefferson Davis reacted to the Emancipation Proclamation with predictable fury. It was, he told the Confederate Congress "the most execrable measure in the history of guilty man." Lincoln wanted "to incite servile insurrection and light the fires of incendiarism," charged Davis. He made this charge even though Lincoln had specifically urged freed slaves to engage in no violence—*except in necessary self-defense.* Frederick Douglass had written that the fear expressed by so many slaveholders "as to the danger of having their throats cut is because they *deserve* to have them cut."[78] Lincoln was becoming converted to the hard-war theory that meant great destruction of rebel *property.* But he gave no support whatever to a slave uprising. The fact that there are no reported cases of murder or rape on Southern plantations speaks volumes of the character of Lincoln and the character of the freed slaves. The "wolf by the ears" so feared by Thomas Jefferson and hundreds of other Southern slaveholders for sixty years did not howl.

Following that "Day of Jubilee"—1 January 1863—there was no more talk of colonizing black Americans. Instead, all attention shifted to determining how quickly and how thoroughly black men might be recruited for the Union armies. Lincoln's administration now was fully committed to employing what Douglass picturesquely referred to as its "Sable Arm" against the rebellion. It was not an easy decision. There had been widespread resistance to black recruitment—even in the army itself. In July of 1862, Union cavalryman Charles Francis Adams Jr. had written to his father in London: "The idea of arming the blacks as soldiers must be abandoned." But just one year later, young Adams could tell his famous father: "The negro regiment question is our greatest victory of the war so far, and I can assure that in the army these [black soldiers] are so much a success that they soon will be the fashion."[79]

One thing that made Northern leaders hesitate was the threat by Confederates to treat black soldiers not as prisoners if they were captured, but as *insurrectionists* meriting only hanging. Their white officers, too, were threatened with death, if taken. General Beauregard, with a grisly French flair, called for their execution by *garrote*. Only after Lincoln issued stern orders for retaliation were the bloodthirsty threats from the South quietly shelved. Following Douglass's impassioned appeals, Lincoln decreed that any black Union soldier who was re-enslaved would be matched by a white Confederate prisoner of war put to hard labor. And any Union prisoner in Southern hands who was put to death would be answered by a Southern POW chosen by lot—*and shot*. Mercifully, Lincoln never had to enforce this grim order.

Still, freedom for black *and* white Americans depended ultimately on the success of Union arms. In the West, General Grant was laying siege to the great Confederate bastion on the Mississippi at Vicksburg. Grant worked in close harmony with Union naval gunboats. But it was a long, drawn-out affair. Grant had won a bloody victory at Shiloh the previous April. There, the Union lost thirteen thousand men (of fifty-five thousand) and the Confederates lost eleven thousand (of forty-two thousand). Confederate General Albert Sidney Johnston—a favorite of President Davis—bled to death from a leg wound covered by his boot. The battle at Shiloh resulted in more casualties in two days than the United States had suffered in its *entire existence* as a nation! When Grant's critics complained to Lincoln, claiming that the general was drinking once again, Lincoln dismissed them, saying, "I can't spare this man; he fights."[80]

In the East, Lincoln had little choice but to confer command of the Army of the Potomac on "Fighting Joe" Hooker. Lincoln was critical of Hooker for the way he had undermined the honorable but incapable Burnside. Lincoln also had heard of Hooker's loose talk about the need for a military dictatorship in the country. Even so, Lincoln gave Hooker the command with these memorable words: "I have heard in such way as to believe it of your recently saying that both the Army and the Government needed a Dictator. Of course it was not for this, but in spite of it, that I have given you the command. Only those generals who gain successes can set up dictators. What I now ask of you is military success, and I will risk the dictatorship."[81]

Hooker ably reorganized the army, improving rations, medical care, and the troops' morale. He energetically moved the army deeper into Virginia. But he could not resist boastfulness. "May God have mercy on General Lee, for I shall have none," he told the press. Then he took his army into another federal disaster on 3 May 1863 at Chancellorsville.

Robert E. Lee's greatest triumph—Chancellorsville—was also the scene of his worst loss. Southern victory was assured when Stonewall Jackson's "foot cavalry" rushed out of the woods, hallooing and giving the terrifying rebel yell. They put the Union troops to panicked flight. Hooker himself was stunned by a Confederate artillery shell that shattered the column upon which he was leaning. But after the day's action, General Jackson rode out on Little Sorrel to inspect his lines and prepare for the next day's fight. Only his aides accompanied him. Confederate pickets thought he was a Union officer and opened fire, wounding Jackson severely. Jackson soon had to have his arm amputated—the standard procedure for almost any serious wound. "He has lost his left arm," a grieving Robert E. Lee said, "but I have lost my right." Within the week, Jackson developed pneumonia and died. In these days before penicillin, almost any infection could prove fatal. The entire South was plunged into deepest mourning. Even in the North, Jackson was honored as the brave and resourceful opponent he was.

Hooker's defeat—he confessed he had "lost confidence in Joe Hooker"—meant Lincoln would have to find another commander in the vital eastern theater. McClellan, Pope, McClellan again, Burnside, Hooker—each had been tried and found wanting in less than a year.

Soon Lee was on the move and heading north. The fate of a nation once again hung in the balance.

EIGHT

A NEW BIRTH OF FREEDOM

(1863–1865)

I. GETTYSBURG: THE CONFEDERACY'S HIGH-WATER MARK

Lee moved north once again in late June 1863, pushing hard into Pennsylvania. With crisis looming, Lincoln accepted the petulant resignation of General Joe Hooker. He turned to General George G. Meade, a native of the Keystone State. Lincoln hoped that Meade could be relied upon to "fight well on his own dunghill."[1]

When Lee encountered the federal main force at Gettysburg, he resolved "to whip them." Lee was hampered by the absence of his great cavalry commander, General James Ewell Brown (J. E. B.) Stuart. Stuart had once humiliated the federals by riding completely around them. Now, he was ranging too far away, capturing badly needed Union supply wagons, but leaving Lee "blind" as to his enemy's movements. Confederate generals Stuart and George Pickett had long since captured hearts throughout the South as dashing cavaliers; the former sported a full red beard, an ostrich plume in his hat, and a brilliant red sash around his middle, while the latter wore his hair shoulder length in perfumed ring-lets. Pickett was the last man in the West Point class of 1846, but he made up for his dismal academic standing by his bravery and energy.

At thirty-four, Union officer Colonel Joshua Lawrence Chamberlain was tall and lean with a flowing mustache. He was a professor of classics in civilian life. He could speak eight languages—English, Greek, Latin, Arabic, Syriac, Hebrew, French, and German.[2] It is doubtful any other man on the field that day was so learned. But many fine minds and brave hearts threw their bodies into the breach on those disputed grounds. Commanding the Twentieth Maine, Chamberlain knew he had to hold Little Round Top on the field at Gettysburg. If the Confederates gained that high point, they could pour artillery fire down onto Union troops below and very likely win the battle—maybe the war.

Chamberlain summoned his Maine farm boys and fishermen to hold off the rebel attack. His company had already lost a third of its men, and he had already been slightly wounded twice during the battle.[3] Facing yet another attack, Chamberlain would later recall, "[M]y thought was running deep. . . . Five minutes more of such a defensive, and the last roll-call would sound for us. Desperate as the chances were, there was nothing for it but to take the offensive. I stepped to the colors. The men turned toward me. One word was enough—'BAYONET!' It caught like fire and swept through the ranks."[4]

When his soldiers ran out of ammunition, Chamberlain could hon-orably have surrendered. Instead, he led his yelling men down from the heights of the Little Round Top, swinging about like a great gate on a hinge. Chamberlain drove the startled Alabamians before him. For his actions that day, the young Mainer was awarded the Congressional Medal of Honor.

Union lines wavered as General Meade's forces were being hard-pressed on the Rose family farm. Places with prosaic names like the Wheatfield and the Peach Orchard there gained immortality in the annals of warfare. Meade was determined to hold. He ordered Major General Winfield Scott

Hancock to support the Third Corps. Among General Hancock's seasoned troops was the famous Irish Brigade. Under their brilliant green flags with their distinctive harps, these Fighting Irish prepared to go into action. Before turning to meet their foe, they turned to their priest for absolution. Standing on a boulder overlooking the earnest, upturned faces, Father William Corby gave the men his blessing. Then he warned them: "The Catholic Church refuses Christian burial to the soldier who turns his back upon the foe or deserts the flag."[5] Today, a monument to Father Corby stands on the boulder where he pronounced those words.

One Irish officer who missed Father Corby's blessing was Colonel Patrick H. O'Rourke. He had graduated first in his class at West Point, just two years earlier. Paddy O'Rourke had bounded off his horse and was leading his Sixteenth Michigan with a hearty shout of "Down this way, boys!" as he was struck in the neck by a rebel bullet and killed. A New York soldier who came upon the pitiful scene said "that was Johnny's last shot." Companies A and G vied with each other to take down the beloved Paddy's killer. That "Johnny Reb" was hit *seventeen times.*[6]

After two days of fierce fighting (July 1 and 2) in the stifling heat of a Gettysburg summer, Lee determined to attack the main body of the Union line. General James Longstreet opposed the move, recalling perhaps the devastation of the Union forces at Maryes' Heights at Fredericksburg. But such was *Marse Robert's* prestige that no one had the courage to challenge his judgment.* Seeing a startled rabbit run off the road, a "Southron" responded with grim good humor. "Run, ol' hare!" the soldier yelled to his brothers lined up in a clump of trees awaiting the order to advance. "If ah was a ol' hare, ah'd run, too."**

When Pickett led his now-famous charge, rank upon rank of Confederates in gray and butternut brown marched straight into the teeth

---

* "Marse" was the Virginia slaves' pronunciation for master. It was eagerly adopted by Lee's adoring men.

** This poignant tale was related by the late Shelby Foote, with a sad chuckle, in Ken Burns's magnificent *Civil War* series on PBS.

of the Union artillery. And they were cut to pieces. Thousands of men died in mere minutes. Union riflemen behind stone walls were completely protected. They marveled at the magnificent sight of the advancing Confederates. As Pickett's charge failed, it broke like a great wave ebbing against the rocks. The cry went up from the Union lines that had held fast: "Fredericksburg! Fredericksburg!" Then the sky was rent with a deep, satisfied roar from the Union ranks. They had saved their country, and they knew it. For the rest of their lives, these Union veterans would pay tribute to the sheer courage and unquestioned dedication of the soldiers in gray.

"Too bad, oh, too bad," cried Robert E. Lee in anguish as the tattered remnants of Pickett's division staggered back to their lines. He rode out to tell his men, "It's all *my* fault."

Instantly, he wired President Davis his resignation. Just as quickly, it was rejected. Lee was that rare figure in war—loved, even *worshipped*, by his soldiers, revered by the people of the South, and deeply admired by nearly all his adversaries in the North. "I wish he were *ours*," said a young Pennsylvania girl who saw him on his ride to Gettysburg. She spoke for millions in the North. Lee had denounced slavery as "a moral and political evil."[7] He had even spoken *against* secession: "The framers of our Constitution never exhausted so much labor, wisdom, and forbearance in its formation if it was intended to be broken by every member of the [Union] at will."[8] Still, when Virginia seceded, Lee could see no other course than to support his state. Hundreds of thousands of brave and honorable Southerners reasoned the same way.

For the defeated Confederates, July 4, 1863, was a most mournful Independence Day, especially since some of them had come to speak of the war as the *Second War for Independence*.[9] On the blood-soaked roads of Pennsylvania, in a drenching rain, Lee's beaten army limped away. Dispirited and expecting a federal attack at any moment, the Army of Northern Virginia rushed to cross the rain-swollen Potomac. Lincoln was desperate for Meade to close with Lee and put an end to the rebellion. When Meade issued an order congratulating his men for driving "the invader" from our soil, Lincoln cried out, "Will our generals never get that idea out of their heads? The *whole* country is our soil."[10]

On this same July 4 came an electrifying message from the West. General Ulysses S. Grant had accepted the surrender of the city of Vicksburg. Grant had conducted a smart, hard-driving campaign against indecisive and divided Confederate defenders. Vicksburg commanded the heights over the Mississippi River. It had been the last Confederate stronghold on the great waterway.

Grant had distinguished himself for bravery in the Mexican War. But then, he did not have responsibility for an army. Now, he was a general. He would later describe his feelings in his first taste of real combat while in command:

> As we approached the brow of the hill from which it was expected we could see [the Confederate] Harris' camp, and possibly find his men ready formed to meet us, my heart kept getting higher and higher until it felt to me as though it was in my throat. I would have given anything to have been back in Illinois, but I had not the moral courage to halt and consider what to do; I kept right on. When we reached a point from which the valley below was in full view I halted. The place where Harris had been encamped a few days before was still there and the marks of a recent encampment were plainly visible, but the [Southern] troops were gone. My heart resumed its place. It occurred to me at once that Harris had been as much afraid of me as I had been of him. This was a view of the question I had never taken before; but it was one I never forgot afterwards. From that event to the close of the war, I never experienced trepidation upon confronting an enemy.[11]

Here we may see the secret of Grant's success: his unadorned style—so clear, so candid—his deadpan humor, his *realistic* view of himself and others. Above all, we see Grant's self-deprecating wit and his bulldog determination: "*I kept right on.*"

After months of Grant's siege, the starving Mississippians gave up. (Vicksburg would not celebrate the Fourth of July again until 1942!) The city's fall gave control of the Mississippi River to the Union—splitting the Confederacy in two. *U. S. Grant!* Could anyone have had more symbolic initials? And to have *united* the upper and lower Mississippi River on the nation's birthday made an indelible impression on the American people. President Lincoln wrote, "The Father of Waters again goes unvexed to the sea."

Back east, the mood was not so celebratory. President Lincoln had hoped for, prayed for General Meade to take the unconditional surrender of Lee's army in Pennsylvania, just as Grant had totally conquered Vicksburg in the West. It was not to be so.

Robert Todd Lincoln had never seen his father cry. But Abraham Lincoln wept bitter tears in the aftermath of the battle of Gettysburg. He could not believe Meade was allowing Lee to escape. Lee's retreat was even blocked by the rain-swollen river, and still Meade did not descend upon him to crush the rebellion once and for all. Porter Alexander, the Confederate artillery chief, described Meade's desultory pursuit: "As a mule goes on the chase of a grizzly bear—as if catching up with us was the last thing he wanted to do."[12]

Lee did escape, but Lincoln did not remove Meade. Meade—called "a goggle-eyed old snapping turtle" by his men—thought himself ill-used by an ungrateful commander in chief after so great a victory. He submitted his resignation. Lincoln immediately wrote a reply which, although he never sent it, reveals so much of his anguish:

Again, my dear general, I do not believe you appreciate the magnitude of the misfortune involved in Lee's escape. He was within your easy grasp, and to have closed upon him would, in connection with our other late successes, have ended the war. As it is, the war will be prolonged indefinitely. If you could not safely attack Lee last Monday, how can you possibly do so South of the river, when you can take with you very few more than two thirds of the force you then had in hand? It would be unreasonable to expect, and I do not expect you can now effect much. Your golden opportunity is gone, and I am distressed immeasurably because of it.[13]

Not only does this unsent letter show Lincoln's deepest yearning to put an end to the bloodletting, but it also reveals his keen strategic sense. Lincoln had become the best strategist either side produced during the Civil War. He alone understood from the earliest days that the destruction of Lee's army—and *not* the capture of Richmond—was the primary objective of Union arms. Where others panicked as Lee invaded the North in 1862 and 1863, Lincoln saw it as a heaven-sent opportunity to cut Lee off from his base of supply and to capture his ragged army of barefoot warriors. "If I had gone up there, I could have whipped them myself," Lincoln told his young secretaries, John Hay and John Nicolay.[14]

In this instance, however, Lincoln may have been wrong. The task of pursuing and crushing Lee's defeated army surely looked easier from Washington than it did to General Meade on the ground at Gettysburg.[15]

If Meade had launched a counterattack to finish off Lee's retreating ranks, he might have been the one surprised. Confederate General James Longstreet rode out after Pickett's failed charge to inspect. "Old Peter," as he was called, was taking a big chance. This was exactly what Stonewall Jackson had done after his great victory at Chancellorsville two months before—and paid for it with his life.

Old Peter was surprised to find an artillery battery in place after he had ordered all his guns pulled back. "Whose are these guns?" he demanded to know, scowling. A pipe-smoking rebel officer came up to the general and answered mildly, "I am the captain. I am out here to have a little skirmishing on my own account, if the Yanks come out of their holes."[16]

Lee had taken great care—as he did in most things—to prepare his line of retreat. But he could not compensate for the terrible losses to his officer corps. In the three days of Gettysburg alone, Lee had lost seventeen of fifty-two generals—nearly a third of his finest officers.[17] This could not last.

Robert E. Lee understood this. But he was also an avid reader of Northern newspapers. He was well aware of the war-weariness of the Northern people. He knew, too, of the outright opposition of many Northern politicians to the war. If only, Lee reasoned, he could win some striking victory—especially one deep in Northern territory—the people of the North might cry out for peace. Some of the Democratic politicians in high offices did exactly that.

Lee was George Washington's step-grandson-in-law. He knew as well as any man in America how Washington had fought many a losing battle only to triumph in the end. Yorktown had been that decisive victory that convinced a war-weary British public they could never subdue America. Lee constantly hoped that he could keep his ragged army going and make the cost of putting down the rebellion too high for the people of the North to bear.

This may explain his determination to win a major battle on Northern soil. He had won spectacular victories in Virginia. Fredericksburg was a triumph. Chancellorsville is still studied in military colleges as a textbook example of courage and skill.[18]

Lincoln in these days began to appreciate what General Meade had accomplished. The people of the North rejoiced in the Gettysburg and Vicksburg victories, and the president seemed to share in their mood. After days of distress, Lincoln sent a dispatch intended for Meade's eyes. This time, he said, "A few days having passed, I am now profoundly grateful for what was done, without criticism for what was not done. General Meade has my confidence as a brave and skillful officer, and a true man." George Gordon Meade would command the Army of the Potomac until the last day of the war.

Lincoln contacted Grant in the same days. Noting that he'd never even met his western commander, Lincoln telegraphed: "I thought you should go down the river and join Gen. Banks; and when you turned

Northward East of the Big Black, I feared it was a mistake. I now wish to make the personal acknowledgement that you were right and I was wrong." Presidents are not always known for such grace, such affecting humility. Not only was Grant a man he'd never met, he was also very possibly a rival for the presidency in 1864!

Despite the victories, Lincoln's immeasurable distress would soon deepen. Within days of winning the ground at Vicksburg and Gettysburg, New York City erupted into the worst riots in U.S. history. The draft—*conscription*—was widely hated in this city of immigrants. Poor Irish laborers had no way to pay the $300 that exempted a man from service in the Union army.*

They lived in crowded, ill-lit tenements. Even their low wages and low-skilled jobs were threatened when Yankee Protestants employed free black stevedores as strikebreakers. The promises of American freedom seemed hollow to these struggling immigrants. New York Governor Horatio Seymour had attacked the Lincoln administration's emancipation and conscription policies in a demagogic Fourth of July speech to city Democrats. When conscription officers began drawing names for the draft on July 11, it was the spark that kindled the flames of rebellion. Mobs attacked black people, lynching six black men and burning a colored orphanage. The editor of the *New York Times* had to defend his offices by installing three newly invented Gatling guns.[19]

Archbishop John Hughes had loyally traveled to Europe to stave off recognition of the Confederacy by Catholic powers, even as he warned against making the war an "abolition war." Now, as rioting began, the archbishop and his Irish priests appealed to their flocks for order. And New York's Finest—its fearless police force (also largely Irish)—battled the rioters. The police were overwhelmed as hundreds died.

Only when troops from Pennsylvania's battlefield arrived in the city

---

* Among those prominent New Yorkers who paid the $300 for a substitute were Grover Cleveland and Theodore Roosevelt Sr., TR's father.

was the worst race riot in American history finally put down.[20] Unfair as it was, the draft proceeded because the government could not afford to let the opposition prevail. It is a tribute to Lincoln that he did *not* clap Governor Seymour in prison for inciting the riot.

When the civic leaders of Pennsylvania decided to dedicate a military cemetery at Gettysburg, they sought America's greatest orator as their leading speaker. Edward Everett, former president of Harvard, former U.S. secretary of state, was the natural choice. Republican Governor Andrew Curtin was then in a tough reelection race, and a major event commemorating the battle could only help him. The battlefield, though, was still a scene of horror three weeks after the battle. The young Gettysburg banker, David Wills, who was to chair the event, reported to the governor: "In many instances arms and legs and sometimes heads protrude and my attention has been directed in several places where the hogs were actually rooting out the bodies and devouring them."[21] Simply to bury the dead among the 22,807 Union and 28,000 Confederate casualties was an overwhelming task. Once Everett had confirmed as the day's primary orator, President Lincoln was asked to make "a few appropriate remarks." The event was viewed primarily as a *state* occasion. Since Washington was only ninety miles away, the president was asked, almost as an afterthought, to attend.[22]

Everett had been the vice presidential running mate on the Constitutional Union ticket in 1860, with John Bell. In effect, event organizers had invited one of the president's *opponents* and had given him star billing. They also invited New York's Democratic Governor Horatio Seymour, whose state had contributed so much to the victory. Lincoln's "remarks" were never thought of as an *address* before he delivered them. Now, when it is recognized as one of the greatest speeches ever delivered in the English language, it is the *Gettysburg Address* that comes to mind whenever the word *address* is used:

> Fourscore and seven years ago, our fathers brought forth upon this continent a new nation, conceived in liberty and dedicated to the proposition that all men are created equal.

Now we are engaged in a great civil war, testing whether that nation, or any nation so conceived and so dedicated, can long endure. We are met on a great battlefield of that war. We have come to dedicate a portion of that field as a final resting-place for those who here gave their lives that that nation might live. It is altogether fitting and proper that we should do this.

But in a larger sense, we cannot dedicate, we cannot consecrate, we cannot hallow this ground. The brave men, living and dead, who struggled here have consecrated it, far above our poor power to add or detract. The world will little note nor long remember what we say here, but it can never forget what they did here. It is for us, the living, rather, to be dedicated here to the unfinished work which they who fought here have thus far so nobly advanced. It is rather for us to be here dedicated to the great task remaining before us—that from these honored dead we take increased devotion to that cause for which they gave the last full measure of devotion—that we here highly resolve that these dead shall not have died in vain, that this nation, under God, shall have a new birth of freedom, and that government of the people, by the people, for the people, shall not perish from the earth.

Here, Lincoln speaks of no North, no South, impugns no man's motives, makes no charges, sounds no note of triumph. But he explains in 266 spare words the meaning of the war. And his words will live as long as the *idea* of America lives.

Lincoln did not "refound" the nation. Nor did he *remake* America. He would have rejected such a notion. Every act of his was simply an effort to defend "the proposition" that had been central to the Founders' vision. If all men are *not* created equal, then they have no God-given right to freedom and no claim to self-government. For Lincoln, this was *axiomatic*.

Happily, the very *Honorable* Edward Everett recognized the genius of Lincoln's speech. He sent the president this gracious note shortly afterward: "I should be glad if I could flatter myself that I came as near to the central idea of the occasion in two hours as you did in two minutes."[23]

II. THE AGONY OF ABRAHAM LINCOLN

We have only to see Lincoln's photographs from 1860 and compare them with those taken at the end of the war to see the effects of those five years on him. He was fifty-one when he was elected. During the war years, he seems to have aged a quarter of a century. Lincoln described himself as "old" in his farewell address to his neighbors in Springfield, Illinois, as he departed on the special train for Washington, D.C.

The ravages of war took their toll on him. The loss of his beloved son, Willy, in 1862 was a cruel blow. After that, Lincoln's relationship with his wife, Mary, suffered. She was driven nearly mad with grief. She even invited spiritualists into the Executive Mansion who claimed to be able to communicate with her dead son. Lincoln attended at least one of these séances. He appears to have placed little stock in necromancy. Avid student of Shakespeare that he was, Lincoln would have read the line in which "the sheeted dead did squeak and gibber in the Roman streets."* Burdened as he was by the cares of the war, it is most likely that Lincoln indulged his emotional, extravagant, and unsteady wife.

Lincoln and his family spent their summers during the Civil War at the Soldiers Home in northeast Washington. Three miles from the President's House, this refuge was cooler and less hectic than the Executive Mansion. There, few office seekers could pursue the overworked president. And overworked he surely was. Lincoln usually breakfasted on coffee and toast and often skipped lunch. He visibly wasted during his presidency. His clothes, always ill-fitting, now seemed to hang on his six-foot-four-inch frame. Often, Lincoln would ride alone the three miles to his office. Ominously, his movements did not go unobserved. He risked death by assassination every day he served as president.

Lincoln faced death with a fatalistic resolve. He believed that anyone

---

* *Hamlet*, act 1, scene 1.

could kill him if he was willing to give up his own life.* Despite the violent emotions that had been unleashed by the war, and by the inflamed political rhetoric that had led to it, many Americans discounted the possibility of assassination. It had never happened in America, after all.

Lincoln was savaged in the press—Northern, Southern, and foreign. Openly racist articles and cartoons were published. A London paper famously cartooned him as a disheveled, uncouth card player about to throw into a losing game the ace of spades. The face on the card was, not surprisingly, that of a young black man. Lincoln's winning opponent in that continental card game was an elegant, confidently smiling Jefferson Davis. It may have been the origin of our term—*playing the race card*. If some hostile newspapers did not show Lincoln as black, he was nonetheless mockingly depicted in the company of black people, dancing and socializing with them. The cartoons were used to stir up racial animosities against the president.

"That giraffe," was the dismissive way the prosperous Pennsylvania railroad lawyer Edwin M. Stanton had referred to the Illinoisan before the war. But when he needed him, Lincoln did not hesitate to bring that able War Democrat into his cabinet. And so he was with most people. He had lived with their condescension all his life—and had used it to master them in the slippery game of politics. Stephen Douglas, William Seward, Roger B. Taney, Charles Sumner, Salmon P. Chase, George B. McClellan—these were but a few of the powerful men who underestimated Abraham Lincoln.

Lincoln sought some relief from his sorrows in humor, his own and that of others. He would always share a funny story or amusing anecdote with visitors to his office. Often, they would come expecting an office or some other favor, then be escorted to the door by the president, pumping their hand and sharing some old "chestnut." Lincoln's penchant for humorous stories was viciously caricatured by the cartoonist who showed

---

* In a famous passage in one of Plato's *Dialogues*, Socrates reminds us that the lowliest citizen of a *polis* can kill the king if he's willing to give up his own life.

the president standing among the Union dead at Antietam, with the caption: "This reminds me of a little story."

The day he assembled his cabinet to hear the Emancipation Proclamation, he tried to break the ice with a clever story from Artemis Ward, his favorite humorist.* Significantly, he told them, "With the fearful strain that is upon me night and day, if I did not laugh, I should die, and you need this medicine as much as I do."[24] There is little indication they appreciated his ministrations that day.

III. LINCOLN TURNS TO GRANT

Lincoln searched with mounting desperation for a fighting general. McDowell had failed him early. McClellan stayed with Lincoln for more than a year but failed him. So did Pope and Burnside. And Hooker. Meade proved more successful, at least on the defensive. But he, too, complained. He never enjoyed Lincoln's full confidence.

Grant was different. Lincoln liked him from the start. Grant was an Illinoisan. He was quiet—and businesslike. Lincoln hoped that Grant shared his ideas for political reconstruction of the Union, but it was far more important that Grant should be on the same page on military matters. Grant had one advantage over all his fellow Union generals: he didn't complain. He took the resources he was given and he fought.

Lincoln had waited so long for a military hero, for someone he could brag about. Even before the fall of Vicksburg, Lincoln was ecstatic about his fellow Illinoisan: "Whether Gen. Grant shall or shall not consummate the capture of Vicksburg, his campaign from the beginning of this month [May 1863] up to the twenty-second day of it, is one of the most brilliant in the world."[25] It wasn't the most brilliant—but it wasn't bad, either. And when compared with the handiwork of Lincoln's other generals, it certainly *looked* brilliant.

---

* It was Ward's "Outrage at Utica" that Lincoln enjoyed.

Lincoln was dismayed to hear renewed complaints about Grant's drinking. Discreetly, he sent Assistant Secretary of War Charles Dana to visit Grant. Ostensibly, Dana was there to inspect Grant's army. Grant soon figured out that Dana was there to look *him* over. Shrewdly, Grant opened up his headquarters to Lincoln's "spy." It proved a smart move. Dana wrote back glowing reports about Grant's intelligence, skill, and devotion to the Union cause.[26]

After the fall of Vicksburg, Lincoln wanted Grant to attend to the situation in Tennessee. After a promising start, Union General William S. Rosecrans had been hit hard by the rebels at the Battle of Chickamauga. To Lincoln, Rosecrans seemed "like a duck hit on the head." Grant quickly dispatched Rosecrans and replaced him with General George Thomas. It was a smart move that would pay off for the Union cause. Thomas, a Virginian, had stood firm during the battle—earning him the title "the Rock of Chickamauga." But his men fondly referred to him as "Pap." Advancing toward Chattanooga, Tennessee, Grant ordered General Joe Hooker to take Lookout Mountain. And Hooker did it in a hard-fought "battle above the clouds." Then Grant directed Thomas to seize the Confederate positions at the base of Missionary Ridge and hold up. Thomas's high-spirited troops took those works—and pressed on to take Missionary Ridge. Grant—and Lincoln—rejoiced.[27]

Always, Lincoln searched desperately for a military commander who could, in his words, "face the arithmetic." By this, Lincoln meant a general who could face the heavy casualties that would be suffered by Union forces as they closed in on Lee's army. The president understood what Lee and some of the Confederate leaders understood: given the vastly superior resources of the North in men and materiel, it would be only a matter of time before the North would grind the South down. Grant was by far the most savvy, the most resourceful, the most courageous of Lincoln's generals. Surely he could face the arithmetic. Lincoln brought him back East and gave him command over all the Union armies. Grant was promoted to lieutenant general, a rank Congress had last bestowed on George Washington.

Grant's manner of taking command of the armies of the United States was typical of him. He came back to Washington and immediately checked into the famed Willard Hotel—just a few blocks from the Executive Mansion. A bored hotel clerk told him that there was only one small room—on the top floor under the eaves—for the general and his fourteen-year-old son. Grant said he'd take it. Only when he signed the hotel register simply as "U. S. Grant and son, Galena, Illinois," did the clerk realize who his powerful guest was. Sputtering, he quickly assigned the new lieutenant general the best room in the house.[28] The other guests in the lobby began to applaud.

In short order, Grant locked horns with Lee in Virginia. It was a rolling, horrific engagement, with wounded men screaming as the woods caught fire and were consumed. Around Spotsylvania Court House, Grant tenaciously pursued Lee, taking terrible casualties and inflicting many more. "If you see the president," Grant told a colleague, "tell him there will be no turning back."[29] And there was no turning back.

Not for Grant.

Or Lincoln.

Or the United States of America.

Initially, the North thrilled to hear this man of few words say, "I propose to fight it out on this line if it takes all summer." But soon, as the long lists of dead and wounded appeared in Northern newspapers, the horror of close engagement in the Virginia woodlands sank in. Hooker and Burnside had traveled this road before him. They had always turned back. True to Lincoln's assumption, Grant faced the arithmetic and pressed on. But at what cost! Doomed Union soldiers sewed their names inside their coats the night before Cold Harbor.* They wanted their bodies identified after the battle.[30]

---

* Cold Harbor is barely ten miles northeast of Richmond.

"I regret this assault more than any I have ever ordered," Grant said of his orders to attack at Cold Harbor. He lost seven thousand Union soldiers killed or wounded *in just thirty minutes* on the morning of 3 June 1864.[31]

Soon, the word *butcher* began to be thrown at Grant. But Lincoln stood by his general. Grant did his job, efficiently and with focused resolve. He did not meddle in politics. He did not demand more support than Lincoln could give him. He even found a new way to handle the pressures—trading his bottle for a knife and whittling stick.

Grant's cool confidence and lack of dramatic flair impressed many. George S. Boutwell, a leading Massachusetts Republican, said, "It is difficult to comprehend the qualities of a man who could be moved by a narrative of individual suffering, and yet could sleep surrounded by the horrors of the battles of the Wilderness."[32]

Horrors they surely were. What must have been the thoughts of young Union soldiers marching, fighting, then bedding down in "ghoul-haunted woodlands" that their older brothers had fought over (and many died in) during the previous two years? Herman Melville captured the eerie feeling in a poem, "The Armies of the Wilderness":

> In glades they meet skull after skull
> Where pine-cones lay—the rusted gun,
> Green shoes full of bones, the mouldering coat
> And cuddled-up skeleton;
> And scores of such. Some start as in dreams,
> And comrades lost bemoan:
> By the edge of those wilds Stonewall had charged—
> But the Year and the Man were gone.

Lincoln grieved at the toll the grinding trench warfare was taking on the Union forces—and the entire Union. For Lincoln did not simply mourn Northern losses. He believed the entire country was one, North and

South. As reports came back of the trenches around Petersburg, Virginia, the whole country understood what it meant. Southern boys as young as thirteen were found dead there, lying next to fallen white-bearded grandfathers. Whose heart could remain untouched at such a loss?

Few families North or South were untouched by the hand of death. The Lincoln family was no different. When Lincoln's favorite sister-in-law, Emilie Helm, was detained at Fort Monroe, Virginia, she refused to take an oath of allegiance to the United States. Ben Helm had married Mary Lincoln's younger half-sister, Emily. He had been killed at Atlanta fighting for the Confederacy. "Send her to me," Lincoln telegraphed the Union officers who had stopped the young widow whom Lincoln and his wife thought of as the daughter they never had.[33] When she arrived at the Executive Mansion, Emilie was embraced by the president and the First Lady. "'You know, Little Sister,'" Emilie Helm later reported his saying to her, "'I tried to have Ben come with me.' Mr. Lincoln put his arms around me and we both wept."[34] In a sense, Lincoln wrapped his arms around the entire country.

IV. "LONG ABRAHAM A LITTLE LONGER"

Despite the great Union victories of 1863, a growing war-weariness among the people of the North was the last remaining hope of the Confederacy. The Emancipation Proclamation had broken the unity of the Northern public. The Democratic Party loudly denounced it. When Democrats captured the legislatures of Illinois and Indiana, they passed resolutions *demanding* the revocation of the proclamation as a condition for their states' continued support of the Union war effort.

After issuing the Emancipation Proclamation, Lincoln opened the ranks of the U.S. military to black soldiers and sailors. Frederick Douglass responded enthusiastically, traveling throughout the North to encourage enlistments. His perennial speech topic: "Why should the colored man enlist?" "You will stand more erect, walk more assured, feel more at ease, and be less liable to insult than you ever were before," Douglass said. "He who fights the battles of America may claim America as his country—and have that claim respected," he told his avid listeners.[35]

Not just self-respect was at stake. Douglass wanted nothing less than full civil and political equality for black people. "Once let the black man get upon his person the brass letters, U.S.; let him get an eagle on his button, and a musket on his shoulder, and bullets in his pocket," he told a Philadelphia crowd, "and there is no power on earth or under the earth that can deny he has earned the right of citizenship in the United States." With his own massive dignity and with the moral force he brought to his cause, he challenged his hearers: "I say again, this is our chance, and woe betide us if we fail to embrace it."[36] Black Americans would heed the abolitionist's call; by war's end, more than two hundred thousand of them would "rally 'round the flag."

Eighteen sixty-four was an election year. Most blacks could not vote, but sullen and resentful whites could. Lincoln had to respond to the rising antiblack sentiment expressed by many Democrats. He did so in a widely circulated letter:

> You say you will not fight to free Negroes. Some of them seem willing to fight for you; but, no matter. Fight you, then exclusively to save the Union. I issued the proclamation on purpose to aid you in saving the Union. . . .
>
> I thought that in your struggle for the Union, to whatever extent the Negroes should cease helping the enemy, to that extent it weakened the enemy in his resistance to you. Do you think differently? . . . . Peace does not seem so distant as it did. I hope it will come soon. . . . [Then] there will be some black men who can remember that, with silent tongue, and clenched teeth, and steady eye, and well-poised bayonet, they have helped mankind on to this great consummation; while, I fear, there will be some white ones, unable to forget that, with malignant heart, and deceitful speech, they strove to hinder it.[37]

Once again, we see Lincoln's use of overpowering logic to deflate his opponents. How could they claim to be loyal to the Union while being willing to leave black Southerners in bondage to harvest the crops that would feed rebel armies?

When Lincoln brought Grant east and gave him overall command of the Union armies, great things were expected. In a strategy conference, Lincoln saw the force of Grant's plan for simultaneous army assaults on the stricken South. The anaconda of the Union blockade was taking its toll by this third winter of war. Lincoln exclaimed at Grant's plan: "I see it. Those not skinning can hold a leg." This frontier metaphor was not lost on Grant, a tanner's son. It meant that even if one or more Union armies were not on the move, they could still help the main thrust by "holding a leg" to prevent the Confederacy from reinforcing by using internal lines of communication.

Yet Grant was seemingly stalemated in the trenches before Petersburg. His assault on Lee's ragged remnant at Cold Harbor had been thrown back with terrible Union casualties.

Some Republicans' dissatisfaction with Lincoln's direction of the war was expressed by the radical wing. They wanted a harder, more punitive prosecution of the war. When Lincoln was renominated by the Republicans in June 1864, the radicals in Congress were unenthusiastic. Desperate to gain support from prowar Democrats, the party nominated for vice president Tennessee's military governor, Andrew Johnson, a Jackson Democrat.

The Democrats nominated Lincoln's former general, George B. McClellan, in the same Chicago convention center—the Wigwam—where Lincoln had himself been nominated in 1860. McClellan had his own problems with party unity. Many Democrats clamored to end the war and sign a peace treaty with the Confederacy. As the election approached, it looked as though Lincoln would go down to defeat.

Military victories changed the political picture. First, U.S. Navy Admiral David Glasgow Farragut steamed through mine-infested waters to seize Mobile, Alabama. "Damn the torpedoes," he said. "Full speed ahead."[38] Then General Phil Sheridan, the Union's greatest cavalry chieftain, put

Virginia's bountiful Shenandoah Valley to the torch. The valley was the "breadbasket of the Confederacy." No longer could the Confederates look to the Shenandoah for their cornmeal and hardtack. Now, said, Sheridan, "A crow flying over it would have to carry its own provender."

Farther south, General William Tecumseh Sherman was on the offensive, pushing from Tennessee into Georgia. Sherman was a tall, red-haired, cigar-chomping West Pointer who brooked no nonsense. Early in the war, he had suffered a nervous breakdown. Many still thought him crazy. He was one of the few who had predicted a long, bloody, very destructive war. Sherman looked like an unmade bed. Although he was older than Grant, and had outranked Grant in the Old Army, he was fully willing to put himself wholly under Grant's command. "Grant stood by me when I was crazy," Sherman said, "and I stood by him when he was drunk. Now we stand by each other always."[39]

Sherman is credited with being the first "modern" warrior in America, the first practitioner of "total war." And destructive he was. His plan was to expose the weakness of the Confederacy for the world to see as he pushed into the South. "My aim [is] to whip the rebels, to humble their pride, to follow them to their inmost recesses, and to make them fear and dread us," he declared.[40]

On September 2 came the news that would reelect Lincoln. Sherman telegraphed: "Atlanta is ours, and fairly won."[41] Sherman then proceeded on his storied "March to the Sea." He left a trail of burned-out, blackened plantation houses sixty miles wide. He burned public buildings. He tore up all railroad lines. His men heated, then twisted the iron rails around telegraph poles—they called them "Sherman bowties." Sherman wanted to make war so terrible that generations would pass before Southerners would resort to it again.*

When election day came, it must have been especially gratifying to

---

* Presidential candidate Jimmy Carter often winced in 1976 as he was greeted by Iowa high school bands playing "Marching Through Georgia," a song celebrating Sherman's March. That's how long these painful memories lasted.

Lincoln that he carried the "soldier vote" against that darling of the Army of the Potomac, General McClellan. Lincoln won 212 electoral votes and 2,213,635 popular votes (55.1 percent). McClellan garnered only 21 electoral votes from Delaware, Kentucky, and New Jersey, and 1,805,237 popular votes (44.9 percent). Eighty electoral votes not cast—representing the states still in rebellion—would not have elected McClellan.

Cartoonists had a field day. One showed an elongated president holding a sheet of paper, labeled "four more years." "Long Abraham a Little Longer" was the caption.

General Sherman wired the president. He presented him with the seaport of Savannah, Georgia, as a Christmas gift. Thankfully, beautiful Savannah had surrendered and was spared the torch. Also spared was elegant Charleston, which had jubilantly greeted the Ordinance of Secession. Columbia, South Carolina's capital, was not so fortunate. There, for thirty years, fire-eating politicians had plotted to break up the Union. When he learned that Columbia had burned, Lincoln's reply was grave and biblical, taken from the gospel of Matthew: "The people who sat in darkness have seen a great light."

He was seeing many things in spiritual terms as this most terrible of all wars ground on. To a friend he wrote in this fateful year of 1864: "I claim not to have controlled events, but confess plainly that events have controlled me."[42] This is an astonishing statement from a man who placed such store in human reason, in an "all conquering *mind*." Lincoln was a driven man. His Springfield, Illinois, law partner, Billy Herndon, said his ambition was a little engine that knew no rest. Lincoln had to know his intellect greatly surpassed that of other men. He was physically strong too. He had been a champion wrestler in his youth. Even as an older man he could still hold a double-blade axe at arm's length. And keep it there. Lincoln also was accused of being a dictator. Even his staunchest defenders concede that no other president ever exercised such great power. Yet here was Lincoln, confessing to a friend his own sense of being controlled by events. It was as if an angel rode in the whirlwind.

V. THE UNION VICTORIOUS

Lincoln's landslide reelection doomed the Confederacy. Now, there was no hope of foreign intervention. The anaconda squeeze of the U.S. Navy blockade was strangling the Southern war effort. The guns of the USS *Kearsarge* remorselessly pounded the great Confederate commerce raider CSS *Alabama*, sending her to the bottom off Cherbourg, France. Everywhere Jefferson Davis looked, the Confederacy was crumbling.

Davis even had to swallow the bitterest pill of all: Robert E. Lee's suggestion that slaves be recruited for the army with the promise of freedom if the South gained her independence. "If slaves will make good soldiers, our whole theory of slavery is wrong," responded Georgia's Howell Cobb.[43]

The famed Massachusetts Fifty-Fourth Regiment had proved itself at Fort Wagner in South Carolina. This "colored" regiment—the U.S. Army would remain segregated until 1948—had been led into battle by the brave young Colonel Robert Gould Shaw, scion of a Boston Brahmin family. When Colonel Shaw fell in the assault, his body was contemptuously thrown into a ditch with those of his dead black troops. Shaw's father was a leading lawyer in Massachusetts. He *declined* an offer to have his son's body disinterred, saying Robert was *honored* to be buried with his men. Stories like this worked a profound change in Northern opinion.*

President Lincoln had been disappointed in many of his generals, as we have seen, until he found the winning team of Grant and Sherman. But he never had occasion to complain of one staunchly loyal Georgian. Montgomery Cunningham Meigs was the Union Quartermaster General. Virginian Winfield Scott had insisted on Meigs's appointment early in 1861 to compensate for the chaos and corruption of Secretary of War Simon Cameron. General Meigs soon brought order to the Union army's procurement of nearly everything from horses to pup tents. He

---

* The story of Massachusetts's famed Fifty-Fourth is admirably told in the Hollywood movie *Glory*. It is accurate in most respects except one: Governor Andrew would never have permitted his brave troops to leave the Bay State without good boots.

constructed massive numbers of hospitals for the wounded.[44] Rigorously honest, tireless, and a brilliant organizer, Meigs had supervised the construction of the Capitol before the war. Then, his boss was Jefferson Davis. Now, it was Abraham Lincoln. Because of Meigs's unstinting efforts, the Union Army was better supplied, better clothed, and better sheltered than any army in history. Everything except food and arms was Meigs's responsibility; among his other achievements, Meigs began the *sizing* of boots and clothing—thus giving a powerful boost to the U.S. civilian economy as soon as the fighting ended.[45]

Because he had to send out the ambulances to tend the hundreds of thousands of Union *and* Confederate wounded, General Meigs understandably became bitter toward his fellow West Pointers who, he believed, had betrayed their oaths as officers. He had once served under Robert E. Lee. Now, when called upon to select a site for a huge new Union cemetery, General Meigs unhesitatingly chose the front lawn of the Custis-Lee Mansion, across the Potomac River from Washington. By putting the Union dead in Lee's front yard, Meigs knew, the Confederate commander's family could never return to their historic home.[46] But in October 1864, General Meigs would face his own family tragedy. Union Major John Rodgers Meigs was killed, and General Meigs saw his own son's body buried in Mrs. Lee's rose garden.[47] Robert E. Lee's magnificent home thus became the site of Arlington National Cemetery. It is hallowed ground.*

Captivity was cruel for the tens of thousands of prisoners taken by both sides in the Civil War. The Confederate prison at Andersonville, Georgia, was the most notorious. Thousands of Union prisoners starved to death there, and the commandant of Andersonville, Henry Wirz, was

---

* After the war, Robert E. Lee's son, George Washington Custis Lee, sued the U.S. government for the return of his parents' home. The U.S. Supreme Court in 1882 ruled 5–4 that the Lee home had been improperly seized and ordered it returned to the Lees. The heirs of Robert E. Lee then sold the property to the United States for $150,000. Ten years later, General Meigs himself was buried at Arlington National Cemetery—*where valor sleeps* ("Arlington House," Arlington National Cemetery, http://www.arlingtoncemetery .net/arlhouse.htm).

the only Confederate soldier convicted and executed for war crimes at the conclusion of the war. But Northern prisons shamed the nation too.

Confederate infantry Captain Jonas Lipps of the Stonewall Brigade was taken prisoner near Chancellorsville, Virginia, in 1864. Taken to Camp Delaware, outside of Philadelphia, Jonas was attacked by a Union guard with a bayonet. The unarmed rebel prisoner jumped back, with the guard's bayonet going through his arm instead of his belly. Jonas pulled out the bayonet and ran the guard through, killing him. A Union captain ordered that Jonas should not be punished. He said the rebel captain acted only in self-defense. At least justice had not died.

Later, Jonas Lipps was tied up outside the Union batteries at Morris Island, South Carolina. Jonas and hundreds of other Southern prisoners were exposed to friendly artillery fire for thirty-one days outside the besieged city of Charleston. This horrible punishment was in reprisal for the Confederates inside the city tying Union prisoners to lampposts to deter the Federal artillery from shelling the beautiful old city. Jonas's diary records that while artillery shells were coming in on him, he saw the gates of heaven open up and he saw himself seated at his father's table. This was war at its worst. Jonas Lipps survived Fort Morris, along with "the Immortal Six Hundred" of his fellow Southerners, only to die of dysentery back at Fort Delaware just five days before the war ended. The Virginian was only twenty-four.

Lincoln approached the inaugural stands for the second time on 4 March 1865. The day was wet and windy. As he arose amid waves of applause, the sun broke through the clouds. Sunbeams shone down on the newly completed dome of the U.S. Capitol. Lincoln had pressed Congress to finish the work of decades, making the Capitol itself a symbol of the completed Union. The Statue of Freedom that topped the dome had originally been brought by wagon to the city of Washington. Many of the teamsters and laborers who hauled the great female figure were, ironically, slaves. By the time she was put in place atop the building where she stands today, they were free.

Lincoln then delivered the greatest inaugural address in American history. Describing the war, he noted that slavery had been the cause of it. Lincoln urged his listeners *not* to claim all righteousness for themselves. He then offered perhaps the most terrible, most thought-provoking idea ever uttered in American public life:[48]

> Fondly do we hope, fervently do we pray, that this mighty scourge of war may speedily pass away. Yet, if God wills that it continue until all the wealth piled by the bondsman's two hundred and fifty years of unrequited toil shall be sunk, and until every drop of blood drawn with the lash shall be paid by another drawn with the sword, as was said three thousand years ago, so still it must be said "the judgments of the Lord are true and righteous altogether."*

Lincoln ended with these immortal words:

> With malice toward none, with charity for all, with firmness in the right as God gives us to see the right, let us strive on to finish the work we are in, to bind up the nation's wounds, to care for him who shall have borne the battle and for his widow and his orphan, to do all which may achieve and cherish a just and lasting peace among ourselves and with all nations.

Lincoln's words were carried in a fine tenor voice—not the baritone so often portrayed by Hollywood. Everyone in the vast crowd could hear him distinctly, including Frederick Douglass.

And John Wilkes Booth.

Later, at the Executive Mansion, Lincoln would greet the celebratory crowd. Frederick Douglass, denied entrance by an usher, climbed through a window and joined the receiving line. Seeing him, Lincoln

---

* "The judgements of the Lord are true and righteous altogether" (Psalm 19:9).

cried out, "Ah, Douglass!" He told the great abolitionist he wanted to know his opinion of the address. "Mr. President, it was a *sacred* effort," Douglass answered. Later, he would say of his relationship with Lincoln that he was the only white man he ever knew who did not instantly make him aware he was a black man.

On 2 April 1865, Richmond fell. General Lee sent a message to President Davis telling him he must abandon the lines. The messenger reached Davis while he was in church. The congregation noted the Southern president's ashen face as he left his pew. The Confederate government frantically packed up and left the city. An attempt to fire key military installations to deny them to the Yankees got out of hand, and the city was soon in flames. Two days later, President Lincoln visited the city. He had his young son, Tad, in tow as he walked to the Confederate White House. Outside, crowds of soldiers and free Negroes cheered as he sat at Jefferson Davis's desk. White Virginians generally looked out glumly from behind shuttered windows. U.S. Army authorities established a quick, firm, but mild control of the old city. And when the invalid Mrs. Robert E. Lee complained of having a black soldier posted as a guard outside her house, he was quickly replaced with a white one. The Stars and Stripes once again flew over the Capitol that Thomas Jefferson had designed.

A week after Richmond's fall, General Lee agreed to meet General Grant at Appomattox Courthouse. Because of a bureaucratic snarl, his hungry soldiers had been sent several boxcars of *ammunition*, not rations. The Southside Virginia countryside could barely feed itself. Lee *rejected* calls by some of his junior officers to take the army into the mountains and fight a guerilla war. Lee had seen how guerilla war degenerated in Missouri. He wanted no part of a merciless, decades-long bloodletting.

Grant had been suffering from a debilitating headache before he received Lee's surrender note. But as soon as he read the welcome news, his headache was gone.[49] General Lee rode Traveler to the Wilbur McLean home in Appomattox Court House, Virginia, where the meeting would take place on 9 April 1865. Attired in his finest uniform, his engraved sword at his side, Lee cut a magnificent figure. When he rode up, General Grant apologized for being late. He was dressed in a private's rumpled jacket, the stars of a lieutenant general incongruously attached to his shoulders. His boots were muddy.

Grant did everything he could to ease Lee's agony. He spoke pleasantly of their Mexican War days. He remembered Lee. Lee could not recall him. When it came to writing out terms for the surrender, Grant asked Colonel Ely Parker, a full-blooded Seneca Indian, to copy out the terms in his beautiful handwriting. Lee froze. He initially thought Colonel Parker was a black man, that his presence might be a way of humbling him. Catching himself, Lee maintained his dignity and military bearing. He asked Grant to amend the terms to allow his men to keep their horses, which most of them owned. Grant declined to change the terms but said it would be understood that any man claiming a horse as his own could keep it. They would be needed for spring planting for "their little farms."

Grant treated Lee with complete tenderness and respect. And when Union troops began to cheer the news of the surrender, Grant immediately ordered it to stop. Nothing should be done to humiliate the rebels who were once again "our countrymen." Grant also ordered tens of thousands of Union rations to feed the "famished rebel horde."[*] General Lee and all of his twenty-eight thousand soldiers of the Army of Northern Virginia were paroled by Grant—allowed simply to go home to live under the laws of their once again *United* States.

Grant would record his thoughts about that day at Appomattox in his memoirs:

What General Lee's feelings were I do not know. As he was a man of much dignity, with an impassible face, it was impossible to tell whether

---

[*] "Fair as the Garden of the Lord / To the eyes of the famished rebel horde," wrote poet John Greenleaf Whittier of the Southern invasion of Maryland in 1862 in *Barbara Freitchie*. Lee's army had been hungry for years.

he felt inwardly glad that the end had finally come, or felt sad over the result, and was too manly to show it. Whatever his feelings, they were entirely concealed from my observation; but my own feelings, which had been jubilant on the receipt of his letter, were sad and depressed. I felt like anything rather than rejoicing at the downfall of a foe who had fought so long and valiantly, and had suffered so much for a cause, though that cause was, I believe, one of the worst for which a people ever fought, and one for which there was the least excuse. I do not question, however, the sincerity of the great mass of those who were opposed to us.[50]

Grant then selected the twice-wounded Union hero General Joshua Lawrence Chamberlain to receive the formal surrender of Southern arms. Chamberlain matched in every way the gallantry and chivalry so long associated with fallen Southerners like J. E. B. Stuart and Stonewall Jackson. As the barefoot, ragged Confederates marched in two days later to lay down their arms and their beloved flags, Chamberlain ordered a smart salute. All along the Union lines, battle-hardened veterans snapped to the call: "Carry Arms!" Confederate General John Brown Gordon wheeled his horse around and executed an elegant response, his horse almost bowing as Gordon touched his saber to his toe: "Honor answering Honor."[51]

Chamberlain would later describe the scene:

On they came with the old swinging route step and swaying battle flags . . . crowded so thick, by thinning out of men, that the whole column seemed crowned with red. . . . In the van, the proud Confederate ensign. . . . Before us in proud humiliation stood the embodiment of manhood; men whom neither toils and sufferings, nor the fact of death nor disaster nor hopelessness . . . could bend from their resolve; standing before us now, thin, worn, and famished, but erect, and with eyes looking level into ours, waking memories that bound us together as no other bond. . . . On our part not a sound of trumpet more, nor roll of drum; not a cheer, nor word, nor whisper or vainglorying, nor motion of man . . . but an awed stillness rather, and breath-holding, as if it were the passing of the dead. . . . How could we help falling on our knees, all of us together, and praying God to pity and forgive us all![52]

Too little credit goes to U. S. Grant for this sublime moment in the history of our wounded world. We need only compare how rebellions in Mexico and Canada had ended just thirty years before. Santa Anna put all the Alamo rebels—both "Anglos" from the North and local Hispanic *Tejanos*—to the sword in 1836. The British in Canada in 1837 had hanged dozens of rebel leaders who demanded nothing more than the same representative government enjoyed by millions of their neighbors in the United States.[53]

In treating his defeated foe with such high regard and compassion, Grant was faithfully reflecting the policies of his commander in chief. Lincoln had vowed to "let 'em up easy." He would have "no bloody work." When asked what he planned to do with Confederate leaders, Lincoln made a "shooing" motion with his hands, as if he were driving geese from the kitchen garden.

Back in Washington, hundreds of Union cannon boomed a joyous salute to the news from Appomattox. President Lincoln appeared at a window of his official residence to acknowledge the cheers of an enthusiastic crowd. His little boy, Tad, excitedly waved a captured Confederate flag to the delight of the spectators. Lincoln requested the band play "Dixie." He said it was always a favorite tune of his, and now, according to the attorney general, it was federal property. When he made some serious remarks about returning Louisiana to the Union on moderate terms, actor John Wilkes Booth bitterly told a fellow conspirator, "That means n——citizenship!" He vowed it would be Lincoln's *last* speech. And it was.

On Friday night, April 14, President and Mrs. Lincoln went to Ford's Theatre to attend a comedy, *Our American Cousin*. The Lincolns were late, but the play was stopped as they arrived and entered the presidential box. The orchestra played "Hail to the Chief," and Lincoln acknowledged the applause of the audience. Then, shortly after 10:00 p.m., a shot rang out and smoke wafted out of the box. A man brandishing a large dagger jumped down to the stage, catching his spur on the bunting that decorated the box. "*Sic semper tyrannis!*"* he cried as he limped toward the stage door exit. Many in the audience immediately recognized him as John Wilkes Booth, one of the most famous actors in America.

The unconscious president was carried through the cold, foggy night to the Peterson house, across from the theater on Tenth Street. There, the six-foot-four-inch giant of a man was placed *diagonally* on a bed in the rear of the house. And the long deathwatch began. Mrs. Lincoln, haunted by the death of their son Willy, in 1862, gave way to hysteria. She could not be consoled by son Robert Todd Lincoln, or even by her good friend, Senator Charles Sumner. Finally, the brusque, autocratic secretary of war, Edwin M. Stanton, ordered soldiers to "get that woman out of here and keep her out."

All through the night, terrible reports came in to the front parlor where Stanton had set up a command post. Vice President Johnson had also been targeted, but George Atzerodt, a German immigrant, got drunk and failed to go through with the attack. Secretary of State William H. Seward was not as lucky. Lewis Powell, one of the Booth conspirators, attacked him in his bed, where he was recovering from a carriage accident. Powell stabbed him repeatedly, lunging for his jugular and nearly cutting off his cheek. Miraculously, Seward survived.

At 7:22 on the morning of April 15, doctors confirmed that the president had breathed his last. Stanton, in tears, arose and said, "Now he belongs to the Ages."[54]

Booth escaped from Washington, riding through Prince George's County into Southern Maryland. There, he hid out at the home of Dr. Samuel Mudd. Dr. Mudd knew Booth well. He set the assassin's broken

---

* "Thus ever to tyrants" is Virginia's state motto.

leg. But Booth and fellow plotter Davey Herold set off at dawn for Virginia. Booth had expected a hero's welcome. Instead, he was shunned.

The North was plunged into deepest mourning. No president had ever been assassinated before. Many people believed that Jefferson Davis—now a refugee in full flight—was behind the foul deed. (There would never be any link found between Davis's government and Booth's conspirators.*) Vice President Johnson was sworn in, but he was an unsteady, inadequate replacement for the slain Emancipator.

Grief was nearly universal. "I never before or since have been with such a large body of men overwhelmed by a single emotion; the whole division was sobbing together," wrote a Union officer in North Carolina.[55] Fearing that the freedmen might take vengeance on fellow Southerners they might hold responsible, Colonel John Eaton was amazed to find not one word of revenge in the black churches he visited in Memphis. "They were in despair . . . but there was no whisper against those who sympathized with all that he opposed," wrote Eaton.[56] General Lee was widely and approvingly quoted when he said the assassination was a calamity for the South and "a crime previously unknown in this country, and one that must be deprecated by every American."[57] One Southern woman told General Sherman she was *glad* Lincoln had been shot. Sherman replied, "Madam, the South has lost the best friend it had."[58]

Lincoln's funeral train retraced much of the same route that had brought him to Washington just four years earlier. Now, many of the same plain people returned who had gathered trackside in 1861 to cheer the elected leader along his route to power. They bore witness in 1865 to the passing of the funeral train as it carried him to glory.

Lincoln's legacy is liberty and union. That which Webster had immortalized in words, Lincoln achieved in word *and* deed. America's poet of

---

* Booth was shot on April 26 by federal troops inside a burning barn near Bowling Green, Virginia. The other conspirators were tried and hanged. Dr. Mudd was imprisoned. No one else was put to death.

the heart, Henry Wadsworth Longfellow, offered his tribute to the Union that Lincoln labored so long to save in "The Building of the Ship":

> Thou, too, sail on, O Ship of State!
> Sail on, O Union, strong and great!
> Humanity with all its fears
> With all its hopes of future years,
> Is hanging breathless on thy fate![59]

NINE

TO BIND UP THE
NATION'S WOUNDS

(1865–1877)

I. PASS IN REVIEW

Out of regard for Robert E. Lee, General Grant had issued strict orders at Appomattox against cheering by victorious Union troops. Nothing but respect to those gallant men in ragged gray was allowed. They were country-men once more. But six weeks later, the people of the North and the armies of the Great Republic were determined to celebrate their victory.

The little southern city of Washington, D.C., would be the scene of the greatest triumphal parade ever seen in this hemisphere. The armed forces of the Union now numbered nine hundred thousand men—white and black.[1] A full two-thirds of that great host, six hundred thousand men of Meade's Army of the Potomac and Sherman's Army of the Tennessee, would pass in review—united as the Grand Army of the Republic. It was not easy bringing these high-spirited young men together, even for a parade.

Riots broke out when the spit-and-polish Army of the Potomac encountered the rangy, rough, almost slovenly veterans of Sherman's "March to the Sea." General Grant soon had to step in and order the two rival Union armies to bivouac on *opposite* sides of the Potomac.[2]

Down Pennsylvania Avenue they marched—sixty abreast—these strong, determined young men in blue. They marched past the reviewing stands in front of the Executive Mansion, the president, the cabinet, the leaders of Congress, and the foreign diplomatic corps. It took all day on May 23 for the Army of the Potomac to pass in review. It took all the next day for Sherman's lean, tough, battle-hardened men to march past the assembled notables. Sherman had apologized to his fellow West Pointer, General Meade, for his men's unmilitary bearing. He needn't have. On this day of days, the Army of the Tennessee stepped off smartly and marched in step with drill parade precision. Hard-bitten, hard-boiled, and sometimes hard-drinking, William Tecumseh Sherman admitted it was one of the happiest days of his life.[3]

That night, a clear and still evening, the men in their camps on a whim put candles in their rifles and began to march on and on. Soon bands joined in. The men cheered and cheered and cheered themselves hoarse. A *New York Herald* reporter wrote that the procession looked "as though the gaslights of a great city had suddenly become animated and had taken to dancing." It had all happened spontaneously. No orders were given.[4]

They would not forget this moment for the rest of their lives. They felt that this time of testing and trial would mark them forever. For many of them, it *was* their life, and they would spend their remaining decades reliving it. Oliver Wendell Holmes Jr.—later a great justice of the Supreme Court—spoke to this sense:

> The generation that carried on the war has been set apart by its experience. Through our great good fortune, in our youth our hearts were touched with fire. It was given to us to learn at the outset that life is a

profound and passionate thing. While we are permitted to scorn nothing but indifference, and do not pretend to undervalue the worldly rewards of ambition, we have seen with our own eyes, beyond and above the gold fields, the snowy heights of honor, and it is for us to bear the report to those who come after us.[5]

And sometimes, Holmes knew, just sometimes, they felt they had more in common with their fallen comrades than with their own unblooded kith and kin: "The army of the dead sweep before us, 'wearing their wounds like stars.'"[6]

II. RECONSTRUCTION AND RENEWAL

The assassination of Lincoln had wrought a profound change in Northern sentiment. Many were now less willing to follow Lincoln's mild policy of reconciliation between the North and South. Massachusetts writer Herman Melville captured the dark mood of the Northern public with his poem, "The Martyr":

> Good Friday was the day
> Of the prodigy and crime,
> When they killed him in his pity,
> When they killed him in his prime
> Of clemency and calm—
> When with yearning he was filled
> To redeem the evil-willed,
> And, though conqueror, be kind;
> But they killed him in his kindness,
> In their madness and their blindness,
> And they killed him from behind.
> There is sobbing of the strong,

And a pall upon the land;
But the People in their weeping
Bare the iron hand:
Beware the People weeping
When they bare the iron hand.[7]

General and Mrs. Grant had turned down a theater invitation from the Lincolns that fateful night. They offered a polite excuse about having to take the train to New Jersey, but the truth was Julia Dent Grant could not stand the often outrageous behavior of Mrs. Lincoln.[8] Mrs. Grant heard a scuffle on the train platform at Havre de Grace, Maryland. The train's brakeman, unlike the Lincolns' police guard that night, was alert to danger. He fought off an assailant who tried to get into the Grants' private car.[9] Only when their train stopped in Philadelphia did General Grant tell his wife the terrible news that Lincoln had been assassinated. Mrs. Grant asked her husband if Vice President Johnson would now assume the presidency. Yes, the general replied, "and for some reason, *I dread the change.*"[10]

No sooner had Andrew Johnson entered the Executive Mansion than he prepared to prosecute General Lee and the Southern leaders. "Treason must be made odious," the new president declared, "and traitors must be impoverished."[11] "Bluff" Ben Wade, the radical Republican Senator from Ohio, advocated punishing the leading rebels. Wade suggested trials for a small number of worst cases—perhaps "thirteen, just a baker's dozen."[12] Johnson replied that he couldn't justify hanging so few, reported James Gillespie Blaine, a congressman from Maine. Perhaps remembering Lincoln's words about "no bloody work," even Ben Wade began to worry that perhaps Johnson would go too far.[13]

When a federal grand jury sitting at Norfolk, Virginia, indicted Lee, Longstreet, and the Confederate high command for treason, Lee immediately wrote to General Grant. How could this indictment be squared with the *parole* Lee and his army had received at Appomattox, Lee inquired with his customary courtesy. It couldn't. And Grant had no hesitation saying so. Grant immediately wrote to Secretary of War Stanton, saying, "The officers and men paroled at Appomattox and since . . . cannot be tried for treason as long as they observe the terms of their parole."[14]*

But Johnson was stubborn. He was determined to exercise his sudden new powers. Grant visited Johnson in the Executive Mansion to press his case. What right, Johnson truculently asked, did a *subordinate* have to "interfere to protect an arch-traitor from the laws?"[15]

Grant was a man famously in control of his emotions. But not now. He was enraged. Lee never would have surrendered if he thought he and his men would be subject to criminal proceedings, Grant told Johnson. And if they hadn't surrendered, the war would have dragged on indefinitely, with far more loss of life to Union and Confederate forces. Then Grant leveled *his* verbal artillery at the stunned Johnson: "I will *resign* rather than execute any order to arrest Lee or any of his commanders so long as they obey the law!" Grant had also secured a similar pledge from his loyal friend Sherman.

Frustrated, Johnson asked Grant, "When *can* these men be tried?"

"Never," answered Grant. "Never, unless they violate their parole."[16]

As willful and bigoted as he was, Andrew Johnson knew when he was outgunned. As a Southern prowar Democrat, he knew he had little support among the Republicans who dominated Congress. He also knew that in any contest between himself and Grant, the country would back its beloved war hero. Johnson's attorney general instructed the U.S. attorneys in Norfolk to quash the indictments.[17]

Grant's trust in Robert E. Lee was well placed. Once he was free from the threat of federal prosecution, Lee moved quickly to assume the presidency of struggling Washington College. He dedicated the remaining five years of his life to education.**

---

* Following Lee's surrender, other Confederate armies surrendered within six weeks on similar terms. Jefferson Davis was captured in Georgia and imprisoned at Virginia's Fort Monroe.

** When Robert E. Lee died in 1870, he was widely mourned in the South *and* the North. Washington College today is thriving as Washington and Lee University.

Johnson claimed to be following Lincoln's mild reconstruction policies, but it soon became clear his motives were entirely different. Johnson had been openly hostile to the aristocratic slaveholders. But this was more a matter of class envy—he could not *afford* slaves—than a matter of justice to the slave. Johnson granted clemency to many former Confederate leaders, *provided that they appeal personally to him*. He soon made his attitudes known. He had no concern for the civil rights of the freedmen. "This country is for the white men," he told the Republican governor of Missouri, "and by God as long as I am President, it shall be governed by white men."[18]

Johnson was eager to accept reconstituted Southern state governments as soon as possible. But Republicans in Congress—not just the radicals—were scandalized when elections in the South returned sixteen high-ranking Confederate officeholders, four Southern generals, and five colonels to Washington.[19] A young French reporter, Georges Clemenceau, put his finger on the trouble: "When anyone has for four successive years joined in a struggle as that which the United States has seen, [he desires] not to lose the dearly bought fruits of so many painful sacrifices."[20*]

Congress had set up a new organization, the Freedmen's Bureau, to help the newly freed black Southerners. General Oliver O. Howard, a brave one-armed hero of the Union army, was named its head.[**]

Many freedmen erroneously thought each family would be given "forty acres and a mule" to begin new lives as independent farmers.[21] Instead, the Freedmen's Bureau tried with varying success to persuade black agricultural workers to return to the fields in return for reasonable wages. In trying to help the freedmen, the bureau often found itself also trying to aid cash-strapped white Southern farmers.

---

* Clemenceau's words were prophetic. This is precisely the view he would take half a century later when, as France's World War I premier, he would strive to retain the fruits of a hard-won victory against the Germans.

** It was to honor General Howard that one of America's great historically black institutions of higher learning was named Washington's Howard University.

This *might have been* the formula for a Southern renaissance. A federal government plan to help both white and black Southerners *might have been* an earlier Marshall Plan. But it was tragically not to be.

For the plan to succeed, Democrats would have to support the Republicans in Reconstruction, and the national Democratic Party was not willing to do so.

When the Republicans who controlled Congress returned to Washington, they were alarmed by what they saw.*

They knew that if Northern Democrats combined with those Democrats from the defeated South, Republicans would be in the minority. Worse, they feared the loss of all they had struggled for. Congress had passed the Thirteenth Amendment to the Constitution early in 1865. This amendment abolished slavery throughout the United States. The Lincoln administration supported it fully. Thus, the *exemptions* that were necessary to issue the Emancipation Proclamation as a war measure were corrected when the amendment was speedily ratified.

Congress overrode Johnson's vetoes of legislation reauthorizing the Freedmen's Bureau and new civil rights laws. Democratic Party newspapers had headlined Johnson's vetoes: "ALL HAIL! GREAT AND GLORIOUS! VICTORY FOR THE WHITE MAN!" Moderate Republicans were deeply disappointed.[22] They had hoped to work with Johnson. They wanted nothing of the radicals' vengeful plans for Reconstruction. But Johnson's intransigence united Republicans against him. The unified votes on overrides were just tokens of an increasing hostility between the new president and Congress.

Meanwhile, throughout the South, racial tensions were rising. Black Southerners had gone on no postliberation sprees of violence, but they quickly became the targets of violence.[23]

In Memphis, Tennessee, in May 1866, two horse-drawn wagons collided on a city street, a common event for any city in America. But

---

* Congress did not meet year-round in this era. The old Congress adjourned in March 1865. The Congress elected in 1864—a much more strongly Republican Congress—did not convene until December 1865.

in this case, one of the waggoneers was white, the other black. White Memphis police arrested the black man, but black veterans of the Union army intervened, charging that he was the victim of prejudice. White mobs quickly formed. Riots broke out across the city.[24] Following were three days of rioting by off-duty white policemen that left forty-six dead in black sections of the city. Hundreds of homes, schools, and churches were burned.[25] City officials did nothing.

That summer in New Orleans, a convention organized to support black suffrage was attacked, and subsequent riots killed forty people. Federal troops had to restore order.[26] President Johnson's policies were seriously discredited by this and other such incidents. Northerners were beginning to see that a firmer hand was required with the defeated South.[27]

Infamous "black codes" were passed in a number of Southern states. These laws severely limited the rights of black workers to contract, to engage in many occupations, to sue, to serve on juries (unless a black person was on trial), even to travel seeking new work. It seemed that the results of the Emancipation Proclamation itself were at risk.

Republicans in Congress struggled to frame an appropriate response. They quickly realized reconstruction would be impossible with the Democrat Johnson wielding presidential powers against them. Initially, defeated Southerners were willing to do what they had to do to regain their full status. But Johnson loudly proclaimed his support for "white man's government," and this encouraged former rebels to resist federal authority.[28]

Soon, congressional Republicans settled on another constitutional amendment to require all states to give freedmen citizenship and to provide "equal protection of the laws" to all citizens. Representative John Bingham (Ohio) and Senator Jacob M. Howard (Michigan), two leading Republicans in Congress, sponsored Amendment XIV. The Fourteenth Amendment also provided that a state's representation in Congress could be limited if it did not comply with the amendment. Republicans made *ratification* of the Fourteenth Amendment a condition of allowing Southern representatives to be readmitted to the Congress.[29]

The danger was a law with no teeth; means to enforce the laws were quickly disappearing. Before the year 1865 was out, the great armies and navy of the Union were demobilized. The number in uniform declined from more than *one million* (a tenth of whom were black) to just 152,000.[30]

Relations between the Executive Mansion and Congress continued to worsen throughout 1866. "Jefferson Davis is in the casemate [prison cell] at Fortress Monroe," complained Massachusetts Senator Charles Sumner, "but Andrew Johnson is doing his work."[31] Johnson received a delegation of black leaders headed by Frederick Douglass. The black leaders were pleading for Johnson's support for Negro suffrage as a part of reconstruction. Johnson remained civil and noncommittal. Afterward, he snarled to his secretary: "Those damned sons of bitches thought they had me in a trap. I know that damned Douglass; he's just like any n——, and he would sooner cut a white man's throat than not!"[32]

Johnson determined to challenge the Republicans in Congress. He set out on a far-flung train trip. He would "swing around the circle" to explain his policies to the people. He persuaded Ulysses S. Grant, then commanding general of the Army, to accompany him. Grant, trying to get along with his commander in chief, agreed to go. It did not take long for things to go sour. The crowds that came out to see Johnson cried out for Grant. And Grant was increasingly disgusted by Johnson's vulgar, vituperative attacks on Congress.

Completely lacking in dignity, Johnson responded to taunts from the crowd by getting into the gutter with his hecklers. He even bawled out that he would hang Congressman Thaddeus Stevens, a leader of the radicals, as well as the famous abolitionist Wendell Phillips.[33] As Grant wrote his wife, he looked upon Johnson's tirades as "a National disgrace."[34] Grant was especially offended by Johnson's fierce hatred of black Americans.[35] Johnson had never been a member of Lincoln's Republican Party; he was put on the ticket as a War Democrat in 1864 only in an effort to bring about greater national unity during the Civil War.

As soon as he could, Grant pleaded illness and left the train. Johnson's speechifying was turning into a disaster, personal and political, for the president. Rejecting Johnson's strident appeals for support, voters in November returned an overwhelmingly Republican Congress.[36]

Republican leaders of Congress now had the bit between their teeth. They were determined to reconstruct the South according to their own plan. They passed a Reconstruction Act that divided the defeated South into military districts. Military governors were appointed who would take their orders from General Grant, not the president. Seeing how Johnson had made clever use of his appointment powers, Congress passed the Tenure of Office Act. Under this clearly *unconstitutional* measure, the president could not remove an official who had been confirmed by the Senate until his successor was likewise confirmed.

The Reconstruction Act was used to remove from office governors of six Southern states and thousands of state and local officials on grounds of "loyalty." An army of occupation suppressed many manifestations of Southern patriotism, including veterans groups, memorial parades, and historical societies.[37] Radicals in Congress were determined to suppress rebellious sentiment in the conquered South.

White Southerners bitterly resisted what they termed Northern despotism. They denounced Northerners who came south to help with the work of reconstruction as "carpetbaggers"—no-accounts and opportunists who had packed everything they owned into a cheap, shoddy carpetbag. Those few Southerners—like former Confederate General James Longstreet—who were willing to cooperate with Union authorities were slammed as scalawags.[38] Able, literate black politicians were denounced as readily as unprepared, illiterate ex-slaves who suddenly found themselves in legislative arenas.

President Johnson tried to obstruct the Fifteenth Amendment to the Constitution. It would give the vote to adult black males. Even his military aide, Colonel William G. Moore, noted in his diary that "the president has at times exhibited morbid distress and feeling against the Negroes." Once, seeing a number of black men working in the Executive Mansion, Johnson angrily asked if all the white men had been laid off.[39]

Johnson deliberately determined to stick his head in the lion's mouth over the power of appointment and removed Edwin M. Stanton as secretary of war. Stanton had been reporting all cabinet discussions to the radicals. But when the order to vacate his position came, the irascible ex-Democrat, whom Lincoln had called *Mars*, barricaded himself in his office and refused to leave![40]*

III. IMPEACHMENT

The radicals were outraged. Representative Thaddeus Stevens even introduced a bill to suspend President Johnson pending the outcome of an impeachment and trial. This was too much for General Grant. He recognized Stevens's move as clearly unconstitutional. He assured Johnson, whom he despised, that he would *resist* any attempt to arrest the commander in chief prior to a properly conducted impeachment and trial. When Grant told Congress he would not participate in anything so unprecedented, Stevens's plans for an arrest fizzled.[41]

Thad Stevens was hardly a reassuring figure for leadership. He had some estimable qualities, to be sure. He had been an early and ardent opponent of racial discrimination. He even refused to sign Pennsylvania's new constitution in 1838 because it failed to extend the vote to black Pennsylvanians. He was one of the first members of Congress to advocate full emancipation and civil and political equality for the four million slaves in the South. But Stevens's postwar plan to confiscate Southern planters' lands and resettle them with Northern migrants and freed slaves was too extreme even for his own fellow radicals![42]** His plan to arrest

---

* *Mars* was the Roman god of war. Lincoln had a sense of humor, even if Stanton did not.

** Stevens, though driven and humorless, had the virtue of sincerity. When he died, his will provided that he be buried in one of Pennsylvania's few racially integrated cemeteries. His epitaph proclaims "the Equality of Man before his Creator" (Foner and Mahoney, *America's Reconstruction*, p. 91).

President Johnson only added to Stevens's reputation as an unforgiving and intemperate man.

Grant's intervention barely slowed the rush to impeachment. The House of Representatives brought eleven charges against the president. Ten of these related to the willful violation of the Tenure of Office Act.

When the trial before the Senate took place in March 1868, the country held its breath. In just three years, the people of the United States had endured the bloody end of the nation's most devastating war, the assassination of its president, a tumultuous reconstruction era, and now *this*—the first presidential impeachment proceeding.

Seven Republican senators saved Johnson from conviction and removal from office. Three of these were well-respected moderate Republicans who did not fear the radicals' wrath: William Pitt Fessenden (Maine), James Grimes (Iowa), and Lyman Trumbull (Illinois). Fessenden spoke for many when he said, "The president is on trial for specific offences charged, and for none other. It would be contrary to every principle of justice . . . to try and condemn any man, however guilty he may be thought, for an offense not charged."[43]

Johnson avoided conviction by one vote in the Senate. He escaped, as Winston Churchill would later write of an opponent, "unsung and unhung." But our bleeding country did not escape Andrew Johnson's vindictive rule.

The radicals can be blamed in three ways for this debacle. First, they should have taken care to elect a more confidence-inspiring figure than Bluff Ben Wade as their Senate president. Second, they should have moved *sooner* to impeach the odious Johnson to avoid entanglement with the presidential election of 1868. Third, they should have impeached Johnson on more substantial grounds. Johnson was doing everything possible to *obstruct* the laws of Congress. The president is constitutionally bound to "take care that the laws be *faithfully* executed." This, and not the flagrantly unconstitutional Tenure of Office Act, might have constituted valid grounds for impeachment.

The Andrew Johnson presidency—just six weeks short of four dreadful years—was a national tragedy.

IV. "LET US HAVE PEACE"

In 1868, Republican Ulysses S. Grant was elected president, defeating Democrat Horatio Seymour, former governor of New York. "Let us have peace," Grant had said after his nomination. The phrase became a byword for the campaign, the Grant presidency, and his life.

The renewal of a united government would not prove an easy task. In the South, resistance was digging in. The Ku Klux Klan arose to terrorize black freedmen and those whites who sympathized with them. Former Confederate General Nathan Bedford Forrest was now the "Grand Dragon" of the Klan. In 1871, in one county alone, 163 black Southerners were murdered. Fully 300 were murdered in parishes near New Orleans.[44*] The Fifteenth Amendment had given the right to vote only to those brave enough to exercise it.

Despite the turmoil in the South, many Americans were now looking in another direction. During the Civil War, Congress had passed a Homestead Act, opening up vast tracts of western lands to farmers. After the war, Secretary of State William H. Seward engineered the purchase of Alaska from Russia. And soon after Grant took the oath of office as president, Americans thrilled to the driving of the Golden Spike at Promontory Point, Utah, on 10 May 1869. The completion of the Transcontinental Railroad knitted the country together, to be sure, but it also emphasized the opening of the West and naturally distracted attention from conditions in the South.

Labor unions began to agitate for higher wages and better working conditions in the North. The sacrifices demanded by the war could no

---

    * In Louisiana, counties are referred to as *parishes*, a holdover from the days of French rule.

longer justify failure to pay attention to the concerns of the workingman. Typical was this appeal of a labor activist: "The workingmen of America will in future claim a more equal share in the wealth their industry creates in peace and a more equal participation in the privileges and blessings of those free institutions defended by their manhood on many a bloody field of battle."[45]

In fact, it was in the same period as Reconstruction (1865–77) that America saw the highest percentage of workers joining unions of any period in the nineteenth century.[46]

Workers, many of them Union war veterans, were increasingly put off by the antics of some Republican politicians who constantly "waved the bloody shirt" to gain their votes.[47*] The Democratic Party descended to blatant racism in many of its election appeals. But that did not change the party's historic appeal to workers.

Republicans were hampered, too, by all-too-credible charges of corruption. Too many of Grant's appointees and close associates had shown themselves eager to dip their spoons in the gravy of corporate largesse. Grant had unwisely given his grasping father, Jesse, an important postmaster job in Kentucky. Dubious characters included even his brother-in-law, Abel Corbin, his appointments secretary, and a few cabinet members. Although Grant was personally honest and profited in no way from the shenanigans, he was too naïve about *appearances*.

Early in his presidency, Grant had spent time socially with Wall Street financiers Jay Gould and Jim Fisk. They tried to get the president to hold off on government purchases of greenbacks for gold. Grant did not realize that they wanted to corner the gold market.

While vacationing, President Grant received a long letter from Corbin. His brother-in-law listed all the reasons why the president should

---

    *   Congressman Ben Butler had waved a bloody shirt—allegedly from an Ohio "carpetbagger" beaten by the Klan—to support the impeachment of Johnson. It was another innovation from the man who invented the term *contraband* for escaped slaves. Ironically, Butler was an ex-Democrat.

suspend government sales of gold. When Grant learned that his brother-in-law was in cahoots with the slippery pair, he was furious. He refused even to reply. But the local telegraph office sent back a message that would be widely misinterpreted. "Letter received all right," wrote the courier. But the message was sent as: "Letter delivered. All right."[48] There's a cruel irony here. As a winning general, U. S. Grant was famous for the crisp clarity of his written orders. No one ever misunderstood a Grant order. But Grant did not write this garbled message.

Quickly, Grant ordered Treasury Secretary George Boutwell to *increase* the sales of gold to $4 million.[49] Fisk and Gould escaped unscathed from the collapse of their scheme, but thousands of gullible investors in their scam were ruined. It was known as *Black Friday* on Wall Street, and it stained Grant's reputation. Jim Fisk brazened it all out, telling his cronies "nothing lost, boys, save *honor*." The results of this misguided attempt to corner the gold market were to cast a shadow over the Grant presidency.

President Grant sincerely sought reconciliation of the sections while upholding the threatened rights of the freedmen. Grant pressed Congress to pass the Ku Klux Klan Act. This act gave the federal government new powers to suppress the "invisible empire." Grant quickly signed the bill and used it to great effect against the white-sheet-wearing nightriders of the KKK. Grant's election and reelection were enthusiastically supported by Frederick Douglass. He complained to dissatisfied freedmen that while the Republicans too often "ignore us, the Democrats kill us!"

Many institutions for higher learning—Fisk, Tuskegee, Atlanta, and Howard—testify to the sincerity of Northern efforts to help educate and uplift the freedmen. Some of the best men in the South encouraged these efforts.

Eventually, the North was worn down by the resistance of a determined few in the South. The formal, constitutional safeguards for equality under the law had been put in place by the Thirteenth, Fourteenth, and Fifteenth Amendments. But these would prove hollow assurances for nearly a century. Reconstruction failed. Americans yearned for an end to ceaseless agitation and recurrent troubles in the South. Exhausted by civil strife and controversy, most Northerners wanted to get on with their lives. They longed to *ignore* politics and to seek the means of happiness in their private pursuits.[50]

While the people of the North turned their attention to economic pursuits, black and white Southerners suffered immeasurably. For the rest of the century, the South was "an economic basket case."[51] It might all have been avoided. Had Northern politicians followed Lincoln's enlightened principles, had they guaranteed equal rights and suppressed terrorists like the KKK, they might have helped restore their prostrate fellow countrymen. It was a failure of imagination not to see the opportunities for renewal in a Union restored with liberty for all; for as Frederick Douglass wrote: "The abolition of slavery has not only emancipated the Negro, but liberated the whites" as well.[52]

As the depression following the Panic of 1873 deepened, President Grant came under extreme pressure to inflate the currency. Debtors, especially in the western states, cried out for relief from Washington.[53]

Republican Party campaign officials panicked too. They pleaded with Grant to sign a measure demanded by farmers and ranchers to print up to $100 million in greenbacks. Grant's cabinet also favored the inflation bill.[54] The president later reflected on the pressures—and his final action:

> The only time I ever deliberately resolved to do an expedient thing for party reasons, against my own judgment, was on the occasion of the inflation bill. I was never so pressed in my life to do anything as to sign that bill—never. It was represented to me that a veto would destroy the Republican Party in the west. . . . I resolved to write a message that the bill need not mean inflation. . . . I wrote the message with great care and put in every argument I could call up to show that the bill was harmless. When I finished my wonderful message, I read it over and said to myself, "What is the good of all this? You do not believe it. I know it is not true." . . . I resolved to do what I believed to be right [and] veto the bill.[55]

Veto the inflation bill he did. And those Republican Party leaders were not wrong about the political consequences of such an act. The party suffered its worst defeat in its history that fall. The House of Representatives went from a Republican majority of 194–92 to a Democratic majority of 181–107.[56] It was a net loss of *eighty-seven seats* for the Republicans. After this, Grant's honest efforts to help freedmen in the South were hampered by divided government.

One obvious and important development in these years after the Civil War: Americans ceased to concentrate their gaze on the South. The South had dominated the nation's politics from 1800 to 1860. After the Civil War, New York and Ohio were the most important states. Whether the focus of attention was on the teeming cities of the North and Midwest, the farm belt of the Great Plains, the embattled frontier regions, or the coalfields, iron ranges, and railroad yards, the South mattered less.

This was a tragedy for black Americans, most of whom continued to live in the states of their birth. It was also a tragedy for white Southerners. While the nation recovered and moved on to greater heights, the South languished. Jim Crow laws that separated the races held *all* of its talented and devoted people down.

V. A TRAGIC DIVORCE IN FREEDOM'S RANKS

Until the Civil War, many reformers worked together to end slavery and to enfranchise women. The leading suffragettes were all antislavery advocates. And abolitionists nearly all favored votes for women. It seemed the two causes were bound together. But the debate over the Fifteenth Amendment would cause a split in the two movements that would have consequences that extend even to our own day. Susan B. Anthony spoke for most of her movement when she dramatically said she would "sooner cut off my right hand than ask the ballot for the black man and not for woman."[57]

When Frederick Douglass left an early women's convention,

Miss Anthony scolded him: "Not one word from you since you suddenly and mysteriously disappeared at Albany."[58] He declined even to show up at another conference.

The reason for the split was simple. Republicans were preparing to extend the vote to black men North and South, but they were unwilling to give votes to women. They thought the move would be too radical for the time. Democrats in Congress were opposed to enfranchising either women *or* black men. In a letter he wrote to a friendly woman reformer, Douglass explained his motives. As usual, his considerations were not only principled but practical:

> The right of woman to vote is as sacred in my judgment as that of a man, and I am quite willing at any time to hold up both my hands in favor of this right. . . . [But] I am now devoting myself to a cause [if] not more sacred, certainly more urgent, because it is one of life and death to the long enslaved people of this country. While the Negro is stabbed, hanged, burnt and is the target of all that is malignant in the north and all that is murderous in the south, his claims may be preferred by me. . . . [Susan B. Anthony and Elizabeth Cady Stanton oppose the Fifteenth Amendment if it fails to include women.] Their principle is that no Negro shall be enfranchised while woman is not.[59]

It was a cruel dilemma. Millions of women throughout the North and the South were fully literate. Unlike Douglass, most of the freedmen were not. In a number of slave states, it had even been against the law to teach a black man to read. Women had contributed substantially to the political debates of the nation. They had sacrificed greatly in the Civil War for the nation's sake. How *could* their just claims be cast aside? At the same time, the chance to give votes to black men seemed to Republicans the only way to ensure that the hard-won gains of the Civil War could be maintained. With their right to vote protected by federal troops, Southern black leaders were sitting in Congress for the first time. Senators Blanche

K. Bruce and Hiram R. Revels and Representatives Benjamin S. Turner, Josiah T. Walls, Joseph H. Rainey, Robert Brown Elliot, Robert D. De Large, and Jefferson H. Long represented Southern constituencies. It was very unlikely they could survive in office if the Fifteenth Amendment was not passed.

Few could have known at the time that the long struggle for women's suffrage would take fully half a century to achieve its goal—or that the period of black male enfranchisement, even *with* the ratification of the Fifteenth Amendment, would prove pathetically brief. Still, the adoption of the Fifteenth Amendment in 1870 provided a logical basis for the eventual passage of the Nineteenth Amendment in 1920. And many states preceded the federal amendment in recognizing women's right to vote.

VI. THE SPIRIT OF 1876

Americans had many reasons to congratulate themselves as they approached their great centennial celebration. They had declared their independence and made it stick in a long but ultimately successful revolution against the British monarchy. They had accepted a French alliance but had been relieved to see the large and powerful French army peacefully sail away.* They had drafted and ratified a Constitution unprecedented in the world that established a "new order of the ages." Their new federal republic in 1789 stretched from the Maine woods to the Florida border and west to the Mississippi River. They negotiated the greatest land deal in history—the Louisiana Purchase. Americans fought the War of 1812. They had repulsed the British invasion from Canada, withstood the enemy burning their capital city, and finally they had

---

* One of General Washington's serious concerns in the War of Independence was that the French would not send enough troops. A second, equally serious worry was that the French would send so many troops that Americans would find themselves colonists all over again. It was a very delicate balancing act.

triumphed over the most serious British threat at New Orleans. Following an extraordinary period of national expansion, Americans carried their democratic institutions across the continent, as far as the Pacific Ocean. And they had saved their Union, with liberty, after a harrowing four years of civil war. They freed four million slaves. By constitutional amendment, Americans abolished slavery, pronounced equal protection of the laws, and proposed votes for men newly freed from bondage. America, it seemed, had truly seen "a new birth of freedom." Following the Civil War, Americans referred to their united *nation* as a singular noun: the United States *is*, not the United States *are*.[60]

And the nation *avoided* a military dictatorship. Grant and Sherman were as daring and inventive on the battlefield as Napoleon had been. They were as single-minded for national unity as Bismarck was. Sherman's opponent, Confederate General Joseph Johnston, said no army since Caesar's had moved with such an irresistible force. But Grant and Sherman both deferred always to the people's *elected* representatives.*

In material terms, America's wealth and power would have astonished even such visionaries as Franklin and Jefferson. Everywhere, sail gave way to steam. Canal building—which had so strongly appealed to future-oriented leaders like Washington—was rapidly eclipsed by railroad construction. Americans followed up the Golden Spike of the Transcontinental Railroad with a rush of tributary lines to bind the country together with rails of steel. Immigrants flocked to the country. Even with 620,000 deaths in the Civil War, America in the 1860s showed a robust *26 percent increase* in population. The population in 1860 was 31,443,321, one-seventh of whom were slaves and 13 percent of whom were immigrants. By 1870, with slavery abolished, the U.S. population was 39,818,449. Immigrants accounted for 14.2 percent of these.[61]

For all the criticisms of a materialistic age, the material changes in

---

* So had Lee and Jackson in the South. The willing subordination of these great generals to civilian authority was doubtless a result of their West Point training, another tribute to "the long gray line" of distinguished graduates of the U.S. military academy.

American life were stunning. Civil War veterans said that it seemed they had grown up in a different *country* than the one to which they returned from the battlefield. For Americans who lived after the Civil War and through the remainder of the nineteenth century, the country they saw must have seemed part of a different *world*.

Breakthroughs in agriculture and industry made it possible to feed more people than at any time in history. America became an important *exporter* of foodstuffs throughout the world. Refrigeration and canning created a continental market for meats and vegetables. Most Americans wanted a greater share of the material abundance that freedom made possible. They didn't turn their noses up at a land of plenty. They agreed with Samuel Gompers when he said his very *American* workers simply wanted "more."

President Ulysses S. Grant looked forward to opening the International Centennial Exhibition at Philadelphia in 1876. He yearned to finish out his two presidential terms with such an honorable and dignified event. The presidency had not been kind to the victor of Appomattox. Corruption tarnished his administration's reputation.

Following its 10 May 1876 opening, nearly ten million people flocked to Philadelphia for the International Centennial Exhibition. President Grant joined Brazil's Emperor Dom Pedro at the opening ceremonies. German composer Richard Wagner pocketed a fee of $5,000 for his heavy, pompous original work, the "Centennial March."[62*] America's Centennial followed the great 1851 London exhibition in the Crystal Palace. That event had been brilliantly organized by Queen Victoria's consort, Prince Albert. Since then, such demonstrations of science, technology, and commerce were the hallmarks of an Age of Progress. The United States' entry into this competition was a signal of the rising power and prestige of the Great Republic. Americans took great satisfaction that their democracy stood on a par with the imperial powers of Europe.

One of the attractions that caused a great stir at the Centennial

---

* Mark Twain may have captured the essence of the great composer's *Sturm und Drang* (storm and upheaval) when he said: "I'm told that Wagner's music is better than it sounds."

Exhibition was the huge extended female arm, its hand holding a giant torch. This was just the first section of a monumental statue, a gift from the people of France. Sent over in advance to spark interest, the statue would be known formally as *Liberty Enlightening the World*. The Statue of Liberty, as we know it, was originally conceived by the noted French friend of freedom, Edouard de Laboulaye. He had courageously opposed the proslavery policy of the tyrannical Emperor Napoleon III. Following President Lincoln's assassination, Laboulaye wanted to pay tribute to the Great Emancipator's vision. He shared his idea with the young Alsatian sculptor, Frédéric-Auguste Bartholdi. Soon, the people of France caught the spirit. They enthusiastically subscribed to a lottery to raise the funds needed to construct the massive monument. Bartholdi brought the arm and the torch to fire Americans' imaginations—and he did. Bartholdi's arrival in New York's majestic harbor gave him the inspiration for the site of Lady Liberty.*

A second marvel at the Centennial Exhibition was a demonstration by Alexander Graham Bell. The young Scottish immigrant brought a working model of his new invention—the telephone. Few had been interested in the telephone until the Brazilian emperor hailed Bell. Dom Pedro had met him at Bell's school for the deaf. Now, at the exhibition, he asked to see the young inventor's new device. As a crowd gathered, they heard passages from Hamlet's soliloquy: "To be or not to be?"

At the time, Bell had to borrow lunch money from his assistant, Watson. He was finally recognized months later by the exhibition's judges for "the greatest marvel hitherto achieved by the telegraph."[63] Bell's telephone was clearly superior to the telegraph. The telegraph never had the capacity for a mass audience, but the telephone would soon spread to thousands of businesses and government agencies, and millions of American homes.

Not everyone was awed by the Centennial Exhibition. With some

---

* Bartholdi's passion for liberty was an intensely personal commitment. By the time he arrived in America, his own beloved province of Alsace-Lorraine had been wrenched from France by Germany following the Franco-Prussian War of 1870–71.

wit and much candor, Japan's commissioner to the event recorded the opening day:

> The first day crowds come like sheep, run here, run there, run every-where. One man start, one thousand follow. Nobody can see anything, nobody can do anything. All rush, push, tear, shout, make plenty noise, say damn great many times, get very tired, and go home.[64]

VII. A DANGEROUS DISPUTE

Ulysses S. Grant doubtless could have won a third term in 1876 had he seriously wanted to contest for his party's nomination. He was only fifty-four years old, still younger than most presidents had been on first entering the office. But he had given his word that he would not seek re-election in 1876, and he resolved to keep it. Not even the Battle of the Little Big Horn shook Grant's determination to leave office. Colonel George Armstrong Custer and 265 men of the Seventh Cavalry were killed on 25 June 1876.* Custer's death led to many cries for retribution against the Sioux. There had been some two hundred clashes between Indians and the bluecoats during Grant's two terms.[65] Grant was particularly con-cerned to deal fairly with the Indians. In this, he did not hesitate to stand *against* public opinion, especially the views of settlers on the frontier.

The presidential election of 1876 was a messy and near-disastrous affair. Democrats nominated Governor Samuel J. Tilden of New York. Republicans turned to Ohio Governor Rutherford B. Hayes, a Civil War hero with a clean if colorless record.

When the votes came in, a dangerous dispute arose. Tilden's victory seemed clear. He had won 4,288,546 popular votes (51 percent). Hayes

---

* No, Custer was not busted from general's rank to colonel. With the vast downsizing of the post–Civil War army and navy, many who wished to remain on active duty had to be willing to serve at a lower rank.

trailed with 4,034,311 popular votes (48.0 percent). But then, as now, it is the *electoral vote* that determines who wins the presidency. What was especially perilous in 1876 was the multiple sets of electors vying for acceptance. In the states of South Carolina, Louisiana, Oregon, and Florida, rival slates had been chosen. Each party claimed those electoral votes. The issue was further complicated by accusations of voter intimidation in the South. With the results in doubt and emotions running high, there was talk of armed conflict.[66]

President Grant was a pillar of strength during the election crisis of 1876. He gave strict orders to his great friend, General Sherman, to guard the election returns and to keep order throughout the disputed states. Grant wrote to Sherman: "No man worthy of the office of President would be willing to hold the office if counted in, placed there by fraud; either Party can afford to be disappointed in the result, but the country cannot afford to have the result tainted by the suspicion of illegal or false returns."[67]

Congress created an electoral commission to decide which slates of electors to accept as valid. In the end, the commission worked out a compromise. Hayes was elected by 185 to 184 electoral votes. In return for throwing the election of Hayes, the Southerners were promised that Union troops would be removed from the South. Reconstruction was over.

For their part, the Republicans received vague assurances that the civil rights of black Southerners would be respected. It was to prove a terrible bargain. Over the next twenty years, black people were driven out of political participation in the South. Not until *1965* did black Southerners have free access to voting.

Many Democratic newspapers denounced Hayes as "His Fraudulency" and "Ruther*fraud* B. Hayes." He entered office under a cloud of suspicion. He continued to suffer attacks on the very legitimacy of his presidency for the first two years of his term.

With Hayes in the White House, Ulysses S. Grant and his wife, Julia, embarked on a world tour that lasted more than two years. A final judgment on Grant's presidency might be rendered by one who knew him well. Frederick Douglass was grateful to the victor of Appomattox:

> To Grant more than any other man the Negro owes his enfranchisement and the Indian a humane policy. In the matter of the protection of the freedman from violence, his moral courage surpassed that of his party.[68]

TEN

AN AGE MORE GOLDEN
THAN GILDED?

(1877–1897)

I. A GILDED AGE?

For generations, American students have been taught that the "driving of the Golden Spike" at the completion of the Transcontinental Railroad was only accomplished at the cost of lining the pockets of compromised politicians with cash. Clearly, there was corruption involved in the building of the great railroad. Still, the project that Abraham Lincoln embraced and promoted achieved its goal in just seven years. In Canada, corruption abounded, too, and it took their government-run rail construction twenty years to complete. Russia's Trans-Siberian Railroad took forty years and was also awash in corruption.

More important, with the Transcontinental Railroad we got a great national institution that helped immeasurably to bind up the nation's wounds from the Civil War. Those trains not only carried freight farther and cheaper, reducing the price of goods, and not only carried immigrants "yearning to breathe free," they also carried newspapers whose headlines deplored the very rails that made them truly national journals.

We have been taught that the last part of the nineteenth century was, in Mark Twain's inimitable phrase, a "Gilded Age." Its glitter, Twain winked, was only on the surface, only a thin veneer of shininess. The *New York Times* slammed the captains of industry who built great corporations as "robber barons." The title stuck. But *Harper's Weekly* saw through the propaganda: "Wherever [Commodore Vanderbilt] 'laid on' an opposition [railroad] line, the fares were instantly reduced, and however he bought out his opponents . . . or they bought him out, the fares were never again raised to the old standard."[1] It was the American people who benefited from those lower fares. "Barons" had never before stooped to so perfectly serve the needs of the little guy.

Railroads were tying the country together. From 1870 to 1900, miles of rail increased from 52,922 to 193,346.[2] Railroads dominated American life for one hundred years. Steel production went from a mere 1,643 tons in 1867 to a phenomenal 7,156,957 tons in 1897. The United States, by the end of the century, outstripped both Germany and Great Britain in steel production—a fact of far-reaching political and military significance.[3] American inventiveness in this period—telephones, light bulbs, phonographs, sewing machines, typewriters, and automobiles—was not only a marvel in itself and not only changed Americans' lives forever, but it helped transform the *world* economy.

In saying all this, we must not lose sight of the fact that all the growth was not equally distributed throughout the country. It never is. The South, devastated by war, suffered from economic backwardness and from unjust Jim Crow laws that kept the races legally separated. They barred the way to progress for black and white Southerners alike. Immigrants piled into slums in the cities of the North. These blighted neighborhoods appalled reformers. The average immigrant family got out of the slums in less than fifteen years, and even these eyesores were often better than the grinding poverty they had known in the "Old Country."[4] There is no denying there was corruption of our political system in the late nineteenth century. But, then as now, free government and a free press unleash the vast engines of reform.

II. HAYES, GARFIELD, AND ARTHUR

President Rutherford B. Hayes was scorned as *Rutherfraud* when an electoral commission handed him the presidency just two days before inauguration day in 1877. Hayes helped his own case with the American people. Nothing about his conduct of his office justified the word *fraud*. Upright, intelligent, and dignified, he formed a distinguished cabinet. He included such reformers as German immigrant Carl Schurz and William Evarts. Evarts's legal skill had saved Andrew Johnson from removal during the impeachment. Republican Party regulars, known as *Stalwarts*, were horrified. They were even more upset when Hayes named a former Confederate to his cabinet. He chose David M. Key of Tennessee as postmaster general. Hayes also elevated Kentucky's John Marshall Harlan to the U.S. Supreme Court. An ex-slaveholder, Harlan began a long and distinguished career committed to equal rights for *all* Americans. Of great symbolic importance was Hayes's nomination of Frederick Douglass to be U.S. Marshal for the District of Columbia.[5] It was the highest and most prominent appointive position yet attained by a black American.

Hayes's clean government record led some of the more cynical believers in the "spoils" system to sneer at him as "Granny Hayes." And these hardened party politicos were even more put off when the beautiful and intelligent First Lady declined to serve alcohol at the Executive Mansion.[6] "Lemonade Lucy" was a gracious and accomplished hostess. Her performance of her official duties was as well respected by Americans as that of Mrs. Julia Dent Grant. During Mrs. Hayes's years in the Executive Mansion, the "water flowed like champagne."

Because he had committed to serving only one term, Hayes did not flinch from fighting with Stalwarts in his own party over patronage positions. Civil service reform was a rising issue in the nation. The federal government had long operated on a spoils system in which civil service jobs went to politicians' friends, supporters, and relatives. Hayes tried to appoint more public officials on the basis of merit and fewer in return for service to the party. Stalwarts who fought to protect the spoils system ridiculed the president's "snivel service reform."[7]

Hayes's last years in office were stormy. Despite anti-Chinese riots in San Francisco and heavy pressure to sign the bill, he vetoed a Chinese Exclusion Act passed by Democrats in 1879. He also vetoed Democrats' attempts to roll back black voters' rights in the South. Hayes's Ohio friend, Congressman James A. Garfield, called this veto message by far the ablest he had ever produced.[8] Hayes also expressed increasing concern for the status of *marriage* in the United States. He went so far as to ask Congress to bar *polygamists* from holding office or serving on juries.[9]

By committing himself in advance to only one term, Hayes limited his political clout. Nonetheless, he took quiet satisfaction in the 1880 nomination of his close friend to succeed him. James A. Garfield was selected by Republican delegates following the collapse of a third-term boom for ex-President Grant. Hayes was even philosophical when the pro-Grant Stalwart faction of the Republican Party put Chester Alan Arthur of New York on the ticket as the vice presidential nominee. Ohio and New York had become the keys to the election of a president, and the Republicans had balanced their ticket with care.

Garfield was elected over a lackluster Democrat, Winfield Scott Hancock. Like old General Winfield Scott, Hancock had been a great general but a poor candidate. The Garfield-Arthur ticket won by a mere 9,500 votes. But at least they had won. The Garfield campaign stressed his stellar war record. They recirculated the dramatic story of Garfield's ride into a panicked crowd on Wall Street. It was the day news came of Lincoln's assassination. Bravely, Garfield had charged into the crowd, calming them with these words: "Fellow citizens! God reigns and the government at Washington lives!" His timely action probably averted a riot or financial collapse. Garfield was a multitalented man. Among large immigrant audiences, he spoke German. He would entertain his friends by having them call out Shakespeare quotations. He would then simultaneously translate them into Latin and Greek, writing them out with both hands.

The country had little chance to embrace this gifted man. On 2 July 1881, barely four months after he was inaugurated, a disgruntled office seeker shot Garfield. Charles A. Guiteau stalked the young president into Washington's Union Station. Crying, "I'm a Stalwart and now *Arthur* is president," he shot Garfield in the back. The president lingered throughout the brutally hot Washington summer. Various doctors came to the Executive Mansion to try their skills. Still, the president weakened. Urgently, they called Alexander Graham Bell to come and use his telephone equipment to locate the bullet. "The whole world watched and hopes and fears filled every passing hour. No one could venture to predict the end so long as the position of the bullet remained unknown," Bell recalled.[10] Bell was frustrated when he could hear nothing but static. Bell even went so far as to buy a slab of meat and fire a bullet into it. His equipment performed flawlessly. But what the president's doctors had *neglected* to tell Bell was that the stricken Garfield lay on a steel-spring mattress. This caused static on the line. Some of those who had put their unwashed fingers into the president's wound now leaked word of Bell's failure to the press. Some in the press even accused Bell of being a faker.[11] Poor Bell was to learn that he had greater freedom in America than in his native Scotland, but he also lacked the protections of Britain's stringent libel laws.

America had survived her second presidential assassination in just sixteen years. Guiteau was soon tried, convicted, and hanged. There were lingering questions about whether President Arthur would align himself with the Stalwarts, or whether he would follow the path of reform laid out in Garfield's all-too-brief tenure.

Tall and distinguished looking, with great, bushy side whiskers, Arthur was a capable public official. His friends in New York knew him as "Our Chet." Fashionable and suave of manner, he soon returned champagne and whiskey to presidential receptions. That's all the Stalwarts got.[12] Arthur stunned them by signing the Pendleton Civil Service Reform Act in 1883. Arthur also committed the nation to a naval rebuilding program.

Arthur had burned too many bridges with the movers and shakers of the Republican Party, however, to be considered for a second term. We now know that he was secretly suffering from Bright's disease, a kidney malfunction. He died soon after leaving the White House. Contemporary Mark Twain put it well: "I am only one in fifty-five million, still in the opinion of this one fifty-five *millionth*, it would be hard to better President Arthur's administration."[13] Actually, Twain spoke for far more than his one voice. As a publisher generously said of Arthur: "No man ever entered the presidency so profoundly and widely distrusted, and no one ever retired . . . more generally respected."[14]

III. GROVER CLEVELAND'S DYNAMIC, TROUBLED AMERICA

In 1884, Americans elected Governor Grover Cleveland of New York, a Democrat, to be the twenty-second president. Cleveland was a large bear of a man, a bachelor with a drooping walrus mustache. He had a reputation for fighting for reform, even if that meant crossing his own party leaders. Publisher Joseph Pulitzer, an immigrant from Hungary, provided Cleveland's strongest appeal when he editorialized in his *New York World*: "There are four reasons for electing Cleveland: 1. He is an honest man. 2. He is an honest man. 3. He is an honest man. 4. He is an honest man."[15]

The country over which Cleveland presided was dynamic but troubled. The Republicans' ideal of free land, free labor, and free enterprise was a compelling one. But a worldwide agricultural depression that began in the 1870s hit the U.S. farm belt hard. Wheat sank from $1.19 a bushel in 1881 to just 49 cents in 1894. Corn slid from 63 cents a bushel to 18 cents during those years.[16] In order to increase their yields, farmers invested heavily in expensive new equipment. When credit contracted, though, farmers were left in perilous straits. That is why they increasingly demanded free coinage of silver, greenbacks, lower tariffs, *anything* to give them some relief. It was called Prairie Populism. It would express itself in the Granger Movement. At one point, as many as eight hundred thousand farmers signed on. Grangers tried "co-ops," schemes for *co-operative* action on storage and marketing of grains.[17] The Grange was a social and intellectual organization whose charter forbade it to engage in political activity. It was a simple matter, though, to gather farmers for a regular Grange meeting and then vote to "adjourn." Organizers would then harangue the assembled crowd on economics and politics. As the farm belt sank deeper into depression, Mary Lease ("the Kansas pythoness") exhorted farmers to "raise less corn and more *hell!*"[18]

The face of urban America was changing rapidly. From his first demonstration of his telephone in 1876 to 1885, Alexander Graham Bell had seen his Bell Telephone Company gain 134,000 subscribers, mostly in cities and towns. This was ten times as many subscribers as Britain recorded.[19] Thomas A. Edison invented the electric lightbulb in 1879 and created a sensation throughout the world. William H. Vanderbilt, one of the great shipping and railroad Vanderbilts, was an early financial backer of the incredible invention. So was banker J. Pierpont Morgan, who wrote about it to his brother-in-law in Paris: "Secrecy at the moment is so essential that I do not dare put it on paper. Subject is Edison's Electric light—importance can be realized from editorials in London Times . . . and the effect upon gas stocks which have declined 25–50% since rumors of Edison's success."[20]

What we see here is the support given by men of great wealth to the brilliant inventor in order to bring his new product to market in a timely manner. We also see the *dynamism* of free enterprise: even a rumor of an electric light depresses gas stocks overnight. They didn't attempt to stifle the electric light in order to "protect" the gas industry. Today, we know that gas suffers not at all from the competition of electricity. Americans now heat their homes with gas. But this episode teaches us that market vitality brings more and better products to more people at lower prices. It offers better lives for millions. Today's General Electric Company was brought into being by the creative genius of Thomas A. Edison.

America was in the middle of a second industrial revolution. U.S. steel production of twenty thousand tons right after the Civil War outstripped Great Britain by 1895, with six million tons.[21] And steel was used in new ways. Not only was it essential for railroad locomotives and, now, passenger and freight cars, steel was increasingly being used for major construction. The magnificent new Brooklyn Bridge that connected Manhattan, a part of New York City, to the independent city of Brooklyn was the creation of engineers John and Washington Roebling. Opened in 1883, the Brooklyn Bridge is still in daily use. Frenchman Gustave Eiffel provided a steel "skeleton" for the Statue of Liberty that would soon grace New York Harbor.* Andrew Carnegie—like Bell, a Scots immigrant—led the way in organizing the steel industry. (An expert *telegrapher* during the Civil War, Carnegie might have been thrown out of work, had he stayed put, by Bell's invention of the telephone.) John D. Rockefeller organized the Standard Oil Trust in 1879. The word *trust* came to describe the new form of industrial organization. But Rockefeller's methods—though they made possible a world transportation revolution that started in America—would arouse a nation against the growing power of trusts. The power the trusts exerted over the U.S. government was a matter of mounting concern in the late nineteenth century. Humorist Mark Twain captured this sentiment when he

---

* French writers denounced the engineer's famous Eiffel Tower when it opened in Paris in 1889. They called it too "American." In a real sense, it was. The steel undercarriage provided the basis for such modern skyscrapers as the Chrysler Building, the Empire State Building, and the now-destroyed World Trade Center.

said, "It is the foreign element that commits our crime. There is no native American criminal class—except Congress."

President Cleveland made no pretense of "running the country." Who could *run* such a vast nation? But he worked away diligently at the elegant *Resolute* desk given to the American people by Queen Victoria.* He braved the enmity of the powerful veterans lobby when he vetoed hundreds of private pension bills for Civil War soldiers. This was particularly *resolute* for one who had himself hired a substitute rather than serve in combat in the war. Yet Cleveland firmly believed that Congress was trying to give "shirkers and skedaddlers" a place at the public trough.[22]

Grover Cleveland was not all work and no play, however. The forty-eight-year-old bachelor found time to court the daughter of the very friend whose reputation he had so nobly guarded—the lovely Miss Frances Folsom. Although a wag might say she was half his age and not quite half his weight, it is a known fact that election as president notably *improves* a man's marital prospects.[23] He and Frances were married in the Executive Mansion on 2 June 1886. "The March King," John Philip Sousa—the son of Portuguese immigrants—led the Marine Band for the ceremony. It was the first such wedding there, but Cleveland thought it an inappropriate place to call a home. So he bought and refurbished a comfortable country house for his new bride and himself. Called Red Top, the house was in what is today the quiet, pleasant Washington neighborhood known as Cleveland Park.

According to a well-circulated story of the day, the new Mrs. Cleveland rousted her snoring husband to tell him there were *burglars* in the house. Sleepily, he reassured her, "No, no, my dear. In the *Senate* maybe, but not in the House."[24]

---

* The double pedestal desk made from the timbers of the HMS *Resolute* remained in the family quarters of the White House until President Kennedy had it moved to the Oval Office. There it remains to this day.

IV. THE GOLDEN DOOR

To the mournful skirl of bagpipes, the Seventy-Ninth New York Cameron Highlanders Regiment marched through the black-shrouded streets of Manhattan. The unit had been formed of Scottish immigrants from New York City. They sported full highland regalia, including kilts, Scottish military caps called *glengarries*, and coats of the highland cut. In July 1885, they marched in the funeral procession for General Ulysses S. Grant. Grieving Americans had waited in line for two days and two nights to file past the bier of the sixty-three-year-old victor of Appomattox. Grant was sincerely mourned throughout the country. General Winfield Scott Hancock led the mile-long procession. President Cleveland led the nation in mourning the departed hero. Luxurious private trains had been ordered up to bring the nation's new industrial elite to the fashionable event. The flashy display of wealth struck many people as tasteless. To them, it was a showy example of the excesses of the Gilded Age. But America's new class of entrepreneurs were proud of the free enterprise system. Grant's military exploits had saved it for them. Just as firmly, they believed that *their* industrial might had given Grant the sinews of victory. In the harbor, ironclad warships boomed a twenty-one-gun salute. Former presidents Hayes and Arthur stood guard at the general's tomb. Union generals Sherman and Sheridan were joined by ex-Confederate heroes Simon Bolivar Buckner and Fitzhugh Lee.[25]

Grant had won his last campaign. He ran a race against death to complete his *Personal Memoirs*. Less than a year before his death, Grant was diagnosed with cancer of the throat. It soon spread to his tongue. For much of the year, Grant was either groggy from pain medication or suffering so that even water felt like fire. Every quality that had made Grant a great general made him a great writer—courage, personal integrity, intense concentration, and a clear and compelling message. No one in war ever misunderstood a Grant order. Not even his enemies. Day after day, while the nation watched the drama, he doggedly wrote on.[26]

He had to. Grant was nearly destitute. In these days before generous pensions for ex-presidents, Grant sank all his money in the Wall Street investment firm of Grant & Ward. Ferdinand Ward, his younger partner, defaulted and defrauded him. As Ward headed off to prison, Grant and his family were ruined.[27]

Samuel Langhorne Clemens, better known to us as Mark Twain, came to Grant's rescue. His new publishing house offered Grant a most generous contract for his memoirs. A year later, Twain was able to hand Julia Grant a check for $200,000. At that time it was the largest royalty check ever written.[28]

In time, the *Personal Memoirs* of Ulysses S. Grant in two volumes sold three hundred thousand sets and earned $450,000 for Grant's heirs. Grant had produced a literary masterpiece. Civil War historian James McPherson has said of them: "To read the *Personal Memoirs* with a knowledge of the circumstances under which Grant wrote them is to gain insight into the reasons for his military success."[29] Robert E. Lee would have been a great man in any country, but U. S. Grant's story showed the unique possibilities of freedom in America.

Americans' attention focused once again on New York City in 1886. President Cleveland returned to lead the dedication ceremonies for the Statue of Liberty. Thousands crowded the shores to witness. As Frédéric-Auguste Bartholdi pulled away the giant French tricolor flag that had shrouded the great statue, the harbor scene erupted with noise and celebration. Naval vessels, passenger ships, and innumerable small boats in the harbor were decked with flags and bunting. Guns boomed, bands played, and horns blared. The president maintained his dignified repose even as the event chairman, New York Senator William Evarts, struggled in vain to make himself heard.

The event almost didn't come off. When the French donors completed the colossal figure, American fund-raising had failed to pay for construction of the solid pedestal on which the Lady would stand. Publisher Joseph Pulitzer did not turn cap-in-hand to the nation's new-rich titans to pay for the pedestal. In a stroke of marketing genius, his *New York World* appealed instead to the *children* of America to donate their pennies to the cause. While denouncing the provincialism of some Americans who had refused to donate to a monument to be sited in New York, Pulitzer also spurred New Yorkers to action by warning them that other American cities—Philadelphia, Boston, even Minneapolis—were bidding for the statue.[30]

Pulitzer's campaign sparked an art auction to raise funds "in aid of the Bartholdi pedestal." For this auction, the thirty-three-year-old poet Emma Lazarus wrote the words that would completely change the way the Statue of Liberty would be understood by succeeding generations. They are worth reading in full:

"The New Colossus"

Not like the brazen giant of Greek fame,
With conquering limbs astride from land to land;
Here at our sea-washed, sunset gates shall stand
A mighty woman with a torch, whose flame
Is the imprisoned lightning, and her name
Mother of Exiles. From her beacon-hand
Glows world-wide welcome; her mild eyes command
The air-bridged harbor that twin cities frame.[*]
"Keep ancient lands, your storied pomp!" cries she
with silent lips. "Give me your tired, your poor,
Your huddled masses yearning to breathe free,
The wretched refuse of your teeming shore.
Send these, the homeless, tempest-tost to me,
I lift my lamp beside the golden door!"

---

[*] The "twin cities" referred to here are New York and Brooklyn, then two separate municipalities. Lazarus's words would eventually be inscribed in the Statue's base.

Our French benefactors had three objectives in mind. First, they wanted to commemorate the centennial of the alliance between France and America. Second, they sought to inspire their fellow citizens of the *Third* French Republic to *emulate* America's republican ideals of *liberty and union*. Finally, they wanted to encourage *other* Europeans to cast off the outmoded idea of hereditary monarchy.

Artfully, Emma Lazarus's poem substituted her own powerful vision. "The New Colossus" made the Statue of Liberty a symbol for immigrants departing from Europe's "teeming shore" to enter America's "golden door." Lazarus's writing was an unparalleled example of what happens under freedom. The power of *words* to express new and different ideas could change what years of effort, hundreds of thousands of dollars of investment, 225 tons of steel, and a 305-foot-1-inch statue represented.[31] In this, too, America was an extraordinary place. Freedom of speech and of the press, freedom of religion—all this was opening new doors—actual doors *and* symbolic doors.

America has had lapses in her attempts to realize the ideals that Emma Lazarus raised on high with her awesome words. Think of the Chinese Exclusion Act that Grover Cleveland signed. Think of the turn-of-the-twentieth-century debates over "desirable" and "undesirable" immigrants. These arguments drew on a vulgarized Social Darwinism. Unjust and restrictive immigration laws were approved in the 1920s. These were followed in 1939 by the shame of turning away the SS *St. Louis*. Hundreds of desperate Jews were thereby doomed to face Hitler's wrath. In our own time, Vietnamese "boat people" have been welcomed. Even as we acknowledge the failure of Americans always to act on our own highest ideals, we must also point out that this nation has welcomed millions of people "yearning to breathe free." No other nation on earth has accorded to so many the blessings of liberty and opportunity. In the same decade during which America accepted the Statue of Liberty, our population soared a full 25 percent. In 1880, official census figures put U.S. population at 50,155,783. Of these, 13.1 percent were foreign-born.

These numbers rose by 1890 to comprise 62,947,714 Americans, of whom 14.5 percent were immigrants.[32] By any account, it is an astonishing record. No other country can match it.

The prominence of Joseph Pulitzer and Emma Lazarus in this story of the Statue of Liberty points to another important change in America's story of freedom. Pulitzer was a recent immigrant. Lazarus hailed from an old and distinguished New York family. Both were Jewish. America had had Jewish immigrants as early as 1654, when twenty-four Sephardic Jewish immigrants came to New Amsterdam.* It was in the latter part of the nineteenth century, however, that the numbers of European Jews would begin to increase significantly. As with so many other groups, Jews were drawn to freedom and opportunity in America, and they were repelled by militarism, political tyranny, and the lack of religious liberty in the old country.

In the case of Jewish immigrants, the spur of increasingly vicious anti-Semitism in Europe made America especially attractive. America was not just the "golden door" of Emma Lazarus's poem. In the Yiddish language of so many European Jews, America was *die goldeneh medina*— the golden land.

V. WINNING THE WEST

The only good Indian is a dead Indian.
—PHILIP H. SHERIDAN, 1869

Phil Sheridan was not a brutal man. He was a tough, battle-hardened Union cavalry commander who had laid waste the Shenandoah Valley. But we tend to remember men by such ill-considered and ugly sentiments. As Shakespeare's Marc Antony says in *Julius Caesar*: "The evil that men

---

* Sephardic Jews came to the New World from Spain and Portugal.

do lives after them; the good is oft interred with their bones." We are less likely to recall this more humane and, we might hope, more considered statement by General Sheridan: "We took away their country and their means of support, broke up their mode of living, their habits of life, introduced disease and decay among them, and it was for this and against this they made war. Could anyone expect less?"[33]

With the nation distracted by the Civil War in 1862, the frontier exploded. When Sioux from the Dakotas carried fire to Minnesota that year, they killed nearly a thousand settlers before being put down by the U.S. Army. Stories of murder, rape, and mutilation chilled the reading public. President Lincoln was beset by Union defeats and the death of his own son. Still, he took time to carefully review the trial records of every one of 303 condemned Sioux warriors. He pared down the list to 38. Even so, his clemency was attacked by Minnesota's Governor Ramsey. When Ramsey later came to Washington as a senator, he berated Lincoln. He blamed his merciful actions for Republican losses in the fall elections. "I could not afford to hang men for votes," Lincoln mildly replied.[34]

Lincoln's moderation was not untypical of presidents in the latter part of the nineteenth century. No president endorsed harsh policies toward the Indians. All presidents called for justice and mercy. But none of the presidents of this period pursued a peace policy with the single-minded determination that Jackson had pursued Indian removal in the 1830s.

With a sudden strike in the Black Hills in Dakota Territory ("There's gold in them thar hills!"), efforts to preserve lands for the Sioux collapsed.[35] When Sitting Bull and Crazy Horse surrounded and wiped out Colonel George Armstrong Custer and hundreds of his Seventh Cavalry troopers at the Battle of Little Big Horn in 1876, many Americans thirsted for revenge.

President Grant hoped that by recruiting religious leaders to help as Indian agents, he might pacify the Plains Indians with mild treatment—a "conquest by kindness." He told a visiting group of the Society of Friends, "If you can make Quakers out of the Indians, it will take the fight out of them." Then he applied his signature line: "Let us have peace."[36] Grant's appointment of Lawrie Tatum was characteristic of his attempt to find capable and honest Indian agents. Even the mild-mannered Tatum, however, eventually came to believe that force was needed. Neither President Grant's peace policy nor even Christian evangelism was the answer to the stubborn ferocity of the Plains Indians, Tatum thought.[37] No one in American history showed greater goodwill toward the Indians than U. S. Grant. Yet his policy was not notably more successful.

Indians were forced off tribal reserves in Montana territory (Crow and Blackfeet) and the new state of Colorado (Utes).[38] Chief Joseph of the Nez Percé Indians struck back when gold-hungry prospectors invaded his lands in the Idaho Territory. He led U.S. Army troops on a long, exhausting chase as he fled toward the Canadian border. His tactics continue to be studied at military staff colleges to this day, but he was eventually brought to ground less than thirty miles from his refuge. Eloquently, he told his disheartened people he would surrender (5 October 1877): "Hear me, my chiefs. I am tired; my heart is sick and sad. From where the sun now stands I will fight no more forever."[39]

The right path eluded leaders of both parties and all segments of society. Railroad men and hunters used the new mobility made possible by the trains to shoot hundreds of thousands of buffalo. They killed far more than they needed to feed construction crews and settlers. It was a shocking spectacle to see hundreds of magnificent bison left to rot in the sun. The buffalo slaughter was *not* unprecedented, however. The Indians themselves sometimes drove whole herds off cliffs, taking only their tongues—a prized delicacy.

An old Sioux spoke for all the tribes when he said, "They made us many promises, more than I can remember. But they never kept but one; they promised to take our land and they took it."[40] Fitfully, the government tried to mend its ways. In 1887, spurred by the protests of such reformers as Carl Schurz, Bishop Henry Whipple, and authors like Helen Hunt Jackson, Congress passed the Dawes Act. President Cleveland signed it. Under this act, the government gave incentives to Indians to become individual homesteaders. But even with title to their lands, Indians were inexperienced in agriculture. They could not afford the increasingly heavy investment required to put land in crops. Thus, they remained prey for unscrupulous land speculators.[41]

In this instance, some of the institutions of American freedom could frustrate justice. Most Americans wanted justice for the Indians. These Americans lived in the burgeoning cities and populous states of the East and Midwest. They were far away from the frontier. Frontier juries were composed of men who could remember horrible Indian raids. In many cases, members of their own families had been slaughtered. It was exceedingly difficult to get such juries to convict settlers accused of crimes against the Indians.

In 1890, ironically, almost at the moment the Census Bureau announced the closing of the American frontier, a tragic clash occurred at Wounded Knee in the Dakota Territory. Five hundred U.S. soldiers attempted to disarm a small band of Sioux led by Chief Big Foot. They ran into resistance. The phenomenon of "Ghost Dancing" had raised apprehension on all sides. Suddenly, a tribal medicine man threw dirt into the air, a signal for warriors to shoot. They would not die, he assured them, because they were dressed in "ghost shirts." Fierce hand-to-hand fighting ensued. A Sioux warrior, firing a Winchester rifle, took off Captain George C. Wallace's head. When the troopers withdrew, other soldiers opened up with deadly Hotchkiss guns. The rapid fire killed at least 150 and wounded 50. Many of the dead included women and children caught in the crossfire.[42] It was a terrible and discreditable episode, but it was not the unprovoked and willful massacre that has been portrayed by Hollywood. The military force in the West was always one-sided, but that did not mean the violence was one-sided. Before he was subdued, the Apache leader Geronimo eluded capture for fifteen years. In that time, he managed to kill 2,500 U.S. citizens.[43]

The Dakota country also beckoned a young New Yorker. Theodore

Roosevelt Jr. had barely begun his political career as an assemblyman in the Empire State when a double tragedy struck. On a single day—14 February 1884—his mother and his beautiful young wife died in the same Manhattan brownstone house. Valentine's Day would never again be mentioned in the Roosevelt family. Overwhelmed by grief, TR "lit out for the territories." He invested a major portion of his inheritance in a ranch in the Dakota Territory. There, the spindly young aristocrat would become hardened by the challenges that made frontier life always a danger. He faced cattle stampedes, floods, and blizzards.

Once, he had himself deputized by the sheriff so he could pursue some shiftless men who had stolen his worthless boat. The wealthy easterner didn't *need* the boat. But the code of the Badlands said that a man was not a man if he let the riffraff trifle with him. TR captured his outlaws and dragged them back to face justice.* Later, he walked into a saloon. There, an armed, drunken bully drew his six-guns and announced that "Four-eyes" would be buying the house a round of drinks. "Four-eyes" was a reference to TR's milk-bottle-thick pince-nez eyeglasses. TR records what happened next:

> He stood leaning over me, a gun in each hand, using very foul language. He was foolish to stand so near, and, moreover, his heels were close together so that his position was unstable. Accordingly, in response to his reiterated command that I should set up the drinks, I said: "Well, if I've got to, I've got to," and rose, looking past him. As I rose, I struck quick and hard with my right just to one side of the point of his jaw, hitting with my left as I straightened out, and then again with my right. He fired his guns, but I do not know whether this was merely a convulsive

---

* Significantly, he did *not* exact his own punishment. Many a horse thief and cattle rustler would be lynched in the West. The institutions of justice were sometimes slow to keep up with the pace of settlement. In Canada, the Dominion government kept a stricter rein on settlement and, hence, the "Wild West" never really applied where the Royal Canadian Mounted Police ("Mounties") held sway.

action of his hands or whether he was trying to shoot at me. When he went down, he struck the corner of the bar with his head. It was not a case in which one could afford to take chances, and if he had moved I was about to drop on his ribs with my knees; but he was senseless.[44]

TR's vivid experiences in the West would change his life and the life of his country. His colorful writing would fire the imagination of an entire generation. He never forgot the Badlands. Nor did he let anyone *else* forget. In this, he was part of the unique American tradition of westward pioneers that stretched from George Washington and Daniel Boone through Lewis and Clark and the Mountain Men.

More than this, TR's experiences in the West made him a lifelong conservationist. Thoughtful Americans read TR as they read the writings of John Muir on "The Treasures of the Yosemite"[*] and John Wesley Powell on the Grand Canyon[**] and resolved to save the vanishing wilderness. From this era of rampant development and often heedless exploitation of natural resources, we can also date the first of America's great national parks.[***] In this, America's Indians may have had their influence. In their native religion, the "purple mountains' majesty" was not simply awe-inspiring, it was *sacred*. TR helped all Americans appreciate the priceless treasure that is the West.

VI. A SOCIAL GOSPEL

At the same time the West was being won, many powerful men thought *they* were God's instruments to modernize their country and bring more

---

* "The Treasures of the Yosemite," *Century Magazine* 40, no. 4, August 1890.

** Powell, J. W. (1875), *Exploration of the Colorado River of the West and Its Tributaries.*

*** President Grant signed legislation as early as 1872 creating Yellowstone National Park, another of his great and too-little-appreciated achievements.

goods and services to more people at cheaper prices. That this vital process also involved child labor and mothers toiling away in "sweatshops" did not trouble these new captains of industry. For industrial workers who worked for ten hours a day, the titans' protestations of God's benevolence soon wore thin. "You'll have pie in the sky when you die" was a bitter and biting commentary on the consolations of religion.

As it always has, the reforming spirit in America called out for *action* to correct abuses. Jane Addams was determined to do something about the conditions she saw in the crowded immigrant slums of Chicago. In 1889 she opened Hull House, a settlement house (named after the building's original owner, Charles Hull) that helped working-class people, many of them immigrants.

Jane Addams's settlement house work would provide shelter and affection for thousands. Everything from maternal care and education to concerts and lessons in citizenship and philosophy could be found at Hull House. Americans complained that the immigrants smelled bad. Jane Addams provided bathtubs—and recorded the eagerness with which they were used. Miss Addams struck to the heart of Americans' profession of Christian principles when she pointed out that we gave the immigrant man the vote, but "dub him with epithets deriding his past or present occupation, and feel no duty to invite him into our homes."[45] She called for a democracy that opened doors.

Decades before child psychologists noted a "failure-to-thrive" syndrome, Jane Addams had it pegged. "We are told that the 'will to live' is aroused in each baby by his mother's irresistible love for him, the physiological value of joy that a child is born, and that the high death rate in institutions is increased by 'the discontented babies' whom no one 'persuades into living.'"[46] Boys' clubs, girls' clubs, meeting places for working mothers to organize—a union! This was Hull House's daily fare. Seeing in her efforts to give practical help to the poor the "spirit of Christ," Jane Addams said: "If you don't take charge of a child at night, you can't feel a scared trembling little hand grow confiding and quiet as soon as it lies within your own. If you don't take little children out in the yard to spend the morning you can't see their unbounded delight and extravagant joy when they see a robin taking his bath."[47]

The meat-packing trust, the railroad trust, the oil trust, the steel trust. It was an age dominated by the *trusts*. Still an older kind of trust was shown by the knot of weary, smoke-stained firemen who crowded into the parlor of Hull House one cold midnight. There had been a fire in the stables. The horses were not all dead. Many were just horribly burned. It took a court order to discharge a firearm within city limits, and the courts were closed until the morning. Meanwhile, the horses were in agony. Could *Miss Addams* authorize these hardened men to shoot the poor horses? "I have no *legal* authority but I will take the responsibility," she said. She didn't go back to bed, but rode with the firemen to stand watch while they put the horses out of their misery.[48]

We tend today to think of such saintliness as very remote, almost unbelievable. Mother Teresa is believable. The Calcutta streets where she ministered to untouchables who were dying in the ditch are half a world away. But such grace was seen here, too, with an American accent, in Chicago.

VII. "A CROSS OF GOLD"

Cleveland's commitment to lower tariffs cost him reelection in 1888. Republicans chose Benjamin Harrison of Indiana. Harrison was the grandson of William Henry Harrison and also a war hero. Skillfully, Republican campaign operatives worked among the Irish Americans in New York. They showed Cleveland doing the bidding of the British Empire in lowering the "protective" tariff. Their campaign literature showed Cleveland wrapped in the Union Jack while Harrison waved the Stars and Stripes. Cleveland, they charged, was "employed by Ireland's cruel enemy to aid her work of enslavement."[49] It worked.

Cleveland actually won *more* popular votes nationally than Harrison did. Harrison had carried New York State by 14,363 votes—a mere 1.1 percent. With New York's 36 electoral votes, Harrison was elected. Only twice since Lincoln in 1860 had New York failed to go with the winner. Often, New York provided the winning margin in the electoral college. The need to carry New York's large contingent of black voters and immigrants, including many Catholics and Jews, gave increased attention to minority concerns. Thus, the Founders' wisdom in creating an electoral college was confirmed once again. The electoral college has usually operated to protect minorities from majority tyranny. And minority rights are essential to freedom.

Cleveland never questioned the result. He did not complain that the election had been stolen from him. Nor did he disavow his views on the tariff. "I would rather have my name [on] that tariff measure," he said of the bill he signed to lower import duties, "than be president."[50]

Republicans sincerely believed that high tariffs were necessary not only to protect young American industries but also to protect the working man. They rejected the arguments of free traders that competition would cause every boat to be lifted by a rising tide of prosperity.

In addition to battles over the tariff, politics came to be dominated by arguments over the currency. Grover Cleveland agreed with many easterners, including most Republicans, that the nation needed to stand squarely on the gold standard—a system in which the government issued gold coins and backed every paper dollar with a dollar's worth of gold. These "goldbugs," however, were opposed by advocates for the free coinage of silver and by those who wanted to inflate the currency by printing "greenbacks." "Why should this Grand and Glorious Country be stunted and dwarfed—its activities chilled and its very life blood curdled by these miserable 'hard coin' theories, the musty theories of a bygone age?" asked Jay Cooke, an opponent of the gold standard.[51]

President Harrison presided over three critically important pieces of legislation, two of which were sponsored by Ohio Republican Senator John Sherman (General Sherman's brother).

The Sherman Anti-Trust Act of 1890 was the first attempt to control "every contract, combination in the form of trust or otherwise, or conspiracy, in restraint of trade or commerce among the several States or with foreign nations." A certain vagueness in the definition of the law's terms would give the U.S. Supreme Court an opportunity to apply its provisions to *labor* unions.[52]

President Benjamin Harrison also signed in 1890 the Sherman Silver Purchase Act. This bill represented some "logrolling" by western state Congressmen who favored *bi-metallism*, which regarded both gold *and* silver as the basis for the currency.[53] In return for easterners backing them on silver, these westerners supported the McKinley Tariff Act that reversed Cleveland's lowering of duties.

The McKinley Tariff of 1890 raised rates to the highest levels in history. It also raised prices sharply even as it raised *havoc* with the Republicans' election prospects that year. Only 88 members of the GOP were returned to the House of Representatives, as opposed to 235 Democrats![54]

These sharp fluctuations in tariffs created a mood of uncertainty in the nation's financial institutions. This instability was felt—*painfully*—in the nation's farm belt. There, the new Populist (People's) Party appealed for votes from desperate farmers. Once again, Mary Lease spoke for many:

> We were told two years ago to go to work and raise a big crop, that was all we needed. We went to work and plowed and planted; the rains fell, the sun shone, nature smiled, and we raised the big crop they told us to and what came of it? Eight-cent corn, ten-cent oats, two-cent beef, and no price at all for butter and eggs—that's what came of it. Then the politicians said that we suffered from over-production![55*]

Overproduction would hardly have been possible for most farming communities before the nineteenth century. Cyrus Hall McCormick's

---

* Mary Lease spoke in a verbal shorthand that farmers readily understood. She meant eight cents and ten cents for a bushel of corn and oats, respectively, and two cents for a pound of beef.

reaper helped make America an agricultural force in world markets by the 1880s.[56]

Cultivation of the rich, loamy soil of the Midwest might not have been possible at all had it not been for "the plough that broke the plains." John Deere was a young Vermont blacksmith who took Horace Greeley's advice to "Go west, young man." Deere settled in Illinois. There, his highly polished steel hay forks and shovels made his reputation. Soon, farmers were coming to him with a serious problem. The cast iron plows they had brought from home were adequate for New England's sandy soil. But here, the rich, fertile soil of the Midwest clung to the mold-board, requiring farmers to stop every few feet to clear it. Deere imported high-grade polished steel from England and developed a "self-scouring" plow that revolutionized agriculture around the world. One hundred fifty years later, the company slogan—"Nothing runs like a Deere"—could be traced to that first John Deere plow.[57]

Plows, combines, reapers—all these required far more cash investment than subsistence farming. It explains why so many immigrants and so many newly enfranchised black Southerners were unable to take advantage of the generous Homestead Act passed during Lincoln's term. Two-thirds of the four hundred thousand who accepted the government's 160-acre land grant eventually gave up on farming.[58] Frederick Douglass knew these daunting odds. He appealed to black Southerners *not* to join the "Exodusters" who fled discrimination for the open prairies. He called on them, instead, to stand and fight for their rights in their home states.[59]

"The Communist is here!" That was the caption on a brilliant Thomas Nast cartoon. As early as 1874, Nast depicted a workingman and his poor family being lured into a parade by a beckoning skeleton. The cartoon is clear evidence of the fear and loathing Communism spread among millions of Americans. That Communism could bring death could hardly be doubted. The world had been shocked and horrified by the bloody uprising of the Paris Commune in 1871 (and the even bloodier suppression of the *communards* by the military forces of the Third

French Republic). Nast's dramatic rendering of the workman, pulled away from his weeping wife and child, included a typically nasty libel: Nast showed the Communist skeleton in the characteristic garb of the Ancient Order of Hibernians—an Irish Catholic fraternal group—decked out for a St. Patrick's Day parade.*

Nast doubtless thought the violence practiced by such unorganized groups as the Molly Maguires in the Pennsylvania coalfields was a trait of all the Irish Americans in labor. Those groups gained sympathy in America with such legitimate tactics as the boycott. When their opposition to brutal conditions in the mines extended to intimidation of other workers and allegedly to the murder of mine company officials, however, they lost public support.[60]

In truth, Irish Americans in particular and Catholics in general were to prove themselves tireless advocates for organized labor and against Communism. The history of American organized labor is replete with such Irish names as Terence Vincent Powderly of the Knights of Labor, John Mitchell of the United Mine Workers, and more recently, George Meany, longtime president of the AFL-CIO. All resisted the siren song of Karl Marx's *Communist Manifesto*.

Samuel Gompers was backed strongly as leader of the rising labor movement by the Irish in the American Federation of Labor (A. F. of L.). Gompers was a Jewish immigrant from England. He fiercely resisted Communist and Socialist influence in the labor movement.[61] He wanted *economic* action only. He rejected any wholesale plan for political action to remake America's democratic form of government. When asked what the workingman wanted, Gompers answered succinctly, "More." More pay, more time off, more protection from dangerous accidents on the job. More benefits for old age. *More.*

Gompers's only interest in politics was to "reward our friends and punish our enemies."[62] His influence is a major reason why the United States never developed a Labor Party as England and so many European

---

* The gifted Nast gave us our modern benign image of Santa Claus—Saint Nicholas. Apparently, Nast was blithely unaware of the good saint's very Catholic antecedents.

states did. Gompers's natural sympathy for the workingman also rejected trade unionism for whites only. Gompers never sought to run the government; he simply wanted *more* for his members.

Henry Clay Frick was an avowed enemy of labor unions. When his boss, Andrew Carnegie, set sail for a sentimental return to Scotland in 1892, Frick used the occasion to slash wages for the Amalgamated Iron and Steel Workers Union. Frick wanted to break the union. He refused even to talk to the union leaders. When the workers went out on strike, he hired Pinkerton Company agents as a private police force to take over the Carnegie Company's steel plant at Homestead, Pennsylvania.[63] The *New York Tribune* reported that the Pinkertons fired first from their boat as it approached the plant's riverside entrance.[64] In the clash that followed, thirteen died and one hundred were wounded. From Scotland, an agitated Carnegie called for federal troops to be called out.[65] He wanted them to break the strike. Frick overcame an anarchist's bullet, so determined was he to teach Carnegie's employees "a lesson they will never forget."[66] Carnegie valued his image as a progressive employer. He was appalled when London newspapers condemned him while he was making his Scottish homecoming tour. Those press accounts of the strike soured what he'd long looked forward to as a triumphal return to the land of his birth.

The Homestead Strike was not the most violent clash of the Gilded Age. But it still echoed throughout the world. It was a problem for Carnegie, who had written of his paternal responsibility in his widely read book, *The Gospel of Wealth*. With his many charitable activities—endowing libraries, concert halls, colleges—he claimed to be exercising an enlightened stewardship of the resources God had given him. He was a world figure. He entertained Russian composer Pyotr Illyich Tchaikovsky. The maestro conducted the opening performance at New York's Carnegie Hall.[67] The capitalist system, Carnegie wrote,

> is best calculated to produce the most beneficial result for the community—the man of wealth thus becoming the sole agent and

trustee for his poorer brethren, bringing to their service his superior wisdom, experience, and ability to administer—doing for them better than they would or could do for themselves.[68]

On the other hand, his workers put in twelve-hour days with only Sundays, Christmas, and the Fourth of July off.[69] A skilled worker might make $280 a month, but unskilled laborers worked for fourteen cents an hour, less than $50 a month. There were rivalries to be exploited between older stock workers—Irish, Welsh, English, and Germans—and newer, less skilled immigrant workers. These hailed from Hungary, Bohemia, Italy, and Poland.[70] Steelworker Andrew Keppler died in one of the terrible industrial accidents. Molten metal had spilled out of a ladle. His friends tried frantically to pry his body loose, but he had to be buried in the slab of steel.[71] There were three hundred such deaths each year in Carnegie's mills.[72]

The irrepressible Mary Lease had this sharp response to Carnegie's *Gospel of Wealth*: "You may call me an anarchist, a socialist or a communist, I care not, but I hold to the theory that if one man has not enough to eat three meals a day and another man has $25,000,000, that last man has something that belongs to the first."[73]

Republican leaders appealed to Carnegie not to slash wages—at least not in an election year.[74] But Henry Clay Frick—acting on Carnegie's orders—won his battle with the union. The steel industry would not be organized for another fifty years. One of Andrew Keppler's friends said later it was the anarchist's bullet that had pierced the heart of the strike.[75]

Grover Cleveland, running for a second term, denounced Henry Clay Frick for "the exactions wrung from [labor] to build up and increase the fortunes" of the very rich. Workers, he said, "have the right to insist on the permanency of their employment."[76]

Benjamin Harrison was intelligent, honest, and hardworking. He was also aloof and colorless. Few Americans were strongly attracted to him. His two most outstanding appointments were rather low-ranking ones:

Frederick Douglass as U.S. minister to Haiti and Theodore Roosevelt as a civil service commissioner.

When Frances Folsom Cleveland left the White House on 4 March 1889, she had told the head usher to take good care of the place because she expected to return. Asked when that would be, she gave him a charming smile and said, "Four years from today."[77]

And so she did.

Carnegie himself said that the Homestead Strike had elected Cleveland in 1892.[78] Grover Cleveland's two nonconsecutive terms make him unique among American presidents.* The Populist Party nominee, James Baird Weaver, polled more than one million votes. He carried several western states that previously had backed the Republicans.

Cleveland would soon have reason to wish he had lost the 1892 election. A series of bank failures resulted in the Panic of 1893 and the country slid into a severe depression.[79] Hard times would shadow Cleveland's unhappy second term. When a wealthy New Yorker brought his son to the Executive Mansion to meet the president, Cleveland patted the boy on the head. "My little man," he told young Franklin Delano Roosevelt, "I am making a strange wish for you. It is that you may never be President of the United States."[80] Faithful to his convictions, he persuaded Congress to *repeal* the Silver Purchase Act of 1890. Farmers felt betrayed.

Worse, Cleveland received a devastating doctor's report: he had cancer of the jaw. In these days before radiation or chemotherapy, surgery was the only hope. But the president's condition had to be kept secret. With the panic at its height, the thought of the president's going under the knife could have wrecked the nation's economy. This was especially the case since Vice President Adlai E. Stevenson was a committed *silver* advocate.**

---

* It's a record unlikely to be repeated, since parties today shun one-term presidents who fail in their reelection bids. Imagine Jimmy Carter running in 1984 or George H. W. Bush making a second bid in 1996.

** Vice President Stevenson was the grandfather of Illinois Governor Adlai E. Stevenson, who twice ran unsuccessfully for president against Dwight D. Eisenhower in the 1950s.

Casually, the president went onboard a yacht owned by one of his wealthy friends. The *Oneida*, anchored in New York's East River, became a floating operating room. He told the yacht's skipper: "If you hit a rock, hit it good and hard so that we all go to the bottom."[81] With part of his jaw removed, the president emerged to an unsuspecting public.

Cleveland would seriously alienate labor by his conduct in the 1894 Pullman Strike. George Pullman had invented the railway "sleeper" car. Pullman envisioned an ideal of industrial paternalism. His company town outside Chicago was a model. The Pullman Company provided rental housing for factory workers. Company literature boasted, "All that is ugly and discordant and demoralizing is eliminated, and all that inspires to self-respect is generously provided."[82] Reality was not quite up to this ideal. High rents forced families to accept lodgers.[83] Pullman's policy of giving hiring preference to residents of company housing meant that a worker who moved out risked losing his job. Rents remained high as wages were slashed during the deepening depression. Families were left with mere pennies after their rent was deducted from pay envelopes.[84]

Eugene Victor Debs's American Railway Union (ARU) went out on strike. With workers refusing to handle Pullman cars, the federal government claimed the U.S. Mail was not getting through. Even though the union tried to make an exception for mail cars, President Cleveland ordered in federal troops to assure delivery of the mails. Debs appealed to the American Federation of Labor's leader for support. Samuel Gompers turned him down. He thought it was a bad time to risk a strike. If Debs persisted, Gompers and the A. F. of L. leadership feared the ARU would be broken.[85]

"If it takes every soldier in the United States to deliver a postal card in Chicago, that postal card should be delivered," Cleveland vowed.[86] The Pullman Strike was broken, and Debs was jailed for violating a court injunction. While in prison, Debs read Karl Marx and became a Socialist.

Gompers was proven right about the strike, but he took little comfort from it. He wrote a strong letter to President Cleveland, protesting against his calling out the troops. "[T]he people have answered at the polls your . . . use of the military power to crush labor," Gompers wrote after Democrats suffered heavy losses in the 1894 congressional elections. "Though the change may benefit us little, the rebuke will nevertheless be appreciated and remembered."[87]

The Pullman Strike was just one of 1,300 strikes in 1894.[88] It was a dramatic example of the use of court *injunctions* against labor. And Gompers's A. F. of L. would continue trying to "reward our friends and punish our enemies."

As in all depressions, black Americans suffered greatly. Added to economic misfortune was the rising power of segregation. Ida Wells had exposed the national shame of lynchings in her writings. Early in her career, Frederick Douglass inspired her. Now, *she* inspired *him*.[89]

In 1894, he rose to the challenge in a speech titled "The Lessons of the Hour."

In it, he denounced the charge of *rape*. Why is it that no one charged rape when white women were alone on Southern plantations during the Civil War?, he asked pointedly.

The real purpose of the spurious charge, he said, was to disenfranchise the black man. The hateful cry of rape was raised, he said, "simultaneously with well-known efforts now being . . . made to degrade the Negro by legislative enactments, and by repealing all laws for the protection of the ballot, and by drawing the color line in all railroad cars and stations and in all other public places in the south."[90]

Frederick Douglass then turned on some in his own community who had sought relief from injustice through emigration to Africa. Douglass didn't even want his fellow black Americans to *identify* with Africa: "All of this native land talk is nonsense. The native land of the American Negro is America. His bones, his muscles, his sinews are all American. His ancestors for two hundred and seventy years have lived, and labored, and died on American soil."[91]

It was to be his last, great effort. Even as the shadow of Jim Crow stalked the land, Douglass never gave in. Asked by a young follower what he should do with his life, he answered fiercely, "Agitate. Agitate. Agitate." In 1895, he collapsed and died at his stately Cedar Hill home in Washington, D.C. He was mourned throughout the world. Elizabeth Cady Stanton, the great leader for women's suffrage, recalled her first meeting with him: "All the other speakers seemed tame after Frederick Douglass. He stood there like an African prince, majestic in his wrath."[92]

Poet Vachel Lindsay wrote of *another* American majestic in his wrath. The election of 1896 presented a fundamental challenge to American democracy. The depression had made men desperate. William Jennings Bryan spoke to that desperation:

> Prairie avenger, mountain lion,
> Bryan, Bryan, Bryan, Bryan,
> Gigantic troubadour, speaking like a siege gun,
> Smashing Plymouth Rock with his boulders from the West.

The thirty-six-year-old Nebraska delegate to the 1896 Democratic National Convention had a chance to reach a great crowd with his address on the party platform. That platform was a direct repudiation of Grover Cleveland, the Democrat then sitting in the Executive Mansion. No matter, all over the country people blamed the gold standard for the worst depression in living memory. As Bryan concluded his speech, the delegates were swept away with emotion. His fiery ending captured their hearts:

> Having behind us the producing masses of this nation and the world, supported by the commercial interests, the laboring interests, and the toilers everywhere, we will answer their demand for a gold standard by saying to them: You shall not press down upon the brow of labor this crown of thorns, you shall not crucify mankind upon a cross of gold.

It was hard to defend a gold standard during times of "tight money"— that is, during a depression or during times of high interest rates.

Essentially, what a gold standard means is that the federal government will use gold as the currency, or issue "notes" that can be exchanged for gold. To go "off the gold standard" creates inflation. Inflation is always favored by people in debt because it means they can pay back what they owe in depreciated dollars.

Barrel-chested and balding, Bryan was fully capable of making the rafters ring with the power of his voice. His "Cross of Gold" speech swept him to the party's nomination for president. (His achievement is not *quite* as impressive as it seems. Many of the party's senior leaders knew that defeat was the usual fate of a political party that holds the presidency in times of great economic hardship.*)

Undeterred by the daunting task of mounting a campaign in opposition to the Republicans *and* the Cleveland Democrats, Bryan won the endorsement of the Populist Party. He then undertook an unprecedented whistle-stop tour of thirteen thousand miles by train to reach the voters.[93] He spoke to hundreds of thousands.

The prairies seemed on fire with Bryan's hot rhetoric. He told the farmers how important they were to the nation's well-being: "Burn down your cities and leave our farms, and your cities will spring up again as if by magic; but destroy our farms and the grass will grow in the streets of every city in the country."

Against Bryan, the Republicans had nominated William McKinley, author of the McKinley Tariff. McKinley had served in Congress from Ohio and now served as governor of the Buckeye State. His campaign presented the perfect contrast to Bryan's frenetic stumping around the country. The Republican Party brought thousands of citizens *to their candidate*. Staging a "front porch campaign," McKinley addressed these polite, orderly crowds, offering them staid homilies and comfortable platitudes. He may have been put down as "a bronze in search of a pedestal,"

---

* If Democratic Party leaders thought they could give Bryan a worthless nomination and thereby be rid of him, they miscalculated. Bryan would be their party's standard bearer in three national contests and a major figure in the party until his death in 1925!

but he presented Americans with a figure of dignity and solidity to compare with Bryan's impassioned rabble-rousing.[94] And given a choice, Americans usually prefer dull to dangerous.

Senator Mark Hanna ran McKinley's campaign for him. Hanna stressed McKinley's respectable Civil War record, always a plus for presidential candidates.* Hanna was a wily political boss who "assessed" Big Business for campaign contributions. Voters were told that McKinley was "the advance agent of prosperity." Some workers got the hint when employers said if Bryan was elected on Tuesday, don't bother showing up for work on Wednesday.[95]

When the votes were tallied, McKinley swept the Northwest and the industrial Midwest. He was elected with 7,104,779 popular votes (50.2 percent) and 271 electoral votes. Bryan got 6,502,925 popular votes (46 percent) and 176 electoral votes. It was a very respectable showing for a young Democrat who had held no significant office. This race would make Bryan a national figure for a generation.

While Bryan was setting the prairies afire, Theodore Roosevelt remained *incombustible*:

> Mr. Bryan is appealing more and more openly to the base malignancy and hatred of those demagogues who strive to lead laboring men to ruin, in order to wreak their vengeance on the thrifty and well-to-do. He advocates principles sufficiently silly and wicked to make them fit well in the mouth of the anarchist leader. For the government of Washington and Lincoln, for the system of orderly liberty bequeathed to us by our forefathers, he would substitute a welter of lawlessness as fantastic and as vicious as the dream of a European communist. . . . Instead of a government of the people, by the people, for the people, which we now have, Mr. Bryan would substitute a government of the mob.[96]

---

* McKinley had served as a young sergeant in the same Ohio unit in which Rutherford B. Hayes had been a general.

VIII. "FROM THE NEW WORLD"

For four hundred years, America had been known to Europe as the New World. America in the late nineteenth century still held a fascination for Old Europe. When Czech composer Antonín Dvořák came to New York in 1892, he was inspired by the legend of Hiawatha. While in New York, he would compose his Symphony No. 9—*From the New World*—for a debut at Carnegie Hall. Jeannette Thurber had engaged Dvořák to make the journey from Prague to New York to lead the National Conservatory of Music. Mrs. Thurber was the wife of a wealthy merchant.[97] The very practical son of Bohemian peasants, Dvořák jumped at the opportunity to make *twenty times* what he had been earning under the Austro-Hungarian Empire. Dvořák was quite taken with what were then called Negro spirituals. Henry Burleigh often sang them for the great composer in his home. He said Dvořák "saturated himself in the spirit of these old tunes."[98] Dvořák appreciated Mrs. Thurber's concern for a distinctively *American* music. "I am convinced that the future music of this country must be founded on what are called Negro melodies," he told her. "These can be the foundation of a serious and original school of composition, to be developed in the United States. These beautiful and varied themes are the product of the soil. They are the folk songs of America and your composers must turn to them."[99]

When he became homesick, Dvořák left New York for Iowa for a working vacation. Dvořák would take a bucket of beer down to the Mississippi River to take in the songs and spirit of manual laborers. There, in the Bohemian immigrant colony of Spillville, he completed the Ninth Symphony. He especially enjoyed seeing Indians perform the music and dance of their people. Conductor Leonard Bernstein would later trace the major themes in Dvořák's *From the New World*. Dvořák had drawn on Czech, French, Scottish, German, and even Chinese sources.[100] In this one powerful work, we see the theme of the American "melting pot."

The new rich elites of America's Gilded Age have many critics, both then and now. It cannot be forgotten, however, that they contributed mightily to the power and dynamism of the great and free republic. They also outdid themselves in acts of charity and high culture. Not only did they seek to preserve the best of European civilization, but in patronizing an artist like Antonín Dvořák, they fostered new and beautiful contributions to world culture.

It is true that there was much political corruption in the Gilded Age. But there was arguably even more corruption abroad in Europe and other parts of the world. We can be proud of those called to the highest office in America during this era. Garfield and Arthur rose above questionable conduct in their pasts to set a fine example in the White House. America's other presidents in this period—Hayes, Harrison, and Cleveland—were honorable, diligent, and serious-minded. Given this era of revolutionary change, and comparing America's development to other countries, this is an estimable record, more glittering than gilded.

ELEVEN

THE AMERICAN DYNAMO— SHADOWED BY WAR

(1897–1914)

I. "A SPLENDID LITTLE WAR"

Commissioner Theodore Roosevelt stalked the streets of New York City at night. As the most visible member of the city's Police Board, he had gained a reputation for surprising members of "New York's Finest" who were not exactly fulfilling their duties. To make sure that his night patrols would not go unnoticed by the press, TR took along his friend Jacob Riis, a Jewish immigrant from Denmark. Riis was a journalist who was making a name for himself as a reformer.

Outside a restaurant late one night, Roosevelt and Riis saw the owner impatiently rapping on the street with his stick. "Where *does* that copper sleep?" the owner barked with irritation. He was not aware that the man he was addressing was in fact the president of the city's Police Board.[1]

The public loved reading the adventures of their night-stalking "com-mish." TR was called "Haroun al Rashid Roosevelt," after the famous vizier of Baghdad who moved in disguise among his people.[2] But he wasn't always loved by his men. Some of the sleeping constables, shown up by TR's antics, tried to get even. One night, they raided a society dinner at which "Little Egypt," an exotic-dancing sensation of the Chicago Columbian Exposition, planned to do her thing. Roosevelt was said to be present, and they hoped to nail him. For once, however, Commissioner Roosevelt was asleep in his New York mansion. TR laughed when told of the renegade policemen's attempt to embarrass him. He had been at home all night with his wife, Edith, and their growing young family.

Jake Riis must have been puzzled when his friend announced that a German pastor—a notorious anti-Semite—would indeed be allowed to give a speech in New York City. Teddy was, after all, a firm advocate of free speech. But to underscore his own feelings about the speaker's hate-filled message, TR took care to provide an escort of large, muscular patrolmen from the NYPD—every one of them Jewish.

When William McKinley returned Republicans to power in Washington in 1897—after the dignified rule of Grover Cleveland—he appointed Roosevelt to be assistant secretary of the navy. Naval affairs were one of TR's passions. A friend had once described him as a many-sided man and "every side was like an electric battery."[3] Teddy the battery soon gave the navy a jolt.

The United States had been viewing developments in nearby Cuba with mounting concern for nearly fifty years. Prior to the Civil War, various proslavery "filibusters" wanted to seize this "Pearl of the Antilles" from the weakening grasp of royal Spain. After the Civil War, the persistence of slavery in Cuba presented a bar to annexation by the United States. But when Cuban rebels seeking independence from Spain began their agitation, American sympathies were all with these freedom-seeking *insurrectos*. When a full-scale revolt broke out in 1895, millions of Americans cried, *"Cuba libre!"* ("Free Cuba!").

Spain sent General Valeriano Weyler to put down the rebellion. The American press went wild. General Weyler reacted to the insurrectos' "scorched earth" tactics by rounding up Cuban peasants in rebel areas and confining them to concentration camps. This *reconcentrado* policy resulted in thousands dead from hunger and disease. Weyler was vilified in the "Yellow Press" (so-called because of the cheap newsprint on which the penny-a-sheet sensationalist newspapers were printed). Atrocity stories from Cuba daily filled the pages of Joseph Pulitzer's *New York World* and the rival *New York Journal*. The bumptious young millionaire, William Randolph Hearst, owned the *Journal*. Hearst and Pulitzer were in a circulation war, and they used Cuban horrors to gain readership. As the old journalistic saw has it: *if it bleeds, it leads.*

Hearst sent the great American artist, Frederic Remington, to Cuba during a lull in the fighting. "There is no trouble here," Remington cabled Hearst. "There will be no war. I wish to return." Hearst quickly responded by telegram: "Please remain. You furnish the pictures and I'll furnish the war."[4] Pulitzer's *World* fanned anti-Spanish sentiment with paragraphs like this: "Blood on the roadsides, blood in the fields, blood on the door-steps, blood, blood, blood! The old, the young, the weak, the crippled—all are butchered without mercy. . . . Is there no nation wise enough, brave enough, and strong enough to restore peace in this bloodsmitten land?"[5]

All these horrors, the reader was led to believe, were committed on the direct orders of General Weyler. When a new ministry came to office in Madrid, it attempted to quiet the storm in Cuba. Weyler was recalled. His *reconcentrado* policy was eased. Soon, it appeared, order and peace would be restored to Cuba.

Just at this moment, the United States sent the battleship *Maine* to Havana, Cuba, to "show the flag" and let pro-Weyler Cubans know that the *Yanquis* would not tolerate abuse of Americans or their property in Cuba. President McKinley did not want to be rushed into war, but soon terrible news came from Havana. The USS *Maine* had exploded in the harbor with heavy loss of American life. More than 250 sailors died instantly, and more would die from burns and wounds. The Yellow Press went wild. "*Maine Destroyed by Treachery!*" screamed Hearst's nationwide chain of papers.[6]

Members of Congress hounded McKinley for war with Spain. A cartoon published in Hearst's *New York World* showed McKinley as a determined old lady, futilely trying to sweep back a hurricane with her broom. The winds were labeled "the people" and the waves were labeled "Congress."[7]

Theodore Roosevelt was disgusted by the president's failure to call openly for war. "McKinley has no more backbone than a chocolate éclair!" Teddy cried.[8] When the official navy board of inquiry reported an external submarine mine had caused the explosion of the *Maine*, it did *not* place the blame on Spain. It didn't have to. Around the country, the cry went up:

Remember the *Maine*
    To Hell with Spain![9]*

Wall Street did not want war. Most Europeans thought America would lose. Business leaders worried what would become of Americans' major investments in Cuba. Roosevelt confronted Senator Mark Hanna bluntly. Hanna, Wall Street's man in the Capitol, dug in his heels against war. "We will have this war for the freedom of Cuba," TR said in a Washington speech. "The interests of the business world and of financiers may be paramount in the Senate," but the American people cared about morality. "Now, Senator," Theodore said, appealing directly to Hanna, "may we please have war?"[10]

Teddy admitted to his sister, Bamie, that he was "something of a jingo." Actually, there was no one in America *jingoer*. What decided the fate of the nation, however, was a speech by Vermont Senator Redfield Proctor. No jingo, the seasoned and highly respected Proctor had actually gone to Cuba. His speech to the Senate, delivered in a calm and deliberative tone, changed minds. He confirmed the atrocity stories. The people there

---

* A 1976 investigation by Admiral Hyman G. Rickover concluded that the battleship *Maine* was destroyed by coal dust's igniting *within* the ship.

were "living like pigs and dying like flies. . . . To me, the strongest appeal is not the barbarity practiced by Weyler, nor the loss of the *Maine* . . . but the spectacle of a million and a half people [of Cuba] struggling for freedom and deliverance from the worst misgovernment of which I ever had knowledge."[11] Congress soon voted for war.

Assistant Secretary of the Navy Roosevelt promptly resigned. Henry Adams, the grandson and great-grandson of presidents, was stunned. "Is his wife dead? Has he quarreled with everybody? Is he quite mad?" Teddy the dynamo was determined to join the fight. TR said he had to "act up to my preachings."[12] Although vigorous and strong, TR could never have been accepted in today's military. Not only had he suffered from asthma as a child, but his vision was so poor that he was virtually blind without his spectacles. And he was nearly forty. No matter. Teddy immediately joined with his friend Leonard Wood to recruit a company of volunteers.

Teddy accepted a commission as a *lieutenant* colonel, modestly taking second in command of the regiment he and Colonel Wood raised. Teddy called on all his Ivy League friends, his fellow cowboys from the Dakotas, and Indian fighters from the prairies. Soon, the regiment was nicknamed the "Rough Riders." TR would later describe them as "Indian and cowboy, miner, packer and college athlete, the man of unknown ancestry from the Western plains, and the man who carried on his watch the crest of the Stuyvesants and the Fishes."[13]

Before the Rough Riders could get to Cuba, however, the navy went into action against Spain in the Philippines. No one expected the Americans to beat the Spaniards. When the U.S. ships weighed anchor in Hong Kong, their British hosts said of them: "A fine set of fellows, but unhappily we shall never see them again."[14] Commodore George Dewey struck hard at Manila Bay. Taking the Spanish fleet by surprise on 1 May 1898, Dewey gave the order to Captain Charles V. Gridley of the USS *Olympia*: "You may fire when ready, Gridley." Gridley *was* ready, and the Spanish fleet that had spanned the globe for four centuries was destroyed in a matter of minutes.* Below decks on the *Olympia*, the temperatures rose to 150 degrees! Still, the sailors were in high spirits. They stripped down to nothing but shoes and sang a popular rag tune of the day: "There'll be a hot time in the old town tonight."[15]**

When the Rough Riders landed in Cuba, they soon found that the war was no lark. The Spanish soldiers who faced them were well trained, highly disciplined, and excellent shots. They were well equipped with 7x57mm-caliber German Mausers, the best rifle in the world. TR said the sound of a Mauser—*a-z-z-z-eu*—was like "ripping silk."[16] Most dangerous was the fact Mausers used smokeless powder. Those firing from the dense jungle undergrowth could not be easily located. On 1 July 1898, the Rough Riders went into action at San Juan Hill. When retreating Spaniards broke into a run, Army General "Fighting Joe" Wheeler, an old veteran of the *Confederate* army, excitedly cried out: "We've got the damn Yankees on the run!"[17]

One of the first Rough Riders killed was New Yorker Hamilton Fish Jr. The nephew and namesake of U. S. Grant's distinguished secretary of state, Sergeant Fish was one of the glamorous "Fifth Avenue boys" TR had recruited.[18] (B. F. Goodrich and the jeweler's son, Bill Tiffany, were other famous names who survived the war. Frank Knox would live to serve as secretary of the navy under TR's cousin, Franklin.)

Another famous Rough Rider was Bucky O'Neill. O'Neill had fought Indians and chased outlaws as sheriff of Prescott, Arizona. As he exhaled smoke from his ever-present cigarette, Bucky boasted that the Spanish

---

* Captain Gridley had little chance to enjoy his worldwide fame. He died of illness in Kobe, Japan, less than a month after his great victory. His name is remembered in a succession of naval vessels. Future senator and presidential candidate Lieutenant John Kerry served on the USS *Gridley*, a destroyer, off Vietnam.

** The American victory at Manila Bay would begin the long association of the U.S. Navy with the Philippines. Many an American sailor would head for the wild liberty port of Alongopo City. It was the location of some of the most notorious saloons and brothels in Asia. To be fair, "Po Town" was also hometown to some of the most enduring marriages in American service life.

bullet hadn't been made that could kill him. At that moment, a German-made Mauser bullet hit him in the mouth and took off the back of his head.[19]

For all the comic opera aspect of this war, once the Americans got to Cuba they found it all too real. Huge land crabs attacked corpses, as did vultures.[20] In the assault on San Juan Hill, Lieutenant Colonel Roosevelt scolded some of the regulars who were hunkered down. "Are you afraid to stand up when I am on horseback?" he asked. Even as one of the crouching soldiers rose, though, the poor man was cut down by a well-aimed Spanish shot.[21] Soon, TR found it more prudent to dismount from Little Texas and proceed on foot.

The war quickly wound down. Half a world away, Americans gratefully accepted British intervention in the Philippines. When Commodore Dewey shelled Spanish shore positions at Manila on August 13, a Royal Navy squadron put itself between the Americans and a German naval flotilla that had attempted to interfere with the American attack. The German battleships actually *trained* their guns on the Americans! Unwilling to risk war with *both* the British and the Americans, the German commander backed down.

Britain was the only European power to openly back the Americans in the Spanish-American War. Young Winston Churchill was a war correspondent. He spoke for many Englishmen when he said, "The Americans should be admired for their action in Cuba . . . though as a nation . . . they always contrive to disgust polite people. Yet their heart is honest."[22] Britain had its own *goo goos*. America's minister in London, John Hay, had worked hard to gain British support for the U.S. position. As a young man, Hay had served as Lincoln's secretary. Then, he saw what horrors war could bring. Now, he called TR's project "a splendid little war."[23] For Spain, which lost 50,000 men—2,000 in combat, the rest to disease—it was a painful experience. For America, the 385 battle deaths and 2,000 lost to disease were the cost of the country's emergence as a world power.[24]

To President McKinley now came the difficult task of deciding what to do about America's conquests. Cuba would be granted independence. That much was sure. But what about Guam, Puerto Rico, and the Philippines? McKinley struggled over the Philippines, in particular. He told a delegation of Methodists he had prayerfully decided it was his duty "to take them all and to educate the Filipinos, and uplift and civilize and *Christianize* them." The Filipinos, under Spanish guidance for three centuries, were mostly Christian.[25] And soon, Americans would have their own *insurrectos* to contend with there. McKinley's decision was widely criticized as an imperialist power grab. The truth is the Philippines cast adrift would have been snapped up by either Germany or Japan in 1898. Under American rule, at least, they would have the *promise* of independence. For good measure, McKinley took the occasion to annex the Hawaiian Islands.

"Japan has her eye on them," he told an aide.[26] Senator Lodge and Captain Mahan, among others, had convinced the president that in the modern world of great ironclad fleets, Hawaii was necessary for the defense of California.

II. ROUGH RIDER POLITICS

Colonel Roosevelt and the Rough Riders came to Montauk, on Long Island's East End, to be "mustered out." After a brief and glorious tour of duty, they were honorably discharged from active service. There, President McKinley came to greet the returning heroes. TR jumped off his horse and struggled to get his glove off to shake hands with the commander in chief. Finally, frustrated at not being able to pull the glove off, he took it in his teeth and yanked it off so he could pump the chief executive's hand. Those prominent teeth, the pince-nez eyeglasses, the slouch hat— all had become the stuff of legend and the delight of cartoonists. Though he hated the nickname, Roosevelt was "Teddy" to the whole country.[27] The Rough Riders gave him a Frederic Remington sculpture, *The Bronco Buster*, and wept as they bade him good-bye.[28]

TR could not have returned at a more politically advantageous time. Senator Thomas Platt was known as New York's Easy Boss for his soft-spoken manner. He saw sure defeat for New York Republicans if they renominated their scandal-tainted governor, Frank Black. Black's administration couldn't explain how a million dollars intended for repairs on the Erie Canal got misdirected.[29] Platt hated to dump a loyal Republican, but he hated losing even more. Respectfully, Theodore went to Platt's headquarters in Manhattan's Fifth Avenue Hotel. There, Platt held court with his group of hangers-on. They were known as the Amen Corner. By going to *him*, Teddy was showing that he could cooperate. Platt insisted that Teddy reject the pleas of enthusiastic reformers that he run for governor as an *independent*. In return, the senator would throw the Republican nomination for governor to the Rough Rider.

TR parlayed his war fame into a run for governor of New York as a Republican. The fall campaign was a whirlwind. Teddy appeared at the back of his train, the Roosevelt Special. He waved his uniform hat and surrounded himself with Rough Riders who announced his speeches with a bugle. One of his sergeants, Southerner Buck Taylor, happily told one crowd, "He kept ev'y promise he made to us and he will to you. . . . He led us up San Juan Hill like sheep to the slaughter—and so he will lead you!"[30]

Despite this *dubious* endorsement, Teddy went on to win the governorship—but narrowly. He won by less than 18,000 votes out of more than 1,300,000.[31] But he had won, and in winning he had kept the critical Empire State in the hands of the Republicans. This was vitally important. President McKinley was surely relieved as he extended his congratulations to "the Colonel." He would need the Empire State's electoral votes when he ran for reelection in 1900.

The president's reelection prospects at midterm did not look so promising. The acquisition of an overseas empire was proving difficult—the Filipino *insurrectos* were no fonder of American rule than they had been of Spanish rule. American soldiers were dying in the fight to put down Emilio Aguinaldo's nationalist forces. The little war had shown the complete lack of preparedness of the American army. Nevertheless, the Treaty of Paris of 1898, which brought an end to the Spanish-American War, signaled the beginning of the era of the U.S. as a military power on the world stage.

It is easy to poke fun at the pretensions of the imperialists. British poet Rudyard Kipling urged us to "take up the white man's burden." Uninformed people spoke of "civilizing the Filipino." These ideas sound absurd to us today. Yet American intervention made a great difference in the lives of Cubans in one important respect. The dreaded yellow fever took thousands of lives there. American troops, Spanish troops, and Cuban nationals all suffered. When U.S. Army doctor Walter Reed investigated the causes, he learned of Cuban physician Carlos Finlay's work. Dr. Finlay's research showed that mosquitoes carried the disease. Dr. Reed advised General Leonard Wood, TR's old commanding officer, to attack the carrier. General Wood took up the challenge and waged "war" on the insect. By 1901, Havana was free of the killer disease.[32]

In the case of the Philippines, American rule would prove brief. Four hundred years of Spanish colonial rule had not equipped Filipinos for self-government. In light of later events in the Pacific, especially three long, brutal years of Japanese occupation during World War II, America's role in protecting and guiding the Filipinos formed the basis for our continuing friendship with that country.

In another way, America's newfound prestige benefited others. McKinley had summoned John Hay home from Britain to become U.S. secretary of state. Hay examined the growing turmoil in China and saw the imperial powers of Europe—and Japan—eager to carve up the ancient Celestial Empire. In 1899, Hay circulated a letter to the European Powers, calling on them to prevent the further disintegration of the country and to treat all of China's trading partners equally. This became known as the "Open Door Policy," for which Hay is justly famous.

Hay's generous sentiments were misinterpreted by one small group of Chinese, however. Young martial arts students, called the Fists of

Righteous Harmony, rose up. They wanted to drive out the "foreign devils" entirely. Called *boxers* by the Europeans, their bloody action in 1900 is known as the Boxer Rebellion. Thousands of Christian missionaries and Chinese Christian converts were slaughtered as the Boxers laid siege to the foreign legations in Peking. When an international force finally rescued the diplomats and other Westerners, the Boxer Rebellion was ruthlessly put down. All over the world, readers of the Yellow Press gawked in horror to see photographs of *Chinese* pyramids. But these pyramids were made of the severed heads of the Boxers. The world shuddered as well when Kaiser Wilhelm II ordered his troops—part of the multinational force—to suppress the Boxers with all the ferocity of the Huns of old. German soldiers would never shake that sobriquet.

Facing the election of 1900, Republicans sought to shift the public's attention to the prosperity of "the full dinner pail." They nominated Governor Theodore Roosevelt to be McKinley's vice president.

The Democrats again chose William Jennings Bryan as their presidential nominee. This time, Bryan shifted ground once more and campaigned *against* imperialism. Charles Francis Adams Jr., another member of the famous Adams family, thought little of McKinley, but he liked Bryan even less: "He is in one sense scripturally formidable, for he is unquestionably armed with the jaw-bone of an ass. He can talk longer and say less than any man in Christendom."[33]

Bryan once again conducted a whistle-stop campaign, barnstorming the country by rail.

This time, however, Republicans sent TR to combat the man who was called the Great Commoner. Teddy's popular appeal proved more than a match for Bryan's. Teddy campaigned in his Rough Rider hat to enthusiastic whoops from his audiences. When the votes were finally counted, the Republicans won in a landslide.

Six months later, the kindhearted President McKinley visited the Pan American Exposition in Buffalo, New York. He was greeting well-wishers. He extended the hand of friendship to a young man whose own hand was wrapped in a large bandage. Leon Czolgosz, an anarchist, fired two shots that struck the president in the chest and abdomen.* "Be easy with him, boys," the stricken president called out as Secret Service agents pummeled the assassin with their fists. For a time, the president seemed to rally. Medical reports were so encouraging that his vigorous vice president thought it safe to take some time off for recreation. He set out to scale New York's highest peak, Mount Marcy. Mount Marcy is near Lake Tear of the Clouds, in Essex County, close to the border with Vermont. Suddenly, below him, TR saw a ranger running toward him, waving a yellow telegram. Teddy knew what it meant.[34] He jumped in a buckboard for the mad dash to the train station. A special train sped him nearly four hundred miles westward to Buffalo, to the stately home of the Roosevelts' wealthy friends, the Wilcoxes, where Theodore Roosevelt was sworn in as president. He was just a few weeks shy of his forty-third birthday, the youngest man ever to take the oath as president.

Riding in the presidential funeral train, Senator Mark Hanna ruefully reflected on his conversation with his dearest friend: "I told William McKinley it was a mistake to nominate that wild man at [the Republican National Convention in Philadelphia the previous summer]. I asked him if he realized what would happen if he should die. Now look, that damned cowboy is President of the United States!"[35]

III. TR IN THE WHITE HOUSE

We are so used to identifying the presidency with the White House that it's hard to believe that the *official* title of the president's residence for more than a century was the Executive Mansion. But that would not last long with TR. By proclamation, he renamed the building the White

---

* Czolgosz was quickly tried, convicted, and sentenced to die in New York State's new electric chair. He was executed on 20 October 1901, barely five weeks after the president died. The electric chair was one of Thomas Edison's less salubrious inventions.

House. This was but one of the whirlwinds of change that Roosevelt brought to the office. He of course presided over the nation's period of deep and sincere mourning for the slain McKinley. But he did not let this tragedy slow him down:

> It is a dreadful thing to come into the Presidency in this way; but it would be far worse to be morbid about it. Here is the task, and I have got to do it to the best of my ability; and that is all there is to it.[36]

Shortly after moving into the White House, the president heard that Booker T. Washington was in the capital. Dr. Washington was the president of the Tuskegee Institute, the leading black college in America. Without hesitation, TR invited the distinguished educator to dinner. Teddy liked to boast of his Southern ancestry. His mother was from Georgia, and his two dashing uncles served on the CSS *Alabama*. But he was completely unprepared for the storm of protest in the South that greeted this first White House dinner given to a black man.* Southern newspapers denounced the president for this "most damnable outrage." Even worse was the reaction of a Democratic senator from South Carolina. "Pitchfork Ben" Tillman said, "The action of President Roosevelt in entertaining that n—— will necessitate our killing a thousand n——s in the South before they will learn their place again."[37] Tillman was not exaggerating. Each year hundreds of black Southerners died at the hands of lynch mobs. To the everlasting shame of the U.S. Senate, Tillman was *not* expelled at that instant!

What made the reaction even more astonishing was that Dr. Washington had gone out of his way to *avoid* challenging the white Democrats who ruled the one-party South. He was an advocate of reconciliation, and he

---

* President Lincoln had famously invited Frederick Douglass to confer man-to-man with him in the White House and to attend the reception following his second Inaugural, but this was the first dinner invitation extended to a black man. Ironically, the White House head waiter, who was black, seemed to disapprove.

accepted the burden of segregation. The U.S. Supreme Court had even approved racial segregation in its appalling *Plessy v. Ferguson* ruling of 1896. Bowing to this reality, Booker T. Washington advocated black self-help. His best-selling autobiography, *Up from Slavery*, urged black Americans to improve themselves through education and training *before* demanding social equality and their constitutional right to vote.

This very "moderate" position led young black intellectuals like W. E. B. DuBois to criticize Booker T. Washington:

> But so far as Mr. Washington apologizes for injustice, North or South, does not rightly value the privilege and duty of voting, belittles the emasculating effects of caste distinctions, and opposes the higher training and ambition of our brighter minds—so far as he, the South, or the Nation, does this—we must unceasingly and firmly oppose them. By every civilized and peaceful method we must strive for the rights which the world accords to men, clinging unwaveringly to those great words which the sons of the Fathers would fain forget: "We hold these truths to be self-evident: That all men are created equal; that they are endowed by their Creator with certain unalienable rights; that among these are life, liberty, and the pursuit of happiness."

Stressing "continuity of government," TR asked a number of McKinley's cabinet members to stay on. He particularly wanted Secretary of State John Hay to remain. TR's father had known Hay in the Lincoln White House. When Theodore Senior got the idea of *allotments* for Union soldiers, Hay whisked *Greatheart* in to see President Lincoln. Lincoln instantly approved the idea.* Now, the slender young man of the Lincoln

---

* Prior to Lincoln's adoption of the Roosevelt allotment system, thousands of Northern families were left destitute. Their young men frittered away their military pay in camp on high-priced snacks, whiskey, gambling, and prostitutes. The Roosevelt system—still in use today—permitted these men to have cash allotments sent home to their needful families before the money was ever paid out to them.

White House was a portly, witty, and wise senior statesman. TR turned to him as to a trusted old family friend. He wanted John Hay to use his excellent contacts with the British to negotiate a better U.S. treaty for a Central American canal. Hay succeeded brilliantly. By the terms of the Hay-Pauncefote Treaty of 1901, the United States now had a free hand to negotiate, build, *and fortify* a canal across the isthmus.[38] And TR fully intended to use that free hand in constructing an *American* canal to link the Atlantic and Pacific Oceans.

An early test of TR's presidency came in 1902 as the United Mine Workers union called a national strike against the anthracite coal owners. The nation was completely dependent upon coal. Homes, factories, and public buildings were heated by coal. Railroad trains and steamships were fueled by it. Without coal, the nation would be crippled.

TR summoned the mine owners to the White House to meet with John Mitchell and other union leaders. "Are you asking us to meet with a set of *outlaws*?" asked John Markle of the owners' group. Infuriated, Teddy said of Markle's arrogance: "If it wasn't for the high office I held, I would have taken him by the seat of the breeches and the nape of the neck and chucked him out of that window!"[39] The attitude of the owners was exemplified by a private letter from owner representative George Baer that soon leaked out: "The rights and interests of the laboring man will be protected and cared for—not by labor agitators, but by the Christian men to whom God in His infinite wisdom has given the control of the property interests of the country."[40] Such a cocksure notion of what the Almighty intended made the owners seem ridiculous to the public at large.

The miners were striking against deplorable working conditions. As Irving Stone would write in his biography of radical lawyer Clarence Darrow: "Six men of a thousand [miners] were killed every year; hundreds were maimed by explosions and cave-ins; few escaped the ravages of asthma, bronchitis, chronic rheumatism, consumption, heart trouble. By the age of fifty the miners were worn out and broken, good for little but the human slag heap."[41]

One of the most frightening hazards miners faced occurred when a bootlace or shirtsleeve became entangled in the gears of a coal-crushing machine and the miner was dragged to a slow and agonizing death. George Baer denied that the miners suffered at all: "Why, they can't even speak English!"[42] Perhaps Teddy could identify with United Mine Worker President John Mitchell because he could remember fighting for breath when he was a sickly boy, stricken with asthma.

TR rattled his saber (something he *loved* doing). He let it be known he was contemplating taking over the coal mines and having the army operate them.

Worried that he might do something rash like that, the owners soon agreed to an arbitration panel. TR quickly named Catholic Bishop John Spalding to the panel. The largely Catholic miners trusted their bishop. In addition, Teddy recruited a willing former president, Democrat Grover Cleveland. Soon, the miners and owners came to a compromise agreement, and the nation was saved from paralysis. It was the first instance of "jawboning" by a president, and it was a great success for Roosevelt.

Mindful of the fierce reaction from the South over his invitation to Dr. Washington, TR decided to visit his mother's homeland for a hunting trip. He wanted to mend political fences. Because of the many death threats TR had received and the recent McKinley assassination, the Secret Service nervously watched the New Yorker president as he descended on Dixie "loaded for bear."* The trip, however, was an embarrassing failure as TR repeatedly failed to bag a catch. Finally, TR's Mississippi hosts cornered a small black bear, wounded it, and called eagerly for the president to come and shoot it. Teddy the sportsman resolutely refused. He had eagerly shot grizzly bears, but he could not bring himself to take unfair advantage of the terrified, trapped animal. *Washington Post* cartoonist

---

* Following the assassination of President William McKinley in 1901, the third chief executive assassinated in just thirty-five years, Congress voted to provide Secret Service agents to protect the president and his family. The irrepressible Roosevelt clan gave their Secret Service detail quite a workout.

Clifford Berry immediately offered a picture he called "Drawing the line in Mississippi." Berry intended it as a commentary on "drawing the line" on *race* in the South. But the country missed the barbed point entirely. Instead, the whole nation thrilled to their Teddy's nobly sparing the poor little bear. In no time, it became the story of "Teddy's bear." That Christmas, New York's posh F. A. O. Schwarz store offered an elegant bear crafted by Germany's Steiff toy company. In Brooklyn's much less swankier precincts, Morris Michtom offered a stuffed toy bear for just $1.50.[43] Instantly, a worldwide craze began that shows no sign of ebbing a century later. The teddy bear captured the hearts of children everywhere.

When TR turned his attention to the powerful railroad trusts, he decided to go after the new Northern Securities Company. Banker J. Pierpont Morgan had brought together controlling shares in the Northern Pacific, Union Pacific, and Burlington Railroads. The board was composed of such titans of industry as Morgan himself, James J. Hill, and E. H. Harriman. Morgan was called *Jupiter* on Wall Street. "The boldest man was likely to become timid under his piercing gaze," men said of him.[44] Wall Street was therefore shocked when TR instructed his attorney general, Philander Knox, to file suit in federal court *against* the Northern Securities Company. TR said they were violating the Sherman Anti-Trust Act of 1890. But what was *this*? The magnates were used to the federal government using the Sherman Act against *unions*. How dare the president wield this club against *them*?

Exhaling clouds of cigar smoke—like an active volcano—Jupiter came to the White House to put the new president in his place. "If we have done anything wrong, [just] send your man [Attorney General Knox] to see my man and they can fix it up."[45] TR did not think he was settling on the sale of a private yacht or arranging the swap of thoroughbred racehorses. He marveled at the way the Wall Street baron talked down to him. "That can't be done," TR responded.

When the Roosevelt administration finally won its case in the Supreme Court in 1904, TR was elated. The Court ruled that the Northern

Securities Company had indeed violated the Sherman Act and ordered that the giant trust be broken up.

Teddy's acts as president had made him wildly popular with the American people, if not with leaders of his party and their friends on Wall Street. Still, Teddy was something of a force of nature. He preached the *strenuous* life—and practiced it. He loved to lead foreign diplomats, military officers, and panting civil servants on his soon-famous "point-to-point" walks through Washington's Rock Creek Park. "Over, under or through," Teddy called out to sweating hikers clambering over boulders and through muddy streams, "*never* around!" It would be a watchword for Roosevelt's style of governance. Commenting on the president's boundless enthusiasm, the British minister reportedly said, "You must remember that Theodore is really a six-year-old boy." Not many six-year-old boys read *Anna Karenina* as they bed down on a saddle under the Dakota stars, or head off in hot pursuit of outlaws. Nor are many six-year-olds conversant with Icelandic *sagas*. TR was the most widely read and genuinely scholarly president to occupy the White House since Thomas Jefferson. (Despite this, TR vocally denounced the Sage of Monticello for his neglect of the navy.) Still, the British minister did capture TR's exuberance, his boyish *love* of action and adventure.

The Roosevelt family, too, made a great splash in TR's White House years. Theodore Jr., Archie, Kermit, and Quentin were always getting in scrapes. One time, Archie and Kermit brought their pony, Algonquin, upstairs in the White House elevator. They wanted to charm their sick brother, Quentin. Another time they loosed a four-foot king snake on a cabinet meeting. The country watched with wonder as the Roosevelts sent their children to Washington, D.C.'s public schools. There, the children of a president sat next to the children of milk wagon drivers, seamstresses, and postal workers. The capital's public schools were then segregated, a fact that TR deplored in a Message to Congress:

> It is out of the question for our people as a whole permanently to rise by treading down any of their own number. The free public school, the

chance for each boy or girl to get a good elementary education, lies at the foundation of our whole political situation. . . . It is as true for the Negro as for the white man.[46]

TR's daughter by his first wife was known throughout the country as *Princess* Alice. Headstrong and spoiled, she defiantly quit school and took up smoking. When friends pleaded with him to rein her in, Theodore, exasperated, responded, "I can govern the country or I can govern Alice. I cannot possibly do both." Over it all, First Lady Edith Kermit Carow Roosevelt presided with intelligence, grace, and patience. A friend once remarked to Mrs. Roosevelt how surprised she was to see all the tusks, heads, and hides TR had proudly displayed at Sagamore Hill, the family's Oyster Bay, New York, home. Mrs. Roosevelt tolerantly showed her friend the only stuffed animal she allowed in the dining room. It was *behind* the chair of the lady of the house, where she would never have to look at it. Mrs. Roosevelt made sure the White House was a genuine cultural center. In the days before Washington, D.C. had any but vaudeville theaters, this was an important achievement.

IV. TR AND THE SQUARE DEAL

Few of America's leaders in 1901 could claim to know *How the Other Half Lives.* That was the title of an 1890 book of photos and text by Roosevelt's friend Jacob Riis. It catalogued the truly deplorable conditions in which hundreds of thousands of slum dwellers lived. Especially poignant were Riis's pictures of homeless little boys. Theodore Roosevelt, almost alone among Republicans, knew. He had investigated slum conditions on excursions through Brooklyn with Riis when he was a police commissioner. His father had founded the Children's Aid Society. The elder Roosevelt had spent Sunday evenings for many years reading stories to the impoverished newsboys. He made sure they had at least one hot, nourishing meal that day.

What TR already knew, the country was soon to learn, when *McClure's Magazine* began the series called "The Shame of the Cities." Writer Lincoln Steffens appealed for reform of the municipal corruption that rested on a rotting foundation of slums. TR called many of the progressive writers who constantly dug up stories of want and wrongdoing "muckrakers," and warned against a fixed focus on what was wrong in society. Nonetheless, he also spearheaded reform.

Teddy was well-born. His family had made millions in glass and real estate. He could "ride to hounds" in the fox hunts the social elite of Long Island thoroughly enjoyed, but then Teddy would ride the fourteen miles back to Oyster Bay to avoid spending the night in the "intolerable companionship" of the *Four Hundred*.* He criticized vain rich people whom he accused of living "lives of ignoble ease."[47]

TR fearlessly took on the all-powerful railroads. With the Elkins Act (1903), rebates to favored customers were outlawed. This was the very technique that John D. Rockefeller of Standard Oil had exploited so effectively. Rockefeller would demand and receive from railroads great rebates based on the huge volume of business he gave them. This comparative advantage over other independent oil producers helped Rockefeller drive his competitors into bankruptcy. Rockefeller excelled at this "cutthroat competition." When Congress balked at passage of the reform bill, TR let it be known that Rockefeller was using his vast wealth to "influence" wavering senators. Congress had little choice but to give the president his reform.[48]

Around this time Upton Sinclair, another muckraking journalist, published *The Jungle*. He hoped it would lead Americans to embrace Marxism. It didn't. But it did lead readers to demand reform of the meatpacking industry Sinclair so vividly exposed. Sinclair wrote of the rats, filth, diseased cattle, and swine that went into the canning process. He even described workers who fell into the open vats: "Sometimes they

---

* The Four Hundred was shorthand for the number of prominent names that appeared in the Social Register, a listing of the best-connected, usually wealthiest New Yorkers of TR's day.

would be overlooked for days, till all but the bones of them had gone out to the world as Durham's Pure Leaf Lard."[49]

Humorist Finley Peter Dunne's Irish character, *Mr. Dooley*, commented on the wild success of Sinclair's novel. "It was a sweetly sintimintal little volume to be r-read durin' Lent."[50] And Mr. Dooley's description of the president at his breakfast table had the country rollicking. "There was Tiddy, readin' the book and, whoop, all iv a sudden, he jumps up an' flings his sausages outer the winder, yellin' 'I'm p'isoned, I'm p'isoned!'"

The result of all this agitation was the Pure Food and Drug Act, which Teddy signed with relish. Now, clearly, TR had broken away from the philosophy of Senator Mark Hanna. Hanna told his fellow Ohioans they could do no better than to "stand pat" with the GOP.[51] Theodore, Rough Rider, cowboy, big-game hunter, was not about to *stand pat* for anything he thought was morally wrong.

Stand-patters in the Republican Party hoped someone would rescue them from their cowboy president, but TR ran for reelection in 1904 by explaining his viewpoint: "My action on labor should always be considered with my action as regards capital, and both are reducible to my favorite formula—a square deal for every man."[52] Americans obviously approved of the Square Deal. They returned TR to the White House by a landslide.

Theodore Roosevelt had just turned forty-six when he was elected overwhelmingly to a full term in his own right. He had every reason to feel that his leadership was vindicated. Then, at the height of his power, he committed a grave error: he announced "under no circumstances" would he be a candidate for reelection in 1908. It was a decision he and millions of his countrymen would come to regret bitterly.

Surely one of TR's most enduring achievements was his passion for conservation. No American president since Washington had spent as much time in the wilderness. Even as a young man, TR had written authoritatively on American birds. Hunting, hiking, rowing, riding: these were all second nature to this intrepid adventurer. He worked closely with his friend Gifford Pinchot, the U.S. chief forester, to set aside vast tracts of woodlands as national parks.

At the time, most other politicians formed an Amen Corner for the blinkered views of the Speaker of the House. Joe Cannon growled "not one cent for scenery!"* Theodore personally intervened with Speaker Cannon to save his National Reclamation Bill for irrigating arid western lands.[53] He appointed an Inland Waterways Commission in 1907 to study the complex interrelation of rivers, soil, waterpower, and transportation. The same year, he convened a White House conference on conservation, an unprecedented act that gave the subject a big boost in publicity.[54]

Where he could not get the desired legislation from a grudging Congress, Teddy would act by Executive Order—as he did in creating national wildlife sanctuaries. And when neither route was possible, Teddy could *preach* conservation. For this, especially, he regarded the White House as his "Bully Pulpit." Teddy's vigor, his enthusiasm, his integrity, and his powerful intellect helped keep Americans excited about the Bully Pulpit concept. Later in the twentieth century, as we shall see, Americans became less eager to be "preached to" from presidents mounting the Bully Pulpit.

As president, Roosevelt used the Bully Pulpit to raise public concerns about what we today call family values. Studying government reports and census statistics, President Roosevelt noted that the birthrate of Americans was dropping for the first time since independence. He comprehended the challenges to family life that were presented by the new industrial order. He viewed economic issues in terms of their impact on the family. As he would later say: "I do not wish to see this country a country of selfish prosperity where those who enjoy the material prosperity think only of the selfish gratification of their own desires, and are content to import from abroad not only their art, not only their literature, but even their babies."[55]

---

* This is the Republican speaker for whom the Cannon House Office Building in Washington, D.C., is named.

Roosevelt practiced what he preached. Not only did he have a large and boisterous family, but his and Edith's family was a "blended family," combining his daughter from his first marriage with *five* children from his second. Even in the White House, the president always made time to romp with his lively brood. More important, he obviously took joy in their life together.

V. WIELDING THE BIG STICK

"I have always been fond of the West African proverb: 'Speak softly and carry a big stick, you will go far,'" TR had said.[56] He proved it again and again during his White House years.

No sooner had he inherited the office, however, than President Roosevelt faced a great moral crisis over U.S. policy in the Philippines. Anti-imperialists got hold of an army report of U.S. atrocities toward Filipino guerrillas. What kind of "civilizing" and "Christianizing" was this, they demanded to know. TR had tried to keep the reports from coming out—always a mistake in Washington. But when the country was sufficiently horrified by the lurid stories, TR counterattacked.

He gave his close friend Senator Henry Cabot Lodge the army files that documented what the Filipino *insurrectos* had done to captured Americans. Our soldiers suffered greatly. They had their eyes gouged. They had been disemboweled, slow-roasted, some even castrated and gagged with their own testicles. Lodge's cool, dispassionate cataloguing of these horrors created a sensation: "Perhaps the action of the American soldier is not entirely without provocation."[57]

Fortunately for the United States, the Philippine insurrection was even then collapsing. More fortunate, still, was the dispatch of the able Ohio lawyer, William Howard Taft, to Manila as governor of the Philippines. Brimming with genuine goodwill, the 350-pound Taft brought intelligence and humanity to his task. He referred to the Filipinos as his "little brown brothers." Although rudely condescending to our ears, that sentiment reassured Americans and Filipinos that our rule in the island territory would be humane and temporary. Soon, major land reform in the islands created a rising middle class. U.S. soldiers still griped, "He may be a brother of Big Bill Taft / But he ain't even a [cousin] of mine!"[58] Taft's success in the Philippines opened up wider vistas to his considerable talents. Americans chuckled at the story of a supposed exchange of telegrams between Taft and TR.

Hearing reports that the indispensable governor was seriously ill, TR was said to have cabled Manila regarding Taft's bulk:

> **TR:** Alarmed you're unwell. Report.
> **TAFT:** Am Fine. Rode 25 miles horseback.
> **TR:** How is horse?

In 1903, Roosevelt used big-stick diplomacy to pull off one of the greatest achievements of his presidency: building the Panama Canal. On the Isthmus of Panama, only thirty miles separated the Atlantic and Pacific Oceans. Panama, at that time, was a colony of Colombia. Secretary of State John Hays negotiated a treaty with Columbia to lease a strip of land to build a canal across the isthmus, connecting the two seas.

When the Colombian senate rejected the deal, TR was outraged. He suspected the Colombians were squeezing the *Yanquis* for more money. Panamanians were also upset. They had revolted fifty-three times in fifty-seven years against Colombian rule. Now, it seemed, the faraway dictator in Bogotá and his corrupt senate were about to derail their best opportunity in years.

TR probably did *not* encourage a Panamanian revolt against Colombia, but he doubtless did nothing to *discourage* such a revolt. In Panama, news arrived that the USS *Nashville* would conveniently arrive off Colón on 2 November 1903. That was assurance enough for the small band of Panamanian rebels. Roosevelt instructed Hay to grant official U.S.

diplomatic recognition to the new Panamanian Republic on 6 November 1903, just three days after the not-wholly-spontaneous revolt took place.[59]

Many in the United States denounced the "indecent haste" with which Teddy had acted.

"Piracy."

"Scandal."

"The most discreditable incident in our history."

These were just some of the criticisms lodged against TR's highhanded action.[60] But Teddy was having none of it. He had resolved to "make the dirt fly" in Panama. He later reflected on it as one of his greatest achievements: "If I had followed the traditional, conservative methods, I would have submitted a dignified State paper of probably 200 pages to Congress and the debates on it would have been going on yet [in 1911]; but I took the Canal Zone and let Congress debate: and while the debate goes on the Canal does also."[61]

Later, when Woodrow Wilson's administration expressed regrets and agreed to pay Colombia $25 million in damages, opponents called the payment *canalimony*.[62]

As loud as TR was over Panama, he exercised *quiet* diplomacy with Germany over Venezuela. When the British and Germans threatened a joint occupation of the South American republic because of a chronic failure to pay just debts, TR let the German ambassador know that any European occupation of an independent nation in the Western Hemisphere would be a violation of the Monroe Doctrine. Any such violation, TR said, would *surely* mean war with the United States. When the British backed away, the Kaiser felt exposed. Roosevelt was careful *not* to let the confrontation leak out. He would give the Kaiser "the satisfaction of feeling that his dignity and reputation in the face of the world were safe," TR later wrote.[63] Thus, Roosevelt showed his subtle understanding of the many uses of diplomacy.

The frequent indebtedness of Latin American nations led to a constant threat of foreign intervention. To forestall such assaults on the

Monroe Doctrine, Theodore Roosevelt asserted his own belief that the United States might, from time to time, be called upon to intervene in order to defend the hemisphere. This "Roosevelt Corollary" to the Monroe Doctrine was highly controversial in its own day and has since been abandoned by the United States. But it did ensure no foreign interventions in this continent during the Roosevelt presidency.

Roosevelt faced another foreign crisis when a North African desert chieftain called the *Raisuli* took hostage the U.S. consul, Ion Perdicaris. The Raisuli was trying thereby to exert pressure against a rival Arab ruler. TR instructed Secretary of State John Hay to send this terse message: "We want Perdicaris alive or Raisuli dead." He got Perdicaris alive.

Roosevelt's reputation for wielding the Big Stick strengthened his hand as a peacemaker. When Japan smashed the Russian fleet in a sudden, overwhelming attack in 1904, a major war broke out. TR called both parties to New Hampshire in 1905 and hammered out the Treaty of Portsmouth to end the Russo-Japanese War. His efforts made him the first American to win the Nobel Peace Prize.[64]

Approaching the end of his presidency, TR resolved to brandish his Big Stick one last time. He sent the large, modern fleet of U.S. battleships on an unprecedented round-the-world cruise. The Great White Fleet—so called because the ships' hulls were painted white—showed the flag in dozens of foreign ports.

The trip was a public relations bonanza for the United States, while demonstrating to the crowned heads of Europe and Japan all the muscle of the brash young republic. At a time of growing Anglo-German naval rivalry, TR forcefully demonstrated that the United States was not a country to be trifled with on the high seas.

Roosevelt was determined to choose his own successor. Throughout his second term, he had come increasingly to rely on his loyal and efficient secretary of war, William Howard Taft. Taft would have preferred to be chief justice, but TR and Mrs. Taft had other ideas. The Republican Party was happy to have the popular, jovial Ohioan at the head of its ticket. Democrats again chose the Great Commoner, William Jennings Bryan. Older now, but not notably wiser, Bryan mounted a *third* vigorous campaign for the White House.

Taft benefited from the great popularity of TR and the progressive record of his administration. When the votes were counted in 1908, Taft bested the Democrat Bryan by 7,678,908 votes (321 electoral votes) to 6,409,104 for the Prairie populist.

As Taft prepared his smooth transition, TR insisted on one more headline grabber as president. When he issued new fitness regulations for the army, some of the desk-bound brass loudly complained that they were too demanding. Nobody can be expected to ride ninety miles in three days, they said. "Nonsense," TR said, taking up the challenge. He assured skeptics he could ride ninety miles *in one day*! With just weeks remaining in office, the fifty-year-old Teddy mounted a succession of horses and took off in the dead of winter for Warrenton, Virginia. His faithful military aide, Major Archie Butt, and a small contingent of hardy souls joined him. He stopped at Warrenton, shook hands all around, and addressed the school-children there. Then he remounted and galloped back to Washington. The presidential party returned to the capital after dark. The ice-covered roads made riding treacherous. Rejecting calls to dismount, TR charged on. When they reached the White House, Edith Roosevelt greeted the ice-covered party and brought them in for a hot meal and warm hospitality.[65]

Taft was inaugurated 4 March 1909, with all pomp and circumstance in the middle of a blinding snowstorm. Theodore wanted to give his man some time to put his own stamp on the presidency. He cooperatively announced he was heading to Africa for a hunting safari.

VI. THE TAFT INTERLUDE

America was ready for a breather. William Howard Taft's 1908 election victory was even stronger than TR's vote of 1904 had been. Americans embraced their large, genial new president with respect and affection. A favorite story of the time said the president stood up on a streetcar to give *three* ladies his seat.[66] But Taft was highly intelligent, loyal, and able. As with any period of revolutionary activity, there is the trailblazer who marks out the new course to be followed. Then there is the necessary period of consolidation. Taft was a consolidator. He enacted *more* of the Roosevelt program than TR had been able to do.[67] During his four years in office, Taft's administration would prosecute *twice* as many antitrust cases as Roosevelt had done in seven and a half years.[68] This was no easy task, since the power of the trusts was daunting. At this time, U.S. Steel *alone* had a greater budget than the entire U.S. government![69] Taft got little credit for this among reformers. They saw him leisurely swinging a golf club in the company of wealthy friends. It was hard to see him as a trust-buster.

It's not surprising that pressures should have risen at the White House during Taft's term. America was undergoing rapid change. Following the Wright Brothers' historic flight in 1903, an aviation industry was born. Henry Ford was putting more and more Americans on the roads with his Model T. (Ford was a pioneer in cutting costs by mass production, putting thousands of cars on America's poorly paved roads. Critics said you could have any color you want, so long as it's black. Ford soon provided consumer choice on color too.) Along with this increased mobility came danger. Highway fatalities for 1911 rose to 1,291.[70]

Theodore Roosevelt thought he had the answer to this quickening pace of change. He delivered a far-ranging speech in Osawatomie, Kansas, in August 1910, in which he called for more regulation of corporations and railroads, a graduated income tax, reform of banks, labor legislation, and direct primaries. He called his program the New Nationalism.[71] It marked a sharp departure from Taft administration policies, and it split the GOP. Democrats, not surprisingly, took over Congress that November.

Taft felt the burden greatly. So did Major Archie Butt of Georgia, Taft's loyal military aide. When he saw TR upon his return from Europe, the gallant Southerner remarked how the old Rough Rider had changed:

"He is bigger, broader, capable of greater good or greater evil, than when he left."[72] Major Butt was deeply devoted to *both* Theodore Roosevelt and William Howard Taft. To give Archie Butt a much-needed break, President Taft sent him on a diplomatic mission to the Vatican. He could relax in Europe afterward and enjoy a homeward cruise on the maiden voyage of the White Star Line's luxurious new liner, the Royal Mail Steamer *Titanic*.

The *Titanic* represented the latest in marine technology. Her steel compartments and watertight doors led many in the press to label her "unsinkable." Her passenger list for her first voyage from Southampton to New York read like the Social Register. Some of the first-class suites went for as much as $4,000—$50,000 in today's dollars.

The magnificent ship struck an iceberg on the moonless night of 14 April 1912. The collision occurred at 11:40 p.m. She sank in less than three hours, at 2:20 a.m. At the end, the ship's orchestra played "Nearer My God to Thee" to keep doomed passengers from panicking. It was not the greatest maritime disaster in history, but it was surely the most sensational.* John Jacob Astor and Benjamin Guggenheim, Mr. and Mrs. Isidore Strauss, and many other very wealthy British and American passengers died. Despite this, the heavy loss of life among third-class passengers— mostly immigrants crammed into the steerage compartments—led to widespread denunciations of privilege in the Yellow Press. In all, more than 1,500 passengers died. A Canadian newspaper estimated at $191 million the net worth of just twelve of the leading first-class passengers who were lost.[73] (That's $2.3 billion in today's dollars.) Owners of the *Titanic* were rightly criticized for the wholly inadequate number of lifeboats provided. J. Pierpont Morgan's holding company owned the White Star Line and was thus ultimately responsible.[74]

---

* For example, 9,343 people died on 30 January 1945, when the German liner *Wilhelm Gustloff* was sunk in the Baltic Sea by a Soviet submarine. The liner was carrying wounded sailors, soldiers, and civilians. They were fleeing Soviet troops advancing into what was then East Prussia (http://in.rediff.com/news/2005/may/09spec1.htm.).

Instead, most press criticism at the time focused on Bruce Ismay, managing director of the White Star Line. Ismay had quietly stepped into a lifeboat at the instruction of a crew member. Many thought Ismay, like Captain Smith, should have "gone down with his ship."[75]

By all accounts, Major Archie Butt faced death in the icy waters with heroic resolution. He and other men of the *Titanic* brought credit to themselves by the stoic way in which they gave preference to women and children. Captain Arthur Henry Rostron, master of the SS *Carpathia*, steamed at a top speed of seventeen and one-half knots through treacherous waters to arrive at the disaster scene. Without Captain Rostron's heroic rescue dash, few of the 712 survivors would have lived in the freezing temperatures. Winston Churchill reflected that "the strict observance of the great traditions of the sea towards women and children reflects nothing but honor on our civilization."[76]

Not entirely. The testimony of Sir Cosmo Duff Gordon at a London inquest revealed he had gotten into a boat designed for forty but which held only twelve. Worse, Sir Cosmo offered each of the seamen in the boat a promissory note for £5 (approximately $312 in today's money). On the witness stand, he maintained that the payment was only offered to reimburse poor seamen who had lost everything when the great ship went down. But critics charged that Sir Cosmo's payment was a bribe to keep the seamen from going back to pull dying passengers out of the frigid waters. Sir Cosmo's reputation, like Ismay's, never recovered. And they seemed a symbol of the callous indifference of the rich to the plight of the poor.[77]*

President and Mrs. Taft were devastated by brave Archie Butt's loss. They had loved him as a son. The president immediately ordered an ice patrol. Soon, U.S. Coast Guard cutters took on the responsibility for safety of life at sea. Mrs. Taft appealed to the women of America to contribute to

---

* Lady Duff Gordon—Lucille—suffered no lasting damage to her reputation. She opened a stylish dress shop in Paris that thrived. The French love a little *soupcon* of scandal.

a *Titanic* memorial dedicated to the men who gave up their lives so that women and children might live. The handsome monument was erected on the banks of the Potomac.*

VII. A BULL MOOSE ON THE LOOSE: THE ELECTION OF 1912

Taft tried hard to avoid a break with his dear friend, Theodore. "I have had a hard time," he wrote the former president. "I have been conscientiously trying to carry out *your* policies."[78] Indeed he had. By early 1912, however, many in the Republican Party were convinced they had to have new leadership if they were to win the White House. The loss of Congress to the Democrats had been a terrible shock to the GOP. Many blamed Taft, even though their party had had an abnormally long run in control of the legislative branch.

"My hat is in the ring, the fight is on and I am stripped to the buff," TR finally told supporters in February 1912.[79] He would challenge the president of his own choice for the Republican presidential nomination

Taft supporters were called Republican regulars or the Old Guard. Roosevelt's backers—*progressives*—heaped scorn on them. In the middle of one pro-Roosevelt rally, some Old Guard Republicans became dispirited. "Oh hell, what's the use?" they said. "Even babies cry for Roosevelt. He is the whole three rings, ringmaster and elephant. Maybe he will let us into the show if we carry water for the elephant."[80]

Most despondent of all was William Howard Taft. He had not wanted to run for president. He did so only out of loyalty to his beloved friend, Theodore. He never relished political combat the way Teddy did. Now Teddy was attacking him most cruelly. "Roosevelt was my closest friend,"

---

* The *Titanic* memorial still stands in Washington, D.C., although it was moved to make way for the Kennedy Center.

Taft told a reporter on the presidential train. With that, he dissolved into tears.[81] But fight he would when TR attacked the independent judiciary. Taft became convinced that Teddy was a menace to the system of checks and balances at the heart of the American system. Taft's supporters went much further, denouncing Teddy as a demagogue and *his* supporters as snake-oil salesmen.[82]

Soon TR's "Dutch" was up. He bitterly attacked Taft in the most personal terms. And he whipped up his troops with this appeal: we are "fearless of the future, unheeding of our individual fates; with unflinching hearts and undimmed eyes, we stand at Armageddon, and we battle for the Lord!"[83]

Armageddon? It's a little hard to believe the rhetoric nearly a century later, yet this is a classic example of how people—even highly intelligent people of undeniable integrity—can work themselves into a lather in the heat of political combat. It gets worse. TR called Taft "a fathead" with "the intellect of a guinea pig." Taft shot back: TR was a "dangerous egotist" and a "demagogue."[84]

Charging bad faith and foul play, Teddy led his delegates in a walkout from the Republican National Convention in Chicago. Several weeks later, they reconvened in the same rented hall, now calling themselves the Progressive Party. When the Progressives took the bunting off the speakers' platform, they were amazed to find that Taft's Republican floor managers had placed *barbed wire* underneath! The Republican regulars had been ready for an assault by Teddy's delegates.

TR gave the new party its name when he said he felt as fit "as a bull moose."[85] Suffragettes—as advocates of women's suffrage were known—embraced the Progressive Party's call for equal voting rights. Jane Addams of Hull House pitched in. She said: "To keep aloof from [politics] must be to lose one opportunity of sharing the life of the community."[86] So did Oscar Strauss, a leading reformer and a Jew, who outsang other Progressive delegates in a spirited version of "Onward Christian Soldiers."[87] TR's soldiers, Christian or not, marched for direct election of U.S. senators, a federal income tax (both soon to be enacted as constitutional amendments), direct primaries and initiative, referendum, and recall (several western states, notably California, would soon enact these reforms). Along with all the earnest social do-gooders, the high-minded intellectuals, and the veterans of grassroots organizing, even TR had to admit the Progressives attracted more than their share of the "lunatic fringe."[88]

Experienced pols knew what the split in the GOP meant: Democrats would win. TR knew it too.[89]

The only question: *Which* Democrat? Incredibly, William Jennings Bryan was making his *fourth* try for the White House. But Democrats looked to Governor Woodrow Wilson of New Jersey. Wilson had been in Trenton little more than a year, but he had built a national reputation as a scholar and reforming president of Princeton University. Theodore Roosevelt respected Wilson and had actually conferred with him in Buffalo in the dark hours following McKinley's assassination. After forty-six ballots in sweltering Baltimore, the tall, angular "schoolmaster in politics" was nominated.

The fall campaign rolled on to its predetermined end. In October, TR's train pulled into Milwaukee, a hotbed of Progressive agitation. While proceeding to the auditorium where he would give another stemwinder of a speech, Teddy was shot once by a would-be assassin. Fortunately, the bullet was slowed by the thick sheaf of papers—Teddy's speech—and an eyeglass case that he carried in his vest pocket. Rejecting medical attention, Teddy mounted the podium and delivered the speech to an audience amazed at his courage and blown away by his endurance.[90]

Harvard's Samuel Eliot Morison, the great historian, cast his first vote that year. He asked a colleague how he should vote: "Vote for Roosevelt, pray for Taft, but *bet* on Wilson."[91]

That proved to be shrewd advice. Although he won only 41.9 percent of the popular vote (6,293,152), Wilson won a huge majority in the electoral college, 435. TR did something never done before or since: he came in *second* running on a third-party ticket. He garnered 4,119,207 popular votes (27.4 percent) and 88 electoral votes. Taft came in third with 3,486,333 popular votes (23.2 percent) and only 8 electoral votes. Eugene V. Debs ran on the Socialist ticket. He campaigned vigorously in a train called "the red special." Debs won over one million votes but carried no state. In effect, TR and Taft had knocked each other out. Wilson was elected with 110,952 *fewer* popular votes than Bryan had won in his disastrous third run for president in 1908.

The Bull Moose Party effort of 1912 is convincing proof, if ever it was needed, that the *only* thing a third-party campaign can do is to break up the ruling coalition and elect a minority president. William Howard Taft might well have lost to Wilson anyway. His administration had been "a series of political explosions," true.[92] But most of them were not of his making. He deserved better of his country. He surely deserved better of his friend, Theodore Roosevelt.

VIII. WOODROW WILSON AND THE NEW FREEDOM

The new president, tall and dignified, mounted the speaker's rostrum in the House of Representatives. There, on 7 April 1913, Woodrow Wilson delivered an address to a joint meeting of Congress.[93] The practice of delivering State of the Union messages and other important speeches *in person* before the assembled lawmakers had been dropped by Thomas Jefferson more than a century earlier. Jefferson said it smacked too much of the English monarch's Speech from the Throne, but it was also the case that Jefferson was a poor public speaker, and he knew it. Wilson was a great public speaker, and he knew it.

Not only did it provide a dramatic setting for the president's messages, but it ensured that the president would thenceforth take the initiative in proposing important legislation. Wilson was the first PhD to win the presidency. His specialty was political science. He was determined to bring major change to the institutions of government that he had studied, taught, and written about.[*]

Wilson was determined as well to bring about major economic reforms. President Wilson was the first leader since Lincoln to go up to the Capitol to confer in person with members of his party.[94] Democrats now controlled both houses of Congress, but even so, success for Wilson's economic program would take hard work. Wilson succeeded in his objectives, achieving a major overhaul of the nation's banking system. The Federal Reserve Act of 1913 divided the country into twelve districts, each with a federal reserve bank to regulate the currency and provide a modern banking system. This measure, authored by Virginia's courtly Senator Carter Glass, remains essentially unchanged to this day and counts as one of Wilson's major achievements.[95]

Wilson plowed ahead with reforms. He appealed to Congress to outlaw almost all child labor (even though the Supreme Court was to strike it down as unconstitutional). He got legislative approval for limiting to eight hours a day the work of railroad workers. He successfully pressed Congress for an income tax and a Federal Trade Commission, and he passed an inheritance tax—over the loud objections of propertied Americans.

The Underwood Tariff stands as another of Wilson's major achievements. It lowered import duties by 10 percent across the board. Wilson took on the manufacturers and lobbyists and prevailed with hard bargaining.[96][**]

The Clayton Anti-Trust Act of 1914 was another piece of legislation Wilson strongly backed. The act was sponsored by Alabama Congressman Henry de Lamar Clayton. Samuel Gompers, president of the American Federation of Labor, called the Clayton Act "labor's charter

---

[*]   Wilson received a doctorate in political science in 1886 from Johns Hopkins University in
     Baltimore, Maryland. He was the first, and to date the last, PhD in the White House.

[**] Tariff issues have always loomed large in American politics. In the years before the 1913
     ratification of the Sixteenth Amendment, which allowed a federal income tax, the tariff was
     the primary means of financing the federal government.

of freedom." Under this act, labor unions would no longer be considered "combinations in restraint of trade," as they had often been under the Sherman Anti-Trust Act of 1890. Labor was specifically allowed to engage in strikes, boycotts, and picketing, although violence against persons and property continued to be against the law. Court injunctions had been a major weapon used *against* unions in labor disputes. The Clayton Act required federal courts to use more restraint in issuing such injunctions.[97]

Wilson challenged the nation to live up to its founding creed when he nominated Louis D. Brandeis to the Supreme Court. Brandeis was a highly respected reformer, beloved of the Progressives. Labor loved him for his "Brandeis briefs," sociological studies that showed the often terrible impact of management decisions on the lives of workers, especially women and child laborers. Although Wilson had passed over Brandeis for a cabinet post, he had looked to him as architect of the New Freedom legislation. Now, Wilson was determined to name the first Jew ever to sit on the High Court.[98] In the face of fierce opposition, some of it anti-Semitic, Wilson backed his man and secured a signal victory for America as an open society. Indeed, this was a New Freedom.

For one group of Americans, however, Woodrow Wilson's New Freedom rang hollow. Although black Americans certainly were helped by Wilson's labor and social legislation, they found no interest among the Democrats in civil rights. As the names of the sponsors of Wilson's landmark reform legislation show, Wilson was highly dependent upon white Southern Democrats to get his program through Congress. Since most black Americans at the time were firm supporters of the party of Lincoln, the Democratic victories in Congress and the presidency meant that hundreds of black federal officeholders would be swept out.[99] One of Wilson's Georgia appointees said it bluntly: "A Negro's place is in the cornfield."[100] The president did not rebuke him.

Segregation in federal government offices was only partially reversed by Wilson, despite his personal claim of sympathy for the plight of black Americans.[101] His speech at the fiftieth anniversary of the Battle of

Gettysburg made no mention of the fact that black Americans were still denied their rights as citizens of the United States. If, as the Declaration of Independence said and Lincoln reaffirmed at Gettysburg in 1863, "all men are created equal," no one listening to Wilson's forgotten Gettysburg Address of 1913 would have thought so.[102]

Worse, Wilson gave a platform to one of the worst examples of racial intolerance in American history. The movie *The Birth of a Nation* may have been a silent film, but it shouted its contempt for black people from the housetops. The epic silent movie depicted the Ku Klux Klan not as terrorists and murderers but as freedom fighters. The movie was the first film ever screened at the White House. Wilson watched it and praised it extravagantly. "It is like writing history with lightning. My only regret is that it is all so terribly true," he enthused.[103*]

Frustrated by the slow pace of change, even by backsliding in Washington, W. E. B. DuBois and other dedicated black and white reformers (including Jane Addams) had banded together to form the National Association for the Advancement of Colored People (NAACP). They resolved to challenge the "go along to get along" attitude they saw in Booker T. Washington's Tuskegee Machine.[104] The NAACP began its half-century fight for full, equal rights for black Americans.

IX. "THE LIGHTS ARE GOING OUT . . ."

As Ellen Axson Wilson lay dying of cancer in the White House in the summer of 1914, the president was bowed down with grief. He and the First Lady had been married for twenty-nine years. She was the center of

---

* President Ronald Regan spoke to a Catholic men's group about *The Birth of a Nation*. The Knights of Columbus were meeting in New Haven, Connecticut, in 1982. The KKK's hatred encompassed not only black Americans, but also Catholics, Jews, and foreigners. Reagan told the knights that he was proud of his Hollywood movie career. "But," he said, "I have never seen that film . . . *and I never will!*" The knights erupted in loud, sustained applause.

his close-knit and supportive family. Aside from Mrs. Wilson, his faithful aide Joseph Tumulty, and his intimate friend and adviser Texas "Colonel" Edward M. House, Woodrow Wilson had few people upon whom he could rely.* Wilson was described as one who loved humanity—in the abstract.[105] Wilson was aware of this trait: "I have a sense of power in dealing with men collectively which I do not feel in dealing with them singly."[106] His own very able secretary of the interior, Franklin K. Lane, said he was "clean, strong, high-minded and cold-blooded."[107] Now, with Mrs. Wilson's untimely death, there would be a terrible void in his life.

Meanwhile, in Europe death stalked the corridors of power in a very different way. In late June, Archduke Franz Ferdinand, the heir to the throne of the unsteady Austro-Hungarian Empire, paid a "goodwill" trip to the beautiful medieval city of Sarajevo in the province of Bosnia-Herzegovina. Young Slavic nationalists in the province resented being ruled from distant Vienna by the Teutonic and mostly Catholic Austrians. Aided by a Serbian underground terrorist group called the Black Hand, some of these students resolved to kill the archduke.

As Franz Ferdinand and his wife, Sophie, were being driven through the narrow streets of Sarajevo on 28 June 1914, a band of young terrorists prepared their bombs. "One was so jammed in the crowd that he could not pull the bomb out of his pocket. A second saw a policeman standing near him and decided that any movement was too risky. A third felt sorry for the archduke's wife and did nothing. A fourth lost his nerve and slipped off home."[108] But nineteen-year-old Gavrilo Princip did not flinch. When a first bomb exploded but failed to injure the imperial couple, Princip thought the plot had failed. Minutes later, he was astounded to see the archduke and archduchess in their official car, just five feet from him. (The car had taken a wrong turn down a narrow side street.) Princip knew he could not throw his bomb; there was no room. So he pulled out his Browning pistol and fired two shots, point blank. He hit Franz Ferdinand

---

* House was given an honorary title as colonel as an adviser to the governor of Texas.

in the throat, severing his carotid artery. His second shot hit Sophie in the abdomen. Both were dead within the hour.[109]

In Vienna, the humorless and harsh Franz Ferdinand had been unloved. Still, the assassination of the heir to the imperial throne had to be avenged. Austria-Hungary decided to use the "outrage" as a pretext to destroy Serbia. For this, though, the Austrians needed the backing of their powerful ally, Germany. The Austrians feared that if they went to war against Serbia, Russia would hasten to protect their Slavic brothers.

At this critical moment, when the life of Europe teetered in the balance, Germany's Kaiser Wilhelm II gave Austria-Hungary a "blank check." Germany would back Austria-Hungary in whatever she decided to do about Serbia, the Kaiser said.[110]

Europe was quite literally sitting on a powder keg. If Austria-Hungary moved against Serbia, Russia would come to Serbia's aid. If Russia came in, Germany would declare war against Russia. If Germany attacked Russia, France was bound by treaty to race to Russia's defense. And if France was attacked, Great Britain would feel honor bound to stand by her. If Britain joined the war, so, too, would Canada, Australia, New Zealand, South Africa, and India. In a matter of days, what began as a localized conflict would become a *world war.*

Worse, Germany's ruler was Europe's "powder monkey." That is, he was running around the continent with explosives in hand. One of Wilhelm II's early acts was to "drop the pilot," to get rid of "the Iron Chancellor" Otto von Bismarck in 1890. Bismarck would never have risked his German Empire on a conflict in the Balkans. "The whole of the Balkans is not worth the bones of a single Pomeranian grenadier," he had said contemptuously. But Bismarck also had played the prophet: "If there is another war in the future," he had said, "it will come out of some damned foolish thing in the Balkans."

Now, even as the president was attending the Georgia funeral for Mrs. Wilson, Europe was sliding into war. Nor would it be a localized, limited war. Europe had seen a score of these in the hundred years since the defeat of Napoleon at Waterloo in 1815. This would be a war more terrible, more total than anything previously seen.

Several years earlier, America was fresh on the world horizon, a land infinite with opportunity and electric with optimism. Now an ocean away, despair gripped the Old World, and the only opportunities seemed for destruction. Britain's foreign secretary, Sir Edward Grey, spoke of the hushed sense of anticipation all truly knowledgeable people felt in August 1914: "The lights are going out all over Europe. We shall not see them lit again in our lifetime."

TWELVE

AMERICA AND THE GREAT WAR

(1914–1921)

I. "HOME BEFORE THE LEAVES FALL"

Germany's Kaiser Wilhelm II was, in many ways, the most important figure in Europe in 1914. A product of royalty's preference for intermarriage, Wilhelm was the grandson of Britain's Queen Victoria. The widowed queen had so many relatives in ruling royal houses she was called "the grandmother of Europe." He proudly wore the uniforms of admiral in the Royal Navy and field marshal in the British Army. He thought he knew Britain well, spoke English fluently, and visited his relatives there often. He could and should have been Britain's best hope for peace on the Continent. Instead, he was the greatest threat.

From his earliest days, Wilhelm had been a troubled and troubling child. He was bright, eager, and energetic. But he seemed to have been born with a chip on his shoulder. He was, in fact, born with a tragic birth defect. His left arm was shorter than his right, a fact about which he was deeply sensitive. He tried to conceal it, with some success, by elaborate military capes and long, elegant kid gloves that he always held in photographs. Wilhelm's willfulness terrified even his own parents.

Wilhelm had read *The Influence of Sea Power Upon History*. This important book by American Admiral Alfred Thayer Mahan had deeply impressed the German ruler. It was also devoured by such naval power theorists as Theodore Roosevelt and Winston Churchill. The leaders of the Imperial Japanese Navy translated Mahan's great work as early as 1896. In the early 1900s, Wilhelm raced to build a powerful fleet of dreadnought battleships and ordered every German warship to carry a copy of Mahan's masterpiece.

The kaiser's throwing his weight around did not stop with building a navy. Soon he was trying to grab colonies in Africa and the Pacific. He demanded Germany's "place in the sun." His rough handling managed to alienate his cousin, Tsar Nicholas. In response, Russia soon concluded an alliance with France. The watchword for the kaiser's rule was *weltmacht oder niedergang* ("world power or decline").[1] It explains the constant pushing and shoving of Wilhelm and his military chiefs that made peace so precarious for a full quarter of a century before the final outbreak of war in 1914.

Americans, shielded by three thousand miles of ocean from the kaiser's bluster, initially felt unconcerned about his militarism and his frequent saber rattling. The interference of the German fleet with Commodore Dewey's Philippine operations in 1898 came as a rude shock. So did the kaiser's meddling in Latin America in the early Roosevelt years. But we had Teddy's Big Stick to keep us safe.

At the turn of the new century, Americans tended to view Kaiser Wilhelm II with a mixture of distrust and amused contempt. A 1903 poem published in *Harper's Weekly* reveals the attitude:

> Kaiser, Kaiser, shining bright
> You have given us a fright!

With your belts and straps and sashes,
And your upward-turned mustaches!
And that frown so deadly fierce
And those awful eyes that pierce
Through the very hearts of those
Whom ill fate has made your foes.
Kaiser, Kaiser, Man of War
What a funny joke you are.[2]

Readers recognized the satire on William Blake's line "Tyger, Tyger, burning bright." When the clash in the Balkans finally came in 1914, Wilhelm relied on his English family connection to avert war with Britain. He sent his brother, Prince Heinrich, to speak to King George V, their first cousin through their grandmother, Queen Victoria. The king said that he hoped Britain would stay out of any continental war. The kaiser mistakenly took that to mean the king would determine British policy. "I have the word of a king," he boasted.[3] Wilhelm apparently learned nothing from his mother or grandmother about the British system of governance. Britain was (and is) a constitutional monarchy. Foreign policy is made by the cabinet, not the Crown.

In July 1914, only days after the assassination of Archduke Ferdinand, the world breathed a sigh of relief as the kaiser went on his annual three-week cruise in the fjords of Norway. It seemed he was disengaging from the mounting crisis between Austria-Hungary, Serbia, and their allies. His magnificent 380-foot, 4,280-ton yacht *Hohenzollern* looked like a giant white swan gliding silently over Norway's dark, cold waters that summer.* But this peaceful image was deceptive. While the kaiser cruised these placid waters, the air was electric with radio traffic to and from the vessel.

Given the nature of Europe's web of alliances, the kaiser virtually guaranteed a world war in 1905 when he approved the military plan

---

* Uncharacteristically for a royal yacht, *Hohenzollern* was heavily armed. She carried three rapid-fire, 105mm cannons and twelve rapid-fire, 50mm cannons.

of General Alfred von Schlieffen, chief of the Imperial General Staff. According to the Schlieffen Plan, German soldiers would have to smash into Belgium and drive deep into France, knocking France out of any future war before her Russian allies could be mobilized in the East. "Let the last man on the right brush the [English] Channel with his sleeve," it was said of the Schlieffen Plan.

Wilhelm carelessly exposed Germany to a dreaded two-front war through his own unskillful diplomacy and his regular threats to his neighbors. Further, Wilhelm seemed oblivious to the fact that the Schlieffen Plan involved violating Belgian neutrality, which Germany as well as Britain had guaranteed for a century. Britain had not clearly warned Kaiser Wilhelm that violating Belgium's neutrality would mean war. In fact, none of the Powers knew exactly what Britain's response would be if Germany marched across Belgium en route to France.[4]

Twenty years later, Wilhelm would tell British historian Sir John Wheeler-Bennett that he never would have invaded Belgium if he had known that such a move would incite Britain to war. Subtle hints and diplomatic nuances were wasted on Wilhelm. If ever there was a case for Big Stick diplomacy, it was here.

Many would later claim that Britain gave insufficient warning to the Germans. This, however, gives too little attention to the reckless conduct of Germany for the previous twenty-five years and ignores the basic fact that aggressor nations have no right to expect hand-sitting by their neighbors.[5]

The kaiser assured his ally that Germany would stand by Austria-Hungary "through thick and thin." Don't worry about Russia, he told the Austrian ambassador. Russia is "in no way prepared for war."[6]

Backed by Wilhelm II, the Austrians rejected Russia's urgent plea for negotiations, even as the German military High Command was pressing the Austrians for war in response to the assassination. Cousin "Nickie," Russia's tsar, desperately wrote to Cousin "Willy," the kaiser, to "beg" him to restrain Austria. Lying, Wilhelm wrote he was doing his utmost to hold his ally back.[7] Similarly, Berlin rejected Britain's call for a Four-Power conference.[8]

As July closed, Germany filled the telegraph lines of Europe with cabled ultimatums—to Russia, to France, to Belgium. A leading member of the British cabinet, Winston Churchill, was the First Lord of the Admiralty. He was responsible for the readiness of the British fleet. He worried that the Powers were sliding into war. "I wondered whether those stupid Kings and Emperors could not assemble together and revivify kingship by saving the nations from hell but we all drift on in a kind of dull cataleptic trance."[9]

Hell was closing in. Germany declared war on France and invaded Belgium.[10] With the mutual declarations of war, Churchill cabled the Royal Navy: "Commence hostilities against Germany."

The invasion of Belgium did everything to justify the name *Hun* that the kaiser had given his troops in 1900. As early as 5 August, General von Moltke admitted that "our advance into Belgium is certainly brutal."[11] He was right. The German army murdered women and children in the towns of Andenne, Tamine, Seilles, and Dinant; more than two hundred civilians in the first days of war. The University in Louvain was burned and pillaged. The senseless destruction of this "Oxford" of Belgium, with its priceless medieval books and tapestries, was denounced by scholars throughout the world as "a crime against civilization."[12]

Millions in France and England who had foolishly predicted their boys would be "home before the leaves fall" were stunned as Germany's ruthless push drove the French forces and the British Expeditionary Force back to the defenses of Paris. That autumn, France was nearly defeated. France's Ferdinand Foch rallied his troops. A message—probably apocryphal—has him saying, "My center is giving way, my right [flank] is in retreat, situation excellent. I attack." Apocryphal or not, that is exactly what Foch did.[13] He was helped when hundreds of Paris taxicabs were pressed into emergency service. They brought every extra French *poilu* who could carry a rifle to the front.* Soon, the world saw "the miracle of the Marne" as the German advance was halted at the river's bank, just outside Paris.[14]

Less of a miracle was the terrible cost to France of this desperate defense. The deadly machine gun put an end to the French tactic of *offensive á outrance*. This tactic called for charging fixed-gun emplacements. It was even more suicidal than the futile rushes at Fredericksburg and Gettysburg had been for the Americans. In the first three months of war alone, 350,000 French soldiers died.[15] Both sides soon dug in for a long, bitter war of attrition. The trenches they built were strung with barbed wire. Between the opposing lines was a deadly "no man's land." Eventually, this ugly scar extended from Switzerland to the North Sea.

Gone were the cheering crowds who had welcomed the war. Gone, too, were the colorful flags and banners. The famous French uniforms—blue jackets with red pants and hats—were quickly replaced by dun-colored shapeless greatcoats as millions of young men descended into the blood and mud of inhuman trench warfare.

II. "TOO PROUD TO FIGHT"

President Woodrow Wilson immediately declared America's neutrality. Reacting to the stories of the "rape of Belgium," Wilson said, "We must be impartial in thought as well as in action, must put a curb upon our sentiments." The stance was very popular with Americans. Even the normally bellicose TR said it would be "folly to jump into the war."[16]

All eyes turned to Europe when a German submarine sank the British luxury liner *Lusitania* on 7 May 1915 off Kinsale, Ireland. The U-boat (*unterseeboot*)** attack claimed more than twelve hundred noncombatants

---

* *Poilu*: literally, "a hairy one." French enlisted men had little time for haircuts and shaves under constant German bombardment in the trenches.

** Literally, an "under the sea boat."

as the great four-stack vessel sank in just eighteen minutes. Of these, 126 were American citizens who ignored the warning notices the German embassy had placed in newspapers in New York and several other major U.S. cities.[17]

The *Lusitania* was carrying munitions, which made her a legitimate target for destruction in German eyes. They had the letter of the law on their side. Even so, Americans felt a shock of horror as survivors described the babies who cried piteously as their wicker basket cradles sank slowly beneath the waves. Americans were further repelled by the German reaction to the sinking. There, editorials boasted of a "joyful pride in our navy," schoolchildren were given the day off in celebration, and a Munich citizen even had a commemorative medallion struck to honor the submariners who had done this act. A pro-British American living in London seized upon the medal and had three hundred thousand copies made. These circulated throughout the U.S. and the British Empire as evidence of German inhumanity.[18*]

President Wilson quickly responded to the outrage and the demands for war with Germany. "There is such a thing as a man being too proud to fight," he said, echoing his previous sentiments about staying out of the war.[19] Such indifference shocked former presidents Theodore Roosevelt and William Howard Taft, both Republicans. Wilson's statement left them appalled.[20] They both called for war. TR's cousin, Franklin Delano Roosevelt, agreed with their outrage.[21] But as Wilson's assistant secretary of the navy, FDR was a loyal Democrat. He could not go public with his disagreement with the president of his own party.

Instead of preparing for war, Wilson sent Germany a diplomatic note. When this produced no discernible reply, the next month Wilson sent a second, sterner note.

TR, of course, was disgusted. He turned the air blue with words of

---

* The American was Gordon Selfridge, the owner of a famous London department store. He was later to become a British subject (Massie, *Castles of Steel*, 534).

contempt for "Professor Wilson," who represented all "flubdubs, molly-coddles and flapdoodle pacifists."[22] Wilson continued sending his feckless diplomatic notes—typed on his own typewriter—for another year.

Americans were horrified by the slaughter in the trenches in France. Not only had the Germans initiated submarine warfare against passenger ships, but they were the first to introduce poison gas.[23] Hundreds of miles of the beautiful French and Belgian countryside were reduced to a hellish moonscape, a "no man's land" where rats fattened on corpses. The Germans used their powerful artillery to batter quaint towns and villages into rubble. "Big Bertha" was a forty-three-ton monster howitzer produced by the Krupp company and incongruously named for Gustav Krupp's wife. It fired a 2,200-pound shell more than nine miles.

The Germans also rained death from the air. Their hydrogen-filled dirigibles—called *zeppelins* after German Count Zeppelin—dropped bombs on civilians in London.[24] In all this, the kaiser's High Command consciously pursued a policy of *schrecklichkeit* ("frightfulness") to terrify their enemies.[25]

Wilson addressed the war in Europe in a controversial speech in 1916 in which he called for a "peace without victory" and offered to mediate.[26] Germany spurned the offer. Once again, Republicans and other supporters of the Allies were deeply affronted.

Wilson's reelection prospects brightened somewhat when the Germans offered the Sussex Pledge in May of 1916. This event followed an attack by a U-boat on the unarmed French channel steamer *Sussex* in which fifty people, including Americans, were killed. In this agreement, the Germans pledged not to attack merchant vessels unless they were carrying war contraband and unless their passengers and crew members had first been allowed to get into their lifeboats.

Wilson was renominated in 1916, but with the Republicans' divisions papered over, it appeared he would be a one-term president. TR urged his Bull Moose Progressives to get behind the Republicans for the sake of national unity.[27] GOP prospects looked good; no Democrat had been reelected since Andrew Jackson.

The Republicans backed Supreme Court Justice Charles Evans Hughes. Despite the fact that the tall, bearded Hughes had once been governor of New York, however, he proved to be an inept campaigner.

Wilson's campaign stressed the theme "He Kept Us Out of War." Privately, Wilson worried that "any little German lieutenant" could put us into the war and the president could not stop it.[28] Wilson knew that relatively low-ranking submarine commanders held vastly destructive power in their hands. Any one of them could create an international incident by killing more noncombatants. What if, for example, a U-boat skipper had sunk an American liner off the shores of the president's home state of New Jersey?* But publicly, Wilson was content to campaign as the peace candidate. Democrats took out full-page ads in newspapers attacking both Hughes *and* Theodore Roosevelt:

YOU ARE WORKING;

—NOT FIGHTING

ALIVE AND HAPPY;

—NOT CANNON FODDER!

WILSON AND PEACE WITH HONOR?

OR HUGHES WITH ROOSEVELT AND WAR?[29]

On Election Day, Hughes swept the Northeast and appeared to have won. According to a story widely circulated at the time, a reporter telephoned the Hughes home and the Republican candidate's son responded that the "president" had retired for the night. "Don't wake him now," said the impish reporter, "but when he gets up, tell him he *ain't* president." The story is probably legend, but it does illustrate the cliffhanger nature of the election and the overly self-assured reputation of the Hughes campaign. When all the votes were counted, Wilson won a narrow victory for a second term.

---

* The Germans would sink American ships within sight of the Jersey beaches in 1942.

The Allies had been bled white by the war in France. Britain alone lost 20,000 men and 40,000 wounded on the first day of the Battle of the Somme.[30] By early 1917, the Allies were near financial collapse.[31] To win the war, the Germans needed only to avoid antagonizing America.

This the reckless kaiser could not do. Early in February, he gave in to his admirals and announced a resumption of unrestricted submarine warfare. The Germans had begun to discount the American reaction to this. Because they had repeatedly provoked America and had faced no serious consequences, they haughtily assumed that America would not fight. Or, if America fought, it would not achieve much.

"They will *not* even come, because our submarines will sink them," Admiral Capelle promised Germany's parliament, the Reichstag, in January 1917. Pridefully, he continued: "Thus America from a military point of view means nothing, and again nothing, and for a third time [I say] *nothing!*"[32]

This contempt was not only an example of the German military's bloody-mindedness, it was also a reflection of President Wilson's policies and his choice of key personnel. Wilson had no military experience. He was certainly well respected as a scholar, but he had no deep knowledge of American diplomacy and warfare. Worse, with the sole exception of Franklin D. Roosevelt, Wilson surrounded himself with advisers similarly unqualified. He had consciously chosen pacifists as secretary of state (William Jennings Bryan) and secretary of the navy (Josephus Daniels).[33] His attorney general (A. Mitchell Palmer) was a noted Quaker, a Christian sect founded on pacifism.[34]* Even his secretary of war, Newton D. Baker, improbably, was a pacifist.[35] German diplomats stationed in Washington could not have failed to point to these incredible facts in their reports to Berlin.

As if unrestricted submarine warfare were not provocation enough, German foreign minister Arthur Zimmermann sent a secret cable to his

---

* Initially known as "the fighting Quaker," Palmer was derided as "the quaking fighter."

ambassador in Mexico. The infamous *Zimmermann Telegram* proposed that Mexico and Japan should be approached to align with Germany to make war on the United States. In return for their support, the Mexicans would be given large parts of the American Southwest that the United States had seized during the Mexican War.

The Hearst Yellow Press—bitterly opposed to war with Germany—cried foul. It was all a trick of British propaganda, they charged. George Viereck was the editor of the largest German-language newspaper in the United States—*Vaterland* ("Fatherland"). Viereck bluntly called the Zimmermann Telegram "a brazen forgery planted by British agents." Actually, it was Viereck and Hearst's Berlin correspondents who were paid *German* agents.[36]

Viereck was right about one thing: the British were involved. British agents had intercepted the Zimmermann Telegram—and they were at pains to keep that fact from becoming known. At first blush, this seems counterintuitive. After all, if the telegram were made known, it would provoke America to war. But it wasn't that simple. Why? President Wilson had foolishly allowed the Germans to use official U.S. diplomatic cables because he wanted to let them discuss peace proposals without British interference. Unknown to Wilson, the British not only tapped the German cables but the American ones too. So proficient was British intelligence that its agents could intercept, decode, and translate German cables *faster* than the Germans themselves could.[37] Americans were surely shocked by the Zimmermann Telegram. But they would have been unwilling to go to war if they had known that the British had uncovered it. They would have suspected a forgery by British intelligence—just as Hearst's men claimed—and that would have effectively kept the United States out of the war.

But then, incredibly, Foreign Minister Zimmermann admitted that the telegram was his![38]

This may have been the greatest diplomatic blunder in history.

Overnight, the American Midwest changed its view of the faraway conflict in Europe. The *Omaha World Herald* wrote, "The issue shifts from Germany against Great Britain to Germany against the United States." Other Midwestern papers, including the influential German-language press, dropped their neutrality.[39]

Theodore Roosevelt wrote to Massachusetts Republican Senator Henry Cabot Lodge. The older Lodge had been TR's friend and political mentor for decades. If Wilson would not fight now, TR wrote, "I'll *skin* him alive."[40]

III. ROOSEVELT TO FRANCE?

Once the lonely decision for war was taken in the White House, Woodrow Wilson's famous gift for oratory did not desert him.

Wisely, he told a joint session of Congress on 2 April 1917: "We have no quarrel with the German people. We have no feeling towards them but one of sympathy and friendship." We were fighting, he said, because "the world must be made safe for democracy."[41]

> The right is more precious than peace, and we shall fight for the things we have always carried nearest our hearts—for democracy, for the right of those who submit to authority to have a voice in their own governments, for the rights and liberties of small nations, for a universal dominion of right by such a concert of free peoples as shall bring peace and safety to all nations and make the world itself at last free . . . the day has come when America is privileged to spend her blood . . . for the principles that gave her birth . . . God helping her, she can do no other.[42]

During this somber Washington Holy Week, the Senate and House voted for war. Most Americans embraced their country's moral cause with eagerness. Irish American composer George M. Cohan soon wrote the lilting song that became the theme of America's first major foreign war:

Over there, over there!
Send the word, send the word, over there!
That the Yanks are coming, the Yanks are coming,
The drums rum-tumming ev'rywhere!
So prepare, say a prayer, send the word, send the word to beware!
We'll be over, we're coming over,
And we won't come back 'til it's over Over There!

Not only was Tin Pan Alley*—as America's music publishing industry was then known—fully behind the war effort, millions of Americans subscribed to Liberty Loans. These were government bonds issued to help fund the war.

Theodore Roosevelt desperately wanted to get into the action. He wanted to be an American Lafayette.[43] TR swallowed his pride and went to see Wilson in the White House. He begged the president, actually *pleaded*, for permission to raise a company of volunteers to join the fight in France. Momentarily moved, the president wavered. He told his trusted aide, Joseph Tumulty, that TR was "a great big boy. . . . There is a sweetness about him that is very compelling. You can't resist the man."[44]

The two men who sat across from each other, the president of the United States and his bitter rival, the former president, could not have been more different in background, temperament, or outlook. Theodore Roosevelt was the descendant of a rich and powerful New York Dutch family who had overcome a frail body and childhood asthma to build a powerful persona. He became America's darling as a cowboy in the Dakotas and the boisterous leader of the Rough Riders. As president,

---

* Tin Pan Alley is located at 28th Street in Manhattan, between 5th Avenue and Broadway. It was home to many popular music publishers. At the turn of the twentieth century, journalist Monroe Rosenfeld wrote that the sound of all the pianos banging out tunes sounded like tin pans crashing. The name stuck. (Rick Reublin, "In Search of Tin Pan Alley," Parlor Songs Association, updated March 2009, http://parlorsongs.com/insearch /tinpanalley/tinpanalley.php.)

he had busted Trusts, wielded a Big Stick in diplomacy, and "made the dirt fly" to dig a canal through Panama. He won a Nobel Peace Prize for bringing an end to the Russo-Japanese War, but he sent his Great White Fleet around the world as a warning to increasingly contentious imperial powers: Don't Tread on Me.

All that was in the past.

Now, on 7 April 1917, just one day *after* President Wilson had signed Congress's joint declaration of war against Germany, the Theodore Roosevelt who sat across the desk was a shadow of the man he had been.

He was still suffering the effects of a 1914 expedition through the Brazilian rain forest to trace the uncharted waters of the River of Doubt. TR and his son Kermit had dashed off on the expedition almost on a dare. He *had* to go, he told doubtful friends: "It was my last chance to be a boy." Teddy left so hurriedly he couldn't even select enough reading matter. He did manage to bring Thomas More's *Utopia*, the plays of Sophocles, two volumes of Gibbons's *Decline and Fall of the Roman Empire*, and the works of Marcus Aurelius and Epictetus.[45] When he ran through these, often consuming them in a dugout canoe or sitting under mosquito netting on a rotting log, the former president seized upon Kermit's book of French poetry. "For French verse, father never cared. He said it didn't sing sufficiently. 'The Song of Roland' was the one exception he granted," his son recounted.[46]

The expedition soon became a nightmare. "I don't believe [Roosevelt] can live through the night," wrote the seasoned explorer George Cherrie in his diary, as TR raved in a delirious fever.[47] At one point, TR was so weakened by infection and starvation that he actually told Kermit to push on and leave him to die. Miraculously, he survived the man-eating piranhas,* the poisonous snakes, the malarial mosquitoes, and the intense heat. He made it home, but barely. Roosevelt limped badly. He lost fifty-five pounds in the rain forest, and his clothes hung on him. He never

---

* Ravenously hungry, TR and his party ate some surprisingly tasty piranhas. In another first, Roosevelt thus became the only former U.S. president who actually was a man eating piranha.

fully regained his youthful vigor. To honor him, the Brazilian government renamed the one-thousand-mile extent of the River of Doubt the Rio Roosevelt.[48]

How could President Woodrow Wilson find common ground with his visitor? Wilson had been raised in modest circumstances in the South, the son of a Presbyterian minister. From his earliest days, he was a man of words, not a man of action. He did not play baseball, but he wrote editorials for the student newspaper, *The Princetonian*, on how the captain of the baseball team should be selected. He urged more attention to oratory, the power of rhetoric, to persuade. As a Princeton undergraduate, he complained about "an excess of visible skin in the gymnasium."[49] What would the mature Wilson have thought of TR's famous "point-to-point walks" as president? During some of these, Roosevelt and his companions (senior military officers, foreign diplomats) would strip to the buff to wade through rushing streams.

Whereas Roosevelt once boasted he was proud he had not "a single drop of English blood," Wilson revered the Great Commoner, Prime Minister William E. Gladstone. Like Hamilton before him, he publicly advocated revamping the U.S. constitutional system to make it more like the British model.[50]

But now it was Teddy Roosevelt who was pleading for a chance to get into the action. He felt that history was passing him by. He may even have sensed his own mortality. Roosevelt did not care, he said, if the war killed him: "If I should die tomorrow, I would be quite content to have as my epitaph, and my only epitaph, 'Roosevelt to France.'"[51]

France's premier Georges Clemenceau was clamoring for TR. He told Wilson that the presence of Roosevelt in the trenches would do wonders for the morale of the battered French soldiers who had been fighting there for three years. "Send them Roosevelt," he pleaded.[52]

In the end, Wilson rejected TR's plea.[53] The army brass remembered TR's brashness in Cuba and wanted no part of him in France. Also, this grim war of attrition was to be no daring dash up San Juan Hill. TR was wasted by tropical diseases contracted from his South American trip; he was in no condition to fight in the trenches.

Roosevelt took it the only way he knew how—hard. Wilson's refusal to let him fight only deepened the former president's hostility toward the man he thought had so unworthily occupied the White House.* Bitterly, he lashed out to Kansas editor William Allen White, a progressive Republican: "The Washington people . . . would rather make this a paper war . . . but if not that they want to make it a Democratic war."[54] TR nonetheless had the satisfaction of seeing all four of his sons bravely volunteer. Even his son-in-law, a physician, and his daughter, a nurse, faced danger in frontline medical units.

IV. OVER THERE!

Very quickly, the Americans proved the Germans wrong about their submarine weapon. FDR moved energetically to supply the U.S. Navy with 110-foot antisubmarine vessels while Navy Admiral William S. Sims soon organized a convoy system that overcame the U-boat threat. Because of FDR and Sims's efforts, only 637 of more than two million American soldiers were lost to U-boat attacks crossing over to France.[55]

American intervention came not a moment too soon for the Allies. Britain suffered the highest loss of tonnage to submarines in *two* world wars in April 1917.[56]

General John J. Pershing was given command of the American Expeditionary Force. He was a resolute and determined leader. The previous year, Pershing had been called upon to quell some trouble with Mexico after outlaw Pancho Villa crossed into New Mexico and murdered

---

* With Wilson's rejection also came the end of "Roosevelt to France" as TR's epitaph. Curiously, he was the second U.S. president to propose putting a reference to France on his own tombstone. A century earlier, another combative man offered this: "Here lies John Adams, who took upon himself the responsibility of peace with France in the year 1800."

seventeen Americans at Columbus.[57] Wilson sent General Pershing and twelve thousand cavalry troopers to pursue the bandit leader three hundred miles into Mexico. Villa only narrowly escaped and "Black Jack" Pershing's reputation was made in the "Punitive Expedition."[58*]

Americans thrilled to stories of heroism from U.S. forces. Flying in French biplanes, the Lafayette Escadrille distinguished itself in the air. Lieutenant Eddie Rickenbacker became America's first air "Ace" by shooting down twenty-six German planes.[59] American infantrymen called "doughboys" captured French hearts too.[**] Colonel Charles Stanton wowed the French at a Fourth of July ceremony in Paris. At the tomb of the Marquis de Lafayette, Stanton stepped forward, saluted smartly, and said, "*Lafayette, nous voici!*" ("Lafayette, we are here!")[60]

U.S. Marines went into action against battle-hardened German troops who soon learned to fear the Leathernecks. They called our Marines *teufelhunden*—devil dogs. When Allied generals called for a temporary withdrawal, Marine Captain Lloyd Williams groused: "Retreat? *Hell*, we just got here!"[61]

It took time for U.S. industry to be converted to a wartime economy. The military was woefully ill-equipped. Secretary of War Newton D. Baker even bragged about it: "I delight in the fact that when we entered this war we were not, like our adversary, prepared for it, and inviting it. Accustomed to peace, we were not ready."[62] As a result, Americans flew in French-built Nieuports, shot British rifles, and fired French 75mm artillery almost until the end of the war.[63]

The Allies gained major support with the arrival of the Americans but would soon lose their Eastern partner. The tsar was overthrown in March 1917 by a democratic uprising against his long and unenlightened

---

*   Pershing's nickname came to him because he had proudly commanded black troops in these days of the segregated U.S. Army.

**   *Doughboy* was the nickname for American infantrymen. There are several theories as to its origin, the most likely of which goes all the way back to the Civil War and the dumpling-shaped brass buttons, or "doughboys," worn on Union uniforms.

rule. The Provisional Russian government led by Alexander Kerensky vowed to stay in the war, which opened an opportunity for Vladimir Lenin, the exiled leader of the Bolsheviks.* The Bolsheviks claimed to be the majority of Russia's revolutionary Communists. The German High Command, eager to knock Russia out of the war, placed Lenin and several top Bolshevik exiles on the famous "Sealed Train"** and sent them to Petrograd, the capital of exhausted Russia.*** Lenin promised "peace, land, and bread" to the starving, war-weary Russian peasants and workers. To the Germans he pledged to pull Russia out of the war. Winston Churchill described this foolhardy German move as "injecting a plague bacillus" into the Russian state.⁶⁴

By November 1917, when Lenin seized control of the Russian government in the Bolsheviks' Red October revolution, the Germans looked forward to transferring a full *fifty* divisions of seasoned veterans to the Western Front.**** Lenin put the democratic government of Alexander Kerensky to flight, plunging Russia into a Communist dictatorship for a full seventy-four years. Lenin soon signed a separate peace with Germany, permitting scores of battle-hardened divisions to join the German ranks in France.

The war produced new strains on the home front in America. The government funded the Committee on Public Information to actively

---

* *Bolshevik*, from *bolshoi*, means "larger" in Russian. The Bolsheviks were, in fact, the *smaller* faction among Russia's revolutionaries. It was the beginning of their propaganda success.

** The German High Command, fearing that the Communists' revolutionary ideas would "infect" their own starving people, allowed no one to enter or leave the Sealed Train. It passed through Germany to Russia and into history.

*** The tsar had changed the city's name from St. Petersburg to Petrograd at the outbreak of the war to give the capital city built by Peter the Great a more Russian-sounding name. It was soon to be renamed Leningrad after the founder of the USSR. In 1991, the name reverted to St. Petersburg.

**** Although the Revolution occurred on 7 November 1917, Russia was still operating under the Julian calendar, which the British Empire had abandoned for the Gregorian calendar in 1752.

promote the war with sophisticated propaganda. George Creel, head of the committee, called the effort "the world's greatest adventure in advertising."[65] Seventy-five thousand "Four-Minute Men" were paid to take to public stages in movie houses and theaters to whip up sentiment against the Hun.[66] Herbert Hoover, a millionaire mining engineer, had distinguished himself by leading an effort to send food to starving people in German-occupied Belgium at the outbreak of the war. Wilson now tapped him to head the Food Administration. The country got used to "wheatless Mondays" and "meatless Tuesdays." All the while, Hoover urged Americans to "clean [y]our plates" and the government posters reminded them that "Food Will Win the War."[67]

As many Progressives had warned, the war unleashed a virulent hatred of all things German. Gone was the respect for German inventive genius—like Dr. Roentgen's X-ray machine and the diesel engine. Mozart and Beethoven were shunned, stupidly. Sauerkraut was renamed "Liberty Cabbage."[68]

Even worse things were to come. German-language books were thrown out of public libraries, and a number of Midwestern states even made it *unlawful* to teach schoolchildren in the German language.* The Sedition Act made any interference with the war effort a crime. More than fifteen hundred people were arrested. Perennial Socialist candidate for president Eugene V. Debs was tried, convicted, and sent to prison. Whipped up anti-German sentiment unleashed a wave of suspicion as neighbors spied on neighbors. It was an opportunity, as Samuel Eliot Morison put it, for "frustrated old women of *both* sexes" to indulge their fantasies.[69]

President Wilson went before Congress in January 1918 to lay out his war aims. He spoke hopefully of the new Bolshevik government in Russia.

---

* The Lutheran Church–Missouri Synod, a church body claiming millions of adherents, used German in its worship services and parochial schools. The Synod fought the language laws all the way to the U.S. Supreme Court, winning vindication there in 1923 in the case of *Meyer v. Nebraska*. The wartime hysteria had subsided by then. *Meyer* remains an important victory for parental rights.

He praised "the new voice" of the Russian people as "thrilling and compelling." Few Western leaders yet understood the violence and oppression that regime would bring, but most welcomed an end to tsarist autocracy. Wilson emphasized again his respect for the German people—as opposed to their brutal leaders. Germans, he said, were distinguished by their learning and enterprise. Their role in the world made their "record very bright and very enviable."[70]

The substance of his speech became known as the Fourteen Points. Wilson called for "open agreements openly arrived at." This was a response to the secret treaties that many blamed for the war. The Bolsheviks had published these from secret tsarist archives. Wilson also called for freedom of the seas. He asserted the principle of national "self-determination." He concluded with a ringing call for a "League of Nations" to defend the peace the Allies sought.[71]

The Fourteen Points represented the high idealism of progressivism. Colonel Edward M. House, Wilson's close advisor, had worked with a group of intellectuals he discreetly called "The Inquiry" to draft the principles Wilson would fashion into his soaring rhetoric.* The president himself typed the eloquent address. Ironically, the group worked in secret. So did Wilson. He did not share his vision with his cabinet, with leaders of Congress, or with the democratically chosen leaders of Britain or France, his chief allies.[72]

Americans began streaming into the Allied lines in great numbers in 1918. The Marines distinguished themselves in major action at Belleau Wood and Chateau Thierry. An American-led U.S.-French assault on German lines at Saint Mihiel in September led to a great breakthrough as the Allies took fifteen thousand Germans prisoner.[73] German forces were at the breaking point.

Americans sang Irving Berlin's catchy tune, "O How I Hate to Get Up in the Morning," and eagerly read stories of battlefield heroism "over

---

* Among the distinguished scholars of the Inquiry who would go on to greater renown were William C. Bullitt, Walter Lippmann, and Samuel Eliot Morison.

there." One most amazing story is that of Sergeant Alvin York. Sergeant York hailed from the hills of Tennessee. A member of a small, pacifist Christian sect, he would not even have been drafted into the U.S. Army of World War II. But the draft board did not recognize York's church, so in he went. Sergeant York overcame his initial doubts about the use of deadly force. He won the Congressional Medal of Honor by saving his platoon from destruction by enemy machine gunners. York's skill with a rifle, honed by twenty years of hunting squirrels and rabbits, was unsurpassed.[74*]

Thousands of American homes received the dreaded telegram from the War Department that fall. One of those homes was Sagamore Hill on Long Island. There, former president and Mrs. Roosevelt learned that their youngest son, Quentin, had been shot down behind German lines in France. Quentin, always the prankster in the White House, had pursued the Germans in the skies with more zeal than skill. Quentin made "repeated attacks" on seven German aircraft, their press agency reported. The Germans, to their credit, buried the twenty-year-old with full military honors. But somewhere a German got hold of a photograph of the dead Quentin and quickly printed thousands of ghoulish postcards. One of these even made its way back to Sagamore Hill.[75] Shaken, but unbowed, TR compared his son to Colonel Robert Gould Shaw, telling reporters, "Those alone are fit to live who do not fear to die."[76**] With similar bravery, Quentin's mother, Edith Roosevelt, said, "You cannot raise your sons to be eagles and expect them to act like sparrows."

The German people and their armed forces expected a quick victory after the Bolshevik Revolution in Russia. They had been assured they would win before the Americans could tip the balance in France. But the failure of the German army's "Big Push" in France filled the ranks with despair. Fresh American troops seemed numberless. The Yanks proved

---

[*] As in every American war, hunters often made the critical difference on the battlefield.

[**] TR was referring to the Colonel Shaw who was killed at Fort Wagner, South Carolina, in 1864 as he led the soldiers of the first all-black regiment in the Union army, the 54th Massachusetts.

themselves again and again during the Meuse-Argonne offensive. When French Marshal Ferdinand Foch, the Supreme Allied Commander, broke the Germans' Hindenburg Line on 1 October 1918, even the German High Command knew it was all over.[77]

When the liberal Prince Max, the new German civilian leader, reached out for an armistice, he communicated directly with President Wilson.[78] He wanted a peace based on the Fourteen Points. Without consulting his allies, Wilson responded that the kaiser must be overthrown before an armistice could be arranged.[79] But when the German military and civilian leaders pressed Wilhelm to abdicate, he resisted. "I wouldn't dream of abandoning the throne because of a few hundred Jews and a thousand workers," he told Prince Max.[80] The kaiser, however, was forced into exile. He fled for refuge in Holland.[81]

Soon, the Germans set up a republic, which sued for an armistice. Marshal Foch forced the Germans to accept harsh conditions for an end to the fighting. The agreement was signed in Foch's railway car at Compiègne, France.

The war ended at the *eleventh hour of the eleventh day of the eleventh month*—November 1918. Captain Harry S. Truman was serving in an artillery battery of the Missouri National Guard. He fired his last round at 10:45 a.m. that day.[82] Finally, after four long years of the worst mass killing in human history, the guns fell silent. An estimated ten million had died in the Great War. Then, at last, it was "all quiet on the Western Front."

That night, Harry complained that the men of the neighboring French artillery battery kept him awake. They had gotten drunk and each one insisted on marching past Harry's bed to salute him and yell, "*Vive President Wilson! Vive le Capitaine d'artillerie américaine!*"[83]

On the German side, Corporal Adolf Hitler received the news in a military hospital; he had been temporarily blinded by poison gas. He cried bitter tears. For his courage under fire, Corporal Hitler was awarded the Iron Cross, First Class. He was recommended for this unusually high honor by Captain Hugo Guttman, a Jew.[84]

In Berlin, Communists attempted to set up a German *soviet* on the model of that in Moscow.* Rosa Luxemburg and Karl Liebknecht led the Red forces there. Viewing these events from the Kremlin in Moscow, Vladimir Lenin was excited.** Germany was "afire" with revolution, he reported.[85] Communists under Bela Kun set up a Soviet government in Hungary. Soon, however, Luxemburg and Liebknecht were overthrown and killed. Bela Kun's attempt, too, failed.

Hitler, writing later in *Mein Kampf* (*My Struggle*), pointed to the involvement of some prominent Jewish Communists in these events. He complained that the bloody repression of the Communists was not nearly bloody enough. He wanted to see poison gas used for "the extermination of that pestilence."[86]

V. WILSON IN PARIS

President Wilson was determined to go to France for a great Peace Conference. He would confer with the leaders of the victorious Allies to craft a treaty that would officially end the war. Wilson spurned calls for him to stay home. The president of the United States had never before left the country for an extended period. The Paris Peace Conference promised to last for months. Was it even *constitutional* for the American president to absent himself? Some offered friendly advice. Journalist Frank Cobb was a strong Wilson supporter. From Paris, he wrote, "The moment the President sits at the council table with these Prime Ministers and Foreign Secretaries, he has lost all the power that comes from distance and detachment. Instead of remaining the great arbiter of human freedom, he becomes

---

* *Soviet* comes from the Russian word that means "to advise." A soviet, therefore, was an advisory council. In practice, the soviets did not give advice; they took it, and from only one source: the Communist Party.

** *Kreml* is the Russian word for "fortress." The Moscow *Kremlin* remains the center of the Russian government to this day.

merely a negotiator dealing with other negotiators." Wilson's secretary of state, Robert Lansing, also urged him not to go.[87] He could let subordinates do the detailed negotiating and take the high ground. No, Wilson objected. He had to go personally to head the American negotiating team.

Arriving in France aboard the troopship *George Washington*, Wilson was invited to visit the battlefields over which so much blood had been shed. Seeing this as an attempt to manipulate him through emotion, Wilson turned down the invitation. When they heard of this, the nearly one million American doughboys were deeply disappointed.[88]

With the end of military combat on the Western front came an even more deadly killer—influenza. The great pandemic of 1918–19 swept across Europe and America and from there, around the world. Between fifty and one hundred million died in a span of mere months. Unlike previous experience with plagues, this so-called Spanish Influenza seemed to carry off the young and the fit. In a recent work on the pandemic, John M. Barry noted that "it killed more people in *twenty-four weeks* than AIDS has killed in twenty-four years, more people in a year than the Black Death of the Middle Ages killed in a century."[89] The disease was especially devastating to soldiers. More than half of the U.S. casualties in World War I were attributable to influenza, not German bullets or gas. Barry also maintains that it was influenza, not a stroke, that laid President Wilson low at a critical point in the Paris peace negotiations. Moreover, Barry contended that Wilson's judgment was affected by the disease.[90]

Early in 1919, the American delegation in Paris received stunning news from home. Theodore Roosevelt had died in his sleep at Sagamore Hill. TR had seen it coming. He told his son-in-law Dick Derby, "We have warmed both hands before the fire of life."[91] Roosevelt's son, Archie, cabled to his brothers in uniform around the world: "The old lion is dead."[92] No further explanation was necessary. Following the funeral party to the graveside in the January cold at Oyster Bay was Theodore's great and good friend, the ever-forgiving William Howard Taft. Once again, Taft wept for his lost friend.

The nation and much of the world mourned the death of the Rough Rider. The normally frosty New Englander, Senator Henry Cabot Lodge, had been TR's colleague and friend for more than three decades. He was older than TR, and he choked up as he concluded his eulogy to Roosevelt. To Lodge, TR was "Valiant-for-Truth," the admired character in John Bunyan's *Pilgrim's Progress*. When he "passed over, all the trumpets on the other side sounded," Lodge said.[93]

In Paris, Wilson realized that death had taken his most formidable adversary. TR had been Wilson's bitter, too often hateful enemy, but the president charitably (and wisely) issued a public statement praising one of America's most beloved presidents.[94]

"A specter is haunting Europe, the specter of Communism." So begins *The Communist Manifesto* by Karl Marx. Although Marx had been dead thirty years when the victorious Allied leaders met at Paris, the specter of Communism haunted their deliberations. A leading member of the British cabinet pointed to the specter in a speech to his Scottish constituents: "Civilization is being completely extinguished over gigantic areas, while the Bolsheviks hop and caper like troops of ferocious baboons amid the ruins of cities and the corpses of their victims."[95] Winston Churchill's listeners cheered lustily as he denounced the violence and brutality of the new Bolshevik regime in Russia. Like the rest of the civilized world, the Scottish had been horrified by the Bolshevik murder of the tsar and his entire family.*

But Scotsmen booed Churchill just as loudly as they had cheered him when he explained that the threat of Communism was why the statesmen should make a moderate peace with Germany.[96] Few people shared Winston's enthusiasm for intervening in the increasingly bloody civil war

---

* Russia's deposed Tsar Nicholas II; his wife, Tsarina Alexandra; their hemophiliac teenage son, Alexei; his four older sisters, Maria, Olga, Tatiana, and Anastasia; the Imperial family doctor; and several faithful servants had been ordered into a basement in Ekaterinburg, Siberia. There, in the early hours of 18 July 1918, drunken Red guards shot, clubbed, and stabbed them to death. Their bodies were dissolved in acid and dumped in a mine shaft.

in Russia. Churchill wanted to "strangle the baby in the bath." War-weary publics in the democracies had no such vision and no such eagerness to confront the Bolsheviks.

Millions of cheering, weeping Englishmen, Frenchmen, and Italians during Wilson's victory tour of Allied capitals cried out for him. In Paris, he rode in an open car through the Arc de Triomphe. In Rome, the city streets were spread with golden sand; Wilson was hailed as "the God of Peace."[97]

President Wilson sat down for talks with Britain's Prime Minister Lloyd George and France's Premier Georges Clemenceau. The Big Three were joined by Italy's Premier Vittorio Orlando. It soon became clear that the Allied leaders did not stand in awe of the American president. These seasoned, wary politicians had come to Paris to claim the fruits of victory.

When Wilson returned to the United States briefly in February 1919, signs were not good at home. Republicans controlled both houses of Congress. Senator Lodge circulated among Republican senators a "Round Robin." It was a document that insisted that the Senate be fully included in treaty-making and sternly warned Wilson that changes would have to be made in his League of Nations before the senators who signed would vote to ratify the final peace treaty.[98] Because there were more signers of the Round Robin than were required to defeat a treaty, Wilson was put on notice of the need for compromise with the Senate.* Lodge told the Senate there must be no "meddling or muddling" in every petty quarrel in Europe, that the U.S. Congress must have the ultimate decision-making authority. Wilson already disliked Lodge. Seeing this as a partisan attempt to embarrass him, the president's hatred of the senator deepened.[99]

Returning to Paris, President Wilson's mood darkened. When his devoted friend, Colonel Edward M. House, briefed him on the status of negotiations in his absence, Wilson was shocked. "House has given away everything that I had won before we left Paris." The president

---

* Before the admission of Alaska and Hawaii, there were ninety-six U.S. senators. Treaties required approval by two-thirds of the Senate to be ratified. Thus, thirty-three senators could demand amendments or the treaty would be lost.

began to be influenced by the deep-seated hostility that his wife held for Colonel House. This, and differences about the negotiations, introduced a strain in the president's relationship with his most faithful and selfless subordinate.[100]

Wilson argued against French Premier Georges Clemenceau with vigor. At one point, he even ordered the *George Washington* made ready to depart. He was prepared to leave Paris and abandon the Peace Conference. Clemenceau privately sneered at this maneuver as Wilson's "going home to mother," but to Wilson's face he said *he* would go home. He stalked out of the conference but soon was back.

Clemenceau said he agreed with Wilson that all men are brothers, but they are brothers "like Cain and Abel." He hammered incessantly at the need for security. Even over lunch, he humorously pointed to the chicken elegantly displayed. "Why is the chicken on this plate? Because it did not have the *force* to resist us. And a good thing, too!"[101]

Finally, Britain's Lloyd George broke the impasse. He persuaded Wilson to give Clemenceau the assurances he sought for French security. In exchange for the Tiger's dropping the French demand for dismembering Germany, Great Britain and the United States agreed to come to France's defense if that country were attacked by Germany.[102] Only with France's safety thus protected would Clemenceau agree to Wilson's proposals for the League of Nations. Clemenceau regarded the Guarantee Treaty as the "crowning glory" of his policy.[103]

The peacemakers agreed to the creation of an independent Polish state. They carved Czechoslovakia and Yugoslavia and an independent Hungary out of the now-dissolved Austro-Hungarian Empire. They banned any union (*Anschluss*) between the small Austrian republic and the larger state of Germany. They forced Germany to turn over the High Seas Fleet to Britain and imposed an undetermined amount of war reparations on Germany. They demanded German disarmament. Most important to many, they inserted into the final treaty a "war guilt" clause that forced the Germans to acknowledge that they had caused the war. The Rhineland was demilitarized and the coal-rich Saar region was stripped from Germany for fifteen years.

Woodrow Wilson's chief goal in coming to Paris was to champion his cherished League of Nations concept. He sincerely believed that many of the concessions he was forced to make to the British and the French on territory, colonies, reparations, and the war guilt of the Germans were necessary in order to achieve his overarching purpose. The League, he thought, could correct any mistakes made by the hard-pressed negotiators in Paris. Wilson had an almost religious faith in the ability of this new "concert of nations" to operate harmoniously. This may explain his rigid refusal to compromise in any way on issues touching on the League. The Treaty of Versailles may have belonged to George and Clemenceau, but the League of Nations was *his*.

Wilson's vision was sometimes compelling but too often vague. Theodore Roosevelt had believed that his son Quentin and all the brave American soldiers had "saved the soul of the world from German militarism."[104] TR wanted an unconditional surrender of Germany to break the pride and will of the German militarists. He wanted the kaiser and his military clique punished. Roosevelt thought a peace based on Wilson's Fourteen Points—which he derided as "fourteen scraps of paper"[105]— would mean unconditional surrender, but for the United States, not Germany.[106] Surely, this last point was hyperbole. But it is no exaggeration to say that Roosevelt's concept of a League of Nations—one that began with Britain and France and that did not threaten the cornerstone of American sovereignty, the Monroe Doctrine—was the more realistic of the two men's postwar visions. But Roosevelt, alas, was dead, and it was the elected President Woodrow Wilson who had the constitutional authority to conduct the Paris negotiations.[107]

In June 1919, the German High Seas Fleet steamed between massed British warships at Scapa Flow, off Scotland. But rather than surrender their magnificent dreadnoughts, German sailors opened the seacocks, set explosive charges, and scuttled their vessels. The kaiser's pride, his magnificent dreadnoughts, sank beneath the waves.[108] The race to build bigger, more powerful battleships had been a leading cause of the First World War. Now, the fleet the British so long feared simply disappeared.

Germans were outraged at the terms of the Treaty of Versailles. They considered them brutally unfair. They pointed out that they had only sought an armistice; they had not offered to surrender unconditionally. The Germans were given no part in the negotiation of the treaty. They were summoned to the great Hall of Mirrors in the historic Palace of Versailles only to sign the treaty. The signing ceremony was held on 28 June 1919. It was, ironically, the fifth anniversary of the assassinations in Sarajevo. The Hall of Mirrors was the very place where Bismarck had announced the creation of the German Empire in 1871. Now, the German delegates even brought their own fountain pens to sign the hated treaty that would end the German Empire.[109] They were unwilling to give the victors any souvenirs.

The leading delegate of the German Republic, Foreign Minister Brockdorff-Rantzau, offered his response:

> We know the power of hatred which we encounter here. . . . It is demanded of us that we shall confess ourselves to be the only ones guilty of the war. . . . Such a confession in my mouth will be a lie.[110]

The Allied leaders were enraged at this German defiance. "The Germans really are stupid people," Wilson said. Britain's foreign minister, Lord Balfour, was normally a placid man. He chimed in: "Beasts they were and beasts they are."[111]

The harsh Treaty of Versailles was dangerous—to the victors as well as the vanquished. Germany was a great power with a great ability to recover her strength. Nothing could stop that. Winston Churchill understood this. He, too, opposed a vengeful peace with Germany. He said the hatred of the French toward the Germans was "more than human."[112] He wrote in unconcealed admiration of his fallen foe:

For four years Germany fought and defied the five continents of the world by land, sea and air. The German armies upheld her tottering confederates, intervened in every theater with success, stood everywhere on conquered territory, and inflicted on their enemies more than twice the bloodshed they suffered themselves. To break their strength and science and curb their fury, it was necessary to bring all the greatest nations of mankind into the field against them.[113]

Wilson had become impatient, intolerant of any criticism of the peacemakers' work. This attitude extended even to the more absurd parts of the treaty. When one of his advisers complained that forcing the Germans to pay Allied soldiers' pensions would double the war reparations bill and was illogical, Wilson responded angrily: "Logic! Logic! I don't give a damn for logic! I am going to include pensions."[114]

Secretary Lansing tried to warn the president. "The terms of the treaty appear immeasurably harsh and humiliating, while many of them are incapable of performance," he wrote Wilson.[115] But Wilson stiff-armed his secretary of state. "The treaty," he said, was the work of "the hand of God."[116]

VI. "A WAR TO END ALL WARS"

In June 1919, when the recently returned president visited the Senate, he bore the Treaty of Versailles in an elegant leather binding. Senator Lodge courteously offered to carry the treaty into the hearing room. "Not on your life," Wilson said, smiling broadly.[117] Everyone laughed at the president's comment, but it was not the kind of jest that breaks tension. It *increased* the tension.

Senator Lodge's goals for American foreign policy were simple. He wanted to win the war and curb Germany's capacity to threaten the peace.[118] He strongly supported the French Guarantee Treaty.[119] In this, Lodge shared Clemenceau's hardheaded, practical approach to peacemaking. In favoring the guarantee to France, Lodge spoke for the Republican leadership.

Senator Lodge was pressing for two amendments, or reservations, to the treaty that Wilson had negotiated. He wanted the new League of Nations to formally acknowledge America's preeminence in the Western Hemisphere by recognizing the Monroe Doctrine. He also demanded a reservation to Article X so that the U.S. Congress, and not a majority vote of the League of Nations in Geneva, would make final decisions on sending American boys to fight in foreign wars. Lodge strongly believed the U.S. Constitution required such congressional authorization.

President Wilson rejected any change to Article X. Revising this article, he said, "cuts the heart out of [the treaty]."[120] Wilson's ideas for the League of Nations represented a sharp break with America's history and traditions. As Henry Kissinger has written, Wilson wanted nothing less than world government and American participation in a global police force.[121] This much the Republicans were not prepared to give him.

Wilson refused to give an inch. He demanded that the Senate accept the Treaty of Versailles as written. "I am an uncompromising partisan," he said.[122] Wilson's unyielding position worried even some of his fellow Democrats in the Senate.[123]

Against the advice of his family and his doctor, the president decided to take his case for the unamended treaty and the League to the American people. He would undertake a lengthy tour of the Western states whose senators led the opposition to the treaty. Wilson planned to deliver scores of speeches on this railroad tour.

Wilson did not use the phrase "a war to end all wars." That unfortunate phrase was Lloyd George's. That was nonetheless the main point of Wilson's case for ratification of the treaty as it was signed in Paris. He told the people of St. Louis what he would have to say to American servicemen *if* the treaty was rejected:

You are betrayed. You fought for something that you did not get.

And the glory of the armies and navies of the United States is gone like a dream in the night, and there ensues upon it . . . the nightmare of dread . . . and there will come some time, in the vengeful Providence of God, another war in which not a few hundred thousand men from American will have to die, but as many millions as are necessary to accomplish the final freedom of the peoples of the world.[124]

His opponents were not merely mistaken, they were disloyal, Wilson was saying. They did not simply oppose him, they opposed God. And if his prescription for peace was not followed without even mild reservations, another war would come and *millions* of Americans would die.

Wilson was emotionally overwrought and physically spent when he came to Pueblo, Colorado, three weeks into his speaking tour. There, on 25 September 1919, President Wilson suffered a severe nervous collapse. The remainder of the speaking tour was cancelled as, with drawn shades, the presidential train sped east toward Washington.[125]

Days later, in the White House, Wilson suffered a massive stroke. His speech and motor skills were seriously impaired. Then, and for many long months afterward, Mrs. Wilson and a handful of aides conspired to keep the nature and extent of the president's debilitating illness concealed from a worried, anxious American public.[126] Wilson held no cabinet meetings for the next critical eight months.[127] The vice president of the United States did not meet with him. Mrs. Wilson barred him from the president's sickroom.[128] She also screened all official documents and limited access to the president to a trusted few. And these few had but minutes to speak to the desperately ill chief executive.[129]

Secretary Lansing, as the senior cabinet member, was rebuked when he suggested the time had come to invoke the Constitution. Lansing wanted the vice president to assume power, at least temporarily, because of the president's disability.* When Wilson learned that the secretary of state had been meeting with the cabinet in an attempt to keep the government functioning, Wilson fired him.[130]

---

* Lansing was clearly right. Today, the Twenty-fifth Amendment provides for cabinet action to declare presidential incapacity if the president stubbornly refuses to step aside.

Wilson's illness had not tempered his intransigence. Partially paralyzed, his speech impaired, he nonetheless ordered Democrats in the Senate to vote *against* the treaty. Why? It was no longer his treaty. Lodge had amended it to require Congress's authorization before U.S. troops could be ordered into combat by the League of Nations. Senator Brandegee was happy to see the treaty and the League go down to defeat. "We can *always* depend on Mr. Wilson," he said to Senator Lodge.[131] Even so, the treaty lost by only seven votes.

Two very important constitutional amendments were ratified in the waning Wilson years. The country adopted the Eighteenth Amendment to ban the sale of alcoholic beverages. Prohibition would be called a "noble experiment." It would deeply divide the country. Women achieved the goal first proclaimed at the Seneca Falls conference half a century earlier. The Nineteenth Amendment gave all adult women the vote. America led the world in this important advance.

As the country prepared for the election of 1920, President Wilson was increasingly disconnected from reality. Incapable of serving out a second term, he absurdly expected the Democratic Party to nominate him for an unprecedented *third* term.[132] Democrats instead nominated Governor James M. Cox of Ohio, who was soundly defeated by the Republican nominee, Ohio Senator Warren G. Harding. President Wilson was shattered: "They have disgraced us in the eyes of the world."[133]

So it had come to this. Estranged from the leaders of the opposition and of his own party, his closest advisers, and his friends, Woodrow Wilson now turned on the American people themselves. It was a sad end for the man who wished to "make the world safe for democracy." He retired to a house on S Street in Washington, D.C. There, he spent his last few years occasionally writing short articles and receiving only a few visitors selected by Mrs. Wilson. He told visitors his principles would eventually win out: "I have seen fools resist Providence before."[134]

America had faced the horror of world war with courage and determination under Woodrow Wilson's leadership. Its armed forces and financial strength saved the Allies when they were at the point of defeat. They stopped the kaiser from imposing the rule of a haughty military clique on the free peoples of Europe.

After the war, however, Wilson's paralysis led to paralysis at the heart of the great American republic. Wilson had called for a war "to make the world safe for democracy." He had a duty at least to help make democracies like France and Britain safe. His failure was as much a failure of character as anything else.

Wilson allowed Clemenceau and Lloyd George to turn an armistice into an unconditional surrender and saddle the defeated Germans with impossibly heavy reparations. At home, he utterly alienated the Republicans. He resisted the entreaties of his closest political allies and personal friends. In refusing to compromise with the Senate, he lost all chance to ratify the Treaty of Versailles. His inflexibility and disdain for others' judgment cost him and the nation dearly.

Had he possessed Lincoln's selfless qualities, or Washington's ability to forgive, he might have been an architect of peace. As it was, no man was more responsible for losing the peace than Woodrow Wilson. That was his tragedy—and ours.

THIRTEEN

THE BOOM AND THE BUST

(1921–1933)

I. THE ROARING TWENTIES

When America sent two million soldiers to France in 1918, high idealism was the order of the day. Americans repeated the verse: "Forget us, God, if we forget, / The sacred sword of Lafayette." Lafayette's sword and many other sacred things took a beating in the brutal trench life of barbed wire, poison gas, rats, and incessant artillery bombardment. America lost forty-eight thousand young men in a short, intense period of violent combat. Another fifty thousand soldiers died from the Spanish Influenza epidemic, which claimed millions of lives worldwide.

As soon as the armistice ending World War I was signed, however, a different call went up among the troops of the American Expeditionary Force:

> We drove the Boche across the Rhine
> The Kaiser from his throne
> O Lafayette, we've paid the debt.
> For Christ's sake, send us home.[1]

The hardened, cynical swagger in that doggerel speaks to the disillusionment millions of Americans felt about our first massive intervention in a foreign war.

The 1920s would regard such jaded sentiments as realism. Unwilling to sacrifice for what President Harding called nostrums, many Americans, especially the young, believed Uncle Sam had been played for Uncle Sap. No one wanted to be taken for a sucker. Americans jumped in their "Tin Lizzies" and headed out for the open road. Jazz music was just one example of the new freedom that was a far cry from Woodrow Wilson's ideals. The proliferation of hip flasks and "bathtub gin" bespoke the attitude of millions to the new restrictions on the sale and manufacture of alcohol under Prohibition.

A new freedom could be seen in art, music, architecture, and everyday fashion. Women had succeeded in claiming the right to vote. The half-century crusade of Susan B. Anthony and Elizabeth Cady Stanton finally achieved the suffragettes' goal with the ratification of the Nineteenth Amendment to the Constitution in 1919. These women prevailed by rejecting the tactics of radicals within their movement. Those militant crusaders who paraded outside the White House with "Kaiser Wilson" banners protesting the president's opposition to a federal suffrage amendment had not helped their cause.[2]

In the Roaring Twenties, however, flappers bobbed their hair and wore dresses that came just below the knee—scandalous for the time. This frivolous form of "liberation" would have stunned many of the sober, thoughtful earlier reformers who thought women's votes would mean a purification of politics. Since the 1830s, Big City political machines had been a raucous caucus, based largely in the saloons. Women's voting and Prohibition were twin reform efforts to end all that. As we shall see, the post–World War I amendments certainly brought change, but change in unanticipated ways. No one captured the spirit of the age better than the irreverent, brassy newspaper columnist H. L. Mencken, who plied his trade at the *American Mercury* and the *Baltimore Sun*. His biting wit and mordant style made him "the god of the undergraduates." After the failure of Wilson's crusade, Americans were ripe for a writer who reveled in the role of intellectual *enfant terrible*.

> Here the general average of intelligence, of knowledge, of competence, of integrity, of self-respect, of honor is so low that any man who knows his trade, does not fear ghosts, has read fifty good books, and practices the common decencies stands out as brilliantly as a wart on a bald head, and is thrown willy-nilly into a meager and exclusive aristocracy. And here, more than anywhere else that I know of or have heard of, the daily panorama of human existence, of private and communal folly—the unending procession of governmental extortions and chicaneries, of commercial brigandages and throat-slittings, of theological buffooneries, of aesthetic ribaldries, of legal swindles and harlotries, of miscellaneous rogueries, villainies, imbecilities, grotesqueries, and extravagances—is so inordinately gross and preposterous, so perfectly brought up to the highest conceivable amperage, so steadily enriched with an almost fabulous daring and originality, that only the man who was born with a petrified diaphragm can fail to laugh himself to sleep every night, and to wake every morning with all the eager, unflagging expectation of a Sunday-school superintendent touring the Paris peep-shows.[3]

II. SUNRISE AT CAMPOBELLO

The thirty-nine-year-old Franklin D. Roosevelt looked forward to his summer vacation at Canada's Campobello Island, just across the U.S. border from Lubec, Maine.* His family had enjoyed the cool ocean breezes and the bracing waters of the Bay of Fundy for many years. In August

---

* The title of this section is taken from the popular three-act play written by Dore Schary. The play was first presented by the Theatre Guild on 30 January 1958 (FDR's birthday) at New York City's Cort Theatre.

1921, however, it would be different. FDR tried to lead his family in a spirited romp after a swim. He was consciously imitating his late cousin Theodore.[4]

Suddenly, the former assistant secretary of the navy found himself stricken, unable to move. FDR had feeling in his arms, although he was temporarily unable to sign his name. (His closest political adviser, Louis Howe, would take over this job.) At the onset of the disease, he lost all feeling in his legs. FDR's wife, Eleanor, and Louis Howe took turns massaging his feet and toes. They even had to insert a catheter and administer enemas so he could eliminate waste. Howe spent weeks calling up and down the East Coast, desperately seeking competent medical advice. Only after Howe wrote to Roosevelt's uncle in New York were capable physicians engaged who could even diagnose FDR's symptoms correctly: he had polio.[5] At the time, there was no known cure. The disease had blighted the lives of thousands. At its worst, polio could leave a person paralyzed from the neck down, condemned to life in an "iron lung," an unwieldy contraption that breathed for the victim. It was a devastating report for a vital man in the prime of life.

At least, it could have been devastating.

From the beginning, FDR was determined to beat polio. When he returned to New York City in the fall of 1921, Louis Howe took pains to make sure that curious reporters didn't get the full picture of FDR's disability.[6] A smiling, buoyant Roosevelt appeared only momentarily. He had his cigarette in its familiar holder, clasped between his teeth at a jaunty angle.[7] He waved cheerily to onlookers. Out of public view, however, he required considerable help to perform even the most mundane tasks—getting dressed, going up stairs, shifting from a bed to a chair.*

Despite this cruel blow, FDR continued to pursue a political career.

---

* FDR's wheelchair had been crafted for him by a trusted Hyde Park village blacksmith. It was made from a simple kitchen chair and had no arms. Of the thirty-five thousand photos in the FDR Library at Hyde Park, only two show him in his wheelchair (Alter, *Defining Moment*, 83).

Democrats had nominated him to be James M. Cox's running mate in the 1920 presidential election, and although they had lost, Roosevelt's future seemed bright. His ex-boss, Josephus Daniels, visited him in the hospital. FDR turned on his famous charm. Daniels was not to think of him as an invalid, he said. He punched the paunchy former navy secretary in the belly to make his point.[8]

Eleanor needed Franklin to succeed politically in order to continue the independent life she had made for herself. She had decided against a divorce when she discovered Franklin's affair with Lucy Mercer in 1918. In her own right, Eleanor had become a major figure in the Women's Division of the New York State Democratic Party in these first years after women received the vote.[9] Eleanor traveled the state, often in the company of two female friends. Journalist Nancy Cook and social worker Marion Dickerman gave her solid support and dismissed the inevitable gossip. Alice Roosevelt Longworth couldn't resist a pointed barb. Teddy's incorrigible daughter and Eleanor's first cousin, Alice called Eleanor's mannish friends "female impersonators."[10]

Roosevelt kept up his political contacts, often entertaining politicos at the family home or on board their houseboat. And against Eleanor's urgings, he invested nearly two-thirds of his savings in a run-down hotel and resort complex in rural Georgia that was soon to become world famous as Warm Springs. Young people in the country were dancing the Charleston and riding around in automobile "rumble seats," but FDR wanted only to walk again. The soothing, sulfurous waters at Warm Springs provided Roosevelt the buoyancy he needed to exercise his withered legs. The waters lifted his spirits. FDR became the cheerleader-in-chief for hundreds of other polio sufferers who flocked to the resort as word of its therapeutic waters spread. Roosevelt's presence was a magnet. He took a personal interest in the progress of each of his patients. His confidence was contagious.[11]

With the help of Eleanor, Louis Howe, his faithful secretary Missy LeHand, and a host of others, Franklin Roosevelt was able to conceal the full extent of his disability. He never denied having polio, but his carefully constructed persona was a denial of reality. Obviously, polio had changed him. He was no longer tall and slender. The rigorous physical therapy he went through gave him massive strength in his neck, shoulders, and biceps. All this was necessary to compensate for his lifeless lower limbs. In his prime, FDR stood six feet two inches tall and weighed 188 pounds. Even when he had to lean on another's arm for support or grip a podium, he was a large, impressive man.

Prior to his attack, FDR was thought of by many fellow politicians as a shallow, rich young man. To them, he was an ambitious striver eager to capitalize on his famous cousin Teddy's name. After contracting polio, however, FDR had a personal story of triumph over adversity even the most hard-bitten critic had to admire. It's worth noting that FDR had won two political contests before he was afflicted with polio, both for the relatively minor post of New York State senator. He had also lost two important races, one for U.S. senator from New York and the other for vice president of the United States. After his onset of polio, however, FDR never lost an election.[12]

III. A HARLEM RENAISSANCE

During World War I, black Americans had migrated north in great numbers. Many looked for work in defense industries. Others sought opportunities in the burgeoning cities. New York's Harlem—named for the Dutch city of Haarlem—had been almost all white in 1900. By 1925, black people were flocking in. It was here that the NAACP established its headquarters and published its important journal, *The Crisis.* Under the leadership of James Weldon Johnson, the NAACP boldly proclaimed its purpose:

> Nothing more or less than to claim for the Negro common equality under the fundamental law of the United States; to proclaim that democracy stultified itself when it barred men from its benefits solely on the basis of race and color.[13]

Politically, the atmosphere of Harlem gave black Americans freedom to speak, to write, to organize, to march. A photo of an early demonstration there shows young black men, smartly turned out in well-tailored suits and fashionable straw hats, bearing a banner with the famous words of the Declaration of Independence: WE HOLD THESE TRUTHS TO BE SELF EVIDENT . . . THAT ALL MEN ARE CREATED EQUAL. Below these words was a legend that read: IF OF *AFRICAN* DESCENT, TEAR OFF THIS COVER.[14]

Because of their concentration and numbers, black Americans could assert themselves freely, without fear, in Harlem. The result was a literary, musical, and social renaissance. James Weldon Johnson, publisher of *The Crisis*, admired the new self-confidence of the emerging black middle class. "The Negro's situation in Harlem is without precedent in all his history in New York. Never before has he been so securely anchored, never before has he owned the land, never before has he been so well established in community life."[15]

Young New Yorkers, including white members of the so-called Smart Set, delighted in Harlem's cultural attractions. Jazz music and the blues— thoroughly unique and vital contributions of black Americans to the wider culture—thrilled these sophisticates. In 1922, Edward Kennedy "Duke" Ellington began a five-year run at Harlem's Cotton Club. There, as the bandleader, he played to all-white audiences. Over the years, he performed such jazz classics as "Take the A Train," "Mood Indigo," "Sophisticated Lady," and "I Got It Bad and That Ain't Good." The "A" Train, as savvy New Yorkers knew, was the subway line that led from midtown Manhattan to Harlem.

Zora Neale Hurston came from a poor Alabama sharecropper's family to graduate from Columbia University's Barnard College in 1928. She became an internationally respected writer, notably for the novel *Their Eyes Were Watching God*, and she concentrated especially on black folklore from her native South. She was fully aware of injustice, but she looked steadfastly to the future. "No, I don't weep at the world," she said. "I am too busy sharpening my oyster knife."[16]

"I don't study the black man," said poet Langston Hughes. "I feel him." Hughes faced the challenges that came inevitably to black writers seeking to carve out literary careers in the years of the Harlem Renaissance. "After all the deceptions and disappointments, there was always the undertow of black music with its rhythms that never betray you, its strength like the beat of the human heart."[17] In this way, the freedom of black music reinforced the yearning for freedom of black writers. And they, in turn, gave poetic expression to the soul of their community.

No small part of Harlem's attraction was the more relaxed enforcement of Prohibition laws north of 125th Street. "Speakeasy" was the name given to after-hours clubs where society "swells" could go if they were "sent by Joe."

To many black Southerners, the life and lure of Harlem beckoned like the North Star. To reach it, some poor sharecroppers fled their fields under cover of darkness. At some railroad stations, black farm workers were met by gangs of young white thugs who forcibly turned them back to their fields. To check this terror, James Weldon Johnson persuaded a Republican congressman from Missouri, L. C. Dyer, to introduce the nation's first federal anti-lynching law. The Dyer bill passed the House of Representatives, but it was defeated when white Southern Democrats filibustered it to death in the Senate.[18]

In Washington, D.C., Commerce Secretary Herbert Hoover signed an order banning racial segregation in his department. Hoover's action placed pressure on other federal government agencies to overturn the Wilson administration's unfair policies on equal employment opportunity in the nation's capital.[19] Soon, Washington would become another Mecca for black Americans seeking work and dignity.

IV. NORMALCY

When Warren G. Harding promised Americans "normalcy," they knew what he meant. Americans had been exhausted by years of tumult, years of reform at home and war abroad. With Harding, people expected a breathing spell.

Harding encouraged Secretary of State Charles Evans Hughes to press for a major international disarmament conference in 1921. When delegates gathered in Washington, D.C., Hughes's bold opening announcement stunned the world. Hughes said that the United States was willing to scrap new naval construction on which the country had already spent $300 million.[20] Partially constructed warships would simply be put in "mothballs."

The Washington Treaties that were quickly negotiated outlawed the use of poison gas in war. They also ruled "piratical" submarine warfare against merchant ships, whether the ships were armed or not.[21] The most important feature of the treaties was the ratio of 5:5:3:1:1 for naval battleship and aircraft carrier construction. The United States and Britain would have the highest tonnage allowed; Japan would be allowed 60 percent of their totals; France and Italy were limited to one-fifth of the U.S.-British ratio.

Naval limitation was widely popular because the naval arms race between Britain and Germany was thought to have led to World War I. Still, the 5:5:3:1:1 ratio the treaties imposed was to have dire consequences when the United States was later in danger in the Western Pacific.[22] Theodore Roosevelt would have been appalled, but few Americans objected at the time. After years of sterile conflicts between the White House and Congress, the new Republican administration seemed to be working smoothly to bring an era of international peace.

Harding was a forgiving man. He quickly moved to pardon Eugene Debs, whom Wilson had imprisoned for violating the Sedition Act. The president even hurried up the signing of Debs's pardon so he could be released from jail in time to spend Christmas with his family.[23] Even Democrat FDR was impressed by Harding's magnanimity.[24]

Harding might have fared better had he left the entire government in the hands of his abler cabinet members—Secretary of State Hughes,

Secretary of the Treasury Andrew Mellon, and Secretary of Commerce Herbert Hoover. He recognized his own limitations: "I can't make a damn thing out of this tax problem," he once said. "I listen to one side and they seem right, and then . . . I talk to the other side and they seem just as right. I know somewhere there is a book that will give me the truth, but hell, I couldn't read the book. . . . God, what a job!"[25]

But not everyone around him was able and trustworthy. When Senator Thomas J. Walsh, a Montana Democrat, relentlessly pursued the source of a $100,000 unsecured loan to Harding's interior secretary, Albert Bacon Fall, he unearthed a great scandal. Fall had allowed the great oil reserves at Teapot Dome, Wyoming, to go to private interests in a non-bid contract. Soon, Fall was tried for corruption, convicted, and packed off to prison—the first cabinet member in history to be so disgraced.[26]

It wasn't the only impropriety. When Alice Roosevelt Longworth wandered upstairs at the White House—her former home—she came upon a recently vacated poker table. It was littered with cigar stubs and half-full whiskey glasses. Poker and tobacco were one thing, but the nation was under Prohibition. She didn't bump into Harding's young mistress, but she might have.[27]

Harding became more troubled, more harried with each passing day. He seemed to sense that his friends were not leveling with him, and he fretted about the consequences of public disclosure of some of their shady dealings. He knew he could not disentangle himself from his questionable friends. They knew too much about him. As Harding himself once confessed in a speech, his father had told him: "It's a good thing you weren't born a girl. You'd be in a family way all the time. You can't say 'no.'"[28]

The president did what so many embattled presidents before and since have done to get away from troubles: he took a long trip. His escape route even took him north to Alaska. But he couldn't outrun his problems. They caught up with him on his return swing, when he collapsed and died 2 August 1923. The country knew little of what Washington insiders had begun to suspect, so Harding was deeply and sincerely mourned.

"Harding was not a bad man," said Alice Roosevelt Longworth. "He was just a slob."[29] That has been history's verdict too.

The new president who was sworn in at 2:45 a.m. on 3 August 1923 could not have presented a stronger contrast with the man he succeeded. When word of Harding's death reached him, Vice President Calvin Coolidge was visiting his boyhood home in rural Plymouth Notch, Vermont. He took the presidential oath by the light of a kerosene lamp. His father, a local justice of the peace, swore him in.[30] It was an image of flinty integrity that Americans would cling to—and soon.

The country smiled when it heard how Calvin Jr. got word that his father had become president. The teenager reported for work at a Western Massachusetts tobacco farm where he had a summer job. The farmer told him that his father had been inaugurated in the dead of night. The boy took the report without comment, then asked, "Which shed do you want me to work today?" Amazed, the farmer said that if his father had been named president of the United States, he surely wouldn't be working twelve-hour days in a tobacco field. "You would if your father were *my* father," responded young Calvin.[31] A chip off the old block!

President Coolidge was famously reticent. His nickname, "Silent Cal," endeared him to millions. Americans delighted in stories of their new chief executive. When a young debutante approached Coolidge, one story had it, she gushed that she'd bet her friends she could get him to say more than two words. "You lose," Coolidge is reported to have replied. TR's daughter, Alice Roosevelt Longworth, typically, was less impressed. She said Coolidge looked as if he had been "weaned on a pickle."[32]

As the roof fell in on the Harding scandals, the new president moved adroitly to distance himself from them. When Attorney General Daugherty balked at providing Congress with documents for an inquiry, Coolidge might have invoked executive privilege to shield him. Instead, he sacked the tarnished Harding appointee.[33]

Coolidge took office at a time when fear of "the foreign element" was on the rise. Legislation by the Republican Congresses in the 1920s sharply restricted the number of immigrants. The main part of the law was to restrict southern and eastern Europeans; the Asian restrictions were secondary. The bill did not ban African immigration though it did impose strict quotas. The first law was passed in 1921, limiting overall immigration and creating quotas of 3 percent of each foreign-born group present based on the 1910 Census. In 1924, the immigration cap was lowered, the quotas were dropped to 2 percent, and the 1890 Census was used. This severely restricted southern and eastern Europeans. The national origins provision did not come into effect until 1929. This provision set out to determine the national origins of the entire American nation and set quotas based on that information. Ironically, the law favored immigration from our recent foe—Germany—because so many German-Americans were already in the country.

The anti-immigrant spirit was fueled by advocates of *eugenics*. Charles Darwin's cousin, Francis Galton, had developed the concept in 1883 that meant, literally, "good genes."[34] Eugenicists believed that physical and mental health came from having good genes. They sought to encourage people with good genes to have more children and discourage people with "inferior" genes from becoming parents.[35]

American William Z. Ripley, a respected economist, had published a book, *The Races of Europe*, in which he divided whites into three groups—Nordics, Mediterraneans, and Alpines. His work helped fuel the anti-immigrant feeling.*

Margaret Sanger, a public health nurse who challenged laws against distributing birth control information, embraced eugenics. Sanger founded Planned Parenthood, ostensibly to encourage poor immigrants and other Americans to limit the number of children they bore. "As an advocate of birth control," she said, "I wish . . . to point out that the unbalance between the birth rate of the 'unfit' and the 'fit,' admittedly the greatest menace to civilization, can never be rectified by the inauguration

---

* German scientists in the 1920s and 1930s would go beyond Ripley's work with lethal consequences for all of Europe.

of a cradle competition between these two classes." She also spoke out in favor of immigration restrictions. Slowing the incoming tide of "unfits" was good policy as far as she was concerned; she did not want to pollute "the stamina of the race." Soon, she would advocate a national plan to "give dysgenic groups [people alleged to have bad genes] in our population a choice of segregation or sterilization."[36]

In the twenties, Americans had a love affair with the automobile. Henry Ford made Detroit into the hub of the nation's auto industry. He introduced advanced techniques of assembly line production. Although Ford employees were not permitted to sit, to talk, or even to whistle while they worked, they could earn as much as $5 a day—considered a very good wage in 1924.* Ford himself became fabulously wealthy. He was probably worth $10 billion in 2004 dollars.[37]

In many ways, Henry Ford was an enlightened entrepreneur. By 1926, he had ten thousand black Americans in his workforce. In the Ford Motor Corporation, black employees could rise into management. Ford also opened his plant doors to workers with disabilities. His assembly line methods enabled blind men, amputees, and others to perform a single, important task. In this, he affirmed the human dignity of thousands.[38]

But Henry Ford had a dark side; his tolerance did not extend to the Jewish community in particular. His newspaper, the *Dearborn Independent*, regularly published violently anti-Semitic articles. So offensive were his attacks on the Jews that President Harding and fellow industrialist Thomas Edison had begged him to knock it off. The *Independent* reprinted the notorious invention of the tsarist secret police called *The Protocols of the Elders of Zion*. This work, long exposed as a forgery, charged there was an international conspiracy of powerful Jews to rule the world. "The International Jew: The World's Problem" was the lead article in the *Independent* that echoed the themes of the discredited *Protocols*.[39]

---

* "Whistle While You Work" was a catchy tune sung by Snow White's friends, the seven dwarfs, in the 1937 Walt Disney animated classic. Could Disney have been satirizing Ford's "no whistle" policy?

In 1922, a foreign correspondent for the *New York Times* visited the Munich headquarters of a new political faction, the National Socialist German Workers Party. Soon, they would be known by the German abbreviation for National Socialists—*Nazis*. The leader of the party was called *der Führer*. A decorated veteran of the Great War, young Adolf Hitler had a large portrait of Henry Ford in his office. Outside, there was a table stacked high with German translations of Ford's book *The International Jew*.[40]

Hitler expressed his admiration for another influential American, Leon Whitney, president of the American Eugenics Society. The Führer requested a copy of *The Passing of the Great Race*, written by a leading member of the American Eugenics Society, Madison Grant. Hitler lavished praise on the book, calling it his "Bible."[41]

V. "KEEP COOL WITH COOLIDGE"

The country was shocked in 1924 by the Chicago trial of Richard Loeb and Nathan Leopold for the murder of fourteen-year-old Bobby Franks. Loeb and Leopold were teenagers, both from very wealthy families, both extremely well educated. Loeb was the son of a Sears Roebuck executive and the youngest graduate in the history of the University of Michigan. There, he had become absorbed in reading Friedrich Nietzsche's *Beyond Good and Evil*. Nietzsche argued that conventional moral codes could not apply to the "superman." Leopold was attracted to Loeb and desperately sought his approval.[42]

Loeb wanted to commit the perfect crime. The boys lured young Bobby Franks into their car, where Loeb killed him with a chisel. The boy's naked body was soon found in a culvert. The families retained the best criminal lawyer in the country, Clarence Darrow. Since evidence of the teens' guilt was overwhelming, Darrow decided to make an impassioned appeal to spare the killers' lives. Darrow recruited the best psychiatrists to testify to the nature of psychological compulsion. The prosecution derided these experts as "three wise men from the East."[43]

Darrow's closing arguments came in a hot Chicago courtroom in August 1924. He explored a world of overwhelming sexual and psychological urges. He argued for a "deterministic" view of the universe. "Nature is strong and she is pitiless." Nature works in mysterious ways over which we have little control, he contended. He made a case for life imprisonment as being even harsher punishment than hanging—"In all the endless road you tread, there's nothing but the night." In pleading for the lives of the two killers, Darrow passionately cried out: "If the state in which I live is not kinder, more humane, and more considerate than the mad act of these two boys, I am sorry I have lived so long!" Many in the courtroom, including the presiding judge, wept openly as Darrow finished his appeal. The novel tactic worked well enough to save the pair from execution. Leopold and Loeb were sentenced to ninety-nine years in prison.[44*]

By the time the election year of 1924 arrived, few Americans tied President Coolidge to the record of Warren G. Harding. Coolidge's own honesty was beyond question. The country was enjoying peace abroad and unprecedented prosperity at home. Or at least it appeared to be. Already, there were warning signs in the farm belt as commodity prices slid. Most Americans, however, were happily experiencing boom times.

When the Democrats met to select a presidential nominee, they faced a hard task and they knew it. The Democratic National Convention of 1924, held at Madison Square Garden, was a rambunctious affair filled with arguments over whether to repeal Prohibition and condemn the Ku Klux Klan. It was the first American political convention to be broadcast on radio. The Democrats chose as their nominee New York Governor

---

* Richard Loeb was killed in 1936 by another inmate who claimed Loeb had made a sexual advance toward him. Nathan Leopold learned twenty-seven foreign languages, served as an X-ray technician in the prison hospital, and reorganized the prison library. Released in 1958, he moved to Puerto Rico and married. He wrote *The Birds of Puerto Rico*. He died in 1971 at the age of sixty-seven.

Alfred Emanuel Smith, who had gained fame in 1911 when he co-chaired a commission to investigate the horrible Triangle Shirtwaist Factory Fire in Manhattan. Scores of young women had been trapped on the upper floors by an inferno. Firemen were unable to reach them because the doors were barred to prevent theft. New Yorkers were shocked by stories of the young women throwing themselves out of the building's windows to escape the flames. As a New York Assemblyman in Albany, Smith had sponsored many reforms to provide for worker safety. Soon, he was elected governor of the Empire State. When reporters quizzed him about his views on Prohibition, the clever Smith smiled and asked them: "Wouldn't you like to have your foot on the rail and blow the foam off some suds?"[45]*

Meanwhile, in those steaming summer days of 1924, at the White House, the life of sixteen-year-old Calvin Coolidge Jr. ebbed away due to a simple blister that had become infected. For a brief moment, the feuding delegates ceased their fighting to pray for the dying boy and to send a message of sympathy to the lad's heartbroken father.[46] Later, Coolidge would write about his son's death in his autobiography. With this grievous loss, Silent Cal became more silent still:

> In his suffering he asked me to make him well. I could not. When he went, the power and glory of the presidency went with him. . . . The ways of Providence are often beyond our understanding. It seemed to me that the world had need of the work that it was probable he could do. I do not know why such a price was exacted for occupying the White House.[47]

Republicans said the election was about "Coolidge or Chaos."[48] When the votes were counted, they suffered no hangover at all from the Harding binge. Coolidge scored a nationwide victory, losing only the states of the Old Confederacy, Oklahoma, and LaFollette's Wisconsin.

---

* Dr. Joseph Walsh, the author's grandfather, was Smith's personal physician, according to Bennett family lore. In any case, the governor must have been a treat to treat.

The election wasn't the only contest that captured national attention then.

The state legislature of Tennessee pondered the often-frightening world conjured up by such events as the Leopold and Loeb trial. The lawmakers saw in the atheistic philosophies of such intellectuals as Charles Darwin, Friedrich Nietzsche, and Sigmund Freud cause for alarm. Nietzsche's statement that "God is dead" was widely quoted and mostly misunderstood. Actually, Nietzsche meant that people's *belief* in God had died. Shocked by such ideas, fearful Tennessee lawmakers found themselves agreeing with Russian writer Fyodor Dostoevsky, whose Ivan Karamazov said if God is dead, then everything is permitted. The lawmakers shouldered the task of making sure that not everything was permitted in Tennessee. The solution was simple and direct. They passed a law banning the teaching of Darwinism or any creed that held that man was descended from a "lower" life form.

A new group called the American Civil Liberties Union (ACLU) saw in this law an excellent opportunity to score ideological points against what they regarded as intellectually backward Christian fundamentalism. The ACLU took out ads in various newspapers and young John T. Scopes responded. The Dayton, Tennessee, science teacher indicated his willingness to test the law. In 1925, he was charged with breaking the new law, and the summer Scopes trial gripped the attention of the entire country. The famous Clarence Darrow guaranteed national focus for the case when he took up the defense.

William Jennings Bryan was eager to serve with the prosecution. Bryan was not a Tennessean, he had never made his living practicing law, and he had no knowledge of the scientific arguments likely to be at the core of the trial. But Bryan earned a good living lecturing and writing articles. Besides, the former secretary of state and the Democratic Party's three-time nominee for president of the United States loved the spotlight.[49]

Bryan succeeded in one important trial maneuver. He gained a favorable ruling from the judge that if Darrow brought in scientific experts to testify in defense of Scopes, these experts would be subject to cross-examination. The ACLU's co-counsel, Arthur Garfield Hays, was distressed. "Cross examination would have shown that the scientists, while religious men—for we chose only that kind—still did not believe in the virgin birth [of Jesus] and other miracles." Hays knew that the testimony of such skeptics would undermine the ACLU's broader agenda for American education. Hays later wrote that the ACLU *needed* the backing of millions of Christians who believed in the basic doctrinal positions of their churches. He did not want the radicalism of the ACLU to be publicly exposed by placing doubting scientists on the witness stand.[50]

Reacting to this victory for the prosecution, newspaper columnist H. L. Mencken sneered, "All that remains of the great cause of the State of Tennessee against the infidel Scopes is the final business of bumping off the defendant."[51] Mencken was just one of hundreds of journalists who had descended on the little town of Dayton for what the press called "the monkey trial." Mencken couldn't pass up the chance to laugh at what he saw as a typical example of Southern backwardness. The South, he had written, was the "Sahara of the Bozart" (Beaux Arts).[52]*

Darrow struck next. He called to the stand "the greatest Bible expert in the world"—William Jennings Bryan![53] Poor Bryan was soon shown to be ill-equipped for the intellectual parry-and-thrust that was the experienced Darrow's courtroom stock-in-trade. And Darrow was the best in the country. Quickly tied in knots of self-contradiction, Bryan pounded his fist and pathetically cried out: "I am simply trying to protect the word of God against the greatest atheist or agnostic in the United States!" The courtroom crowd wildly applauded this statement, but it was in fact an admission of defeat.[54]

When the jury found John T. Scopes guilty of having violated Tennessee's law, the judge prudently levied a fine of only $100. Bryan, unwisely again, took the verdict as a vindication and announced plans to

---

* French for "the fine arts."

carry the cause to other states. His wife, Mary, expressed her doubts. She did not want to see him lead an effort that would be seen as an assault on intellectual freedom. Within days of the trial's end, however, the Great Commoner died in his sleep. Mencken gloated that "God aimed at Darrow and hit Bryan!"[55]

The trial came to be seen as a watershed moment in American life. An entire mythology grew up around it. The Broadway play (later a film) *Inherit the Wind* helped spread the misconceptions. Joseph Wood Krutch, a careful journalist and later a distinguished literary critic, helped to untangle the story. "The little town of Dayton behaved on the whole quite well," he wrote. "The atmosphere was so far from being sinister that it suggested a circus day. The authors of 'Inherit the Wind' made it . . . a witch hunt." Krutch pointed out that the defense, not the prosecution, sought the trial. "Thus it was a strange sort of witch trial, one in which the accused won a scholarship enabling him to attend graduate school and the only victim was the chief witness for the prosecution, poor old Bryan."[56]

There would be no such spectacular trials over troubling books in Europe. In the same year that Americans debated Darwin, German presses rolled out a new tome. Adolf Hitler published *Mein Kampf* following his release from prison. The Nazi party leader had been tried and jailed for his attempt to overthrow the government of his home state of Bavaria. Hitler spent his brief, easy sentence dictating his book.*

If Darwin described a struggle among the species in which only the fittest survive, Hitler applied that struggle to the relations between nations. In his ponderous work, Hitler laid out in chilling detail his plans for the new Germany. *Aryans*—that is, those whose genes gave them fair skin, light hair, and blue eyes—were nature's fittest. They were the *Herrenvolk* ("master race"). And the only reason they had lost the First World War is that they were betrayed by Jews. Hitler referred to the

---

* Hitler's Nazi Party celebrated the anniversary of the failed 1923 Munich Beer Hall *putsch* every year.

armistice agreement as "the stab in the back" and those Germans who signed it as "the November criminals."

VI. "THE LONE EAGLE"

Charles A. Lindbergh was determined to make his mark. The young aviator was self-confident but did not like to hustle. He didn't like having to ask businessmen and bankers for money. The twenty-four-year-old college dropout was an unlikely figure in the 1920s. He didn't smoke or drink. He avoided the girls who hung around the flight line. He set high standards for himself—even setting up categories of perfection as Benjamin Franklin had done: Alertness, Altruism, Balance, Brevity, all the way through to Unselfishness and Zeal.[57]

A more unrepresentative figure for the "lost generation" could hardly be imagined. But Lindbergh, son of a Minnesota congressman, did have one characteristic that he shared with F. Scott Fitzgerald's Jay Gatsby: he had an eye for the Main Chance. He knew how to get what he wanted.

Worldwide fame awaited the man who could fly nonstop across the Atlantic Ocean. Not only fame, but fortune: the $25,000 Orteig Prize led men to risk their lives. Navy Commander Richard Byrd, the famous pilot who first flew over the North Pole, had crashed in April 1927 in his large trimotor plane, *America*. Byrd, only slightly injured, was followed two weeks later by two other navy pilots who died in the crash of their trimotor.[58]

The prize could be won by a flight in either direction, so two French pilots started at Paris, flying westward to New York on 9 May. When the great Charles Nungesser and Francois Coli were reported off the New England coast, Lindbergh's heart sank. Crowds were already cheering in Paris.[59] Suddenly, the plane carrying Nungesser and Coli went missing.

As Lindbergh watched his single-engine monoplane, *The Spirit of St. Louis*, being prepared for takeoff, the drizzling rain and deeply rutted muddy road combined with the recent deaths of Nungesser and Coli to create a somber, not a celebratory, scene. "It's more like a funeral procession than the beginning of a flight to Paris," Lindbergh thought.[60] He had stripped the plane to the barest of necessities. Everything not essential had to give way to fuel. The lanky aviator took only five sandwiches for the trip. Asked if this would be enough, he answered laconically: "If I get to Paris, I won't need any more. And if I don't get to Paris, I won't need any more, either."[61]

On the morning of 20 May 1927, Lindbergh took off from Long Island's Roosevelt Field.* The fuel-heavy plane missed a tractor by only ten feet, telephone wires by barely twenty as it struggled to get airborne. The country held its breath. Will Rogers did not attempt humor:

A . . . slim, tall, bashful, smiling American boy is somewhere over the middle of the Atlantic Ocean, where no lone human being has ever ventured before. He is being prayed for to every kind of Supreme Being that ever had a following. If he is lost it will be the most universally regretted loss we ever had.[62]

Except he was not lost. And he wasn't really alone. Harold Anderson of the *New York Sun* wrote one of the most widely circulated newspaper columns of the era, "Lindbergh Flies Alone":

Alone? Is he alone at whose side rides Courage, with Skill within the cockpit and Faith upon the left? Does solitude surround the brave when Adventure leads the way and Ambition reads the dials? Is there no company with him for whom the air is cleft by Daring and the darkness is made light by Emprise?[63]**

---

* It was not a good omen, for people who paid attention to such things. Roosevelt Field had been named for Quentin Roosevelt, the brave young American aviator who met his death in the skies over France.

** "Emprise: an adventurous, daring, or chivalric enterprise" (Merriam-Webster's Dictionary, https://www.merriam-webster.com/dictionary/emprise).

Delirious crowds of Frenchmen swept onto Le Bourget airdrome in Paris when Lindbergh landed, following a flight of thirty-three hours and thirty-nine minutes.[64] In an age fascinated by technical details, it was pointed out that the engine of *The Spirit of St. Louis* had to fire 14,472,000 times—without a skip or a miss—to cover the 3,735 miles from New York to Paris.[65]

Charles Augustus Lindbergh became the greatest hero of the age. He was worshipped in Paris. He received a hero's welcome and a ticker tape parade down Broadway in New York. He became such a celebrity that he could no longer send his shirts out to be laundered. They would be cut up for souvenirs. Nor could he write a check. His signature was worth more than the amount on the slip. Flying around the United States afterward, Lindbergh was feted everywhere. At one dinner, George Gershwin played his famous *Rhapsody in Blue* for the young man, only to stop midway to ask about the dangers of the flight.[66]

When the man the press dubbed "the Lone Eagle" flew nonstop from Washington, D.C., to Mexico City, the people went wild with joy. Thousands had slept on the runway to get a glimpse of the hero. Many prayed as Lindbergh, who had lost his bearings, arrived more than two hours late. "*Viva Lindbergh!*" they cried. Mrs. Morrow thought they might tear the young aviator's clothes off in their excitement.[67] It was, and remains, the greatest moment in U.S.-Mexican relations.

VII. PEACE AND PROSPERITY

Charles Lindbergh was not the only American who looked to Paris to make his mark. In the twenties, expatriate authors like Ernest Hemingway and F. Scott Fitzgerald flocked to the City of Light. There, Gertrude Stein and her companion Alice B. Toklas kept a literary salon that was the gathering place for young American writers eager to make their reputations. "Remarks, Hemingway, are not literature," was Stein's blunt assessment of the young American's gritty style.[68] Despite her often acerbic comments, Stein's advice was respected among writers. Even that quintessential Southerner, William Faulkner, and aspiring playwright Eugene O'Neill made their way to this home of *belles lettres*.

American Secretary of State Frank B. Kellogg also looked to Paris. He responded to an offer of a treaty from the French foreign minister, Aristide Briand. The proposed treaty would ensure that the two nations would never go to war against one another. It was Briand's attempt to get U.S. backing in case France was attacked. Kellogg broadened the scope of the offer to fashion a treaty whose avowed purpose was to "renounce war as an instrument of national policy" and invited all states to sign it. The Kellogg-Briand Pact would win the Nobel Peace Prize for its two authors. Sixty-two nations would in time subscribe, including Japan, Germany, and Italy.[69]

But the Kellogg-Briand Pact was a mixed bag. In the long term, it provided the legal basis for the eventual war crimes tribunals for the makers of aggressive war. In the short term, however, it dangerously lulled the democracies into thinking they could rely on a piece of parchment for their security. Senator Carter Glass, Democrat of Virginia, said he was not "simple enough to suppose it was worth a postage stamp."[70] Nonetheless, Glass voted to ratify the so-called Pact of Paris. It sailed through the Senate on a vote of 81–1.[71] The *New York Evening Post* ridiculed the pact when Congress approved construction of fifteen new naval cruisers. How many cruisers would we need, the *Post* editorialized, "if we *hadn't* just signed a peace treaty with twenty-six nations?"[72] Apparently, the *Post* had forgotten TR's dictum: Speak softly, but carry a big stick.

Kellogg-Briand was so popular in part because Americans preferred not to think about foreign troubles. And troubles there were. In Germany, the liberal Weimar Republic struggled to maintain democracy in the face of challenges from the Communists and the Nazis. In Soviet Russia, the Bolsheviks had completely extinguished freedom. In the struggle for power that followed Lenin's death in 1924, Josef Stalin emerged victorious. Stalin played various factions of the ruling Communist Party of the Soviet Union off against one another.[73] His successful attacks on his enemies left him a free hand to bring the Ukraine under his thumb. In this "breadbasket of Europe," the Communists intentionally starved six or seven million peasants to death after expropriating their land.

While most Americans knew nothing of Stalin's atrocities in the Ukraine, one American did—Walter Duranty, Moscow correspondent of the *New York Times*. He would win a Pulitzer Prize for his sympathetic coverage of Josef Stalin. He chose not to report on the brutal famine. Apparently not all the news was fit to print.

In America, the love affair with the automobile proceeded apace. General Motors did not try to compete with Ford through lower prices but by giving the consumers more car for their money. The Chevrolet came with a self-starter feature that vastly increased the popularity of driving, especially among women.[74]

On the silver screen, 1927 saw the first "talkie" produced. Al Jolson starred as *The Jazz Singer*. The plot centered on the son of a Jewish cantor who uses his great voice to make a fortune as a popular singer. His parents grieve because they think he has prostituted his God-given talents. Most Americans were thrilled when Al Jolson spoke his signature line: "You ain't heard *nothin'* yet!"[75] But black Americans could not have been flattered by the fact that Jolson's Jazz Singer was performed in blackface.

Coolidge was at the height of his popularity in the summer of 1927. Vacationing in the Black Hills of South Dakota, the president held one of his regular not-for-attribution press conferences. As the reporters filed into a high school gym, Coolidge handed each one a slip of paper on which was typed the curt message: "I do not choose to run for President in nineteen twenty-eight."[76] Brief, blunt, direct. It was Coolidge's style.

There followed a short but intense period of speculation. Did he really mean it? Did he want to be drafted? Few insiders who had seen the president staring longingly out of the White House window at the tennis courts where Calvin Jr. had played his last game could have been surprised.

Others who heard Grace Goodhue Coolidge's whispered words to her friends ("Poppa says there's a depression coming") would have been in no doubt of his sincerity.[77] Coolidge may have sensed his own mortality. A distinguished doctor later said of him, "I have rarely known a man to have the type of heart condition such as that from which President Coolidge suffered without himself having had some of the danger signs."[78] To those who knew the president slept as many as twelve hours a day, angina may have been an explanation—perhaps even depression.

Whatever his reasons, Calvin Coolidge did his country a service in leaving office with such dignity. After the rigor mortis of Wilson and the flaccidity of Harding, he dignified his office. The title that Kansas editor William Allen White gave to his book on Coolidge neatly summed up this quiet man's presidency: he was *A Puritan in Babylon*.

One American who did choose to run that year was George Herman Ruth—known to millions of baseball fans as the Babe. Babe Ruth in 1927 ran the bases an astounding sixty times to set a home run record that lasted more than thirty years. Little wonder that Yankee Stadium was called "the House that Ruth built."

Americans also thrilled that year to the exploits on the links of Bobby Jones. In his 1927 biography, *Down the Fairway*, Jones wrote, "I wish I could say here that a strange thrill shot through my skinny little bosom when I swung at a golf ball for the first time, but it wouldn't be truthful." Even so, Robert Tyre Jones began to teach himself to play golf at age six and entered his first professional championship at fourteen.[79] He would come to dominate the game and represent the model of a Southern gentleman and sportsman.

The Republicans felt confident about 1928. Peace and Prosperity always favors the "in" party. The obvious choice to succeed Coolidge was Commerce Secretary Herbert Hoover. President Harding had called him "the smartest gink I know."[80]

Americans admired Herbert Hoover's story. Born in poverty in Iowa, orphaned as a young boy, he had gone to Stanford University and become a world-renowned mining engineer. He made millions and could easily have retired in luxury. Instead, he threw himself into projects like Belgian Relief, Russian famine relief, and, finally, service for eight years as commerce secretary during a time when, as President Coolidge said, "The chief business of the American people *is* business and the chief ideal of the American people is idealism."

Hoover's campaign promised to keep the good economy going. At times he reached for the rhetorical heights like Icarus reaching for the sun: "We in America today are nearer to the final triumph over poverty than ever before," he said. "The poorhouse is vanishing. . . . [Given] a chance to go forward with the policies of the last eight years, we shall soon with the help of God be in sight of the day when poverty will be banished from the nation."[81]

New York Governor Al Smith was the Democrats' nominee. Smith's fondness for cigars gave him a gravelly voice. He joked about his humble origins. He could not afford to go to college, but he said he had earned his FFM degree (from the Fulton Fish Market). Al Smith was certainly very bright, and he had a natural dignity, but his rough accent grated on Americans' ears. He was the *foist* to address them on the *raddio*. It didn't help that candidate Smith sounded a lot like the mobsters who were being hauled before congressional committees and grand juries all over the country.

Then, there was the religion factor. Hoover would not countenance any bigotry. That didn't restrain his followers, however, for whom Smith's Catholicism was frightening. A Methodist bishop from Smith's own New York State fought Governor Smith as president of the state's Anti-Saloon League. He bluntly said, "No Governor can kiss the papal ring and get within gunshot of the White House."[82] Kansan William Allen White was the editor of the *Emporia Gazette*. He had been a Progressive. Even so, White wrote, "The whole *Puritan* civilization which has built a sturdy, orderly nation is threatened by Smith."[83]

No Democrat could have beaten "Peace and Prosperity." When the votes rolled in, Hoover overwhelmingly defeated Smith. If Hoover could have seen what lay ahead, he probably would have traded places with Smith in a heartbeat.

VIII. CRASH!

All Quiet on the Western Front was the literary sensation of 1929. For his classic story of the brutal impact of war on young men, German author Erich Maria Remarque was hailed throughout the Allied countries. The book sold almost half a million copies by Christmas. While French critics praised the work, saying every copy sold was "a plebiscite in favor of peace," Remarque was denounced by German army officers. Later, when the Nazis came to power, his works would be burned. Remarque was forced to flee Germany and his sister, Elfriede, was killed by the Nazis.[84]

In America, Ernest Hemingway's *A Farewell to Arms* also spoke to the disenchantment so many young people felt with the failed promises of a world made safe for democracy.[85]

In Chicago, Prohibition enforcement was a sometime thing. Alfonse ("Scarface Al") Capone's gang was deep into bootlegging, speakeasy shakedowns, illegal gambling, and prostitution. All over the country, the government struggled to keep up with the bootleggers and rumrunners. In Rhode Island, for example, the U.S. Coast Guard chased the speedy rumrunner *Black Duck* in Narragansett Bay. When after repeated warnings the *Black Duck* failed to stop, the coast guardsmen opened fire, killing three of four crewmen and seizing five hundred cases of whiskey.[86] In nearby Boston, thirsty crowds were so incensed that they rioted outside Faneuil Hall and beat up a coast guard recruiter.

On Wall Street, the Roaring Twenties roared on. Millions of people rushed to get into a Bull Market, often buying stock on a "margin" as little as 10 percent of face value, then reselling as a speculative "bubble" was created. In this way, stocks in poorly managed companies could nonetheless be artificially bid up in value. Hundreds of thousands acted on "hot tips" and rushed to invest their money in stocks without having any idea of their real worth. Everyone wanted to "get rich quick."

Harvard economist William Z. Ripley had warned of the Wild West atmosphere on Wall Street. He colorfully denounced the "honeyfugling, hornswoggling and skullduggery" of the corporate boardrooms.[87] Ripley's party-pooping went unheeded.

A warning tremor of hard times came in early October 1929, when the price of wheat plummeted. This would have devastating consequences not only for American farmers in the Midwest but also for Canadians and Australians.[88]

Later in the month, the New York Stock Exchange recorded a serious sell-off, taking prices back to their 1927 levels. President Hoover hastened to issue a reassuring statement. The "fundamentals" of American prosperity, he said, were sound.[89]

President Hoover's message could not have been more ill-timed. On that day, 24 October 1929, the stock market collapsed. It would forever be known as "Black Thursday." A month before, the average price of thirty leading American industrial shares was $380. When trading ended on Black Thursday, it was only $230.[90] Overnight, the investments of millions of American families were virtually wiped out.

Americans were plunged into the worst Depression they had ever known. It was an experience that scarred millions. This had always been the Land of Opportunity. And that opportunity was based in no small part on bountiful harvests. Even in the midst of civil war, President Lincoln's Thanksgiving Proclamation praised the Almighty for sending us fertile fields and bulging granaries. No more. For millions, these were the "Hungry Years."[91]

For those Americans who did not put their savings into Wall Street stocks and bonds, and they were legion, the Great Depression was felt in the unemployment figures. As more and more people lost their jobs, fear stalked the land. Was there no turnaround, no recovery in sight? In 1932, unemployment rose to a full 24 percent—twelve million out of work.[92]

Bank failures also frightened many of the most stable citizens. Trust is essential to enterprise, as Americans back to Alexander Hamilton knew. When hundreds of banks "went under," the Depression deepened. Work and thrift had always been the basis for American economic strength. Now, both work and thrift seemed to avail Americans little.

President Hoover tried manfully to buck up Americans' sagging spirits. "Any lack of confidence in . . . the basic strength of business is foolish," he said in November. "We have now passed the worst," he declared on 1 May 1930.[93] "May Day," ironically, is the international distress call. The president was hurt badly in public esteem as it soon became obvious that the corner had not been turned at all.

Many Americans thrown out of work took to the roads. "Okies" from Oklahoma piled into overburdened trucks to make the passage to Southern California, where there was said to be work. Oklahoma's Native Son, Will Rogers, ruefully joked that America was the first country ever to "drive to the poor house in an automobile." Many a young man hit the rails, hitching rides on slow-moving freight trains.

John Steinbeck would later immortalize the experience of the stricken Joad family in his gritty novel, *The Grapes of Wrath*. Soup kitchens and shanty towns sprang up around the country. The shanty towns were dubbed "Hoovervilles" in a cruel riposte to the president's invincible view that "prosperity is just around the corner."

> Hoover is our shepherd
> We are in want
> He maketh us to lie
> Down on the park benches
> He leadeth us beside the still factories
> He disturbeth our soul.[94]

With the deepening Depression, Americans looked to the man in the White House for answers. President Hoover continued to maintain as much of a normal routine as he could, hoping to build confidence in recovery. He dined each night at the White House wearing formal attire. He attended the opening of the baseball season (and had to endure the indignity of being roundly booed by fans in Philadelphia). When a reporter asked Babe Ruth how he could justify earning more than the president of the United States, he replied, "I had a better year than Hoover did."

In June 1930, Congress left President Hoover with an important decision: whether or not to sign the Smoot-Hawley Tariff Bill. Herbert Hoover had never been identified with isolationism, nor with a narrow, "beggar thy neighbor" view of America's economic place in the world.[95] Nonetheless, he signed Smoot-Hawley. It was to prove perhaps his worst mistake.* High tariffs on imported goods led immediately to other nations raising *their* tariffs in retaliation. Thus, at a time when all countries needed to stimulate international trade, they were choking it off.

The disastrous impact was felt almost immediately with our closest neighbor and biggest trading partner, Canada. One thousand economists had appealed to the president to veto this bill, as had the American Bankers Association. As a direct result, Canada retaliated against American goods, and eighty-seven branches of American factories opened up north of the 49th parallel.[96] This hurt American workers, who lost jobs and the ability to export their manufactures.

To many, Hoover seemed callously indifferent to the suffering of the common man. Although this was far from true—Hoover had in fact been a great humanitarian throughout his life—this shy, reserved man was the butt of endless bitter jokes. When out-of-work men pulled

---

* The farmers led the demands for protection and their appeal outweighed the 1,028 economists who appealed to Hoover to veto the tariff bill. The Depression deepened and lengthened as a result. (Taranto, James, and Leonard Leo, *Presidential Leadership*, Wall Street Journal Books, New York: 2004, p. 221.)

their empty pockets inside-out, they were said to be flying "Hoover Flags." A story circulated that the president had asked Andrew Mellon, his secretary of the Treasury, for a nickel to call a friend. "Here's a dime," the Pittsburgh millionaire purportedly told Hoover. "Call *all* your friends."[97]

The team of Mellon and Hoover were singled out for abuse in a thousand rhymes and satires:

> Oh, Mellon pulled the whistle, boys,
> And Hoover rang the bell,
> Wall Street gave the signal,
> And the country went to hell.[98]

When Hoover vetoed a bill to pay out early the bonus promised to veterans of World War I, a "bonus army" descended on Washington in 1932. The president quietly ordered tents and medical units to be made available for members of the Bonus Expeditionary Force (BEF, a clever play on the name of the U.S. force in WWI, the American Expeditionary Force, AEF). When Communist agitators prodded a small number of the men to throw bricks and stones at police, however, Hoover was determined to preserve order in the nation's capital.[99]

Hoover ordered the army to quell the riots that were breaking out downtown. He specified that the regular troops should *not* be armed and that the BEF men were simply to be escorted to their tent camps or turned over to Metropolitan Police.[100]

General Douglas MacArthur, the army's chief of staff, took personal command of his troops. He used tanks, tear gas, and soldiers with fixed bayonets to clear the streets of rock-throwing bonus marchers. MacArthur's aide—Major Dwight D. Eisenhower—was surprised and disappointed to see his chief preparing to storm the bonus marchers' camps. Major George S. Patton, however, eagerly led U.S. cavalry down Pennsylvania Avenue in what was to prove to be one of the last charges of mounted soldiers.[101]* Two of the bonus marchers were killed in the resulting melee. The *Washington News* was aghast. "What a pitiful spectacle is that of the great American Government, mightiest in the world, chasing unarmed men, women and children with Army tanks. . . . If the Army must be called out to make war on unarmed citizens, this is no longer America."[102]

Conditions were so desperate in the election year of 1932 that thousands of prominent writers and intellectuals openly called for Communism. F. Scott Fitzgerald, author of the vastly popular *Great Gatsby*, yearned to "bring on the revolution." Other famous writers drawn to Marxist ideas were Upton Sinclair, Edmund Wilson, Sherwood Anderson, Erskine Caldwell, Malcolm Cowley, and Lincoln Steffens.[103] Many of these writers lived and worked in New York City, giving a strong leftist tilt to the state's intellectual climate, and, in effect, to the nation's atmosphere as well.

IX. "HAPPY DAYS ARE HERE AGAIN"

In the election year of 1932, Americans were suffering their worst economic conditions since the Panic of 1893. This virtually guaranteed that the Democrats would win the White House. Republican insiders all expected Hoover to lose.

Franklin Delano Roosevelt was hardly the unanimous choice of the fractious Democrats. Many of the serious thinkers of the country dismissed him. Columnist Walter Lippmann said he was "a pleasant man who, without any important qualifications for the office, would like very much to be President." Supreme Court Justice Oliver Wendell Holmes chimed in, saying FDR had "a second class intellect, but a first class temperament."[104]

They all underestimated the New Yorker. In a dramatic move, FDR

---

* It may have been the last charge of U.S. cavalry, unless one counts the remarkable pictures of U.S. troops in Afghanistan in 2001, pursuing the Taliban on horseback.

flew from Albany to the Democratic Convention in Chicago, breaking with the tradition that said a candidate never appears before the convention that nominates him. "Let it be symbolic that I broke traditions. Let it be from now on the task of our party to break foolish traditions. . . . I pledge you, I pledge myself to a new deal for the American people."[105]

The power of the appeal was mighty. Here, a man crippled by polio had dared to take to the still-hazardous skies to carry his message of hope to millions who heard him via radio as he confidently addressed the party faithful. The day after FDR delivered his acceptance speech, the *New York World-Telegram* published a cartoon by Rollin Kirby. A hard-pressed farmer was shown looking up hopefully at Roosevelt's airplane. On its wings were the words "New Deal."[106]

President Hoover bravely soldiered on. He campaigned harder than he had in 1928. But he spoke in a listless, uninteresting fashion. At some of his campaign stops, he faced unfriendly audiences.[107]

If Hoover was dour but dutiful, FDR was radiant. He beamed the smile that drove his opponents crazy. He looked out at the world near-sightedly from behind *pince-nez* glasses that were already out of fashion when cousin Teddy wore them. He wore a cape instead of an overcoat. It was a concession to his polio, but it gave him a rakish air. Roosevelt complained about "centralization" and called Hoover a "big spender." These were laughable charges then and hilarious now given how FDR actually governed. But he could have teamed with Walt Disney's little friend Mickey Mouse as his running mate and it wouldn't have made a difference in the outcome.*

Roosevelt won 22,821,857 popular votes (57.4 percent) and 472 electoral votes. Hoover suffered the greatest repudiation ever dealt to a sitting president. He won 15,761,845 popular votes (40.0 percent) and just 59 electoral votes. Most interesting, Socialist Party candidate Norman Thomas got only 2.2 percent of the popular vote. When the stakes were

---

* The Walt Disney studios were launched in 1928 with a black-and-white cartoon feature called "Steamboat Willie." It was Mickey Mouse's silver screen debut.

this high, few voters wanted to risk "throwing their votes away" on a futile third-party protest.

"The little fella' felt that he never had a chance, and he didn't until November the eighth. And *did* he grab it!"[108] That's how Will Rogers described the popular earthquake that overthrew not only Hoover, but the Republican majority coalition that had governed for most years between 1896 and 1932. Roosevelt not only carried a Democratic Congress in with him, he swept away Republican majorities in a score of state legislatures. Governors, mayors, even winning candidates for recorder of wills in Sleepy Eye County, Minnesota, owed their victories to Franklin Delano Roosevelt. More important, they *knew* it. For the Democrats and their millions of newly won friends, Happy Days were indeed here again.

By Inauguration Day 1933, the country longed for an end to the *interregnum*. (Americans, typically, rejected the fancy Latin word in favor of the more folksy term: *lame duck*.) FDR rode down Pennsylvania Avenue with the outgoing president. That was the only *outgoing* thing about poor Herbert Hoover. When he failed to engage his defeated rival in conversation, Roosevelt turned to the happy crowds cheering along the parade route. He smiled his radiant smile and waved his top hat.[109] The extraordinary scene was captured—and exaggerated—by a cartoon published in the *New Yorker* magazine. FDR was buoyant, optimistic, Hoover tight-lipped and grim. Unfortunately for the Republicans, that was to be their image for years.

"Let me assert my firm belief that the *only* thing we have to fear is fear itself"—Roosevelt intoned from the Inaugural platform—"Nameless, unreasoning, unjustified terror which paralyzes needed efforts to convert retreat into advance." Then he signaled his intention of summoning Congress into special session, saying: "I shall ask the Congress for the one remaining instrument to meet the crisis—broad Executive power to wage a war against the emergency, as great as the power that would be given to me if we were in fact invaded by a foreign foe."[110]

Roosevelt's opponents seized upon the opening notes of his

administration. Why were they so *fearful*? Why did FDR's appeal seem to them like a desperate power grab? To answer that, we must understand that in 1933 constitutional democracies were on the retreat all around the world. Stalin in the Soviet Union was ever tightening the vise of Communist terror and tyranny on the masses of Russians. In Germany, Adolf Hitler had no sooner been named chancellor of the Weimar Republic than a suspicious fire in the Reichstag building gave him the opportunity to blame the Communists. By outlawing the German Communist Party, Hitler's Nazis dominated elections for the new parliament. The only story related to foreign news on the front page of the *New York Times* on the day following FDR's inauguration informed readers: "Victory for Hitler Expected Today." When the new Reichstag reconvened, it passed a law allowing Hitler to rule by decree. Opposition to Hitler, the *Times* noted, was now *verboten*.[111]

The liberal Weimar Republic effectively died just weeks after Hitler came to power. Dictatorships in Hungary, Poland, and Italy had taken the place of democracies. In Japan, a prime minister who had opposed the aggressive designs of young military officers was assassinated as a warning to others not to interfere.

President Hoover, in one of his few memorable phrases, had dismissed FDR as a "chameleon on Scotch plaid."[112] To Hoover, the detail-oriented engineer, Roosevelt was shockingly unprepared for the office he had won so overwhelmingly. And here was Roosevelt, talking about asking Congress for war powers in a country still at peace. Small wonder, then, that his opponents feared Roosevelt.

FOURTEEN

FDR AND THE NEW DEAL

(1933–1939)

I. THE HUNDRED DAYS . . . AND AFTER

When Franklin Roosevelt took the oath as the thirty-second president of the United States on 4 March 1933, trucks that delivered the mail had to be accompanied by armed guards in some cities. An air of crisis pervaded the country. The new president moved immediately to declare a "bank holiday," closing the nation's savings institutions for a week. He needed to stop a run on the banks, which had spread panic during the long period from his election in November until his March inauguration. Will Rogers joked that Americans were happy at last: "We have no jobs, we have no money, we have no banks; and if Roosevelt had burned down the Capitol, we would have said, 'Thank God, he started a fire under something.'"[1]*

---

* Burning down the nation's legislature was no laughing matter in Germany, where just weeks prior the Reichstag had been burned down by a Dutch anarchist. Hitler seized upon the incident to outlaw the Communists and many of their left-wing allies. From this early moment in 1933, Hitler's Germany was effectively a dictatorship.

When Congress assembled, the new president submitted a flurry of legislative proposals that were enacted into law so quickly that few lawmakers had even read them. Fifteen major laws were enacted between 9 March and 16 June 1933. Their very titles give us an idea of the incredible range and extent of the new powers being assumed by the federal government: Emergency Banking Act, National Industrial Recovery Act, Civilian Conservation Corps, Leaving the Gold Standard, Emergency Relief, Agricultural Adjustment Act, Emergency Farm Mortgage, Tennessee Valley Authority, Truth-In Securities, Home Owner's Loan Corporation, Glass-Steagall Banking Act, and the Farm Credit Act.[2] This fecund period was to be known as the Hundred Days, setting a standard of legislative accomplishment never again to be equaled.*

One of the measures easily passed by the new Congress was the Twenty-First Amendment to the Constitution: the repeal of Prohibition. Even though FDR's landslide made Prohibition's repeal a dead certainty, Congress was taking no chances. For only the second time in history, a constitutional change was submitted to state ratifying conventions rather than to the state legislatures.** At 3:32 p.m., mountain time, on 5 December 1933, Utah became the thirty-sixth state to vote for repeal of the Eighteenth Amendment; Prohibition thus became the only constitutional amendment ever repealed.[3]

Wet in both principle and practice during Prohibition, H. L. Mencken partook of his first *legal* beer in thirteen years at Baltimore's Rennert Hotel. "Here it goes," he said after accepting a frothy stein from barkeep Harry Roth. He tossed it back and adjudged its contents: "Pretty good,

---

* The Republican minority was overwhelmed in both Houses. To have filibustered against New Deal legislation at a time when everyone recognized an unprecedented national emergency would have labeled them obstructionist. Still, we can hardly claim that FDR's proposals were seriously debated in Congress. "The Hundred Days" previously had referred to Napoleon's return from Elba. Comparing an American president's agenda to that tyrant could hardly have been comforting to FDR's legions of critics.

** The original Constitution was ratified by state conventions, and in 1933, this method was employed to ratify the Twenty-First Amendment.

not bad at all."[4] He similarly adjudged repeal: "It isn't often that anything to the public good issues out of American politicians. This time they have been forced to be decent."[5]

Thumping Democratic majorities in both Houses of Congress provided "a rubber stamp" to FDR's proposals. So many of the members had ridden into office on FDR's coattails that it was unthinkable they would seriously oppose him.

A single paragraph from Samuel Eliot Morison is worth volumes in our understanding of the cultural and political world we inhabit, to a great extent, seventy years after the New Deal:

> A feature of the WPA [Works Progress Administration] which caught the public eye and became nicknamed "boondoggling," was the setting up of projects to employ artists, musicians, writers and other "white collar" workers. Post offices and other public buildings were decorated with murals; regional and state guides were written; libraries in municipal and state buildings were catalogued by out-of-work librarians, and indigent graduate students were employed to inventory archives and copy old shipping lists, to the subsequent profit of American historians. The federal theater at its peak employed over 15,000 actors and other workers, at an average wage of $20 a week. Under the direction of John Houseman, Orson Welles, and others, new plays were written and produced, and the classics revived.[6]*

Here, in a nutshell, we see the origins of many of today's political alignments. Hollywood, academia, the press, libraries, the public universities—all are inhabited by tens of thousands of people who could trace the existence

---

* Interestingly, the same John Houseman who started off in the federal WPA later became known to Americans as the curmudgeonly TV pitchman for the Wall Street investment firm of Smith-Barney. "They make money the old fashioned way," Houseman intoned. "They *earn* it."

of their jobs or their institutions to a federal program begun under FDR. By bringing into government a "Brain Trust," FDR assured the allegiance of what we today call the "knowledge class" to the Democratic Party. One thing can always be assured: if you take from Peter to pay Paul, you can generally rely on the vote of Paul.

During the 1930s, the ideas of communism appealed to some on the American left. The Communist Party of the United States of America (CPUSA) was politically agile and adept at advancing its aims through progressive issues. In the first half of the thirties, American Communists supported the New Deal. CPUSA agitators could be seen in a host of labor clashes, particularly where violence was employed. Textile workers in Gastonia, North Carolina, and coal miners in Harlan County, Kentucky, found their legitimate grievances being taken up by Communists sent in by the party to stir things up.[7]

While many liberals mistrusted Communists, some considered them simply "liberals in a hurry." A popular slogan of the day explained away Stalin's crimes by saying "you can't make omelets without breaking a few eggs." Many liberals agreed with veteran muckraker Lincoln Steffens who had visited the new Soviet Union in 1919. Steffens said, "I have seen the future—*and it works!*" What Stalin was breaking was not eggs, but heads; and there were millions of them, not a few. We now know that the CPUSA was controlled throughout its existence by Moscow.

Some of the legislation of the Hundred Days was intended only to be temporary; other laws remain on the books to this day. One of the temporary measures was the Civilian Conservation Corps (CCC). Under the CCC, thousands of young men camped out in tents, worked on projects such as completing the long, snaking Appalachian hiking trail, and received three square meals a day. They earned little, but they had health care and, importantly, a sense of achievement.[8] FDR himself stressed the spiritual and social benefits of conservation work for unemployed, restless young men. Roving bands of out-of-work, out-of-luck young men have often created combustible conditions in a nation's urban centers. Roosevelt seemed to sense this instinctively.* The Public Works Administration (PWA) dedicated itself to large projects like New York City's Triborough Bridge—still in daily use.[9]

Tens of thousands looked to the jobs provided by the Works Progress Administration (WPA) to get them through the Depression. When John Reagan became an administrator for the Dixon, Illinois, WPA, it helped the family stay afloat (and not incidentally made his son, Ronald, a firm supporter of the New Deal).

The National Industrial Recovery Act was also not intended to be long term. But that did not mean it was insignificant. Congress appropriated the then-huge sum of $3.3 billion to set up an elaborate, nationwide system to manage the stricken economy.[10] FDR chose West Pointer Hugh Johnson to run the National Recovery Agency (NRA) set up by the legislation. The NRA provided codes for wages, hours, and working conditions, and it discouraged women and child labor in hazardous industries. Johnson designed an Art Deco Blue Eagle as the NRA's symbol. He also organized parades and other events to rally mass support. To FDR's opponents, the NRA's symbol looked shockingly like the Nazi eagle, and Johnson's marchers looked like the Hitler Youth. When Johnson unwisely praised Mussolini's Fascist "corporatist state," even many conservative *Democrats* took alarm. They were worried about the survival of freedom in a world menaced by tyrannies of the left and the right. Both John W. Davis (1924) and Al Smith (1928), the only living former Democratic presidential candidates, joined the Liberty League to organize opposition to Roosevelt's New Deal.

---

* FDR's praise for the spiritual impact of the CCC is one of the quotes chosen for his memorial in Washington, D.C. "I propose to create a Civilian Conservation Corps to be used in simple work. More important, however, than the material gains will be the moral and spiritual value of such work" (Message to Congress on Unemployment Relief, Washington, D.C., 21 March 1933).

II. HITLER'S GAMES: THE BERLIN OLYMPICS

On 7 March 1936, Adolf Hitler told his rubber-stamp legislature that he would reoccupy the Rhineland. Even as he spoke in the Reichstag, German troops were entering this historically German region.[11]* This was a bold challenge to the Western Allies. Under the terms of the Treaty of Versailles, Germany was forbidden both to rearm and to reoccupy the Rhineland. Now, Hitler was throwing down the gauntlet. France reacted as if an electric shock had gone through Paris. Just as quickly, however, the conservative government of Prime Minister Stanley Baldwin in London called on France to "wait in order that both countries might act jointly and after full consideration." Winston Churchill called this move "a velvet carpet for retreat."[12] And so it was Hitler shrewdly coupled his Rhineland takeover with an offer of a twenty-five-year peace pact with the Western democracies. Leading British appeasers immediately wired Prime Minister Baldwin. He should "welcome Hitler's declaration wholeheartedly," they swooned.

Americans wanted desperately to stay out of Europe's quarrels. Because the United States had not ratified the Treaty of Versailles, FDR had little influence over events on the Continent. Moreover, Congress had passed a series of Neutrality Acts that would sharply reduce the president's ability to help threatened democracies in Europe. This, and their own worried electorates, prompted British and French leaders to try to keep Hitler at bay by making timely concessions to him. They realized they could not rely on American help and vainly hoped that they could satisfy Hitler's demands. Clemenceau's nightmare had sprung to life. Germany moved menacingly closer to France and the "Anglo-Saxons" did not lift a finger to stop it.

---

* The Rhineland was always German, but it was Catholic—Germany was largely Protestant. Thus, the French had hopes that the Rhinelanders could be persuaded eventually to form their own *Rhenish* state as a buffer between France and the more powerful, largely Protestant power of Germany. The Rhineland is located on the West Bank of the Rhine River and borders France and Belgium.

With the successful remilitarization of the Rhineland, Hitler was eager to redirect the world's focus. The 1936 Olympics had been awarded to Germany long before he established his Nazi dictatorship. Hitler planned to use the Games as a showcase for his regime. It was to be a propaganda blitz.

The Nazi regime stressed physical fitness, especially for the young. "Your body belongs to your country," said one fitness book that was required reading in German schools. "You are responsible to your country for your body."[13] Hitler wanted to show off the athletic prowess of German youth as a model of what National Socialist ideology taught about Aryan superiority.

Tall and statuesque, the green-eyed German Helene Mayer was living in California when the 1936 Olympics were being prepared in Berlin. She had won the gold medal for fencing while representing her native Germany in the 1928 games. Would she compete again now? Because her father was Jewish, under Hitler's new Nuremberg Laws she was officially designated as a *mischling* (person of mixed race).[14] Despite the fact that Jews had had their citizenship revoked by Hitler and were suffering all forms of political, civil, economic, and social persecution in the Nazi state, Helene was still eager to compete under the swastika flag.* She soon became immersed in a great political controversy over what some called "the Hitler Games."[15]

Predictably, Hitler's actions were producing deep unease across the Atlantic and many Americans urged a boycott of the games.[16] But Avery Brundage, head of the U.S. Olympic Committee, wanted his countrymen to compete in Berlin. He told the pro-Nazi, German-American Bund that the Olympics were "a religion with universal appeal, which incorporates all the basic values of other religions, a modern, exciting, virile, dynamic religion." Brundage opposed any talk of boycott: "Politics must not be brought into sports. I have not heard of anything to indicate discrimination of any race or religion."[17]

---

* The *swastika* was called "*Hakenkreuz*" (Hooked Cross) in German. Adolf Hitler personally adopted the ancient mystical sign as the symbol of his Nazi movement. It was incorporated into the German flag and was seen everywhere in Germany under the Third Reich.

Brundage had not read the signs in hundreds of German towns: *Juden unerwuenscht*—"Jews Unwelcome." But thousands of others had read them and could have informed the USOC boss. Nor, apparently, was he aware that Jews had been excluded from all German sports clubs, although everyone else in the world of sports knew about this. Helene Mayer had even been excluded, but Hitler's government recognized the propaganda value of letting Helene compete for the *Vaterland*. "Helene is a good German and has nothing to do with the Jews," cabled the German consulate in San Francisco to the German Foreign Office in Berlin.[18]

Helene went on to win a silver medal in Berlin. The crowd roared as Helene stood rigidly at attention on the winner's platform, giving the stiff-armed "Heil Hitler" salute.

Not all Jewish competitors were so fortunate. American athletes Marty Glickman and Sam Stoller were yanked from their race just a day before they were to run—to appease Hitler. Frank Metcalfe and Jesse Owens would run in their place, their American coach told them. "Coach, I have won my three gold medals," Owens protested. "I have won the races I set out to win. I'm tired. I'm beat. Let Marty and Sam run." Coach Dean Cromwell pointed his finger at Owens and said: "You will do what you are told." Owens went on to win his fourth gold medal.[19]

Owens's "sunny demeanor" won him fans and friends wherever he went.[20] German crowds took up a cry of "*Oh-vens! Oh-vens!*" whenever he appeared to compete. Hitler, already having made up his mind to stop shaking each Olympic medal–winner's hand, was asked by an aide if he wanted to make an exception for Jesse.[21] Hitler shouted at him: "Do you really think I will allow myself to be photographed shaking hands with a Negro?"[22] Much has been made of the fact that Hitler would not shake hands with Jesse Owens. But the reality was that Jesse Owens was spared the indignity of having to shake hands with Adolf Hitler.[*]

"No matter how Hitler and other Nazi leaders felt," writes one

---

[*] Lifelong Republican Owens spunkily pointed out that FDR never shook hands with him either. But there was never a doubt that Roosevelt would have been proud to shake Owens's hand.

author, "the Germans embraced Owens and his incredible performance. Altogether, African-American athletes won almost one-quarter of all the U.S. medals in the games. Their performance brought honor to themselves, their team, and their nation—and were a slap in the face of Hitler's racist policies."[23]

When the games opened with much fanfare, two of the surprise guests were American exiles, Charles Lindbergh and his wife, Anne. The first words that the Lindberghs heard in Germany after a short flight from England were "Heil Hitler!" Lindbergh had come to Germany as an official guest of Hitler's new air force, the *Luftwaffe*.* Anne's biographer would write of the world famous aviator: "Adolf Hitler was certain that Charles Lindbergh personified [the future of the Third Reich]. His tall frame, his sandy-haired boyishness, his piercing blue eyes, made him the quintessential Aryan. The Nazis could not have constructed a more eloquent embodiment of their vision."[24]

Lindbergh was especially impressed with the advanced state of German aeronautics. He appreciated the appearance of order and discipline he saw everywhere he went. The German press was not permitted to pester him and his wife. "Lindbergh had found the atmosphere fraternal, the people congenial, the press under control, officials deferential, discipline good, morals pure and morale high," wrote Tom Jones, a British civil servant close to Prime Minister Baldwin, of Lindbergh's reaction. "It was a refreshing change . . . from the moral degradation into which he considered the United States had fallen, the apathy and indifference of the British, the decadence of the French."[25]

Jones pointed out that Lindbergh liked what he saw because he never asked to see the concentration camps where, already, Jews, Communists, social democrats, Socialists, and any other people whom the regime chose were packed away.[26] The Nazis had opened Dachau in March 1933, just weeks after Hitler came to power. It was the first of many concentration

---

* According to the Versailles Treaty, Germany was forbidden to have an air force. Hitler more or less openly defied the treaty's disarmament provisions.

camps that immediately began filling with opponents of the regime. By the end of the year, the Nazis had taken as many as one hundred thousand Germans away to these camps.[27]

III. "AS GOES MAINE . . ."

FDR's reelection in 1936 was by no means assured. The country had not fully recovered from the effects of the Depression. Economic conditions were nowhere near their pre-Crash 1929 levels. "Happy Days Are Here Again" was the Democrats' theme song, but it remained to be seen if they could capitalize on their victories of 1932 and 1934. Still, leading indicators *were* improving. The number of working Americans increased from thirty-eight million to more than forty-four million. Unemployment numbers declined from thirteen million to eight million. And the economy was adding 150,000 new jobs for each month in 1936.[28]

Black Americans historically had found themselves backing the party of Lincoln. By 1936, however, many were beginning to question their ties. One black WPA worker put it this way: "I don't think it is fair to eat Roosevelt bread and meat and vote for Governor Landon."[29] Black Americans had suffered as greatly in the Depression as anyone; they looked to Washington, and FDR, for relief.

Eleanor Roosevelt was particularly sympathetic to the concerns of black Americans. In 1936, she invited the distinguished opera singer Marian Anderson to entertain at the White House. She was the first black artist to do so. While there was as yet no black cabinet member, FDR had named a record number of black appointees to subcabinet positions. When some of these officials came together under the leadership of Mary McLeod Bethune, they constituted themselves as FDR's "black Cabinet."[30] This group raised issues that the federal government might address, first to Bethune, then to the First Lady, and from there to FDR's breakfast table.

Mrs. Roosevelt's special sympathy gave rise to ugly stories and hateful attacks from racists threatened by such deliberate attempts to address racial imbalance in leadership. One vicious rhyme had FDR saying to his wife over breakfast:

> You kiss the Negroes and I'll kiss the Jews
> And we'll stay in the White House as long as we choose.[31]

In truth, FDR was building a new coalition that included *many* minorities. Catholics, Jews, blacks, Westerners, Southerners, labor union members—all were welcomed into the New Deal new majority.

When the Republicans nominated Kansas Governor Alf Landon, they spurned former president Hoover and his increasingly strident opposition to everything FDR had done. Most significantly, Republicans endorsed the Social Security Act FDR had introduced and Congress had quickly enacted in 1935. They also endorsed the right of labor to organize and certain forms of business regulation.[32] It was not a platform designed to appeal to conservative Republicans, and it didn't.

The press weighed in. FDR charmed the White House reporters who met regularly with him for off-the-record "background" briefings. Many of their editors, however, were solidly against Roosevelt. Colonel Robert McCormick, owner of the *Chicago Tribune*, despised FDR. He instructed his switchboard operators to answer every call with the number of days until the country was freed from Roosevelt's misrule.[33]

FDR reveled in the opposition of Big Business. He loved to tell the story of the "nice old gentleman" who had fallen into the water while wearing an expensive silk hat. In the story, the gentleman's friend ran down the pier, jumped into the water, and pulled him out. But the hat floated away on the tide. At first, the old gentleman thanked his friend and praised his courage. Four years later, though, the old gentleman had begun to complain about losing that fine hat![34] FDR's telling of this story fit the caricature of the Big Businessman that even then was being popularized by the best-selling board game, *Monopoly*. People could see the "old gentleman" who wore the shiny top hat.*

In a more serious vein, FDR accepted his renomination in Philadelphia with an eloquent call: "This generation of Americans has a rendezvous with destiny."[35]

The well-respected *Literary Digest* attempted a public opinion poll. The science of polling was then in its infancy. The *Digest* polled those with telephones. In the depths of a Depression, this meant the views of millions of poverty-stricken Americans were not considered. The *Literary Digest* confidently predicted a Landon win. "A *Landon*-slide" boasted GOP campaign operatives when Maine's vote came in. The Down East State traditionally had voted in September. The old saying was, "As goes Maine, so goes the Nation."

Not this year. When the votes came in, FDR had triumphed again. He won reelection with an unprecedented 27,476,673 popular votes—a stunning 60.6 percent. Landon got 16,679,583 popular votes, just 36.8 percent. In the electoral college, Roosevelt swept the nation with 523 votes to Landon's derisory 8. Democratic National Chairman Jim Farley, one of FDR's savvy Irish political lieutenants, jibed that in view of Roosevelt's forty-six-state sweep, the old adage would have to be changed: "As goes Maine, so goes Vermont."[36] Abashed, the *Literary Digest* soon ceased publication.

IV. FDR'S "RISKY SCHEME"

Overwhelmingly reelected and with even stronger majorities in both Houses of Congress, FDR prepared to take on the U.S. Supreme Court.

He had reacted angrily to the Court's 1935 decision in the famous "sick chicken" case. By a vote of 9–0, the Court ruled in *Schechter Poultry Corp. v. United States* that the National Industrial Recovery Act was

---

* *Monopoly* was invented in 1934. Originally rejected as too complex, it has now sold more than two hundred million copies in more than eighty countries.

unconstitutional. The Court then proceeded to strike down the Agricultural Adjustment Act and other New Deal legislation. Roosevelt felt that none of his administration's achievements could be secure as long as the "nine old men" on the Supreme Court had unchecked power. He responded with a plan that soon came to be known as his "court-packing scheme."

FDR was worried that the major legislation of his first term was in jeopardy—including the Wagner Act, which governed labor relations; the Social Security Act; and his agriculture laws.[37] Roosevelt criticized Chief Justice Hughes for saying, "We are under a Constitution, but the Constitution is what the judges say it is." No, said the president, "We want a Supreme Court that will do justice under the Constitution, not *over* it. In our courts, we want a government of laws and not of men."[38]

FDR might have succeeded with his judicial reorganization plan had he been straightforward, direct, and candid with the American people. Instead, he presented his bill as an attempt to help old or infirm judges. He would add a justice for every member of the Supreme Court who passed age seventy and did not resign. Despite its lofty-sounding justification, Americans were not taken in. FDR's scheme was a transparent plan to pack the court with compliant justices.

Congressional Democrats rebelled. "Boys, here's where I cash in," said the Texas chairman of the House Judiciary Committee to Southern colleagues.[39] Southern Democrats had come to view the Supreme Court as their bulwark against civil rights legislation. The Supreme Court's *Plessy v. Ferguson* decision of 1896 had permitted racial segregation. *Plessy* was still the "law of the land."

The Court, perhaps recognizing it was under assault, surprised everyone by *upholding* both the Wagner Act *and* the Social Security Act. When one of the older justices resigned, FDR was given his first opportunity to name a member of the Supreme Court.

"How do you find the Court situation, Jack?" the president asked Vice President John Nance Garner about the status of the court reorganization bill.

"Do you want it with the bark on or off, Cap'n?" asked Garner.

"The rough way," said FDR.

"You are beat," said the vice president. "You haven't got the votes."[40] Roosevelt would remember that Garner said *you* and not *we*.

When Senator Robinson of Arkansas, the Democratic majority leader, died of a heart attack, FDR's last chance of winning on his court-packing scheme also died. Still, the Supreme Court *did* come around. It would later be called "the switch in time that saved nine." Very soon, however, FDR would make key appointments to the Supreme Court. Roosevelt would have no more trouble with the Court for the rest of his presidency. If that is defeat, he was a lucky loser.

V. "ONLY THE BEGINNING OF THE RECKONING"

"It was the pride of Germany, the way Germany showed her new aggressive flag—the swastikas on her tail. . . . It was the wonder of awed millions in cities the world over . . . a silver whale, the symbol of luxury and speed in transatlantic travel. . . . It was landing."[41]

The great German airship *Hindenburg* approached the mooring station at the Naval Air Station at Lakehurst, New Jersey. Announcer Herb Morrison of Chicago's station WLS was describing its arrival to radio listeners around the country.

Suddenly, the great zeppelin burst into flames.

"It is burning, falling. . . . Oh! This is one of the worst. . . . Oh! It's a terrific sight," Morrison cried out in anguish. Radio announcers had not yet learned to mask their feelings behind a façade of professional *cool*. "Oh . . . the humanity!"[42]

The hydrogen-filled airship's explosion was one of the great disasters of the thirties, not because of the loss of life (amazingly, only thirty-five died), but because it was so public. Americans were as yet not accustomed to disasters occurring in "real time"—recorded by newsreel cameras and carried "live" by radio announcers.

The *Hindenburg* disaster also alerted Americans to another grim reality: even though the swastika-emblazoned airship's voyage ended in flames, it demonstrated Hitler's reach. If German engineering could send a zeppelin across the ocean, might it in time send aircraft or even missiles? Thoughtful Americans realized that the broad Atlantic could no longer protect them.

Air travel was beginning to shorten distances once considered vast. Eleanor Roosevelt grasped this. She took up the cause of women in aviation. Eleanor even invited noted aviatrix Amelia Earhart to the presidential inauguration. Once, Eleanor hosted a small dinner at Hyde Park that included Earhart and Britain's first female member of Parliament, Lady Astor. A local newspaper hailed the dinner party as a gathering of "three of the world's outstanding women." Earhart was an outspoken pacifist. As the first woman ever to lecture the midshipmen of the Naval Academy, she spoke on the need for peace. Along with movie stars Katharine Hepburn and Marlene Dietrich, she popularized the wearing of slacks by women. She even wore them—shockingly—downtown.[43]

Earhart had won her wings, and public adulation, by flying across the Atlantic on the fifth anniversary of Lindbergh's historic flight. Granted, she flew only from Newfoundland to Ireland—a far shorter flight than Lindy's—but she still braved the forbidding North Atlantic alone. She invited the First Lady to go up flying with her, and Eleanor quickly took her up on the offer.[44]

The American people admired young fliers like Lindbergh and Earhart because they were incredibly brave and highly skilled. Flight was still very dangerous. That fact was underscored in newspaper headlines many times throughout the decade of the 1930s. America's beloved humorist Will Rogers and journalist Wiley Post had been lost in 1935 in an air crash in Alaska.

When in 1937 Amelia announced her daring "Round the World"

flight, Eleanor admitted in her syndicated column that she was anxious. "All day I have been thinking about Amelia Earhart somewhere over the Atlantic," she wrote.[45] As Amelia and her navigator Fred Noonan headed out over the Pacific, the Coast Guard cutter *Itasca* had been detailed to send weather reports to the courageous young flier.

As the First Family gathered at Hyde Park for a Fourth of July picnic and a wedding, the Roosevelts' holiday was overshadowed, as was that of the whole country, by reports that Amelia Earhart had gone missing. The *Itasca* joined four thousand men in ten ships to search an area of the Pacific the size of Texas. It was all in vain. Amelia was lost, just twenty-three days short of her fortieth birthday. She had said, "When I go, I would like to go in my plane. Quickly."[46] Rumors continued for years—none of them substantiated—about Amelia Earhart. Had she been taken captive by the Japanese on Saipan Island? Was she spying for the Roosevelts? Especially after Japanese planes attacked the USS *Panay* in China—an act for which they quickly apologized—Americans were jittery about the Rising Sun flag of Japan in the Pacific.

Boston's Joseph P. Kennedy wanted to become the first Irish-American ever named as ambassador to the Court of St. James—that's how the U.S. Embassy in London is known. Kennedy had been Roosevelt's first chairman of the Securities and Exchange Commission. On the theory that "it takes a thief to catch a thief," FDR named a man known for his sharp dealing to ride herd on the sharp dealers.[47] Kennedy was an important supporter for FDR in the Catholic community.

"When I passed it to Father," said Jimmy Roosevelt, the president's son, of the Kennedy-to-London idea, "he laughed so hard he almost toppled from his wheelchair."[48] But the more the president thought about it, the more he hoped it might work. Kennedy came from Boston, where Irish-American opinion was strongly against *any* help to Britain in the event of another war. FDR thought having Kennedy in London might help to overcome that resistance should war threaten. But he also wanted to have some fun with "Old Joe."

He summoned Kennedy to the White House and told him to drop his trousers. Stunned, Kennedy complied. "Joe, just look at your legs," the president said. He explained to Kennedy that all ambassadors to Britain have to wear knee breeches and silk stockings. It's tradition. "You are the most bowlegged man I've ever seen," FDR said. "When photos of our new ambassador appear, we'll be a laughing stock." Unfazed, Joe Kennedy hitched up his suspenders and appealed to the president: if he could get the British to let him present his credentials in striped pants and cutaway coat, could he go to London as ambassador? "Give me two weeks," Kennedy told the president.[49]

Roosevelt needed Joe Kennedy's help more than ever. Kennedy's friend Father Charles Coughlin had soured on the president. Father Coughlin's radio broadcast reached an astonishing forty million homes.[50] Initially well-disposed to FDR and the New Deal, Father Coughlin increasingly criticized Roosevelt's Brain Trust and his policies. Father Coughlin even began to sound more anti-Semitic as he attacked bankers and banking in terms not very different from those used by Henry Ford.

With Kennedy on his side, FDR would have a valuable ally should war come. Or so FDR thought at the time. As soon as Kennedy had installed his large family in the ambassador's quarters in London, he marked out an independent course. With him, he brought Rose, his wife, and his children: Rosemary, Kathleen, Eunice, Patricia, Jean, Joe Jr., John Fitzgerald, Robert, and Edward (Teddy).

Initially, the lively Kennedy clan was very popular in Britain. Joe wanted to make a social splash and kicked up an association with the socially prominent "Cliveden Set." Lady Astor's country home, Cliveden, was the social center for appeasement in Britain. The appeasement policy was based on the belief that the Treaty of Versailles had been too harsh and vindictive (which was very likely) and that better relations with Germany could be had by appeasing Hitler's territorial and economic demands (which was just as unlikely).

Hitler was unsatisfied with reoccupying the Rhineland in 1936. Early in 1938, he threatened and bullied his native Austria into submission.

When he marched into Vienna on 12 March 1938, the swastika flag replaced the bold red-and-white striped Austrian flag at every flagpole. Hitler's power and prestige within Germany and Europe had never been higher. He had accomplished without war what not even the Iron Chancellor, Otto von Bismarck, had achieved.

The Treaty of Versailles had forbidden Germany to unite with Austria. Few of the treaty's provisions seemed to matter to him—why this one? The Austrian-born Hitler was determined to achieve this union, what he called his *anschluss*. He not only wanted to bring his homeland under his control, he also wanted to show his opponents inside Germany and outside that the victors of World War I were powerless to stop him. This made him even more powerful at home and abroad.

Hitler's every aggressive move seemed only to bring more attempts of appeasement from the British government of Prime Minister Neville Chamberlain. As soon as Nazi troops moved into Austria, they brought with them their *Gestapo*. This dreaded state police hunted down Jews, prominent Socialists, intellectuals, and Catholic opponents of Hitler.[51] One of those who fled from Nazi-ruled Vienna was Sigmund Freud, the father of psychoanalysis.

No sooner had Hitler swallowed Austria than he began to threaten Czechoslovakia. The free, democratic state created by the Allied leaders at Versailles contained a small German-speaking minority in the border region known as the *Sudetenland*. Hitler had sent money, arms, and agitators to stir up these *Sudeten* "Germans" against the Czech government in Prague. Now, he demanded that the Czechs cede the Sudetenland to him. If they wouldn't, there would be war.

Hitler spoke to a huge Nazi Party rally in Nuremberg in 1938.* He

---

* Leni Riefenstahl, who had been in some disfavor since her Olympic film did not conform to Nazi racist notions, filmed the Nuremberg party rally. Her movie—*Der Triumph des Willins* (*The Triumph of the Will*)—remains a classic example of effective propaganda. It shows the awesome power unleashed by new techniques of cinematography. The Nazis were delighted with Leni's creative effort.

demanded that "civilized" Germans be liberated from the backward Czechs. French Prime Minister Edouard Daladier and foreign minister Georges Bonnet were alarmed. They flew to London to plead with Chamberlain to stand firm against this new threat. They explained to Chamberlain that if Hitler gobbled up the Sudetenland, he would also get the formidable Czech border defenses and the world-famous Skoda arms works. Their meeting in No. 10 Downing Street—the official residence of all British prime ministers—was a stormy one.[52]

Chamberlain would not bend. He could not bear the thought of war with Germany. "How horrible, fantastic, incredible it is that we should be digging trenches and trying on gas-masks here, because of a quarrel in a faraway country between people of whom we know nothing."[53] He was determined to do everything, *anything*, to avoid war. He dramatically proposed to meet Hitler to discuss peace—dramatic because he'd never flown and air travel was still dangerous. Nonetheless, he flew into Munich for a meeting with Hitler, Italy's Fascist dictator Benito Mussolini, and France's Premier Daladier. President Eduard Benes of Czechoslovakia was not even invited to the conference that would determine his brave little country's fate.

The Western democracies were not helped by Mussolini's presence at Munich. The Italian Fascist dictator always struck a pose of being more reasonable, less fanatic, than Hitler. As time would show, Mussolini's promises were as worthless as Hitler's.

Chamberlain agreed to give Hitler what he wanted. When he returned to London, he told an enthusiastic airport crowd that Britain would have "peace in our time." He was given the unprecedented honor of appearing on the balcony of Buckingham Palace with King George VI and his wife, Queen Elizabeth. Hundreds of thousands of weeping, cheering Britons hailed Chamberlain as the bringer of peace.

Few disagreed, but Winston Churchill was one of them. He gripped the attention of a hushed House of Commons, insisting that the British people should know the truth:

They should know that there has been gross neglect and deficiency in our defences; they should know that we have sustained a defeat without a war . . . they should know that we have passed an awful milestone in our history, when the whole equilibrium of Europe has been deranged, and that the terrible words have . . . been pronounced against the Western democracies: "Thou art weighed in the balance and found wanting."*

And do not suppose that this is the end. This is only the beginning of the reckoning. This is only the first sip, the first foretaste of a bitter cup which will be proffered to us year by year unless by a supreme recovery of moral health and martial vigor, we arise again and take our stand for freedom as in the olden time.[54]

Churchill was heard, but not heeded. He had been out of the cabinet for nearly a decade. To most Britons he was a spent force. He seemed an irrelevant old warmonger, "a man of a bygone era."

One of those who mistrusted Churchill was U.S. ambassador Joe Kennedy. He spoke on Trafalgar Day to a dinner hosted by the Navy League in London. This anniversary celebrated Britain's victory over the continental tyrant, Napoleon. Joe Kennedy used the occasion to urge ever more appeasement. "It has long been a theory of mine that it is unproductive for both the democratic and dictator countries to widen the divisions now existing between them by emphasizing their differences which are now self-apparent," he said. "[T]here is simply no sense, common or otherwise, in letting these differences grow into unrelenting antagonisms. After all, we have to live together in the same world whether we like it or not."

Kennedy's speech provoked a firestorm of controversy. He directly contradicted the president's powerful call to "quarantine the aggressors." FDR responded calmly that there can be no peace if some nations use the

---

* Winston Churchill was a man rarely found in church, but his powerful rhetoric owed much to the sonorous cadences of the King James Version of the Bible. This familiar phrase is from Daniel 5:27.

threat of war as a "deliberate instrument of national policy."[55] This meant Hitler, without a doubt.

Ambassador Kennedy couldn't take a hint. He ostentatiously invited Lindbergh to visit him in London. America's leading appeaser found Joe Kennedy's views on the European situation "intelligent and interesting." They were exactly like his own. Lindbergh's wife described Kennedy as "an Irish terrier, wagging his tail." FDR's press secretary Steve Early knew that Kennedy had his eye on the 1940 Democratic presidential nomination: "Joe wants to run for President and is dealing behind the Boss's back at the London Embassy."[56]

After the Munich conference, the irrepressible Kennedy bumped into the Czech diplomat, Jan Masaryk, in London. "Isn't it *wonderful?*" Kennedy asked the heartbroken man. "Now I can get to Palm Beach after all!"[57]* To his friends, Kennedy said, "I can't for the life of me understand why anyone would want to go to war to save the Czechs."[58]

It was easier for the wealthy, socially prominent businessman-turned-diplomat to share the world with Nazis. For one, he wasn't Jewish. Just weeks after Kennedy's speech, Hitler's Nazis went on a rampage throughout Germany. Hitler had taken the measure of the leaders of Britain and France at Munich. He knew he had little to fear from them. On 9 November 1938, his Nazi thugs smashed Jewish-owned shop windows, looted merchandise, burned synagogues, beat up innocent Jews, and terrorized others. *Kristallnacht* or "night of the broken glass" was a chilling announcement that the Third Reich would brutalize any Jews who came within its grasp—and defy the opinion of the world. The hostility began to spread to sympathizers of the Jews: the Nazis roughed up Cardinal von Faulhaber and smashed windows in his Munich study in an attempt to shock him into silence.**

---

* This was a reference to the Kennedy family vacation home in the fashionable Florida community. The family still owns this estate.

** Cardinal von Faulhaber had a mixed record. He gave off-and-on-again support to the Hitler government, but he did loudly protest the Nazi euthanasia program. After the war, he ordained Joseph Ratzinger, the future Pope Benedict XVI, as a priest.

Joe Kennedy responded not with outrage against the Nazis, but with a plan to relocate all of Germany's Jews to Africa and Latin America. So impressed was *Life* magazine with the ambassador's ideas it editorialized that, if successful, the Kennedy Plan "will add new luster to a reputation that might well carry Joseph Patrick Kennedy into the White House."[59]

It was not to be. Kennedy's open clash with the president and his eagerness to appease Hitler ended his hopes for the Democratic presidential nomination—and his public career. FDR was not surprised. He had given the wily Boston pol "enough rope." Privately, Roosevelt said he was "not a bit upset over [the] final result."[60]

VI. REBUILDING AMERICA

Americans in the thirties vastly preferred to concern themselves with projects closer to home.

The dynamiting of thousands of tons of stone at South Dakota's Mount Rushmore captured the nation's imagination. Danish American sculptor Gutzon Borglum had studied under the great French artist Auguste Rodin. He envisioned a mammoth memorial to America's greatest leaders—Washington, Jefferson, Lincoln, and Theodore Roosevelt. Selecting the site himself, Borglum declared, "American history shall march along that skyline." This great work reaffirmed Americans' belief in themselves, and in the appeal of democracy in a world increasingly threatened by bloody dictatorships. Miners who at first saw the project only as steady work soon caught the spirit of the monument. Even decades later, driller "Happy" Anderson boasted, "I put the curl in Lincoln's beard, the part in Teddy's hair, and the twinkle in Washington's eye. It still gives me a thrill to look at it."[61]

New York's elegant Empire State Building was the brainchild of Al Smith after his failed presidential bid. It crowned the Big Apple's skyline as the world's tallest building until it was topped by the World Trade Center's twin towers in 1972.[62]

In California, Depression-era voters showed their confidence in the future by authorizing a bond issue to construct the graceful Golden Gate Bridge. Construction engineers stressed safety, using hard hats and safety goggles for the first time. Even as FDR's policies were creating a "safety net" for American workers nationwide, workers on the Golden Gate Bridge had an actual safety net that protected them from the high winds and dizzying heights. Nineteen men who were caught by the safety net formed a group they jokingly called the Halfway-to-Hell Club.[63]

The federal government also added to the brick-and-mortar spirit of the decade. The Grand Coulee Dam in Washington State and the massive Tennessee Valley Authority are just two examples of Depression-era projects that changed the American landscape and not incidentally brought hydroelectric power to rural communities. Rural electrification had massive social, economic, and political consequences. The cultural isolation of rural America ended when power lines made radio reception possible. Electrifying the countryside made possible a huge increase in agricultural output. Politically, and FDR was certainly not unaware of this, rural electrification wired millions of farmers to the New Deal.

It's worth pointing out that Stalin's Belomor Canal, built by slave laborers in the Soviet Union, claimed tens of thousands of lives and soon silted up, becoming useless. Hitler's gargantuan Reich Chancellery was destroyed in World War II. His grotesque plans for *sportspalasts* (giant sports stadiums) and all-new planned cities never got off the drawing board. "Stalin Gothic" architecture disfigures many an urban landscape in Eastern Europe today. Hitler proudly displayed the work of his favorite architect, Albert Speer. The huge German pavilion at the Paris World Exposition of 1937 was a tower of stone and light, crowned by a Nazi eagle. This overbearing, inhuman structure, one prophetic critic said, looked "like a crematorium and its chimney."[64] Both Stalin's and Hitler's architectural visions were ugly monuments to the soullessness of their authors.

Americans also rejoiced in sports in the thirties. In 1938, boxer Joe Louis had a return match with Max Schmeling, the great German boxer who had defeated Louis in 1936. This time, Nazi ideology could not brag about another Germanic triumph over the Brown Bomber. Jimmy Carter recalled the reaction of poor black tenant farmers on his father's rural Georgia peanut farm. Allowed to approach the front porch of the big house by Carter's father, the black fans listened to the radio report Joe Louis's pounding victory. They thanked "Mr. Earl" Carter politely and quietly returned to their modest shacks. But from there, Jimmy recounted, he could hear an eruption of shouts of joy and "Bless the Lord" that he remembered all his life.[65]

Americans had much else to occupy their attention. The New Deal had sputtered into a recession in 1937. Roosevelt could point to major legislative achievements. The Social Security Act of 1935 changed American society and politics for generations. The Wagner Act is viewed as the Magna Carta of organized labor. But Americans are result-oriented. And when FDR faced restive members of his own party in the 1938 elections, his attempts to punish conservative Democrats who opposed the New Deal were singularly unsuccessful.

Despite all this, FDR dominated the political landscape. He did so by the force of his personality. He was—as one of his biographers noted in the subtitle of his book—both "The Lion and the Fox." In Niccoló Machiavelli's classic work of 1513, *The Prince*, he famously pointed out that the prince must know how to play the part of the lion and the fox; in other words, he had to be both strong *and* clever. Franklin D. Roosevelt—while driving his critics to distraction—proved he had learned to play both parts.

FIFTEEN

AMERICA'S RENDEZVOUS
WITH DESTINY

(1939–1941)

I. MAN OF THE YEAR

As 1939 dawned, *Time* magazine stunned the world by naming Adolf Hitler as its "Man of the Year" for 1938.[1] Editors of the popular newsweekly hastened to remind readers that their selection did not imply *approval* of the Nazi dictator. As they would say again and again over the decades, the "Man of the Year" (later, "Person of the Year") designation merely meant that this individual, more than any other, had influenced events for good or evil.

Hitler had assured Chamberlain and Daladier at Munich that he had "no further territorial demands in Europe." With the consent of the democracies, he had torn the German-speaking Sudetenland from a wounded Czechoslovakia. Nervous Westerners hoped it would take Hitler time to absorb his latest, almost bloodless, conquest. Still, the Nazi juggernaut showed no signs of slowing. In 1938, Hitler had expanded

Germany's territory from 186,000 to 225,000 square miles and swelled the population under his control from 68 to 79 million.[2]

Whatever their rationale, *Time*'s editors gave Hitler a huge propaganda boost. Surely they knew of his brutal campaign of murder and intimidation against the Jews. And it was well known that the Nazis were pressuring parents to pull their children out of their Catholic and Lutheran church groups, and to put their young people under the control of the HJ—*Hitler Jugend*. This Hitler Youth was a state-run organization that indoctrinated the young of Germany and the occupied lands in anti-Christian beliefs.

In March 1939, Hitler tore up the agreement he had signed the previous September. It was the paper Prime Minister Chamberlain proudly displayed at his airport news conference, the one with "Herr Hitler's name on it." On 15 March, the Ides of March, Hitler marched into Prague. The stricken Czechs were too stunned to resist. Hitler now made no pretense of "liberating" Germans. The Czechs were Slavs. "Shamefully abandoned," as Churchill said of them, they had put their faith in their fellow democracies and had been utterly betrayed. Fascism's march seemed unstoppable. By April, Franco had prevailed in Spain.

Pressured by members of his ruling Conservative Party, Chamberlain at last responded to Hitler's aggression by offering assurances to Poland. Britain would back the endangered nation and declare war on Germany if Hitler attacked. But this appearance of spine did not mean that Chamberlain had renounced appeasement. To the contrary, he asked U.S. ambassador Joseph Kennedy to intervene with President Roosevelt. Chamberlain's purpose: to get FDR to secretly pressure the Poles to make concessions to Germany! Frustrated, FDR asked his ambassador to "put some iron up Chamberlain's backside." Kennedy answered that the British had no iron to fight with.[3]

The following month, FDR delivered the first address ever broadcast on the new invention—television—at the opening of the New York World's Fair on 30 April 1939. Roosevelt used the occasion to celebrate the 150th anniversary of George Washington's First Inauguration. He spoke of "the vitality of Democracy and of democratic institutions." "Yes, our wagon is still hitched to a star," he said. "But it is a star of friendship, a star of progress for mankind, a star of greater happiness and less hardship, a star of international good will, and, above all, a star of peace."[4] With those words, the world's most famous scientist, Albert Einstein, threw a switch to light up fountains and floodlights. The fair was officially open.[5]

Two of the most famous fairgoers that year were King George VI and his spirited wife, Queen Elizabeth. They had never expected to sit on England's ancient thrones. But when Edward VIII abdicated rather than give up his American fiancée, his younger brother resolved to overcome his childhood stammering and do his duty.

FDR planned every detail of this first visit ever made by British monarchs to North America.[6] Snubbing Joe Kennedy in London, the president worked through William C. Bullitt, his ambassador in Paris, to bring off this historic event.[7] FDR saw this visit in many ways as a response to upper-class Americans who considered him a "traitor to his class." Their attitude was jocularly expressed in the *New Yorker* cartoon that showed well-heeled theatergoers headed off to the movies. They call in to a dinner party of fellow swells: "Come on—we're going to the Trans-Lux to hiss Roosevelt." Now, FDR would play host to the biggest society "catch" in the world—the king and the queen. FDR grandly greeted the royal pair at his Hyde Park home. As soon as the royal couple had changed for dinner, FDR appeared with a pitcher of martinis that he had mixed himself. "My mother thinks you should have a cup of tea—she doesn't approve of cocktails," the president said. The king replied, "Neither does mine," as he grabbed the martini. Imagine the horror of the Roosevelt hissers when they learned that FDR and Eleanor had offered the royals a picnic lunch of hot dogs and beans at Hyde Park![8]

It was not all social. FDR talked long into the night with the young king and with Canadian Prime Minister MacKenzie King about the looming danger of war.* Finally, FDR tapped the king on the knee. "Young man," he said, "it's time for you to go to bed."[9] No one seemed to notice that FDR had broken one of the oldest taboos associated with the British monarchy—that they were never to be touched by a commoner. Staring at the grim prospect of war—and the even more terrible possibility of invasion by Hitler's Germany—perhaps the young monarch was happy to have Roosevelt's reassuring touch.

The royal visit sent a vital message of Anglo-American unity as the world hurtled toward another war. For millions of Americans, however, the democracies of Europe were weak and decadent and the dictatorships were strong and dangerous. Better to stay out of the fray entirely. To the 480,000 members of the German American *Bund*, this stance seemed especially appealing. Fritz Kuhn brazenly led twenty-two thousand members of his pro-Nazi group at a rally in Manhattan's Madison Square Garden. A giant banner held aloft a picture of George Washington, but on the floor *bundists* wore swastika armbands and offered the "Heil Hitler" salute.[10] As far as Madison Square Garden events went, it was small. Given New York's large number of Jews, Catholics, Poles, Eastern Europeans, and black Americans, however, it was an incredibly provocative act.

Charles A. Lindbergh was no *bundist*. But he was equally determined to keep America out of Europe's troubles. He joined with others to form the Committee to Defend America First. Lindbergh had returned home from three years of self-imposed exile in Britain. He was at one time the most famous advocate for American isolation and possibly the most controversial: he had visited Hitler's Germany no less than six times while living in Britain. Lindbergh had even accepted a Nazi medal from Hermann Goering, chief of the Luftwaffe, the German air force. "If we fight [Germany]," Lindbergh had said, "our countries will only lose their best men. We can gain nothing. . . . It must not happen."[11]

---

* U.S. reporters resented the famously close-mouthed Canadian prime minister. Veteran newsman David Brinkley wrote that they made up this disrespectful doggerel: "William Lyon MacKenzie King/Never gives us a G—d—thing."

457

Like Ambassador Kennedy, Lindbergh had found the Cliveden Set the most congenial of Englishmen. He had urged his English hosts not to resist Germany but to make an alliance with Hitler. At one of Lady Astor's parties, which included Joe Kennedy and the U.S. Ambassador to France, William C. Bullitt, Lindbergh "shocked the life out of everyone by describing Germany's strength."[12] Back in the United States, Lindbergh threw himself into opposition to President Roosevelt's plans.

Meanwhile, others were also trying to influence Roosevelt's plans. Leo Szilard and Eugene Wigner were atomic scientists. They had fled Germany with the rise of the Nazis. Now, in the summer of 1939, they were in America trying to find Albert Einstein. Einstein had taken a summer cottage in Peconic, Long Island, where he enjoyed sailing. Wigner and Szilard, unfamiliar with American roads (or with American towns), got lost. They confused Patchogue on the South Shore, with Cutchogue, on Long Island's North Fork. Unable to locate Einstein's summer cottage, Szilard and Wigner almost gave up. Finally, Szilard leaned out of his car window and asked a little boy, "Say, do you by any chance know where Professor Einstein lives?" The eight-year-old promptly took the émigrés to Einstein's cottage. There, the scientists quickly persuaded Einstein to send a letter to President Roosevelt.[13]

They almost miscalculated disastrously when they planned to ask Charles Lindbergh to be their courier to carry the Einstein letter to the White House.[14] These politically naïve men did not yet realize that Lindbergh's sympathies were not at all theirs. Instead, they asked Alexander Sachs, a man friendly to FDR.

The Einstein letter explained to the president that nuclear fission could create a chain reaction that would release vast amounts of heat and radioactivity. A bomb might be created using uranium. And, he wrote, the *Germans* were known to be working on atomic fission.[15] Einstein knew all the top German scientists. Until Hitler's rise to power, Einstein had been a respected member of the German-Swiss intellectual community. As a Jew, however, he could never be accepted in the new Germany Hitler was fashioning.

FDR received Einstein's letter from scientific gadfly Alexander Sachs. Waving away the complex scientific jargon, FDR told Sachs: "Alex, what you are after is to see the Nazis don't blow us up."

"Precisely," Sachs answered.[16]

With that, FDR summoned General Edwin "Pa" Watson, his trusted appointments secretary. "Pa, this requires *action*."[17] With those spare words, the largest secret weapons project in history began—the race to build an atomic bomb.

II. AMERICA ON THE ROAD TO WAR

The world awoke to a shock on 24 August 1939. News came from Moscow and Berlin of the signing of the Nazi-Soviet Non-Aggression Pact. After the Munich agreement the previous year, Stalin had decided to protect the USSR and come to an agreement with his declared enemy, Hitler. To ease the transition, Stalin sacked his Jewish foreign minister, Maxim Litvinov, and replaced him with Vyacheslav Molotov. Molotov's name means "hammer," and the signing of the Nazi pact struck the Western democracies like a terrible blow. Now, Hitler was free to go to war in the West—free from the worst fear of all German leaders, a two-front war.

Hitler wasted no time. On 1 September 1939, the armored divisions of his *Werhmacht* crashed across Poland's borders even as his Luftwaffe bombed military and civilian targets from the air. Hitler's forces showed no mercy toward hospitals, schools, or churches. He waged a war of terror designed to destroy his enemy's will to resist. This was *Blitzkrieg*—lightning war.

Poland lasted just a month. Overrun and overwhelmed, the Polish army fought bravely, often on horseback. German propaganda films emphasized the futility of Polish cavalry charging against *Panzer* tanks.*

---

* Three years later, however, the Soviets would use cavalry against the Germans to devastating effect. Their swift horses could attack when the Panzer tanks were immobilized by-50° F temperatures in the dreaded Russian winter.

Prime Minister Chamberlain, facing the ruin of all he had worked for, reluctantly declared war on Germany, but not for three days. At the end of Chamberlain's dispirited, lugubrious war announcement on the British Broadcasting Company (BBC), air raid sirens began to wail in London. Armed with a bottle of brandy, Winston Churchill accompanied his wife, Clementine, into the air-raid shelter.[18] Realizing the need for broader support in the House of Commons, Chamberlain invited Churchill, his sharpest critic, once again to become First Lord of the Admiralty. On 3 September 1939, the Board of Admiralty signaled to ships in every corner of the globe: "Winston is back."[19]

Within a week, FDR was writing a personal letter to Churchill. He had taken the trouble to "clear" the communication with Prime Minister Chamberlain, he explained. But he wanted to write directly to the man who would command the world's largest navy. From then on, Chamberlain would be "out of the loop." So, not incidentally, would Ambassador Joseph P. Kennedy. FDR would do his own diplomacy with his fellow "former naval person."

Poland's agony was extreme. When the teenager Karol Wojtyla and his ailing father joined millions of refugees fleeing bombardment by Nazi *stukas*, their flight was halted by even more terrible news: the Soviets had invaded Poland from the East. Under the barbarous rule of Nazi Governor-General Hans Frank, Poles were shot for the slightest offense, such as failing to step into the street when a German soldier passed.[20] Young Karol, the future Pope John Paul II, returned to his home to face the rigors of Nazi occupation.

In just one month, Poland was torn apart. The Soviets attacked her from the East, the Nazis from the West. With Poland's collapse, a curtain of silence descended on this ancient land. The rule of murder and repression went largely unreported in the Western press. Stalin ordered the massacre at the Katyn forest of 3,500 captured Polish army officers.[21] The West knew nothing of this until well after the war.

In the West, Britain and France settled down to a "phony war," a conflict marked by no action. The French placed their greatest reliance on a string of very modern forts known as the Maginot Line. After the bloody exhaustion of World War I, their mindset was thoroughly defensive.[22] They gave no thought to invading Germany's lightly defended Western front. Journalists mockingly called this war of preparations a *sitzkrieg*—a sitter's war.

Americans, public opinion polls showed, were strongly *opposed* to taking any part in Europe's new war. Senator William E. Borah, an Idaho Republican, was a leader of the isolationists. When the Germans attacked Poland, Borah told reporters: "Lord, if I only could have talked with Hitler, all this might have been avoided."[23]

As the 1930s ended, the movie *Gone with the Wind* reminded millions of the costs of war in death and destruction. The great Hollywood epic of the Civil War premiered in Atlanta. American matinee idol Clark Gable starred with two English actors, Leslie Howard and Vivien Leigh. Two of the movie's most memorable performers, however, did not attend. Hattie McDaniel ("Mammy") and Butterfly McQueen were not invited to the all-white Atlanta premiere.[24]

Hitler struck on 10 May 1940 in the North and West. He invaded neutral Holland and tiny Denmark, crushing those peaceful little kingdoms in hours. His armored divisions, backed by air power, smashed into France. When Britain's Labour Party leaders said they would *not* join a coalition government headed by Neville Chamberlain, Chamberlain offered the king his resignation. Now, the choice was between the foreign secretary, Lord Halifax, and the First Lord of the Admiralty, Winston Churchill. Halifax told his best friend, Chamberlain, that he did not think he could lead the House of Commons from his position in the House of Lords. Winston, uncharacteristically, remained silent as his only possible rival took himself out of contention.

When the king called Churchill to Buckingham Palace, Churchill was invited to form a national unity government to include all of Britain's parties. He would later write of his "profound sense of relief" at that moment:

At last I had authority to give directions over the whole scene. I felt as
if I were walking with destiny, and that all my past life had been but a
preparation for this hour and for this trial.[25]

As French and British forces in France retreated before the armored
German onslaught, Churchill went before the House of Commons to
offer "blood, toil, tears and sweat." His aim was simple: victory.

Victory at all costs, victory in spite of all terror, victory however long
and hard the road may be, for without victory there is no survival.[26]

To many in Britain then, and in the United States, Churchill's stirring speeches didn't stir. He seemed a reactionary man, unacquainted
with the realities of modern life. But in his understanding of the mind of
Adolf Hitler, it was Churchill who was right and the sophisticates who
were wrong. Churchill knew that no negotiation was possible with such a
warped and hateful man. He also knew the kind of war Hitler was determined to wage—a total war.

Sumner Welles, FDR's undersecretary of state, warned that Churchill
was only a "third or fourth rate man," and a "drunken sot" to boot.[27] Joe
Kennedy didn't trust him.

As France collapsed, the British army in France retreated before the
onrushing Germans. Within mere weeks, they had fallen back on the
French port of Dunkirk. There, with their backs to the English Channel,
the entire British force in France was surrounded by the triumphant
Germans. They would either be driven into the sea, annihilated where
they stood, or taken prisoner.

Dunkirk is located just ten kilometers west of the Belgian border,
along the English Channel.* In a maneuver code-named Operation
Dynamo, Britain's Royal Navy managed the evacuation of some 620,000

---

* Dunkirk's un-French sounding name is really Flemish, a language closer to Dutch.
Dunkirk is just a two-hour trip by ferry from the English port city of Dover.

soldiers—the bulk of the entire British Expeditionary Force (BEF) and many French and Allied units, as well. This incredible feat was accomplished between 26 May and 4 June.

As he was to do on a number of other occasions, Hitler misjudged his enemy. The sight of the soldiers coming home from Dunkirk did not demoralize the British. They were dirty and ragged. Some were missing teeth. Many still had oil over their faces from where they had been plucked out of the sea. Yet, they were cocky. They grinned and gave thumbs-up signals. They said: "I'm all right, Jack." The mere sight of them thrilled the people of Britain.*

France surrendered three weeks later. On 22 June 1940, the French signed the so-called armistice. Hitler, with a dramatic flair, demanded that the French meet him in the same railway car that had been used when the Germans were defeated less than twenty-two years before! He came to the clearing at Compiègne, an hour's drive northeast of Paris.[28]

FDR viewed the events in Europe with mounting concern. He spoke at the University of Virginia on 10 June 1940. Without mentioning Mussolini or Italy by name, he said of the *Duce's* unprovoked attack on France: "the hand that held the dagger has struck it into the back of its neighbor."** He criticized those Americans who thought the United States could exist as a "lone island in a world dominated by the philosophy of force."[29] Clearly, FDR was talking about Defend America First, Lindbergh's group dedicated to keeping the United States out of the war.

The stunning series of events of the past weeks clearly *reversed* the outcome of World War I. On 23 June, Hitler even conducted a predawn tour of the city of Paris. He admired the architectural wonders and vowed to remake Berlin on an even grander scale. Americans saw Hitler's early

---

* Not all got off. Tens of thousands of valiant British and French soldiers faced capture or death forming a perimeter defense. Some of those captured by the SS were massacred.

** *Il Duce* is Italian for "the leader." Mussolini was Europe's first Fascist dictator. He seized power in 1922. Hitler's title—*der Führer*—was the German translation of *Duce*. *El Caudillo* was the variant adopted by Spain's general, Francisco Franco.

morning victory tour in their weekly newsreels and remembered that more than 350,000 young Frenchmen had died keeping the Germans out of Paris in World War I. This time, there was no "Miracle of the Marne." For millions of Americans, this only confirmed the futility of "entanglements" in Europe's affairs.

Churchill's opponent in Britain's war cabinet was Lord Halifax, the foreign secretary. This quiet, austere aristocrat was unimpressed with Winston's flowery rhetoric. To this refined man, Churchill's gravelly voice "ooze[d] with port, brandy, and the chewed cigar."[30] Americans who supported Britain, however, warmed to "Winnie's" bulldog persona. They loved his V-for-Victory salute, the cigars, the Homburg he always wore. And for this influential group, his 1940 speeches were stirring. Consider such a speech, delivered five days before Hitler toured Paris:

What General Weygand called the Battle of France is over. I expect that the Battle of Britain is about to begin. Upon this battle depends the survival of Christian civilization. Upon it depends our own British life, and the long continuity of our institutions and our Empire. The whole fury and might of the enemy must very soon be turned on us.

Hitler knows that he will have to break us in this Island or lose the war. If we can stand up to him, all Europe may be free and the life of the world may move forward into broad, sunlit uplands. But if we fail, then the whole world, including the United States, including all that we have known and cared for, will sink into the abyss of a new Dark Age made more sinister, and perhaps more protracted, by the lights of perverted science.

Let us therefore brace ourselves to our duties, and so bear ourselves that if the British Empire and its Commonwealth last for a thousand years, men will still say, "This was their finest hour."[31]*

---

* General Charles de Gaulle broadcast from London on the same day. His "Appelle de l'honneur" (Appeal to Honor) was carried by the BBC to a prostrate France. He rejected the Armistice and called on the "Free French" to join him in resistance to Hitler. It was de Gaulle's "finest hour" too.

III. "SAIL ON, O UNION STRONG AND GREAT"

"This . . . is London." That staccato message, recited in a chain-smoker's baritone, brought the war into American living rooms. CBS's chief London correspondent, Edward R. Murrow, brought his Yankee accent and his reporter's eye for detail to the heart of London in the midst of the Blitz.

America listening to the CBS *World News Roundup* could hear the *pom-pom-pom* of London's anti-aircraft (AA) guns going off. Londoners reacted differently to the sounds of the AA guns. One man said, "You can't sleep with the guns, but it's a good sound." One elderly cleaning woman groused: "Them damn guns, I could kill 'em." "It's worse than the bloody Jerries," complained a grandmother soothing a frightened child in an air-raid shelter. Men, in general, liked hearing the guns giving the Germans back "some of their own." One reported: "The louder it was, the more confidence we had."[32]*

Mass circulation publications like *Time, Life, Look, Collier's,* and the *Saturday Evening Post* printed dramatic photographs and written copy detailing every aspect of the war. The local movie theater ran newsreels of war footage from the front. At the same time that Americans desperately wanted to stay *out* of Europe's war, the mass media was inexorably drawing them *in*. Day after day, Americans sensed that the events overseas could not be kept at bay much longer. The very speed and range of the Nazi juggernaut threatened Americans' sense of security, of being set apart from European conflicts.

Even schoolchildren became familiar with the datelines of war stories—London, Paris, Berlin, Warsaw, Moscow, Prague, Oslo, Copenhagen, Amsterdam. Never before had Europe's affairs been so much a part of Americans' daily consciousness.

---

*   In the BBC series *World at War*, a Cockney veteran of one of these AA crews was asked years later how many "Jerries" he had shot down. "Nary a one. Never 'ad a chance uv 'ittin' one," he said with a laugh. Why did they fire off those AA guns then? "It gave great 'eart to the people in the Underground!"

It would not have been possible in World War I to *feel* the war in all its immediacy and danger. Radio now made this possible. The distance between London and New London had become negligible.

Just months before, many Americans would have agreed with Joe Kennedy that Britain was washed up. Now, in the summer of 1940, the Battle of Britain took place in the skies above "This England" that Americans remembered from their poetry books and their high school literature classes as written by Shakespeare:

> This royal throne of kings, this sceptred isle,
> This earth of majesty, this seat of Mars,
> This other Eden, demi-paradise,
> This fortress built by Nature for herself
> Against infection and the hand of war,
> This blessed plot, this earth, this realm, this England.

The Royal Air Force scrambled every day to beat off wave after wave of attacks from Hitler's Luftwaffe. "Never in the field of human conflict has so much been owed by so many to so few," Churchill said in tribute to the young men who faced death daily. Some of them may well have been among the Oxford University undergraduates who had voted overwhelmingly as recently as 1936 *against* fighting "for King and Country." Now, *everyone* had but one goal: to fling defiance in the teeth of the Hun, to resist with every ounce of human strength the "nozzie [Nazi] beast."

The Royal Air Force saved Britain from invasion that summer. In June 1940, the operational strength of RAF's Fighter Command was 1,200 planes. By November, that number had *increased* to 1,796. The German Air Force's single-engine aircraft had *decreased* from 906 at the beginning of the Battle of Britain in June to 673 in November.[33] Why this discrepancy? Many British fighters were shot down, it is true, but many of their planes could be repaired, and surviving pilots would go back into action. Also, British aircraft production was setting records with factories working around the clock. Any planes that were not destroyed landed in British fields, where they could be retrieved. All German planes and pilots knocked out of the skies over southern England were either captured or destroyed.[*]

Churchill laid down concertina wire all along the threatened coastlands, creating a sharp-barbed obstacle for enemy landings. He planned to light off precious gasoline if the Germans came ashore. They would be met with a furious uprising of the whole people, he swore.

Murrow brought it all to Americans listening captive at home. He quoted William Pitt, the famous opponent of Napoleon: "England will save herself by her exertions, and Europe by her example."[34]

The bombs that fell on London killed and maimed thousands of civilians. Murrow broadcasted the sounds of fire engines racing through the night, the sound of flames crackling around St. Paul's Cathedral, the sound of Cockneys digging through the rubble of their apartment buildings.

The pleasant, shy, young king and his lively wife did not escape. Buckingham Palace was bombed. The prime minister's office let it be known that the queen was taking shooting lessons with a revolver. Resisting pleas from Canada to send the young princesses across the ocean, the queen said: "The Princesses could not leave without me—and I could never leave without the King—and, of course, the King will never leave."[35]

FDR agreed to send Churchill fifty old World War I destroyers. These were desperately needed for convoy escort duty. Britain was wholly dependent on her seaborne lifeline for most of her food and war materiel and all her oil.

In return, Britain leased to the United States a number of New World bases for ninety-nine years. Some of these, as in Gander Bay, Newfoundland, and in the British West Indies, served the U.S. Navy for decades. FDR pledged "all aid short of war."

---

[*] The Battle of Britain is generally thought of as the aerial duel between British and German fighters over southern England from late summer to early autumn 1940. "The Blitz," Hitler's nighttime bombing raids over English cities, lasted until 10 May 1941 and resumed with V-1 and V-2 rockets in 1944.

As sympathetic as Americans were to the plight of the British, polls confirmed that they were determined not to become involved. Still, FDR boldly proposed Lend-Lease and the first peacetime draft in American history.[36] Lend-Lease was a new policy that allowed Britain to borrow war materiel for the length of the emergency. Typically, FDR explained his policy in down-to-earth terms. He compared it to lending our "neighbah" a length of garden hose to put out a fire. In other words: We don't want the money. We just want our hose back when the fire is extinguished.[37]

As war raged in Europe, Roosevelt waged a campaign for an unprecedented third term in the White House. In deciding to run, he challenged the "two term" tradition established by George Washington. If he lost, his entire record would be tinged with failure. Ulysses S. Grant had tried and failed to win a third term. So had Cousin Theodore. But these attempts followed a period out of office. FDR was breaking new ground.

The Republican nominee, Wendell Willkie, campaigned vigorously throughout the country. On the night of the election, 5 November 1940, the normally gregarious FDR closeted himself away from everyone at Hyde Park. Grim-faced and sweating, he waited out the long hours alone until victory was assured.[38] It's a good thing for the leaders of this great republic to fear the people.

The 1940 election brought an event which had never occurred before—and likely will never occur again. A president of the United States was reelected to a third consecutive term. FDR's electoral vote total of 449 from thirty-eight states gave him a commanding, convincing victory. It was a demonstration of popular appeal and political skill never to be equaled.

President Roosevelt closed out the eventful year of 1940 with one of his famous "fireside chats" to the American people. *Time* magazine reported, "The President came in five minutes before the broadcast on a small rubber-tired wheelchair."[39*] He called on America to become

---

* *Time* was the largest circulation weekly newsmagazine in the United States. The matter-of-fact tone of this sentence shows once again that Americans were never in doubt that their president was paralyzed from the waist down.

"the great arsenal of democracy."[40] The speech was memorable and politically successful. An arsenal provides vital means of defense, but it does not take part in armed struggle. That was the policy Americans favored.

When his defeated rival, Wendell Willkie, planned a trip to embattled Britain, FDR invited him to the White House for a friendly chat. He gave Willkie a handwritten message and genially asked him to deliver it personally to Prime Minister Churchill. It was a favorite Longfellow poem the two "former naval persons" would surely appreciate, "The Building of the Ship":

> Sail on, O Ship of State!
> Sail on, O Union, strong and great!
> Humanity with all its fears,
> With all the hopes of future years,
> Is hanging breathless on thy fate.[41]

Isolationists had by no means dropped their efforts when Roosevelt was reelected. Early in 1941, the Defend America First Committee stepped up its efforts to keep the United States out of the war. Although the group clearly attracted what Teddy Roosevelt had referred to as "the lunatic fringe," it would be a mistake to think that this was the *only* support America First received. Joe Kennedy Jr., a politically ambitious young *Democrat*, proudly signed up. So did Sargent Shriver, eventually to be a *Democratic* nominee for vice president and a candidate for president (and a Kennedy in-law). Kingman Brewster went on to become president of Yale University.* Republican Gerald Ford also joined America First, as did Olympic chairman Avery Brundage, Alice Roosevelt Longworth, and World War I flying ace Eddie Rickenbacker.[42]

---

* In one of the most bizarre of diplomatic postings, President Jimmy Carter sent Brewster to London as his ambassador. It might have been argued that had the young Brewster had his way, London would have been under German occupation.

Charles A. Lindbergh reached out to his friend Henry Ford. Lindbergh, as *Life* magazine pointed out, did not even express a hope that Britain would win.[43] It might be seen as singularly ungrateful to the country that had generously provided him a safe haven in 1935, but veteran diplomat Sir John Wheeler-Bennett thought Lindy was not really anti-British; he had simply concluded that Britain was a "bad bet."[44] Ford agreed with Lindbergh. He even predicted in *Scribner's* magazine in January 1941 that the Germans would win.[45]

Lindbergh's high profile in America First gained him the attention of one young cartoonist named Theodore Geisel. Geisel lampooned the aviator as "the Lone Ostrich":

> The Lone Eagle had Flown
> The Atlantic alone
> With fortitude and a ham sandwich.
> Great courage that took
> But he shivered and shook
> At the sound of the gruff German landgwich.[46]

Geisel would become familiar to millions of Americans as the inimitable Dr. Seuss. Geisel's put-down of Lindbergh became public only following the aviator's death. When President Roosevelt publicly criticized *Colonel* Lindbergh, he reacted with anger. Unwisely, he resigned his army commission.[47]

It was a fateful move. It would alter Lindbergh's life. Never again would he have the complete trust of his government or his fellow Americans. Roosevelt's supporters pointed out that Lindbergh had never resigned as a German Knight of the Eagle. It was a distinction he shared with Henry Ford. But he had thrown back his U.S. Army commission. Defenders of the famed aviator said he had innocently received the Nazi medal and didn't know what to do with it. Unimpressed, FDR shot back: "*I* would have known what to do with it!"[48]

IV. "IF HITLER INVADED HELL . . ."

Americans and Britons did not know it at the time, but Hitler had decided *against* an invasion of Britain in 1941. Herman Goering's Luftwaffe had failed to destroy the Royal Air Force. He had failed to break the will of the British people by means of the Blitz. German fliers could not establish air superiority in the skies over southern England. And the German Navy could not provide safe passage for invading troops, even though the English Channel at its narrowest was only twenty-two miles.

Instead, Hitler looked East. In April, he attacked Yugoslavia and Greece. Once these states were taken down, Hitler would put into place his Operation Barbarossa: the invasion of the Soviet Union.

Churchill learned about these plans from the now-famous Enigma decrypts. These were British intercepts of Germany's coded messages. When Churchill tried to warn Stalin, the Soviet dictator brushed him off. The "Great Leader of the Peoples" had trusted only one human being in his entire life: Adolf Hitler.

Before dawn on Sunday, 22 June 1941, the full might of the German war machine was unleashed on unsuspecting Russia. The ever-so-cynical Nazi-Soviet Non-Aggression Pact signed with such ceremony on 23 August 1939 had lasted barely twenty-two months. Stalin had allowed Hitler a free hand in Poland, France, the Low Countries, and Britain. Now, his people would pay for his treachery.

Churchill hesitated not at all. His private secretary, who had once been skeptical of Churchill's leadership, now recorded the prime minister's irrepressible wit. Even at such a perilous moment, Churchill joked: "If Hitler invaded Hell, I would at least make favorable reference to the Devil" in the House of Commons.[49] He immediately bet his advisers "a Monkey to a Mousetrap that the Russians are still fighting, and fighting victoriously, two years from now."[50]* He spoke on the BBC that night:

---

* Churchill's colorful phrase was not nonsense to his hearers. A Monkey is racetrack shorthand for 500. A Mousetrap, similarly, means a gold Sovereign, a valuable British coin. Churchill would win that bet, even giving 500:1 odds! (Gilbert, *Churchill*, 701.)

No one has been a more consistent opponent of Communism for the last twenty-five years. I will unsay no word I have spoken about it. But all this fades away before the spectacle which is now unfolding. . . . Any man or State who fights on against Nazism will have our aid. . . . [We] shall give whatever help we can to Russia.[51]

The most noticeable change in the American scene was the way Communist Party of the United States of America (CPUSA) members and their fellow travelers changed on a dime. Ever attentive to the "party line" emanating from Moscow, Communists went from being fierce opponents of the "Imperialists' War" to clamoring for immediate U.S. entry into the war.

Meanwhile, the German thrust into Russia was opening the door to the Holocaust. The vast majority of Europe's Jews in 1941 lived in Poland, Russia, and the Ukraine. Tens of thousands of Jews were massacred as the Wehrmacht rolled almost unopposed deeper and deeper into Russia.[52] All Jews were soon to be targeted for destruction. Hitler wanted land in the East as *lebensraum*—"living room"—for his rapidly expanding population of Germans. To achieve this, he intended to make this huge region a *judenrein*—a territory "cleansed" of Jews.

Late that summer, Churchill decided to visit President Roosevelt in North American waters. Boarding the HMS *Prince of Wales* in Scotland, Churchill steamed through U-boat-infested waters to meet Roosevelt at Placentia Bay, Newfoundland.[53]

En route, Churchill watched a movie, *That Hamilton Woman*. It starred Vivien Leigh and Lawrence Olivier. As Olivier, playing England's great naval hero, Lord Nelson, lies dying on the deck of the HMS *Victory*, he is told that he has won the Battle of Trafalgar. "Thank God!" whispers Nelson. Churchill was seen to wipe his eyes with his handkerchief. And this was the *fifth* time he had seen the movie.[54]

FDR, for his part, let reporters and family members think he was just going out on the presidential yacht for his annual fishing vacation.[55]

Roosevelt, it must be admitted, loved pulling dramatic surprises of this sort. He soon transferred to the USS *Augusta* and headed for the frigid waters of Newfoundland.

Aboard the *Augusta* at 11:00 a.m. on 9 August 1941, Churchill approached President Roosevelt. He bore a personal letter of introduction from the king. He gave the president a slight bow.[56] He was, after all, the head of government, but Roosevelt was the chief of state.

The president stood under an awning, leaning on the arm of his son, Elliott. He smiled his broadest smile: "At last—we've gotten together." Churchill's answer: "We have."[57]

It was indeed a rendezvous with destiny. Freedom's champions met in the sheltered waters of Placentia Bay. Together, over the next four years, these two remarkable men would chart the course for the world struggle of freedom against tyranny.

SIXTEEN

LEADING THE
GRAND ALLIANCE

(1941–1943)

I. 1941: "A YEAR OF HOLDING OUR BREATH"

On 6 January 1941, Franklin D. Roosevelt rose to deliver his State of the Union message. He was determined that, in the United States, the lamp of freedom would be held high. He pledged the United States to Four Freedoms:

> We look forward to a world founded upon four essential human freedoms. The first is freedom of speech and expression—everywhere in the world. The second is freedom of every person to worship God in his own way— everywhere in the world. The third is freedom from want . . . everywhere in the world. The fourth is freedom from fear . . . anywhere in the world.

In time, these ringing phrases would be depicted in posters by the popular American illustrator, Norman Rockwell. With *Freedom from Fear*, Rockwell depicted a typical American couple looking in on their peacefully sleeping children, tucked in under the covers in an attic bedroom. Mom and Dad are a picture of loving protectiveness. In his left hand, Dad trails a newspaper whose headline tells of the aerial bombardment of civilians in a faraway corner of the world. The newspaper might have told of Hitler's bombing of Rotterdam or Warsaw or a thousand Russian towns. Or it might have related the horrors of Japan's "Rape of Nanking." There, Japanese soldiers killed more than a quarter million Chinese civilians. Many were raped. Thousands were used for bayonet practice, hung up by their tongues, and eaten by vicious dogs.[1] Freedom's enemies have rarely shown themselves to be friends of mercy.

From the Arctic Circle to the Greek Isles, Europe was under the Nazi thumb. Americans sang "The Last Time I Saw Paris" and "God Bless America" with special fervor. Italy, allied with Germany, was poised to move against Albania and Greece. Inaugurated for a third term, FDR quietly ordered U.S. naval vessels to occupy Iceland and to extend ever eastward the boundaries within which American destroyers escorted convoys of merchant ships bearing supplies for embattled Britain.

In March 1941, Roosevelt finally succeeded in winning congressional approval of Lend-Lease for Britain. Churchill had told Roosevelt secretly that Britain could no longer pay for war materiel. Britain, in a word, was broke. Lend-Lease was FDR's ingenious response to keep our ally supplied. It had been touch and go. Isolationists, especially Republican senators Robert Taft of Ohio and Gerald Nye of North Dakota, bitterly opposed the measure. FDR had compared it to the garden hose one lends the neighbor whose house is burning. Taft answered the homely homily by saying that lending war supplies to a combatant was more like lending chewing gum. "We certainly do not want the same gum back."[2]

If Charles Lindbergh's historic transatlantic flight in 1927 proved anything, it was that America could not be isolated from Europe. Still, America's great aviation hero was a relentless foe of any aid to the Allies. Lindbergh mobilized the America First Committee. "I would sooner see our country traffic in opium than in bombs," he told fellow isolationists at one massive rally.[3] America Firsters, as they soon became known, flooded Congress with telegrams, petitions, and letters against U.S. aid to Britain.*

Confronted with flaming opposition from isolationists across the nation, FDR even had to face brushfires within his own party. Joe Kennedy, just returned from his duty as U.S. Ambassador to Great Britain, dramatically broke with his party's leader. He even testified in Congress against providing aid. Four years earlier, FDR had sent Kennedy to London in the hope that he would help him sell aid to the Allies should that become necessary. FDR needed the influential Kennedy's help among American Catholics. But his patience was wearing thin. When FDR invited Speaker of the House Sam Rayburn and his young protégé, Texas representative Lyndon Johnson, to visit him at the White House, the president took a call from Ambassador Kennedy. As usual, Kennedy complained bitterly of mistreatment by the State Department. While trying to smooth Kennedy's ruffled feathers over the phone, however, FDR drew his finger across his throat in a gesture that could mean only one thing: the president was about to drop the troublesome Boston politician. Kennedy quit as ambassador and explained that he was opposed to any and all U.S. involvement in what FDR was now calling the Second World War. "[I]f I am called an *appeaser* because I oppose the entrance of this country into the present war, I cheerfully plead guilty," Kennedy said.[4] Although he didn't know it at the time, Kennedy's public clash with FDR would prove fatal to his own political prospects. He never again held any public office.

FDR's supporters on Capitol Hill numbered the bill H.R. 1776—a clear patriotic rallying point. This maddened critics, who said the effect of Lend-Lease was to bind the United States and Great Britain ever closer

---

* Friends of democracy in France point out that the United States never even considered sending aid there, to our World War I ally. Even when the Third Republic was in its death throes, even when Premier Reynaud publicly pleaded with President Roosevelt to send "clouds of aeroplanes," the American response was a stony silence. Roosevelt's defenders argue, however, that only after the shock of the Fall of France would Americans listen to arguments for Lend-Lease. Even at that, the bill passed only with great difficulty.

together. In this they were right, although it was Britain who became dependent on the United States. Roosevelt's supporters countered, saying America's independence could be guaranteed only by propping up democracy in Britain as a counter to the Nazi menace to freedom everywhere.

William Allen White was the Republican editor of the *Emporia* (Kansas) *Gazette*. He founded the Committee to Defend America by Aiding the Allies. The group's ungainly name lacked the zing of America First. But it didn't lack clout. Soon, Americans would be wrapping bandages, folding blankets, and packaging foodstuffs for shipping. These were the famous "Bundles for Britain." It was a PR campaign that caught on. White's committee successfully fought back against America First.

With some amending and a lot of arm-twisting and horse trading on Capitol Hill, Speaker Sam Rayburn and South Carolina's Jimmy Byrnes pushed the Lend-Lease measure through a reluctant Congress. FDR signed the bill 11 March 1941. It provided for $7 billion in aid to Britain, an astonishing figure considering that the entire federal budget in 1940 was only $10 billion.[5]

Even more difficult was the decision to aid the Soviet Union after 22 June 1941. Missouri's Democratic senator, Harry S. Truman, spoke for millions of Americans when he said he would just as soon see the Soviets and the Nazis finish each other off.

Hitler dubbed his invasion of the Soviet Union Operation Barbarossa, after the famous crusading German emperor of the Middle Ages, Frederick Barbarossa ("Red Beard").[*] German troops raced toward Moscow and Leningrad, overrunning the ancient cities of Kiev in the Ukraine and Minsk in Byelorussia (now Belarus). Millions of Red Army soldiers were captured. Most of these men starved to death in Nazi POW camps.

The Germans besieged Leningrad (now called St. Petersburg). The German stranglehold on Tsar Peter the Great's beautiful "window on the

---

[*] Hitler had named his abortive plan to invade England *Operation Seeloewe*. As historian John Lukacs points out, the sea lion is not a very fierce beast.

West" began in 1941 and lasted nine hundred days. Millions of defenders starved to death or fell to disease. In Leningrad alone, more than two million Russians died. This dreadful death toll exceeded the sum of all U.S. and British losses in World War II.[6]

When FDR and Churchill met secretly aboard the USS *Augusta* in Newfoundland waters in August 1941, they agreed to the Atlantic Charter. This document was unprecedented. It was not a treaty, because it contained no provisions for an alliance. (And FDR would not have wanted to submit it to a fractious Senate for ratification.) It was not the U.S. Declaration of War on Germany that Churchill had hoped for. Only Congress had that power. Yet it was a joint statement of goals the two leaders embraced. Both leaders said their nations sought no territorial aggrandizement from the war. Both asserted the right of all peoples to live under a government of their own choosing.

The meeting was high drama. Churchill planned a joint religious service aboard HMS *Prince of Wales*. British and American sailors and marines together joined the two leaders in singing "Onward Christian Soldiers" and "O God Our Help in Ages Past." Churchill chose the hymns. He was playing on FDR's American sensibilities. Afterward, awed young American sailors followed their British counterparts on a ship's tour. The Yanks gawked at the still unrepaired shell damage done to *Prince of Wales* in its recent deadly clash with the German pocket battleship *Bismarck*. It had taken all the Royal Navy's might to sink the *Bismarck*. Churchill posed with U.S. Marines. FDR presided as U.S. Marines heaved over his own "bundles for Britain." They were gift boxes from the commander in chief of the U.S. Navy to each of the men on board the British and Canadian warships. The boxes contained cigarettes, fresh fruit, cheese, and candy.[7] They were highly prized by the battle-hardened young British and Canadian sailors. Wartime rationing had deprived them of most luxuries.*

---

* For hundreds of these young British sailors, FDR's box would be their last gift. HMS *Prince of Wales* and her sister ship HMS *Repulse* were sunk by the Japanese off Singapore, with heavy loss of life, barely four months later.

II. A DAY OF INFAMY

If Roosevelt was concerned to stop Hitler from overrunning all of Europe, the immediate threat to the United States came in the Far East. Japan's military rulers were enraged by the oil embargo the United States had imposed. The Roosevelt administration hoped to prevent Japan from attacking the Dutch East Indies (present-day Indonesia). In this instance, *economic* sanctions led directly to war.[8]

America's relations with Japan had been strained for decades. It was the United States, probably unwisely, that had pressured the British to end their treaty of cooperation with Japan following World War I. When young militarists assassinated Japanese democratic officials, the way was cleared for Japan's assault on China. Americans were outraged by Japan's unprovoked aggression against its weaker neighbor and especially horrified by the hundreds of thousands of civilians murdered during the 1937–38 "Rape of Nanking." During this attack on China's then capital, Japanese naval aircraft struck the USS *Panay*.

The U.S. Navy's gunboat was sunk with three sailors killed and more than forty injured. The Japanese would apologize and pay reparations, but feelings between the two Pacific powers were further embittered.

While Japan sent special emissaries in late 1941 to talk peace with Secretary of State Cordell Hull in Washington, Japan's Admiral Isoroku Yamamoto was planning a strike against the U.S. fleet anchored at Pearl Harbor on the Hawaiian Island of Oahu.

On the morning of 7 December 1941, waves of Japanese Zeroes swept in among the verdant hills of Oahu and struck without warning at the Navy ships tied up along "battleship row." "Pearl Harbor was asleep in the morning mist," Commander Itaya reported as his torpedoes shattered the Sunday calm of the harbor.[9] In little more than one hour, attacking Japanese aircraft had sunk the USS *Arizona*, the USS *Oklahoma*, and seriously damaged four other battleships. In all, eighteen U.S. warships were sunk or seriously damaged. One hundred eighty-eight aircraft were destroyed, most of them on the ground at Hickam Army Airfield.[10]*

Worst of all, America lost 2,403 killed and suffered 1,178 wounded. Nearly half of the deaths occurred when the *Arizona* blew up.[11] In the coming days and years, details of the sneak attack would enrage and horrify Americans. The doomed men banging on pipes with wrenches in capsized warships wrung our hearts. But the story of navy yeoman Durrell Conner aboard the stricken *California*, engulfed in flames, lifted our spirits. When many of his fellow crewmen jumped overboard, it became impossible to fight the fires. Yeoman Conner hoisted the American flag from the battleship's stern, and sailors returned to keep her afloat.[12] *Don't give up the ship, indeed!*

An entire generation of Americans would remember where they were when they heard the shocking news of Pearl Harbor. Reverend Peter Marshall was the chaplain of the U.S. Senate. He had just preached a sermon at the Naval Academy, "What Is It Like to Die?" After the service, the young Scottish immigrant gave a lift in his car to a midshipman, only to do a U-turn and return him to duty when they heard the news on his car radio.**

Brigadier General Dwight D. Eisenhower's name was known only to his many friends, fellow West Pointers, and a few thousand troops in the shrunken U.S. Army. He was sleeping in on this Sunday after weeks of grueling training exercises in the field. Despite orders to let him sleep, he was awakened with the news. He dashed out of his quarters at Fort Sam Houston, in Texas, telling his wife, Mamie, he was going to Washington and did not know when he would return. Senator Henry Cabot Lodge, a Republican from Massachusetts, learned of the attack as he stopped to get gas. Just as his father had done with President Wilson, young Cabot Lodge

---

* Until 1947, America's air force was part of the U.S. Army.

** The inspiring story of this Presbyterian minister was told in the book *A Man Called Peter* by Catherine Marshall.

now offered President Roosevelt his full support in prosecuting the war.* So did the leader of Senate isolationists, Michigan Republican Senator Arthur Vandenberg. Vandenberg was pasting press clippings about his fight *against* U.S. involvement in the war in his scrapbook when word came.[13]

The next day, President Roosevelt appeared before a joint session of Congress. The attack had forged national unity as nothing else could. California Senator Hiram Johnson, who had been TR's running mate on the Bull Moose ticket in 1912, had strongly opposed intervention. Now, he marched into the chamber arm-in-arm with a Democratic colleague and voted for war.[14]

The president approached the speaker's rostrum, leaning heavily on son Jimmy's arm:

Yesterday, December 7, 1941—a date which will live in infamy—the United States of America was suddenly and deliberately attacked by naval and air forces of the Empire of Japan.[15]

Roosevelt wore a somber expression to match the black armband he bore for the fallen. He related the lightning strikes Japanese forces had made the same day against Hong Kong (a British Crown Colony) and the U.S. dependencies of Guam, the Philippines, and Wake and Midway Islands. He concluded his call for a declaration of war with these words: "With confidence in our armed forces—with the unbounding determination of our people—we will gain the inevitable triumph—so help us God."[16]**

Few Americans realized at the moment how perilous was the condition of America's armed forces. Our army ranked in size below that of Romania.

---

* The man who would eventually defeat Senator Lodge in Massachusetts, twenty-three-year-old John F. Kennedy, spent the morning of December 7 playing touch football on the grounds of the Washington Monument (Renehan, Edward, *The Kennedys at War: 1937–1945*, Doubleday, New York: 2002, 200).

** These last four words of President Roosevelt's sentence were, inexplicably, dropped from the engraved quotation on the World War II Memorial.

Our navy had just been dealt a near-fatal blow. Providentially, however, the U.S. aircraft carrier fleet was out to sea when Pearl Harbor was struck.

The main reason the sneak attack on Pearl Harbor was such a shock is because it was so stunningly *irrational*. As Samuel Eliot Morison has written: "One may search military history in vain for an operation more fatal to the aggressor."[17] Almost immediately, the planner of the Pearl Harbor attack realized how fatal that error had been; Admiral Isoroku Yamamoto reportedly said: "I fear we have awakened a sleeping giant and instilled in him a terrible resolve."[18] While America lost some 2,400 on that day of infamy, the conflict begun by Japan's warlords on 7 December 1941 would eventually cost two million of their own countrymen's lives.[19]

Hitler declared war on the United States on 11 December 1941. It was an act of suicidal folly equaled only by the Japanese decision four days earlier to attack Pearl Harbor.

In 1941, however, it did not look like suicide. Powerful Japanese forces were immediately unleashed on the Philippines. Churchill responded to the Japanese attacks on the Americans and British possessions by declaring war on the Japanese Empire. Churchill had gained not only a powerful ally in the United States but also a dangerous and determined enemy in the Far East, where Britain's colonial empire was ripe for the picking.

Adolf Hitler's treaty with Japan required him to help his ally only if Japan was attacked. But Japan was the aggressor at Pearl Harbor. Frustrated at not being able to take Moscow in that first, bitterly cold Russian winter, Hitler lashed out at the United States: Roosevelt was controlled by the Jews, he said. Speaking from his headquarters at Rastenburg, in the German state of East Prussia, Hitler explained to an aide why he had declared war on the United States.* "[In Japan,] we now have an ally who has never been vanquished in three thousand years."[20]

---

* East Prussia was a historically German region between Poland and Lithuania. Soviets overran the capital, Königsberg, and surrounding territories in 1945. The Germans were killed or expelled. East Prussia was divided between the Russians and the Poles. Today Königsberg is the Russian city Kaliningrad. On the Polish side, the East Prussian city of Danzig is now called Gdansk.

FDR had called 7 December 1941 "a date which will live in infamy." His words were prophetic in another way. On that very day, Hitler began gassing the Jews of Poland.[21] His troops near Chelmno took trucks with 700 Jews and transferred them in groups of eighty to a specially modified van. The van's exhaust had been rerouted into the cargo compartment. By the time the van reached Chelmno, all eighty Jews inside were dead. It was to be the first, crude attempt at mass murder that would be known as Hitler's "Final Solution" of the "Jewish problem" in Europe. On this day of infamy, all 700 were killed. In time, 360,000 Jews from 200 surrounding villages—called *shtetls*—were killed using mobile killing vans.[22]

Hastening to Washington, Churchill spent a month in the White House in close consultation with his friend, FDR. His response to the attack on Pearl Harbor, he admitted, was not altogether mournful: that night, Churchill said he "slept the sleep of the saved and the thankful."[23] He addressed a joint meeting of Congress. There, he received a thunderous ovation. Even in the midst of these "stern days," Churchill could not resist a witticism:

> I cannot help reflecting that if my father had been American and my
> mother British, instead of the other way around, I might have got here
> on my own. In that case, this would not have been the first time you
> would have heard my voice.[24]

He was an important guest in the White House—and memorable. Stories began to circulate about his eccentricities.

"Now, Fields," Winston told the White House usher, "we had a lovely dinner last night, but I have a few orders for you. We want to leave here as friends, right? So I need you to listen. One, I don't like talking outside my quarters; two, I hate whistling in the corridors; and three, I must have a tumbler of sherry in my room before breakfast, a couple glasses of scotch and soda before lunch and French champagne and ninety-year-old brandy before I go to sleep at night." For breakfast, Churchill ordered "eggs, bacon or ham and toast, two kinds of cold meats with English mustard and two kinds of fruit plus a tumbler of sherry."[25] We don't know what Fields thought of this—except that for the White House staff it was already a long war. They had become used to the prime minister padding around the living quarters in his "siren suit," a one-piece blue affair, flight gear for the Royal Air Force.[26]

On New Year's Day 1942, Churchill cosigned with Roosevelt a joint statement of war aims that spoke of the *United Nations'* desire to win a complete victory over Germany, Italy, and Japan. It was the first reference in American history to the United Nations as the formal name of the alliance of the twenty-six nations that were fighting the Axis powers.

When he saw the newsreels of the two leaders' press conference, Hitler pronounced FDR "truly mentally ill!" and said the whole event had degenerated into a theatrical performance—"Truly Jewish," he said of it.* "The Americans are the dumbest people that one can imagine," the Führer snorted.[27]

The Allies' situation was grim. In the Philippines, U.S. Army and Philippine national forces under General Douglas MacArthur were increasingly isolated on the Island of Bataan. There, Japanese forces under General Homma tightened the noose. From January to April 1942, the situation worsened. Unable to relieve the fortress of Corregidor, President Roosevelt ordered MacArthur to evacuate his family and immediate staff to Australia. The Australians were an important ally. But they were shocked to suddenly find themselves in the path of the Japanese juggernaut. FDR sent MacArthur there to reassure them. As he left the Philippines by Patrol Torpedo (PT) Boat, MacArthur declared, "I shall return."

---

* Hitler's party rallies—orchestrated by Albert Speer and recorded on film by Leni Riefenstahl—were nothing but theatrical. Only his hatred of Jews could blind the Führer to the fact that his enemies had an even greater sense of history's drama than he did.

American G.I.s felt abandoned.* Bombed day and night by the Japanese, they sang a mournful tune:

> We're the Battling Bastards of Bataan
> No mama, no papa, no Uncle Sam,
> No aunts, no uncles, no cousins, no nieces,
> No pills, no planes or artillery pieces.[28]

When the American surrender finally came in April 1942, horror awaited the U.S. and Filipino POWs. Nearly 78,000 of them—the largest mass surrender in American history—were force marched to a prison camp more than sixty-five miles away. The starving, sick Americans and Filipinos were clubbed, bayoneted, and shot to death if they fell out of the line of march. It has ever after been known as the Bataan Death March.[29] (For his part in ordering the march, Japanese General Homma would later be tried, convicted, and hanged for war crimes.[30])

To lift American morale after the disastrous defeat in the Philippines, FDR ordered an air raid on Tokyo. Colonel Jimmy Doolittle led sixteen USAAF B-25 bombers from the deck of the USS *Hornet*. Doolittle's bomber pilots practiced takeoffs from an airfield lined to the exact dimensions of a carrier deck, but they had never actually taken off from a real carrier pitching and rolling in the always stormy waters of the northern Pacific. Never before or since have bombers been launched from an aircraft carrier. Vice Admiral William F. ("Bull") Halsey's task force carried the planes to within five hundred miles of Japan's home islands. Doolittle's raid—those famous *Thirty Seconds Over Tokyo*—did little damage to Japan's war machine. But it did cause the military leaders to "lose face" among the Japanese people. They now realized they were not immune to air attacks. The Doolittle Raid also electrified Americans. Just

---

*   *G.I.*—short for Government Issue—was a nickname for American soldiers during World War II, just as *doughboy* had been the preferred usage in World War I.

four months after Pearl Harbor, the Doolittle Raid demonstrated that the United States could strike back. Nine of the eighty American flyers died in the raid, some being executed by their vengeful Japanese captors—a clear violation of the Geneva Convention.* The military felt the pressure to do something dramatic. An impatient public and an equally impatient FDR demanded action.[31]

Some Americans gave in to their fears during World War II. Widespread rumors of Japanese American disloyalty led to panic, especially on the now-vulnerable West Coast. Responding to cries from California's Republican attorney general Earl Warren among others, President Roosevelt signed Executive Order 9066 on 19 February 1942. EO 9066 is now generally conceded to be one of FDR's worst mistakes. It provided for the internment of some 110,000 persons of Japanese descent. These included not only Japanese citizens but also those who were *Nisei* and *Sansei*, second- and third-generation Japanese Americans. Fully 64 percent of these were American citizens.[32] They were sent to internment camps in remote parts of the vast West. In no way can such camps be fairly compared with Nazi death camps or Stalin's *Gulag*, but the terrible fact remains that Americans who had done no wrong lost their property and, temporarily at least, their liberty because of the hysteria and hatred of their neighbors.

Fortunately, the heroic combat record of the Army's all-Nisei 100th Battalion in Italy did much to bank the flames of prejudice. The 100th was integrated into the 442nd Regimental Combat Team. It was in this unit that Daniel K. Inouye, a Hawaiian Nisei, won the Congressional Medal of Honor. Years later, he was sworn in as the first Japanese

---

* "A set of eighty silver goblets, each one inscribed with a Raider's name, has been kept on display at the U.S. Air Force Academy in Colorado Springs, Colorado, and flown to each reunion. There, in a private ceremony, the survivors raised their cups in a toast to Raiders departed and inverted the cups of those men who died since the previous get-together. When the last man is gone, his goblet, too, will be reversed" (https://www.historynet.com /jimmy-doolittle-and-the-tokyo-raiders-strike-japan-during-world-war-ii.htm).

American member of Congress. When Speaker Sam Rayburn intoned the usual "raise your right hand," an awed hush came over the House of Representatives; Congressman, now Senator, Inouye had lost his right arm in service to America.[33]

FDR wasted no time or sympathy on those German Americans who were suspected of being "fifth columnists."* Or on spies. Two parties of German saboteurs were landed by U-boat on America's shores. One came ashore in Florida, the other on Long Island, intercepted at first by a young Coast Guardsman, John Cullen, near Amagansett, New York. Seaman Cullen soon alerted his superiors and all the Germans were quickly apprehended. FDR ordered a trial by military tribunal. Though ably defended by government attorneys, the German saboteurs were prosecuted by Francis Biddle, attorney general of the United States. They were convicted as spies. Six members of the group were sentenced to death; two who had turned themselves in received life sentences.[34]

Roosevelt similarly turned a stern face toward Charles A. Lindbergh, whom he suspected of disloyalty. After Pearl Harbor, America First had folded and Lindbergh made it known he wanted to return to the army. Lindbergh was fully willing to fight the non-white Japanese, but he hadn't changed his mind about the desirability of coming to an agreement with Hitler. FDR was in no mood to negotiate with Lindbergh. Nor would he make any concessions to Lindbergh's oft-repeated notion that a war by Britain and America against the German *Aryans* would be suicide for the white race. Roosevelt stonily rejected Lindbergh's bid for an air force commission. "I'll clip that young man's wings," FDR told several senators.[35] And he did. Lindbergh never again enjoyed the public's trust.

FDR was sensitive to racial unrest at home. Millions of black Americans were moving North to work in war industries. They faced discrimination in housing and in many daily activities. Race riots threatened

---

* The term "Fifth Column" was in widespread use during World War II. It was first used during Spain's civil war (1936–39) to describe a subversive element within a besieged city that would help an attacking general take it. It became shorthand for disloyalty.

national unity at a critical time. In one of the worst of these riots, in 1943, thirty-four people died in Detroit.

Young black men were subject to the draft, but they served in all-black units. In one such unit, the Tuskegee Airmen gained lasting fame in the skies over Germany. President Roosevelt promoted Benjamin O. Davis Sr. as the first black general in the army, a historic breakthrough.[36] The government publicized boxer Joe Louis's wry response to racial injustice in America: "There's nothing wrong with this country that Hitler is going to cure."[37]

Still, there *was* much wrong with the country. Union leader A. Philip Randolph was determined to use the war emergency to press for greater equality for black Americans. Before the outbreak of the war, Randolph had urged a great march on Washington for justice if the president did not address the issue of hiring discrimination by government defense contractors. FDR responded by creating the Fair Employment Practices Commission (FEPC). He had been urged on by Eleanor. Randolph led the Brotherhood of Sleeping Car Porters. His members were known as "civil rights missionaries on wheels."[38] Randolph would become a leading figure in the civil rights movement.

"Freedom is never granted," he said. "It is won."[39]

III. A WORLD AT WAR

By 1942, the whole world was at war. For millions, defeat would mean not only a loss of freedom, it would mean *annihilation*. This was certainly true for the Communist commissars of Soviet Russia. Hitler had issued a "commissar order" that called for the immediate murder of any of these Communist Party officials who fell into German hands. Slavs were endangered as well. Hitler wanted Poland and the Ukraine for *lebensraum*, or "living space," for the rapidly expanding population of Germans. Slavery, followed by starvation and sterilization, would be the fate of the Slavs who were in his way.

Of course, Hitler's "New Order in Europe" threatened Jews most of all. Although Allied intelligence did not know it yet, the 20 January 1942 conference held in the Berlin suburb of Wannsee planned the "Final Solution of the Jewish Problem in Europe." This *solution*—a chilling euphemism for a nonexistent problem—was to be nothing less than the murder of all eleven million European Jews. The mass shootings of Jews in Russia and the gassings at Chelmno, as destructive as they were, only convinced the Nazi high command of the need for "industrial" methods of slaughter if they were to destroy all the Jews in Europe. Thus, at Wannsee, they planned to use rail transport to forcibly relocate all the Jews they could capture. Surrounding populations would be told the Jews were merely being "relocated in the East." But at remote places like Auschwitz, far from prying eyes, the monstrous mechanism of mass murder would accelerate beyond anything previously known in human history. It was the beginning of the *Holocaust*. In many of the occupied states of Europe, Hitler would find willing accomplices for his plans. He sought to make all Europe *judenrein*, a land free of Jews. Hitler had publicly warned the Jews that if "they" plunged the world into another great war, they would be exterminated. Few in the West imagined he really *meant* or thought it.

Hitler spoke to a conference in Berlin, boasting that anti-Semitism was on the rise throughout the world. In this, he was correct. "In Germany, too, the Jews once laughed at my prophesies. I don't know if they are still laughing," the Führer said with malicious sarcasm. Meanwhile, several hundred miles to the east, at a remote Polish village, Jews from France, Belgium, and Holland were arriving in cattle cars. Many had died en route. In one group, 957 Jews had arrived from Paris on the morning of 2 September 1942. By that afternoon, 918 had already been gassed.[40]

Hitler welcomed the Grand Mufti of Jerusalem—Muslim leader Haj Amin al-Husseini—to Berlin at the outbreak of the war. There, the mufti broadcasted militantly anti-Jewish messages to the Arab world. He had helped the Germans to recruit Muslims in the Balkans—the 13th *Waffen SS* Handschar Division.[41] These were certainly not Aryans. Thousands of Jews from Palestine joined the British Army in Egypt. They knew too well that if Rommel's powerful Afrika Korps crossed the Suez Canal, Hitler would call upon the Muslims to rise up and exterminate the half million Jews living precariously under the British mandate in Palestine. A distinguished Jewish educator in Jerusalem pleaded for enlistments: "If the men of the Hebrew University do not realize the urgency of this hour, who will?"[42]

FDR and Churchill had agreed on a "Germany First" strategy since both viewed Germany as the greater menace. This decision was to have profound consequences for the course of the war and for the shape of the postwar world. But agreeing on fighting Germany first did not mean that the two leaders would always agree on strategy. Nor would they find their alliance with Soviet Russia's Josef Stalin an easy one.

"I feel damn depressed," wrote Harry Hopkins from the prime minister's residence at No. 10 Downing Street in London. He said Churchill was like a cannon: great to have on your side, but devastating when he was firing away at you.[43] Hopkins had been engaged in some hard dealing with Churchill on the subject of Britain's colonies.

Churchill did not agree with Roosevelt about the future of the British Empire. FDR was not willing to spend American blood and treasure to shore up what he saw as a collapsing imperial power. He would fight to save the British home islands from Hitler's ruthless tyranny, but that was all. "Billions for Britain," FDR was saying, in effect, "not a penny for Empire."

American schoolchildren of those days were used to seeing maps of the world that had great, broad bands of red (actually pink) to indicate British dominions. Canada, Australia, New Zealand, India (including modern Pakistan), as well as extensive territories in Africa, the Middle East, and Asia—all these were tied to the British Crown.

In 1942, it was still true that the "sun never set on the British Empire." With the loss of Hong Kong, Singapore, and Malaya to the Japanese, with India threatened, and with Germany's Afrika Korps moving east toward the Suez Canal, how much longer would this be true?

It must have seemed ironic indeed to Churchill that he had to battle his English-speaking ally for the sake of his king. Hitler had pledged *not* to interfere with the British Empire. Now, here was the great democrat, Roosevelt, demanding self-government for the British colonies. Churchill doubtless had FDR in mind when he declared defiantly in Parliament: "I have not become the King's first minister in order to preside over the liquidation of the British Empire."[44]

America in World War II mobilized in a way never seen before—or since. "Hitler should beware the fury of an aroused democracy," said U.S. General Dwight D. Eisenhower.[45] Hitler probably had little understanding of the vast numbers that would soon come against him. With the aid of prewar military conscription (which had been reauthorized by a single vote in Congress), the United States quickly built up a huge military. Soon, the United States would have over twelve million men and women in uniform—surpassing all other powers, even Russia by a slight margin.[46]

Nation	Troops Fielded
Britain	4,680,000
Japan	6,095,000
Germany	10,000,000
USSR	12,300,000
U.S.	12,364,000[*]

These numbers meant that one in eleven Americans was serving in the military. (By comparison, in 2018, roughly one in two hundred and fifty Americans was on active duty.) This incredible mobilization represented a monumental investment for a democracy—never before seen and never since surpassed.

---

[*] Ambrose, *World War II.*

Americans sang along with pro-military songs like the Andrews Sisters' "Boogie Woogie Bugle Boy." Irving Berlin's plaintive "God Bless America" had lifted hearts when Kate Smith sang it in the darkening years before the war. Now, in 1942, Berlin used humor to keep up morale:

> This is the Army Mister Jones,
> No private rooms or telephones,
> You had your breakfast in bed before,
> But you won't have it there any more.

Millions of young men were swept up in the draft. Few even dreamed of staying out. Conscientious objectors were shunned as "shirkers."

On the home front, Americans lived with the rationing of many daily necessities. Meat, gasoline, automobile tires, and women's nylon stockings were but a few of the essentials in short supply. FDR let his interior secretary, Harold Ickes, mount a drive to collect rubber to repurpose for the war. The White House announced that the president's Scottish terrier, Fala, would donate his already-been-chewed rubber bones.[47] So enthusiastic was Ickes for his new assignment that he grabbed the rubber doormat outside the president's office and put it in the trunk of his limousine!

Americans were exhorted daily to raise their own vegetables in backyard "victory gardens." They collected used cans and "tin" foil for reuse. With automobile production converted into tank and aircraft production, Americans could not buy new cars. Many other consumer goods were likewise unobtainable. As the government's slogan for wartime austerity put it:

> USE IT UP
> WEAR IT OUT
> MAKE IT DO
> OR DO WITHOUT

Victory gardens, victory loans, everywhere you looked, people were being exhorted to victory. Hard-to-read V-mail (victory mail) was accepted as a matter of course. Every letter to and from America's twelve million men and women in uniform was opened, photocopied, and censored. The addressee got only the photocopy. There was barely a peep of protest at this unprecedented government intrusion.

In major cities of the East Coast, a wartime blackout was in effect. New York's "Great White Way"—the heart of the thriving theater district—went dark. Americans were told that nighttime blackouts were necessary, especially along the Eastern Seaboard. There, Nazi U-boats had been able to pick off U.S. merchant ships silhouetted by the lights of beach town boardwalks.

Of course, war-weary Americans could always go to the movies. Hollywood threw itself wholeheartedly into the war effort. Movie stars appeared at war-bond rallies, encouraging Americans to help finance the war. Tinseltown churned out endless movies designed to bolster morale on the home front. There were several excellent movies, but hundreds of duds. *Casablanca* and *Mrs. Minniver* remain classics today. In *Desperate Journey*, Errol Flynn, Arthur Kennedy, and Ronald Reagan played three American pilots forced down behind enemy lines. It was certainly not a great role for the future president, but it did enable him to joke that he was used to people trying to upstage him. As Reagan himself would say of the producers of some of these clunkers: "They don't want it good; they want it *Tuesday*."

Ronald Reagan would have felt quite at home in North Platte, Nebraska. The town was a typical Midwest hamlet of 12,000 at the outbreak of the war. But something very special happened there. Beginning on Christmas Day in 1941 and continuing through the end of the war, the town offered itself as the North Platte Canteen. There, for 365 days a year from dawn until the last troop train pulled out, volunteers from this remote Great Plains community provided hot coffee, donuts, sandwiches, and sympathy for young soldiers shipping out.

The whole effort started by mistake. Townsmen had heard that Company D of the Nebraska National Guard would be stopping over on its way to the Pacific.[48] Young Miss Rae Wilson wrote to the North Platte *Daily Bulletin* to describe what happened at the depot:

> We who met this troop train which arrived about 5 o'clock were expecting Nebraska boys. Naturally, we had candy, cigarettes, etc., but we very willingly gave those things to the Kansas boys. Smiles, tears, and laughter followed. Appreciation showed on over 300 faces. I say get back of our sons and other mothers' sons 100 percent. Let's do something and do it in a hurry. We can help this way when we can't help any other way.[49]

What began as a mistake—Kansas National Guardsmen taken for Nebraskans—ended five years later. By war's end, more than six million G.I.s had been served at the North Platte Canteen.[50]

Millions of Americans were swept into war industries. Many were prevented from leaving jobs in critical fields. When the United Mine Workers' John L. Lewis planned a strike in the coalfields that would cripple war production, FDR threatened to seize the mines and *draft* the miners.[51]

Millions of women entered the workforce for the first time in World War II. "Rosie the Riveter" became a legend. "She's a WOW," declared one poster showing an attractive young woman looking up from her assembly line at the imagined picture of her man as he headed into combat. As a Woman Ordinance Worker, she was told, she was freeing a man for the fight.[52]

Women and all other defense workers knew they were not just performing a hard, dull, routine task. They were the sinews of victory. To a stricken world, America's productive capacity seemed unlimited.

IV. THE BATTLE OF THE ATLANTIC

Shipbuilding was a critical element in the victory of the Allies. The Nazi U-boat menace threatened Britain's very lifeblood in 1942. If Britain could not be supplied by sea, she would starve and lose the war.

FDR embarked on an ambitious plan to build a fleet of cargo ships that came to be known as Liberty Ships. An astounding 2,751 of these vessels were built during World War II; one of these was built in the record time of four days, fifteen and a half hours from the time the keel was laid.[53] As plucky merchant marine sailors boasted ever after: "We could launch 'em faster than Hitler could sink 'em."

It was a brave boast, but it was the Allied seamen, not their ships, that could not be replaced. From 1939, when Britain and Canada entered the war, to 1945, some 36,000 Allied sailors were killed in the Atlantic, almost all of them by U-boats. And an equal number of merchant seamen were killed.[54] Shortly after Hitler declared war on the United States, the East Coast became a hunting ground for U-boat "wolf packs." By the middle of 1942, the Germans had sunk more Allied tonnage in the Atlantic than the Japanese had done with their more spectacular attacks on Pearl Harbor, the Philippines, Wake, Guam, and other U.S., British, and Dutch possessions in Asia.[55] Hitler never allowed more than a dozen U-boats to operate at one time off America's Eastern seaboard, yet the damage they inflicted was frightening.

The United States and Britain did not rely, however, merely on the overpowering productivity of their shipyards. The convoy system, destroyer escorts, submarine-destroying inventions like SONAR (ASDIC to the British, who invented it), patrol seaplanes, and dirigibles equipped for anti-submarine warfare together put an end to the U-boat menace. The U.S. Coast Guard was especially active in anti-submarine warfare in World War II. Perhaps the greatest of anti-submarine warriors was Britain's Captain F. J. "Johnnie" Walker. He sank *twenty* U-boats, employing his own tactic, the "Creeping Attack." Johnnie Walker gave the Germans no chance to surrender. He would use one ship to locate the U-boat with its sonar while he "crept" up on it silently. Then he ordered the depth charges. No submarine ever survived Walker's hammering blows. Before the war, he had been a boxer. Pity his opponents in the ring.[56]

By May 1943, the "happy time" the U-boat sailors fondly remembered off the coast of North Carolina was over. By war's end, three-fourths of Germany's 40,000 U-boat sailors had been killed. Little wonder, however, that Churchill feared the U-boats above everything. "The U-boat attack was our worst evil. It would have been wise for the Germans to stake all upon it."[57]

V. AMERICA STRIKES BACK

Following the Japanese sneak attack on Pearl Harbor, Navy Admiral Chester W. Nimitz was itching to hit back. The Japanese Imperial Navy had never known defeat. Each of its warships bore the sixteen-petaled chrysanthemum, the Imperial seal. A clash in May between Japanese carrier-based aircraft and American and Australian naval units became known as the Battle of the Coral Sea. The Japanese were attempting to land troops at Port Moresby, New Guinea. It was the first naval battle in history in which neither fleet sighted the other. Although the Americans lost the USS *Lexington*, the Japanese were prevented from landing. They withdrew under pounding from carrier-based aircraft.[58]

The Australians and New Zealanders regard this battle as key to securing their freedom from Japanese invasion.

A Japanese attempt to take Midway Island in the North Pacific in June 1942 was turned back. American carriers that had escaped the attack on Pearl Harbor launched attacks on their Japanese counterparts. Miraculously, an air squadron that was headed the wrong way spotted the wake of a Japanese destroyer. They turned ninety degrees and followed the destroyer all the way back to the carrier task force. There, the U.S. Navy torpedo bombers caught Admiral Nagumo's carriers while they were preparing to receive their own planes. The Japanese decks were covered with bombs and snaking hoses for aviation fuel. When the Americans struck, Nagumo suffered a catastrophe. The carriers that had carried out the sneak attack on Pearl Harbor—*Kaga, Akagi, Hiryu,* and *Soryu*—were sent to the bottom. Americans were thrilled to deal the Japanese such a stinging defeat, just six months after Pearl Harbor. What Doolittle's Raid did in spirit, the Battle of Midway did in reality. The Miracle at Midway punctured the myth of Japanese invincibility. Midway was not won without suffering, however. The USS *Yorktown* was sunk. And out of forty-one planes launched by Admiral Spruance against the enemy, only six returned.[59]

Britain also enjoyed a singular victory later in 1942. Churchill was desperate to stop the "Desert Fox," Field Marshal Erwin Rommel. Rommel's Afrika Korps had pushed the British back to within just sixty miles of the Suez Canal. Not only was the canal vulnerable, and with it Britain's vital oil supply from the Persian Gulf but so, too, was Britain's Mandate in Palestine. Jews the world over shuddered as Rommel's *panzer* tanks sped ever closer to Jerusalem.

To stop the charismatic Desert Fox, Churchill chose the equally color-ful Field Marshal Bernard Law Montgomery. "Monty" and his "Desert Rats" of Britain's 8th Army defeated Rommel at El Alamein in November 1942. Britain was overjoyed. Over his wife Clementine's "violent" objec-tions, Churchill ordered that church bells that had been silent since 1 September 1939 should now ring out all over Britain to mark the victory.* Churchill said it was not the end. "It is not even the beginning of the end. But it may be the end of the beginning." It was.

As he spoke, Hitler's unstoppable armies were stopped in North Africa and at Stalingrad in the USSR. These two Allied victories were to have worldwide consequences.

Meanwhile, in Europe, the Jews were targeted for physical annihi-lation under the Final Solution. Christians were to be terrorized into submission, according to documents compiled by Gen. William Donovan

---

* The church bells were to be rung to signal a Nazi invasion. By this time, the danger of invasion had passed, but "Clemmie" feared further British defeats that would make Winston's impulsive act looks rash. She was always trying to protect him—from himself. (Soames, *Clementine Churchill*, 419).

of the Office of Strategic Services (OSS). Donovan assembled evidence of Hitler's plan to destroy Christian churches and organizations. "Under the pretext that the Churches themselves were interfering in political and state matters, [the Nazis] would deprive the Churches, step by step, of all opportunity to affect German public life." As writer Charles A. Donovan notes, Adolf Hitler and his Nazis were "at war with God."[60*]

El Alamein was followed immediately by Operation Torch. The joint U.S.-British invasion of French North Africa was commanded by General Dwight D. Eisenhower. Although Operation Torch was hugely successful for the Allies in North Africa, it led to Hitler's retaliation by occupying *all* of Metropolitan France.

Now, France was completely at the mercy of Germany's secret police, the *Gestapo*. Hundreds of thousands of young French men and women were swept up and transported across the border as forced laborers in the Third Reich. French Jews were hunted down—often in *collaboration* with Vichy police—and shipped off to German death camps.

To bolster Allied morale, Eleanor Roosevelt visited Britain late in 1942. Clementine Churchill wrote to FDR on the amazing impact of the First Lady's tours on the young servicewomen in the British military—and of the way she handled reporters: "I was struck by the ease, friendliness and dignity with which she talked with the reporters, and by the esteem and affection with which they evidently regarded her."[61]

"Clemmie" later reported that Eleanor and Winston "had a slight difference of opinion" about Spain over dinner. Clementine was on hand to mediate differences, but she gave the president's outspoken wife little hint of her own deeply held views. In the end, Winston realized he had to stay on Eleanor's good side. He wooed her with his old-fashioned charm. "You have certainly left *golden footprints* behind you," he wrote as Eleanor departed England.[62]

---

* Charles A. Donovan is the son of James R. Donovan, Sr., who served in the OSS in 1944–45. (These Donovans are no relation to OSS founder "Wild Bill" Donovan.)

President Roosevelt flew seventeen thousand miles for another secret summit conference with Churchill at Casablanca in French Morocco in early 1943. The president flew aboard a commercial Boeing 314 clipper—a "flying boat." He thus became the first president to fly while in office.[63] Americans were thrilled by the danger and mystery of his dramatic wartime flight.*

Allied prospects had suddenly brightened. American soldiers, sailors, and Marines were in the final stages of taking Guadalcanal, in the Solomon Islands. Despite heavy casualties, including 1,752 dead, the Americans showed that the die-hard Japanese could be beaten, even in the steamy jungles of the South Pacific.[64] By contrast, in sub-zero cold, a major German army was surrounded at Stalingrad.

The most important result of the Casablanca summit was the demand for "Unconditional Surrender." Although the words do not appear in the Allies' joint communiqué, suggesting that Churchill might have been less than enthusiastic, FDR understood that the American people had to have an easily understood war aim.[65] Roosevelt has been criticized for this demand. Critics say he lengthened the war and undercut anti-Nazi elements within Germany and thus cost American lives. Roosevelt knew, however, that Americans were bitterly disillusioned after World War I. He agreed with Cousin Theodore, and not with Wilson, on this point.[66] He had to reassure the American people that no "deal" would be struck with the Nazis. Churchill later softened the Allies' demand by saying: "We are no extirpators of nations, or butchers of peoples. . . . We remain bound by our customs and our nature."[67] The Allies would treat defeated Germany with humanity.

Churchill suffered from pneumonia at the Casablanca summit conference. When he recovered, he ordered a picnic at a rugged retreat in the famed Atlas Mountains. Typically, he scampered down a steep gorge

---

* The straight-line distance between Washington, D.C., and Casablanca is just 3,794 miles, but due to wartime security and heavy load requirements, Boeing's *Dixie Clipper* made the trip in stages. FDR celebrated his 61st birthday on his return trip.

and tried to clamber up the biggest boulder. "Clemmie said nothing," reported a friend, Lady Diana Cooper, "but watched him like a lenient mother who does not want to spoil her child's fun nor yet his daring."[68] Later, Lady Diana spoke to Clemmie about what they would do when the war was over. "I never think of after the war," Clemmie said calmly. "You see, I think Winston will die when it's over. . . . We're putting all we have into this war, and it will take all we have."[69]*

When on 30 January 1943, Hitler promoted General Friedrich von Paulus to field marshal, he reminded his commander at besieged Stalingrad that no German field marshal had *ever* been captured. Temperatures in Russia that winter had plunged to *minus* 30° C (-22° F). Starving *Wehrmacht* soldiers had to eat their horses. They even dug up dead horses to stew their bones. Over and over, the Soviets broadcast to the German troops: *Stalingrad—Massengrab* ("Stalingrad—Mass Grave"). Von Paulus surrendered his new field marshal's baton on 31 January.[70] With him, ninety thousand German soldiers, sick, cold, and hungry, passed through "the gates of Hell" into Stalin's slave-labor camps. They were all that was left of an army of a quarter million. Fewer than five thousand of these men would ever see their homes again.[71] The invading Germans had shown no mercy to the Russians. Now, they received none.

Back in Germany, state radio played dirges for days. The Nazi propaganda machine could not conceal the magnitude of the disaster and for once did not try. The brittle steel of the German *schwerpunkt*—spear tip—had broken. Hitler had determined to take Stalingrad not because of its intrinsic military value, but because of its symbolic name. For that very reason, Stalin was determined to hold it.

The city on the Volga River was little more than rubble when the Germans finally surrendered. Today, its significance is seen as the highwater mark of the German floodtide. From this point, the Germans beat a long, lugubrious but orderly retreat, harassed and pursued every step of

---

* Winston Churchill survived a full twenty years after World War II. His beloved, vivacious Clementine lived until 1977.

the way by the Red Army and by thousands of partisans. And as always, the Russians had on their side their great commander whom not even Stalin could intimidate—General *Winter*. Churchill enjoyed taunting Hitler. As he told the British people:

> Then Hitler made his second grand blunder. He forgot about the Winter. There is a Winter, you know, in Russia. For a good many months the temperature is apt to fall very low. There is snow; there is frost and all that.
>
> Hitler forgot about this Russian Winter. He must have been very loosely educated. We all heard about it at school, but he forgot it. I have never made such a bad mistake as that.

This, barely three months after El Alamein, truly *was* the beginning of the end. The vaunted Nazi war machine was now seen by all to be vulnerable and headed for defeat. That did not mean, however, that the dying cobra had lost its deadly bite.

General Dwight D. Eisenhower—soon known as *Ike* to millions—followed up his North Africa success with an invasion of Sicily. Americans had gone along reluctantly with Churchill's vision for striking the "soft underbelly" of Hitler's Europe and knocking Italy out of the war. Italy did fall, but Hitler's legions soon occupied most of the Italian Peninsula. There was nothing soft about Field Marshal Kesselring or his battle-hardened German troops. The fighting up Italy's rocky spine was brutal and bloody. Fortunately, Rome was declared an open city, so the Eternal City and its architectural treasures were spared. Not so Monte Cassino—which was demolished by Allied bombardment. The Allies stiff-armed protests from Pope Pius XII, believing the Germans had taken refuge in and around the historic monastery. The Allies regarded the lives of their troops as more sacred than even the greatest of monuments.* When the

---

* In 1969, American investigators conceded that the Germans had not, in fact, invested the monastery at Monte Cassino. Its loss, therefore, was a tragic instance of "friendly fire" in warfare. The Pope had been right (Dear and Foot, *Oxford Companion*, 756).

Fascist regime of Benito Mussolini collapsed, *Il Duce*—the leader—was taken prisoner. Hitler sent his commandos on a daring and successful mission to rescue him from his captors. Hitler proved loyal to his ally and mentor until the end.

Franklin Roosevelt lost no opportunity to remind Americans that freedom itself was at stake in the war they were fighting. On 13 April 1943, the bicentennial of Thomas Jefferson's birth, FDR spoke at the dedication of the Jefferson Memorial in Washington, D.C.:

Today, in the midst of a great war for freedom, we dedicate a shrine to freedom. . . .

[Jefferson] faced the fact that men who will not fight for liberty can lose it. We, too, have faced that fact. . . .

He lived in a world in which freedom of conscience and freedom of mind were battles still to be fought through—not principles already accepted of all men. We, too, have lived in such a world. . . .

He loved peace and loved liberty—yet on more than one occasion he was forced to choose between them. We, too, have been compelled to make that choice. . . .

The Declaration of Independence and the very purposes of the American Revolution itself, while seeking freedoms, called for the abandonment of privileges. . . .

Thomas Jefferson believed, as we believe, in Man. He believed, as we believe, that men are capable of their own government, and that no king, no tyrant, no dictator can govern for them as well as they can govern for themselves.

He believed, as we believe, in certain inalienable rights. He, as we, saw those principles and freedoms challenged. He fought for them, as we fight for them. . . .

The words which we have chosen for this Memorial speak Jefferson's noblest and most urgent meaning; and we are proud indeed to understand it and share it:

"I have sworn upon the altar of God, eternal hostility against every form of tyranny over the mind of man."

Roosevelt understood that Jefferson, "an Apostle of Freedom," had seen man's inalienable rights as a gift of the Creator. This was the belief that FDR knew was threatened by the worldwide rise of Fascism and Japanese militarism.

SEVENTEEN

AMERICA VICTORIOUS

(1943–1945)

I. OVERLORD

President Roosevelt employed every aspect of his powerful office to advance the American war effort. He was photographed personally decorating brave young warriors with the Congressional Medal of Honor. One of the more interesting of these was Lieutenant Commander Edward "Butch" O'Hare. This young naval aviator had led his squadron against Japanese bombers that were headed for his carrier, the USS *Lexington*. Butch shot down four enemy bombers in five minutes, risking his life and earning the nation's highest award for heroism. After a U.S. tour speaking at war-bond rallies, O'Hare returned to the South Pacific where he was to die during the famous "Marianas Turkey Shoot" in 1944, possibly a victim of friendly fire. After the war, Chicago's O'Hare Airport was named to honor this intrepid young Naval Academy graduate.[1] Soon, Butch O'Hare would be joined by other genuine heroes like army lieutenant Audie Murphy and Marine Gunnery Sergeant John Basilone. Their stories are worth retelling here. "On January 26, 1945, near Holtzwihr,

France, Murphy's Company B was attacked by six [German] tanks and waves of infantry. Second Lieutenant Murphy ordered his men to withdraw to prepare positions in a woods, while he remained forward at his command post to direct the artillery. One of his company's tank destroyers received a direct hit and began to burn. Lieutenant Murphy climbed on the burning tank destroyer and trained its machine gun on the enemy, killing dozens and causing their infantry attack to waver. He held his position for more than an hour, received a leg wound, but continued the fight until his ammunition was exhausted. He then made his way to his company, refused medical attention, and organized the company in a counterattack which forced the enemy to withdraw."[2]*

Sergeant Basilone's record is similarly amazing: "Basilone was awarded the Medal of Honor during World War II for holding 3,000 Japanese soldiers at bay for 72 hours at Guadalcanal with only 15 men, 12 of whom died. Following this act of heroism, he was sent to the States to promote War Bonds. He later requested return to his unit to 'be with my boys.' Basilone was posthumously awarded the Navy Cross and Purple Heart for destroying a Japanese gun emplacement at Iwo Jima. He was killed there during a shelling attack."[3]

The government made sure that verified stories of sacrifice like those of the five Sullivan brothers were widely circulated. The Sullivans, all young sailors, were lost on the USS *Juneau*.** Also nationally known was the inspiring story of the Four Chaplains—Reverend George Fox, a Methodist minister; Rabbi Alexander Goode; the Reverend Clark Poling, a Dutch Reformed minister; and Father John Washington, a Catholic priest. These brave clergymen gave up their life jackets to young soldiers

---

* Audie Murphy would go to Hollywood to star in his own story, *To Hell and Back*. The movie colony then turned out many a story of wartime heroism.

** This Waterloo, Iowa, family's loss was greater than that which prompted President Lincoln to write his famous letter to Mrs. Bixby during the Civil War. The tragedy also led the War Department to discontinue the practice of allowing brothers to serve in combat together, as the tight-knit Sullivan brothers had requested.

and crewmen aboard the USS *Dorchester* as the overcrowded troop transport went down in the frigid waters off Greenland, the victim of a Nazi U-boat.[4]

FDR undertook another arduous journey in November 1943. He agreed to meet Churchill and Stalin in Tehran, the capital of Iran, for the first summit meeting of what was soon dubbed "The Big Three." Stalin feared to leave the USSR, always mistrustful, always seeing betrayal lurking everywhere. FDR turned down Churchill's invitation to stay at the British Embassy. He didn't want it to appear that the democracies were "ganging up" on Stalin. The U.S. Embassy was too far out of the city, so FDR accepted Stalin's invitation to use an entire house within the Soviet Embassy compound. Stalin told Roosevelt he had intelligence that the Germans would attempt to kidnap the American president. Later, FDR's roving ambassador, Averell Harriman, said he doubted the plot. Instead, he thought Stalin wanted the American president to stay in quarters that had already been bugged by his secret police, the NKVD.[5]

Roosevelt turned down a meeting request by Churchill and met first, instead, with Stalin. When the Big Three finally gathered, it became clear that Stalin shared Roosevelt's disdain for French General Charles de Gaulle because France had collapsed so quickly in 1940.* Stalin had an additional reason to dismiss de Gaulle. A vibrant, non-Communist France would impede his plans for a postwar European settlement. De Gaulle was an obstacle to the Soviets' plan of domination.[6] FDR seemed to go out of his way to tease Churchill in Stalin's presence. Harry Hopkins noted that Stalin was elegantly dressed in a field marshal's uniform, that he smoked his pipe and doodled—constantly drawing wolves—and that he spoke in a barely audible whisper.[7]

The main business of the meeting was a commitment by the United States and Britain to open a "second front" in Western Europe. Stalin

---

* Conveniently forgotten was the fact that French Communists, under orders from Stalin himself, had obstructed the French defense effort both in the army and in key industries. This was because Stalin in 1940 was still Hitler's ally.

continually returned to the theme that the Red Army was doing all the fighting against the Nazis. In terms of numbers of troops engaged, this was largely true. He said he would be willing to break his neutrality toward Japan (the USSR was alone among the United Nations in *not* being at war with Japan), but he would be able to come into the war in the Pacific only *after* the Germans had been defeated. Roosevelt was satisfied with this. Even then, General MacArthur was brilliantly "island-hopping" in the Pacific, bringing the war closer to the Japanese home islands every day. When FDR and Churchill committed early in 1944 to "Overlord," the planned invasion of France, the mistrustful Stalin demanded to know the identity of the Allies' Supreme Commander: "What is his name?"[8]

Stalin would know soon enough. On his long way home from Tehran, FDR met with General Dwight D. Eisenhower in Tunis, North Africa. Almost casually, the president leaned over and said, "Well, Ike, you are going to command Overlord."[9] Not all of FDR's commanders relished the president's breezy informality. When he tried to call the dignified chief of staff of the army by his first name, the very able General George C. Marshall visibly recoiled. "[H]e called me 'George'—I don't think he ever did it again."[10]

Everyone revered General Marshall. Churchill called him "the noblest Roman of them all." It was said of him that even if he entered his Washington office in civilian clothes, the young newsboys might not know *who* he was, but they would sure know *what* he was.[11]

Far from being put off by General Marshall's cool reserve, FDR trusted him and kept promoting him. Marshall far outranked Ike and could have had the command of Overlord simply by asking for it. Still, he told the president he would serve *wherever* the commander in chief needed him. FDR moved decisively to name Ike to command Overlord, telling Marshall, "I didn't feel I could sleep at ease if you were out of Washington."[12*]

---

* The man who said "The only thing we have to fear is fear itself" did have one fear: a White House fire in the night. He regularly practiced rolling himself out of bed and propelling himself along the floor with his powerful arms.

Churchill feared the cross-Channel invasion would fail. "We might be giving the enemy the opportunity to concentrate . . . an overwhelming force against us and to inflict on us a military disaster greater than . . . Dunkirk. Such a disaster would result in the resuscitation of Hitler and the Nazi regime."[13] He spoke darkly of "the tide running red" with the blood of young American, British, and Canadian soldiers.[14]

Ike had to contend with troubles in England. General George Patton, who began the war as Ike's senior but who was now his difficult subordinate, had given a speech to a local English group in which he said the British and the Americans would together rule the world after the war. Moscow fumed and congressmen back home flamed. Newspapers demanded that Patton be fired. Ike let Patton stew for a week before telling him he could stay:

> When I gave him the verdict, tears streamed down his face and he tried to assure me of his gratitude. He gave me his promise that thereafter he would be a model of discretion and in a gesture of almost little-boy contriteness, he put his head on my shoulder as he said it.
>
> This caused his helmet to fall off—the gleaming helmet I sometimes thought he wore while in bed. As it rolled across the room I had the rather odd feeling that I was in the middle of a ridiculous situation. . . . I prayed that no one would come in and see the scene and that there were no news cameras at the window.[15]

"OK, let's go!" That was Dwight D. Eisenhower's order when his staff meteorologist gave him a brief break in the stormy weather that had forced a twenty-four-hour postponement of D-Day. Ike had prepared a statement to be issued in the event the invaders were thrown back into the chilly waters of the English Channel. In it, he took complete responsibility for the failure of Overlord.[16] Fortunately, that statement was never issued.

Ike commanded a larger invasion force than the world had ever seen. He had assembled 150,000 men, 1,500 tanks, 5,300 ships, and 12,000 aircraft.[17]

The Allies had gone to elaborate lengths to disguise their intended target—the beaches of Normandy. They created a false impression among the Germans that they would invade France at Calais—the closest point from Dover on the English side. Allied intelligence shuddered when, by pure coincidence, the word *Overlord* appeared in a crossword puzzle so beloved of the English newspaper readers.[18] More seriously, Ike withheld his invasion plans from General de Gaulle and the Free French until mere hours before launch.*

As Supreme Commander, Ike could give orders to millions—but not to Churchill or FDR. When the prime minister insisted on joining the invasion fleet on D-Day, Ike tried to dissuade him. Ike admired the cigar-chomping, sixty-nine-year-old leader's courage, but he didn't want him interfering. And he didn't want to bear the responsibility if Churchill were killed. Failing to dent Winston's resolve, Ike appealed to King George VI. Only when the king told Winston that he would join him on the beaches was the irrepressible Churchill finally repressed.

Ike proclaimed the expedition "a great crusade." He issued a General Order telling his men, "The eyes of the world are upon you." And so they were.

As army rangers scaled the cliffs at Pointe-du-Hoc on Omaha Beach, a toehold on the European continent was seized.** On the night of 6 June 1944, after what many called "the longest day," President Roosevelt asked the nation to join him in prayer:

> Almighty God: Our sons, pride of our Nation, this day have set upon a mighty endeavor, a struggle to preserve our Republic, our religion, and our civilization, and to set free a suffering humanity.

---

* It was their country, after all, that was being liberated, but the Free French had a bad reputation for leaks. This was not from any sympathy for the Axis but because a passionate people could not resist telling loved ones they would soon be home.

** President Reagan would immortalize "the boys of Pointe-du-Hoc" in his speech on the fortieth anniversary of D-Day in 1984. The Normandy landing beaches, code-named Omaha and Utah (American), Juno (Canadian), and Sword and Gold (British), retain those names to this day.

Lead them straight and true; give strength to their arms, stoutness to their hearts, steadfastness in their faith.

They will need Thy blessings. Their road will be long and hard. For the enemy is strong. He may hurl back our forces. Success may not come with rushing speed, but we shall return again and again; and we know that by Thy grace, and by the righteousness of our cause, our sons will triumph.

They will be sore tried, by night and by day, without rest—until the victory is won. The darkness will be rent by noise and flame. Men's souls will be shaken with the violences of war.

For these men are lately drawn from the ways of peace. They fight not for the lust of conquest. They fight to end conquest. They fight to liberate. They fight to let justice arise, and tolerance and good will among all Thy people. They yearn but for the end of battle, for their return to the haven of home.

Some will never return. Embrace these, Father, and receive them, Thy heroic servants, into Thy kingdom.

And for us at home—fathers, mothers, children, wives, sisters, and brothers of brave men overseas—whose thoughts and prayers are ever with them—help us, Almighty God, to rededicate ourselves in renewed faith in Thee in this hour of great sacrifice.[19]

The cost of freedom was indeed great. Of the 75,215 British and Canadian troops who landed on D-Day, 4,300 became casualties. The losses suffered by Americans were even greater. The United States suffered 6,000 casualties among the 57,500 troops who stormed the beaches. President Roosevelt's prayer also went out for his own relatives. His cousin Brigadier General Theodore Roosevelt Jr. was on the beach. When told that he had landed at the wrong point on Utah Beach, the son of President Theodore Roosevelt gamely said, "No, we'll start the war from right here." General Roosevelt had come ashore with his son, the only father-and-son team to land that day. Exhausted by his exertions, Theodore Roosevelt Jr. was dead of a heart attack three weeks later.

The seemingly impregnable Fortress Europa, which had been strengthened substantially by Field Marshal Rommel, could not be held. Rommel knew that the only way to defeat the Allied invasion was to beat it on the beaches. But he could not persuade Hitler that the invasion was actually coming in Normandy. Hitler persisted in believing that the main invasion force would come at Calais. General George S. Patton headed up Operation Fortitude for precisely that purpose—to deceive Hitler.[20] And it worked.

Soon, the Allied Expeditionary Force met stiff resistance in the hedgerow country of Normandy. These thousand-year-old obstructions were a thick undergrowth of tree roots and hedges that could hardly be bulldozed by attacking tanks. Sometimes six to eight feet high, they formed a perfect defensive works for the retreating Germans. The leading city in Normandy, Caen, was supposed to be taken on D-Day+3; it was not liberated until D-Day+31. Allied soldiers took thousands of Germans prisoner but also lost many to the Germans. When word of the murder of Canadian POWs by SS troops spread, it fired the Allies' anger.

Americans were gratified by the response of the Norman peasants. One story of the loss of an American "fly-boy" speaks across the decades. Ten days after D-Day, Lieutenant Conrad J. Netting III went into action against a German truck convoy. Lieutenant Netting and his wife were expecting their first child back in the States. He even put his unborn son's name on the nose of his plane, a P-51 Mustang. He dove down on the convoy in his "Con Jon IV," but the fighter failed to pull out of a steep dive. What happened next was related years later in a letter from a French villager: "My grandfather ran with some neighbors to the cemetery, just by the place of the crash to help the pilot, but unfortunately it was too late. . . . My grandfather [the village cabinetmaker] made the casket and took care of your father. . . . On his grave was a mountain of flowers."[21] In the village of Saint Michel, a plaque today commemorates the brave young American's sacrifice: "Lt. NETTING, CONRAD J., 8th U.S. Air Force No. 0694174. Mort pour la liberté le 10.6.1944." He died, as did all our brave men, for *liberty*.

On 20 July 1944, as German troops were retreating from Russia and fighting a losing battle in Normandy, a German officer attended a meeting at the *Wolfsschanze*—the Wolf's Lair.* It was Hitler's secret headquarters in East Prussia, near the Russian border. The officer was Colonel Claus von Stauffenberg. He was everything Hitler hated—a devout Catholic, an aristocrat, and a man of moral scruple. Stauffenberg had asked his bishop if it was permissible to kill a tyrant. Told that it was licit, Stauffenberg left a bomb in a briefcase under the table at the Wolf's Lair and left the Führer's staff conference, supposedly to take a phone call. A huge explosion destroyed the building, killed several generals, and left Hitler wounded—but not dead. The widespread plot on Hitler's life soon fell apart. Stauffenberg quickly faced a firing squad. Hitler's revenge was terrible. He ordered Himmler's SS to arrest thousands of actual or suspected conspirators—including all their family members. Thousands simply disappeared into *nacht und nebel* ("night and fog"). Show trials were staged to humiliate elderly generals and aristocrats. The victims were hanged from meat hooks, dying of slow strangulation. Hitler had their deaths filmed. Afterward, his health was shattered, and his arm shook uncontrollably, but his death grip on Germany continued.**

Once the Allies were ashore in Normandy, the overwhelming power of America's economic strength began to be felt by the Germans. One of their area commanders expressed his sense of futility to his superiors. It took courage to commit these words to paper in a Wehrmacht shadowed by Himmler's SS. He might have been arrested and shot for "defeatism":

---

* Stalin's constant doodling of *volky*—wolves—and Hitler's obvious fascination with the ravening animals was hardly the only similarity in the character of these homicidal dictators.

** Hitler's poisonous vengeance—the key to his character—knew no bounds. He forced Field Marshal Rommel to commit suicide even though Rommel was only remotely connected with the July 20th plot. And Hitler made sure the heroic Lutheran pastor Dietrich Bonhoeffer was hanged just days before the whole Nazi regime collapsed in 1945. Bonhoeffer had been a leader of the "Confessing Church" movement—Christians in Germany who refused to bend the knee to Hitler. Bonhoeffer's writings, including *The Cost of Discipleship* and *Life Together*, are classics of Christian literature.

I cannot understand these Americans. Each night we know that we have cut them to pieces, inflicted heavy casualties, mowed down their transport. But in the morning, we are suddenly faced with fresh battalions, with complete replacements of men, machines, food, tools, and weapons. This happens day after day.[22]

II. "THE SUN GOES DOWN ON MORE SUFFERING . . ."

The railroad trains filled with Jews bound for the extermination camp at Auschwitz accelerated their pace as even the most fanatical Nazis must have seen the war was lost. Many Jews died of suffocation en route. The terrified survivors who emerged from the packed freight cars were marched through the gates of Auschwitz. Guards beat stragglers with truncheons or sicced dogs on them. Above the entrance gate was a sign that said ARBEIT MACHT FREI ("work makes you free"). It was just another of the Nazi regime's lies. Millions entered those gates never to return.

The sad history of the world is replete with mass murder, sporadic persecutions, massacres, outbreaks of hatred, even genocide. Most of these, like the anti-Semitic pogroms of Tsarist Russia, were deadly outbursts of short duration. Hitler's Final Solution, however, was a systematic nightmare that applied the techniques of the factory assembly line to the project of mass murder. Hitler's willing accomplices calculated the value of the gold they could extract from the teeth of their victims. Vast gas chambers were supplied with deadly Zyklon B by seemingly legitimate German firms like I. G. Farben. Huge crematoria were constructed to dispose of the remains.

In a rare moment of sorrowful introspection, Churchill considered the world stage on which he played so colorful and important a part: "I do not suppose that at any moment in history had the agony of the world been so great or so widespread. Tonight the sun goes down on more suffering than ever before in the world."[23]

The Allied sweep into Germany bogged down in the summer of 1944. General Eisenhower was pressed by French General de Gaulle to divert his forces to aid in the liberation of Paris. Ike did *not* want the burden of three million extra mouths to feed.[24] But de Gaulle emphasized that if the Allies failed to free Paris, the Germans might destroy it or else the Communists among the Resistance forces might seize the city and establish a Soviet government in the heart of Western Europe. And, please, de Gaulle added, let *French* troops enter the city first. "You may be certain," Ike replied, "I wouldn't dream of taking Paris without French soldiers."[25]

True to his word, Ike magnanimously approved General Omar Bradley's decision to let French General Leclerc enter Paris first. He would allow Free French soldiers the honor of retaking their capital after four long years of German occupation.* Fulfilling a pledge to Eisenhower, de Gaulle specifically disapproved the attempt of Colonel Rol-Tanguy, the Communist leader in Paris, to claim equal credit for the surrender of the German garrison.[26] To an outburst of Gallic joy and affection, the Americans marched smartly down the Champs Elysée through liberated Paris—and right back into battle![27]

Not so happy was the fate of Warsaw. The Poles hoped to free themselves from German cruelty, just as the Parisians were doing. But Ike was nowhere near. Instead, it was the Red Army that was pressing the Germans from the East. When Warsaw rose up, however, Stalin ordered his troops to halt just outside the city. The Germans ruthlessly destroyed what was left of the beautiful medieval city, the jewel of Slavic culture and sophistication. Stalin deliberately held back while the Poles were annihilated by vengeful Germans. When Churchill and Roosevelt appealed to Stalin to allow Allied flyers to land and refuel within Soviet lines after air-dropping supplies to the desperate Polish Resistance, he bluntly refused.[28] It was the first crack in Allied wartime unity.

---

* Ike's sensitivity to wounded French pride would be gratefully remembered when de Gaulle came to power as president of France in 1959 and Eisenhower was serving as president of the United States.

Britain came under renewed German attack in the summer of 1944. By this time, the vaunted Luftwaffe was almost destroyed. The few German planes that could get into the air were limited to a few minutes of flying by the shortage of fuel. Too late, Hitler introduced the world's first jet fighter aircraft. The *Messerschmitt* ME-262 could have turned the tide of war had it been employed one year earlier. Now Hitler unleashed his new Vengeance weapons, the V-1 and V-2 rockets. Launched from a site in Germany called Peenemunde, thousands of these deadly weapons landed on London, Southampton, Portsmouth, and Manchester. The vast majority of the 3,500 rockets that escaped being shot down landed on London, causing great devastation and killing 6,184 people.[29]*

During this fateful summer of 1944, the Allies began to get reliable word on Auschwitz. Allied bombers that had flown resupply missions over Warsaw were bringing back photographs of the death camps at Auschwitz and Treblinka.

Churchill favored bombing the railroad junction that led to Auschwitz. He told his foreign minister, Anthony Eden, "This is probably the greatest and most horrible single crime ever committed in the whole history of the world."[30] Churchill called for action. "Invoke my name," he told Eden.

FDR spoke out publicly against the Holocaust and did not hide his contempt for Hitler:

> In one of the blackest crimes in all history . . . the wholesale, system-
> atic murder of the Jews of Europe goes on unabated every hour. . . .
> None who participate in these acts of savagery shall go unpunished [a
> clear warning of postwar tribunals]. All who knowingly take part in

---

* The V-1 and V-2 were the work of the ingenious young German rocket scientist Wernher von Braun. Not only was von Braun *not* charged with war crimes for developing and deploying this indiscriminate terror weapon, he and his Peenemunde team were welcomed into the United States at the war's end. At the end of the war, von Braun led his team of rocket scientists West, hoping to surrender to the Americans. He succeeded. Von Braun would later lead America's race to the moon.

the deportation of the Jews to their death in Poland or Norwegians and French to their death in Germany are equally guilty with the executioner himself.... Hitler is committing these crimes against humanity in the name of the German people.[31]

Roosevelt and Churchill were moved to outrage, but FDR had to consider Stalin's reaction. What would the grim Soviet dictator think about a joint Anglo-American action in Poland? Stalin was increasingly viewing Poland as a Soviet sphere of influence. Would he be moved by humanitarian concerns? Not likely.[32]

FDR thought his demand for unconditional surrender was the surest way to end the mass murder of the Jews. After all, he may well have reasoned, Hitler did not want to murder only the Jews of Poland; he wanted to murder *all* the Jews. If he broke out into Palestine or counterattacked in Russia or, worse, if he developed an atomic bomb to place on one of his V-2 rockets, the death toll could be even greater. To many, it seemed the quickest way to kill a venomous snake was to go for the head. Hitler was the head.

In the summer of 1944, FDR was distracted. He would have to run for another term, an unprecedented *fourth* campaign for the White House. And he was seriously ill. Once, in his railroad car, he begged his son Jimmy to help him get out of bed to lie flat on the floor. He refused to summon a doctor and attributed the shooting pains he suffered to indigestion. We now know he was suffering from angina—a form of heart disease.[33]

FDR chose Senator Harry Truman of Missouri to be his running mate for his fourth term. Truman was reluctant. He knew Roosevelt was desperately ill, and he didn't *want* to be president of the United States.

When Democratic National Chairman Bob Hannegan brought Harry to his suite in Chicago's Blackstone Hotel, he called the president on the phone. FDR was in San Diego, inspecting the naval base there. The president's familiar rich tenor voice boomed out in the hotel room. "Bob, have you got that guy lined up on the Vice Presidency?"[34]

Hannegan's rough answer may have been intended to shake loose the reluctant Truman. "No," he growled into the receiver, as he looked directly at Harry. "He is the contrariest g—d—mule from Missouri I ever dealt with." FDR fairly shouted back, "Well, you tell the Senator if he wants to break up the Democratic Party in the middle of the war, that's *his* responsibility!" With that, Roosevelt slammed down the phone. Harry's reaction, reportedly, was very human. "Oh s—!" he exclaimed.[35] It was done. Truman's resistance wilted in the face of the president's displeasure.

From the naval base at San Diego, FDR proceeded to Hawaii for an important war council with General Douglas MacArthur and Admiral Chester Nimitz. Nimitz wanted to drive straight for Japan. MacArthur disagreed. He proceeded to warn the president of the dangers of bypassing the Philippines: "I dare say the American people would be so aroused that they would register most complete resentment against you at the polls."[36] Once again, a leading general could not resist lecturing the commander in chief on his political responsibilities—just as McClellan had tried to instruct Lincoln. But the Philippines had been an American colony since 1898, so the case for liberating the islands from Japanese occupation—and the tens of thousands of U.S. and Filipino POWs in enemy hands—was a strong one.

Following the Pacific conference, FDR decided to visit a military hospital in Hawaii. He asked to be taken to the wards where the young amputees were. Ordinarily, Roosevelt took care *not* to be seen being wheeled about in his wheelchair. This time, however, he had himself pushed, slowly, deliberately past the bedsides of the wounded men. "He insisted on going past each individual bed. He wanted to display himself and his useless legs to those boys who would have to face the same bitterness," reported FDR's aide, Sam Rosenman. Rosenman marveled that "this man who had risen from a bed of helplessness ultimately to become President of the United States and leader of the free world was living proof of what the human spirit could do."[37]

FDR was actually trailing in the polls going into the 1944 campaign.[38] The Republicans had nominated the energetic, youthful Governor Thomas

E. Dewey of New York. Dewey was given credit as a crusading district attorney for putting behind bars many members of "Murder, Inc.," an offshoot of the Mob. He was intelligent and sharp-tongued. Republicans attacked what they called the "Roosevelt Recession." Americans were clearly tired after twelve years of Depression, reform, and now war.

Economic conditions were clearly better in 1944. War production had led to high employment and improved wages, to be sure. But the tight controls and strict rationing grated on people's nerves. There was widespread resentment and suspicion that people were skirting the regulations on the black market.* Rumors spread through every town that the well heeled or the well connected were eating T-bone steaks behind their drawn blackout curtains.

Roosevelt waited until late in the season to enter the campaign. He was at this point working shorter days, tiring easily. When he did weigh in, however, the old campaigner proved a masterful politician. To dispel rumors of his fragile health, FDR took a four-hour campaign ride through the boroughs of New York City in an open car.[39] Hundreds of thousands of Americans lined his route to cheer themselves hoarse. Blue-collar workers, in particular, yelled their heads off. FDR beamed and waved and rode through a freezing rain. He was drenched to the skin. It was a bold and dangerous gamble. If anything, however, the dying Roosevelt seemed to draw strength from the love of the people. It was to be for him his last hurrah.

Roosevelt could not bring together all the elements of his coalition, however. The irascible Joe Kennedy, threatening to endorse Dewey, met with FDR in the White House in late October. Bluntly, he told the president his advisers were disserving him. "They have surrounded you with Jews and Communists," Kennedy said angrily.[40] Later, he complained to Harry Truman about Roosevelt: "That cripple . . . killed my son Joe."[41] In

---

* A *black market* is the term given to any "underground" or illegal market in goods or services. Whenever rationing or government price-fixing occurs, a black market springs up almost automatically.

fact, Joe Kennedy Jr. had volunteered for the dangerous mission of flying over the English Channel in a plane loaded with explosives. The death of Joe Jr. would mean that all of Joe Kennedy's ambitions would come to rest on his surviving twenty-seven-year-old second son, John Fitzgerald Kennedy.

On Election Day, Roosevelt triumphed a fourth time. He won 25,602,505 popular votes (53.3 percent) and 432 electoral votes to Dewey's 22,006,278 popular votes (45.8 percent) and 99 electoral votes.

Freedom triumphed when the United States held national elections in the midst of World War II. No longer were people thinking that dictatorships were more efficient and clearly the wave of the future. Italy was out of the war, Germany and Japan were on the defensive, and the democracies were on the rise. The democracies *plus* the Soviet Union, that is. Few could deny that the Red Army was playing a major role in bringing down Hitler. And few could argue that Stalin was a democrat. "When are you going to stop killing people?" asked the audacious Lady Astor of the Soviet dictator at a Kremlin dinner. She was Britain's first woman member of Parliament, and it took courage to ask Stalin that question in his own den. His Communist comrades froze, but Stalin simply pulled on his pipe and mildly replied, "When it is no longer necessary."[42] "Democracy," as Churchill said, "is based on the idea that it is better to count heads than to bash them." It is not an idea Stalin the head basher ever understood.

Roosevelt was reelected and France was largely liberated by late 1944. The German rocket ranges at Peenemunde were overrun. It seemed that only "mopping up" was required to cross the River Rhine and end the war in Europe. When Allied troops advanced to Hitler's Siegfried Line, Germany lay open to invasion. Churchill visited the supposedly impregnable defensive position. He winked at the men—military and civilian journalists—who had accompanied him. Then he led them all in urinating on Hitler's famous line!

If Americans thought that the war in Europe was over, Hitler did not. He secretly planned a major counteroffensive against the Western Allies.

In fact, he stripped his Eastern divisions, fatally weakening his defense against the onrushing Red Army.

Hitler's Ardennes campaign began on 16 December 1944. Taking advantage of the heavy snow and low visibility, German Panzer tanks came crashing through the forests. Americans were taken by surprise. The Battle of the Bulge, as it quickly became known, was the Germans' last thrust in the West. The second day of the battle, eighty American POWs were murdered in cold blood outside the Belgian town of Malmédy. This Malmédy Massacre was the bloody work of the SS.

The Americans suffered greatly at the Bulge, and not merely from German Panzers. The merciless winter claimed casualties of its own. Night fell by 4:45 p.m. in these northerly latitudes. Even Americans from the Dakotas found the cold numbing. "Riding in a jeep through the Ardennes," recalled Colonel Ralph Ingersoll, "I wore woolen underwear, a woolen uniform, armored force combat overalls, a sweater, an armored field jacket with elastic cuffs, a muffler, a heavily lined trench coat, two pairs of heavy woolen socks, and combat boots with galoshes over them—and I can never remember ever being warm."[43] Thousands came down with frostbite and "trench foot," a deadly disease that came from having the foot exposed to dampness for long periods. G.I.s typically hung their wet socks around their necks to provide a spare pair that would be warm and dry.[44]

The tough, battle-hardened U.S. 101st Airborne Division had landed on D-Day. Now, it was surrounded by advancing Germans in the little Belgian town of Bastogne. But when the German commander demanded surrender, the leader of the 101st, General Anthony McAuliffe, replied eloquently, "Nuts!"[45]

Ike ordered General Patton to disengage and head north to relieve Bastogne. By Christmas Eve, the cloud cover lifted. Eisenhower was able to bring to bear his overwhelming air power. That night, two thousand Allied aircraft attacked thirty-one German targets, destroying them. Along with the critical shortage of fuel and the spirited American counteroffensive, the German drive was soon blunted. The Germans suffered more than a hundred thousand casualties in the Battle of the Bulge.[46]

America's victory in the Battle of the Bulge was a tribute to Eisenhower's cool courage, Patton's dash, and McAuliffe's defiance. Most of all, it was a tribute to the soldiers of democracy. The Americans' resourcefulness under the severest conditions of battle and weather was completely underestimated by Hitler and his generals.[47]

III. YALTA

The next Big Three summit meeting was in Yalta. Stalin could not have chosen a *worse* place for the leaders' conference "if we had spent ten years on research," Churchill complained when he learned of the destination.[48]

Yalta was in the Crimea, a region of the Ukraine only recently liberated from German occupation. It was the seaside summer resort of the tsars. The meeting would be held in the Livadia Palace. For FDR, it would be torture. He would have to fly for long hours in his presidential plane from the Mediterranean island of Malta.* Then he would have to drive by car for eight hours. It was a grueling trip for the rapidly failing chief executive.

Meeting with Stalin on his home territory meant, once again, that the quarters assigned to the Allied leaders would be bugged. The maids, butlers, cooks, guards, and all others who came into contact with the Westerners would be employees of the NKVD. Stalin himself made no bones about that. In a jovial mood, he pointed out to Roosevelt one of the Soviet delegates. "That's my Himmler," he said.[49] He was speaking of Lavrentii Beria, the grim head of Stalin's secret police.

FDR knew it would be difficult to deal with the Soviet dictator,

---

* The four-engine, propeller-driven plane had few of the amenities we have come to associate with today's *Air Force One*. Slow, cramped, and stuffy, the president's plane was called *The Sacred Cow*. The name was given by cynical members of the press corps. Some things never change.

especially now that the Red Army was poised for the final assault on Berlin. He had confided in Francis Cardinal Spellman, the Catholic archbishop of New York, that he expected the Soviets to dominate Eastern Europe after the war. He hoped to use diplomacy and generous U.S. aid to guarantee a mild rule.[50]

Roosevelt had to contend not only with Stalin but also with his legions of Soviet supporters in the United States. Walter Duranty, the Moscow correspondent of the *New York Times*, spoke for many of those supporters when he wrote that the "Russians are not less free than we are."[51] Americans were eager to finish the fight and bring the boys home. With twelve million in uniform, there was hardly an American family that did not have an empty place at the supper table. FDR had to consider this powerful sentiment as he sat down with Churchill and Stalin in the ornate palace of the tsars.

Churchill wanted France restored to power and influence. It was not that he found General de Gaulle easy to deal with. He said the "hardest cross I've had to bear is the Cross of Lorraine."* But Churchill wanted a strong France as a counter to rising Soviet power in Europe. Pressing hard, day after day, Stalin finally threw his hands up and said, "I surrender."[52] Stalin, ever the realist, let the British and the Americans give France a Zone of Occupation in Germany *provided it was carved out of the territory already allotted to the Western Allies.* His willingness to let the French sit on the European Advisory Council that would administer occupied Germany was not as generous as it seemed. He had already shown that he could influence the French through his control of the powerful French Communist Party.

If Churchill successfully held out for a restored France, FDR similarly pumped for China to be treated as a Great Power.[53] In the United Nations

---

* General de Gaulle had made the Cross of Lorraine the symbol of his Free French movement. This contrasted strongly with the atheism of the Communists who greatly influenced the French Resistance.

Organization the leaders were planning for the postwar settlement, both France and China would have permanent seats on the Security Council.

Poland was the great issue. Stalin promised "a strong, free, independent and democratic Poland."[54] The difficulty was how Stalin defined democracy. As he had said, it doesn't matter who casts the votes; what matters is who *counts* them. Wouldn't the pope be upset if atheist Communist rule were imposed on Catholic Poles? Stalin had a ready answer: "The Pope? How many divisions has he got?"[55]

Roosevelt hoped he could press the Soviets to respect the agreements they had signed on the treatment of "liberated Europe." But he believed he *had* to have Stalin's help in the coming invasion of the Japanese home islands. Stalin had held out throughout the war, claiming the urgency of defeating Hitler. Now, with the Nazis clearly on their last legs, Stalin finally agreed. The Soviets would join the war against Japan "two or three months" after the Germans surrendered. FDR and his military chiefs were jubilant. Admiral Ernest King enthused, "*We just saved two million American lives!*"[56]

Yalta was—and remains—a highly controversial summit. British Field Marshal Montgomery may have been the first to call it another "Munich," suggesting that Roosevelt and Churchill deliberately sold out Poland and Eastern Europe to Stalin for the sake of peace. Many Roosevelt defenders try to excuse the Yalta agreements by saying FDR was deathly ill, that he really cannot be held responsible. But Averell Harriman, a Roosevelt confidant and a shrewd judge of Soviet intentions, said the president was "worn, wasted, but alert."[57]

The reality was Stalin's hundreds of divisions. No one remotely contemplated war with Stalin to force him back inside the USSR's prewar boundaries. Thus, other than attempting to ply him with Lend-Lease and demonstrations of American and British goodwill, what else could the Allied leaders have done?

There is little doubt that FDR's attempt to forge a personal relationship with Stalin was—as conservative scholar Robert Nisbet has called it—"A failed courtship."[58] Franklin Roosevelt seemed to have little appreciation of the radical threat posed by aggressive, subversive Communism. There is good reason to think that Roosevelt himself recognized this courtship as failed. Two weeks before his death, FDR exclaimed in anguish, "[Stalin] has broken every one of the promises he made at Yalta!"[59]

Critics rightly point to the presence at Yalta of Alger Hiss, a Soviet agent. Hiss was a top State Department official, an FDR appointee, who would travel to Moscow after Yalta and secretly receive the Order of the Red Star.[60] And he was not the only one. Lawrence Duggan of the State Department and Harry Dexter White, a top Treasury Department official, were also Soviet agents.[61]

The shocking reality is that the government of the United States was dangerously penetrated by Soviet agents. To many at the time, however, this was no more sinister than the presence of many British sympathizers in high federal office.

The Soviet people were widely admired for their stubborn, brave resistance to the Nazi invaders. Stalin was seen as a stern, avuncular figure, a Russian authoritarian, but not as the ruthless, homicidal monster subsequent historical research has proved him to be. Americans had sympathy for the twenty million lives lost in the Soviet Union's "Great Patriotic War." They never saw the millions of returning Soviet POWs who were sent directly to the Gulag. If this seems insane to us, it must be remembered that these prisoners of the Nazis knew how unprepared Stalin had been for war and how much better everyone in Europe lived than the people of the Soviet Union. To Stalin, anyone who was captured was a traitor. He made no attempt to gain the release of any of the millions of Russian captives. He even let his own son, Yakov, die in a German POW camp rather than exchange him for the German Field Marshal von Paulus.

Returning from Yalta, President Roosevelt went immediately before Congress. There, he addressed a joint session to deliver a report on the summit. For the first time, he spoke while sitting down. It was also the first time he ever referred to his infirmity in public, referring to the "ten pounds of metal braces" on his legs. He made a point of telling the members that he had fully briefed the other participants on the U.S. Constitution and how it required Senate approval for all treaties. Wisely, he appealed to Congress for its help. He avoided the confrontational posture President Wilson had assumed after World War I.* He said there was not room in the world for "German militarism and Christian decency."[62] He spoke quite openly of the compromise on the Polish border question. The Soviet Union had been given hundreds of miles of formerly Polish territory in the East; Poland was "compensated" by being given vast German lands in East Prussia. (The Poles were not consulted on this swap.) Roosevelt showed himself committed to free elections in Eastern Europe and to a new international organization, the United Nations, to take the place of the League of Nations.[63] Few Americans would have complained if the Yalta agreements had actually been carried out.

Meanwhile, in the Pacific, General MacArthur had liberated the Philippines and was moving ever closer to Japan. Increasingly desperate, the Japanese military leaders unleashed *kamikaze* pilots. The word means "divine wind." In truth, it was a deadly wave of suicide pilots who crashed their planes into U.S. Navy ships. During the U.S. invasion of the island of Okinawa, in April 1945, kamikaze attackers destroyed thirty-six U.S. warships and inflicted damage on 368.[64] Thousands of U.S. sailors and marines were killed in these brutal attacks.

Although all the summit conferences focused primarily on the European Theater, as the war against Germany was called, the tens of thousands of casualties in the Pacific guaranteed American interest in the war against Japan. Young Lieutenant (Junior Grade) John F. Kennedy found his Patrol Torpedo boat (PT-109) cut in half one dark night by a Japanese destroyer. Kennedy swam to a nearby island, pulling a wounded crewman with him and leading the others to safety. He was decorated for valor.

Another lieutenant (Junior Grade), George H. W. Bush, had dropped

---

* Of course, Wilson faced a Republican-controlled Congress. FDR's fellow Democrats were in firm control of *both* Houses.

out of Yale to become the youngest naval aviator in history. When his plane was shot down near Chichi Jima, his two crewmen were lost. Bush frantically paddled his life raft away from the Japanese-held island. He desperately wanted to avoid capture by the savage Japanese who were known to behead downed American fliers and consume their flesh.[65] Soon, Bush was relieved to see the submarine USS *Skate* surfacing to rescue him. The suicidal resistance of the Japanese and the widely circulated stories of atrocities from prisoners of war liberated in the Philippines made a deep, deep impression on millions of Americans.

IV. HARRY TRUMAN: "THE MOON, THE STARS, AND ALL THE PLANETS"

Still exhausted from his strenuous journey to Yalta and back, FDR went to Warm Springs, Georgia, for some rest in the balmy April breezes. There, Lucy Rutherfurd brought the painter Elisabeth Shoumatoff to do a portrait of the president. Rutherfurd had been Franklin's mistress nearly thirty years before.[66] As a condition of Eleanor's agreeing not to divorce him, FDR had promised never to see Lucy again. But here, lonely and sick, he had asked his daughter Anna to invite Lucy back. FDR needed companionship; he needed a warm, accepting friend. Eleanor, with her constant causes, projects, and endless petitioning for the less fortunate, wore Franklin out.

On the morning of 12 April 1945, while sitting for the portrait, President Roosevelt put his finger to his temple, saying, "I have a terrific headache." With that, he collapsed and died.[67] Eleanor immediately learned of Lucy's presence, but the country knew nothing of it. Eleanor coldly dismissed her daughter, whom she knew had helped her father arrange for Lucy's visit. In time, though, Anna and Eleanor were reconciled. And Eleanor later even exchanged forgiving letters with Lucy.

The country was shocked by the president's death. For millions, Franklin Delano Roosevelt had been the only president they had ever known. As he had wished, the funeral ceremonies were very simple. His casket was carried by horse-drawn caisson through Washington, D.C., and thence by train to Hyde Park, New York. America heard the news late on that Thursday afternoon. By Sunday, he had been buried. Four hundred thousand watched tearfully as the funeral caisson passed by. At the moment of interment, West Point cadets fired a rifle salute from the gravesite. Planes waited on runways, trains came to a halt, and all of America observed two minutes of silence.[68] Local newspapers carried a simple death notice just as they did for hometown boys: "Roosevelt, Franklin D., Commander-in-Chief, died at Warm Springs, Georgia." Even many Republicans who had called him "That Man" for years stilled their criticism. The famed editor of the *Emporia Gazette*, Kansan William Allen White, spoke for many of these when he wrote of FDR: "We who hate your gaudy guts salute you."[69] The country was united in grief.

The war could not wait. Aboard the USS *Tirante*, an American submarine cruising through mine-infested waters south of Japanese-occupied Korea, Lieutenant Commander George Street hunted down enemy cargo ships. Street had to take his sub into the harbor on the surface, since it was too shallow to dive. At four in the morning of 14 April 1945, Street hit a huge ammunition ship with his torpedoes. "A tremendous, beautiful explosion," Street reported, "a great mushroom of white blinding flame shot 2,000 feet into the air. . . . [At first, it was silent, but then] a tremendous roar flattened our ears against our heads." But the huge explosion exposed the *Tirante* "like a snowman in a coal pit." Instead of beating a hasty retreat, however, Street turned and coolly picked off two enemy warships, frigates of the *Mikura* class that were bearing down on his vulnerable little boat. Street and his crewmen had heard the news of President Roosevelt's death as they entered the enemy harbor. His message back to Pacific submarine command read tersely: "That's three for Franklin . . . sank ammunition ship and two escorts."*[70]

---

* Captain George Levick Street III (USN Ret.) received the Congressional Medal of Honor for this action.

"Jesus Christ and General Jackson!" Those were Harry Truman's first words upon hearing of Roosevelt's death. He had been having an after-session drink in the Capitol Hill office of the gruff, blunt Speaker of the House, Sam Rayburn of Texas. He hurried out of the Speaker's office, brushing past Texas Congressman Lyndon B. Johnson as he headed for the White House.[71] Here, he was quickly sworn in as the thirty-third president of the United States. Later, when President Truman met with the press for the first time, he said, "Boys, if you ever pray, pray for me now.... [W]hen they told me yesterday what had happened, I felt like *the Moon, the stars, and all the planets had fallen on me.*"[72]

Hitler had a much different reaction. "Fate has removed the greatest war criminal of all time," he said of FDR's death.[73] Fate, it would seem, disagreed. The Red Army was soon closing in on Berlin. Ten thousand Soviet artillery pieces let loose an incredible barrage, reducing the historic capital to rubble.

As the ground shook above him, Hitler received news on 28 April that his mentor and friend, Benito Mussolini, had been captured. Italian partisans quickly tried *Il Duce* and shot him and his mistress along with several of his henchmen. Then they strung up their bodies heels first in a Milan gas station. Hitler was horrified and resolved never to be taken alive. He quickly married Eva Braun, his dim-witted mistress. Then, on 30 April 1945, he poisoned his favorite Alsatian dog, Blondi, and he and Eva committed suicide. Goebbels and his wife first killed their six little children by lethal injection and then joined Hitler in death.

The SS burned the bodies in the courtyard of the ruined Reich Chancellery. The grandiose Reich Chancellery, built by Hitler to over-awe terrified visitors, was to have lasted a thousand years. It lasted barely twelve. The next day, 1 May, amid the stench of burning flesh, Red Army soldiers raised the Soviet hammer-and-sickle banner atop the remains of the Chancellery building. They were just in time to celebrate the international workers' holiday.

The hunt now began for fleeing Nazi leaders. Many were rounded up, but SS leader Heinrich Himmler was able to bite down on a cyanide capsule while in British captivity.

Determination to bring to trial all the leaders of the Third Reich stiffened as Nazi death camps were overrun and their thousands of surviving victims were liberated. Auschwitz, Treblinka, Ravensbruck, Dachau, Mauthausen—all became household words for savagery in April 1945. General Eisenhower forced enemy POWs to bury the piles of bodies that were stacked like cordwood at all the death camps in the American sector. He ordered German prisoners to watch newsreel documentation of the Holocaust.[74] He further ordered army photographers to record everything to guard against future efforts by some in the West to deny the Holocaust ever happened.* "I visited every nook and cranny of the camp," said Eisenhower, stunned by the barbarity of it all, "because I felt it my duty to be in a position from then on to testify at first hand about these things in case there ever grew up at home the belief . . . that 'the stories of Nazi brutality were just propaganda.'"[75]

President Truman pledged to carry out Franklin Roosevelt's policies. Unconditional surrender was the first among these. Within a week, German resistance collapsed. Gross Admiral Karl Dönitz, whom Hitler had designated as his successor, authorized the surrender of all German forces. On 7 May, Supreme Commander Eisenhower received the unconditional surrender of all German forces in the French city of Reims. *Received* was the carefully chosen word that described Ike's victory. So furious was the general at what he had seen in the concentration camps that he refused personally to attend the surrender ceremonies, designating a subordinate to meet the defeated Germans.[76]**

---

* Despite mountains of evidence—some of those mountains in the form of eyeglasses, human hair, and children's shoes—some Holocaust deniers began their incredible work within days of the discovery of Hitler's death camps. They seem to be saying to their credulous hearers what Groucho Marx said, "Who are you going to believe—me or your own eyes?" The Iranian regime in Tehran continues to debate it to this day.

** Ike's son John recalled in 1976: "Dad hated the Nazis so much that he didn't want anything to do with them. He never forgot the horrors of the concentration camps" (Neal, *Harry and Ike*, 49).

The next day, 8 May, was Harry Truman's sixty-first birthday. To the world, though, it was V-E Day—Victory in Europe Day. In London, with hundreds of thousands gathered in Trafalgar Square, Winston Churchill appeared with the king, the queen, and Princess Elizabeth on the balcony of Buckingham Palace. Throughout the West, the peoples of the Allied and liberated countries celebrated the end of the greatest threat to freedom the world had ever known. In Moscow, a thousand-gun salute was fired off on 9 May to celebrate victory in "the Great Patriotic War."

The following month, Eisenhower would be given the keys to the city of London. His acceptance of the honor was the first major public speech of his life. Characteristically, in his Guildhall Speech of June 1945, he stressed his own roots in the American Midwest. In doing so, he spoke volumes about the kind of country that had sent him there. It was Ike's New World that had "stepped forth to the liberation and rescue of the Old," as Churchill always knew it would:

> Humility must always be the portion of any man who receives acclaim earned in blood of his followers and sacrifices of his friends.
>
> Conceivably a commander may have been professionally superior. He may have given everything of his heart and mind to meet the spiritual and physical needs of his comrades. He may have written a chapter that will glow forever in the pages of military history.
>
> Still, even such a man—if he existed—would sadly face the facts that his honors cannot hide in his memories the crosses marking the resting places of the dead. They cannot soothe the anguish of the widow or the orphan whose husband or father will not return.
>
> The only attitude in which a commander may with satisfaction receive the tributes of his friends is in the humble acknowledgment that no matter how unworthy he may be, his position is the symbol of great human forces that have labored arduously and successfully for a righteous cause. Unless he feels this symbolism and this rightness in what he has tried to do, then he is disregardful of courage, fortitude and

devotion of the vast multitudes he has been honored to command. If all Allied men and women that have served with me in this war can only know that it is they whom this august body is really honoring today, then indeed I will be content.

This feeling of humility cannot erase of course my great pride in being tendered the freedom of London. I am not a native of this land. I come from the very heart of America. In the superficial aspects by which we ordinarily recognize family relationships, the town where I was born and the one where I was reared are far separated from this great city. Abilene, Kansas, and Denison, Texas, would together equal in size, possibly one five-hundredth of a part of great London.

By your standards those towns are young, without your aged traditions that carry the roots of London back into the uncertainties of unrecorded history. To those people I am proud to belong.[77]

Despite all the celebrations, however, all was not rosy with the wartime coalition. Passing through Washington en route to the opening of the San Francisco organizational meeting of the United Nations, Soviet Foreign Minister Vyacheslav Molotov—"The Hammer"—stopped by the White House to meet the new president. When Truman expressed concern that the Soviets were *not* keeping their agreements in Poland, Molotov interrupted. He said the Poles were acting *against* the Red Army. Truman cut him off, telling him to inform Marshal Stalin that the United States expected the Soviets to keep their agreements. Molotov, offended, replied he'd never been talked to that way. "Carry out your agreements and you won't get talked to like that," Truman said sharply. Molotov normally was a man of pasty complexion. It was called the Kremlin pallor. Now, he looked ashen.[78] It wasn't a cold war—not yet—but there was a chill wind blowing through the corridors of power.

One of the first things Truman learned on becoming president was about the Manhattan Project. During his Senate days, Truman had repeatedly bumped up against the top secret project to develop an atomic bomb. He wasn't sure what it was, but he knew it was big. Now, twelve days after "the moon, the stars, and all the planets had landed" on him, the new president received his first full-length briefing on the atomic bomb from Secretary of War Stimson. The sole possession by the United States of the atomic bomb was about to change everything. So, too, was the apparent willingness of the Soviets to tear up the agreements Stalin had solemnly inked at Yalta.

V. THE FLAG OF FREEDOM

On the brink of victory, Americans could be confident that their arms and their materiel had tipped the balance of the war. All the Allied peoples had performed amazing feats of labor and devotion. Their soldiers, sailors, and airmen had performed incredible acts of heroism and sacrifice. For all that, America was the indispensable country. America made all the difference. Alistair Cooke was then a young correspondent in the United States, working for the British Broadcasting Company (BBC). In the foreword to Cooke's World War II memoir, we see in dramatic terms the American contribution to victory:

> The Allies would not have won the war in the West and the other war in the East without the way the American people, with amazing speed, created an arsenal no coalition of nations could come close to matching. Britain trebled its war output between 1940 and 1943, a ratio surpassing both Germany and Russia, who doubled theirs, though Japan excelled with a fourfold increase. And America? America stepped up its war output by a staggering twenty-five times. Instance, in 1942 a Liberty cargo ship of British design required 200 days to launch. Henry Kaiser, the dam builder from Spokane, had never before built a ship or airplane or handled steel, but he experimented with prefabrication and cut the time to 40 days. For his next trick he finished the *John Fitch* 24

hours after laying the keel. Without the fleets of Kaiser's ships carrying supplies, Britain would no doubt have starved.[79]

Truman agreed to go to Potsdam for another Big Three summit. With Roosevelt gone, it was important for the new president to establish his own relationship with Churchill and Stalin. Potsdam was a relatively undamaged, fashionable suburb of Berlin. It was behind the Soviet lines. Once again, Stalin would take pains to surround the Allied leaders with spies.

At Potsdam, attention centered on what to do about defeated Germany. Stalin was determined to loot the Soviet sector—soon to be known as East Germany. The Red Army had been allowed, even encouraged, to rape its way across Germany. Some two million German women—everyone from eight-year-old girls to eighty-year-old nuns—were raped in the final assault on Germany. As many as 130,000 German women were raped in the capture of Berlin; 10,000 of these committed suicide.[80]

When the victorious Big Three allied leaders finally met at Potsdam, President Truman assumed his duties as chairman with brisk efficiency. Prime Minister Churchill had arrived with his partner in the wartime coalition, Deputy Prime Minister Clement Atlee. Churchill's Conservative Party and Atlee's Labour Party had just met in an election contest. The votes had been cast, but it took weeks for the "soldier vote" to be counted from across the world. Few expected Churchill to lose.

Churchill had a sudden premonition. On 25 July 1945, he told of a dream he'd had. "I dreamed my life was over. I saw—it was very vivid—my dead body under a white sheet on a table in an empty room. I recognized my bare feet projecting from under the sheet. It was very life-like. . . . Perhaps this is the end."[81]

It was not the end, not the end of Churchill's life nor of his remarkable political career. Still, it must have felt like that. The world was stunned by the Labour Party's landslide victory. Clementine, Churchill's loving and ambitious wife, tried to soothe him. "It may well be a blessing in disguise," she told him. "At the moment," Churchill said glumly, "it seems to be very *effectively* disguised."[82]

Churchill's replacement by Atlee left Stalin with two less experienced summit partners. But Truman had just received a coded message that let him know that the world's first atomic test had gone off perfectly at Alamogordo, New Mexico. One thing Truman knew he had to do at Potsdam if he was to have any hope of holding the wartime Alliance together: he must tell Stalin about the atomic bomb.

At the end of a session in which all sides had bickered, Truman casually approached Marshal Stalin. In a conversational tone, he told Stalin that the United States had developed a very powerful new weapon. Stalin did not react, at least visibly. "All he said was he was glad to hear it and hoped we would make 'good use' of it against the Japanese," Truman later remarked.[83]

Of course, Stalin already knew. Klaus Fuchs, a German-born refugee from Hitler's Germany, was a keenly intelligent nuclear scientist. He was a British subject who had been assigned to work on the Manhattan Project with the Americans. He was also a dedicated Communist and Soviet spy.[84] The Manhattan Project had probably been compromised from the beginning.

As the Potsdam conference concluded, the Allies issued another call for Japan to surrender unconditionally. The Soviets did not take part in this call, since they were not yet at war with Japan.

There was never any thought that the atomic bomb would *not* be used. It was not then seen as a weapon of a different order. Citizens had become accustomed to the terrible "thousand bomber raids" over Hamburg and Tokyo in which hundreds of thousands died. The firebombing of beautiful, ancient Dresden had raised a cry of alarm in some quarters. Churchill, viewing films of the attacks, bolted from his chair: "Are we *beasts*?" he cried out in anguish. But he did not order a cessation of the bombing.[85]

The indiscriminate German bombing of London and Coventry, Warsaw and Rotterdam, had hardened the hearts of the Allies toward the Germans. Similarly, stories of Japanese atrocities in Southeast Asia and the Philippines fired a vengeful mood among Americans.

The devastating American losses at Iwo Jima and Okinawa steeled American resolve to do whatever was necessary to force the Japanese to surrender. Associated Press photographer Joe Rosenthal captured an incredible scene of six American servicemen raising the Stars and Stripes above Iwo Jima.* While Americans thrilled at the raising of the flag over Mount Suribachi by five marines and a navy corpsman, the casualty lists sobered millions. The campaign took nearly three times as long as planned—thirty-six days. And it cost 5,931 marines killed and 17,372 wounded.[86]

The assault on Okinawa was even worse. Wave upon wave of kamikaze planes—1,900 in all—cost 4,900 American sailors their lives. Wounded sailors numbered 4,824. U.S. Marine casualties were heavier—7,613 dead and 31,807 wounded. Further, 763 aircraft were lost. The invasion of Okinawa occurred on 1 April 1945. It was not finally secured until 22 June, three of the bloodiest months of the entire war.[87]

When the Japanese military leaders stubbornly held out against the entire civilized world, Truman ordered the use of the atomic bomb. Given the events of that spring, it is hard to imagine any other president coming to any other decision. Truman feared that as many as 300,000 Americans or more could die in an invasion of the Japanese home islands. The mass suicide attacks at Okinawa, the continuing unwillingness of the Japanese military to consider surrender, and the death each month of as many as 100,000 Allied prisoners held by Japan convinced U.S. war planners of the need to drop the atomic bomb.[88]

On 6 August 1945, a USAAF bomber dropped a single atomic bomb on Hiroshima, Japan. Colonel Paul Tibbets piloted the B-29 and named it for his mother, *Enola Gay*. The powerful aircraft was able to record the

---

* Rosenthal's Pulitzer Prize–winning photograph has been converted into a massive statue across the Potomac River from Washington D.C., known now as the Marine Memorial.

event and escape the horror to return safely to base. Because the bomb was untried, there was a serious danger the atomic blast might consume aircraft and crew as well as its intended target. To guard against this happening, the bomb's descent was slowed by a parachute. The bomb resulted in 140,000 deaths. When the Japanese still had not surrendered, a second bomb was dropped on Nagasaki on 9 August 1945. An estimated 73,884 people were killed instantly. An additional 74,909 were horribly injured, alerting the world to the continuing nightmare of radiation poisoning.[89]

Keeping his word this time, Stalin declared war on Japan. Speaking on nationwide radio for the first time, the Japanese emperor Hirohito called upon his people to "endure the unendurable" and surrender. It was 15 August 1945. In all the Allied countries, the people burst forth in an outpouring of unrestrained joy known as V-J Day—Victory over Japan Day.

On 2 September 1945, the USS *Missouri* entered Tokyo Bay. There, the representatives of the Allies received the Japanese emissaries. Nothing was done to humiliate the Japanese signatories to the Instrument of Surrender. General Douglas MacArthur made sure of that. "Let us pray that peace may be now restored to the world, and that God will preserve it always."[90]

It was not just peace that was secured in Tokyo Bay. Freedom was victorious. People all over the world had seen the democracies bounce back from the depths of defeatism and decadence in the late 1930s. Isolationism in the United States and appeasement in Britain and France were discredited. Democracy had won the war. The Great Republic of the United States had indeed become the "arsenal of democracy." American productivity overwhelmed Japanese and German industry.

To the war-weary peoples of the world, the lessons of the war should have settled forever the question of whether free people can also summon the will and the courage to defend themselves. It was the United States and Britain that held out. The United States and Britain defended the ideals of democracy to a watching world.

Even one of the most painful incidents of the war afforded an important lesson.

Winston Churchill was deeply hurt to be so unceremoniously kicked out of office by the British voters. In time, though, Churchill's famous wit would return. When King George VI offered to make him a Knight of the Garter, he replied impishly: "How can I accept the Order of the Garter, when the people of England have just given me the Order of the Boot?"[91]

The important thing is that the people were *free* to give their leaders the boot. This is what freedom is all about. It is the sovereign right of the people to say who will rule over them. It was a message Americans broadcast to a watchful world. The star-spangled banner those marines and that corpsman raised above Mount Suribachi was not just a victorious battle ensign. It was the flag of freedom.

EIGHTEEN

TRUMAN DEFENDS
THE FREE WORLD

(1945–1953)

I. A COLD WAR BEGINS

When peace finally came in September 1945, the country was exhausted. American boys in uniform who sang "Don't Sit Under the Apple Tree with Anyone Else but Me" strained to get back under that apple tree. Their mothers and fathers, their wives and girlfriends wanted them home. Just as a warship's crew cannot be held to "General Quarters" without relaxing, the American people demanded a stand-down from the rigors of war mobilization. No democratic government could have ignored these pressures. Demobilization became the urgent task of the Truman administration.

In these years of an uneasy peace, however, Americans would come to accept a leadership role in the postwar world. The defense of freedom at home, most Americans believed, required a worldwide network of alliances. America's new prominence as the world leader for freedom focused a brilliant and sometimes unflattering spotlight on American institutions and practices. Racial segregation clashed with the ideal of Americans as defenders of human dignity. It was hard to celebrate the great victory over Hitler's vicious racism and then allow millions of Americans to be degraded by public water fountains labeled WHITE and COLORED. The widespread denial of the right to equal public accommodations and basic civil rights like voting and holding office seemed closer to Hitler's Nuremberg Code than to the ideals of the Founders and Abraham Lincoln. Repeatedly during this period, American presidents would point to the watching world in their appeals to Americans to live up to their highest ideals on civil rights.

Progress on civil rights, ironically, was both delayed and then, finally, accelerated by the pressures of a new, worldwide struggle with Communism. Americans in the wake of World War II were split in their views of their wartime ally, Josef Stalin. To many liberals, Stalin represented the brave Soviet people. He was tough, they granted, and his methods were not our methods. But he had to be tough to survive in a world endangered by Fascists and their sympathizers in the West. Besides, they believed, Stalin's Communist system represented something hopeful for the world. Soviet propaganda regularly denounced racism and anti-Semitism. Few Americans had any knowledge of racism and anti-Semitism in the USSR.

American conservatives had never been comfortable with the wartime alliance of convenience with Soviet Russia. In the months immediately following V-E Day, Americans whose parents had come from Poland and Eastern Europe began to cry out against Stalin's iron grip on the "old countries." Throughout the Catholic Church in America, prayers were regularly offered for coreligionists whose freedom of worship was increasingly endangered in Eastern Europe.

President Truman struggled to maintain friendly relations with the Soviets, even as his rapid withdrawal of troops from Europe daily lessened his influence. Against conservatives' advice, he ordered U.S. troops to withdraw from advanced positions they had seized in the closing days of the war. Truman would honor FDR's wartime agreements and hope that the Soviets would honor theirs.

Stalin gave a speech in Moscow's Bolshoi Theater in February 1946 that signaled a return of the old ways. Almost matter-of-factly, Stalin rehearsed the themes he had often echoed in the prewar years: capitalism was inevitably imperialist, imperialism led to war, and the Soviet Union had to rearm to avoid being encircled and overwhelmed. There are indications as well that Truman's straightforwardness in telling Stalin about the atom bomb at Potsdam may have prompted Stalin to be more, not less, truculent. Stalin may have concluded that only a tough and unyielding stance would convince the West he could not be intimidated by the American monopoly on the bomb.

In March 1946 Truman invited former prime minister Winston Churchill to speak at a small liberal arts college in the president's home state of Missouri. Westminster College was proud to host the most famous man in the world—and happy to see Harry too. Churchill and the president rode by special train from Washington to the college town of Fulton. They had plenty of time to discuss the speech during the day-and-a-half train ride.

Churchill called his address "The Sinews of Peace." As he had promised, Truman introduced the distinguished visitor. Churchill, then seventy-one, seemed to have lost none of his intellectual or physical vigor. He drew out his theme, appealing to what he called the "special relationship" between Britain and the United States in the defense of liberty.[1] He outlined the Magna Carta and England's other great documents of political liberty. With a bow to his hosts, he said these ideals "found their most famous expression in the American Declaration of Independence." Together, these English language documents constituted, he said, "the title deeds of freedom."[2]

There was much for Americans to ponder in Churchill's brilliant and profound speech, but few would ever read it in its entirety. That is because

Churchill chose that moment to rivet the attention of the world by his use of a single arresting phrase:

> From Stettin in the Baltic to Trieste in the Adriatic, an iron curtain has descended across the Continent. Behind that line lie all the capitals of the ancient states of Central and Eastern Europe. Warsaw, Berlin, Prague, Vienna, Budapest, Belgrade, Bucharest and Sofia, all these famous cities . . . lie in what I must call the Soviet sphere, and all are subject . . . to an increasing measure of control from Moscow.[3]

The reaction to Churchill's "Iron Curtain" speech came like a thunderclap in a calm summer sky. Moscow was enraged, denouncing Churchill as a warmonger. Back home in Britain, the Labour government faced rebellion among its more left-wing "backbenchers."* In the United States, the speech was attacked by liberals and conservatives. How dare this foreigner propose a permanent alliance between Britain and the United States, critics howled. Liberals were incensed that that old imperialist Churchill was trying to stir up yet another world conflict. Former Vice President Henry Wallace, leader of the Progressives, was especially upset.[4] Few actually read what Churchill said. He called for no military or even diplomatic action to "roll back" the Iron Curtain. Instead, he urged the Western democracies to maintain their military and economic strength—and then to negotiate a better settlement with the Soviets.[5] Instead of war, Churchill wanted peace through strength. Soon, people began to speak of the "Free World," to distinguish democratic countries (and even some non-Communist autocratic states) from the vast regions behind the Iron Curtain.

Truman should not have been so surprised. He had just received "the

---

* A backbencher is a member of Parliament who is not part of the cabinet but a member of the governing party. His support is usually necessary for the majority party to stay in office. Labor's backbenchers were, and are, largely Marxist. The Conservative (Tory) backbenchers were often strong supporters of the Empire, unwilling to make any concessions to the left wing. Churchill was a Tory backbencher during his "wilderness years" in the 1930s.

Long Telegram" from George F. Kennan in the U.S. Embassy in Moscow. Kennan had detailed the deep roots of Soviet behavior and recommended a policy of "containment" to keep them from bringing all of Europe under their sway.[6]

Not all Americans disapproved of Churchill's electrifying speech, to be sure. Republican representative Claire Boothe Luce of New York had publicly criticized Truman's failure to free the countries of Eastern Europe from Soviet domination.[7] Mrs. Luce was not only a powerful figure in her own right—one of the few women in Congress—but she was also the wife of Henry R. Luce, the publisher of *Time, Life,* and *Fortune* magazines.

The Grand Alliance of World War II still had work to do in 1946. Even as Churchill warned of an Iron Curtain, Soviet military judges sat alongside American, British, and French jurists in the German city of Nuremberg. The city had been the scene of Hitler's monstrous Nazi Party rallies in the 1930s. It was also infamous because of the Nuremberg Code, which had deprived Germany's Jews of their citizenship and had prescribed the death penalty for a Jew having sexual relations with an Aryan. Truman wanted the International Military Tribunal (IMT) to try the leading Nazis. He wanted a full airing of the evidence against the German leaders so that no one could ever say, "Oh, it never happened— just a lot of propaganda—a pack of lies."[8]

Truman selected Justice Robert H. Jackson, FDR's former attorney general and then a member of the U.S. Supreme Court, to lead the U.S. prosecution team at Nuremberg. The International Military Tribunal was not without critics in the United States. Senator Robert A. Taft, leader of the isolationist bloc, said the proceedings smacked of a "spirit of vengeance" and said, "The hanging of the eleven men will be a blot on America which we shall long regret."* Chief Justice Harlan Fiske Stone privately even complained about "Jackson's high-grade lynching party."[9]

---

* Senator Taft's opposition to trying the Nazi leaders earned him praise in Senator John F. Kennedy's best-selling book, *Profiles in Courage,* even though Kennedy made clear he did not share the Ohioan's views.

The Nuremberg Trials were no lynching. Overwhelming evidence was presented on the guilt of the accused Nazis. Hitler, Himmler, and Goebbels had avoided trial by committing suicide. But Hermann Goering, Rudolph Hess, Foreign Minister Joachim von Ribbentrop, Generals Keitel and Jodl, Admirals Raeder and Dönitz, and Albert Speer were among twenty-four key defendants who were confronted by irrefutable evidence of their crimes. Each of the defendants was afforded legal counsel. Each was permitted to summon witnesses to refute the charges against him. In the end, the Nuremberg Trials established an important precedent: that "following orders" was no defense against charges of mass murder, genocide, and gross violations of human rights.

At home, November 1946 meant a political shakeup. "Had enough?" was the Republican slogan in the off-year elections. Americans were impatient that the most rapid demobilization in world history was not more rapid still. As wartime price controls eased, inflation shot up. Even ground beef became too expensive for the average American dinner table. With the spike in consumer prices came wage demands from labor. The year 1946 saw the most strikes in American history.[10]

President Truman's very high approval ratings during the euphoric days of victory over Germany and Japan took a tumble. His broad Missouri twang and flat delivery were compared unfavorably with FDR's elegant phrasing and patrician Hudson River accent. Normally tolerant folks who philosophically said "to err is human" now became irritable and repeated the current slam: "to err is Truman." Republicans rode this tide of voter dissatisfaction into a strong victory in both Houses of Congress. In California, Republicans elected young Richard Nixon to the House. Bucking the GOP trend, though, was Massachusetts Democrat John F. Kennedy, a decorated war hero. The unelected Truman was widely dismissed as a single-termer. Now, he would face an 80th Congress dominated by his political opponents.

His opponents underestimated the resourceful Missourian, however. Truman was a fierce political fighter, but no blind partisan. He invited former president Herbert Hoover to the White House; the much vilified Republican hurried to an Oval Office meeting. When Harry asked him to undertake a survey of world food resources, Hoover bolted and ran from the office without saying a word. Shocked by the Californian's rudeness, Truman turned angrily to his agriculture secretary for an explanation: "Don't you realize, Mr. President, the man *couldn't* answer? There were tears in his eyes." Composing himself, Hoover quickly phoned Harry to accept the assignment. He apologized for his sudden flight, saying, "Mr. President, since 1932 no one has asked me to do anything for my country. You are the *first* one."[11] It was simple human gestures like this that won Harry the tribute from Dean Acheson: "The Captain with a Mighty Heart."[12]

Truman was decisive. He even had a sign placed on his desk: "The Buck Stops Here." He never saw a problem he didn't tackle, or a hornets' nest he didn't whack. For example, when General de Gaulle was too slow in removing French troops from the American Occupation Zone of Germany, Truman bluntly told him to get out or risk an immediate cutoff of U.S. aid. The prickly de Gaulle got out.[13]

Truman was determined that the United States would meet the growing Communist threat in Greece and Turkey. His address to the Congress in 1947 was unprecedented for a nation at peace. He wanted to help the Greek government resist subversion by Communist guerrillas. The Turkish situation was somewhat different: there, that nominally Muslim country was faced with Soviet pressure to gain access to the Mediterranean through the Dardanelles. Stalin demanded bases on Turkish soil.

Truman's appeal took on added weight because the Labour government in Britain had announced it would pull troops out of the Mediterranean as a cost-saving measure. Truman and his advisers feared the Soviets would fill the vacuum the British would leave. The Truman Doctrine pledged the United States to give financial aid to those countries struggling to resist subversion by antidemocratic forces.

Truman's political opponents blamed him for the Cold War. But we now know that Stalin had his own view of East-West relations. While he was not the reckless warmonger that Hitler was, Stalin by no means wanted peace with the West. His foreign minister, Vyacheslav Molotov—"The Hammer"—was a man Churchill described as having the "smile of a Siberian winter." Molotov candidly described his boss's attitude: "Stalin looked at it this way: World War I wrested one country from capitalist slavery [the USSR]. World War II has created a socialist system [the Soviet satellites in Eastern Europe]; and the third will finish off imperialism forever." So long as Stalin—or anyone else in the Soviet Union—saw security as a "zero-sum game" in which the USSR could only be secure by threatening or destroying potential adversaries, the Cold War was unavoidable.[14]

Truman showed remarkable humility in adopting the policy of his secretary of state, George C. Marshall. He had admired the five-star general for years. Even as a senator, Truman had called Marshall the "greatest living American."[15*] When Marshall delivered the commencement address at Harvard in 1947, he called for U.S. aid to stricken Europe. Only if America helped rebuild their shattered economies, Marshall said, could democracy be restored. Truman embraced the policy wholeheartedly. To prevent Republican opposition to him from blocking the necessary good work, he immediately dubbed the program "The Marshall Plan." Secretary Marshall had extended the offer of aid not only to the nations of Western Europe, but he also generously held out a helping hand to the Soviet Union and Eastern Europe. Stalin rejected the extended hand—and forced his satellites to refuse it as well. Nonetheless, the Marshall Plan was, and remains, one of the greatest achievements of the Truman administration. If it was not "the most unsordid act in history"—Churchill had reserved that title for Lend-Lease—it was surely the *second* most unsordid act in history.

While Truman tried, with some success, to frame a bipartisan foreign policy, he continued to appeal to liberals for support of his domestic initiatives. The G.I. Bill of Rights enabled millions to go to college, buy

---

*   That selfless comment *almost* prevented Harry's nomination as vice president. FDR was not pleased (Ferrell, *Harry S. Truman*, 253).

homes, and start farms and businesses. It was an unprecedented government effort to assist returning veterans. Truman even worked with the conservative Senator Robert Taft—"Mr. Republican"—on public housing bills designed to relieve the postwar shortage.

Republicans soon responded to labor troubles, however, by passing the Taft-Hartley Bill, one of the most important pieces of labor legislation in American history. Taft was very concerned about Communist penetration of labor unions.[16] So were labor leader Walter Reuther and Minneapolis Mayor Hubert H. Humphrey. They were unwilling, however, to endorse Taft's harsh medicine. Truman had little choice but to veto the Taft-Hartley Bill.

Congress—with many Democrats joining the majority Republicans—soon overrode Truman's veto. The Taft-Hartley Act of 1947 banned the closed shop, a requirement that only union members could be hired. It mandated an eighty-day "cooling off" period if a threatened strike would affect health or safety nationwide. The law made it illegal to donate union dues to political candidates. It also required union officers to affirm under oath that they were not Communists.[17] When Taft-Hartley became law, it placed a permanent check on the growth of unions in America.[18]

With the powerful United States acting against Communist expansion in Europe and even blocking Communist influence in the American labor union movement, Stalin decided in early 1948 to apply pressure where he could. He backed a Communist *coup* in Czechoslovakia in February. Two weeks later, on 10 March 1948, Foreign Minister Jan Masaryk's body was found on the pavement outside his Prague apartment. Was the anti-Communist Masaryk—son of Czechoslovakia's first president, Tomas Masaryk—a suicide or had he been thrown from his apartment window? History's third Defenestration of Prague sent a shiver down the spines of all friends of freedom everywhere.*

---

* Defenestration—throwing someone to his death out of a window—had a long history in Czechoslovakia. In 1419, radical followers of Jan Hus had thrown imperial counselors out of a Prague window. Again in 1618, a second Defenestration of Prague led to the Thirty Years War in Europe.

II. RED STARS IN HOLLYWOOD

The collapse of the wartime alliance with the Soviets depressed and disappointed millions of Americans who had high hopes for postwar cooperation for peace. No group of Americans was more dismayed by the turn of events than the Hollywood film community. During the war, no one had been more enthusiastic to win a victory than Hollywood producers, directors, and stars. It's not surprising why. Adolf Hitler's rise in Germany had horrified liberals everywhere. His violent anti-Semitism was clear to thoughtful people. When the Communist Party's chief Hollywood recruiter, Otto Katz, came calling, doors opened for him. "Columbus discovered America," Katz would say, "but I discovered Hollywood."[19] With "Uncle Joe" Stalin as a wartime ally of America and Britain, recruitment for the Communist Party USA (CPUSA) in Tinsel Town was not difficult. Many Hollywood people were especially drawn to the Communist Party's open condemnation of anti-Semitism and racial bias. Thus, there was great anxiety when French Communist party boss Jacques Duclos publicly declared there was a *Cold War* between the United States and USSR.[20] Duclos was an obedient servant of the Kremlin. This new clash would test the loyalties of thousands of Americans.

Olivia de Havilland was known to millions of moviegoers world-wide as the beloved "Melanie" in the huge 1939 movie hit, *Gone With the Wind*. (Even Hitler had watched the movie—and liked it.) Miss de Havilland tossed away the pro-Soviet part of a speech she was scheduled to give in Seattle in June 1946. It had been written for her by Communist screenwriter Dalton Trumbo.[21] Instead, she delivered new lines written for her by James Roosevelt, an anti-Communist liberal and son of the late president. De Havilland's tough speech was denounced by Hollywood's left wing. When a young actor, Ronald Reagan, spoke up in defense of Olivia de Havilland's right to express her own ideas, Reagan was denounced as "fascist scum."[22] Soon, Reagan, de Havilland, and other stars left the Communist-dominated Hollywood Independent Citizens Committee of the Arts, Sciences, and Professions, known as HICCASP.*

Communist Party members were very active in the Conference of Studio Unions (CSU), a collection of support staff—cartoonists, office workers, and skilled filmworkers—whose jobs involved low pay, long hours, and no glamour. At times, violence marked their strikes. CSU founder Herb Sorrell, a Communist Party member, told Ronald Reagan, then president of the Screen Actors Guild, that "when it ends up, there'll be only one man running labor in Hollywood, and that man will be me."[23]

The fight over Communism in Hollywood went on for many years and continues to roil the film industry to this day. Communists and ex-Communists battled over the Hollywood "blacklist"—a list of those writers who could not find work because of their ties to Moscow. It was, in fact, Communists themselves who first introduced the practice of blacklisting. Edward Dmytryk was a talented movie director and Communist. He was walking across the studio lot at RKO pictures in 1945 when he mentioned to a producer friend, Adrian Scott, an interesting new book, *Darkness at Noon*.[24] Scott, also a Communist, shushed Dmytryk, telling him party members were not allowed to read anything written by Arthur Koestler. Koestler was a disillusioned Communist, and his works lampooned the Soviet dictator. The Hungarian-born Koestler used Stalin's real name—Dzhugashvili—to satirize the heavy-laden jargon of Communist writing: *Dzhugashvilese*.[25] (As it happened, it took Hollywood a full ten years—until 1955—to make a film of Koestler's powerful book. By that time, Stalin was dead and many of the "blacklisted" Hollywood Communists were writing again.)

---

* In an age of acronyms, HICCASP may have been the most unwieldy. Ronald Reagan, after quitting it, joked that it sounded like "the cough of a dying man" (Radosh and Radosh, *Red Star*, 114).

III. *HA TIKVA*—THE HOPE OF ISRAEL

With tensions rising in Eastern Europe, suddenly Americans and Jews throughout the world looked to the Middle East for a stunning development. On 14 May 1948 a new state was born and an ancient people restored to their land: Israel. The Jewish state had been authorized by the United Nations and created by Zionists—a movement of mainly European and American Jews who sought nationhood for the millions of Children of Israel who had been exiled for two thousand years in the *Diaspora.*

When David Ben-Gurion, the new prime minister, announced the birth of Israel, he presented their Declaration of Independence. As with the American document, the Israeli charter offered to a candid world the reasons for the new nation's being: "Here [the Jews'] spiritual, religious and political identity was shaped. Here they first attained to statehood, created cultural values of national and universal significance, and gave to the world the eternal Book of Books."[26]

Truman had to overcome the strenuous objections of the man he admired most in the world—Secretary of State Marshall.[27] During a face-to-face meeting in the Oval Office, Marshall warned the president that recognizing Israel would endanger U.S. objectives in the Middle East. Resisting Communist infiltration in that critical region would be harder if we antagonized fifty million Arabs, the State Department feared. Truman's secretary of state told him he would vote against him for president if he recognized the State of Israel.[28] This must have pained Truman deeply. Still, Harry was a shrewd Kansas City politician too. He knew that millions of Jewish voters in America's cities would be especially relieved and grateful. Truman was in a tough contest with the Progressive Henry Wallace for the support of this traditionally liberal, very Democratic group of voters.[29]

---

    *   *Diaspora* (die-AHS-poor-ah), from the Greek, means "a scattering."

Truman also listened to the earnest pleas of Eddie Jacobson, his partner in his first, failed haberdashery store in Kansas City. Jacobson brought Chaim Weizmann—who would become Israel's first president—to see his old friend. This time, Truman overrode General Marshall's objections.

Psalm 137 was one of Truman's favorites. "By the rivers of Babylon, there we sat down, yea, we wept, when we remembered Zion." Truman as a U.S. senator had given strong support to the World War I–era Balfour Declaration of the British Government.[30] That 1917 document had promised the Jews a "national homeland in Palestine." Now in 1948 Truman felt it was time that that promise was honored.* He extended the United States' official recognition eleven minutes after Ben-Gurion's announcement. America was the first nation in the world to recognize Israel as a *de facto* state.

Truman had been influenced by a higher authority—the Bible. Very simply, Truman came to believe that after the Holocaust, the Jews "deserved a home."[31] It was a view he shared with most Americans of the time. U.S. Supreme Court Justice Felix Frankfurter was a man normally not given to emotional outbursts. He wrote to Chaim Weizmann: "Mine eyes have seen the glory of the coming of the Lord; happily, you can now say that. . . ."[32] Truman's announcement came not a minute too soon. As soon as Israel declared her independence, she was invaded by five Arab neighbors. She was soon fighting for her very life.

IV. THE BERLIN AIRLIFT OF 1948

The postwar settlement in Germany had created two rival systems. Western Germany, occupied by U.S., British, and French troops, comprised more than two-thirds of Germany's territory and population. This

---

    * Waffling on the issue of a Jewish homeland by Britain's postwar Labour Party government had led the Jews in Palestine to joke ruefully that theirs was not only "The Promised Land" but the "Twice-Promised Land."

zone was free and was quickly rebuilding a vibrant economy. Eastern Germany was a grim, totalitarian police state wholly under Stalin's heavy thumb. The Soviets had looted their occupation zone. There was little recovery in the vast, gray, dreary realm. Hitler's capital of Berlin was also divided. East Berlin was Soviet. West Berlin was free. But West Berlin was precariously located 110 miles *inside* Communist East Germany.

On 24 June 1948, Stalin applied the screws to West Berlin. He initiated a blockade by cutting off all rail and road traffic to the surrounded Free City of Berlin. Stalin was not known to be the poker player that Truman was. But he nonetheless found a way to force Truman to "put up or shut up." Here was Stalin's clever challenge to Truman's famous decisiveness. Would Harry force his way into the city, using tanks or bulldozers to knock down Soviet barriers? This would guarantee World War III, less than three years after the most terrible war in human history. Or would he surrender two and a half million West Berliners to Communist aggression and thus show the world America's powerlessness to defend freedom abroad?

General Clay was Truman's military governor in Germany. He reported that he had food stocks for only thirty-six days; coal reserves would last only forty-five days. Clay said Stalin's move "was one of the most ruthless efforts in modern times to use mass starvation for political coercion."[33]

Truman decided. He would not have war *or* surrender. He refused to accept either of Stalin's forced choices. Instead, he brought the incredible power of America to bear on this most dangerous of postwar crises. Truman immediately ordered that West Berlin would be supplied *by air*. Harry would go the extra mile to keep freedom alive in its most exposed outpost.

Thus began the Berlin Airlift. Over the next nine months, the United States and Britain conducted 277,804 flights into Tempelhof Airport carrying a total of 2,325,809 *tons* of supplies into the besieged city, more than a ton for every man, woman, and child. So successful was the airlift that rations for each Berliner actually *rose*.[34] Nearly one hundred U.S. and British servicemen lost their lives keeping Berliners free. Just three years earlier, American and British bombers had been pounding Berlin to rubble. Now, U.S. C-47 cargo planes were dropping candy by parachute to little German children, who scrambled to retrieve it. As a result of the Berlin Airlift and the heroic struggle of the West Berliners, the free sectors of that great city were transformed in Western eyes from a citadel of Nazism to a courageous outpost of freedom.

V. "GIVE 'EM HELL, HARRY!"

As the election year of 1948 arrived, President Harry Truman should have been a strong candidate for reelection. Millions of G.I.s had returned home to find jobs, buy homes, or start college with the assistance of the G.I. Bill. They married and—this is often a sign of public optimism—fathered a huge "baby boom." The long-feared postwar depression did not occur. The American economy dominated the world. The United States, with only 6 percent of the world's people, produced more than one half of the world's goods and services.[35] Truman's Fair Deal programs, it is true, were largely frustrated by the Republican 80th Congress. Medicare, for example, was first proposed by Truman but was rejected. Despite this, millions of veterans were benefiting from the G.I. Bill, and they gave Truman and the Democrats credit for it. The generous allowances it provided often made it possible for a young married man to support a family while he went to college. Others bought homes and started farms and businesses with the help of veterans' benefits. Henry R. Luce, publisher of *Time*, labeled this "the American century."

Looking abroad, Germany had been defeated and occupied; the Western Zone was peaceful and rapidly developing as a free and democratic state. Japan, similarly, under the enlightened administration of General Douglas A. MacArthur, was quiet. MacArthur authorized war crimes tribunals that carefully excluded the Emperor Hirohito. The general introduced women's suffrage, economic and educational reforms, and even promulgated a new democratic constitution that outlawed militarism.[36] America had developed the atomic bomb but had not threatened to use it after Japan surrendered. Western Europe was enthusiastically accepting American leadership through the Marshall Plan.

Truman should have been a sure bet for reelection. In fact, few besides Harry himself thought he would win. Former Vice President Henry Wallace had left Truman's cabinet and would run for president as a Progressive Party candidate. Although Wallace could not win, he could cost Truman critical support in states like New York, Illinois, and California. Democrats feared defeat with Truman. The popular song "I'm Just Wild About Harry" had not been written to honor the Missouri Plain-Speaker. Many politicos now said, tongue-in-cheek, "I'm just mild about Harry."

If Henry Wallace spelled trouble among Progressives, civil rights meant trouble in the South. For eighty years, the Democrats had relied on "the solid South" for their electoral victories. Now, however, millions of returning veterans found the antiquated strictures of racial segregation were not what they had fought for.

In 1948, both parties saw civil rights as a pressing matter. Truman had named a Civil Rights Commission the previous year whose report, *We Hold These Truths*, demanded far-reaching change.[37]

Many doubted the sincerity of Harry's commitment to civil rights. He was the proud grandson of Confederate veterans. He represented Missouri, where segregation was the law. His own mother, it was known, hated the Great Emancipator so much that she was quoted as saying she'd rather sleep on the floor than sleep in the Lincoln bed in the White House. And there was Harry's appalling habit of referring to black people as n——s in private conversation.

Harry Truman as president soon dispelled any notion that he would not stand up for black Americans' civil rights. At a White House luncheon, a Democratic committeewoman from Alabama pleaded with him not to "ram miscegenation" down the throats of Southerners. Harry pulled a copy of the Constitution out of his pocket and read her the Civil War amendments. "I'm *everybody's* President," he said with steely determination. "I take back nothing of what I propose and I make no excuse for it." A black White House waiter was so moved he accidentally knocked the president's coffee cup out of his hand. Mississippi's Democratic senator James Eastland was stunned. Why, he sputtered, if Harry is right, then "Calhoun and Jefferson Davis were wrong."[38] Exactly.

The Republicans meeting in Philadelphia called for action on civil rights. They demanded the abolition of the poll tax, long used to deny black Americans access to the ballot in Southern states.[39] Governor Thomas E. Dewey of New York was again the Republicans' choice for president. Dewey was a sincere advocate of civil rights. He had done well among black voters in the Empire State.

Minneapolis's young mayor, Hubert H. Humphrey, was also a strong supporter of civil rights. He was the nominee of Minnesota's Democratic-Farmer Labor Party for the U.S. Senate in 1948. Humphrey and his fellow liberals were pressured to support *anybody but Truman* for president. Naturally, Humphrey wanted the strongest candidate possible at the head of the ticket to help him win his Senate race. Few people thought Harry Truman was the strongest candidate.

James Roosevelt, son of the late FDR, was sure Truman could not beat Dewey. He was leading a campaign to draft General Dwight D. Eisenhower as the *Democratic* Party nominee. Early in his term, Truman himself had offered to run for vice president if only Eisenhower would run for president as a Democrat.[40]

But now, Truman's fighting spirit was up. He took a train to Berkeley, California, where he confronted the younger Roosevelt: "Your father [FDR] asked me to take this job. I didn't want it. . . . But your father asked me to take it and I took it." Jabbing his finger into the younger Roosevelt's chest, Harry said, "But get this straight: whether you like it or not, *I am going to be the next President of the United States.*"[41]

It seemed to many of the professional politicians who gathered in Philadelphia for the 1948 Democratic National Convention that the Wallace campaign would cost Truman liberal support in the North. They reasoned that if Truman had any chance at all, that chance would be destroyed by any further defections from the Roosevelt coalition. That meant they had to avoid trouble on civil rights.

Hubert Humphrey didn't see it that way. He thought the Republican civil rights plank was "relatively forward looking."[42] He and his allies conducted a "floor fight" at the Democratic National Convention to adopt a strong platform plank on civil rights. Only with such a strong commitment, Humphrey reasoned, could Democrats compete with Wallace in the electoral-vote-rich states in the North, the Midwest, and most importantly, California. When Humphrey arose to speak, he appealed to the Democrats to move out of the "shadow of states' rights and into the bright sunshine of human rights."[43] The adoption of the Humphrey plank offended South Carolina's Democratic Governor J. Strom Thurmond. Thurmond walked out of the convention, taking with him dozens of other Southern delegates. Thurmond pledged to run for president as the candidate of the States' Rights Democratic Party. Instantly, the press dubbed Thurmond's faction the "Dixiecrats." Thurmond vowed to maintain racial segregation.*

All public opinion polls showed Dewey easily beating Truman. The *Chicago Tribune* published a mocking tribute to the embattled Harry: "Look at little Truman now / Muddy, battered, bruised—and how!"[44]

In August, *Time* magazine editor Whittaker Chambers electrified Capitol Hill and the nation with his sensational testimony before the House Un-American Activities Committee. Chambers admitted that he had once been a Communist agent and that he had carried highly classified State Department documents to his Soviet "handler." Chambers

---

* Thurmond must have known that, in demanding segregation for black Americans, he was consigning his own daughter to second-class citizenship. We learned after his death that he had fathered a daughter by the family's black maid.

said he obtained these secret documents from Alger Hiss, a top official of the Roosevelt and Truman administrations.[45] Speaker Sam Rayburn, a Texas Democrat, shrewdly saw "political dynamite" in Chambers's charges, but President Truman bobbled the issue badly. He agreed with a reporter's description of the issue as a "red herring."[46] It was to prove one of Truman's worst political mistakes.

Republicans fairly saw the White House as theirs for the taking. They had been out of office since 1933. They ached to return to power. Thomas Dewey was now the popular and Progressive governor of New York, the biggest electoral vote prize in the nation. Dewey realized that his slashing attacks on FDR in 1944 had turned voters off.[47] In his second run for the presidency, he would maintain a dignified "above the fray" pose. He would behave as if he were already president. The problem with this strategy is that it only reinforced voters' impression of Dewey as a pompous, stiff, standoffish candidate. "You have to know Mr. Dewey really well in order to dislike him," said one Republican lady, somewhat unhelpfully.[48*]

Truman followed his August blunder over Alger Hiss with what must be seen as one of his most far-reaching decisions. Instead of going hat-in-hand to Strom Thurmond's Dixiecrats, Harry boldly issued an Executive Order *desegregating* the U.S. Armed Forces.[49**] Truman's order would take years to implement fully, but, for the first time in U.S. history, all those who risked their lives for America's freedom would do so under conditions of equality and dignity.

Harry battled through the Midwest aboard his campaign train. He had

---

* Years later, a young legal intern in Governor Dewey's law firm would take a ride with the New Yorker in the elevator of the Manhattan skyscraper where both worked. When the two men were alone, the New Yorker asked Jim Compton if he was going to lunch. Excited at the prospect of dining out with the famous leader, New Mexico native Compton eagerly responded, "Yes, sir!" "Without your hat?" Dewey asked coldly and stalked out alone.

** "I was able to rise to the top of the Armed Forces because of those who went ahead and proved we could do it," said General Colin Powell fifty years after Executive Order 9981 was issued, "and Harry Truman who gave me the opportunity to show I could do it" (Neal, *Harry & Ike*, 104).

to borrow money to keep the train chugging ahead. Truman denounced the Republican Majority on Capitol Hill as the "do nothing Eightieth Congress." Senator Taft complained that the president was denouncing Congress at every whistle-stop in the West. And even *that* statement came back to haunt the luckless Republicans. It was said to show their contempt for the people in small towns. In a fight for his political life, Truman threw away prepared texts. He was a flat speaker with a text, anyway. From the back of his train, Truman rose to the occasion. "Give 'em Hell, Harry!" yelled delighted listeners in the partisan crowds he addressed with increasing vigor. Truman's train, the *Ferdinand Magellan*, became the command center of the American government. Harry traveled an unprecedented 21,928 miles in that Whistle Stop Campaign of 1948.[50] Just as bluntly as he attacked Republicans, Harry scalded "Wallace and his Communists."[51] In fact, Wallace's campaign *was* dominated by Communists who secretly took their orders from Moscow.[52]

The last minute hustle paid off.

"Dewey Defeats Truman" read the headlines in the early edition of the *Chicago Tribune*. It remains one of the greatest embarrassments in the history of journalism. Harry's grinning picture as he holds the *Tribune* up for the crowd's delight is one of the classic American political photographs. Truman won 24,179,346 popular votes (49.8 percent) and 303 electoral votes to Dewey's 21,991,291 (45.1 percent) and 189 electoral votes.

Truman pulled off a victory few but him had predicted. A huge turn-out of black voters and liberal supporters of civil rights had given him the edge. Friends of Israel proved grateful for Truman's timely help. And organized labor was thrilled by Harry's veto of the Taft-Hartley law. That veto won for Truman the strong support of Ronald Reagan and most of the non-Communist Hollywood Left. Generally, Truman was too conservative for the liberals and too liberal for the conservatives.[53] Still, his inspired leadership in foreign policy and his frenetic, aggressive campaign style enabled him to defy all pollsters and pundits and score a knockout.

VI. UNDER THE CLOUD OF WAR

The Soviets' aggressive moves in Eastern Europe convinced Truman that the United States had to ally more closely with the democracies of Western Europe. Truman persuaded General Dwight D. Eisenhower to take a leave of absence as president of Columbia University to lead the military effort of the North Atlantic Treaty Organization (NATO). Truman recognized that only a formal U.S. commitment to defend Western Europe from external aggression could prevent dangerous Soviet inroads. NATO was built on the idea of "collective security." An attack by the USSR on any one of the members of NATO was to be regarded as an attack on all of them. No more would dictators be able to carve up Europe piecemeal, as Hitler and Mussolini had done.

Truman knew Eisenhower was skilled at diplomacy as well as military planning. He felt that only Eisenhower's prestige as the conqueror of Hitler would bring the Europeans into full cooperation. As with his outreach to Herbert Hoover and General Marshall, Truman once again showed keen insight and humility in promoting Ike. Under Truman, West Germany (the Federal Republic of Germany) was formed by uniting the Occupation Zones of France, Britain, and the United States. West German rearmament would lead, eventually, to a free and democratic German state as the second largest military member of NATO (1955). Never before had a victorious power sacrificed so much to restore and rebuild—*and defend*—a defeated enemy.

As successful as Truman's defense of freedom in Europe was, however, the U.S. position in Asia looked all the more precarious. In 1949, success with NATO was matched by the disastrous defeat of the U.S.-backed Nationalist government in China. Communist guerrilla leader Mao Zedong succeeded after nearly twenty years of civil war in driving Jiang Kai-Shek's *Kuomintang* forces out of Mainland China and onto the tiny island of Formosa, known today as Taiwan.

"Who lost China?" came the anguished cry. The obvious answer, that Jiang Kai-Shek had lost China, did not satisfy. The former U.S. ambassador to Nationalist China, conservative Patrick J. Hurley, had resigned in protest. He complained that there were too many Communists in the State Department's China Desk.[54] Many Democrats and Republicans were appalled by the Communist takeover. It was an especially jarring event coming just weeks after President Truman had announced that the Soviet Union had exploded its first atomic bomb. Truman's statement was meant to reassure Americans:

> We have evidence that within recent weeks an atomic explosion occurred in the U.S.S.R.
>
> Ever since atomic energy was first released by man, the eventual development of this new force by other nations was to be expected. This probability has always been taken into account by us.[55]

Whether or not the top leaders of the government had always expected the Soviets to develop the atomic bomb, the American people were shocked that the Soviets had seemingly "caught up" in just four years. This, the Communist takeover in China, and the revelations about Alger Hiss contributed to a pervasive sense that perhaps it was not just Soviet strength but Communist perfidy that explained these disturbing events.

Congressman Richard M. Nixon had made a reputation as a tough Communist hunter when he served on the House Un-American Activities Committee (HUAC). Nixon summoned Hiss to testify. Alger Hiss denied he even knew Whittaker Chambers, although he hedged by saying he *may* have known him under another name. Chambers for his part produced microfilm copies of top secret State Department documents he said Hiss had given him. Dramatically, Chambers retrieved these microfilm copies from a pumpkin patch. He had hidden these "pumpkin papers" on his Westminster, Maryland, farm. Chambers's microfilmed documents seem all (with one exception) to have been typed on a Woodstock typewriter—specifically, Woodstock #N230099 owned by the Hisses.

Hiss's friends—and he was *very well connected*—struck back. Rumors circulated broadly about Chambers's alleged homosexuality, insanity, imposture, and criminal behavior.[56]

Despite Hiss's firm denials he had ever cooperated with Chambers, Chambers seemed to know him very well indeed. Chambers had told HUAC of Hiss's excitement at seeing a rare bird, a *prothonotary warbler*. Later, in what seemed a relaxed interlude, a congressman asked Hiss if he'd ever seen a prothonotary warbler in the Washington area. When Hiss's eyes brightened and he confirmed his rare find, a strong link in the chain binding him to Chambers seemed to be forged. Hiss would deny for the rest of his long life what the *Venona* decrypts later proved: that he was an active Soviet agent.[57*]

Americans also worried about Communist influence in the movies. When HUAC subpoenaed several movie stars to testify, a number complied. Screen Actors Guild President Ronald Reagan testified that, yes, there *was* considerable Communist influence in Hollywood. But he urged no witch hunt. Instead, he said, "democracy is strong enough to stand up and fight against the inroads of any ideology."[58] Reagan knew what he was talking about. He had been anonymously threatened with a disfiguring acid attack if he persisted in his anti-Communist campaign. Undeterred, Reagan told the Members of Congress:

> I never . . . want to see our country become urged by either fear or resentment of this group that we ever compromise with any of our democratic principles. . . . I still think democracy can do it. . . . I believe that, as Thomas Jefferson put it, if all the American people know all of the facts they will never make a mistake.[59]

The Cold War was splitting not only Hollywood but many American institutions. The universities, journalism, organized labor, and the military each felt pressures in different ways.

---

* The Venona Project is the name given to a super-secret U.S. intelligence effort to intercept, decode, and translate thousands of messages from Soviet agents in America to their superiors in Moscow. Only in 1995, following the collapse of the Soviet Union, did this material become available to the world.

In the civil rights movement, the staunch anti-Communist Walter White exerted firm leadership in the National Association for the Advancement of Colored People (NAACP). White had rejected Henry Wallace's Communist-backed Progressive campaign and backed Harry Truman in his come-from-behind victory of 1948. When the gifted black singer-actor Paul Robeson and the famed black intellectual W. E. B. DuBois supported a Communist-inspired petition to the UN called "We Charge Genocide," White denounced the petition.[60] Yes, some state governments engaged in invidious discrimination. Some outlaw organizations like the Ku Klux Klan even engaged in lynching and other forms of terrorism to prevent black Americans from exercising their constitutional rights. But this was not the same thing as a U.S. government–backed policy of genocide, White argued. White stated forcefully that "measurable gains have been made in reducing racial bigotry." Anyone who doubted that had only to look at the now-integrated U.S. military or go to a baseball game and see Jackie Robinson slam a home run. (Robinson's triumphal entry into the major leagues proved to be a major turning point in a cultural revolution in America.) White made sure that the NAACP backed the Marshall Plan, rejecting "the most savage imperialism of our time: the road of Moscow and Peiking [Beijing]." Walter White was not alone in fearlessly advocating freedom for black Americans at home while strongly resisting the siren song of Communism abroad. He enlisted the support of Mary McLeod Bethune, Roy Wilkins, Congressman Adam Clayton Powell Jr., and a host of other black civil rights leaders.[61] Together, they gave unyielding support to America's increasingly anti-Communist foreign policy.

VII. THE KOREAN CONFLICT

Harry Truman might not have imagined how soon he would have to test the resolve of the integrated military force he had created. In addition to *racially* integrating the U.S. military, Truman was responsible for uniting *all* the armed services, except the Coast Guard, under the newly created

Department of Defense. No longer would cabinet-level War and Navy Departments jockey with each other for a president's support.

In January 1950, Secretary of State Dean Acheson gave a fateful speech. The precise, elegant Acheson did not suffer fools gladly. His prep school background, neatly trimmed mustache, and British mannerisms were easy to caricature. Acheson was a highly capable, very dedicated diplomat. But when he addressed Asia, he made a mistake of catastrophic proportions. He spoke of a "defensive perimeter" in the Far East that pointedly did *not* include Taiwan or South Korea. "It must be clear that no person can guarantee those areas against military attack," he said.[62] To compound this grievous error, Texas's Tom Connally, the Democratic chairman of the Senate Foreign Relations Committee, announced in May that Russia might seize the Korean peninsula without U.S. response because Korea was "not very greatly important."[63]

Stalin followed these events closely. In a Kremlin meeting with the North Korean Communist ruler Kim Il-Sung, Stalin gave grudging approval to Kim's plan to invade South Korea. But Stalin warned Kim, "If you should get kicked in the teeth, I shall not lift a finger to help. You have to ask Mao for all the help."[64] That was all the word Kim needed.

Ninety thousand North Korean troops crossed the 38th Parallel into South Korea on 25 June 1950. Truman, stung by charges his administration had "lost" China to the Communists, knew he had to resist this naked aggression. General of the Army Douglas MacArthur was then in charge of the occupation of Japan as what some called a "Star-Spangled Mikado [Emperor]."* MacArthur advised Truman to send U.S. air cover from Japan to help the retreating forces of the Republic of Korea (ROK).

Only because the Soviet delegate was boycotting a UN Security Council session over another issue was it possible for the United States

---

* Enormous prestige went with the exalted five-star rank held by MacArthur and only four other generals in U.S. history: George C. Marshall, Dwight D. Eisenhower, Henry H. ("Hap") Arnold, and Omar Bradley. The navy lists only four five-star Admirals of the Fleet: William D. Leahy, Ernest J. King, Chester W. Nimitz, and William F. ("Bull") Halsey.

to get the UN to authorize action to repel the North Korean aggression. Now, just five years after MacArthur had stood on the deck of the USS *Missouri* in Tokyo Bay to proclaim the return of peace, the United States was involved once again in a land war in Asia.

General MacArthur was seventy years old in 1950. He might easily have begged off from yet another combat assignment and asked Truman to select a younger man. He was highly respected in the United States, not only as the victor in the Pacific war but also for his enlightened rule in occupied Japan. Why take a dangerous assignment on the Korean peninsula? For MacArthur, the answer was one word, the most important word: *duty.*

The North Korean invasion had shocked the world. The newly created Central Intelligence Agency (CIA) failed seriously in not detecting the buildup of "Red" tanks and infantry north of the 38th Parallel. ROK forces retreated pell-mell. American troops performed badly. Poorly trained and equipped, soft from easy occupation duty in Japan, some of our soldiers allowed themselves to be overrun and taken prisoner. Within weeks, the Reds had encircled American and ROK forces in a narrow band around the South Korean port city of Pusan. MacArthur was determined to break out of this "Pusan Perimeter."

His plan was audacity itself. MacArthur planned a seaborne invasion *behind* the Red lines near Inchon, the seaport for the South Korean capital of Seoul. "We drew up every conceivable natural and geographic handicap, and Inchon had them all," said one of MacArthur's military aides.[65] Not the least of the hazards were *deadly* thirty-foot tides. MacArthur's naval chief could muster no better endorsement of his plan than that it was "not impossible." MacArthur kept his own counsel, puffing constantly on his trademark corncob pipe. He remembered the words of his own father, who like his son was a Medal of Honor winner: "Doug, councils of war breed timidity and confusion."[66]

MacArthur's Inchon landing succeeded brilliantly. It was one of the greatest turnarounds in American history. For breathtaking boldness, it ranked alongside Washington's crossing of the Delaware, Grant's descent on Shiloh, and Patton's relief of Bastogne. South Korea's aged President Syngman Rhee accepted the return of his liberated capital of Seoul with tearful gratitude: "We love you," he told MacArthur, "as the savior of our race."[67]

Because this was the UN's first attempt to resist aggression, the United States had the support of troops from Britain, Australia, New Zealand, Canada, and even France.[68] Truman refused to call the Korean War a war. It was a "police action," he insisted, trying to emphasize that the United Nations was being tested by international Communism. If we allowed the Reds to get away with it in Korea, then Communists would be encouraged to probe Western defenses elsewhere in Asia, Europe, and Latin America, Truman argued.

When MacArthur met Truman at Wake Island (the scene of bitter fighting in World War II) on 14 October 1950, UN forces had thrown the Reds back and were advancing toward the North Korea–China border on the Yalu River. MacArthur assured President Truman at Wake Island that there was "very little chance" of a massive intervention by Communist Chinese forces.[69]

But two hundred thousand Communist Chinese "volunteers" defied MacArthur's prediction and stormed across the frozen Yalu River. Americans were shocked and dispirited.* U.S. Marines caught by the sudden invasion took heavy casualties at the Chosin Reservoir. It was Korea's coldest winter in a century. The "Frozen Chosin" was the name this Marine "band of brothers" took for themselves. Samuel Eliot Morison calls Marine General Oliver Smith's "fighting retreat" from the Chosin Reservoir "one of the most glorious in the annals of that gallant corps, recalling Xenophon's retreat of the immortal 10,000 to the sea."[70] In less flowery terms, the "grunts" on the ground called the long retreat "bugging

---

* The idea that anyone could volunteer for anything in the ruthlessly regimented Communist Chinese regime ruled by Mao Zedong was another example of the "black is white, day is night" Communist doublespeak. It left Americans deeply distrustful of Communist statesmen, methods, and motives.

out." Nonetheless, their courage and discipline under the harshest conditions should earn undying praise.

MacArthur wanted to carry the war north of the Yalu River, bombing the bridges and the staging areas inside Mainland China. Britain and France vetoed this idea. Britain was fighting a Communist insurgency in Malaysia; France, likewise, was bogged down battling Communists in Indo-China.[71]

Truman remembered George F. Kennan's "Long Telegram" (his lengthy and influential cable of 5,363 words). *Containment* was the policy it recommended. Containment meant holding free territory and not yielding it up to the Communists. It did *not* mean using force to liberate territories already under Communist control. Now that Stalin, too, had the atomic bomb, that strategy might bring a nuclear World War III.

Kennan, meanwhile, had begun to see dangers *within* the West. He saw the return of the fear that had stalked free nations before World War II. He spoke to that same sense of dread that had made George Orwell's grim prophecy in his novel *1984* an international bestseller. Kennan said nuclear weapons "reach backwards beyond the frontiers of western civilization, to the concepts of warfare which were once familiar to the Asiatic hordes.[72] In a memo to his State Department superiors that was promptly ignored, Kennan quoted Shakespeare's *Troilus and Cressida*:

> Power into will, will into appetite
> And appetite, a universal wolf,
> So doubly seconded with will and power,
> Must make perforce a universal prey
> And last eat himself up.[73]

The imperious MacArthur wanted to threaten the Chinese with the atomic bomb if they did not agree to negotiate a peace in Korea. General MacArthur then committed the act that led to his summary dismissal. He released a "military appraisal" that explained why he had to carry the war to the North. He went further, writing to the Republican leader in the House of Representatives to show why his, MacArthur's, view, and not Truman's, was the correct one. "There is no substitute for victory," was MacArthur's ringing declaration.

Truman immediately fired MacArthur. It did not matter to many that Secretary of Defense George C. Marshall and Army Chief of Staff Omar Bradley—also five-star generals—recommended this course of action for rank insubordination. Truman had to endure a firestorm of protest and abuse. California Senator Richard Nixon called for MacArthur's immediate reinstatement, and Wisconsin Senator Joseph McCarthy, a notorious boozer, accused the commander in chief of sacking MacArthur while he, Truman, was drunk![74]

"Old soldiers never die," General MacArthur told a joint meeting of Congress, "they just fade away." It was an emotional moment. American soldiers were dying in frigid Korea. One of our greatest generals stated that the president and his team were not trying to win. And some strident voices were saying that that was because they didn't *want* to win, that they were influenced by Soviet agents. Small wonder that Truman's approval rating sank to an historic low of 23 percent!

Yet, it is precisely in such moments that a president's strength of character is tested. However brilliant and insightful MacArthur was, this country can never tolerate a military commander going over the head of the civilian authority. George Washington *wouldn't* do that. George McClellan *didn't* do that. It can *never* be allowed.

Fortunately for the country in this desperate hour, a number of leading Republicans, including Governors Thomas E. Dewey and Harold Stassen and Senators Henry Cabot Lodge Jr. and John Foster Dulles, boldly spoke up in support of the president's right as commander in chief to give orders to his military subordinates.[75] Once again, Thomas Dewey put principle above narrow partisanship.

Also critical to consider is how important the patriotic stance of

Walter White and the NAACP leadership was at this juncture. Had there been any crack in national unity along a racial fault line, America's military position might have become untenable.

Communist propaganda tried to paint Americans as racists for fighting nonwhites in Korea. Walter White was having none of it.

VIII. THE MAN FROM INDEPENDENCE

Heading into the election of 1952, President Harry Truman confronted a long, grinding, bloody war in Korea. General Matthew B. Ridgeway, his replacement for the ousted MacArthur, had solidified the UN front roughly at the 38th Parallel, the prewar border between North and South Korea.

The result could hardly appeal to Americans on the ground: "Why die for a tie?" G.I.s complained. But a negotiated settlement at the 38th Parallel would at least *contain* Communism on the peninsula. And containment was the Truman administration's goal. Truman was committed to "limited war" or, as he sometimes called it, a "police action." Needless to say, such a stance was deeply unpopular in his time.

Inflation had hurt the president's domestic record. Strikes were a nagging problem. When Truman seized the steel mills to prevent a strike from crippling production during wartime, the U.S. Supreme Court handed Harry his hat. The Court struck down Truman's action by a stunning vote of 6–3 in the case of *Youngstown Sheet & Tube Co. v. Sawyer* (1952). The Supreme Court was then composed of FDR and Truman appointees, a fact that made the rejection of Truman's actions an even more stinging rebuke.

Then there was the two-term limit, passed by a Democratic-controlled Congress. Congress had passed and the states had ratified the Twenty-Second Amendment to the Constitution, limiting the president to only two terms. The terms of the amendment specifically exempted the current occupant of the White House, but many saw its quick passage as a vote of no confidence in Harry Truman.*

Harry Truman prized his reputation for "Plain Speaking" honesty. Once, when a *Washington Post* music critic panned the president's daughter's singing, Harry Truman responded as an outraged, protective *father*. Harry immediately wrote the offending critic a letter, saying, "You're an eight ulcer man on four ulcer pay." He even threatened him. When I meet you, he wrote, "you'll need a new nose, a lot of beefsteak for black eyes, and perhaps a supporter below!"[76] Then, in typical Truman fashion, he affixed his own three-cent stamp to the envelope. He wouldn't abuse his presidential franking privilege when threatening a columnist with a punch in the nose!

For all his flinty personal integrity, Truman was embarrassed by attempts by some of his appointees to cash in on their offices. He had to let General Harry Vaughan go when he took up with perfume smugglers. Gifts of freezers and mink coats tainted the entire administration's reputation. By the standards of the past—the Tweed Ring, the Credit Mobilier scandal, Teapot Dome—the Truman-era corruption was "small beer." Still, his party had been in power for twenty years, and people sensed a certain laxness. Truman had pulled off the most stunning political upset in history with his 1948 win. He did not want to jeopardize that feat by losing in a failed bid for a third term. So he decided not to run.

Despite his widespread unpopularity in 1952, President Truman soldiered on. While most Americans strongly disapproved of *his* performance, Winston Churchill came to Washington again and provided—as usual—a deeply insightful assessment of the Man from Independence.

Churchill had just led his Conservative Party to victory in Britain.

---

* The Democratic Party, going back to Jefferson and Jackson, had championed the two-term limit. It was Republicans Ulysses S. Grant and Theodore Roosevelt who seriously challenged that tradition by seeking third nonconsecutive terms (1880 and 1912, respectively). But it was the Democrat FDR who sought and won third and fourth consecutive terms. Roosevelt dominated not only the Republicans but also many conservative Democrats. The Twenty-Second Amendment was their response.

Relaxing with Truman aboard the presidential yacht, *Williamsburg*, the seventy-seven-year-old prime minister was unusually blunt. He confessed to Harry's face that he had initially held him in "low regard" and "loathed your taking the place of Franklin Roosevelt."[77] But, he continued, that view changed:

> I misjudged you badly. Since that time, you, more than any other man, have saved Western Civilization. When the British could no longer hold out in Greece, you, and you alone, sir, made the decision that saved that ancient land from Communists. You acted in similar fashion . . . when the Soviets tried to take over Iran. . . . [Your] Marshall Plan . . . rescued Western Europe wallowing in the shallows and easy prey to Joseph Stalin's malevolent machinations. Then you established the North Atlantic Treaty Alliance. . . . Then there was your audacious Berlin Airlift. And, of course, there was Korea.[78]

It's fair to say that half a century after that chilly January cruise on the Potomac, most Americans today view Harry Truman the way Winston Churchill did—and not the way our own parents did in 1952. In refusing to allow MacArthur to use—or even threaten to use—an atomic weapon, Truman vastly increased the power of his presidency. He also reversed what had been an irreversible pattern in history: that when new weapons had been developed, they would be used.[79] And used again and again.

When Harry Truman returned with his devoted wife, Bess, to their home in Independence, Missouri, he prepared for life as a former president. There was no pension in the 1950s. There were few opportunities for him. But he returned uncomplaining to the community that had nurtured him. Asked by a television reporter what was the first thing he did on returning to the family home, Harry, plainspoken as ever, said, "I took the grips [suitcases] up into the attic."

NINETEEN

EISENHOWER AND HAPPY DAYS

(1953–1961)

I. "I LIKE IKE!"

The Republicans could smell victory in 1952. President Harry Truman's broad unpopularity made the GOP prospects bright. Many Republicans hoped Dwight D. Eisenhower would be their nominee, but the general resisted. Time and again, he said he would not seek office.

Yet as a "Draft Eisenhower" movement got going, Ike did nothing to scotch it. He could have reached back to the nineteenth century for a quote from his fellow West Pointer. General William Tecumseh Sherman knew how to squelch a draft: "If nominated, I will not run. If elected, I will not serve." Ike issued no such statement. Further, he was increasingly aware that he had an obligation to run. Ohio Senator Robert A. Taft was calling for the United States to bring the troops home from Europe, and Eisenhower realized such a move would be disastrous given the power vacuum it would create for the Soviets to fill. He would have to run.

Fifteen thousand people gathered in New York's Madison Square

Garden for an Eisenhower rally. "I Like Ike" read their signs.[1] It was a slogan that would soon sweep the country.

When Eisenhower finally spoke out on political issues, he declared that he was opposed to Big Government, high taxes, inflation, and the "Kremlin menace."[2] Clearly, he was a Republican. Delegates at the 1952 Republican National Convention in Chicago gave him the nod. California Senator Richard M. Nixon became his running mate. Democrats, meanwhile, chose the witty, urbane governor of Illinois, Adlai E. Stevenson, as their nominee. Across the country, liberal intellectuals went "Madly for Adlai."

Eisenhower proved a powerful campaigner. His smile dazzled millions of Americans. His war record was admired throughout the world. But Ike was leaving nothing to chance: his special train racked up its own whistle-stop record: 51,276 miles of nonstop campaigning, more than doubling Harry Truman's 21,998 miles in the *Ferdinand Magellan* in 1948.[3]

Eisenhower's campaign train was almost derailed, however, when it was revealed that his running mate had been supported by a "secret fund" raised for him by a small circle of California businessmen. Nixon went on national television to defend himself in a tearful performance. Particularly effective was his defiant refusal to return to donors the gift of a little dog. His young daughters called the Cocker Spaniel "Checkers," and they loved him. Nixon's "Checkers Speech" saved his political life. Public reaction was positive and overwhelming.

Eisenhower was an approachable man of the people, a son of the American prairie. His detractors characterized him as uncultured and anti-intellectual, but his associates knew that just wasn't so. C. D. Jackson, a protégé of *Time*'s Henry Luce, said Ike "moved young" and was highly literate. Eisenhower is "cultured well beyond innate gentlemanliness," he said. "His classical, Biblical, and mythological allusions come tumbling out when he is working with words. Even [speechwriter] Emmett John Hughes would have to agree that his capacity for unscrambling an involved paragraph and fixing it so that it says what it was supposed to say in the first place, is sometimes uncanny."[4]

Ike led in the polls throughout the campaign, but he "put it away" in October with a simple announcement: "I shall go to Korea." Americans had confidence that Ike's military and diplomatic experience would enable him to find a way out of the bloody stalemate that then existed in that war-torn country. With that, the campaign effectively ended. Eisenhower rode to victory in November on a tidal wave of "I Like Ike."

It's commonplace to say Eisenhower had no political experience before entering the White House. While it is certainly true he had held no elective office, it is also true that he had operated with distinction in the highly political atmosphere of the prewar army and had superintended the greatest international wartime coalition in history. He knew Churchill, Roosevelt, Truman, Marshall, de Gaulle, and the Soviet military leaders on a personal basis. In the dangerous new world the United States faced in the 1950s, few Americans could equal his breadth and depth of experience.

II. THE KREMLIN'S LONG SHADOW

Taking the oath at the Capitol on 20 January 1953, President Eisenhower was the first Republican in twenty years to form an administration. Americans cheered and sophisticates sneered as Ike led the nation in prayer:

> Give us, we pray, the power to discern clearly right from wrong, and allow all our words and actions to be governed thereby, and by all the laws of this land. Especially we pray that our concern shall be for all the people, regardless of station, race, or calling.[5]

Cynics were quick to point out that Ike had never joined a church prior to his coming to the White House. True, but he had never joined a political party, either. The young evangelist Reverend Billy Graham did not agree with the cynics' view of Ike. Graham knew Eisenhower well. Ike had invited him to come to Paris when Ike was the head of the Supreme Headquarters Allied Powers Europe (SHAPE). Eisenhower had even invited the young evangelical leader to come to his Chicago hotel when he was nominated for president to advise him on his acceptance speech. Graham recalls, "Eisenhower was a very religious man."

Many changes were in store. Eisenhower would speak of "moral rearmament" to meet the threat of atheistic Communism and would urge Congress to add the words "under God" to the Pledge of Allegiance. The Knights of Columbus, a Catholic men's group, had been lobbying tirelessly for the change. With Ike's backing, Congress readily complied.

Eisenhower was presented with a horrible decision on becoming president. Would he allow the execution of convicted atomic spies Julius and Ethel Rosenberg to proceed, or would he grant executive clemency?

The Truman administration had prosecuted the Rosenbergs. Judge Irving Kaufman, who presided at their trial, was a Democratic appointee, not a Republican.

Time magazine reported the verdict in its 16 April 1951 issue. In sentencing them to death, Judge Kaufman had sternly told the Rosenbergs:

Plain, deliberate, contemplated murder is dwarfed in magnitude by comparison with the crime you have committed. . . . I believe your conduct in putting into the hands of the Russians the A-bomb . . . has already caused the Communist aggression in Korea . . . and who knows but that millions more of innocent people may pay the price of your treason.[6]

World figures like Pope Pius XII and Albert Einstein appealed to the new president for clemency. Leftists around the world soon accused Eisenhower of anti-Semitism. International Communism raised a hue and cry against Ike personally. Communist novelist Howard Fast wrote that the "stale smell of fascism" was detected around Eisenhower by "the Jewish masses of our country."[7]

This was an obscene charge against the man who had forced German civilians to walk through liberated Nazi death camps and who had ordered army filmmakers to record for posterity the irrefutable evidence of the Holocaust. Ike maintained a dignified silence as the convicted spies went to their deaths in the electric chair at Sing Sing Prison in New York.[8]*

President Eisenhower was able to announce the ceasefire in Korea on 27 July 1953. This uneasy truce has lasted until the present day. The Korean War killed 36,000 Americans, 600,000 Chinese, and some 2,000,000 North and South Koreans.[9] The Demilitarized Zone (DMZ) separating North and South Korea along the 38th Parallel remains one of the most volatile borders on earth.

In this early Cold War atmosphere of real treason, rumored treason, and fear of espionage, Senator Joseph McCarthy of Wisconsin rose to power and prominence by accusing people—sometimes viciously—of being communists. McCarthy gained sudden prominence when he told a Republican audience in Wheeling, West Virginia: "I have in my hand [a list of] . . . cases of individuals who would appear to be either card-carrying members or certainly loyal to the Communist party" in the State Department.[10] The exact number McCarthy used remains controversial to this day. Thus was born "McCarthyism." McCarthy addressed a real problem: disloyal elements within the U.S. government. But his approach to this real problem was to cause untold grief to the country he claimed to love.

President Eisenhower invoked executive privilege to keep McCarthy from going on a "fishing expedition." Whether it's fishing to "hook" embarrassing details or legitimate legislative oversight is sometimes in the eye of the beholder, but Ike had a growing number of supporters using

---

* French Communist Party boss Jacques Duclos was a hard-line Stalinist. He attacked America, explaining that the conviction of the atomic spies in America was anti-Semitism but that the execution of *eight* Communists, all Jews, in Czechoslovakia was not (Radosh and Radosh, *Commies*, 46).

the tools at their disposal to oppose the senator. Veteran CBS newsman Edward R. Murrow opposed McCarthy on his popular television broadcast *See It Now.* "We cannot defend freedom by *deserting* it at home," he said.[11] The Senate's only woman, Maine's Republican Margaret Chase Smith, fearlessly took on McCarthy.

When McCarthy dragged Ike's beloved army before his committee, the same television cameras that had aided McCarthy's rise would become his undoing. His constant badgering of witnesses, his unstable personal conduct, and his general recklessness went on full display. He interrupted a witness to make sure that some damaging information about a young lawyer was put in the record—and broadcast on national television. The lawyer in question had once belonged to the Communist-backed National Lawyers' Guild. Now he worked for the same law firm that represented the army at the Army-McCarthy hearings. The army's attorney, the proper Bostonian Joseph Welch, skewered McCarthy with this famous retort:

> Until this moment, Senator, I think I never really gauged your cruelty or your recklessness. Let us not assassinate this lad further, Senator; you've done enough. Have you no sense of decency, sir? At long last, have you left no sense of decency?[12]

Eisenhower always thought McCarthy was more interested in hunting headlines than catching Communists.[13] He surely knew the old saw: "Give a man enough rope and he'll hang himself." He gave McCarthy enough rope in the Army-McCarthy hearings, as he took command of the administration's efforts to clip McCarthy's wings.[14]

The rope this time was the coaxial cable of the television camera. Like the mythical Icarus, McCarthy flew high on wings of his own fashioning. Flying too close to the sun—in this case the glare of national publicity— the wax melted and he plummeted to earth.

McCarthy was soon censured by the full Senate by an overwhelming

67–22.[15]* The vote was taken 2 December 1954, less than two years after Eisenhower came to office. Behind the scenes, Ike urged Republicans to back the censure motion.[16] It was an outstanding example of what has been called "The Hidden-Hand Presidency."

Three years later, still drinking heavily, Joe McCarthy died. He was, at forty-nine, a burnt-out case. As Michael Barone writes of him, he was "utterly unscrupulous, untethered to any truth, unhampered by any sense of fairness, and undisciplined by any desire to accomplish a concrete goal."[17] Worst of all, McCarthy besmirched the honorable cause of anti-Communism. He discredited *legitimate* efforts to counter Soviet subversion of American institutions. From this point on, it would only be necessary for disloyal people or groups to yell "McCarthyism" to distract public attention from real problems. For too long, McCarthy had operated with the active cooperation of mainstream Republican politicians like Senator Robert A. Taft and Senator William F. Knowland. He was even defended by the brilliant young William F. Buckley Jr. Unfortunately, McCarthy's fall did not serve as a cautionary tale to all Americans. Robert Welch, founder of the fiercely anti-Communist John Birch Society, became convinced that President Eisenhower was "a conscious agent of the Communist conspiracy."[18]

This ridiculous charge was made against the man who had written in his memoir, with evident horror, of the Soviet method of clearing a minefield *by marching right through it*! Marshal Zhukov personally confirmed this method when Ike visited Moscow in 1945.[19] The Soviets' blatant disregard for human life—like the Nazis' concentration camps—made a deep impression on the humane Eisenhower.

---

* Conspicuously not voting was young Senator John F. Kennedy. JFK had been hospitalized for a life-threatening back operation. Thus he avoided voting to censure the man whom his father had befriended, a man who had been a guest in his home and who had dated his sister. Jack Kennedy would later joke that if reporters quizzed him while he was being wheeled into surgery on a gurney, he would cry out, "O! My back!" Mrs. Eleanor Roosevelt was not amused. She would later say JFK needed to show more courage, less *profile*.

III. FREEDOM RISING

Communism inspires and enables its militant preachers to exploit injustices and inequity among men. This ideology appeals, not to the Italian or Frenchman or South American as such, but to men as human beings who become desperate in the attempt to satisfy common human needs. Therein it possesses a profound power for expansion. Wherever popular discontent is founded on group oppression or mass poverty or the hunger of children, there Communism may stage an offensive that arms cannot counter. Discontent can be fanned into revolution, and revolution into social chaos. The sequel is dictatorial rule. Against such tactics exclusive reliance on military might is vain.[20]

Volumes have been written on the appeal, the danger, and the appropriate responses to international Communism. No one understood its challenge better than Dwight D. Eisenhower. This passage from his bestselling war memoir, *Crusade in Europe*, makes this clear. Ike was a man widely lampooned as unintellectual, lazy, and doddering by members of an adversary culture. But this revealing passage shows his penetrating grasp of the issues and his keen insight into Communism's mesmerizing and dangerous appeal.

In this context, Eisenhower's refusal to repeal the New Deal and his encouragement of policies that brought greater material abundance to average Americans can be seen as the most effective defense of freedom. Let workers earn that new car, a television, and a summer cabin by the lake and there will be nothing to fear from Red agitation. America and Western Europe in the Eisenhower years enjoyed unprecedented prosperity.

Eisenhower went to Geneva in 1955 to meet with the new Soviet Communist leaders, Nikolai Bulganin and Nikita Khrushchev, who came to power after Joseph Stalin died in 1953. Ike was joined by his British and French allies. He boldly offered an "Open Skies" proposal—an attempt to ease international tensions by allowing both sides to fly over each other's countries. Khrushchev, quickly emerging as the real power in the Kremlin, turned down Ike's idea. But the "thaw" in the Cold War brought about by "The Spirit of Geneva" soothed raw nerves on both sides of the Iron Curtain.

At home, Eisenhower's appointee as chief justice, Californian Earl Warren, moved quickly to respond to the issue of racial segregation in schools. What Warren lacked in legal background and constitutional subtlety he more than made up in skillful personal relations. Warren steered the Supreme Court to produce the landmark *Brown v. Board of Education* decision during his first term. By a vote of 9–0, the U.S. Supreme Court struck down racial segregation in public education.* Freedom was rising.

Eisenhower has been much criticized for his failure to publicly endorse the Court's decision. But he felt that doing so would set an undesirable precedent. If a president endorsed decisions he agreed with, might he feel compelled to oppose decisions he did not agree with? And what would that do to the rule of law? "The Supreme Court has spoken and I am sworn to uphold . . . the constitutional processes. . . . I will obey."[21] Another reason for Eisenhower's restrained response was his concern that some Southern states might close down their public school systems altogether rather than integrate them. In that event, Ike feared that all students, black as well as white, would be handicapped.[22]

For lead attorney Thurgood Marshall and other leaders of the NAACP, who had fought for so long for freedom, it was an incredible victory. Thurgood Marshall had counted no more than *four* votes for desegregation on the Court when Harry Truman's good friend, Fred Vinson, was chief justice.[23] Now, in 1954, Ike's nominee, Earl Warren, had seemingly wrought a miracle.

Freedom is contagious. Instead of resting on the hard-won victory

---

* The pre-Warren Court might have rendered a ruling favorable to integration, but strategists worried that a divided Court would strengthen resistance. The unanimous ruling Warren engineered was considered essential to popular acceptance of the Court's decision in *Brown*.

of the NAACP in *Brown v. Board*, leaders pressed for more. Civil rights was in the air. The very next year, a black seamstress in Montgomery, Alabama, refused to give up her seat on a city bus. The young Reverend Martin Luther King Jr. immediately protested the arrest of Mrs. Rosa Parks. Her tax dollars paid for those buses too. So did Dr. King's. Quickly, Dr. King organized a boycott of the city bus lines. He held the boycott under a tight discipline. Citing the Prophet Amos, King assured everyone there would be no violence:

> I want it to be known throughout Montgomery and throughout this nation that we are—a Christian people. . . . And we are determined here in Montgomery to work and fight, until justice runs down like water and righteousness as a mighty stream![24]

One reason Dr. King felt he had to emphasize the Christian and *constitutional* nature of his crusade for civil rights was that the civil rights movement had been dogged by charges of Communist infiltration. His statements of faith did not offend liberal supporters. The Democratic Congress had just passed and Eisenhower quickly signed a bill to make "In God We Trust" our official motto. The Republican president and Democratic congressional leaders believed—as Truman did before them—that it was important to draw a line between America's commitment to religious freedom and Soviet atheist propaganda. The Reverend Dr. King emphasized his Christian principles. He returned again and again to the Declaration of Independence and the Constitution as his sources of authority.*

The Montgomery Bus Boycott lasted more than a year, with hundreds of volunteers supplying rides to people who ordinarily needed bus transportation to get to work, to go to church, or even to shop. The city

---

* This author once received a compliment from Coretta Scott King for taking care to emphasize the fact that Martin Luther King Jr. was a *Reverend*.

appealed to the courts to stop the carpooling. Several black churches, including that of the Reverend Ralph David Abernathy, King's closest friend, were firebombed. A white Lutheran pastor who served a black parish had his home bombed. Dr. King, shaken by the violence, stunned his congregation with his tearful prayer: "Lord, I hope no one will have to die as a result of our struggle for freedom.... But if anyone has to die, let it be me!"[25]

With a stroke of the pen, the U.S. Supreme Court handed down a ruling declaring all segregation on public buses unconstitutional.[26]

Overnight, Dr. Martin Luther King Jr. became *the* recognized leader of the civil rights movement. He was profiled in the *New York Times* and put on the cover of *Time* magazine. President Eisenhower invited him, with other leading black Americans, to a meeting in the Oval Office. This was the first such meeting since President Lincoln had invited Frederick Douglass to confer on civil rights during the Civil War.[27*]

Most adult black and white Americans were wage earners in 1955. Whether or not they were members of organized unions, the amalgamation of the American Federation of Labor (AFL) and the Congress of Industrial Organizations (CIO) was big news for them. George Meany and Walter Reuther were both strongly anti-Communist. They were firm advocates for civil rights. They knew that workers in the Soviet bloc enjoyed no right to strike and no right to bargain collectively. The new AFL-CIO would prove to be a bulwark *against* Communist expansion, both in the United States and around the world. Free labor could be relied upon in the worldwide struggle for freedom.

Suddenly, the nation was stunned to learn in the autumn of 1955 that President Eisenhower had suffered a serious heart attack. Contrasting sharply with the experiences of Wilson, Harding, and FDR, however, Ike resolved to tell the American people *everything* about his illness. His press

---

* TR had famously invited Dr. Booker T. Washington to dinner at the White House in 1901—and suffered great abuse from white racists for it. But that was a social invitation, not a formal conference on civil rights.

secretary, Jim Hagerty, gave full and detailed descriptions of the president's medical condition.[28] Hagerty's briefings calmed the jittery public, but they did more: they set the standard for full disclosure of the people's right to know. "Sunshine," as Justice Brandeis said, "is the best disinfectant." Never was this wise saying truer than in the matter of presidential health.

In 1956, Eisenhower was willing to challenge politics-as-usual. He even explored the idea of running with Ohio's *Democratic* Governor, Frank Lausche. The president admired Lausche's common sense and wanted to be the first to put a Catholic on a Republican ticket.[29]

Not surprisingly, the man who was just one heartbeat away from the presidency in 1956 did not take kindly to being nudged aside. Vice President Richard M. Nixon wasn't biting when Ike tried to lure him away. The president urged Nixon to take four years as secretary of defense to give him "executive experience." Ike prized it. Nixon prized power more and refused to step down. It is little wonder that Eisenhower responded to his doctors with irritation. They warned him to avoid "frustration, anxiety, fear, and above all anger." Ike shot back: "Just what do you think the Presidency *is*?"[30]

Frustrated or not, Eisenhower ran on a slogan of "Peace and Prosperity" in 1956. His opponent, once again, was Adlai E. Stevenson. The election returns showed another landslide for the invincibly popular Eisenhower. With typical wit, Adlai Stevenson quoted Lincoln's story of the little boy who stubbed his toe in the dark: "I'm too big to cry," said the lad, "but it hurts too much to laugh." Ike swept every region outside the Deep South. And he even won several Southern states, including Virginia, Tennessee, Kentucky, Louisiana, Texas, and Florida. It was the best showing ever for a Republican.

Eisenhower's popularity was not shared by his party, however. Unlike the Republican sweep of 1952, this time the Democrats retained control of *both* Houses of Congress. Political commentators speak of "the coattail effect" (when a candidate for president or governor pulls in candidates for lesser offices and other candidates just hang on to their leader's coattails). Political humorists were quick to jibe in 1956 that the famed Eisenhower jacket—the military style Ike made famous in World War II—"has no coattails."

Privately, Ike did not even *want* some of his fellow Republicans elected. Of the GOP Senate leader William F. Knowland, for example, Eisenhower wrote that in his case there seemed to be no final answer to the question: "How *stupid* can you get?"[31] He was impatient with some Republicans who called for eliminating Social Security, abolishing the minimum wage, and repealing farm programs and labor legislation, including unemployment compensation. Ike wrote his brother Edgar *opposing* that businessman's conservative ideals. To attempt what Edgar proposed, he said, would be political suicide.[32] Eisenhower promoted what he called "Modern Republicanism." His "flaming middle of the road" positions led conservative Barry Goldwater to dismiss Eisenhower's administration as "a dime store New Deal."

Young conservatives rallied to the standard of *The National Review*. This brash, new journal was founded in 1955 by William F. Buckley Jr. Buckley took pains to avoid the extremism of the John Birchers and the anti-Semites. He rejected the racism of some who claimed to be conservatives. His feisty publication lost money, but it gained a following. And conservative books became bestsellers too. More than six hundred thousand readers had pored over Friedrich A. Hayek's *The Road to Serfdom* since its publication in 1944. Hayek showed with admirable clarity and logic how even *democratic* socialism would lead to a loss of fundamental freedoms. Hayek was never a popular author to the extent that everyone was reading him at the corner newsstand. But the Austrian refugee showed how the *roots* of Hitler's tyranny and the bases of Marxist collectivism were one and the same. His work had a profound influence on a generation of freedom-loving young conservatives.

Even Hayek might have approved of Eisenhower's pet public works projects. Early in his presidency, Ike overruled Pennsylvania and Ohio steel interests in approving the Saint Lawrence Seaway Project. Canada, impatient with decades of delay, was planning to go ahead alone with the massive effort to make the ports of the Great Lakes accessible to ocean-going vessels. President Eisenhower soon recognized the national defense implications of the project.[33] Looking beyond the narrower economic interests, Ike opted for full cooperation with the Canadians. The project is one of the world's greatest examples of peaceful international cooperation. The Soviet Union could point to no similar example of trust and mutual respect with any of its threatened neighbors.

In 1956, President Eisenhower persuaded the Democratic Congress to support his plan for an Interstate Highway System. Ever since 1920, when Major Eisenhower led an army truck convoy on a two-month expedition across the Continent, he had known that the world's richest country was hampered by seriously inadequate roads.[34] As the Supreme Allied Commander in World War II, he saw the advantages Hitler had from the excellent German autobahns. As president, he was determined to bring America into the twentieth century. Congress authorized Ike's plan, a massive road-building project. The forty thousand miles of Eisenhower's Interstate Highway System was the largest public works project in our history.[35] It was comparable to the Roman roads, the pyramids, and the Great Wall of China.* It changed America forever.

President Eisenhower faced two major crises in 1957. The locally elected school board of Little Rock, Arkansas, voted to comply with the *Brown* ruling. They began to *desegregate* the city's schools, if slowly, beginning in the fall of 1957. Nine black students were registered for classes at the city's Central High School. When some whites protested, Democratic Governor Orval Faubus called out the Arkansas National Guard to block the black students' registering. President Eisenhower ordered the Justice Department to go into federal court to demand the

---

* The Romans built more than 50,000 miles of roads; the Great Wall of China is 4,500 miles long (*World Book Encyclopedia*, 2004 ed., vol. 16, p. 361; vol. 8, p. 349, respectively). Both projects, of course, required *centuries* to complete. And neither project was built by *free* men.

governor withdraw his state's troops. Faubus gave in, but riots by white protesters broke out as the black students began their classes. Quickly, Ike sent in the 101st Airborne Division to protect the black students and enforce the law. The 101st remained at the school for several months to ensure order.

Ike knew well the splendid fighting qualities of the 101st Airborne: he had ordered "the Screaming Eagles" to lead the Normandy invasion thirteen years before. The president went on national television to explain his action. Pointing to the watching world, he called on all Americans to show respect for the laws. His goal was to restore "peace and order and a blot upon the fair name and high honor of our nation in the world will be removed." Eisenhower knew that Little Rock was being exploited by Soviet propaganda.[36]

Eisenhower sent in the troops to Little Rock knowing it might cost his Republican Party dearly in elections in this region. But duty came first for Ike. Leading Democrats criticized President Eisenhower's use of federal troops. Georgia's senator Richard Russell compared Eisenhower's actions to Hitler's. Also, ironically, among those condemning Ike's use of force were Senators John F. Kennedy and Lyndon B. Johnson.[37]

Little Rock was knocked off the front pages by a chunk of heavy metal. The Soviet Union stunned the world by launching *Sputnik*, the first earth satellite. In Russian the word means "fellow traveler," but for Americans it meant trouble. For two hundred years, Americans felt sheltered by thousands of miles of open ocean. After Sputnik, the heartland of America was vulnerable to nuclear attack by Intercontinental Ballistic Missiles (ICBMs). Americans shuddered.

A reporter asked Eisenhower if the launch of the Sputnik didn't prove the superiority of Communism over capitalism. After all, he said, Khrushchev was boasting that the hammer-and-sickle flag was flying on the moon. "I think it's crazy," Ike responded. "We should not be hysterical when dictatorships do these things."[38]

Khrushchev saw it differently.

IV. "WE WILL *BURY* YOU!"

"We will *bury* you!" shouted the ebullient Nikita Khrushchev in 1956. Khrushchev presented a new challenge to America's political, military, and diplomatic supremacy. Unlike the cautious, secretive Joseph Stalin who rarely left his Kremlin apartments, it seemed Khrushchev was everywhere. He traveled extensively outside the USSR, especially to the nonaligned countries in Asia and Africa. The "winds of change" that followed decolonization of the British and French Empires were blowing strongly in favor of socialism.

Khrushchev exercised a rough, peasant charm and a crude sense of humor. A highly intelligent, shrewd survivor of numberless Kremlin purges and plots, he was a short, roly-poly bald man with prominent warts and a fifty-two-inch waistline. But he moved like a thin man. Khrushchev moved vigorously, creating the impression of a Soviet Union leading the way into the future. When Sputnik bleep-bleeped its way across the skies every ninety minutes, Khrushchev pointed to this coup as evidence of Soviet technological superiority. The Soviets, he said, would win the space race.

Americans did not know they were even *in* a space race. The Soviet satellite program was launched in total secrecy. That contributed to the shock. America's response was total openness. It would invite the world to watch the United States launch its own earth satellite. The decision was surely right, but it had disastrous consequences for American prestige—at least in the short run. As the world looked on, several U.S. rockets blew up on the launchpad. "Kaput-nik" teased irreverent headline writers. A cartoonist showed a golf ball trailing Sputnik in orbit. Maybe the president, an enthusiastic golfer, could put that in orbit! It was an international embarrassment. Senator Kennedy and Governor Nelson Rockefeller, a dissident Republican, began speaking of the "missile gap." They said the United States had fallen behind the Soviets during Eisenhower's watch. The charge was untrue.

Ike knew it was untrue. When Khrushchev had shot down Ike's "Open Skies" proposal at Geneva in 1955, the president authorized secret flights over the USSR. The high-flying American U-2 jets provided U.S. intelligence with a treasure trove of information. Ike was angry that his political opponents were taking advantage of his enforced silence.[39]

Similarly, the United States had a great advantage in submarines. In 1958, the USS *Nautilus*, the world's first nuclear-powered submarine, went from the Pacific to the Atlantic *under the polar ice cap*. (Later *Nautilus* would surface at the North Pole to claim the prize of centuries.) At last, the Northwest Passage had been discovered! Led by the genius of Admiral Hyman G. Rickover, the United States' nuclear submarine force provided America and the world with the means of "massive retaliation." In a dangerous and violent world, Rickover's "boomers" and attack submarines would provide the "nuclear umbrella" that sheltered America's freedom.

President Eisenhower named Admiral Rickover as his personal representative for New York City's ticker-tape parade down Broadway to welcome home the USS *Nautilus*. It was a gracious invitation for the old West Pointer to give to a graduate of rival Annapolis. And Admiral Rickover, as usual, promised not to be an easy guest in the Big Apple. The navy brass wanted all participants to appear in sharply creased dress whites. Rickover, a three-star admiral, claimed not to have any dress whites—and, besides, he preferred his working khaki uniform.[40] It was vintage Rickover.

The "father of the nuclear navy," Rickover had been putting tacks on the chairs of navy bigwigs for nearly four decades. He had arrived at Ellis Island as a six-year-old immigrant child. His mother and siblings already had their papers marked "Deported" when his father arrived at the last minute to claim them.[41] At the Naval Academy, weighing barely 125 pounds, young Rickover had to fight with other midshipmen who insulted his Jewish background. A fellow Jewish "mid" had suffered the indignity of having his page of the Academy yearbook perforated—for easy tearing out.[42] But Rickover prevailed over pride, prejudice, and pressure.

Admiral Rickover probably wasn't kidding when he said he didn't own the ceremonial dress whites the navy loves. He typically showed up for the maiden cruises of "his" nuclear submarines in a business suit. The submarine's crew had been instructed by their skipper to provide the admiral's uniform and all toilet articles he would need. Rickover's bags contained crisp, official stationery and the prototype of a word-processing machine.

When the new submarine performed up to his most exacting standards, the admiral would unlimber his equipment and print out scores of letters from the bottom of the sea to influential members of Congress and captains of industry.[43] Rickover became a legendary figure in the navy. He rose on the basis of smarts and dedication—and carefully maintained connections on Capitol Hill. Rickover stepped on hundreds of toes. "They called me that ugly SOB; they called me that mean SOB," Rickover told his longtime aide Bill Bass, "but they never called me that dumb SOB."

Thanks to Rickover's genius and ceaseless demands for rigorous safety standards, America quickly developed a submarine force to prevail over any possibility of a sneak attack by the Soviets using nuclear weapons. It was done at comparatively low cost and with the greatest regard for the human lives of America's nuclear sailors. There would be no "marching through minefields" under Dwight D. Eisenhower.

Ike knew America was ahead of the Soviets, and he refused to give in to politically inspired panic for a raid on the Treasury. Eisenhower alone had the military expertise and prestige to stand fast. It took strength and courage. Rudyard Kipling could have been describing Ike in his poem "If":

> If you can keep your head when all about you
> Are losing theirs and blaming it on you. . . .

V. IKE'S LAST YEARS

Eisenhower's "New Look" in defense increased America's reliance on nuclear weapons. His secretary of state, John Foster Dulles, spoke of

"Massive Retaliation" against the Soviets if they invaded Western Europe. This reliance on nuclear supremacy also enabled Eisenhower to reduce federal spending. Ike used the new CIA to destabilize or topple left-wing regimes he considered hostile to U.S. interests. He was determined not to allow Communism to expand into the Western hemisphere.

Nonetheless, many people worried about war. Hollywood produced in 1959 *Pork Chop Hill*, a movie starring Gregory Peck. Just as *All Quiet on the Western Front* had done twenty years earlier, *Pork Chop Hill* stressed the futility of war.[44] It was based on the hill in Korea that had been taken by American forces, lost to the Chinese, retaken, and finally evacuated, all at the cost of 314 American lives.

Vice President Nixon was confronted by Premier Khrushchev at a U.S. trade exhibit in Moscow in 1959. Khrushchev "debated" Nixon about the gleaming American consumer goods that were displayed. Amid dishwashers and televisions, Khrushchev said the Soviets would move on past the United States in economic development. Waving his hand "bye-bye" and grinning, Khrushchev mugged for the news cameras. One Soviet citizen—and we must hope the KGB never recognized his handwriting—spoke for millions when he wrote in the U.S. guestbook: "Drop me off in America as we pass them by."

When Khrushchev shot down an American U-2 jet days before a scheduled East-West summit conference in Paris in May 1960, Eisenhower fell into an embarrassing trap. At first, the administration issued a cover story—that CIA pilot Francis Gary Powers was actually a weather reconnaissance flyer who'd been blown off course. Khrushchev then let the world know that the pilot had been taken alive, and he had confessed to spying. Ike was caught in a direct lie. When Khrushchev demanded Ike apologize as a condition for going ahead with the summit, Eisenhower refused.

This time, Britain's Prime Minister Harold MacMillan, France's President Charles de Gaulle, and West German Chancellor Konrad Adenauer—the democratic leaders of NATO—fully supported President

Eisenhower. Senator Kennedy stumbled when he suggested that Eisenhower apologize for the sake of peace.

The 1960 Paris summit collapsed as Khrushchev and the Soviet delegation walked out. It was Khrushchev's way of trying to tip the coming American election to the Democrats. Americans, as they so often do in crises, backed President Eisenhower completely.

Eisenhower was criticized by many writers of the adversary culture. Smart, "hip" young comedians like Mort Sahl and Lenny Bruce mercilessly lampooned the fractured syntax and confusing grammar of the old general. Serious social analysts deplored what they saw as stultifying conformity and soulless materialism. John Kenneth Galbraith derided *The Affluent Society* and Sloan Wilson's *The Man in the Grey Flannel Suit* questioned: "What price success?" Cars with wraparound chrome and outrageous fins for mom and dad, a Davy Crockett coonskin cap for Junior, and a Hoola Hoop for sister—all this represented what some saw as the mindlessness of Eisenhower's "Happy Days." Television was denounced as "a vast wasteland" by Federal Communications Commissioner Newton Minow, Adlai Stevenson's law partner. Comedian Fred Allen called television "bubble gum for the eyes."

But television was not just the well-scrubbed version of family life represented by *Ozzie and Harriet*. Host Ed Sullivan presented not only Elvis Presley's "Hound Dog" but also serious opera arias by Richard Tucker and Leontyne Price, the light wit of Victor Borge, and the artistry of mime Marcel Marceau.* Today, we view the 1950s as television's "golden era." Ronald Reagan's weekly announcement of the high-toned *GE Theater* surely contributed to television's popularity—and his.

Those same television sets transmitted Dr. Martin Luther King Jr.'s

---

* Few who watched Marceau's silent antics on TV would have guessed that his greatest acting role was with the French Underground during World War II. He impersonated a scoutmaster who was taking children on "hikes" into the Alps. In fact, he was helping these Jewish children escape to neutral Switzerland (https://www.history.com/news/marcel-marceau-wwii-french-resistance-georges-loinger).

powerful cry for freedom. In not a few years, those grainy black-and-white TV news pictures of vicious dogs attacking peaceful civil rights demonstrators would help mightily to form the new *national* consensus for justice and freedom.

Ditto Eisenhower's beloved highway system. Before Ike, hundreds of American communities really were literally isolated. As soon as those four-lane "Interstates" were laid down, however, they could convey buses carrying Freedom Riders to remote towns. The revolutions in communications and transportation that Eisenhower promoted by his policies meant freedom rising. Quietly, Eisenhower filled the benches of the federal judiciary with judges who would fearlessly put an end to racial segregation.[45] Will future generations see these changes, too, as part of the Hidden-Hand Presidency?

The late Stephen Ambrose sums up Ike best for us today:

> He was so comforting, so grandfatherly, so calm, so sure of himself, so skillful in managing the economy, so experienced in insuring America's defenses, so expert in his control of the intelligence community, so knowledgeable about the world's affairs, so nonpartisan and objective in his above-the-battle posture, so insistent on holding to the middle of the road that he inspired a trust that was as broad and deep as that of any president since George Washington.[46]

Eisenhower himself once responded to a complimentary letter from Henry Wallace. FDR's second vice president had made a number of speeches comparing Ike favorably with George Washington. Flattered, Ike sent this courteous reply: "My sense of pride is all the greater because I've never [agreed] with those who so glibly deprecate [Washington's] intellectual qualities. I think too many . . . confuse facility of expression with wisdom; a love of the limelight with depth of perception. I've often felt the deep wish that The Good Lord had endowed me with [Washington's] greatness of mind and spirit."[47]

Eisenhower's own assessment of his two terms was typically pithy: "[After Korea], the United States never lost a soldier or a foot of ground in my administration. We kept the peace. People ask how it happened—by God, it didn't just happen, I'll tell you that."[48] With the major exception of Cuba's falling prey to a stealthy Communist revolution, Ike's defensive reaction is basically true. To top it all off, millions of Americans who grew up under his wise and good leadership can still say with genuine conviction: *I like Ike!*

TWENTY

PASSING THE TORCH

(1961–1969)

I. THE NEW FRONTIER

John F. Kennedy's image was everywhere in 1960. Americans saw his tanned, handsome face; his beautiful, elegant wife; and their lovely little girl smiling down from thousands of magazine covers. Kennedy was in the newsreels, in the newspapers, on television. His Pulitzer Prize–winning book, *Profiles in Courage*, was reprinted for the campaign season. No one had ever campaigned so vigorously for the presidency before. *Vigah*—as he pronounced *vigor* in his Boston accent—was the key to the Kennedy magic. Another new word—*charisma*—came into general usage. Americans eagerly anticipated change.

Jack Kennedy had been planning his presidential run from the moment that he narrowly lost the Democratic vice presidential nomination to Estes Kefauver in 1956.* But it would not be an easy run for

---

* Kefauver, a liberal U.S. senator from Tennessee, had made a name for himself investigating gangsters in televised hearings regarding organized crime in America. Stevenson had thrown open the selection of a vice presidential nominee to the convention delegates, who had narrowly selected Kefauver. Later, when the Democratic ticket lost in a landslide, Jack Kennedy considered himself fortunate not to have been on it.

the nomination. He beat three Democratic titans—Adlai Stevenson of Illinois, Hubert H. Humphrey of Minnesota, and Lyndon B. Johnson of Texas—for the party's nomination to face Republican Richard M. Nixon in the general election.

In his campaign, Kennedy urged a stronger response to the Soviets and a greater federal government role in domestic programs. He eloquently called for Americans to advance toward "a New Frontier." Nixon was hampered by his pledge to visit all fifty states.* In these days before regular jet travel, flying to Alaska and Hawaii was a long, long process.

Kennedy, a Catholic, took up the religion issue head-on in a meeting with the Protestant Ministerial association in Houston, Texas. He said he believed no Catholic president should allow a Catholic bishop to tell him how to act. He pledged to *resign* if his Church ever attempted to dictate his conduct of his office. This was intended as much as a signal to the Catholic Church to give him room as it was to the attentive Protestant pastors in the hotel ballroom. He told the ministers he did not speak for the Catholic Church and, significantly, the Catholic Church did not speak for him. The key issue then was not, as it later became, abortion or federally funded birth control, but federal aid to education. Kennedy favored federal aid that *excluded* students in Catholic parochial and other religious schools.[1]**

When Senator Kennedy met Vice President Nixon for a series of televised debates, most people expected the senior, more experienced Nixon to win convincingly. However, the tanned, articulate Kennedy performed with cool competence and flashes of wit. Nixon recently had

---

* The election of 1960 was the first to include fifty states. The admission of Alaska (1959) and Hawaii (1959) had been the first to include noncontiguous territories as states. Hawaii's admission had been delayed by Senate segregationists who resisted admitting a state with a nonwhite majority.

** Abortion was then illegal in all fifty states, as were suicide and homosexual sodomy. No-fault divorce was illegal in forty-nine states, with only Nevada allowing for an easy end to a marriage. All of this was to change in the following decade.

been released from the hospital for a knee infection. He looked haggard. His much lampooned and cartooned five o'clock shadow gave him a grim appearance. Those who *heard* the debate on radio scored it for Nixon, but *viewers* gave the contest to the young Kennedy.[2]

On Election Day, Kennedy eked out an incredibly narrow victory. He won 34,227,096 popular votes (49.7 percent) and 303 electoral votes to Nixon's 34,107,248 popular votes (49.5 percent) and 219 electoral votes. Just 119,848 votes (two-tenths of 1 percent) separated the two candidates.

On a sunny, frigid January day in 1961, the youngest man ever to be elected president delivered his Inaugural Address.* In a world threatened by atheistic Communism, Kennedy reaffirmed his commitment to the ideals of the Declaration of Independence: "[The] rights of man come not from the generosity of the state, but from the hand of God." He included a ringing call to service and sacrifice that thrilled millions: "Ask *not* what your country can do for you; ask what you can do for your country."[3] He concluded with these powerful words: "With a good conscience our only sure reward, with history the final judge of our deeds, let us go forth to lead the land we love, asking His blessing and His help, but knowing that here on earth God's work must truly be our own."

He was to find no "honeymoon period" in the onrush of crises foreign and domestic. When the Eisenhower-initiated action by the CIA to overturn Cuba's Communist dictator Fidel Castro was presented to the new president, he allowed it to go forward. But, at the last minute, he withdrew the U.S. air cover for the Cuban exile army that was storming ashore. Probably, the Cuban exiles never had a chance of toppling Castro, but taking away the air cover *guaranteed* failure. The fiasco at the Bay of Pigs seemed to confirm what JFK's critics had charged: he was too young, too inexperienced, too hasty in his judgments.

When Kennedy met Khrushchev in Vienna in June 1961, the whiff

---

* JFK was elected at age forty-three. TR was forty-two when he *succeeded* the assassinated McKinley. This author was seventeen in 1961, a student at a Washington, D.C., Catholic high school, and attended John F. Kennedy's inauguration.

of failure in the Bay of Pigs debacle was still in the air. Khrushchev told his Kremlin comrades, "Berlin is the testicles of the West. Every time I want to make the West scream, I squeeze on Berlin."[4] Behind closed doors, Khrushchev berated and bullied the young president. Threatening war, Khrushchev did his best to intimidate his adversary. He would sign a separate treaty with his East German satellite to force the Western Allies out of Berlin, he warned. Kennedy said he could sign anything he liked with the East Germans so long as Western occupation rights were respected. "Force will be met with force," Khrushchev replied menacingly.[5] Trying to break the ice, Kennedy asked Khrushchev about a medal he was wearing. Told that it was the Lenin Peace Prize, JFK could not resist quipping: "I hope you keep it."

The Soviet ruler ended the summit conference by saying that in six months he would sign the treaty with the East German regime. Kennedy believed that would mean war. "If that's true, it's going to be a cold winter," he said grimly.[6]

It was a baptism by fire. It was the struggling young president's first direct encounter with the brutality of the Soviet system. "He just beat hell out of me," JFK confessed to associates.[7] Kennedy told James Reston, a *New York Times* columnist—on deep background—that the Bay of Pigs fiasco had emboldened Khrushchev: "Most important, he thinks I have no guts."[8*]

Khrushchev had another important reason to feel buoyant at Vienna. The Soviet Union had only recently launched the first manned spaceflight in history. On 12 April 1961, Major Yuri Gagarin orbited the earth three times in his *Vostok* space capsule. Vostok, which means "East," put the Eastern bloc far ahead in the race into space.

Soviet gains in space presented Kennedy with a serious challenge.

---

* When a president, or other high government official, gives an interview "on background," it means he cannot be directly quoted. "Deep background" meant the journalist could not even quote the *substance* of the conversation. JFK learned to use this technique to enlist the support of influential journalists.

He had come into office pledging to "get America moving again." Now, the Soviets seemed to be passing America by. Khrushchev had seen the great excitement in the West created by the appointment of seven Project Mercury astronauts.[9] The clean-cut, buttoned-down, young military pilots had what was called "the right stuff."* The U.S. media made them heroes before they set foot in space. Khrushchev was determined to steal Kennedy's thunder. And, with Gagarin's flight, he did.

Americans worried that with *Lunik 3* flying past the moon, taking photographs of the dark side, the Soviets were planning to put a man on the moon. With a cosmonaut on the moon, what would come next? Moon colonies? Missile bases on the moon that could threaten U.S. cities? Some of these fears were fanciful, to be sure, but there was no denying that the Soviets appeared to be moving far ahead of the United States.

Khrushchev thought the success of Soviet space efforts would prove the validity of Marxism-Leninism. Not the least of this system was its militant atheism. Cosmonaut Gagarin was a committed Communist. Asked what he had seen in the heavens during his first orbital flight, he grinned in reply: *"Nyet boga!"* ("No God!")

Kennedy's response to this challenge was ingenious. Informed that there was no way the United States could catch up with the Soviets in space for the next few years, JFK demanded answers from leaders of NASA.** "Is there any place we can catch them? What can we do? Can we go around the moon before them? Can we put a man on the moon before them?"[10] The new president's science advisers told him they could beat

---

* The Project Mercury astronauts were to become America's first men in space. They were: Capt. Donald ("Deke") Slayton (USAF), Lt. Cmdr. Alan B. Shepard (USN), Lt. Cmdr. Wally Schirra (USN), Capt. Virgil I. ("Gus") Grissom (USAF), Lt. Col. John Glenn (USMC), Capt. Leroy Gordon ("Gordo") Cooper (USAF), and Lt. Scott Carpenter (USN). "Deke" Slayton would be grounded for a decade for a minor heart condition, finally flying on the orbiting Apollo-Soyuz space station in 1972.

** The National Aviation and Space Administration (NASA) was Eisenhower's civilian space agency. Ike was determined to avoid militarizing space.

the Soviets to the moon. That was all Kennedy needed to hear. We'll do it, he said.

Instantly, Kennedy redefined the Space Race. From this point on, every Soviet first—the first woman in space, the first space walk, the first long-term orbital flight—would be measured against the over-arching goal: Have they landed on the moon yet? Kennedy took a long stride toward winning the Space Race: *he moved the finish line!* Soon, Americans would be able to hail their own space heroes, as first Navy Lieutenant Commander Alan B. Shepard and then Air Force Captain Virgil I. "Gus" Grissom rocketed into space.

Here on earth, Khrushchev was still a dangerous antagonist. In August 1961, when many Western leaders were on vacation, Khrushchev moved to seal off East Berlin. He had to do something. The grim, Stalinist rump regime the Soviets had created was called the German Democratic Republic. It was neither democratic nor republican. And it wasn't even German. It was merely a puppet state set up by the occupying Soviets. Many of the Germans who ran it for Moscow had themselves spent the Second World War in Moscow. Now, in 1961, this Soviet Zone of Germany was hemorrhaging. Thousands of trained doctors, teachers, engineers, and scientists—especially young people—were streaming into West Berlin seeking a better life. They could take an elevated tram or simply walk across the dividing line between East and West Berlin. No one dared to joke, "Will the last German to leave the Soviet Zone please turn off the searchlights?" Still, that was what was behind Khrushchev's belligerence over divided Berlin.

In late August, Khrushchev struck. The Soviet ruler ordered East Germans to string barbed wire along the entire perimeter between East and West Berlin. This was soon followed up by bulldozers and concrete sections of a long and ugly wall surrounding the entire free city of West Berlin. Kennedy, expecting another Berlin Blockade, breathed a sigh of relief. Maybe there would not be a "long, cold winter" after all. As long as Khrushchev did not block Allied access to West Berlin, the United States could protest, but it could not justify knocking down what people now called the Berlin Wall.

German families were cruelly separated. Brutal East German guards even shot their countrymen as they tried to escape from "the workers' paradise." The world watched in horror as seventeen-year-old Peter Fechter was shot by border guards. The lad lay bleeding, dying, crying out for mercy in the no-man's-land the Communists had created. East German *Volkspolizei*, or VOPOs, were said to be the "people's police." The VOPOs trained their guns on West Berliners, threatening to shoot any of them who tried to rescue young Fechter. Over the next three decades, hundreds of others would be shot down in cold blood while trying to escape.

II. "GODSPEED, JOHN GLENN!"

Marine Lieutenant Colonel John H. Glenn seemed like a figure out of central casting. Lean and strong, his "high and tight haircut" marked him as the straight arrow he was. He had met his wife, Annie, in the playpen in New Concord, Ohio. There had never been another girl in the world for him but this dark-eyed beauty. And just as Annie overcame the handicap of a speech impediment, John bested graduates of the nation's elite service academies. At the press conference where the original *Mercury 7* astronauts were announced, Glenn stole the spotlight by speaking out about his religious faith. Even in those more religiously demonstrative times, Glenn's televised profession of faith appeared to many sophisticates as "uncool."

He almost got blackballed by his fellow astronauts when he bluntly told them to "keep it zipped." NASA officials were worried that a sex scandal might ground the famously high-flying jet jocks.

President Kennedy liked the gutsy combat pilot from the Buckeye State. He invited Glenn to the White House a few weeks before his scheduled flight in *Friendship 7*. It was to be the first U.S. effort to send a man into orbit around the earth. Kennedy had a great deal of his own political prestige riding with the Marine. Kennedy asked Glenn to roll out his charts, models, and maps in the Cabinet Room. He quizzed Glenn for more than an hour on every aspect of the flight.[11] The president was insatiably curious.

Glenn and his fellow Mercury astronauts often evoked strong feelings in Americans. Many yearned to beat the Russians and genuinely loved these brave young men who were willing to risk their lives doing it. Tax attorney Leo DeOrsey was no exception. He had agreed to represent the astronauts with the media *pro bono*.* As John Glenn prepared to rocket into space, it was revealed to his circle of family and friends that he had very little life insurance. DeOrsey told John and Annie Glenn that Lloyds of London had agreed to cover the astronaut for the expected six hours of his maiden flight—for a premium of $16,000![12] Several days later, however, DeOrsey called back to recommend they turn down the Lloyds deal. He felt bad about it, he said. "I'm not going to bet against you," DeOrsey told Glenn. Instead, he gave a mutual friend a check for $100,000, made out to Annie Glenn, just in case anything should happen to John.[13]

Astronaut Scott Carpenter, Glenn's backup, was obviously moved as the Atlas rocket's 367,000 pounds of thrust roared into action for liftoff. "Godspeed, John Glenn," Carpenter cried out. Tom O'Malley, the General Dynamics Corporation's project director, added his prayer: "May the good Lord ride with you all the way."[14]

Glenn could hear none of this encouragement over the sound of his rocket engines. A heart-stopping moment occurred while Glenn was in orbit when mission control began to suspect that mysterious light "butterflies" Glenn reported meant the space capsule's heat shield had deployed too soon. To test it in flight was dangerous too. When Glenn was instructed to throw the switch, he gingerly complied—after only a slight hesitation. The temperatures outside his capsule rose to 9500°F as

---

* *Pro bono*: "for free."

he reentered the earth's atmosphere—lower, but not much lower, than the surface of the sun! Without the heat shield, Glenn would be incinerated. The world held its breath.

There was a period of radio silence during reentry. It was anticipated, but now it only increased the tension. Finally, after what seemed an eternity, John Glenn showed the right stuff as his calm, professional voice broke through the static. The heat shield held! Once again, America had fired a shot heard 'round the world.

III. "EYEBALL TO EYEBALL" OVER CUBA

Forty thousand Soviet troops were in Cuba in 1962. We now know that. When New York's Republican senator, Kenneth Keating, spoke out against the Soviet buildup "just ninety miles from our shores," President Kennedy was outraged.[15] He thought government leaks were enabling the Republicans to embarrass him and make him look weak.

In the middle of a campaign trip, the president was summoned back to Washington, D.C. There, he received confirmation from U-2 flights over Cuba that the Soviets were installing Intermediate Range Ballistic Missiles on the island fortress. These Soviet IRBMs were capable of delivering a nuclear strike against the entire Eastern Seaboard of the United States. Texas, Oklahoma, and Louisiana, in a single, secret stroke, were now also in grave danger of a nuclear Pearl Harbor.

Instantly, President Kennedy summoned his top advisers to a crisis conference. Some of his military chiefs warned him that staging a preemptive assault on Cuba to wipe out the missile bases before they could be made operational could lead to nuclear war.[16] Kennedy rejected that option. But he knew the Soviet missiles could not be allowed to stay in Cuba. The Kremlin turned a stony face to the world and flatly denied they had placed their offensive missiles in Cuba.

President Kennedy went on national television on 22 October 1962 to inform the American people and the world that the United States knew of the Soviets' deception—their "clandestine" and reckless nuclear arms buildup in Cuba—and to demand that the missiles be removed.

> Neither the United States of America nor the world community of nations can tolerate deliberate deception and offensive threats on the part of any nation, large or small. We no longer live in a world where only the actual firing of weapons represents a sufficient challenge to a nation's security to constitute maximum peril. Nuclear weapons are so destructive and ballistic missiles are so swift, that any substantially increased possibility of their use or any sudden change in their deployment may well be regarded as a definite threat to peace.

Kennedy then ordered a "quarantine" of Cuba.* He would use the vast U.S. naval superiority to surround the island and intercept Soviet freighters bound for Havana with more missiles.

The British were then supplying the United States with high-level intelligence from deep within the Kremlin. Colonel Oleg Penkovsky, an officer in Soviet military intelligence, was secretly spying for Britain.** Kennedy received full support from the American people, Britain's conservative Prime Minister Harold MacMillan, and, surprisingly, France's President de Gaulle. When Kennedy's special envoy, Dean Acheson, entered de Gaulle's magnificent office in the Elysée Palace, he offered to show the austere Frenchman the U-2 photographs the United States had obtained from flights over Cuba. "Put your documents away," de Gaulle said dramatically. "The word of the President of the United

---

* He avoided the term *blockade*, which is an act of war under international law. In choosing to call his action a *quarantine*, he harkened back to FDR's famous "quarantine the aggressor" speech. It was a comparison JFK welcomed.

** Penkovsky was caught and executed by the KGB. For years, the story circulated in Moscow that he had been rolled into the city's Donskoi crematorium—still alive. Recently, doubt has been cast on that part of the story, but it served its purpose.

States is enough for me. Tell your President that France supports him unreservedly."[17]

At the UN, Ambassador Adlai Stevenson showed the U-2 reconnaissance photos and confronted the Soviet ambassador with his lies. The Soviet claimed he had trouble with the interpretation of Stevenson's comments into Russian. "I am prepared to wait, Mr. Ambassador, *until hell freezes over* for your answer!" It was Adlai's finest hour. Watching on television, President Kennedy said, "Terrific! I never knew Adlai had it in him."[18]

When he received *two* distinct cables from the Soviet government, Kennedy ignored the harsher one and focused on the more accommodating one. He presumed that the former had been drafted by the Soviet *apparatchiks*, while gambling that Khrushchev himself had written the softer line.

Khrushchev offered Kennedy a *quid pro quo*—removal of Soviet missiles from Cuba in exchange for removal of U.S. missiles from NATO ally Turkey. Kennedy had to reject this, at least publicly. But he followed up another Khrushchev suggestion: that the United States agree to guarantee Cuba's territorial integrity. That meant the United States would have to drop its support for the anti-Communist Cuban exiles and agree not to invade Cuba with U.S. forces.[19]

As a Soviet freighter steamed toward the U.S. ring of steel surrounding Cuba, tension mounted around the world. Would she turn back? Would she refuse to allow an American inspection party to board her? Would there be bloodshed? Was this the opening act of World War III? Finally, the Soviet freighter turned away.

Khrushchev was unwilling to initiate a nuclear war over Cuba. Claiming that all he ever wanted was to protect Cuba from invasion, Khrushchev publicly backed down. On 28 October 1962, he agreed to remove his missiles from Cuba.[20] Cuba's Castro reacted with obscene abuse of his Soviet ally. Saying Khrushchev was a *maricón*, a homosexual, Castro kicked the wall and broke a mirror in his anger and frustration.[21]*

---

* Castro's hatred of homosexuals is well-known. He regularly condemned homosexual Cubans to imprisonment on the Isle of Pines.

Kennedy had prevailed. As Secretary of State Dean Rusk put it, "we were eyeball to eyeball and the other guy just blinked."[22] But Rusk's comment was delivered on background. Kennedy ordered no public gloating over Khrushchev's *apparent* humiliation. Nor did JFK want it revealed that he had indeed agreed quietly to remove the U.S. missiles from Turkey.[23] Perhaps we went eyeball to eyeball over Cuba and *our* guy blinked!*

"Appearances contribute to reality," Kennedy often said. And to all appearances, the brave young president had courageously backed the Soviet adversary down. Khrushchev's private letters to Kennedy now contained the word *détente*. He looked to a general relaxation of tensions, he said. Accordingly, he okayed a new "hotline" between Moscow and Washington, D.C. This was actually a teletype machine between the two capitals that would permit a more rapid communication in the event of a crisis. Kennedy was deeply concerned that a miscommunication might bring nuclear war. Khrushchev also dropped his opposition to the Nuclear Test Ban Treaty. It would become one of the stellar achievements of the Kennedy administration.

JFK worked to break down barriers. When he addressed the Alfred E. Smith Memorial Dinner in New York, he reminded his audience of the famous telegram Smith had supposedly sent the pope following his disastrous defeat in the presidential election of 1928: "Unpack." With a wink, Kennedy said he just received the Vatican's response to his education bill: "Pack." The audience of distinguished Catholics, Protestants, and Jews— New York's elite—laughed uproariously. A Catholic president making fun of one of the most sensitive issues in politics delighted everyone.

While the joke enhanced the president's popularity, it didn't help his education bill. Kennedy's proposal excluded any aid to children attending Catholic schools. Like so much of Kennedy's legislative program, the bill stalled in Congress.

---

* Those missiles in Turkey are routinely described as "obsolete" in media accounts of the Cuban Missile Crisis, but they certainly weren't obsolete when they were installed, just months before Khrushchev demanded their removal.

Meanwhile, *National Review* (*NR*) criticized the Vatican for its seeming willingness to do business with the Communist occupiers of Eastern Europe. Such dissent from positions embraced by the Roman Catholic Church coming from both the liberal JFK and the conservative and largely Catholic editors of *NR* helped put to rest fears of Catholic dominance of American political life.

War and peace were not the only issues to command attention in those heady days. A new concern, perhaps sparked by the discussion on the impact of atmospheric nuclear testing, raised questions about humans' care of the earth. "We are challenged, as mankind has never been challenged before, to prove our maturity and mastery not of nature but of ourselves," wrote Rachel Carson in her best-selling 1962 book, *Silent Spring*.[24] Americans showed renewed regard for the impact of industrialization and modernization on their surroundings. A movement arose to protect the *environment*. At first, it was a voluntary movement of individual citizens. In time, it would express itself in legislation.

IV. FREEDOM ON THE MARCH

The fact that Americans were enjoying continuing prosperity during the affluent 1960s made the Kennedy administration seem all the more successful. JFK was generally frustrated in his attempts to get legislation he backed through Congress. He pressed the Democratic-controlled Congress to cut taxes. He was the first of his party to embrace the idea that cutting taxes could actually stimulate economic growth and increase government revenues. Kennedy failed to get Medicare approved. This government program to socialize medicine for the elderly had been on the agenda since Teddy Roosevelt's failed Bull Moose effort in 1912.[25]

JFK did succeed in sending thousands of idealistic young Americans around the world in his Peace Corps. His *Alianza para Progreso* (Alliance for Progress) promised a new overture to America's long-neglected allies in Latin America.

Jacqueline Kennedy was a vastly popular First Lady. She redecorated the White House and invited leading artists to grace the old mansion. Spanish cellist Pablo Casals offered a concert for a sparkling reception. French writer André Malraux read. And always, the dashing young president and his lady brought off the ceremonial side of the White House with style and ease. Mrs. Kennedy's love of culture and refinement added immeasurably to the appeal of this engaging young couple. The public delighted in pictures of young Caroline Kennedy riding her pony, Macaroni, and little John-John (JFK Jr.) peeking out from the kneehole of his dad's historic desk.[*] The popular Broadway show *Camelot* captured the imagination of the times. And Kennedy's New Frontiersmen would not have strenuously objected to any comparison of their young vibrant administration with the mythical Knights of the Round Table. We do know that Kennedy, quoting Shakespeare's *Henry V*, often used the phrase "we happy few, we band of brothers."[**]

The booming economy made conditions seem all the more intolerable for black Americans who were denied equal accommodations in hotels and restaurants, who faced discrimination in jobs and housing, and who were disqualified from voting in wide areas throughout the South. People talked about the "revolution of rising expectations." The Fifteenth Amendment to the Constitution had asserted the right of the freedmen to vote, but federal enforcement was woefully lacking. Poll taxes, literacy

---

[*] This author's uncle, Dr. John W. Walsh, was the obstetrician who delivered John F. Kennedy Jr. John Walsh was the son of Dr. Joseph Walsh, who was said to be "Al Smith's personal physician." Both doctors would treat Republicans too. Their Hippocratic oath required it.

[**] Only years later, after Kennedy's death, were the tawdry tales of JFK's womanizing known to Americans. Only then might it have been pointed out that the beauty and justice of Camelot were lost because of adultery at its heart. So is the fine legacy of John F. Kennedy tinged with sorrow.

tests, and grandfather clauses were devices routinely employed in the former Confederate states to disenfranchise black voters.*

President Kennedy's administration asked the Interstate Commerce Commission (ICC) to ban segregation at lunch counters engaged in interstate commerce along the new interstate highways. Freedom Riders from the North took buses into the South to claim the right to eat at integrated lunch counters. Some of these buses were firebombed, and the Freedom Riders were beaten. President Kennedy hesitated to endorse the Freedom Riders' effort, but he demanded order. And the ICC did ban segregation in interstate commerce.[26]

Dr. King decided to make Birmingham, Alabama, the center of his freedom movement. He called Birmingham "the most thoroughly segregated big city in the United States."[27] The local, mostly white, chamber of commerce was eager to avoid confrontation, but Police Chief Eugene "Bull" Connor vowed resistance.[28] Connor was also Alabama's Democratic National Committeeman, a man of considerable influence. Rioting broke out in Birmingham the night after Dr. King's home was hit by a bomb. Bull Connor used fierce police dogs to make sure crowds were kept in check. Television images of Bull Connor's dogs attacking demonstrators made the city notorious around the world. Alabama's Democratic governor, George Wallace, in his 1963 inaugural address, breathed defiance. This was his understanding of freedom:

> I have stood, where once Jefferson Davis stood, and took an oath to my people. It is very appropriate then that from this Cradle of the Confederacy ... that today we sound the drum for freedom as have our

---

* The poll tax required citizens to pay a tax for the supposed maintenance of the election machines and payment of the election officials. The tax had a disparate impact on poor black sharecroppers, most of whom could not afford to pay it. The so-called grandfather clause exempted some citizens from the literacy test if their grandfathers had been registered voters. Prior to Emancipation, of course, black people in the South could not vote. Thus, the grandfather clause was an ill-disguised ploy to let illiterate whites vote while keeping black voters from enjoying their constitutional rights.

generations of forebears before us done, time and time again through history. . . . I draw the line in the dust and toss the gauntlet before the feet of tyranny . . . and I say . . . segregation today . . . segregation tomorrow . . . segregation forever.[29]

Clearly, Governor Wallace did not consider Birmingham residents and taxpayers like Dr. King and his congregation to be "his people."

When Wallace, as he had pledged, "stood in the schoolhouse door" to prevent two black students from enrolling at the University of Alabama, President Kennedy had no choice but to send in federal troops. Although he had criticized Eisenhower's use of federal troops at the time of Little Rock, Kennedy addressed the country on television. He called on every American to "stop and examine his conscience" about these acts of lawlessness.[30]

Kennedy praised the people of the South for their patriotism and service in peace and war, but he was determined to stand up for the civil rights of all. And he was under unremitting pressure from Roy Wilkins of the NAACP, Whitney Young of the Urban League, and A. Philip Randolph of the train car porters' union. The senior leadership of the civil rights movement expressed their frustration over the slow pace of change. Kennedy had boasted during the campaign that discrimination in housing could be ended "by a stroke of the pen." Black Americans began sending thousands of pens to the White House.

In Birmingham, though, progress would bring problems. A Nazi Party member jumped onto the stage and attacked Dr. King. King was unhurt, but there was a ceaseless drumbeat of violence directed against him and his nonviolent movement. King had already been stabbed by a deranged black woman, beaten on an airplane flight by an enraged white passenger, and pummeled at a newly integrated hotel in Selma, Alabama.[31] The thirty-three-year-old minister had to live every day as if it would be his last.

The president went on television 11 June 1963 to address the nation on civil rights. His powerful words are worth remembering today.

If an American, because his skin is dark, cannot eat lunch in a restaurant open to the public, if he cannot send his children to the best public schools available, if he cannot vote for the public officials who represent him . . . then who among us would be content to have the color of his skin changed? Who among us would then be content with the counsels of patience and delay? We face a moral crisis as a country and as a people. . . . A great change is at hand, and our task is to make that revolution peaceful and constructive for all.[32]

In Mississippi, Byron de la Beckwith did not wait to hear Kennedy's appeal for peace and justice. He shot NAACP leader Medgar Evers as the civil rights leader was returning to his home. Evers bled to death in the driveway of his home, in the presence of his wife and children.[33]

When Dr. King was jailed in Birmingham, he wrote a memorable letter that has ever afterward served as a key text of the civil rights movement. In it, he explained the need for action. "We have waited for more than 340 years for our constitutional and God-given rights," he said. "The nations of Asia and Africa are moving with jet-like speed toward gaining political independence, but we still creep at horse-and-buggy pace toward gaining a cup of coffee at a lunch counter. Perhaps it is easy for those who have never felt the stinging dart of segregation to say, 'Wait.'"[34]

Dr. King emphasized that respect for law was essential. He wrote that when he was forced to resist an unjust law as a last resort, he had to be willing to submit to the punishment that was meted out. In this, Dr. King was well within the American tradition—and the Christian tradition—of civil disobedience. King also coupled his determination to engage in civil disobedience with a firm respect for higher law and lawfulness. As a result, he obediently accepted jail sentences when courts found him in violation of law.

Kennedy's Civil Rights Bill was introduced on 19 June 1963. The Senate's famous Rule XXII had prevented meaningful action for decades. Rule XXII meant a determined minority of senators could filibuster a bill to death.* Kennedy was frustrated at the slow pace of legislation. Senator Hubert Humphrey, the prime sponsor of the Civil Rights Bill, agreed. The Constitution makes no provisions for a cloture rule in the Senate. Under Rule XXII, a bill needed the support of two-thirds of the senators in order to be voted upon. But the Constitution, Humphrey argued, states clearly that only a majority shall be necessary to conduct business.[35] However, the legislative process was about to get a shove.

The long-promised March on Washington was the cherished idea of A. Philip Randolph, leader of the train car porters' union. He had urged this action for more than twenty years. Earlier, however, FDR had talked him out of it. Now, in 1963, Dr. King joined the national civil rights leadership to urge hundreds of thousands to come to Washington in a blazing August sun. To Randolph's pioneering vision of a Great March was added the organizational skill of civil rights activist Bayard Rustin. Labor joined the effort, with George Meany and Walter Reuther of the AFL-CIO giving the March their full endorsement. Hundreds of church leaders and Jewish groups joined in.

President Kennedy's reaction was guarded. He worried that any disorder in such a huge crowd would be seized upon by Senate opponents of civil rights. He declined to meet with March organizers before the event. He did not want them to present him with any list of demands, and he wanted to keep his distance in case there was violence. But he held open the possibility of a White House meeting after the March.[36]

Gospel singer Mahalia Jackson introduced Dr. King with the words of an old Negro spiritual:

---

* A filibuster was the title given to the Senate's tradition of "unlimited debate." In practice, senators did not have to address the merits of a bill and could even read a telephone directory of all those they claimed would be adversely affected by the pending legislation. All they had to do was keep talking. Strom Thurmond held the filibuster record of twenty-four hours and eighteen minutes for speaking against a civil rights bill in 1957. He had the help of a "Motorman's Friend"—a device that enabled him to stand and speak so long without going to the men's room.

I'm going to tell my Lord when I get home
Just how long you've been treating me wrong.
I've been 'buked and I've been scorned
Trying to make this journey all alone![37]

Most white Americans had never heard the great power of the black preachers of this country. So when Dr. King mounted the podium in front of the massive, brooding statue of Abraham Lincoln, he asked that his children be judged "not by the color of their skin, but by the content of their character." Most of his hearers that day were unprepared for the force and the emotion that King's biblical cadences could evoke:

> I have a dream . . . I have a dream today! So let freedom ring. . . . Let freedom ring from Stone Mountain of Georgia. Let freedom ring from every hill and molehill of Mississippi, from every mountainside. And when this happens—when we allow freedom to ring from every town and every hamlet, from every state and every city, we will be able to speed up that day when all God's children—black men and white men, Jews and Gentiles, Protestants and Catholics—will be able to join hands and sing in the words of the old Negro spiritual, "Free at last, free at last, thank God Almighty, we are free at last!"[38]

So rarely can it be said that speeches change things. *Rhetoric* or *mere rhetoric* is the way knowing insiders dismiss the power of public address. But Dr. King's speech changed things. It changes things still.

And President Kennedy had inspired King and all his brothers. "Freedom is indivisible, and when one man is enslaved, all are not free," Kennedy had told hundreds of thousands in West Berlin, just weeks before the Civil Rights March on Washington. Kennedy had said, "Ich bin ein Berliner!" I am a Berliner.

If freedom truly were indivisible, as JFK said, why did it make sense to defend freedom in West Berlin but not to let freedom ring in

Birmingham, Alabama? America in the 1960s still had military conscription. If young black men could be drafted and sent to West Berlin or to the Demilitarized Zone separating North and South Korea, how could anyone justify segregation at home? Why should such young Americans be denied freedom in their own home towns?

The vast throng, hot, thirsty, and tired, left in a quiet and orderly way. According to most accounts, some two hundred thousand marchers dispersed, leaving not so much as a piece of litter behind. Hundreds of mass demonstrations would follow in Washington, D.C. Hardly a weekend goes by without some march for this or that. None of them—arguably, not all of them combined—has had the impact that that great 1963 March on Washington had.

V. 22 NOVEMBER 1963

President Kennedy's political prospects looked bright in the fall of 1963. He expected his Republican opponent in 1964 to be either New York Governor Nelson A. Rockefeller or Arizona's conservative Senator Barry Goldwater. Kennedy dismissed "Rocky" as having no guts; Barry, he thought, had "no brains."[39] Though confident, he was leaving nothing to chance. Texas Democrats had split in a nasty feud between liberal Senator Ralph Yarborough and conservative Governor John Connally. JFK thought a presidential visit might help mend political fences. He was especially pleased that Jackie would go with him. Normally, the First Lady found politics a crushing bore. Texas politics was even more so. But she recognized the importance to her husband of this vital state.

The president and the First Lady rode in an open limousine down a main thoroughfare in Dallas, Texas, on a clear November day. Nellie Connally, the governor's wife, turned around in the car to comment on the large crowds who lined the way, cheering lustily. "You sure can't say Dallas doesn't love you today, Mr. President," she said.

Then shots.

They had just passed the Texas Schoolbook Depository. The shots came from behind. "I looked back and saw the president's hands fly up to his throat. He made no sound, no cry—nothing," she wrote. "I had a horrifying feeling that the president had not only been shot, but could be dead." Years later, she recalled the terrifying details as if they had just happened. "It's the image of yellow roses and red roses and blood all over the car . . . all over us," she said. "I'll never forget it. . . . It was so quick and so short, so potent."[40]

Governor Connally, riding in the "jump" seat, was struck and pitched forward. Another shot destroyed the president's skull as the limousine blazed ahead, racing for the hospital. Mrs. Kennedy, risking her own life, crawled over the seat and out of the vehicle to help a Secret Service man get on board.

Kennedy was dead as soon as the second bullet struck him, but doctors at Parkland Memorial Hospital tried feverishly to revive him nonetheless.

The nation heard the news within moments. Walter Cronkite, CBS's veteran anchorman, broke down as he announced the president's death. The entire world seemed to stop as the casket containing the president's body was loaded onto Air Force One—as the presidential jet was now called. Mrs. Kennedy seemed stunned as she entered the plane, her brilliant pink suit still stained with her dead husband's blood. Lyndon Johnson asked her to stand next to him in the jet's forward cabin. With the plane still on the runway, he was sworn in as the nation's thirty-sixth president by Federal District Court Judge Sarah T. Hughes. Judge Hughes was a longtime Johnson ally. LBJ had been instrumental in having the Dallas lawyer named to a lifetime appointment as a federal judge.

Daniel Patrick Moynihan, then a young Kennedy appointee in the Labor Department, spoke for most when he said, "I don't think there's any point in being Irish if you don't know the world is going to break your heart eventually." During those four cold, bleak November days, *all* Americans were Irish.*

---

* Moynihan told columnist Mary McGrory, also an Irish Catholic, "We will laugh again, but we will not be young again."

The assassination and funeral were the first televised event that fused the American people together. The entire Baby Boom generation would share the memory—just as their parents' generation had been brought together by the attack on Pearl Harbor and a more recent generation by the terrorist attacks of 11 September 2001. Millions of American homes had photographs of President Kennedy. Millions bought and saved for their children the commemorative editions of *Time*, *Life*, and *Newsweek* that rolled off the presses.

The accused assassin, Lee Harvey Oswald, was quickly apprehended in Dallas. He was himself shot to death by Jack Ruby, the operator of a sleazy Dallas nightclub, as Oswald was being transferred from one prison to another. The fact that Oswald had defected to the Soviet Union, taken a Russian wife, and then returned to the United States to be employed by the Fair Play for Cuba Committee, a Communist front group, seemed to make no impression on the media of the day. Dallas was blamed, even though Judge Hughes and Mrs. Connally could have testified that they felt no fear from the good people of Dallas. In the years since the assassination, a vast right-wing conspiracy was blamed in countless articles, books, and Hollywood movies.

Conspiracy theories of the Kennedy assassination soon cropped up. President Johnson attempted to put these to rest by appointing Chief Justice Earl Warren and Republican House Conference Leader Gerald Ford to head a commission to investigate the killing. A persistent, vocal minority would not be convinced by the Warren Commission Report, issued the next year. The report said JFK was assassinated by one man— Lee Harvey Oswald—and not by a conspiracy.

VI. "AN IDEA WHOSE TIME HAS COME"

President Lyndon B. Johnson spoke at a somber joint meeting of the 88th Congress on 27 November 1963. "Let us continue," he told the lawmakers in a nationally televised broadcast. Then he gave them his number-one priority for the session.

> [No] memorial oration or eulogy could more eloquently honor President Kennedy's memory than the earliest possible passage of the civil rights bill for which he fought so long. We have talked long enough in this country about equal rights. We have talked for one hundred years or more. It is time now to write the next chapter, and to write it in the books of law.[41]

Lyndon B. Johnson was widely distrusted by many supporters of civil rights. They feared his Texas origins. They distrusted his close ties to Senator Richard Russell of Georgia, Senator Harry F. Byrd of Virginia, and other segregationists among the Senate Club. Now Johnson would prove that those ties of many decades would serve him well in the White House. He would prove with deeds his sincere commitment to civil rights. In publicly committing himself to JFK's Civil Rights Bill, Johnson would go far to secure the Kennedy Legacy. His first address to the nation came just five days after the tragic events in Dallas. LBJ claimed the mantle of John F. Kennedy as he fully embraced civil rights. Passage of Kennedy's bill would be the test of his sincerity. He would not fail.

Johnson and his Senate allies had to overcome the Southern Democrats' filibuster. That required sixty-seven votes.* He could only do that with Republican support. "Everett, we can't pass this bill without you," Minnesota's Hubert Humphrey told Senator Everett McKinley Dirksen of Illinois over and over.[42] Dirksen, whose honey-coated speaking voice earned him the nickname "the Wizard of Ooze," was proud of the GOP's heritage of civil rights. He took seriously his role as Illinois's favorite son. Illinois is, after all, "the Land of Lincoln." Dirksen would remain staunch for civil rights at every turn.

---

* Today, it requires only sixty votes to invoke *cloture*, to break a filibuster. But it remains a formidable hurdle.

Senator Humphrey threw himself into the effort to pass the bill, which required equal access in all public accommodations. It also prohibited discrimination in hiring, promotion, and firing on the basis of race, color, religion, or sex. It was the most far-reaching civil rights legislation since Reconstruction.

Humphrey had to fend off criticism that the Civil Rights Bill would lead to racial quotas. He memorably shot back at his antagonists: "If the Senator can find in Title VII . . . any language which provides that an employer will have to hire on the basis of percentage or quota related to color, race, religion, or national origin, I will start eating the pages one after another, because it is not in there."[43]

In the midst of this great debate, Humphrey received word that his younger son, Bob, was headed into surgery for a cancerous tumor in his neck. Unable to leave his post at this critical moment, the weeping floor leader was consoled by his Senate colleagues.[44]

The bill went forward. Sensing his opponents had talked themselves out, Senator Humphrey brought the great Civil Rights Act of 1964 to a floor vote. Senator Dirksen, true to his word, moved for adoption of the bill. Quoting the great French liberal, Victor Hugo, Dirksen said, "Stronger than all the armies is an idea whose time has come. The time has come for equality of opportunity, in sharing in government, in education, and in employment. It will not be stayed or denied. It is here!" Hundreds of young seminarians, both Catholic and Protestant, prayed in the halls of Congress. Americans called and sent telegrams to Capitol Hill urging passage. Hundreds of organizations—religious, civic, business, professional, labor, and liberal—wrote letters of support.

Dirksen led twenty-six Republicans in voting yes. Barry Goldwater joined only five other Republicans in voting no. Among Senator Russell's segregationist supporters were Senator Robert Byrd of West Virginia, Albert Gore Sr. of Tennessee (father of the future vice president), and Strom Thurmond, then a Democrat. The vote on final passage in the

Senate was 71–29. Republicans voted 27–6 in favor of the bill; Democrats approved it 44–23.*

On 2 July 1964, President Lyndon B. Johnson signed the most far-reaching Civil Rights Act in American history. Invited to the White House for the signing ceremony were Martin Luther King Jr., Roy Wilkins of the NAACP, Whitney Young of the Urban League, A. Philip Randolph, and other major leaders of the civil rights movement. Senator Everett Dirksen, Senator Thomas Kuchel of California, and other key Republicans who had given their indispensable support to pass the bill were seated in the front row of distinguished guests.

For the rest of their lives, millions of black and white Americans would remember this day as the moment when the long-delayed promise of American freedom at last became real. One of the great tragedies in modern American life is that too many critics who viewed the Civil Rights Act of 1964 as "only the first step" have diminished the epoch-making achievement of Senator Hubert Humphrey, Senator Everett Dirksen, and their colleagues. It had taken one hundred years to achieve what they achieved that day.

VII. A CHOICE, NOT AN ECHO

For generations, political scientists and commentators had called for two broad parties based on philosophy—a liberal party and a conservative party. In 1964, the country got that choice. Barely two weeks after LBJ signed the Civil Rights Act, Senator Barry Goldwater accepted the Republican nomination for president. Goldwater's rise had been as stunning as it was unexpected.

Goldwater was the standard bearer for the newly assertive conservative

---

* Among those voting against the Civil Rights Act on final passage were well-known Senators J. William Fulbright (Democrat of Arkansas) and Sam Ervin (Democrat of North Carolina).

movement. Despite the fact that some young conservative thinkers had doubts about Barry's intellectual depth, Goldwater's wildly successful book had won him thousands of eager volunteers.[45] *The Conscience of a Conservative* sold more than seven hundred thousand copies and went through twelve printings.[46] This was unheard of for a political book. With characteristic candor, Goldwater would later disavow some parts of his bestseller ("Hell, I didn't write that . . . [Brent] Bozell did," he would say in exasperation). This mattered little to the legions of loyal young conservatives who enlisted in Barry's movement. Against liberal charges that he was hopelessly outdated, a relic from an earlier time, Barry eloquently stated, "The laws of God and of nature have no dateline." Against Lyndon Johnson, whose standard of achievement was to run up the legislative scoreboard with bills enacted, Goldwater boldly said, "I don't aim to pass laws, *but to repeal them.*"[47]

The editorial writers constantly implied that Goldwater was a Fascist. In reality, though, he was a principled champion of freedom. He had been influenced by Friedrich A. Hayek's *Road to Serfdom* and the free-market ideas in the work of Adam Smith.[48] He was, he often said, a *Jeffersonian* who believed that that government is best that governs least. "Politics is the art of achieving the maximum amount of freedom for individuals that is consistent with the maintenance of social order," he wrote.[49]

At a raucous GOP national convention in San Francisco's Cow Palace, delegates chose Goldwater to be their candidate. Members of the party's liberal wing, such as New York Governor Nelson A. Rockefeller, looked on in dismay.

"I would remind you that extremism in the defense of liberty is no vice!" said Goldwater upon accepting the nomination. "And let me remind you also that moderation in the pursuit of justice is no virtue!"[50] The words were crafted by young Professor Harry Jaffa, and there was nothing in it that Thomas Jefferson or Abraham Lincoln would not have endorsed, but it was seized upon by the media and cast as a dangerous expression of radicalism.

Barry Goldwater was an enormously attractive figure. A trim, tanned, athletic Westerner, he could ride and hunt, loved skiing and camping. Goldwater was a capable pilot and had risen to the rank of brigadier general in the air force reserve. "In your heart, you know he's right" was the slogan quickly adopted by his followers. "In your guts, you know he's *nuts,*" his liberal critics fired back.[51]

Liberals were especially concerned with what they considered his nuclear saber rattling. As a senator, Goldwater had argued that NATO's commander should have the power to initiate a nuclear response if the Soviets invaded Western Europe. Goldwater thought we could trust solid men like Eisenhower and General Lauris Norstad with that decision. But the very idea was treated as if it were radioactive. Goldwater was widely described as recklessly advocating nuclear war. The charge was that he had once joked about "lob[bing] one into the Kremlin men's room."[52] This was at a time when leading air force generals like Curtis LeMay talked about "bombing them back to the Stone Age." Goldwater, a man's man, was blunt, direct, and funny. But presidential candidates do not joke about nuclear war, not if they hope to get elected.*

The Johnson team knew exactly how to handle the Goldwater threat. Johnson's young campaign aide, Bill Moyers, approved what was, and still is, the most vicious television ad in American history. A lovely little girl is shown pulling petals off a daisy, counting "1-2-3...." Then, a man's voice reverses the count, "6-5-4 ..." giving the unmistakable impression of a *countdown* to a missile launch. Americans had grown very familiar with this rocket launch sequence because of Eisenhower's decision to broadcast our space program. But the ad showed the little girl dissolve into a

---

* The only known exception to this rule was the wisecrack Ronald Reagan offered in 1984. Warming up for his weekly radio address, Reagan said he had just signed legislation abolishing the Soviet Union and the bombing would begin in five minutes. The White House quickly put out a statement saying the president was only joking and didn't know the microphone was live. Reagan had been president for four years at that point and had gained a reputation for calm, steady leadership. Even so, it was a heart-stopping moment for his campaign managers.

picture of a nuclear explosion. Johnson's voice was heard saying, "We must love one another or die," suggesting outrageously that Goldwater's election meant death. "Vote for President Johnson" came the white words on a funereal black screen. "The stakes are too important for you to stay home."[53] The Johnson campaign ran Moyers's Daisy ad only once, but in those days before cable and satellite, most American homes had only three or four television channels. Thus, fifty million people saw this classic negative ad. For the rest of the campaign, the networks ran the ad *for free* as they discussed the issue of nuclear responsibility in the election.

Goldwater met with Johnson in the White House. He agreed not to make an issue of riots in Harlem. He wanted to avoid injecting race into the campaign. When his campaign team produced a film called *Choice* that depicted drunken white teens cavorting naked and young black men rioting, he kept his word and rejected its use. It would inflame race relations, he said.[54]

Johnson showed no such restraint in attacking Goldwater. He chose Hubert Humphrey as his running mate and encouraged the Minnesota senator to go after Goldwater with vigor. Humphrey's point-by-point dissection of the Goldwater voting record demonstrated why senators are so rarely nominated for president. Humphrey treated the delegates at the Democratic National Convention with his litany of measures supported by both Republicans *and* Democrats. "But not Senator Goldwater" was Hubert's refrain, as the delighted delegates took up the response.[55] Humphrey's attack was hard-hitting and effective, but not out-of-bounds. Goldwater enjoyed his reputation for flinty independence of mind. But his often-eccentric voting record made it easy to depict him as an extremist.

Politics ain't beanbag.

The same could not be said for *Fact* magazine. "1189 Psychiatrists Say Goldwater Is Psychologically Unfit to Be President," blared the editors' alarming headline.* They neglected to tell their readers that 12,356

---

* To be sure, *Fact* was not *Life* magazine. Still, its sensationalized story was picked up by the mainstream news organizations and given far broader circulation.

psychiatrists had been questioned, that only 2,417 had responded, that 571 of these had said they couldn't properly diagnose the senator without ever speaking to him.[56] (After the election, Barry Goldwater sued *Fact* for libel and won. The federal court found the article so false, so defamatory, so malicious, it awarded Goldwater $75,000 in punitive damages. The U.S. Supreme Court upheld the judgment.)[57]*

Goldwater approved one campaign broadcast that was to have vast consequences for American history. When every poll showed Goldwater about to get buried in almost every region, he okayed a speech by Californian Ronald Reagan. The popular former actor and television host addressed a nationwide audience with "A Time for Choosing." The speech was the great success of the campaign. Reagan articulated smoothly, convincingly, and nonthreateningly the ideals of freedom, limited government, military strength, anti-Communism, and patriotism that Goldwater had tried without success to defend in his speeches. Goldwater's campaign was cruelly cartooned as a San Francisco cable car crashing down a steep hill: "A Streetcar Named Disaster."** Reagan's speech brought a flood of donations to a campaign rapidly running out of money.

More importantly, overnight, it made Reagan the bright hope of the conservative movement. From the date of "the speech," Ronald Reagan became the *de facto* head of the conservative movement in America.

Even as he caricatured Goldwater as a warmonger, Johnson rushed through the Gulf of Tonkin Resolution through Congress when North Vietnamese gunboats attacked two U.S. destroyers in August 1964 in the Gulf of Tonkin. The resolution blamed the North Vietnamese for the clash and authorized the president "to take all necessary measures

---

* The American Medical Association denounced the magazine article when it was written. Afterward, the American Psychiatric Association adopted the Goldwater Rule, calling it a violation of professional ethics to diagnose without meeting a subject.

** The caption was a satirical reference to the play by Tennessee Williams titled *A Streetcar Named Desire.*

to repel any armed attack against the forces of the United States and to prevent further aggression." He discouraged any extensive debate and demanded immediate action. Only two senators—Wayne Morse of Oregon and Ernest Gruening of Alaska—voted no.

Vietnam was rarely discussed in the 1964 campaign. Yet it loomed, like Banquo's ghost at MacBeth's banquet, behind the seated guests.[*]

Goldwater tried to raise the issue of war and peace. The Democrats, he charged, had led the nation blindly into "Lyndon Johnson's war in Vietnam.... American sons and grandsons are being killed by Communist bullets and Communist bombs. And we have yet to hear a word of truth about why they're dying."[58] His point was legitimate. But by this stage in the campaign, no one was listening.

Election night 1964 produced one of the most lopsided landslides in American history. LBJ won 486 electoral votes and 42,825,463 popular votes (60.6 percent) to Goldwater's 52 electoral votes and 27,175,770 popular votes (38.5 percent). Johnson's popular-vote percentage exceeded FDR's in 1936. He swept all regions except the Deep South. Johnson's coattails produced a huge Democratic majority in the 89th Congress.

Critics accused him of wanting every vote and stopping at nothing to gain an overwhelming victory. Surely, Johnson's vanity was famous. He named his Texas ranch "LBJ" for himself. His wife, Lady Bird, bore the same initials, as did his daughters, Luci Baines and Linda Bird Johnson.[**] Only his pet beagles—whom he yanked up by their ears—escaped the Texan's brand. They were called *Him* and *Her.*

The president's very practical reasons for wanting to bury Goldwater

---

[*] The Kennedy administration had okayed the ouster of South Vietnam's authoritarian president Ngo Dinh Diem. President Kennedy was shocked when military plotters not only removed Diem and his powerful brother, Ngo Dinh Nhu, but murdered them both on 1 November 1963. This left the U.S. planners working, uneasily, with the homicidal conspirators who had seized power in Saigon. The grim story, however, was overshadowed by JFK's own assassination just three weeks later.

[**] Johnson did not name his wife. Born Claudia Alta Taylor, as a baby she was said to be "as purty as a lady bird." The nickname stuck.

were simple: he wanted to break the power of conservative Southern Democrats and Republicans who resisted big spending programs. Johnson knew he would need a huge victory in 1964 to make up for expected losses in the South. He had seen the FDR, Truman, and JFK administrations frustrated on Capitol Hill. He had Texas-sized plans for legislation. Only a Texas-sized victory would produce the majority he needed to enact his programs.

Johnson wanted to achieve what FDR had outlined in his 1944 State of the Union address. FDR was his political mentor and hero. Johnson wanted to expand federal programs to give the government extensive new powers in housing, education, welfare, and medical care. Nor would that be enough; he knew that great presidents were patrons of culture. Personally, he cared nothing for literature, music, or art, but he believed he could win the support of refined people by treating their artistic interests the way he treated other congressional colleagues' desires for a new bridge or post office. He was not entirely wrong.*

In private, Johnson railed against "all those high-falutin' Harvards."[59] At one of Jackie Kennedy's elegant White House cultural soirées, Johnson was seen in the hall with his foot up on the immaculate wall, paring his fingernails with a pocketknife, bored to death. In fairness, JFK found Jackie's cultural evenings boring too.[60]

VIII. "WE SHALL OVERCOME!"

Johnson wasted no time in applying his greatly expanded new congressional majority. Calling his program for the country "The Great Society," he pressed for new federal legislation on education and health care. Congress passed the landmark Elementary and Secondary Education Act

---

* The patrons of the arts proved to be very supportive of federal spending on their special interests, but Johnson miscalculated in thinking they would be grateful to *him* for the generous endowments he created.

on 9 April 1965, and the president signed it into law two days later. LBJ broke a logjam that had lasted for decades. As a Protestant, he was politically able to provide funding for students attending parochial schools (mostly Catholic). Johnson also overcame Southern opposition. With desegregation now inevitable, Southern members of Congress wanted all the federal aid they could get.

The election victory the previous November, and the Deep South's choice of Goldwater, only emphasized to Dr. King and his supporters how powerless they were without the vote. A planned march on the state capital at Montgomery began in Selma, Alabama, on a cold, blustery Sunday in March. "It's not just Negroes, but really *all* of us who must overcome the crippling legacy of bigotry and injustice. *And we shall overcome,*" King told supporters in Selma.[61] The march was interrupted by club-swinging, mounted police who barred the way to the Edmund Pettis Bridge.

Other violence broke out as well. A white minister from Boston, James Reeb, was attacked by a mob of white youths for joining in the demonstrations. He died of his wounds. Later, Viola Liuzzo, a Detroit housewife, was gunned down attempting to help young black volunteers register voters.[62]

Dr. King was joined in Selma by hundreds of marchers, including leaders of the AFL-CIO, religious groups, and national civil rights organizations. With three thousand marchers in Selma demanding civil rights, President Johnson went on national television to announce his support for a far-reaching Voting Rights Bill.

When the Voting Rights Bill swept through the 89th Congress, Johnson signed it on 6 August 1965. With his signature, Johnson put an end to the political order that had dominated his native region since Reconstruction. With voting rights enacted into law, segregationist politicians "turned on a dime." Strom Thurmond, Jesse Helms, George Wallace, and hundreds of other office seekers dropped their support of racial segregation.[63] As Senator Dirksen would say of his errant colleagues, "When I feel the heat, I see the light."

Voting rights for black Americans transformed politics. America could stand before the world and assert to be, indeed, the home of freedom. No longer could Communist and unaligned delegates at the UN taunt America for hypocrisy.

Johnson did not rest on his laurels. He pressed Congress to enact Medicare, which it dutifully did. LBJ traveled to the Truman Presidential Library in Independence, Missouri, for the bill-signing ceremony. Generously, Johnson paid tribute to Harry Truman's vision—and promptly signed up the frail senior citizen as the *first* enrollee in the vast new medical program for the elderly. LBJ demanded and got new federal departments of Housing and Urban Development (HUD) and Transportation. For HUD, he tapped Robert C. Weaver as secretary. Weaver was the first black man to serve in a president's cabinet. Johnson also named Thurgood Marshall to the Supreme Court. Marshall was the first black member of the high court.

The president greatly expanded welfare. If he had read Daniel Patrick Moynihan's warnings on the crisis in the black family, he apparently paid them no mind. Moynihan warned that the illegitimacy rate among black families—then at 22 percent—posed a serious threat to community stability. But in LBJ's Great Society, marriage would no longer be the centerpiece of federal family policy. Many federal bureaucrats questioned whether marriage had any significance anyway. A husband, it seemed, could be replaced by a check. Johnson's "War on Poverty" resulted in billions of dollars going to Appalachian and Inner City projects. Some of these proved worthy, but many were, as their Republican critics called them, "boondoggles."

Lady Bird Johnson gained great credit for her drive to beautify federal highways. Commercial interests, including billboard advertisers, groused, but Mrs. Johnson's views prevailed.

LBJ used his vast appointive powers to give positions to consumer advocates. He also created the National Endowment for the Arts and the National Endowment for the Humanities. He created the Corporation for Public Broadcasting (CPB), which in time spawned the Public

Broadcasting System (PBS) for television and National Public Radio (NPR). These never created a federal government monopoly on broadcasting—as is so often the case in Europe—but they helped to further institutionalize Johnson-style Big Government liberalism.

IX. VIETNAM

At first, the Vietnam War was not Lyndon Johnson's war. The Truman Doctrine had committed the United States to help nations trying to resist Communist subversion. Accordingly, Truman sent U.S. aid to the French and anti-Communist forces in Indochina. Despite the vigorous attacks on containment by Vice President Richard Nixon, President Eisenhower committed the United States to contain Communist expansion. Ike was the one who first used the analogy of the dominoes to explain why the United States had to support South Vietnam.[64] According to the Domino Theory, if South Vietnam fell to the Communists, so, too, would Laos, Cambodia, and very likely Thailand, Malaya, Singapore, and all of Southeast Asia. Given the Cold War experience with Poland, Czechoslovakia, Hungary, and the rest of Eastern Europe, it seemed a compelling theory.

As president, John F. Kennedy backed the South Vietnamese government. He increased U.S. forces from 3,164 in 1961 to 16,263 by the time of his death in 1963.[65]

When Johnson came into office, he failed to make the case for the Vietnam War to the American people. He also failed to gain the support of America's allies. British voters had turned out the Conservatives just weeks before Goldwater was buried. The new Labour Prime Minister Harold Wilson wanted no part of armed intervention in Southeast Asia. Johnson tried to give his famous "treatment" to Canada's Prime Minister Lester B. Pearson. He treated that nation's most respected diplomat with such contempt that the Canadian press published cartoons showing Johnson lifting "Mike" Pearson by his ears—just like a Johnson beagle!

When Johnson visited American forces in Vietnam, he told our soldiers to pursue victory, to "nail the coonskin to the wall."[66] Because he could give Americans no overarching reason to fight and sacrifice, Johnson himself increasingly became the object of opposition to the war. His coarseness and his tendency to make outrageous displays of his emotions made his critics angrier with his policies. Johnson self-pityingly decried all of this criticism as disdain for him *as a Texan.*

Johnson's personality and his administration's record became the focus of the Republican campaign of 1966. In response to *three* "long, hot summers" in which race riots had broken out in many cities, Hubert Humphrey told the NAACP convention that if *he* had to live in a ghetto, "he might lead a pretty good revolt" too. With this statement, Humphrey seemed to condone rampant lawlessness and caused many Americans to believe that liberals were "soft on crime" and disorder. Thirty-four people had died in riots in the Watts section of Los Angeles in 1965.[67] Richard Nixon came out of his four-year retirement to lead the GOP attack in 1966. The Republicans gained forty-seven seats in the House of Representatives and three new U.S. senators. One of these was Massachusetts's Edward Brooke, the first black senator elected since Reconstruction.

In California, voters gave Ronald Reagan a *million vote* margin over incumbent Governor Edmund G. "Pat" Brown. Brown's campaign had stupidly compared Reagan's acting career to that of John Wilkes Booth. Students who grew their hair long, smoked marijuana, and protested the war in Vietnam, the draft, and almost everything else about American life were the butt of Reagan's campaign humor. They were known as "hippies." They "act like Tarzan, look like Jane, and smell like Cheetah," Reagan said good-naturedly.[68] Californians loved it.

Johnson's typical habit of exaggeration was seen in inept defenses of his war policy: we won't "pull back our defenses to San Francisco."[69] LBJ himself seemed not to understand clearly what Americans were fighting for. He relied heavily on Defense Secretary Robert S. McNamara, one of the so-called "whiz kids" from the Ford Motor Company. McNamara was one of JFK's brilliant New Frontiersmen whom Johnson had retained.*

The president began to face a large and growing antiwar movement. Because he had never taken his case to the American people and because he had never asked Congress for a declaration of war, Johnson relied too heavily on public opinion polls. These showed support for U.S. involvement, at least until 1966. Most of the American press, especially the "prestige press," backed the Johnson administration's position on the war as late as 1966.[70]

While campaigning against Goldwater, Johnson had charged the conservative senator with being reckless. Now, LBJ boasted that he kept such a tight rein on his generals "they can't bomb an outhouse" in North Vietnam without his approval.[71] The only unbelievable part of that statement is that Johnson would have said "outhouse" and not something cruder. Although he could rightly say he had not initiated the war, he was unquestionably the one who escalated American involvement and increased American forces "in country" to more than five hundred thousand. Most of these were draftees.

Vietnam kept American policymakers distracted. When, in June 1967, Egypt's dictator Gamal Abdel Nasser expelled UN peacekeepers from the Sinai Desert, President Johnson used the hotline Kennedy and Khrushchev had established to argue that both nuclear superpowers should avoid direct involvement in a Mideast war. Soviet Premier Alexei Kosygin gave Johnson assurances, but the Soviets had armed Egypt and other Arab states to the teeth.[72]

When Nasser closed off the Straits of Tiran, blocking Israel's freedom of the seas, Israel decided to act. "Our basic objective," Nasser stated publicly, "will be to destroy Israel."[73] The Israelis struck back, destroying

---

* LBJ was mightily impressed by that fellow "with the sta-comb in his hair." When he told Speaker Sam Rayburn how bright McNamara and his fellow intellectuals were, Mr. Sam reportedly responded, "Maybe, Lyndon, but I'd feel a hell of a lot better if even *one* of them had ever run for sheriff."

the Arab air forces on the ground and unleashing a lightning assault on the Egyptians, Jordanians, and Syrians. In six days, the Israelis threw back their Arab enemies, gaining extensive territory on the West Bank of the Jordan River, the Sinai Desert, and the Golan Heights of Syria.

Israeli jets also attacked the USS *Liberty*, killing 34 American sailors and wounding 172. President Johnson accepted Israel's formal apology. They said they had misidentified the clearly marked intelligence ship. Israel agreed to pay $13 million in damages.

Jews around the world—and particularly in the Soviet Union—were thrilled by the State of Israel's brilliant campaign to smash the Arab armies. Friends of Israel rejoiced that the Jewish state would now have a territorial "buffer" to protect it from terrorist attacks. East Jerusalem, with its famous Western Wall, the site of Solomon's Temple, now came under Israeli control.* The occupation of the West Bank and Gaza— with more than three million Palestinian Arabs—would create massive problems for Israel that persist to this day.

The American news media wrote about "hawks" and "doves" in the administration and on Capitol Hill. *Life* magazine published three hundred photographs of young Americans who had been killed *in just one week* of fighting in Vietnam. And there were many such weeks. The media harped on Johnson's "credibility gap," accusing him of lying to take the country into war. To many Americans, the press seemed to relish its "adversarial" pose *vis à vis* the administration. Some thought the media friendlier to North Vietnam's Communist rulers than to their own government.

Woodrow Wilson had been able to defend his war policies. FDR gave eloquent expression to the need to sacrifice. Truman's defense of his Korean War policies faltered. Eisenhower had avoided a land war in Asia, or anywhere else. Judging from his World War II statements, he could have led the country in war. JFK excelled in public communication. ("Any spot is tenable if brave men will make it so" was a typical piece of Kennedy

---

* The Israelis allowed Muslims to control the Dome of the Rock mosque, a holy site of Islam.

eloquence.) But none of them ever encountered the kind of bitter, intense, personal hatred that LBJ did. An example:

Hey! Hey! LBJ!
How many kids have you killed today?

Keenly aware of the American domestic front, North Vietnamese Communist leaders staked all on a single attack in January 1968—the Tet Offensive. They pushed their Vietcong allies to stage a suicidal series of attacks across South Vietnam.* Militarily, it was a disaster for the Vietcong as thousands were killed. But the sight of the U.S. Embassy in Saigon being invaded, of hundreds of American casualties all over the South, showed that we were nowhere near "the light at the end of the tunnel." Johnson's policy of graduated escalation seemed to millions of television viewers to be a total and bloody failure.

Tet was planned to take place during a holiday truce. But Tet was a Buddhist holiday, not an *American* one. Communists in Hué, a city in northern South Vietnam, killed between two thousand and three thousand civilians. Many of these were clubbed to death or buried alive.[74]

Little of this was shown on American television. The city was under Communist control. But when South Vietnam's police chief, General Loan, shot a Vietcong colonel in the head, the photo was shown around the world. It won a Pulitzer Prize. General Loan seemed the very picture of a brutal tyrant to shoot an unarmed man, a man whose arms were tied behind his back. We now know that Loan *knew* the man, caught him in the act of terrorizing a Saigon neighborhood, and captured him in civilian clothes.[75] The man Loan shot had just killed a close personal friend of the police chief's and murdered the friend's entire family. None of this mattered then to the protesters.

---

* *Vietcong* was the name given to black-pajama-clad Communist guerrillas in the South. We now know that they were not independent of the North, but wholly subordinate to it.

Antiwar protests grew in breadth and intensity. Demonstrators burned American flags and draft cards. Three Americans, doubtless influenced by the horrific pictures of a protesting Buddhist monk in Saigon, actually *burned* themselves to death.[76] Communist agitators in the United States urged resistance to government policy. The national antiwar group, the Mobilization to End the War (known to activists as "the Mobe") was taken over by Communist followers of the violent ideas of Leon Trotsky.[77]

Writer Susan Sontag said that North Vietnam *deserved* to be idealized.[78] Actress Jane Fonda went to Hanoi and posed on North Vietnamese antiaircraft guns. This, at a time when American pilots were being shot down, killed, or imprisoned and tortured. American antiwar activists took at face value North Vietnamese claims that they actually fed U.S. prisoners *more* than they fed their own people "because they are bigger than we are."[79] Prisoner of war Jeremiah Denton was brought before television cameras. Unable to speak openly, he nonetheless sent a message. It was daring. He blinked his eyes in Morse code, and the message he sent was chilling: "t-o-r-t-u-r-e."

Defense Secretary McNamara stepped down in January 1968. He has since written a widely criticized memoir in which he claimed that he always harbored grave doubts about the U.S. involvement in Vietnam.* Johnson replaced him with Clark Clifford, who undertook a total review of U.S. policy.

Following Tet, thousands of young antiwar activists went "clean for Gene." They cut their hair and volunteered in the New Hampshire campaign of Senate dove Eugene McCarthy, who had entered the Democratic presidential primaries on an antiwar platform. McCarthy, a poet and former semi-pro baseball player, had had an undistinguished career in the

---

* Secretary of State Dean Rusk and National Security Advisor Walt Rostow believed in the U.S. mission in Vietnam all their days. McNamara gave no indication of his private doubts to the two presidents he served, nor to the American people, nor to the young men he sent to fight and die in Vietnam. His attempt to curry favor with the antiwar elites only further damaged his tainted reputation.

Senate. Now, though, the press lionized him. *St. Gene* became the great hope of activists for bringing down LBJ.

When McCarthy carried 42 percent of the vote in the New Hampshire Democratic primary, the press proclaimed him the winner.* New York Senator Robert F. Kennedy now came under increased pressure to enter the race against Lyndon Johnson.

Kennedy had held back. He said he didn't want to split the Democratic Party. He said he didn't want his challenge to look like a "grudge match." (The mutual loathing between Kennedy and Johnson was famous.) At first, he didn't think Johnson was vulnerable. After New Hampshire, however, McCarthy had shown that Johnson could be brought down— maybe not by McCarthy, however. Leading antiwar Democrats feared that the aloof, scholarly McCarthy could never win a general election.

When Robert Kennedy announced that he, too, would challenge LBJ, many old Kennedy supporters were thrilled. Some of McCarthy's backers, however, were outraged. They admired their man for having had the courage to take Johnson on. Now, they resented "Bobby" for butting in. During his brother's administration, Robert Kennedy had earned a reputation for playing hardball. Now all the old stories of his political ruthlessness were revived.

X. 1968: ANNUS HORRIBILIS

Americans greeted 1968 with trepidation. In just five years, the nation had had to endure a nuclear showdown over Cuba, the assassination of a beloved president, and a seemingly endless and bloody war. No sooner

---

* Actually, Johnson won with 49 percent of the vote. McCarthy's achievement was all the more amazing since he did not campaign and his name was not even on the ballot. But, as JFK said, appearances contribute to reality. In a short time, the public believed that Senator McCarthy had in fact won the New Hampshire primary election. It would not be the last time that a second-place showing in New Hampshire "spun" into a win. Bill Clinton managed that feat in the Granite State in 1992.

had Americans rallied to support the great Civil Rights Act of 1964, the Voting Rights Act of 1965, and a host of other measures designed to secure equal rights in housing, education, and employment than a number of major cities faced racial rioting. Los Angeles, Detroit, and Newark were among the worst of these "urban disorders," as the dominant media euphemistically called them. Hundreds of lives were lost; millions of dollars of property damage occurred.

A naturally optimistic people, Americans hoped for a better new year. It was not to be. The year 1968 would prove to be one of the most discouraging in our history.

Lyndon Johnson's approval rating, on which he set much store, had plummeted. After McCarthy's strong showing in New Hampshire's primary, LBJ could not bear to be bested by Bobby Kennedy, whom he despised. Johnson felt embittered and hurt. He had never wanted the Vietnam War, he told intimates. He had followed Jack Kennedy's policies—urged on by Jack Kennedy's advisers. When he entered the White House, Bobby Kennedy was still a "hawk" on Vietnam. There was a Green Beret—the symbol of America's anti-guerrilla elite warriors—on JFK's grave. And the Green Berets had no greater champion in Washington than Robert Kennedy.

Meanwhile, President Johnson's Commission on Civil Disorders reported that America was becoming two societies "increasingly separate and unequal." Despite the major civil rights bills that had been passed and signed—with broad popular support—the Commission's majority blamed the urban riots on the racism of the white majority in the United States.

Johnson announced a national television address for 31 March 1968. The White House said the speech would be a review of U.S. policy in Vietnam. It was—but there was more. At the end, Johnson stunned the world by announcing that he would withdraw from the presidential race. The country was shaken. What did this mean to the troops then fighting in Vietnam? Did it mean Johnson had abandoned the policies that sent them there? Did it mean he had abandoned *them*?

Hard on the heels of this news came an even more shattering word from Memphis. Though he'd received death threats continually since 1955, Dr. Martin Luther King Jr. never shied from making public appearances. On the night of 3 April 1968, he spoke to a large crowd in a church: "I've been to the mountaintop. And I don't mind. Like anybody, I would like to live a long time. . . . But I'm not concerned about that now. I just want to do God's will. He's allowed me to go up to the mountain, and I've looked over and I've seen the Promised Land! . . . Mine eyes have seen the glory of the coming of the Lord!" It was his last public address. The following day, Dr. King leaned over the railing at the Lorraine Motel and asked a friend to "sing *Precious Lord* for me tonight as you've never sung it before."[80]* At that moment, he was cut down by an assassin's bullet.

Robert Kennedy shared the news with a largely black crowd as he campaigned in Indiana. Crying and embracing, the crowd dispersed peacefully after he spoke these words:

> So I shall ask you tonight to return home, to say a prayer for the family of Martin Luther King . . . but more importantly to say a prayer for our own country . . . a prayer for understanding and that compassion of which I spoke.
>
> We can do well in this country. . . . It is not the end of violence; it is not the end of lawlessness; it is not the end of disorder. But the vast majority of white people and the vast majority of black people in this country want to live together, want to improve the quality of our life, and want justice for all human beings who abide in our land.
>
> Let us dedicate ourselves to . . . tame the savageness of man and

---

* A memorial plaque has been placed at the site of Dr. King's assassination. It says, "They said one to another,
  Behold, here cometh the dreamer . . .
  Let us slay him . . .
  And we shall see what becomes of his dreams."
  Genesis 37:19–20
  The biblical inscription challenges each of us to "see what becomes of his dreams."

make gentle the life of this world. Let us dedicate ourselves to that, and say a prayer for our country and for our people.[81]

Bobby Kennedy's words on that mournful occasion touch us down to our own day. But across America that night, riots broke out in hundreds of cities and towns. Reminiscent of the New York draft riots of 1863, rioting, looting, and burning continued for days in many cities. Hundreds died as National Guard troops had to be called in to restore order. In Washington, D.C., the Capitol looked like St. Paul's Cathedral had looked during the London Blitz. Smoke and flames rose up across the country.

America in 1968 felt like a runaway train ride. When Vice President Humphrey declared his candidacy, he spoke of "the politics of joy." The learned Humphrey was only quoting from John Adams, but he was roundly criticized for it. Who could talk about *joy* in such a year?

And it only got worse.

Early in June, Robert Kennedy battled Gene McCarthy in the California Democratic Primary. As Kennedy went down to claim victory in Los Angeles's Ambassador Hotel, he was shot by Sirhan Sirhan, a young Palestinian immigrant who hated Senator Kennedy for his support of Israel. RFK died early the next morning.*

With King dead, the Kennedys dead, three hundred a week dying in Vietnam, our cities in flames, many of our campuses in an uproar, inflation rampant, authority itself seemed to be breaking down. The foundations of the Great Republic were tottering. Would there be no end to the horrors of this *annus horribilis*?

When the 1968 Democratic National Convention met in Chicago, Vice President Humphrey had most of the delegates' support. Humphrey

---

* Oceans of ink were spilled in these years describing the United States as a "sick" society because of these horrific assassinations. But JFK was killed by a man who had renounced his U.S. citizenship. The Reverend Dr. King was murdered by a drifter, a marginal man who spent most of his life in jail. And here, Bobby Kennedy was assassinated by a foreigner. Sirhan's vengeful act deserves to be described as the first instance of Arab terrorism in America.

later reported that his wife and children had been threatened by antiwar protesters. [82] No politics of joy here. Protesters were determined to break up the convention. Chicago police were just as determined to prevent that. The Democratic Party was itself bitterly divided, over the war, over the draft, over the crisis in the cities and on campuses, over the nomination of a candidate who had contested no primaries.

Only four years before, Lyndon Johnson had celebrated his fifty-sixth birthday at the Democratic Party's 1964 National Convention in Atlantic City, New Jersey. Then, throaty Carol Channing had sung "Hello, Lyndon" to the tune of "Hello, Dolly." Now, the repudiated Johnson dared not show his face at his party's nominating convention.

The riots that occurred in Chicago's Grant Park and throughout the city were fully televised to the American people. Liberal Connecticut Senator Abe Ribicoff denounced the head-knocking conduct of the Chicago Police as the city's mayor, Richard J. Daley, yelled obscene abuse from his seat in the middle of the Illinois delegation. Waiting to deliver his acceptance speech, Humphrey was almost overcome by tear gas in his hotel room. Outside, demonstrators chanted "Dump the Hump!" Jerry Rubin, one of the "Chicago Seven" later tried for their activities at the convention, said his group was "guilty as hell." Rubin added, "We wanted . . . to make the city react as if it was a police state and force the attention of the whole world on us."[83]

Following the uproarious Democratic National Convention in Chicago, it is small wonder Republican nominee Richard Nixon was more than thirty points ahead in the polls in the summer of 1968. Alabama Governor George C. Wallace jumped into the race as an independent. At the time, Wallace's entry was expected to hurt Humphrey. Many blue-collar workers sympathized with Wallace's hawkish position on the war and his threat to "run over" demonstrators if they blocked his limousine. But as temperatures and tempers cooled in the autumn, Humphrey and his running mate, Maine's Democratic Senator Edmund Muskie, rose in the polls.

There were no debates. Nixon coasted. He exuded calmness and command. "I'm not going to campaign for the black vote at the risk of alienating the suburban vote," he told campaign associates.[84] This, combined with Goldwater's stance in 1964, helped to alienate black voters from the GOP from that point on.* Burned by his experience in 1960, Nixon's goal was *not* to lose.[85] And he didn't. Despite Humphrey's resurgence in the polls, Nixon won with 31,710,470 popular votes (43.4 percent) and 301 electoral votes. Claiming victory, he told the television audience of the little girl who had held up her hand-lettered sign: "Bring Us Together." Americans prayed for that.

To close out this horrible year, Americans at last had an event to bring them together. Ever since the fire on board that killed three astronauts at Cape Kennedy during a launch pad test in January 1967, it seemed doubtful that America could keep John F. Kennedy's promise to land a man on the moon by the end of the 1960s.

Now, however, in December 1968, there were concerns that the Soviets might try a "figure eight" flight to circle the moon and claim the prize. It would be a disaster for U.S. prestige at any time, but it would have been especially dispiriting after Americans had endured such a year.

President Johnson ordered NASA to go ahead with *Apollo 8.* Astronauts Frank Borman, Jim Lovell, and Bill Anders prepared to be the first human beings to leave earth's orbit and head out to the moon. Their wives were told by NASA that their husbands' chances of making it back alive were no better than 50–50.[86] They would not land, but their voyage would take them to within one hundred miles of the lunar surface, over the Sea of Crises, the Marsh of Sleep, and on to the Sea of Tranquility.[87] Frank Borman did not ordinarily wear his religion on his sleeve, but he said he was seized by the spiritual impact of being the first human being to see the earth as God saw it. He and his fellow astronauts broadcast to the world from sixty-nine miles above the lunar surface. They had gone

---

* As recently as 1960, Nixon had been able to win 30 percent of black voters' support. Far from a majority, to be sure, but a respectable showing.

where no men had gone before. And they chose to read from Genesis on Christmas Eve.

> In the beginning, God created the heaven and the earth; and the earth was without form and void, and darkness was upon the face of the deep; and the spirit of God moved upon the face of the waters.
>
> And God said, "Let there be light," and there was light.
>
> And God saw the light, that it was good.
>
> And God divided the light from the darkness.[88]

After a year of death and destruction, of tumult and war, and rumors of war, the *Apollo 8* astronauts' brave journey and their healing gesture were like a balm in Gilead. The world stood in awe of the pictures of an "earth rise" coming up over the horizon of the moon. We marveled at the beauty of this bright blue orb set in a black night. As one telegram of thanks to the astronauts put it: "You saved 1968."[89]

For Americans, *Apollo 8* held the promise that a free people and free institutions would not fail after all. Americans coming together could still achieve wonders.

TWENTY-ONE

NIXON'S THE ONE

(1969–1974)

I. "THE EAGLE HAS LANDED!"

Between 750,000 and one million people crowded Florida's Cape Kennedy in the ninety-degree heat of July 1969 to witness the launch of *Apollo 11*.[1] Foreign journalists joined the throng. "This is the America we love, one so totally different than the one that fights in Vietnam," wrote a Czech reporter, whose country had the previous summer been overrun by Soviet tanks. *Pravda,* the official Soviet paper, hailed "these three courageous men." *France-Soir*'s special edition of 1.5 million copies sold out while Germany's *Bild Zeitung* noted, with proud precision, that seven of the fifty-seven *Apollo* managers, or 12 percent, were born in Germany.[2]

President Nixon planned to have dinner with the *Apollo 11* astronauts the night before their historic flight to the Moon. NASA's chief physician, Dr. Charles A. Berry, scotched that plan when he told the press that Nixon comes into contact with hundreds of people and might unknowingly communicate a disease to the spacemen. "Totally ridiculous," was Astronaut Frank Borman's response to the doctor's exaggerated concern, but he didn't call for Berry to be countermanded. Borman thought that if "anyone sneezes on the Moon, they'd put the blame on the President."[3] Such was the atmosphere of mistrust the *Apollo* astronauts would leave behind as they departed for man's first landing on an extraterrestrial body.

Astronaut Mike Collins had the job of orbiting the Moon alone in *Columbia*, the *Apollo 11* command module. On Sunday, 20 July 1969, almost casually, he said farewell to mission commander Neil Armstrong and Buzz Aldrin as they detached in the lunar lander, an ungainly craft named *Eagle*. Armstrong and Aldrin headed for man's first landing on the surface of the Moon.

"You cats take it easy on the lunar surface," Collins coolly warned his fellow astronauts. "If I hear you huffing and puffing I'm going to start bitching at you."[4] Within minutes, Armstrong would be struggling to control his spacecraft to avoid a huge crater with its jagged rocks. The rockets that slowed the *Eagle*'s descent were kicking up huge clouds of dust, obscuring his view. The efforts required to maneuver around dangerous obstacles had consumed precious fuel, leaving Armstrong within one minute of having to abort man's first landing on the Moon.[5] NASA's flight director, Gene Kranz, recalled: "There was no response from the crew. They were too busy. I got the feeling they were going for broke. I had this feeling ever since they took over manual control: 'They are the right ones for the job.' I crossed myself and said, 'Please, God.'"[6]

Almost imperceptibly, Armstrong touched down, shutting off his rockets. Without a hint of concern, he reported to a waiting world: "Houston, Tranquility Base here. The *Eagle* has landed."[7]

A decade earlier, the elite fraternity of American test pilots had laughed at the astronauts as "spam in a can." The astronauts were compared, not always favorably, with Ham, the chimp that NASA launched into space and returned safely.* Here, however, Armstrong proved he

---

* Not only had Americans been shocked by the Soviets beating the U.S. into space with *Sputnik*, but they were horrified when they learned that Laika, the Soviet space dog, would die when he consumed the last portion of his food. The Soviets had put poison in it.

had that most admired, most elusive quality of America's best test pilots: the right stuff.* That night, at Arlington National Cemetery, someone placed a bouquet on John F. Kennedy's grave with an unsigned note: "Mr. President, the *Eagle* has landed."[8]

In Houston, Texas, Armstrong's fellow astronaut, Charlie Duke, answered Armstrong's calm voice: "Roger, Tranquility, you got a bunch of guys about to turn blue. We're breathing again. Thanks a lot."[9] Duke knew what the world did not: that the *Eagle*'s landing on the Moon was a close call. Had Armstrong failed to find a level landing site, had the *Eagle* keeled over on its side, he and Buzz Aldrin would have been condemned to die a slow, painful death as their oxygen ran out. And that nightmare would have happened in the full view of 600 million people.[10]

The landing on the Moon was a victory for the United States of America—and for freedom. President John F. Kennedy had taken up Premier Nikita Khrushchev's challenge of a space race just eight years earlier. The president redefined the space race by shooting for the Moon. "This Nation has tossed its cap over the wall of space, and we have no choice but to follow it," he said of the huge Apollo program on the last full day of his life.[11]

A landing on the Moon by the Soviets would have had incalculable results. Everything they achieved was done in secret, with the massive and single-minded redirection of resources that can only be ordered by a ruthless dictatorship. Anyone who dared to question the Soviet space program would hear the knock of the KGB at his door. Setbacks were covered up. Grudgingly, the Soviets admitted that Cosmonaut Vladimir M. Komarov had been killed in 1967 when the first planned Soyuz spacecraft crashed to earth, but they quickly spread the blanket of secrecy over their failure.[12]

America, in contrast, had been much more open about its efforts. The world knew it when Astronauts Virgil Grissom, Edward White, and Roger Chafee were killed by a fire on the launch pad in Florida on 27

---

* *The Right Stuff* was taken as the title of the great book on America's early astronauts by Tom Wolfe.

January 1967. It was supposed to be a routine test, but a spark in the all-oxygen command module soon became an inferno. Temperatures rose in seconds to 2,500 degrees Fahrenheit.[13] The world followed the detailed investigation of the disaster that forced an eighteen-month delay in the Apollo program. The entire program had to be redesigned. It was as if the United States had broken a leg eighty yards into a hundred-yard dash.

Kennedy was dead and Khrushchev had been overthrown, but the super-power rivalry had continued. Soviet Communist chief Leonid Brezhnev had sought access to Western technology through the new policy of *détente*—a French word that means "an easing of tensions." It was an implicit confession of weakness. To his fellow Communists in the USSR, however, Brezhnev boasted that space would lead the Soviet economy into the twenty-first century. Throughout 1968, with America distracted by riots and assassinations at home, the Soviets had sent *Zond* rockets around the Moon.[14]

If the Soviets had reached the moon first, Communist atheist ideology would have won a great victory. "When man conquers the universe," Marxist historian Zheya Sveltilova had said, "he will learn to believe in himself. It will simply be ridiculous to rely on any force other than himself. People who now believe in God will reject him. Such belief won't be logical or natural. *Man will be stronger than God*."[15]

With Armstrong's safe landing, however, the United States' victory was assured. As he descended the ladder to the lunar surface, Armstrong calmly observed: "That's one small step for man, a giant *leap* for Mankind."[16]

Meanwhile, Buzz Aldrin, inside the Lunar Excursion Module (LEM), was quietly observing the historic occasion in his own special way. Aldrin had been impressed to read that Tenzing Norgay, the Nepalese sherpa who accompanied Sir Edmund Hillary to the peak of Mt. Everest, had cleared away snow to make room for an offering of thanks to his God. Now, Aldrin poured out wine that nearly overran his little cup in the one-sixth g-force of lunar gravity.[17] Holding a wafer, Aldrin read silently from a small card as he celebrated communion with these words from the Book of John:

I am the vine and you are the branches
Whoever remains in me and I in him will bear much fruit;
For you can do nothing without me.[18*]

In the midst of a long, drawn-out, and inconclusive war in Vietnam, in a nation beset by seemingly irreparable divisions at home, the landing on the Moon seemed to be the one really big thing that went right. Dr. Wernher von Braun had once been Hitler's rocket scientist. Now an American citizen, he spoke with confidence of the future: "I think . . . that the Ten Commandments are entirely adequate, without amendments, to cope with all the problems that the Technological Revolution not only has brought up, but will bring up in the future."[19]

II. THE COUNTERCULTURE

Not all Americans agreed with Dr. Wernher. "You've been *drunk* all summer," said radical writer Norman Mailer, "and they have taken the Moon."[20] Mailer seemed to be scolding his fellow members of what was increasingly called the counterculture. This was a subculture that rejected the world of discipline, achievement, and drive. The radicals claimed that world was leading America to Fascism. Significantly, Mailer had said that "they have taken the Moon." He did not share the sense of satisfaction and pride that millions of Americans felt. He was speaking to that sense of alienation that was the banner of the rebellious youth movement.

By 1969, Norman Mailer had been speaking for an *alien nation* for more than a decade. This talented novelist wrote an influential essay called "The White Negro" in 1957. In it, he said,

---

* Atheist Madalyn Murray O'Hair had sued NASA following the *Apollo 8* crew's reading from the Book of Genesis during their lunar flyby the previous Christmas Eve. Skittish NASA officials had ordered *Apollo 11* astronauts to not say anything religious from the lunar surface. But CBS's Walter Cronkite soon got word of this first communion on the Moon and told the world. The Supreme Court later dismissed O'Hair's suit (Hansen, *First Man*, 487–488).

the only life-giving answer is to divorce oneself from society, to exist without roots, to set out on that uncharted journey with the rebellious imperatives of the self. . . . One is a rebel or one conforms, one is a frontiersman in the Wild West of American night life, or else a Square cell, trapped in the totalitarian tissues of American society. . . . Whether the life is criminal or not, the decision is to encourage the psychopath within oneself."[21]

Mailer was not issuing some abstract call to alienation, to make oneself a *philosophical outlaw*.

No, Mailer laid it out bluntly and brazenly: "It takes little courage for two strong eighteen-year-old hoodlums . . . to beat in the brains of a candy store keeper. . . . Still courage of a sort is necessary, for one murders not only a weak fifty-year-old man but an institution as well, one violates private property, one enters into a new relation with the police and introduces a dangerous element into one's life. The hoodlum is therefore daring the unknown, and no matter how brutal the act, it is not altogether cowardly."[22] Two hundred years before, such notions created a *frisson* of excitement in the salons of Paris. They led then, as they would in the years after 1969, to rivers of innocent blood. Ideas do indeed have consequences. Mailer's malevolent writings made him an American Marat.[*] Mailer wrote extensively about the Moon shot. His book, *Of a Fire on the*

---

[*] Jean Paul Marat was an especially vicious writer in revolutionary France. His daily demands for blood made him a "street corner Caligula." His *Ami du Peuple* (Friend of the People) "defined the language of Jacobinism." Marat wrote in his bathtub, where he spent hours daily treating some undiagnosed skin disorder. Marat was stabbed to death in his tub by the young Charlotte Corday on the eve of the revolution's holy day on 13 July 1793; the lovely *Girondist*, a moderate republican, willingly gave her life to put an end to his. Norman Mailer was not stabbed, but he stabbed his second wife. She survived and so, in hip society, did he. He went on to win a Pulitzer Prize and marry the daughter of a duke. In 1980, he successfully campaigned for the release of convicted murderer Jack Abbott. Out of prison, Abbott murdered again. Alice Kaminsky, mother of the man Abbott murdered, wrote the unforgettable *Victim's Song*. She damned Mailer forever. Is she America's Charlotte Corday? (Furet and Ozouf, *A Critical Dictionary of the French Revolution*.)

Moon, explored what he saw as the deeper meaning of the event. Mailer was widely quoted as saying the landing on the Moon was a triumph of the WASP mind. Like a laser, it could go incredible distances because it was so narrow.*

When Norman Mailer spoke of a drunken summer, he doubtless had in mind the emblematic counterculture event of the time. In August 1969, on Max Yasgur's upstate New York dairy farm, 250,000 young people flocked together to hear the leading rock bands and artists of the day. *Woodstock* was the name of the concert, even though that tiny town was some fifty miles away.[23] The huge throng reveled in the rain and mud, smoked pot, and cheered every cry of defiance that came from the stage. The artists who performed at Woodstock were a virtual Who's Who of American rock 'n' roll, from Joan Baez to Jimi Hendrix.[24] Critics dismissed this huge gathering as "rutting in the mud."**

Many "Middle Americans," those stable and solid folks who paid their taxes and obeyed the laws, had very different tastes in entertainment. They favored *Rowan and Martin's Laugh-in*, *Hee-Haw*, *Gomer Pyle USMC*, and *Bonanza* for evening viewing. When they saw the mud-spattered rock fans rejecting bedrock American values, they were put off. Lurid stories of free love and free drugs further alienated the straight from the hip. Yale Law Professor Charles Reich published a dreamy book, *The Greening of America*.[25] The reviews were rapturous. A cultural revolution was coming, Reich asserted, a new American civilization based on feeling. Reich's definition of freedom was to cast off all the old sexual and moral restraints. Sobriety and industry were for squares. "If it feels good, do it," was the cry of the radicals. And their paean to feeling good made millions of Middle Americans feel very bad indeed.

---

*   WASP was the acronym the waspish Mailer used for White Anglo-Saxon Protestant. It was only partly true of the NASA scientists and engineers then and is much less true of them now.

**   In a Forrestal Lecture to the Brigade of Midshipmen of the U.S. Naval Academy in 1998, this author pointed out that if Woodstock was the defining act of an entire generation of Americans, then D-Day—a quarter century earlier—was the defining act of their parents' generation.

The counterculture felt justified in its contempt for American institutions when reports of the My Lai Massacre surfaced in 1969. First Lieutenant William Calley was court-martialed by the Army for the murder of twenty-two civilians in the South Vietnamese hamlet of My Lai.[26] The killings had occurred in 1968 in the wake of the murderous Communist Tet offensive, but nothing could excuse the direct targeting and killing of unarmed women, children, and old men. Radicals tried to make Calley the poster boy for mainstream society. He was the inevitable result, these critics charged, of going along with the system. Some Americans even refused to believe the story.* Most Americans were deeply troubled by the credible charges of war crimes against our own soldiers. Still, some charged that My Lai was not an aberration, but typical of the conduct of U.S. forces in the Mekong Delta.** These critics, however, reckoned without Army Warrant Officer Hugh Thompson. It was Thompson who saw the killings and landed his helicopter *between* Calley's men and the endangered villagers. Thompson risked his own life and those of his crewmen to save hundreds of South Vietnamese villagers from certain death.[27]

Posters, in full color, that showed the My Lai dead crumpled in a ditch bore the legend: Q: AND BABIES? A: AND BABIES. It was a quote from the transcript of Calley's court martial. Thousands of these posters found their way to the walls of college dorms as opposition to the war took on the cast of a moral crusade. No posters of the thousands of South Vietnamese buried alive by the Communists in Hué are known to exist. And no posters extolled the heroism of Warrant Officer Thompson.

Another casualty of that drunken summer was the reputation of the surviving Kennedy brother. Senator Edward M. Kennedy had turned down pleas to enter the 1968 presidential race following the assassination

---

* "It never happened and, besides, they deserved it," was the way one clever writer satirized the confused, disbelieving response to My Lai.

** Testimony before Congress by young Lt. (junior grade) John F. Kerry, a future secretary of state and presidential candidate, would charge that "war crimes" had been committed routinely by U.S. forces fighting in South Vietnam.

of his older brother, Robert. Now, in 1969, he attended a raucous party on Martha's Vineyard. Five single women and six married men—all of whom had taken part in Bobby Kennedy's presidential campaign—came together for a night of barbecue and drinks. Ted Kennedy left the party with young Mary Jo Kopechne, headed for the Edgartown Ferry. In the early hours of 19 July, Kennedy's car veered off the bridge at Chappaquiddick and sank in the dark waters.[28] Kennedy swam clear but delayed summoning police for ten hours. Kopechne was one of the "Boiler Room Girls" who had worked on brother Bobby's presidential campaign. She drowned in Kennedy's dark blue Oldsmobile.

The news hit on the same day that Neil Armstrong landed the *Eagle* on the lunar surface, so the world was distracted from the full import of what had happened on Martha's Vineyard. This "lunar eclipse" prevented a penetrating media analysis of the incident. No probing questions were asked about Kennedy's unconscionable delay in calling for help, the curious decision of authorities *not* to perform an autopsy on Kopechne's body, and the "tread lightly" reaction of local Massachusetts law enforcement. What a contrast with the intense scrutiny that the errant senator, Joe McCarthy, received from Edward R. Murrow's *See It Now* broadcast of the previous decade. Clearly, Kennedy benefited from this. His pitiable speech to the people of Massachusetts was drafted for him by the protector of JFK's legacy, Ted Sorenson. It avoided as many questions as it answered. Kennedy's conduct at Chappaquiddick would not be extensively examined for another decade, until he ran for president. Even then, much of the questioning would not get to the heart of the matter.

III. THE SILENT MAJORITY

Richard Nixon never said he had a "secret plan" to end the war in Vietnam. That was the charge of one of his critics. Instead, Nixon pledged to bring America out of direct involvement in combat in South Vietnam without allowing the country to fall to Communism. When Nixon took the presidential oath, there were 535,000 young Americans "in country." This huge force had been built up from 16,000 by President Lyndon B. Johnson. LBJ followed a policy of gradual escalation devised by Defense Secretary Robert Strange McNamara.

Facing massive protest demonstrations, Nixon went before the American people in November 1969 to offer his plan for *Vietnamization* of the war in Southeast Asia. By Vietnamization, Nixon meant that the Army of South Vietnam would be required to take up the defense of its own country. The United States would continue to offer air support, naval support, and, of course, a strong financial commitment to keep South Vietnam from falling to the Communist North.

General Douglas MacArthur had spoken for millions of Americans during the Korean War when he said "there is no substitute for victory." Still, top U.S. policy makers knew that there was always a danger of the "limited war" they were fighting becoming a world war, with the United States pulled into a direct conflict with a nuclear-armed Red China or Soviet Union, or both. It was to avoid this danger that both the Johnson and Nixon administrations sought the limited objective of protecting Southeast Asia.

Nixon spoke of a "silent majority" of Americans who backed his policy of gradual withdrawal from Vietnam. Nixon had ordered the return of twenty-five thousand U.S. troops in June of that year, followed by another thirty-five thousand ordered home in September. A Gallup Poll showed that fully 75 percent of Americans approved of Nixon's Vietnamization policy.[29]

That fact did not dissuade antiwar protesters. It seemed only to implicate the American people in what more extreme war resisters saw as the guilt of the U.S. leaders. The radicals wrote of *Amerika*. By using the German spelling of their country's name, they sought to tie the United States to the odious Hitler regime. Giant antiwar demonstrations became an attempt to impede the carrying out of government policy. "Shut it down!" cried the youthful rebels as they ringed the Pentagon and block-aded streets in Washington, D.C. They burned American flags and even used blazing draft cards to light joints.

President Nixon found it hard to understand the youth rebellion that engulfed him. Only once, in 1971, did he attempt to reach out to the protesters who besieged his White House. He went out at dawn to talk to the demonstrators who spent the night on the grounds of the Lincoln Memorial. He tried to shoot the breeze with some of them, talking about football, talking about their hometowns—anything except why they had come to Washington.[30] Shy and awkward, Nixon tried, but he never could comprehend his foes.

When President Nixon invaded Cambodia in 1970, the antiwar movement howled. It was to them an insane escalation of the war. They charged that Nixon had expanded the war into another sovereign nation. The truth was the opposite. The North Vietnamese had been using Cambodia for years as a staging area for their attacks on South Vietnam. London's prestigious journal, *The Economist*, saw straight through the double standard, flagging the fact that the rest of the world made "barely a chirp of protest" about Communists violating Cambodian neutrality.[31] From these Cambodian "sanctuaries," Communist forces had invaded the South, killing thousands, including many Americans. Nixon told the country that his move was only an incursion, not an invasion—only an effort to "clean out" pockets of enemy activity. American forces would leave as soon as they had achieved their aim.

The same liberal leaders who had thought Kennedy clever for using the word *quarantine* at the time of the Cuban Missile Crisis now jumped on Nixon's use of *incursion* as evidence of his duplicity. Men who had been silent, or who had muted their criticism of war policy as the Democrat Lyndon Johnson built up a huge force in Vietnam, now felt liberated as U.S. combat deaths mounted.[32] They attacked Nixon without restraint. Maine's Democratic Senator, Edmund Muskie, charged that Nixon had decided to "seek a military method of ending this war rather than a negotiated method." Normally mild-mannered Senator Walter Mondale lashed out at Nixon. "This is not only a tragic escalation, which will broaden the war and increase American casualties," he said, "but it is an outright admission of the failure of Vietnamization." Mondale was proven wrong when, following the successful U.S. operation in Cambodia, American casualties actually went *down*.[33] The incursion enabled Nixon to accelerate U.S. withdrawals from South Vietnam.

But the critics were not interested in facts. Passions rose to a fever pitch. At Kent State University, Governor James Rhodes ordered Ohio National Guardsmen to contain a student uprising against the Cambodian operation. There, jittery young guardsmen fired on an advancing crowd of protesters, killing four. The country was horrified—and deeply divided over the killings.

Nixon could rightly claim that most Americans backed his war policy. He viewed the struggle in great power terms. He did not want America to become a pitiful, helpless giant.[34]

In his "Silent Majority" speech, Nixon argued strongly for a new course in Vietnam. But he warned against what he called "a precipitate withdrawal":

> The precipitate withdrawal of American forces from Vietnam would be a disaster not only for South Vietnam but for the United States and for the cause of peace.
>
> For the South Vietnamese, our precipitate withdrawal would inevitably allow the Communists to repeat the massacres which followed their takeover in the North 15 years before; they then murdered more than 50,000 people, and hundreds of thousands more died in slave labor camps.
>
> We saw a prelude of what would happen in South Vietnam when the Communists entered the city of Hue last year. During their brief rule there, there was a bloody reign of terror in which 3,000 civilians were clubbed, shot to death, and buried in mass graves.

With the sudden collapse of our support, these atrocities of Hue would become the nightmare of the entire nation—and particularly for the million and a half Catholic refugees who fled to South Vietnam when the Communists took over in the North.

For the United States, this first defeat in our nation's history would result in a collapse of confidence in American leadership, not only in Asia but throughout the world.

Three American presidents have recognized the great stakes involved in Vietnam and understood what had to be done.

IV. NIXON TO CHINA

Nixon was at this point preparing to play the China card. Even before he entered the White House, Nixon had written of the need for a new approach to what was then called Red China. By 1971, Nixon had determined to send National Security Advisor Henry Kissinger on a secret mission to Beijing. He wanted to take advantage of the bitter split between the Chinese and the Russians in the hope of getting China to cut off aid to the North Vietnamese. Dubbing the mission *Polo*, after the famed Italian explorer Marco Polo, the Nixon administration sent Kissinger to Pakistan. From there, Kissinger could approach Beijing more discreetly. Kissinger's July meetings with Mao Zedong and Zhou En-lai took place in strictest secrecy. China was then barely recovering from years of madness known as the Great Proletarian Cultural Revolution. The Cultural Revolution had led to the death and disgrace of millions. Mao had unleashed young Red Guards to humiliate China's intellectuals. The Red Guards brandished copies of Mao's *Little Red Book*. It was the only guide they needed, the young rebels said, to rule great China.

Kissinger stunned the world and its leaders when he announced *rapprochement* with China. Nixon had pulled off a coup. But not all were happy about it. None was more shocked and alienated than America's faithful friend, the Republic of China—the non-Communist Chinese government exiled on Taiwan. "No government less deserved what was about to happen to it than that of Taiwan," Kissinger admitted. "It had been a loyal ally; its conduct toward us had been exemplary. Its representatives . . . had behaved with that matter-of-fact reliability and subtle intelligence characteristic of the Chinese people."[35]

Kissinger the realist believed that the United States could no longer hold off majorities in the UN General Assembly who yearly voted for China to replace Taiwan in the world body and to hold a permanent seat on the Security Council. He thought that the United States could not continue to maintain the fiction that the Republic of China on Taiwan was the sole legitimate government of a billion mainland Chinese.

Soon, Nationalist China, as Taiwan had been known for decades, would be stripped of its seat on the UN Security Council, its seat in the UN General Assembly, and even abruptly downgraded from embassy status in the United States of America.

President Nixon's 1972 visit to the People's Republic of China was the media highlight of his administration. He and Mrs. Nixon were shown walking on the Great Wall and toasting Mao at a splendid Beijing state dinner. Nixon had been the one who built his career denouncing liberals for "losing" China to the Communists. Now, he had come full circle. Henceforward, "Nixon to China" would be the name given to any clever political ploy in which only those who had most strenuously opposed a given policy could suddenly turn about-face to embrace it.

Nixon and Kissinger pursued a policy of *détente* with the USSR. Nixon signed an Anti-Ballistic Missile Treaty, which prohibited both nations from deploying an antimissile defense system (except around the two superpowers' capital cities). Thus, the Republicans believed they were returning to the policies of Eisenhower and Dulles, a policy known as "Mutual Assured Destruction." Fittingly, it was abbreviated MAD. Security in a dangerous world with tens of thousands of nuclear weapons held by the United States and the USSR would come to rely on what

Churchill called the "balance of terror." Nixon also approved the Strategic Arms Limitation Treaty with the Soviets.

Nixon told Americans he was determined not to *bug out* of South Vietnam. To the Chinese, however, he seemed to be saying that the United States would do exactly that. Kissinger and Nixon learned that the Chinese wanted the United States to stay in Asia as a counterweight to the "hegemony" of the Soviet Union. With some bitterness, Kissinger noted, the Chinese seemed to have a better understanding of American policy than the professors in Harvard Yard did.[36]

Nowhere was Nixon's penchant for shocking his opponents and stunning his friends more evident than in his economic policy. Nixon had agreed with conservative economist Milton Friedman that Lyndon Johnson's 10 percent surtax on incomes would be ineffective in wringing inflation out of the economy. By 1971 the problem was spinning out of control.[37] Inflation ate away the savings of the middle class, and it presented a special threat to the reelection of a president who depended on conservative support.

Montana's Democratic Senator Mike Mansfield pushed legislation through both congressional houses to allow the president to set up wage and price controls. Surprisingly, Nixon backed the legislation. "We are all Keynesians now," said Nixon blandly.[38] He seemed not to care that the doctrines of British economist John Maynard Keynes were anathema to his conservative supporters. Keynes had advocated increased government spending in times of economic downturn as a means of "priming the pump" for recovery. Americans enthusiastically embraced the idea of wage and price controls and gave Nixon more than 70 percent approval for his economic policies in public opinion polls.[39] But while the good feelings helped Nixon in the short term, it wasn't long before the economy took a dive.

The American economy in the 1970s suffered from overregulation and underinvestment. The recession of 1973–75 was the worst since the Great Depression, and it would, in time, help to undermine Nixon's standing with the American people when he faced troubles over Watergate. The bleak prospects convinced millions of Americans that their children's futures would be poorer, that there would be fewer economic opportunities for the rising generation. All of this created a sour mood in the country, and many took out their frustrations on President Nixon.

Nor were China and the economy the only areas where Nixon distressed his most loyal supporters. A presidential commission on pornography predictably recommended dropping most legal restrictions. Though many of the laws remained on the books, enforcement lagged. Soon, the nation was flooded with pornography.*

Another Nixon-appointed commission, headed by Laurance Rockefeller, studied the issue of population growth. The Rockefeller Commission backed federally funded birth control and the repeal of the laws against abortion. Nixon *opposed* abortion-on-demand, he said, but he signed the 1970 Family Planning and Reproductive Health Act, which has sluiced billions of tax dollars to Planned Parenthood ever since.**

Nixon also attempted to change federal welfare policy. He supported the initiative of his Domestic Policy Advisor, Daniel Patrick Moynihan. Moynihan was a liberal Democrat who flattered Nixon with the idea that he could be the conservative who implemented a major liberal policy—as Benjamin Disraeli had done in Britain in the nineteenth century. Moynihan pressed for the Family Assistance Plan that would have given poor families cash subsidies from the government in place of welfare. Conservative economist Milton Friedman even spoke up for a Negative Income Tax. If the government could tax higher incomes, Friedman reasoned, why not supplement the incomes of the poor?[40]

---

* POWs returning from Vietnam were latter-day Rip van Winkles. A number of them recorded their shock at seeing—and hearing—obscenities in films, in books, and on stage. New York theater critics gushed over such offerings as the nude scenes in *Hair* and *O Calcutta!*

** The Family Planning and Reproductive Health Act of 1970 was approved by Democratic majorities in Congress. It was cosponsored by Houston's young Republican congressman, George H. W. Bush. His support provided moderate "cover" for what was essentially a radical change in federal policy toward the family. Bush's key role in the bill's passage earned him the lasting mistrust of grassroots conservatives.

Democrats who controlled the Congress blocked any action on Nixon's assistance plan. (Perhaps they agreed with Moynihan and feared that if Nixon became the American Disraeli, their majority would dissolve.) Average working Americans did not like welfare, but they disliked even more the notion that others should be paid for not working. Many asked what would happen to the breadwinners if their work was not needed.*

Nixon supported, or at least did not oppose, the rising environmental movement. The movement was inspired by Rachel Carson's 1962 book *Silent Spring* and given a great boost by photographs of the Earth as a "big blue marble" as taken from the Moon. Senator Edmund Muskie became a leader on Capitol Hill. Muskie crafted major legislation on Clean Air and Clean Water. Nixon dutifully signed these bills and approved creation of a new Environmental Protection Agency.[41] Some conservatives griped that the first Earth Day—22 April 1970—was also the centennial of the birth of the leading Communist revolutionary, Vladimir Lenin. The new movement was not red, however; it was *green*.

The Nixon years also saw major gains by the new feminist movement. Both parties now endorsed an Equal Rights Amendment (ERA) to the Constitution. Nixon's GOP had been supportive of it for generations. When the great Civil Rights Act of 1964 was amended by Virginia's Democratic segregationist Congressman Howard W. Smith, it also banned discrimination on the basis of sex. "Judge" Smith had hoped that outlawing sex discrimination would be a "killer amendment" that would slow down or even derail the Civil Rights Act. It did no such thing. Instead, it provided the basis *in law* for the new feminism.

In addition to the ERA, the new feminists wanted abortion-on-demand.**

---

* Some of the strongest evidence for a powerful effect of welfare on marriage comes from the SIME/DIME experiments (Seattle and Denver income maintenance experiments, respectively). In response to a guaranteed income, divorce increased 36 percent among whites and 42 percent among blacks (Murray, Charles, *Losing Ground: American Social Policy, 1950–1980*, Basic Books, New York: 1994, 151–152).

** Many of the nineteenth-century feminists and suffragettes were strongly *anti-abortion*, most notably Susan B. Anthony.

Several state laws were amended to legalize what the statutes of every state had previously deemed manslaughter. Governor Nelson Rockefeller signed a radical law in New York that permitted abortion for any reason up to six months of pregnancy. California Governor Ronald Reagan agonized, but signed a bill to permit abortion for the life or health of the mother. In Washington State, voters approved a referendum to legalize abortion. Governor Dan Evans approved the change. Rockefeller, Reagan, and Evans represented a broad spectrum of the Republican Party.

Democrats were split on the abortion issue. Many black and Hispanic leaders opposed it, as did some elected Democrats. Seeing a growing *resistance* at the grassroots level to abortion-on-demand, liberal organizers recommended a strategy of going through the federal courts instead of going to the state legislatures or even directly to the voters. As one abortion advocate wrote, the U.S. Supreme Court represented "the only road to rapid change."[42] On such a fundamental matter, activists seemed to reason, democracy could not be trusted.

The most extreme feminists challenged not just American democracy. Radical writer Shulamith Firestone said the assault on traditional values must go further. "Feminists have to question, not just all of *Western* culture, but the organization of culture itself, and further, even the very organization of nature."[43]

V. THE ELECTION OF 1972

President Nixon approached the election year of 1972 in a strong position, but he didn't *feel* strong. With his success in drawing down U.S. forces in South Vietnam and his replacement of the military draft with a draft lottery, he had brought a measure of quiet to the nation's cities and campuses. He might have been the most successful of postwar presidents but for his personal characteristics. As Bryce Harlow, his close associate of many years, noted about him: Nixon was not liked by people, because he did not like people.[44]

Even so, he faced only token opposition for renomination in the Republican Party. Conservative Congressman John Ashbrook of Ohio and liberal Congressman Pete McCloskey of California got no support in their quixotic challenges to Nixon in the GOP primaries. All attention focused, instead, on the Democrats.

The Democrats' nominee, Senator George McGovern of South Dakota, had become a leader of liberal antiwar activists. He was an unusual head of what came to be called the Peace Movement. McGovern's earliest public service had been as a twenty-two-year-old bomber pilot in World War II. He commanded respect and affection from the even younger crew members who flew on his B-24 Liberator. They had named her the *Dakota Queen*, in honor of his wife, Eleanor.[45] Married and mature, McGovern was almost a father figure to his crewmen. Mission after mission, he guided them through German flak and deadly 88-millimeter antiaircraft fire and brought them safely back to base in Italy.

On one of his missions, with several B-24s badly shot up, there were loud complaints and radio chatter about those "blasted n——s," a racist reference to the Tuskegee Airmen whose job it was to protect the slower, more vulnerable bombers. The gripes were quickly cut short when the black squadron commander of the P-51 Mustangs—who had been hovering protectively over them all the while—broke in to say: "Why don't you all shut up, white boys? We're all going to take you home."[46] The Mustangs drove off the German fighters and McGovern's squadron made it home safely. Ever after, George McGovern would be one of that great generation of World War II veterans who would oppose racial discrimination wherever they saw it. As a congressman and U.S. senator, McGovern would be a strong backer of equal rights for black Americans.

In his acceptance speech before the Democratic National Convention in Miami, McGovern gave an impassioned call to "come home, America." It was seen as an appeal to come home from the Vietnam War. The problem for McGovern was that Nixon's policy was bringing Americans home from Vietnam. McGovern spoke to the urgent desire of his supporters for change: "We reject the view of those who say, 'America—love it or leave it.' We reply, 'Let us change it so we may love it the more.'"[47] McGovern's critics countered that he and his backers seemed to be saying they would love America only when they had transformed it in their image.

McGovern's record in World War II is one of undoubted heroism. He braved death daily for years as he fought to take the continent back from Nazism. Little of this was known, however, to the American public in 1972.* The Democratic Party was not just against the Vietnam War; it diminished the American role as the champion of freedom that FDR, Truman, and JFK had embraced.

On Tuesday, 7 November 1972, McGovern suffered one of the worst defeats in the history of presidential politics. Just eight years after LBJ had buried Goldwater, the Republican Nixon carried *every* state except Massachusetts and the District of Columbia. Ever afraid, Nixon had run up the score. He won 520 electoral votes and 46,740,323 popular votes (60.3 percent). McGovern won a scant 17 electoral votes and 28,901,548 popular votes.

Basic insecurity always led Nixon to overcompensate. Unsatisfied with the mess Democrats were obviously making of their 1972 campaign, he apparently wanted to "get something" on them. On 23 June 1972, during the campaign, his operatives broke into the Democratic National Committee headquarters in Washington's Watergate Hotel. When the relatively low-level team of burglars was caught entering the building, Nixon denied any knowledge of the affair. However, audio tapes recorded at the White House make it undeniably clear that he knew of the break-in after the fact, and knew of it long before he ever admitted it to the American people. He lied about it for two full years. Thus was born the Watergate Affair.

---

* By contrast, Nixon's campaign wrapped itself in the American flag. Nixon served on a navy supply ship in the South Pacific. He won the considerable sum of five thousand dollars playing poker. McGovern led the antiwar movement, and therefore benefited not at all from his status as war hero. His WWII story was finally told in Stephen Ambrose's best-selling *Wild Blue*.

Early in his administration, Nixon had installed a new voice-activated audiotape system in the White House. In doing so, he would provide the documentary evidence of his own lawlessness and deceit. Presidents like FDR, Kennedy, and Johnson obviously had taped certain telephone conversations, but Nixon's system could pick up all discussions in the Oval Office.

Immediately after Nixon's joyless victory over McGovern, the president demanded the resignations of all his cabinet officers.* Elliot Richardson tried to break through Nixon's wall of reserve: "I wish somehow deep down inside yourself you could come to believe that you have really won . . . you won by an overwhelming margin."[48] Richardson would serve Nixon as secretary of health, education and welfare, defense secretary, and, most significantly, as attorney general. In the end, however, he couldn't penetrate the *carapace* with which Nixon surrounded himself.

Kennedy had summoned Americans to the great adventure of space exploration, but Nixon now shut the program down. He had spoken of America's need for the "lift of a driving dream." What else was space but that? Nonetheless, he announced in December 1972 that *Apollo 17* would land on the Moon for "the last time in this century."[49] Historian Andrew Chaikin tells us:

> [Astronaut Jack Schmitt] couldn't believe his ears. . . . He hated the words—hated them for their lack of vision. These words from the leader of the nation! Even if Nixon really believed them, he didn't have to say so in a public statement, taking away the hopes of a generation of young people. Schmitt was furious that in the moment of triumph he

---

* It was an unprecedented move for a triumphantly reelected president. Such reshuffles are standard practice under the British Parliamentary system, but they don't import well. Nixon had similarly tried to outfit the White House guards in new comic opera uniforms when he returned from a trip to Paris. He had been overly impressed by the grandeur of President de Gaulle's resplendent *garde républicaine*. For his pains, Nixon's new guard uniforms were laughed out of town.

had been jolted out of the work of the mission to listen to a statement like that. He would fume silently about it for the rest of the flight.[50*]

Immediately following reelection, Nixon had to face a near breakdown of the Paris Peace talks, where the United States was trying to negotiate an end to the Vietnam War. Not only was peace *not* at hand, it seemed more elusive than ever. Nixon reacted by unleashing a fierce bombing campaign against Hanoi, the capital of North Vietnam. Convinced he had been lying (again) just to win reelection, his critics denounced his "Christmas bombing campaign" of 1972.[**] American POWs held in what they jestingly called "the Hanoi Hilton" cheered the bombing campaign. They later reported it had given them hope.

Release of these prisoners of war had become a central objective of the U.S. war policy. With the aid of Texas entrepreneur H. Ross Perot, the POW issue became more important during the Vietnam War than in any previous American conflict. Perot, a graduate of the U.S. Naval Academy, used his wide-ranging relationships with former classmates to attempt a rescue of the POWs. Although that effort failed, Perot made sure the POWs and their families were not forgotten. The U.S. POWs from the Vietnam Era—men like Jim Stockdale, John McCain, Jeremiah Denton, and Bill Lawrence—brought honor to themselves and their country.

Americans have come to honor the Vietnam POWs as no previous war's prisoners have been honored. This is, in part, a tribute to their loyalty and endurance. It is also a commentary on the fact that when many people questioned the old verities of duty, honor, country, these members

---

* Ironically, it is the failed *Apollo 13* mission that is probably most familiar to Americans. *Apollo 13* almost ended disastrously when an onboard explosion forced Astronauts Jim Lovell, Fred Haise, and Jack Swigert to circle the Moon and come back to Earth on auxiliary power. The heart-stopping story of their safe return is a tribute to Yankee ingenuity—and the Ron Howard movie is Hollywood at its best.

** Many of those who cursed Nixon for violating the spirit of the Christmas season in 1972 had offered not a word of criticism of the North Vietnamese when they launched an assault on the South in 1968 during Tet—*their* holiday.

of the U.S. military proved themselves true. They might have felt themselves abandoned by America, but they did not abandon her. They saw other young Americans burning the flag, but they cherished it. They fully merit the accolades a grateful nation has showered upon them.

President Nixon deserves credit for the attention his administration focused on the release of the POWs. Though viciously assailed for his December 1972 bombing campaign, Nixon never lost faith that the POWs would be released. By contrast, Senator George McGovern had said he would be willing "to crawl on his knees to Hanoi" if that would secure their release. Can there have been a more self-defeating verbal image in the history of American presidential campaigning?

As strongly as most Americans identified with the POWs, the reaction of many to actress Jane Fonda's travels to Hanoi, her posing on a North Vietnamese antiaircraft gun, and her confrontational meeting with U.S. POWs exposed a deep and yet-unhealed wound in the nation's soul. Fonda and her fellow travelers were never charged with treason, except in the hearts and minds of millions of Americans.

Meanwhile, Nixon's critics in Congress and in Europe erupted in denunciation of him as a "mad bomber." The Democratic leader in the Senate, Mike Mansfield, called his 1972 bombing campaign "a Stone Age tactic." The Swedish government likened it to those of the Nazis.* America's NATO allies offered no help.[51] Media critics charged Nixon with "carpet bombing" civilian targets in North Vietnam. Only later, much later, did honest journalists survey the damage and report. When almost no one was paying attention, Peter Ward of the *Baltimore Sun* wrote: "Hanoi has certainly been damaged but evidence on the ground disproves charges of indiscriminate bombing."[52]

The U.S. bombing campaign worked. The North Vietnamese signed the Paris accords in January 1973. Kissinger had to press the South

---

* The Swedes in their high dudgeon conveniently forgot how their "neutral" government had provided critical assistance to Hitler in his drive to conquer their peaceful European neighbors.

Vietnamese government, our reluctant ally, to accept the peace agreement he had hammered out with the North Vietnamese representative, Le Duc Tho.

As Nixon prepared for his second inauguration as president, the world marveled at the end of the Vietnam War—or at least, the end of U.S. involvement in that war. American POWs were released to a spontaneous outburst of joy.*

VI. *ROE V. WADE*: "RAW JUDICIAL POWER"

In Texas, Lyndon B. Johnson died of a heart attack on 22 January 1973. He was sixty-four years old. The former president had lived in virtual seclusion since leaving Washington four years earlier, rarely venturing forth from his LBJ Ranch or his presidential library. He did witness the *Apollo 11* launch, a project he had so enthusiastically supported.

Johnson's death, the Paris Peace Accords, and the release of the POWs overshadowed what otherwise would have been the major news story of 22 January 1973: the U.S. Supreme Court's 7–2 ruling in *Roe v. Wade*. The ruling struck down the abortion laws of all fifty states. It allowed abortion for any reason for the first three months of pregnancy. In the second three months of pregnancy, only restrictions designed to safeguard the mother's health were permitted. Only in the final three months of pregnancy, said Supreme Court Justice Harry Blackmun (a Nixon appointee), could the states restrict abortion, so long as the life and the health of the mother were protected.

In a companion case, *Doe v. Bolton*, decided on the same day, however, Blackmun made clear that the definition of the mother's health (including mental health) would be so broad as to provide grounds for striking down any law that placed an undue burden on a woman's choice of abortion.

---

* The North Vietnamese Communists released those officially listed as POWs, but there has never been a full accounting of the MIAs—those "missing in action."

Henceforth, fathers would have no rights, parents of minor girls only very limited rights, and the unborn child no rights at all under the *Roe* and *Doe* line of cases. Thus, the procedure that had been a felony in most states for more than a century now became a fundamental constitutional right due to the new judicial reasoning and line of cases. Justice Byron R. "Whizzer" White, a JFK appointee, dissented, calling *Doe* an act of "raw judicial power," as it took these decisions from the states and enshrined their determination in the Supreme Court's reasoning.

The Court's action would drive a deep wedge between Americans. In its determination to short-circuit democratic processes, the Supreme Court would further undermine Americans' confidence in the judiciary. In the quarter of a century before *Roe*, the proportion of Americans who had "great confidence" in the judiciary plunged from 83.4 percent to just 32.6 percent.[53] And Roe was another self-inflicted wound from which the courts have not recovered. Too many people saw the Court overreaching in its jurisdiction and power with its abortion decisions.

Liberals and feminists hailed the Court's ruling in *Roe v. Wade*. It was, as Lawrence Lader wrote, "central to everything in life and how we wanted to live it."[54] Lader was a founder of the National Association for the Repeal of Abortion Laws. Mainline Protestants, in general, approved the ruling. Liberal church bodies like the Presbyterian Church USA, the Protestant Episcopal Church, and the United Methodists endorsed *Roe*. Many Jewish groups also supported what they viewed as "reproductive rights."

Opposition to the Court's ruling continues to this day. For millions of Americans, the Court illegitimately stripped away the inalienable right to life from the unborn and threatened America's role as a leader of human rights in the world. The National Right to Life Committee rose up to convert opposition into lawful constitutional, legislative, and social action. Major religious groups—including the U.S. Catholic Conference, the Southern Baptist Convention, the National Association of Evangelicals, and the Lutheran Church (Missouri Synod)—would rally against the

Court's rulings. Liberal and feminist groups, in turn, would rally in favor of the Court's ruling—seeing it as a litmus test for their favored brand of constitutional interpretation and as fundamental to the rights of women. Many have boiled it down, simply, this way: those opposed to *Roe* believe the Court should protect life, or the states' rights to protect life; those in favor of *Roe* believe the Court should protect a woman's right to choose an abortion—hence the terms "pro-life" and "pro-choice" have served to identify people's positions on the issue of abortion.

VII. WATERGATE SPILLS OVER

In the spring of 1973, as the Watergate affair unraveled, President Nixon's political stock plummeted. Judge John J. Sirica, an Eisenhower appointee, began to apply pressure to the small fries in the burglary. They, in turn, began to implicate higher-ups, who implicated still higher-ups. Nixon aide John Ehrlichman suggested that L. Patrick Grey, the hapless director of the FBI, be allowed to "twist slowly, slowly in the wind." This graphic phrase soon applied not only to Grey but to the entire Nixon administration.

The press hated Nixon. His increasingly rare press conferences challenged the notion that bearbaiting had been made illegal in America. Nixon had always had a hostile relationship with the press corps.[55] The *Washington Post*'s lead cartoonist, Herbert Block, gave Nixon a "shave" for his 1969 inauguration—a one-day reprieve. He immediately returned to savaging Nixon and his five o'clock shadow *daily* on the editorial page of the capital's hometown paper. Now, with the wolves closing in around him, Nixon was so upset, he would throw up before press conferences.[56]

By October 1973, America faced "a perfect storm." The Senate Watergate Committee had exposed widespread abuses that seemed sure to lead to the president's impeachment. The national media made a hero of the committee's Democratic chairman, North Carolina Senator Sam

Ervin.* Americans were impressed by the cool, lawyerly questioning of Tennessee's Republican Senator Howard Baker. "What did the President know and when did he know it?" Baker asked every witness. (When the answers came to that question, the trap would be sprung.)

Vice President Spiro T. Agnew could not succeed Nixon because he was being investigated for taking massive bribes from highway contractors when he served as governor of Maryland. Agnew pleaded *nolo contendere* ("I do not contest") in Baltimore's Federal Courthouse on 10 October 1973. He resigned to escape a jail sentence.

At the same moment, Israel was invaded by Egypt. The fourth Arab-Israeli War was launched by Egypt on the Jewish High Holy Days, specifically to take advantage of the time when the Jews would be worshipping. Initially, Israeli forces were thrown back. Israel suddenly faced annihilation. The Soviets had armed the Arabs to the teeth and were egging them on

Besieged as he was, President Nixon immediately placed U.S. armed forces around the world on full alert. Following a practical suggestion from Governor Ronald Reagan and an urgent appeal from Prime Minister Golda Meir, he ordered American military transports to fully resupply Israel with the military equipment she so desperately needed.[57] He would not allow the Soviets to take advantage of the desperate political crisis in Washington to let their Arab clients crush Israel. Without the Nixon resupply, Israel might well have fallen.

The ceasefire that Secretary of State Henry Kissinger negotiated in the Middle East bought little time and no credit for Richard Nixon. When he demanded that Attorney General Elliott Richardson fire Special Prosecutor Archibald Cox, Richardson refused and resigned. Deputy Attorney General William Ruckelshaus also refused and resigned. Finally, Solicitor General Robert Bork agreed to fire Cox, if only to keep

---

* Ervin got a pass on his decades of opposition to civil rights. The canonization of this "simple country lawyer" illustrates the rule that the enemy of my enemy is my friend. So long as Ervin pursued the hated Nixon, his past sins were absolved.

the executive branch from melting down at a time when there was no vice president. The press quickly labeled the uproar that greeted this action a "firestorm" and the firing and resignations "the Saturday night massacre."

It was an exaggeration. The Israelis could tell desk-bound reporters something about real firestorms and real massacres. Still, Nixon's authority trickled away like the sands of an hourglass. He named Michigan's Republican Congressman Gerald R. Ford as vice president to replace the disgraced Agnew. Although a strong partisan, Ford was well-liked on both sides of the aisle. He was readily confirmed as the first vice president chosen under the Twenty-fifth Amendment to the Constitution.

The Arabs retaliated against the United States by imposing an oil embargo that caused sharp, severe gas shortages throughout North America and Europe. Prices skyrocketed.

To most Americans, their cars are their freedom.[58] With long gas lines, with odd/even days for purchase of fuel, things seemed to be falling apart. Those in charge, inevitably, were blamed.

Nixon had made no effort to share his 1972 victory with his fellow Republicans. Now, he faced a hostile Congress that did not like and did not fear him.[59] Richard Nixon's political end might actually have come months before he finally resigned. In an effort to appease the pursuing investigators, he released carefully edited transcripts of the White House tapes. These, he argued, would prove him innocent. They proved no such thing. His antagonists sneered at them. The transcripts seriously undermined Nixon's support in Middle America.

When he read the edited transcripts, the Republicans' Senate leader, Hugh Scott of Pennsylvania, called them "shabby, disgusting, immoral."[60] The silent majority that had unswervingly supported Nixon when hundreds of thousands of long-haired demonstrators converged on Washington was appalled by the foul-mouthed Nixon revealed on the transcripts. Hardly a sentence was transcribed without a damning "[expletive deleted]." Nixon had always presented himself to straight Americans as a nice man. He had even prissily confronted JFK in their debates about how Ike had restored decent language to the White House.* Now, Nixon was shown to be a base, mean-spirited manipulator and, worse, an inveterate liar. "I am not a crook," he pathetically told newspaper editors. He might as well have worn a sandwich sign saying I AM A CROOK.[61]

Because of the deepening crisis of Watergate, Nixon's historic visit to the Soviet Union of 27 June–3 July 1974 was overshadowed by the imminent threat of his impeachment.

This first visit by a U.S. president to the Soviet Union nonetheless produced a serious debate about *détente*. Washington's Democratic Senator Henry Jackson strongly opposed the Soviets' anti-Semitic policies, including the Soviet refusal to allow Russian Jews to emigrate to Israel or the United States. Victims of this policy were called *refuseniks*. Senator Jackson cosponsored the Jackson-Vanik Amendment, which limited U.S.-Soviet trade until the Jews were allowed to leave. The Nixon administration, which had very likely saved Israel during the Yom Kippur War, nonetheless strongly opposed Jackson-Vanik.

Opponents of Nixon's policy of *détente* charged that it obscured the distinction between freedom and tyranny. Ironically, the man who began his career as a fierce foe of "atheistic Communism" now seemed to see the U.S. and USSR as morally equivalent.

The House Judiciary Committee proceeded to vote out three articles of impeachment against President Nixon in June 1974. Hillary Rodham was one of the eager young Democratic staffers who helped draft the articles. Though it would avail them little, the Republican members of the committee put their country before their party and voted overwhelmingly to impeach Nixon. Veteran liberal journalist Jack Germond called the House Republicans' defense of the Constitution "magnificent."[62]

When the U.S. Supreme Court unanimously ruled in *U.S. v. Nixon* that the president had to surrender his White House tapes, the end was

---

* Candidate Jack Kennedy, with typical flair, easily fended off Nixon's attack on Harry Truman's barnyard language that Nixon voters could go to hell. Jack quipped, "I don't think we should bring up the religion issue."

not long in coming. The tape that showed "what the President knew and when he knew it" was quickly ferreted out. It was called "the smoking gun," and it showed that Nixon had known all about the break-in at the Watergate virtually since it happened. The tape provided irrefutable evidence that Nixon had tried to get the CIA to pressure the FBI to call off its Watergate investigation. Nixon wanted the CIA to tell the FBI it was for "national security" reasons. Furious at what Nixon had put the Congress, the country, and the Republican Party through for two years, Senator Barry Goldwater telephoned General Alexander Haig, the White House Chief of Staff. "Al," the plainspeaking Arizonan growled, "Dick Nixon has lied to me for the very last time. And to a hell of a lot of others in the Senate and the House. We're sick to death of it all."[63] Goldwater never asked Nixon to resign when he joined the Republican leaders of the House and Senate in a last meeting with the president. But the trio made it clear Nixon had *no* support among Republicans in either House of Congress.

Nixon resigned the presidency at noon on 9 August 1974. In an emotional appearance before his White House staff, he struggled to maintain his composure. This tortured man became the first president in 185 years to resign. He was also the only one to have his name engraved on a gold plate on the Moon. As Charles de Gaulle, one of the few public men Nixon admired, had said when Khrushchev was overthrown: *"Sic Transit Gloria Mundi"*—"Thus passes the glory of this world."

TWENTY-TWO

THE YEAR THE LOCUSTS ATE*

(1974–1981)

I. "I'M NOT A LINCOLN, I'M A FORD"

Gerald R. Ford took the oath of office as president just as Richard Nixon's hel-icopter was leaving the South Lawn of the White House. "Our long national nightmare is over," he said to a relieved country. To millions of Americans, Nixon's forced resignation proved that the system of checks and balances the founders had devised two hundred years before actually worked.[1]

The first order of business for President Ford was the selection of a vice president. Quickly, he named former New York Governor Nelson Rockefeller. The country had been stunned by the resignations of an elected vice president and president. Ford wanted to reassure a worried nation and a doubtful world that Americans could competently deal with

---

* "The years that the locust hath eaten" (Joel 2:25, KJV). The British Minister of Defense, Sir Thomas Inskip, used this phrase to describe the period of 1931–35, during which Britain fell further and further behind Germany in rearmament (quoted in Churchill, *Second World War*, vol. 1, 52). This title was chosen for the period of the mid-70s to 1981 in the U.S. because the forces of freedom were in retreat and Soviet Communism was advancing.

questions of governance and legitimate succession. Many people disliked Rockefeller's liberalism, but no one doubted his competence.

Ford came into the White House on a wave of public approval. Americans welcomed the plain-speaking Midwesterner with genuine affection. "Jerry" Ford had modestly and truthfully said, "I'm not a Lincoln, I'm a Ford." Few Americans could say that Lyndon Johnson or Richard Nixon were basically decent, honorable, trustworthy men. Few Americans doubted that about Jerry Ford.

If he had not been elected to the office, he had the advantage of representing Grand Rapids, Michigan, in Congress for a quarter century. Grand Rapids is virtually synonymous with the American work ethic, solid virtue, and neighborly goodwill. There, and at the University of Michigan, where he was a star football player, Jerry Ford learned to hit hard, but help his opponent up. Nixon brooded over his ever-lengthening "enemies list"; Ford could have kept his on a postage stamp. The media gave him a "honeymoon." The fit, trim sixty-one-year-old was shown diving into his swimming pool. He toasted his own English muffins for breakfast.

But the honeymoon was brief. When he issued an unconditional pardon for Richard Nixon, he hoped to end the divisions and hatreds of Watergate. Instead he just mired himself in it. His approval rating dropped from 71 percent in August to 50 percent in September.[2] His presidency never fully recovered.

"Whip Inflation Now" was Ford's response to the dizzying rise in consumer prices. He wore a lapel button that said WIN. He urged Americans to limit their buying and their demands for wage hikes. He vetoed as inflationary the big-spending bills Congress put on his desk. Ford's WIN buttons provoked hoots of derision. They revived all the old, ugly LBJ stories about Ford's playing football too long without a helmet.[*]

---

[*] "Jerry Ford is so dumb," Johnson had said of the House Republican Leader, "he can't fart and chew gum at the same time." Johnson's crude and funny characterizations of his opponents were Washington legend. But a career of such cruel put-downs left Lyndon Johnson a lonely and dejected man in the end. The media sanitized this to have LBJ say Ford couldn't walk and chew gum at the same time (Reeves, Richard, *A Ford, Not a Lincoln: The Decline of Political Leadership*, Harcourt Brace Jovanovich, New York: 1975, p. 25).

The Democrats used the Nixon pardon and the worsening economic conditions to gain historic victory in the mid-term elections. The "Watergate babies" who composed the new Congress—young, smart, aggressively liberal candidates—would make substantial changes in America.* Ford's repeated attempts to use his veto were frustrated by Congress's new assertiveness. Democrats campaigned for a "veto-proof" Congress and got it.**

First to feel the impact of the liberal Democratic majority on Capitol Hill were the people of Southeast Asia. Without substantial U.S. aid to the non-Communist government in Saigon, South Vietnam could not survive. This was reality, regardless of the guarantees offered by North Vietnam in the Paris Peace accords of 1973.

Seeking to rehabilitate himself after Chappaquiddick, Senator Edward ("Ted") Kennedy had become the most outspoken leader of the liberal opposition to any aid to South Vietnam. His two older brothers, Jack and Bobby, had done much to entangle the United States in South Vietnam. Now, Ted resorted to such devices as refusing even to allow the Pentagon to spend surplus appropriated funds in Vietnam.[3] Following Kennedy's lead, the new Democratic majority voted to cut off all aid to South Vietnam in March 1975.[4] "Do you *want* Cambodia to fall?" asked a worried Ford administration official. "Yes," said liberal Democratic Representative Don Fraser of Minnesota, "under controlled circumstances to minimize the loss of life."[5]

Sensing their opportunity with the "peace" Congress in Washington, North Vietnamese army leaders shredded their agreements and invaded

---

* Patrick Leahy (D-Vermont) was first elected to the Senate in 1974. Among those first elected to the House that year were Sen. Tom Harkin (D-Iowa), Sen. Max Baucus (D-Montana), Rep. George Miller (D-California), Rep. Henry Waxman (D-California), Rep. James Oberstar (D-Minnesota), and Rep. John Murtha (D-Pennsylvania).

** A veto-proof Congress is one in which the president's opponents have more than two-thirds of the seats in both Houses. It has rarely occurred in American history and, even under Ford, could be invoked only on a limited range of usually economic issues.

the South. In short order, Americans watched while the under-equipped South Vietnamese military fell back before the armored onslaught of regular North Vietnamese army units. For decades, it had been argued that the war in the South was a civil war, that the Vietcong were "indigenous" forces. Now, the Communists of the North brazenly rolled over their Southern neighbors.

The U.S. Embassy in Saigon—soon to be renamed Ho Chi Minh City after the founder of Communist North Vietnam—was surrounded by invaders. The U.S. ambassador and his staff had to be airlifted by helicopter from the embassy roof. The ambassador bore a neatly folded U.S. flag under his arm. This was 30 April 1975, the last day of American involvement in Southeast Asia. "This is not a day for recriminations," President Ford said. Ronald Reagan reportedly answered, "What *better* day?"*

Henry Kissinger records the response of a pro-American leader of Cambodia. Distraught at the collapse of American will and American allies in Southeast Asia, Kissinger offered to rescue Sirik Matak from certain death. Matak's response, in elegant French, is memorable:

> I thank you very sincerely for your letter and your offer to transport me towards freedom. I cannot, alas, leave [Cambodia] in such a cowardly fashion. As for you, and in particular your great country, I never believed for a moment that you would . . . [abandon] a people which have chosen liberty. You have refused us your protection, and we can do nothing about it. You leave, and my wish is that you and your country will find happiness under the sky. [If I die here] I have committed only this mistake of believing you.[6]

When the Communist Khmer Rouge seized Phnom Penh, they shot Matak in the stomach. Unattended, it took him three days to die.[7]

---

* A replica of the ladder used by the fleeing ambassador is on display at the Gerald R. Ford Presidential Library in Grand Rapids, Michigan. It has to be one of the strangest mementos of any presidency (Taranto, *Presidential Leadership*, 185).

It would take several years longer for masses of Matak's countrymen to die in a protracted horror known today as Cambodia's "Killing Fields." The French leftists who wrote *The Black Book of Communism* explain the numbers. When the Khmer Rouge's chief, Pol Pot, ordered all residents of Phnom Penh out into the countryside, it resulted in "400,000 deaths." The average number of all executions carried out by the Khmer Rouge forces, the *Black Book* authors find, "hovers around 500,000." Another 400,000 to 600,000 died in prison. And, of course, there was the hunger and disease that overtook city dwellers. People were suddenly thrust into the countryside with no provisions made for them, leaving another 700,000 dead.[8]

Nothing in Sirik Matak's haunting letter proved to be wrong—except perhaps the addressee. He should have sent his letter to Senator Kennedy and Congressman Fraser.

President Ford's ability to help America's abandoned South Vietnamese allies had been seriously impaired by the congressional leadership. They cut off all funding, and Ford respected Congress's constitutional power of the purse. Still, that did not stop him from ordering the Navy to rescue as many as 130,000 "boat people," as storm-tossed refugees from the Communist terror in Southeast Asia were known.

II. 1976: A BICENTENNIAL ELECTION

"My name is Jimmy Carter and I'm runnin' for President," said the grinning peanut farmer from Georgia. Carter himself acknowledged that he was an unlikely candidate for president. He was a one-term governor of a midsized Southern state, a Naval Academy graduate who had worked under the tempestuous Admiral Hyman Rickover in the nuclear submarine program, and Carter's family income was based on the lowly "goober pea."

He was not a lawyer, not a member of Congress, not a Washington, D.C., insider. Instead of these "nots" being demerits, Carter shrewdly made them the centerpiece of his 1976 outsider campaign for president. He communicated to voters very cleverly, perhaps especially when he chose to use only his nickname. He had several reasons for this. He wanted to emphasize a simpler, less "imperial" view of the presidency. He wanted to stress, not hide, his Southern roots. Besides, he could not use his formal name in any event. Key to Carter's quest was his strong support in the black community. *James Earl Carter Jr.* would never do in a country that had just seen the trial and conviction of *James Earl Ray Jr.* for the assassination of the beloved Dr. Martin Luther King Jr.

Carter also emphasized his evangelical Christian faith. For many Americans, their first introduction to a "born again" Christian would come through the campaign of Jimmy Carter.* In many Southern states, and in many other states with large rural populations—like Iowa, Minnesota, Wisconsin, and Pennsylvania—Carter's evangelical tone would strike a responsive chord with millions of voters.[9]

Carter took care to seek out the leading members of the liberal journalistic elite. Who was this "jasper from Georgia," asked the *Baltimore Sun*'s Jack Germond dismissively.[10] Even the hard-boiled Germond, however, could not resist Carter's thoughtfulness. When Germond's fourteen-year-old daughter lay dying of leukemia, Carter sent her a gift. He gave her Indian arrowheads he had found on his family's peanut farm—and a handwritten note asking her to share one with her sister.[11] It was a beautiful gesture.

Based on his outsider status, and his fresh appeal ("I'll never lie to you"), Carter swept past his primary opponents in the spring of 1976. As he captured the Democratic nomination for president, he even became the first candidate in history to refer publicly to his sexual drive. In an interview with *Playboy* magazine, something else unprecedented, Carter

---

* Chuck Colson had also attracted a wide audience with his best-selling book, *Born Again.* Colson went from heading Nixon's "dirty tricks" operation to serving a term in prison. From there, amazingly, he rose to lead Prison Fellowship Ministries. His is an inspiring story of conversion and commitment.

admitted he had "lusted" in his heart, but that he had never broken his marriage vows.

President Ford, meanwhile, faced a stiff challenge for the Republican nomination from former California Governor Ronald Reagan in 1976. Reagan came within 1,317 votes of defeating Ford in the New Hampshire primary. Without a cheering section in the liberal press, however, this near-win was played up as an embarrassing defeat.

Reagan had turned down a third-party challenge to Ford by backers who wanted him to run with Alabama Governor George Wallace. Reagan appreciated the populist style in politics that both Wallace and Carter, both Southern governors, appealed to, but the Californian rejected Wallace's history of support for racial segregation.[12] Reagan also rejected a campaign flyer someone had prepared that featured a newspaper story speculating that President Ford would likely choose Massachusetts Senator Edward Brooke as his running mate. To mainstream conservatives, Brooke was unacceptable because he was a Massachusetts liberal. But Reagan realized that the flyer would be used by the liberal press to suggest the Reagan forces opposed Brooke because he was black. Reagan ordered the flyer shredded.

Reagan was proud of his record as governor of California. He had appointed more than 250 black officials, more than any other governor of the Golden State.[13] And he fondly recalled the story of his Eureka College football team. When bigoted hoteliers refused to let his black teammates stay in their establishments, young Ron took his friends to his home in Dixon—not far from the game. His parents would never turn away a friend in need of a bed and a hot meal.[14]

Reagan suffered several other defeats that spring. He was running out of campaign funds. Even Senator Barry Goldwater—the conservative standard bearer from 1964—urged him to drop out of the race. Journalists at a North Carolina press conference pressed Reagan, badgered him actually, to say when he was going to get out of the race.[15] Reagan's then campaign manager, John Sears, worried that Reagan's image with voters was that of a Republican George Wallace. Thus, Sears deemphasized Reagan's strong conservative stances and ran, instead, a "résumé campaign," which stressed Reagan's experience as California's governor. Sears had actually been secretly talking to President Ford's campaign manager about Reagan's expected departure from the race.[16]

A meeting held in Senator Helms's Washington office proved to be crucial. There, the North Carolina conservative pressed the Reagan campaign team to run on principle—"No pale pastels."[17] It may have been the first of many meetings whose theme was to be "Let Reagan be Reagan." They knew what many would-be "handlers" would later learn—that Reagan was at his best when hard-pressed. He thrilled to the clash of ideas. He fought hardest when his back was to the wall. Reagan's pollster, Dick Wirthlin, put it best: "His enthusiasm would soar, his sights would focus and his passion would stir. He was one of the few leaders I've ever known who actually derived pleasure from confrontation."[18]

Reagan soon struck fire with the Panama Canal issue. Ford and Kissinger were preparing a treaty to turn over the canal to Panama. Reagan stood against leaders of *both* parties—and all of the Establishment press.

"We built it, we paid for it, it's ours!" was Reagan's populist cry of opposition to the giveaway. The canal negotiations represented more than they seemed. The Panama Canal issue struck millions of Americans as symbolic of America's declining power and prestige in the world. Reagan sensed this and rode the issue all the way to the Republican Convention in Kansas City, Missouri.

Jerry Ford had a blessed diversion from his political woes in the celebration of the nation's Bicentennial. Burdened by the memories of Vietnam and Watergate, the American people saw 4 July 1976 as a chance to celebrate two hundred years of freedom and independence. President Ford conducted himself with dignity and good humor at the birthday bash. With ceremonies in Washington, D.C., and Philadelphia, the president basked in the goodwill of a nation on the mend. He told bicentennial celebrants at Independence Hall:

The world is ever conscious of what Americans are doing, for better or for worse, because the United States today remains that most successful realization of humanity's universal hope. The world may or may not follow, but we lead because our whole history says we must. Liberty is for all men and women as a matter of equal and unalienable right. The establishment of justice and peace abroad will in large measure depend upon the peace and justice we create here in our own country, for we still show the way.[19]

In New York City, Ford presided over Op Sail, a magnificent parade of tall ships from all over the world on the Glorious Fourth. Two million people lined the shores of the Hudson River to cheer the stately procession of square-rigged sailing ships led by the U.S. Coast Guard's training ship *Eagle*.* The largest fireworks display in history crowned Lower Manhattan and New York harbor as the nation rejoiced. In a blessed respite, there were no homicides in the Big Apple that historic day.

President Ford's celebratory sojourn was brief. Reagan attacked Ford's foreign policy. *Détente*, Reagan charged, ignored "the overriding reality of our time—the expansion of Soviet power in the world."[20]

Reagan tried to shake loose enough Ford delegates to capture the nomination by selecting Pennsylvania's liberal Republican Senator Richard Schweiker as his running mate. It was either a bold move or a disastrous one. Schweiker's voting record gained him the same liberal rating as George McGovern, but Schweiker had resolutely opposed gun control and abortion and had been an outspoken defender of the "Captive Nations" held down by the USSR. Still, it was an unlikely coalition.

Reagan was trying, haltingly, to reach out to a new constituency. A

---

* What the sailors of the Soviet Tall Ship *Tovarisch* or those of the Polish and Romanian entries—those *captive* nations—thought of this American celebration of two hundred years of freedom would make a fascinating story. Similarly, young sailors of the Chilean Tall Ship *Esmeralda* took part, even though Chile was then under the right-wing dictatorship of General Augusto Pinochet.

year before he challenged President Ford, he broadcast a radio commentary saying abortion was justified only in "self defense" and in which he spoke of unborn children's "human right."[21] In choosing Schweiker for vice president, he showed he wanted to embrace the blue-collar, pro-labor stance Schweiker represented. Reagan understood that blue-collar workers were becoming disenchanted with social liberalism and accommodation of the Soviet Union as represented by *détente*.

President Ford's team used all the advantages of incumbency in beating back the Reagan challenge. Though Ford was a modest man, there was nothing modest about the Ford reelection effort. Once, when wooing some undecided Republican delegates from New York's Long Island, Ford's campaign managers invited the party wheel horses to a splendid White House State Dinner for the visiting Queen Elizabeth II. These "undecideds" quickly decided—and for the president.[22]

With such tactics, Ford beat Reagan for the nomination in 1976—barely. Ford had 1,187 delegates to Reagan's 1,070. Wistfully, Reagan told his son Michael he was not bitter but he would miss not being able to sit across from the Soviet dictator at a summit, listening to his arms control demands, and then walking around to his side of the table to whisper the word "nyet" into his ear.[23]

Despite Ford's victory, Reagan stole the show when President Ford pleaded with him to come down to the victory stage and address the Republican Convention. Ford had dumped Nelson Rockefeller, taken on Senator Bob Dole as a running mate, and made major concessions to the Reagan forces on abortion and *détente* in the party platform. He needed Reagan's support. He was then behind Jimmy Carter by as much as thirty points in some polls.[24] Smiling and gracious, the tanned Californian spoke of a letter touching on world peace he had prepared for a time capsule that would be opened for the nation's *Tricentennial*:

> Those who would read this letter a hundred years from now will know whether those missiles were fired. They will know whether we met our

challenge. Whether they have the freedoms that we have will depend on what we do here.

Will they look back with appreciation and say, "Thank God for those people of 1976 who headed off that loss of freedom, who kept our world from nuclear destruction"?

And if we fail, they probably won't get to read the letter at all because it spoke of individual freedom and [they] won't be allowed to talk of that or read of it.[25]

Here was a sixty-five-year-old man talking of freedom and its future. He concluded with a stirring call to tell the world that "we [Americans] carry the message they're waiting for."[26] Delegates wept openly. Biographer Edmund Morris would later write of Reagan's "off the cuff" remarks: "The power of the speech was extraordinary. And you could just feel throughout the auditorium the palpable sense among the delegates that [they had] nominated the wrong guy."[27] Reagan consoled his heartbroken followers: "Though I am wounded, I am not slain. I shall arise and fight again."[28] Indeed, he would.

Ford campaigned vigorously. He traveled the country frenetically and narrowed the margin between himself and Carter in every poll. He was hampered, however, by his poor communication skills. His message was muddled. Was he for the Nixon-Kissinger policies on *détente* he faithfully implemented or for the newer, more assertive Reagan policies his platform endorsed? Ford let his popular wife, Betty, speak for him on abortion—and Betty quickly disavowed the party's pro-life platform.[29]*

Ford stumbled badly during a presidential debate when he said "there is not Soviet domination in Eastern Europe and there never will be in a

---

* Significantly, the Republican National Platform in 1976 *opposed* the *Roe v. Wade* ruling, offered respectful treatment of both sides in the abortion debate, but firmly endorsed "efforts of those who seek a constitutional amendment to restore protection of the right to life for unborn children." This was the party's first opportunity to respond formally to *Roe*. Although this "plank" provokes a fight—mostly in the press—every four years, the Republican Party has affirmed the right to life of unborn children ever since.

Ford administration."[30] It was a statement so out of line with reality, many Americans concluded that he was simply not up to the job. The Ford campaign never recovered from the gaffe.

Carter received 40,830,763 popular votes, a surprisingly narrow 50.1 percent. Carter and his running mate, Minnesota's liberal Senator Walter "Fritz" Mondale got 297 electoral votes. This was a sharp falloff for the man who once led Ford by thirty points in the polls. Ford received 39,147,793 popular votes (48.0 percent) and 240 electoral votes.[*]

III. "MORAL EQUIVALENT OF WAR"

Carter was, in a sense, a member of a distinct minority. He was the first Southerner elected president since Zachary Taylor in 1848.[**] He was more popular with evangelicals than JFK had been, but less popular with Catholics. His strong appeal to black voters masked his relative weakness among Jews.[31]

In his Inaugural Address, President Carter renewed America's commitment to freedom. "Because we are free, we can never be indifferent to the fate of freedom elsewhere. Our moral sense dictates a clear-cut preference for these societies which share with us an abiding respect for individual human rights," Carter said. But he also warned against defining freedom in terms of material advances: "We have learned that 'more' is not necessarily 'better,' that even our great nation has its recognized limits, and that we can neither answer all questions nor solve all problems."[32]

---

[*] This was one electoral vote fewer than Ford normally would have received. Washington State's "faithless elector," Mike Padden, cast a single vote for Ronald Reagan. Padden checked to make sure Ohio's electoral vote would assure Carter's election before voting his heart. It was to be a harbinger of Reagan's coming electoral vote harvest.

[**] Woodrow Wilson, though born and raised in the South, was governor of New Jersey when elected president. Harry Truman, a Missourian, was from a border state. Lyndon Johnson was from Texas, but he acceded to the presidency only upon the assassination of JFK. Sensing the nation's reluctance to elect Southerners, Johnson liked to stress his Western ties.

Following his address, Carter surprised and delighted the thousands who thronged the inaugural parade route by getting out of his limousine and walking the length of Pennsylvania Avenue. He held hands with First Lady Rosalynn Carter and their daughter, Amy, as they waved to the crowds. Carter was determined to do away with the elaborate ceremony of the presidency. Like Thomas Jefferson, he wanted to bring the presidency to the people. He dispensed with the playing of "Hail to the Chief" and sold the presidential yacht, the USS *Sequoia*.

Jimmy Carter entered office with the great advantage of nearly 2–1 Democratic majorities in both houses of Congress. At least, it would have been a great advantage had Carter not campaigned so assiduously against Washington, D.C. His party, after all, was the party of Franklin D. Roosevelt and Lyndon B. Johnson. His was the party of Big Government. Congressional barons were not amused when he called the tax system they had so carefully crafted "a disgrace to the human race."[33]

Carter was determined to bring the Democratic leaders on Capitol Hill under *his* leadership. To show he meant business, he had Chief of Staff Hamilton Jordan consign House Speaker Thomas P. "Tip" O'Neill and his family to the farthest reaches of the inaugural banquet. It was a studied insult—and a foolish one too.[34] Carter made the mistake of telling Tip O'Neill that he had gone over the heads of Georgia's legislature when its members blocked his programs as governor. "I can talk to your constituents easier than you can," Carter said. O'Neill could not believe Carter was comparing the part-time Georgia legislature with the U.S. Congress. "Hell, Mr. President, you're making a big mistake," Tip told the new chief executive.[35]

The real reason the 1976 election had been so close was the falling away of millions of Carter's early supporters by Election Day. That summer, Carter had led Ford by more than thirty points in most polls. He beat the incumbent in November by barely 2 percent of the vote (50.1 percent to 48.0 percent).

Carter vigorously supported the Equal Rights Amendment (ERA) to the Constitution. First Lady Rosalynn Carter was especially energetic in pushing the ERA. Conservative leader Phyllis Schlafly denounced the ERA and Mrs. Carter's role in pressing for it. ERA foes were angered to see a First Lady exercising political pressure when the American people had not elected her to any office.

Schlafly argued that because the ERA was so vague, it could mean anything. Would young women continue to be exempt from the draft? Would they be forced into combat? Would mothers lose custody of minor children? Would child support and alimony be stripped away? Would the federal government and the states be forced to subsidize abortion-on-demand? Would homosexuals demand the right to marry? All of these questions were raised by the open-ended ERA.

Advocates of the ERA scorned Mrs. Schlafly and her grassroots activists. "Little old ladies in tennis shoes," was a familiar put-down. "They're worried about unisex public toilets," ERA supporters sneered. Well, yes, they were worried about those too.

President Carter addressed the American people on what he called the Energy Crisis. Sitting in front of a fireplace, the president wore a cardigan sweater. He warned that the United States would run out of oil by 1987 and that conservation measures were desperately needed. He called this Energy Crisis "the moral equivalent of war," urging Americans to get used to an era of limits.[36] Soon, windmills and roof-mounted solar panels would qualify for federal tax breaks. Carter strongly backed the 55-mph speed limit that seriously antagonized Westerners. In the vast open spaces of the American West, a "sagebrush rebellion" was sparked first by Washington, D.C., telling residents of sparsely populated states how fast they could drive.

If Carter's policies displeased liberals, they seriously upset conservatives. During Carter's term, groups like Paul Weyrich's Free Congress Foundation, the Heritage Foundation, and the American Enterprise Institute spearheaded serious opposition to the Carter administration's domestic and foreign policies.

Defenders of free-market economics thrilled to the Nobel Prizes awarded to Friedrich A. Hayek (1974) and Milton Friedman (1976).[37] Both of these distinguished scholars showed how socialism not only failed to enrich common people but also sacrificed their freedom too. Socialism was just a shabby way station, as Hayek put it, on "the road to serfdom." As usual, Churchill had gotten right to the nub: "The inherent vice of capitalism is the unequal sharing of blessings," he said. "The inherent virtue of Socialism is the equal sharing of miseries."[38] Except, in practice, it was never even that.

The continuing "stagflation" (stagnant growth, high unemployment, and high inflation) distressed average Americans. Moreover, Americans were frustrated that after billions of dollars spent in Lyndon Johnson's "War on Poverty," the percentage of poor people (12.4 percent) remained essentially what it had been in 1965.[39]

Looking abroad, President Carter soon made clear his unwillingness to press the Soviets very hard on human rights. "We are now free of that *inordinate fear of communism* [emphasis added] that once led us to embrace any dictator who joined us in that fear," Carter told graduates of the University of Notre Dame in 1977.[40] From the earliest days, Carter's administration would place pressure on anti-Communist authoritarian regimes while taking a somewhat relaxed view of Soviet expansion in what was now called the third world.*

Carter chose Cyrus Vance as secretary of state. Vance told *Time* magazine in 1978 that President Carter and the Soviet Communist Party boss, Leonid Brezhnev, "share similar dreams and aspirations about the most fundamental issues."[41] Apparently agreeing with his secretary of state, Carter kissed Brezhnev during their Vienna Summit Meeting.[42] Vance was described by the seasoned New York Democrat Morris Abrams as

---

* Third-world countries generally meant "developing" countries in Asia, Africa, and Latin America. If, however, some of these countries prospered by resorting to free markets—as Singapore, South Korea, and Taiwan did—then they no longer qualified as third world. In practice, therefore, "third world" came to mean wretchedly poor countries in those regions.

"the closest thing to a pacifist the U.S. has ever had as secretary of state, with the possible exception of William Jennings Bryan."[43]

Carter's view sparked alarm, even by some in his own party. Washington State's Henry M. "Scoop" Jackson led the opposition in the Senate to the Strategic Arms Limitation Treaty (SALT II). Jackson was convinced that Soviet cheating made enforcement impossible. Daniel Patrick Moynihan, New York's junior senator, accused Carter of "trying to divert our attention from the central political struggle of our time—that between democracy and totalitarian communism."[44]

Jimmy Carter had to work hard to get his Panama Canal Treaty through the Senate in April 1978. Voting for the "giveaway," as critics called it, were many Republicans, as well as most Democrats. The Republican Senate leader, Howard Baker of Tennessee, would sacrifice his presidential hopes because he inflamed the party's conservative grassroots over the Canal. Nine senators went down to defeat, with opponents attacking them for supporting the giveaway.[45] Reagan had made the Canal giveaway a powerful symbolic issue; his position was supported by most conservatives.

Carter scored his greatest, arguably his *only*, foreign policy success with the Camp David Accords of 1978. Carter succeeded in bringing Egypt's president, Anwar Sadat, and Israel's Prime Minister, Menachem Begin, to the presidential retreat at Camp David for long and tiring negotiations on an Israeli pullout from Egypt's Sinai Peninsula. (Sadat had dramatically flown to Jerusalem to get the talks started.) He was alarmed at Carter's insistence that the Soviets be included.[46] Carter yielded on this point, and the Soviets were not invited. Sadat and Begin would win the Nobel Peace Prize for their roles in the Camp David Accords.*

Exiled Russian writer Aleksandr Solzhenitsyn spoke to Harvard's graduating class in 1978. He warned of the "loss of will" in the West to

---

* Jimmy Carter would have to wait twenty-four years for his Nobel Peace Prize. His selection in 2002 was seen as a slap at President George W. Bush's plans for war against Saddam Hussein's regime in Iraq, a war Carter vehemently opposed.

resist Soviet aggression. Intentionally provoking his audience, Solzhenitsyn said he could not recommend the West as a model for civilization to the enslaved peoples behind the Iron Curtain: "After the suffering of decades of violence and oppression, the human soul longs for things higher, warmer, and purer than those offered by today's mass living habits, introduced as a calling card by the revolting invasion of commercial advertising, by television stupor, and by intolerable music."[47] As Ethiopia, Angola, Mozambique, and Grenada slipped under Communism, Solzhenitsyn's words sparked a wounded reaction from America's liberal elite. The *New York Times*, the *Washington Post*, and even First Lady Rosalynn Carter criticized Solzhenitsyn.[48]

IV. AMERICA HELD HOSTAGE

By 1979, it was apparent that President Carter was in serious trouble. The "misery index" (derived by adding the unemployment figure and the inflation figure) which he had invented and used against Jerry Ford so effectively now weighed heavily against him. Americans had to resort to "odd and even" days to get gasoline, thanks to the Energy Crisis. Carter had grown a huge new bureaucracy in the Department of Energy, but he was unable to assure a plentiful supply of gasoline at the pump—where it counts.

Advised by his brilliant young pollster, Pat Caddell, that Americans were seriously alienated, Carter summoned groups of leaders, academics, and journalists to the scene of his great triumph, Camp David. Carter then came down from the mountain, Moses-like, to fire most of his cabinet officers. He left his inexperienced young White House staffers in place. "Good grief," said a senior Democratic congressman. "He's cut down the tall trees and left the monkeys!"[49] Carter then went on national television to deliver a major speech. In it, he deplored the "crisis of confidence" across the country that he charged was a "fundamental threat to democracy."[50]

To most Americans, the president's performance was profoundly unsettling. Gone was the toothy Carter grin. Gone was the cocky optimism of the nuclear engineer who asked, "Why not the best?" Soon, his speech became known as the *malaise* speech. Though Carter never used that French word, it stuck.

Jimmy Carter and the First Lady tried to bring the country together on the growing concern about the family in America. Following the passage by many states of so-called no-fault divorce laws, divorce rates shot up. The out-of-wedlock birthrate continued to rise alarmingly. Contrary to confident predictions, the widespread availability of abortion did not reduce these numbers. The Carters genuinely sought to find common ground on these and a host of troubling issues in a series of White House Conferences on the Family. The title of these conferences was soon changed to *Families*. And therein lies a story.

Still pressing her campaign against the ERA, Mrs. Phyllis Schlafly put her organizing genius to the task of raising awareness of the implications of that word *families*. With her legal background, she recognized that the White House was on the verge of extending official recognition to a variety of domestic arrangements. She knew that the Census Bureau's decades-long definition of a family as a group of individuals joined by marriage, birth, or adoption was in jeopardy. She and other conservatives, like Paul Weyrich of the Free Congress Foundation and Dr. James C. Dobson of the evangelical organization Focus on the Family, rallied supporters. They urged their followers to get involved in the delegate selection process and take part in the substantive issues that would be raised at the local and regional preparatory meetings for the White House Conferences. Thus was born what participants call the pro-family movement. Those critical of its goals—which were clearly a defensive reaction to rapid social changes—either dismissed this grassroots movement or labeled it "the religious right." Soon, perhaps unavoidably, this movement would have an impact on national politics.

The Reverend Jerry Falwell (head of the newly formed grassroots

Moral Majority), Paul Weyrich, and Mrs. Schlafly were responding, in a sense, to the vacuum created on the conservative side of the political spectrum by the media's decades-long fascination with radical groups on the left. Students for a Democratic Society (SDS), the Congress of Racial Equality (CORE), and the Student Nonviolent Coordinating Committee (SNCC) had been formed in the sixties to generally positive media reaction. Stokely Carmichael (SNCC), H. Rapp Brown (SNCC and the Black Panthers), and Tom Hayden (SNCC and SDS) often flouted the law. Insatiable, they pushed a list of sharp demands on society. Bobby Seale and Huey Newton were leaders of the Black Panthers, one of the most militant of the left-wing groups. The Black Panthers had been implicated in extensive violence and several murders.

The Carters did not lack conviction. Jimmy and Rosalynn both rushed to the scene of the Three Mile Island nuclear power plant breakdown, calming fears.[51] Still, presidents, if they are wise, do not confess to presiding over a malaise

Looking abroad, many Americans found Communist advances in Africa and Latin America disturbing. While publicly embracing Carter, Leonid Brezhnev's sponsorship of terrorists like Italy's Brigadi Rossi, France's Action Direct, and West Germany's Baader-Meinhof Gang was an open secret. Nicaragua's Sandinista regime was taking a menacing turn, cracking down on freedom in that Central American republic while exporting revolution to neighboring El Salvador.

In response, many Democrats who had supported Scoop Jackson and Hubert Humphrey joined with New York writer Midge Decter to form the Committee on the Present Danger. Political science professor Jeane Jackson Kirkpatrick wrote "Dictatorships and Double Standards," a powerful critique of Carter's foreign policy. Her article appeared in *Commentary*, and Ronald Reagan read it. In this era of limits and malaise, who would stand up for freedom? If America was crippled by doubt and guilt, who would lead the Free World? These events and concerns combined to give rise to a new movement called neoconservative, of which

Commentary was the leading journal. Dr. Kirkpatrick blamed President Carter's ineptitude for the fall of many pro-American leaders, including the Shah of Iran.

On 4 November 1979, swarms of "students" in Tehran, Iran, overran the United States Embassy. They took as hostages all the Americans—diplomats and civilian employees of the embassy, even the Marine guards—fifty-two in all.* Not only did the Ayatollah Khomeini not condemn the action, he praised the hostage takers for defying America, that "Great Satan." Perhaps expecting an early resolution of the crisis, television's Walter Cronkite began ending each broadcast of the *CBS Evening News* with the number of days the Americans had been held hostage. Rival *ABC News* weighed in with Ted Koppel offering a late-night program called *America Held Hostage*. Now, Jimmy Carter would have a real malaise to contend with.

The Americans held hostage were beaten, tortured, and threatened with death as the days stretched into months. When Iranian "diplomats" came to New York City for UN sessions, they were allowed to come and go unimpeded. They had diplomatic immunity.

Initially, Americans rallied behind their commander in chief. But it soon became clear that he had no command of the situation. Carter resorted to asking his brother, Billy, a Plains, Georgia, filling station owner, to use his contacts with Libya's Muammar Khaddafi to try to get the U.S. hostages released.[52] Carter sent former U.S. attorney general Ramsey Clark on a mission to Tehran to try to gain the release of the hostages. Clark had gained notoriety for his outspoken criticism of U.S. foreign policy during the decade since he had served as LBJ's attorney general. Carter may have thought that Clark's "Third worldism" would gain him entrée to the Ayatollah's inner circle. Khomeini, apparently

---

* The number of hostages might have been even larger had it not been for the actions of the Canadian Ambassador Ken Taylor and his staff. The Canadians risked their lives to help six Americans escape.

unimpressed by Clark's increasingly anti-American radicalism, refused even to meet with Carter's emissary.[53]

When the Soviets saw that Carter would not use force to free the American hostages in Tehran, they were emboldened. Just after Christmas 1979, Soviet agents overthrew and murdered the ruler of Afghanistan. They installed a puppet ruler, Muhammed Najibullah, in Kabul, and he, obediently, invited Soviet troops to enter the country.* Carter said he was shocked by the Soviet invasion. His ambassador to the Soviet Union, Malcolm Toon, was shocked that Carter was shocked. "Apparently, he hadn't been reading the messages I had been sending him," Toon later said.[54]

As the new decade dawned, America faced a more threatening world, and despite some victories, things only seemed to worsen. Americans went wild with joy when the U.S. hockey team beat the favored Soviets at the Winter Olympics in Lake Placid, New York. "*USA! USA!*" The crowd's chant was defiant and proud. Misjudging the moment, Carter announced a U.S. boycott of the Summer Olympics, scheduled for the following July in Moscow. Sports fans were in a blue funk, but America's highly trained Olympic athletes were devastated.

Carter also cut off U.S. grain shipments to the USSR, a move that soured American farmers in the Midwest. The Soviets were not hurt by this move, since they could always buy grain from Australia, Canada, and Argentina. Only American farmers in the Midwest felt the brunt of it. Carter had begun his presidency with a walk down Pennsylvania Avenue, as Thomas Jefferson had done. Now, he adopted the worst of Jefferson's policies. Then, as in 1807, the embargo hurt Americans more than our adversaries.

When Ronald Reagan announced his candidacy in 1979, he was sixty-eight years old. He was the oldest man ever to run for the presidency, but his health seemed buoyant. He kept in shape clearing away the thick undergrowth on his California ranch—Rancho del Cielo. "People who

---

* Najibullah met his fate at the end of a rope in Kabul's soccer stadium in 1996. He was hanged by the Taliban.

talk about an age of limits are really talking about their *own* limitations, not America's," Reagan said.[55] He didn't mention Jimmy Carter. He didn't have to. Reagan didn't believe in an age of limits or in the limits of age.

Carter viewed it as a "positive" sign when the U.S. hostages in Tehran were transferred from the students to the direct control of the Iranian revolutionary Islamic government. Their captivity didn't end. The threats of summary execution didn't end. Their danger didn't end. What could have been positive? "He is beating on an empty drum," Khomeini mocked. Secretary of State Cyrus Vance took an almost relaxed view: "Most Americans recognize that we cannot alone dictate events. This recognition is not a sign of America's decline. It is a sign of growing maturity in a complex world."[56] So the Ayatollah Khomeini and his Islamic revolutionaries could dictate events but the United States of America could not?

Carter finally roused himself to action in April 1980. Finally. For six months, Americans in Tehran had been tortured. Carter ordered a secret rescue mission, but mournfully, it failed. Several U.S. helicopters collided. Several American commandoes died. *Desert One* became a symbol of the fecklessness of the Carter administration. Cyrus Vance, outraged at the American resort to force, resigned his office.[57]

V. "USA! USA!"

Americans demanded an assertion of their country's interests and honor. The chant that arose spontaneously from the hockey crowds at Lake Placid, New York—"*USA! USA!*"—soon spread across the land. Four years earlier, Jimmy Carter had pledged "a government as *good* as the American people." Now, the American people demanded a government as *strong* as they were.

In the 1980 presidential contest, conservatives flocked to Ronald Reagan, "the Gipper."* Pro-lifers pledged themselves to him. Grassroots activists

---

* Reagan had played doomed football star George Gipp in *The Knute Rockne Story*. Referring to himself, he loved to ask followers to "win one for the Gipper."

were furious with the Panama Canal giveaway. They rejected Kissinger's *détente*. They cheered Reagan's support for California's Proposition 13, the beginning of a tax revolt. Ronald Reagan had been the titular leader of the conservative movement ever since he gave that strong speech for Barry Goldwater in 1964. Nineteen eighty would be Reagan's moment.

Reagan swept the spring primaries and went to the party's convention in Detroit as the tested leader of the Republicans. With the GOP united behind him, Reagan was almost trapped in the selection of his vice president. A movement on the floor of Detroit's Joe Louis Arena—fanned by a bored media—took up the idea of naming former president Jerry Ford to the ticket for vice president. For Reagan to choose Ford would have been a concession that he really wasn't up to the job. The "talking heads"— the network television commentators—loved the idea. Walter Cronkite of CBS even described it, alarmingly, as a "co-presidency." But Reagan's presidency would not have training wheels. He gracefully sidestepped that booby trap by choosing George Bush as his running mate. The party's northeastern wing was mollified by the choice. Happy Republicans would beat Jimmy Carter "like a drum," vowed Party chairman Bill Brock. Brock was the highly organized and combative party leader who had helped rebuild the GOP after the debacle of Watergate.

Democrats were glum as they gathered in New York to nominate Carter to a second term. Walter Cronkite's nightly tally of the hostages' days in captivity in Iran haunted the convention. Surely he never intended it, but Cronkite's signoff became a nightly commentary on Carter's inability to free the hostages—and a constant reminder of the administration's failures.

Carter's managers knew their only chance was to convince voters that Reagan was too dangerous to allow him to have access to nuclear weapons. Meanwhile, Carter's team urged industrialist Armand Hammer to make the case to his Soviet friends for concessions on the Jewish emigration issue.[58] Carter's National Security Advisor, Zbignieuw Brzezinski, signaled to Soviet Ambassador Dobrynin that Carter needed their help and would remember it. "[His] message was clear: Moscow should not do anything to diminish Carter's chances in the election and might even help a bit," Dobrynin reported in his memoirs.[59] They were looking for the Soviets to bail them out. Hammer, we now know, had laundered money for the Communist Party USA and was a key source for Soviet intelligence agencies.[60]

Carter and Reagan prepared for their single debate—the only time the two major party nominees would share the same stage in the 1980 presidential campaign. The Democrats' daily charges that Reagan was reckless were having an impact. Unlike all other presidential campaigns, the number of undecided voters was *increasing*. Voters knew they didn't want Carter again, but they couldn't commit to Reagan.

Onstage in Cleveland, Ohio, Carter was tense, unsmiling, Reagan relaxed. Throughout the ninety minutes, Carter tried to rattle Reagan with constant barbs. He described Reagan's views as *disturbing* six times. Reagan threw the "misery index" back at Carter. It had been 12.5 in 1976 when Carter jabbed at Ford that "no man with a misery index that high had a right to seek reelection." On that October night in 1980, Jimmy Carter's misery index stood at 20![61] Late in the debate, Carter again tried to provoke Ronald Reagan. The former actor looked bemused. He cocked his head to one side, shook it genially, and said: "There you go again."

Ronald Reagan's final statement that night was also memorable. "Are you better off than you were four years ago? Are you safer than you were four years ago?" Reagan's liberal critics thought it was a base appeal to self-interest. But they didn't recognize Reagan's source: he had taken those lines from a Fireside Chat FDR delivered in 1934! They were as powerful in 1980 as they had been when they were first used.

The 1980 election took place on 4 November, the one-year anniversary of the seizure of the U.S. Embassy in Tehran. Fifty-two Americans had been held hostage for 365 days. The cascading returns shocked and awed the liberal media. Network election maps turned "Reagan blue."* Pollsters only belatedly saw the tidal wave coming.

Carter conceded the election shortly after 8:30 p.m. eastern time. It was only 5:30 p.m. on the Pacific Coast, where several tight House and Senate races were to be decided. He had been warned by Pat Caddell he would be swept out of office. He did not want to face the humiliation of a nationwide rejection as the evening wore on. Speaker of the House Tip O'Neill screamed and cursed in his fury.[62] Carter apparently did not understand the impact his premature announcement would have on the party's candidates "down ballot." Hundreds of Democratic candidates would now lose, as millions of the party's voters in the Midwest and Far West—where the polls were still open for another hour and a half—decided not even to bother voting.

Reagan carried 489 electoral votes in 44 states. He claimed an absolute majority of all voters—43,898,770 popular votes (50.8 percent). Jimmy Carter won his home state of Georgia, Fritz Mondale's Minnesota, and just four others (Rhode Island, West Virginia, Maryland, and Hawaii) for an electoral vote tally of 49. He received 35,480,948 popular votes (41 percent). It was the worst defeat for a sitting president since Herbert Hoover in 1932. Congressman John Anderson of Illinois, who mounted an ineffective run as an independent, won just 5,719,222 popular votes. Reagan brought in a Republican Senate and made major gains in the House. It was called the Reagan Revolution.

In Britain, Margaret Thatcher had won an unexpected landslide in 1979. She had to stare down the Communist trade unionists and beat back the battered Labour Party. Most of all, Thatcher had to overcome the weak knees of her fellow Tories. Often at Conservative Party gatherings, it was said, Thatcher was "the only *man* in the room." Her policy was as

---

* The networks had assigned the colors blue and red for their election night maps to the Republicans and Democrats, respectively. In the years since, they've reversed the colors. But around the world, parties of the left are assigned the color red, conservatives are denoted by blue (except in Germany, where they are black).

simple as it was urgent: she wanted to restore freedom. She wanted to put the *Great* back in Great Britain.

Behind the Iron Curtain, Poland's Lech Walesa had started the only free labor union anywhere in the Soviet bloc. *Solidarity* boldly challenged the Polish Communist regime—and the Soviets who propped it up. When Pope John Paul II returned to his native Poland in 1979, he held an open-air Mass for a million Poles. Walesa was there, wearing a lapel pin of the Blessed Virgin. "We want God! We want God!" cried the Poles. Watching on television, his eyes misting up, Ronald Reagan the candidate said of the new pope: "I want to work with him." In the coming decade, these four—the Pope, Thatcher, Reagan, and Walesa—would take their stand for freedom. They and their loyal, liberty-loving followers would change the world.

The Freedom Revolution that began in the late 1970s knocked fatalism into a cocked hat. People who are free can choose to take history by the tail and give it a good yank. And so they did. America, and hope, were coming back.

TWENTY-THREE

REAGAN AND REVIVAL

(1981–1989)

I. 1981: A NEW BEGINNING

When Ronald Reagan mounted the inaugural stands on 20 January, he looked out on a vast throng from the west front of the Capitol. It was the first time an Inauguration had been held there. It was singularly appropriate that this Californian should look westward.

The U.S. economy was in serious trouble at that moment. "Stagflation" meant high unemployment and punishing interest rates. Americans grumbled as they lined up for rationed gasoline. The Iranian militants had been holding fifty-two of America's fellow citizens in cruel captivity for 444 days.

Reagan took the oath and quoted from Dr. Joseph Warren. Warren is among the least-known of the Founding Fathers because he was killed at Bunker Hill in 1775. Yet Warren, the president of the Massachusetts Congress, had told his fellow patriots: "Our country is in danger, but not to be despaired of. . . . On you depend the fortunes of America. You are to decide the important questions upon which rest the happiness and liberty of millions yet unborn. Act worthy of your-selves."[1] Reagan spoke of his confidence that Americans were indeed ready to act worthy of themselves. As he stepped from the Inaugural platform, Reagan signed an Executive Order. With that stroke of his pen, he dismantled the price controls on oil that had stood for a dec-ade. The next day, he went further. He abolished the Council on Wage and Price Stability. The energy crisis that had consumed the Carter presidency ended that day.[2]

At an Inaugural luncheon, President Reagan made the momentous announcement: Finally, the American hostages had been freed! He asked former president Carter to fly to Wiesbaden, West Germany, as his per-sonal representative. There, Reagan's defeated rival would welcome the former hostages to freedom.

President Reagan soon announced his plan for the largest tax cut in American history. Speaker Tip O'Neill, Democrat from Massachusetts, vowed to block it. Massachusetts' other powerful liberal, Senator Edward Kennedy, also opposed Reagan's move. This, despite the fact that his late brother had slashed taxes for business and top earners. "In the 1960s, President John F. Kennedy proposed a cut of the top rate to 70 percent from 91 percent," wrote economist Dan Mitchell. "Between 1961 and 1968, as the economy expanded by more than 42 percent and tax reve-nues rose by one-third, the rich saw their share of the tax burden climb to 15.1 percent from 11.6 percent."[3]

Reagan defended his economic plan before a labor union audience at the Washington Hilton on 30 March 1981. After the event, he walked to his waiting limousine. Bursting out of the crowd, a deranged young man fired six shots at the president. John Hinckley Jr. grievously wounded the president's press secretary, Jim Brady, but it was not immediately clear that the president had been hit. Hinckley also hit a police officer and a secret service agent. Reagan thought he had just broken a rib when his secret service agent shoved him into the limo and jumped on top to shield him with his body. As the president arrived at George Washington

University Hospital, he forced a wan smile. Once inside, however, his knees buckled and he was rushed into surgery.

It would be years before Americans learned how close Ronald Reagan came to dying that day, barely two months into his presidency. The assassin's bullet lodged within just an inch of his heart, and he suffered terrible blood loss.* But that night a relieved country laughed as Reagan's words to First Lady Nancy were quoted on every news broadcast: "Honey, I forgot to duck." Even at the point of death, the affable trouper could not resist cracking a joke.**

The new president's spiritual side showed as well. At one point, Reagan requested a visit from a clergyman. Deaver summoned New York's Terence Cardinal Cooke. When the eminent Catholic leader hurried to Reagan's bedside, the president told him: "I have decided whatever time I may have left is left for Him."[4]

Reagan rebounded from the assassination attempt and spoke to a joint session of Congress to press his economic recovery plan. He was the first president ever to survive after being shot. "He reacted better to being shot," one writer noted, "than most politicians do to a bad headline." "There he stood, Lazarus-like," said Tip O'Neill's young aide, Chris Matthews. "He ran his vote total over the top that night."[5]

Even though Reagan had to wrestle the Democratic Speaker O'Neill for every vote in the House, he never let their competition become personal or bitter. When the time came to celebrate Tip O'Neill's seventieth birthday, Reagan invited him to the White House to apply the soft soap. Toasting the Speaker with champagne, the Irish American president saluted his very Irish American sparring partner:

---

* Surgeons at George Washington University Hospital who opened the president's chest marveled at his musculature. One said he'd never seen a seventy-year-old man with such well-developed pectorals.

** Avid boxing fans knew that Reagan's quote—like so many of his best lines—was not original. Heavyweight Champion Jack Dempsey had first used that line half a century earlier. Just as appropriate at this grim moment in history was another classic Dempsey line: "A champion is someone who gets up when he can't."

If I had a ticket to heaven
And you didn't have one, too
I'd sell mine, Tip
And go to hell with you![6]

In August 1981, President Reagan signed the Economic Recovery Act—a combination of massive tax cuts and spending cuts—at the "Western White House," his Rancho del Cielo near Santa Barbara, California. The law was also known as the Kemp-Roth Bill for its two Republican sponsors, Congressman Jack Kemp of New York and Senator William Roth of Delaware. Kemp was an enthusiastic proponent of supply-side economics. The act was based on the simple idea that when taxes are too high, they discourage enterprise and constrict economic activity. Thus, as the supply-side model shows, lowering taxes stimulates economic growth and generates more revenue in the long run. While Presidents Kennedy and Johnson had shown that the theory worked in practice years before, in those early days of the Reagan administration there was bitter disagreement over the theory.

In the summer of 1981, the Professional Air Traffic Controllers Union (PATCO) went out on strike. Reagan had been proud to claim the support of this union in 1980. He bragged about having been the only union president ever to run for the White House. But now he issued a stern warning: if PATCO members—government employees—violated federal law by walking off the job, he would fire them all. Few people believed the president would carry out that threat. But he did. It was an incredibly daring move. If even one midair collision had occurred, Reagan's presidency might have been fatally damaged.[7]

At the time, it was not clear what impact firing PATCO workers would have. There had been 795,000 workers in all fields on strike in 1980; by 1987, that number declined nationally to 174,000.[8] Not only did the reaction to the PATCO strike give Americans a measure of labor peace at home, but many in the chanceries of Europe and in the Kremlin watched and marveled that Reagan really meant what he said. Even the KGB noted it. With Reagan, they wrote in a background paper for the Soviet Communist leadership, "word and deed are the same."[9]

Reagan also had to contend with international terrorism. On 13 May 1981, the young, vigorous Pope John Paul II was shot in St. Peter's Square. Mehmet Ali Agca, the Turkish would-be assassin, was widely believed to be an agent of the Bulgarian secret police. That meant he was an agent of the Soviet KGB. Reagan wrote to the pope, assuring him of his prayers for a quick recovery. Though grievously wounded, the pontiff did recover. Both leaders would attribute their survival of these near-death experiences to God's protection. It would form a bond between them.

When Libya's dictator, Muammar Khaddafi, sent several Soviet-made MiG jet fighters to threaten U.S. Navy jets in the international waters of the Gulf of Sidra, Reagan ordered them shot down.[10] Reversing Carter-era policies, Reagan told his military chiefs they could pursue harassing Libyan jets. When asked if they could pursue them into Libyan territory, he responded: "You can follow them into their damned hangars."[11] His answer was repeated throughout the Pentagon and, indeed, throughout the entire military.

Stories of Reagan's resolve—coupled with the largest peacetime military buildup in American history—spread through the ranks of the nation's military like an electric current. Reagan greatly improved military pay. Under Carter, in the years of "the hollow military," enlisted men and their families had had to resort to food stamps to make ends meet.[12] Now, morale in the military soared.

At least the military had jobs. For nearly ten million unemployed Americans, *Reaganomics* was proving to be a cruel joke. It seemed Reagan had gambled on tax cuts stimulating the economy and lost. On the other hand, inflation was coming down rapidly as Carter's appointee, Paul Volcker, and the Federal Reserve Board applied a tourniquet to the money supply. Gasoline prices, after an initial spike, were coming down and supply was plentiful. Reagan pledged to "stay the course" and resisted advice to raise taxes again. The loud demands of his opposition on Capitol

Hill were to be expected. The contempt of the liberal press for Reagan and his policies was palpable. Reagan's problem was that most members of his own party, even most members of his own administration, counseled retreat. Reagan stubbornly refused.

By 1982, the recession deepened, and Reagan looked like a one-termer. "The stench of failure" was rising above the Reagan White House, wrote the editors of the *New York Times* with obvious *schadenfreude*. That German word precisely captures their hand-warming "malicious joy." Still, Reagan soldiered on. He did what so many embattled presidents do when domestic crises threaten to overwhelm them. He changed the subject—and the scenery.

In June 1982, President Reagan became the first U.S. president to address both houses of the British Parliament. Of the 225 Labour Party members, 125 boycotted the historic speech.[13] He was undeterred:

> In an ironic sense, Karl Marx was right. We are witnessing today a great revolutionary crisis, a crisis where the demands of the economic order are conflicting directly with those of the political order. But the crisis is happening not in the free, non-Marxist West, but in the home of Marxist-Leninism, the Soviet Union.... [T]he march of freedom and democracy ... will leave Marxism-Leninism on the ash heap of history as it has left other tyrannies which stifle the freedom and muzzle the self-expression of the people.[14]

Many of the British members of Parliament were stunned by Reagan's toughness—and his mastery. They had been led by the U.S. news media to expect something of a dodderer, an elderly and confused man. Reagan in Parliament was in command. And he employed a new style of teleprompter that the British had never seen. They thought he had committed the entire speech to memory. One Labour Party leader, David Owen, was impressed: "Maybe he'll go down as a much better President than any of us are yet prepared to admit."[15]

Reagan also had a chance during this trip to meet with Queen Elizabeth II. The president and the queen were both avid riders. Reagan's men were especially eager to get "visuals" of the president and the queen riding at the royal estate at Windsor. As the two heads of state galloped up a steep hill, however, the queen's horse let out a long, loud blast of gas.

"Oh, I'm so sorry, Mr. President," the queen said.

Without hesitation, Reagan responded: "It's alright, Your Majesty; I thought it was the horse."[16]

Back home, Republicans in the House and Senate were little interested in the clash between East and West. They feared embracing Reagan's staunch stand against Communists. Those facing reelection were skittish about his economic plans. They worried about high rates of unemployment. Although inflation was being wrung out of the economy, interest rates were still painfully high. They dreaded facing the voters.

Tip O'Neill was ready to take back Reagan's victory over taxes. He hammered away at the Reagan record in the months before the mid-term elections. In November 1982, the Republicans barely hung on in the Senate and lost twenty-seven seats in the House.[17]

II. AN EVIL EMPIRE

Reagan did not trim or backtrack on his core principles once he entered the White House. He made no attempt to "run to the middle," as conventional political commentators argued he must do. Most journalists continued to be stunned by Reagan's stubborn commitment to his bedrock beliefs.

Central to those beliefs was his anti-Communism. At one time a "bleeding-heart liberal," Reagan became an unyielding opponent of Communism while serving as president of the Screen Actors Guild. He soon saw Communism's violence, its hostility to democracy, its hatred of God. He knew the Communist record of crushing human rights—and its undeniable record of mass murder.

When Leonid Brezhnev died in 1982, Reagan recognized that the new Soviet Communist Party general secretary, Yuri Andropov, was a more dangerous figure. Unlike Brezhnev, Andropov was known to be highly intelligent. He was the former head of the Soviet secret police, the KGB.* Western liberals welcomed his appointment. Some press profiles gushed over Andropov's supposed fondness for jazz and American movies.

Andropov was determined to block the U.S. effort to put Cruise and Pershing II missiles in Europe. He hoped to split forever the NATO alliance. The KGB supported the Western Peace Movement that called for a nuclear "freeze." No more missiles would be built; none would be placed in Europe to counter the Soviet SS-19 and SS-20 missiles that had already been put in place. Ronald Reagan offered his Zero Option. If the Soviets would only withdraw their offensive missiles, the United States would hold back. Ironically, the Cruise missiles were not a Ronald Reagan initiative. Jimmy Carter had pledged to supply them when nervous NATO allies feared Soviet advances. Now, however, millions in Europe and the United States worried that the "cowboy" Reagan would blunder into war. The president was determined to follow through on Carter's pledge. He pressed wavering European governments to stand by their commitments.

British Prime Minister Margaret Thatcher stood firmly with Reagan on this. So did West German Chancellor Helmut Kohl. Even France's Socialist president, Francois Mitterrand, came around. The NATO alliance held.

Reagan's rhetoric frightened many liberals on both sides of the Atlantic. That didn't slow him down. In March 1983, he spoke to the convention of the National Association of Evangelicals. Warning of the growing trend in religious circles to see moral equivalence between the two Super Powers,

---

* Komitet Gosudarstvennoy Bezopasnosti—the Committee for State Security—was the last name of the dreaded secret police apparatus first established by Lenin in 1918. It went by various names throughout Soviet history—the *Cheka*, the OGPU, the NKVD among them—but its signature was always the single bullet at the base of the skull. The KGB is responsible for taking literally *millions* of innocent lives.

Reagan asked the delegates not to turn a blind eye to the aggressive acts of an "evil empire."[18]

Those two words ricocheted around the world. Reagan used them only once. But they were picked up and repeated endlessly. Deep within the bowels of the USSR, where he was held as a prisoner, Natan Anatoly Sharansky learned of Reagan's words. He tapped them out in prison code on the sewer pipes. Reagan had said what they all knew to be true! "One word of truth can move the world," says an old Russian proverb. *Two* words of truth shook it to the foundations.

Later in March, President Reagan addressed the nation on the subject of ballistic missile defense. He proposed a new Strategic Defense Initiative (SDI), urging a technological breakthrough that would allow the United States to defend itself and its allies from a Soviet missile attack, or, importantly, from a stealth attack by a "rogue" state like Iran or North Korea. "Isn't it better to defend lives than to avenge them?" Reagan asked. Some conservatives approved SDI, but only as a "bargaining chip" to trade away for Soviet concessions on arms control. Liberals uniformly detested the idea. "How high do you want to make the *rubble* bounce?" asked Senator Ted Kennedy. He immediately derided SDI as "Star Wars"—a sly reference to Reagan's Hollywood background and a suggestion that the president was once again confusing fantasy with reality.*

On 1 September 1983, the anniversary of the outbreak of World War II in 1939, a South Korean passenger airliner strayed into Soviet territory over the Kamchatka Peninsula. Soviet MiGs scrambled to intercept it. The jet was clearly marked. Soviet pilots reported they could see the civilians inside. They made no attempt to force the airliner to land.

---

* Conservatives were furious with Kennedy's attack on SDI, but President Reagan never complained. *Star Wars* was one of the most imaginative and popular movies ever made, he knew, and it featured brave warriors of the Republic fighting and winning against an unquestionably evil Empire. Reagan believed that the same advances in computer technology that could produce *Star Wars* could also outmaneuver the "Heavy Metal" of a ponderous, bureaucratic war machine in the USSR.

Instead, they shot it down, killing 269 men, women, and children, including U.S. Congressman Larry MacDonald of Georgia.

Reagan flew back to Washington from California. His military and civilian advisers recommended a wide array of defensive measures. Trade and cultural sanctions against the Soviet Union, condemnation in the UN, and heightened military alerts were among the suggestions. "Fellas," Reagan interrupted, "I don't think we need to do a damned thing. The entire world will rightly and vigorously condemn the Soviets for this barbarism. We need to remember our long-term objectives."[19] Shrewdly, Reagan now knew that those who had praised the jazz-loving movie fan in the Kremlin were the ones who looked foolish. The Soviet bear had shown his fangs for all the world to see. Who could deny it was an evil empire?

The following month, a suicide truck bombing of the Marine barracks in Beirut, Lebanon, shocked America. Killed in their sleep were 241 Marines and Navy corpsmen. They had been sent to the war-torn city to keep peace between the Lebanese, the Palestinians, and the Israelis. Reagan ordered U.S. battleships to shell terrorist strongholds but quickly ordered remaining U.S. forces out of the bomb-cratered Arab capital. It was to be the deadliest attack and the worst failure of the Reagan years.

Reagan continued Carter's aid to the Afghan Mujahaddin. He sent aid to the Nicaragua anti-Communist Contras. He also worked with anti-Communist forces in Poland. Reagan met with the Polish-born pope and pledged to aid Poland's Solidarity movement. Lech Walesa, an electrician, led the first free-trade union behind the Iron Curtain. He had been imprisoned by Poland's Communist government. Reagan delivered stern warnings that the United States would react sharply if Walesa was harmed. Secretly, Reagan supplied Solidarity with Xerox machines and fax machines. Not so secretly, Reagan worked with the AFL-CIO to bolster the role of free-trade unions behind the Iron Curtain.

Unlike the secular elites of the United States and most of Europe, President Reagan took seriously the role of faith in people's lives. He strongly believed in God. He spoke out in defense of freedom of religion everywhere. Under Reagan, the United States government's *Voice of America* began to broadcast religious programs into the Soviet bloc. Catholic Masses from U.S. parishes were beamed into heavily Catholic Poland. Father Viktor Potapov, a Russian Orthodox priest, broadcast his program into Russia. "Religion in Our Lives" was carried to believers in the USSR six times a week in seven languages.[20]

Nor did Reagan doubt the role of faith in Americans' lives. He met with leaders of the Right to Life Movement on 22 January, the anniversary of the Supreme Court's *Roe v. Wade* ruling. Reagan maintained close ties with Rev. Billy Graham, the leading evangelist in the country, and he had an especially close relationship with New York's Catholic leader, Terence Cardinal Cooke. Cooke, dying of cancer, was often welcomed to the Reagan White House. So was Mother Teresa, the Nobel Peace Prize winner who had served the poor of Calcutta for decades. Reagan took care to send many church conventions videotaped messages of support and empathy. It was a way for him to bypass the major television networks whose anchors and reporters were often biased against him.

Reagan's Office of Public Liaison repeated the drill with business groups and friendly professional associations. Reagan earned the title of Great Communicator because of his skill on television, but his detractors hardly realized the manifold ways he would reach out to Americans through such traditional organizations as the Boy Scouts, 4H, and the Future Farmers of America.

New organizations, collectively dubbed "the religious right," appealed to conservative Catholics, Jews, and evangelicals in the Reagan years. Rev. Jerry Falwell's Moral Majority worked on voter registration. Paul Weyrich's Free Congress Foundation and Phyllis Schlafly's Eagle Forum specialized in grassroots organization. Schlafly undertook to defeat the Equal Rights Amendment (ERA). When it was originally approved by more than two-thirds of Congress, the ERA had the support of both parties, the national news media, corporate and labor leaders, professional groups, and virtually all the nation's colleges and universities.

Nonetheless, Schlafly rallied other women against this feminist objective. Specifically, she appealed to women as wives and mothers.

A Harvard graduate with a law degree from St. Louis's Washington University, Schlafly did not suffer fools or feminists gladly. She showed how the ERA's open-ended and purposely vague language could be used by liberal activist judges to force Congress and the state legislatures to pay for abortions with tax dollars and how the ERA would require women to be drafted if the United States ever reinstituted conscription. She showed how child custody and alimony would be affected, to the likely disadvantage of women. Despite the fact that thirty-five of the required thirty-eight states had ratified the ERA, Schlafly reversed the trend and blocked further ratifications.

III. "MORNING IN AMERICA"

The autumn of 1983 marked the beginning of a comeback for Reagan's political fortunes. The economic renewal that he had long proclaimed began sparking to life, and a land held in the icy grip of recession felt a thaw. Housing starts went up. Laid-off workers moved back to work.

Still, Democrats eagerly looked forward to the 1984 presidential elections. To them, 1980 was an aberration—more a factor of Jimmy Carter's great unpopularity than anything innately appealing about Ronald Reagan. As to Carter's low esteem, many Democrats themselves despised him. To them, he was the most conservative Democrat since Grover Cleveland.

Carter's former vice president, Walter "Fritz" Mondale, became the Democrats' nominee. He had an impressive command of facts and figures, a skill honed from nearly twenty years in the Senate and in Carter's White House, but he lacked charisma. He picked as his running mate Congressman Geraldine Ferraro of New York—the first woman on a major party national ticket.

President Reagan had had no primary opponent. He bided his time.

On 6 June 1984, he spoke at the Ranger Monument on a cliff overlooking Omaha Beach at Normandy. There, he pointed to the grizzled veterans of that fateful day forty years before, and he paid tribute to the courage and dedication of those "boys of Pointe du Hoc":

> Behind me is a memorial that symbolizes the Ranger daggers that were thrust into the top of these cliffs. And before me are the men who put them there.
>
> These are the boys of Pointe du Hoc. These are the men who took the cliffs. These are the champions who helped free a continent. These are the heroes who helped end a war.
>
> Gentlemen, I look at you and I think of the words of Stephen Spender's poem. You are men who in your "lives fought for life . . . and left the vivid air signed with your honor. . . ."
>
> Forty summers have passed since the battle that you fought here. You were young the day you took these cliffs; some of you were hardly more than boys, with the deepest joys of life before you. Yet you risked everything here. Why? Why did you do it? What impelled you to put aside the instinct for self-preservation and risk your lives to take these cliffs? What inspired all the men of the armies that met here? We look at you, and somehow we know the answer. It was faith, and belief; it was loyalty and love. . . .
>
> You all knew that some things are worth dying for. One's country is worth dying for, and democracy is worth dying for, because it's the most deeply honorable form of government ever devised by man. All of you loved liberty. All of you were willing to fight tyranny, and you knew the people of your countries were behind you.[21]

Reagan's stirring "Boys of Pointe du Hoc" speech bears comparison with Churchill's tribute to the Royal Air Force ("Never . . . was so much owed by so many to so few."), Pericles' Funeral Oration, and even the Gettysburg Address.

It must be remembered that Reagan was then in the midst of a great transatlantic debate on the defense of freedom against Soviet tyranny. His political and media opponents not only wanted to freeze the production and deployment of nuclear weapons to match the Soviets' attempts to intimidate free societies, they also wanted to chill his moral indictment of totalitarianism. Consequently, national defense played a vital role in Reagan's reelection bid. Opponents bitterly denounced his huge defense buildup. It was contributing to the ballooning deficit, they charged. The defense buildup was undoubtedly expensive, but it was never more than a 6 or 7 percent increase. Reagan sided with his staunch defense secretary, Caspar "Cap" Weinberger, in every administration battle over defense spending. Faced with the choice between balancing the federal budget and, for example, building a six-hundred-ship Navy, Reagan opted for the Navy.

National defense was also the subject of one of the most successful campaign ads in history. The Reagan campaign presented "The Bear" in 1984. The announcer informed viewers that there was a bear in the forest. Some people don't see the bear. Some don't believe there are bears in the woods. All the while, viewers can hear but not see a huge bear, rustling in the branches, grunting. As the camera panned out and showed a very threatening-looking grizzly faced by a single resolute man, the announcer asked if it was not a good idea to be prepared—*"If there is a bear."* Not since the infamous "Daisy" commercial of 1964, which had savaged the supposed recklessness of Barry Goldwater, had a campaign ad achieved so much notice. The ad played on what viewers already knew: Republicans thought Mondale was naïve and weak on defense. The bear, of course, was the historic symbol of Russia. That only made the ad more pointed.

Another memorable television ad showed Americans going back to work, raising the flag, celebrating at the Olympics. The announcer said it's *Morning in America*. It evoked a mood of golden reverie, of renewal, of optimism and growth.

Entering the fall campaign, Reagan was well ahead of Mondale in all the polls. But, when the two candidates met for their first debate in

Louisville, Kentucky, the seventy-three-year-old Reagan seemed slightly confused. He had to correct himself in midsentence once or twice—a rarity for the smoothly articulate old Hollywood pitchman. To make matters worse, Reagan ran overtime in his closing statement, leaving viewers stranded as he spoke about the Pacific Coastal Highway.

Democratic campaign aides handed Fritz a baseball bat, a "Louisville Slugger," as they claimed victory in the debate. The Mondale-Ferraro campaign was infused with new life as the press took up the "buzz" of Reagan's age for weeks. No president had ever run for reelection in his seventies before. Politely, and sometimes bluntly, columnists began to ask if the president had begun to show signs of dementia.

When the two candidates met for a second debate in Kansas City, it was late in the campaign. One of the panel of journalists posed the question to the president—delicately. Henry Trewhitt of the *Baltimore Sun* had asked the *Sun*'s liberal pundit, Jack Germond, how to frame the question that would highlight Reagan's greatest vulnerability. Germond worked with Trewhitt for "several hours" crafting a question that would be hard for Reagan to avoid:

> Mr. President, I want to raise an issue that I think has been lurking out there for two or three weeks, and cast it specifically in national security terms. You already are the oldest President in history, and some of your staff say you were tired after your most recent encounter with Mr. Mondale. I recall, yes, that President Kennedy had to go for days on end with very little sleep during the Cuba missile crisis. Is there any doubt in your mind that you would be able to function in such circumstances?

Germond, watching the debate on a television pressroom monitor, saw the windup and the pitch, but he recalled: "I could see the hint of a smile on Reagan's face, and I thought, Oh, s—, he's all ready for it and he's going to hit it out of the park." And, of course, that is what the president did.

"Not at all, Mr. Trewhitt," answered Reagan. "And I want you to know that I will not make age an issue in this campaign. I am not going to exploit, for political purposes, my opponent's youth and inexperience."[22]

Trewhitt laughed. The panel of journalists laughed. The country laughed. Even Mondale laughed—as his only hope of winning the election went up in smoke.*

Reagan's joke was played and replayed on every television station. Often, it was the only "clip" from the debate that was featured. Reagan's wit was taken as a sure sign that the Old Gipper was mentally agile and fully capable of conducting the affairs of state.

Soviet Communist Party boss Yuri Andropov had died earlier that year, only to be succeeded by the moribund Konstantin Chernenko. Challenged by U.S. reporters for being the first president since Hoover who had failed to meet with the leader of the Soviet Union, Reagan good-naturedly responded: "How can I? They keep *dying* on me!"[23]

Reagan used humor as a weapon. He knew such quips pointed to the larger truth about the USSR: it was a dying empire. It was the Communist system that was sclerotic, ossified. But Reagan knew that even a grizzly bear dying of stomach cancer could be dangerous.

Election Day in Washington, D.C., was blustery and gray. The mood among Reagan's team was somber as they waited for the returns. They were scared. All the public opinion polls looked favorable, but no one can ever be completely sure who will show up at the polling stations or what will motivate them. Voter turnout is everything. Recalling FDR hunkered in Hyde Park during the uncertain election of 1940, the fact bears repeating: in a democracy, it is good for the governors to fear the people.

As the vote tally mounted, sighs of relief and then broad smiles of joy broke out in the White House. Reagan won 54,451,521 votes (58.8 percent)

---

* Jack Germond's honest relating of this campaign story shows the often intimate connection between liberal journalists and their preferred candidates. Would Germond have spent three hours prepping one of the debate panelists with a well-honed question to exploit Mondale's greatest weakness?

to Mondale's 37,566,334 votes (40.5 percent). He won every state except Mondale's Minnesota, giving him 525 electoral votes and, at that time, the greatest popular vote total in history.*

IV. "WE CAN DO BUSINESS . . ."

Ronald Reagan had barely been sworn in for a second term when the Soviet Union once again buried a leader of the Communist Party. Konstantin Chernenko died 10 March 1985 of emphysema. He was seventy-four years old. Three Soviet rulers had followed each other to the grave in less than three years. Nothing better symbolized the hardening of the arteries of the Soviet Communist order.

This would change—abruptly. Mikhail Sergeivich Gorbachev was only fifty-four when he was elected to lead the Communist Party of the Soviet Union. He had been groomed by a dying Yuri Andropov for his intelligence, his polished manners, his youthful vigor, and his affability. If Communism was to survive, if the USSR was to survive, an infusion of new blood was desperately needed. Gorbachev and his educated, stylish, articulate wife, Raisa, were that new blood.**

Even before his selection, Gorbachev had shrewdly made a visit to London. If he could make headway with Prime Minister Margaret Thatcher—Britain's *Iron Lady*—Gorbachev felt confident that would enhance his prestige in Moscow and would later help him deal with Ronald Reagan. Not since Churchill and FDR had there been such a

---

* President Reagan came within 3,100 votes of carrying Minnesota too. That state had only 3,200 election precincts; thus, Reagan lost it by less than one vote per precinct. Reagan had spent only forty-five minutes in the state at an airport rally.

** Raisa Gorbachev's PhD dissertation had advocated national, state-run childcare centers because too many working Soviet mothers were leaving their children in the care of grandparents who were religious. This author had occasion to use this information in congressional hearings where committee members demanded action on day care from the Reagan administration.

close transatlantic partnership as that between Thatcher and Reagan. Gorbachev succeeded brilliantly. Thatcher was duly impressed. She announced after their first meeting: "I like Mr. Gorbachev. We can do business together." From the no-nonsense, all-business Margaret Thatcher, there was no higher compliment.*

President Reagan knew he would have to meet with Gorbachev, but he was not willing to appear too eager. Aides privately pressed the president to meet. Gorbachev was different from all those other Communist Party hacks, they said. Gorbachev was interested in relaxing tensions. There was no time to lose.

Reagan had domestic business to attend to before meeting with Gorbachev. For example, during his first term, the Department of Education warned of "a rising tide of mediocrity" in American schools. The administration responded with a call for greater emphasis on "the basics" in education. It also backed a voucher proposal for students languishing in ineffective federally financed programs for lower income families.

The death of actor Rock Hudson in 1985 introduced the general public to Acquired Immune Deficiency Syndrome (AIDS). The Reagans, of course, knew Rock Hudson from their Hollywood days. They also knew of his homosexuality. Socially tolerant, the Reagans had never shunned friends because they were gay. But when the disease spread, claiming thousands of lives, President Reagan faced a rising chorus of criticism for not delivering a major address on the issue.

The criticism illustrated a striking change in Americans' expectations of their presidents. Millions had died of influenza in 1919 and 1920 and President Wilson never spoke out on the subject. FDR at Warm Springs

---

* The press was right to play up this Thatcher comment, since her closeness with Ronald Reagan was already the stuff of legend. So close were they that Ronald Reagan had a gag film poster in the tack room of his Rancho del Cielo. The poster showed Reagan as Rhett Butler carrying Margaret Thatcher as Scarlett O'Hara upstairs to the bedroom of their Atlanta mansion. Reagan would not bring the satirical poster into the ranch house, he said blushingly, because Britain's first female prime minister, a frequent visitor to the ranch, might see it. A special relationship, indeed! (Morris, *Dutch*, 592.)

contributed mightily to the treatment and acceptance of polio victims, but he did not deliver presidential addresses on the disease. Eisenhower never spoke about heart disease, even after suffering two heart attacks. JFK never admitted he had Addison's Disease. Still, Reagan's silence about AIDS for nearly two years was charged against him by liberal critics as cruel indifference to the plight of sufferers.

It was not that the federal government was not spending huge amounts on research and treatment of the disease. When young Ryan White, a hemophiliac, contracted AIDS through a blood transfusion, Congress moved quickly to fund research and education on the subject. Reagan supported this legislation. Additionally, the second leading cause of AIDS was intravenous drug use. Mrs. Reagan's spirited and effective promotion of the "Just Say No" campaign against drug use was given added urgency by the epidemic.

Meanwhile, back in the USSR, Mikhail Gorbachev became "the new broom that sweeps clean"—or at least he tried to. He denounced alcoholism and absenteeism in the workplace. He spoke out against corruption in the Communist Party *apparat*. He recognized that the USSR must reform or collapse. Pressed hard by Reagan's military buildup and especially concerned about the Strategic Defense Initiative (SDI), Gorbachev started two simultaneous initiatives—*perestroika* ("restructuring") and *glasnost* ("openness"). Under glasnost, horrifying stories that had been suppressed since the founding of the Soviet state began to flood the Soviet media. One of these stories made it into print in the West:

> Tens of thousands of people, perhaps even a quarter of a million, were executed in the prisons of Kiev with a bullet through the temple, brought to Bykivnia by the truckload, and cast into quicklimed pits. Four official commissions have investigated this annihilation in the last forty-five years. Yet the full story of who the victims are, who killed them, and how they came to be buried here has yet to be exhumed.[24]

Gorbachev allowed these stories to come out because he needed to undercut his hard-line Communist opponents in the Kremlin's perennial power struggles. He may not have realized that in so doing, he was undermining the legitimacy of the Soviet state in the eyes of its own people.

When he met Ronald Reagan in Geneva in late 1985, the Western media fairly swooned for Gorbachev. There was little doubt that the Western press was pulling for the vigorous new Soviet party leader to succeed.

The get-acquainted summit produced no diplomatic breakthroughs, nor was it intended to. It did, however, melt the ice between the two heads of government. For the first time since Carter met Brezhnev in Vienna nearly a decade earlier, the Soviet and American chiefs were talking. Some in the American delegation worried that the seventy-four-year-old president would be outmaneuvered by his much younger rival. But Reagan appeared hatless and coatless in the chill air to welcome the Soviet general secretary to the American Embassy. Gorbachev fiddled uncomfortably with his muffler as he got out of his *Zil* limousine.[25] Reagan mixed personal warmth and good fellowship with a tough, almost aggressive negotiating style. "Let me tell you *why* we mistrust you," he said in a one-on-one session.[26] Soon, though, Reagan was insisting that they address each other as "Ron and Mike." Many of Reagan's strongest supporters worried that he would allow personal relationships to blind him to the Soviets' seventy-year record of bad faith. This attempt to build a personal rapport had been the source of FDR and JFK's difficulties in dealing with a shrewd and unscrupulous foe, they believed.

Events beyond improved Soviet relations demanded Reagan's attention then. Early in the new year, the president was alerted to a tragedy unfolding on national television. In a mere seventy-three seconds, the Space Shuttle *Challenger* was launched into a chilly blue sky only to explode spectacularly. Seven *Challenger* astronauts, including the teacher-volunteer Christa McAuliffe, were instantly killed.* Their family

---

* This author had the privilege of meeting Christa McAuliffe and teaching her New Hampshire class.

members witnessed in horror from the reviewing stands, and children throughout the nation watched in their classrooms. President Reagan went on national television that night—28 January 1986—to console and comfort a grieving people. He explained to the frightened children that courage is required to face the dangers of space exploration. We honor those brave astronauts and men and women in every field whose daring and personal sacrifice alone make progress possible. Then, he quoted from "High Flight," a poem written in honor of World War I aviators: "We will never forget them, nor the last time we saw them, this morning, as they prepared for the journey and waved goodbye and 'slipped the surly bonds of earth' to 'touch the face of God.'"

House Speaker Tip O'Neill was moved to tears by the president's eloquence. "He may not be much of a debater," O'Neill observed, "but with a prepared text he's the best public speaker I've ever seen. . . . I'm beginning to think that in this respect he dwarfs both Roosevelt and Kennedy."[27] This was high praise from the fiercely partisan Democratic speaker.

Reagan captured—or perhaps he shaped—a national mood of firm resolve. Public opinion polls recorded that Americans strongly supported continuing the space program, despite the worst disaster in its history. Significantly, despite the trauma of a nationally televised explosion of a space shuttle, NASA remained committed to the policy of openness first mandated by President Eisenhower in 1959.

The year 1986 marked more joyous events, including the centennial celebration of New York's Statue of Liberty. Reagan had used the upcoming hundredth anniversary of the Lady in the Harbor to recruit Chrysler Corporation president Lee Iacocca to lead a private fund-raising drive. Reagan hoped to commemorate the event by restoring the worn, storm-stressed statue. A joint French-American team took on the work of restoration, carefully replacing every one of thousands of individually-wrought steel support struts. The great symbol of "Liberty Enlightening the World" had been in danger of collapse.

On 3 July 1986, President Reagan invited French President Francois

Mitterrand to join him and Mrs. Reagan for the statue's rededication. It was to be a tribute, as well, to American ideals of liberty. Reagan treated the Socialist Mitterrand with elaborate courtesy—even as he was doing his best to consign socialism "to the ash heap of history."

Oddly, Reagan was indebted to Mitterrand. The French leader had collaborated with France's powerful Communist Party in 1981–82. He tried to impose Marxism democratically on the French people. This Gallic effort was widely viewed as the polar opposite of Reagan's renewed commitment to free enterprise. The success of Reagan's policies contrasted powerfully with the soon-abandoned disaster of Mitterrand's policies. The failure of this attempt at democratic Socialism had deeply impressed the free peoples of Europe and the world.

For the celebration, President Reagan strode the deck of the USS *Iowa*, a World War II–era battleship retrofitted for service in the nuclear age. In New York's darkened harbor, he sent a laser beam to the tip of the Statue of Liberty, dramatically signaling the unveiling. With Solidarity alive in Poland, with the Mujahaddin harassing the Soviets in Afghanistan and the Nicaraguan Contras pressing the Communist Sandinistas in Central America, Reagan felt confident in saluting "the cause of human freedom" and relighting Lady Liberty's torch.*

With peace and prosperity, Reagan could be forgiven for thinking he had restored America's rightful place of leadership in the world.

V. REYKJAVIK: THE CLASH

The Soviet Union was not just going to collapse, said the leading experts on the Kremlin. Former president Richard Nixon had spoken of seeking

---

* When the majority of House Democrats in 1986 voted against aid to the anti-Communist Nicaraguan contras, this author, a lifelong Democrat, finally switched parties and became a Republican.

"hard-headed *détente*" as the best we could realistically hope for.[28] But Reagan saw things differently.

His critics always accused him of being *simplistic*. Veteran Washington wise man Clark Clifford called the president "an amiable dunce."[29] They did not know what Reagan had told Richard Allen a decade earlier. Allen would become Reagan's national security advisor in the White House. Years before Reagan was elected, he told Allen: "My idea of American policy toward the Soviet Union is simple, and some would say simplistic. It is this: We win and they lose."[30] The problem was that Reagan's critics mistook clarity for simplicity.

The hastily called summit at Reykjavik, Iceland, in late 1986 was Gorbachev's idea. If Hollywood had searched for a location in which to dramatize visually the East-West clash, it could not have chosen a better one. Iceland is a volcanic island midway between Europe and North America. Instead of green grass, there is black volcanic ash. The island's capital city is surrounded by dark gray crags. The two superpower leaders would meet at Höfdi House, a modest, nineteenth-century mansion. It is an unadorned, white building with a dark slate roof. Some local residents even claim that Höfdi House is haunted.[31]

In mid-October the stark Icelandic landscape was almost devoid of color. The scene was dominated by black and white. It was like the Hollywood movies that Reagan had starred in, the ones that sharply contrasted good and evil. Those were the films that nauseated the sophisticates. To make the contrast even more compelling, Gorbachev showed up in his black limousine, wearing a heavy black overcoat and a black snap-brim fedora. Reagan arrived wearing a light tan raincoat, which on television appeared to be white.

Very quickly, both summit participants went far beyond the agenda. Gorbachev, we now know, was desperate to end the arms race. Perestroika was not working. The Soviet system was being crushed by the burden of keeping up with the U.S. military buildup. If he could cut defense spending, Gorbachev could divert desperately needed funds to perestroika and his effort to save the Communist system. "He has a nice smile," the grim-faced Foreign Minister Andrei Gromyko said of their young champion, "but he has *iron* teeth."[32]

Like two poker players, the leaders faced each other across a table. Gorbachev made daring offers about major weapons cutbacks. Everything Reagan had offered five years earlier in his Zero Option proposal, he could now have. Reagan suggested that both sides scrap all offensive missiles within ten years. Soon the two men found themselves talking about nuclear arms reductions that went far beyond anything ever proposed, ever even imagined, in the entire history of arms-control negotiations between the United States and the USSR. The progress seemed breathtaking. But Gorbachev had a condition: the United States would have to agree not to continue work on the Strategic Defense Initiative.[33]

Ronald Reagan could have the most successful summit in American history. He could sign the most far-reaching agreement ever with the Soviets. He could return home—just in time for the midterm congressional elections—as the Peacemaker. All he had to do was give up SDI. He could explain to the American people that it had *always* been his intention to use SDI as "a bargaining chip" and that he had held out for the best agreement the United States had ever won.

He would not do it. He had eerily described this scene fully ten years earlier. In 1976, he told his son Michael that he was not so sorry he had lost the Republican nomination for president. His only regret was now he would never have the chance to hear out a Soviet ruler's arms control demands. These demands would surely have left the free countries at a disadvantage. Then, Reagan said, he would quietly walk around the table and whisper *nyet*. Here, that scene, exactly as Reagan had described it, was being played out. And as president, Ronald Reagan whispered *nyet*.

With hopes dashed, the two unsmiling leaders left Höfdi House. "I don't know what else I could have done," Gorbachev told Reagan through an interpreter as they parted. "You could have said yes," Reagan answered with uncharacteristic bitterness. At the time, Reykjavik seemed to be a failed summit. In the off-year elections of 1986, the Republicans lost control of the Senate. For the rest of Reagan's term, he would face an increasingly fractious Congress.

VI. IRAN-CONTRA

"Do whatever you have to do to keep the Contras alive," President Reagan had told his National Security Staff.[34] Gung-ho figures like Admiral John Poindexter and Marine Lieutenant Colonel Oliver North were prepared to carry out that order.

Reagan wanted to help the anti-Communist Contras fighting in Nicaragua weather the seesawing efforts in Congress to cut off their funding. Liberals were determined to avoid a Vietnam in this hemisphere. They made repeated runs at defunding the Contras, occasionally succeeding in passing amendments to appropriations bills. Congressman Eddie Boland, a Democrat from Massachusetts, offered an amendment that prevented U.S. intelligence agencies from seeking to overthrow the government of Nicaragua. The Reagan administration narrowly interpreted this amendment as applying to the Central Intelligence Agency and the Defense Intelligence Agency, but not to the National Security Council where Poindexter and North worked. They were deemed free to seek outside support for the Contras. "Ollie" North was thus left free to solicit funds from such anti-Communist stalwarts as the Sultan of Brunei.

Beirut came back to haunt the administration. The Marines and Navy Corpsmen who died in 1983 were deeply mourned in the Reagan White House. CIA Station Chief William Buckley had been kidnapped, tortured, and murdered by Hezbollah terrorists. So had Navy diver Bobby Stethem. Reagan anguished over these deaths. He was incapable of putting these American captives out of his mind and regarding them as casualties of war.[35] Reagan had spoken wistfully of the days when an American had only to put an American flag in his lapel to be able to walk safely anywhere in the world. He yearned to intervene on behalf of endangered Americans—especially those who were serving the United States.

Reagan was persuaded that there were "moderates" in Iran. These moderates were jockeying for power in a post–Ayatollah Khomeini regime. They said they wanted better relations with the United States. But they would be strong-armed out of power unless they could buy weapons. If they were armed, they claimed they could influence the hostage takers in Beirut.

Thus was born the fateful linkage between the sale of arms to Iran, the ransoming of hostages in Beirut, and the diversion of profits from the arms sales to support the Nicaraguan Contras.

What is so clear to critics now was not so clear then. Americans have repeatedly joined civilized nations all over the world in negotiating for the release of hostages held in the Middle East. Hostage taking and ransom demands are a highly developed art in the Mideast. As long ago as the eighteenth century, no lesser figures than President Washington and President Adams became involved in paying for the release of American sailors held captive in North Africa. They did it because the Europeans did it. Jefferson determined to use force rather than pay ransom. He sent U.S. warships and Marines "to the shores of Tripoli."

The day before the 1986 midterm elections in the United States, a Beirut newspaper reported that the United States was involved in paying for the release of hostages. Initially, the Reagan White House dismissed the notion as ridiculous. When White House Chief of Staff Donald Regan first informed President Reagan that the profits from arms sales were being diverted to support the Contras, Reagan became pale. "Why would they do that?" he asked, apparently forgetting his orders to Poindexter and North.[36]

Iran-Contra, as the burgeoning scandal was soon known, erupted. Reagan was described in the press as culpable if he was aware—and thus liable to impeachment. Or, if he really did not know what his subordinates were doing, then he was clearly disengaged. The famous Reagan management style was to sketch the broad outlines of policy in clearly communicated terms and then let subordinates handle the details. This style had been highly successful in the first term. Now, especially with Donald Regan making many of the day-to-day decisions himself, Reagan's hands-off management style was seen as a failure.

President Reagan suffered a loss of twenty points in his approval rating by the American people. He was dispirited. When he finally agreed to fire Chief of Staff Donald Regan, he did not realize how close he was himself to being deposed. Regan's departing assistants told staffers for the incoming White House chief of staff, Howard Baker, that Reagan was incapacitated. Baker should be prepared, they said, to invoke the Twenty-fifth Amendment to the Constitution. Reagan was too old, too forgetful, too passive to serve in the nuclear age.[37]

On arriving for work, former senator Baker stationed various staff members at different points in the Cabinet Room. Their assigned task was to observe closely how the president interacted with others.

They found Reagan stimulated by the new faces, fully engaged, and with a total grasp of the issues at hand. The president rose to the occasion. He may never have known he was being measured for a political casket when he gamely refused to die. Senator Baker concluded that he was "fully competent" and the crisis passed.[38] When the president went on national television to take responsibility for Iran-Contra, his approval rating buoyed up once again.*

VII. "TEAR DOWN THIS WALL!"

Reagan was scheduled to visit West Germany again in June 1987. He wanted to speak there as part of Berlin's 750th anniversary celebration. Less interested in history, the media were obsessed with Iran-Contra.

---

* This author had encouraged the president to take this course that day.

Commentators spoke of Reagan as a "lame duck." There was a sense that his trip to Europe was merely an effort to avoid the political heat at home.

The president was determined to make a strong statement about divided Berlin. Nothing could be worse, the State Department thought. Prepping for the president's trip in May 1987, White House speechwriter Peter Robinson traveled to the divided city and met with John Kornblum, the top U.S. diplomat in West Berlin. Don't bash the Soviets, Kornblum counseled. Don't come off as a "cowboy." And whatever you do, don't mention the Berlin Wall. Berliners, Kornblum advised, are worldly, sophisticated, and left-wing. And besides, they've grown *used* to the Berlin Wall.[39]

Robinson listened carefully. Then he took a ride in a U.S. Army helicopter.

The sixty-mile-long wall didn't just separate a city, Robinson later wrote, but "separated two different modes of existence. On one side . . . lay movement, color, modern architecture, crowded sidewalks, traffic. On the other side, all was drab."[40] In East Berlin, buildings still showed evidence of bomb and bullet damage from World War II. In 1987, the war had been over for forty-two years. Two hundred fifty people had been killed by East German border guards since the wall went up in 1961.[41]

That evening, Robinson went to a dinner party hosted by Dieter and Ingeborg Etz. Herr Etz had lived in Washington when he worked at the World Bank and Frau Etz taught German at Georgetown Prep in suburban Bethesda, Maryland.[42] Emboldened by his helicopter ride, Robinson asked his hosts and their German guests if West Berliners had, as he had been told, "gotten used to the Wall."

The dinner party became very quiet. Robinson thought he'd committed a faux pas even asking the question. Then, one of the German men looked very serious and said: "My sister lives twenty miles in that direction. I have not seen her in more than two decades. Do you think I can get used to that?" Another German described his morning walk to work, past a guard tower where a soldier—always the same soldier—stared at him through binoculars. "That soldier and I speak the same language. We share the same history. But one of us is a zookeeper and the other is an animal, and I'm never certain which one is which."[43] Finally, Ingeborg Etz broke in, her face reddening. She pounded a fist into her palm and said: "If this man Gorbachev is serious with his talk of *glasnost* [openness] and *perestroika* [restructuring], he can prove it. He can get rid of this wall!"[44]*

Returning to Washington, Peter Robinson was determined to put a line in the president's speech about the Berlin Wall. But it would not be easy. Robinson put in a line urging General Secretary Gorbachev to tear down the wall. Robinson met in the Oval Office with Reagan and the speechwriting team. Robinson told the president that the speech would be heard on radio, not just in West Berlin, but in East Berlin, East Germany, and as far away as Moscow. "That wall has to come down," Reagan reiterated. "That's what I'd like to say to them."[45]

The State Department, the National Security Council, even Secretary of State George Schultz all weighed in *against* putting that line in the president's speech.

Grudgingly, they suggested that Reagan might say something vague, like "some day this ugly wall will disappear." Some day?

Reagan knew the Western media was swooning over Mikhail Gorbachev. He also knew something about upstaging a rival. If Gorbachev really meant *openness*, he could start by opening the Brandenburg Gate.

> General Secretary Gorbachev, if you seek peace, if you seek prosperity
> for the Soviet Union and Eastern Europe, if you seek liberalization:
> Come here to this gate! Mr. Gorbachev, open this gate! Mr. Gorbachev,
> tear down this wall!

Though Reagan's speech at the Brandenburg Gate stands today as one of history's great speeches, at the time, the American press paid little

---

* The story of Ingeborg Etz and her role in Reagan's historic speech has been related by Peter Robinson and by Dr. Stephen J. Ochs, history instructor at Georgetown Preparatory School in Bethesda, Maryland. Ochs taught both the author's sons.

attention. It seemed almost rude to mention Gorbachev's connection to the Iron Curtain. There was far more interest in the Senate's Iran-Contra hearings. But the drive to criminalize policy differences was dealt a serious blow when Colonel Oliver North used his testimony before the committee to vigorously defend his actions. Appearing ramrod straight in full uniform, with a chestful of combat ribbons, North thrilled the country. "Olliemania" swept the land.[46] Not only did he not repent, he intimidated and flummoxed committee members. Even North's attorney, the redoubtable Brendan Sullivan, managed to back down the committee. When one senator tried to elicit a statement from witness North without advice of his counsel, Sullivan shot back irreverently: "I'm not a potted plant!"

The summer of 1987 also saw a great fight over a vacancy on the U.S. Supreme Court.

President Reagan had named the first woman to the high court. Justice Sandra Day O'Connor was a keen disappointment to the president's conservative backers. They were happier when he elevated Associate Justice William Rehnquist to Chief Justice and named Federal Judge Antonin Scalia to fill the Rehnquist vacancy in 1986. Of course, all three of those nominations had been made while the Republicans controlled the Senate.

Reagan's opponents, led once again by Senator Kennedy, were determined to deny him his choice of Supreme Court justices. When Reagan named the controversial Federal Judge Robert Bork, Kennedy lit up the Capitol with his impassioned rhetoric. "In Robert Bork's America," Kennedy roared, women would have to resort to back-alley abortions. Even worse, he claimed, "In Robert Bork's America . . . blacks would sit at segregated lunch counters; rogue police would break down citizens' doors in midnight raids."[47]

Never before had a Supreme Court nomination been made the subject of such a vast, well-financed public campaign of vilification and character assassination. Lifelong friends of the scholarly, bearded former Yale law professor could not recognize the devilish figure Kennedy had created.

The idea of a single member of the Supreme Court having the power Kennedy conjured was ridiculous on its face, but Bork's opponents would stop at nothing to discredit the witty, learned man. Liberal activists who had virtually invented the constitutional doctrine of privacy found nothing wrong with invading the judge's privacy, even records of his video rentals were gone over for evidence to use against him. (The judge, it seemed, had a predilection for Broadway musicals.)

On 17 September 1987, the day of the Bicentennial of the U.S. Constitution, Bork had to endure being grilled by Senator Kennedy before the Judiciary Committee. Kennedy asked the judge hostile questions about his ruling in an interstate trucking decision.*

In a gross violation of the Constitution's provisions on a religious test, Judge Bork was asked by Alabama's Democratic Senator, Howell Heflin, to discuss his religious beliefs—under oath. Robert Bork, then a conventional Protestant, had married a Jewish woman. Following her death from cancer after a long and devoted marriage, Bork had married a former Catholic nun. If ever a man had demonstrated his complete lack of religious bigotry, it was Robert Bork. The mere asking of such a question directly violated the Constitution's prohibition. Had the committee chairman, Senator Joseph Biden, a Democrat from Delaware, cared about fairness, he would instantly have ruled the question out of order.**

Bork was rejected 58–42 by the Senate. This entire ugly and discreditable episode was dragooned by Edward M. Kennedy. The country's politics and jurisprudence continue to be poisoned by the dishonorable methods used in that Bicentennial summer of 1987 by Robert Bork's opponents.

---

* One wag at the time suggested that it was the judge who should be arraigning the senator from Chappaquiddick on *his* driving safety record.

** Article VI, Section 3 of the Constitution says, "[B]ut no religious test shall ever be required as a qualification to any office or public trust under the United States." Heflin's improper grilling of Judge Bork may have been the most public and flagrant flouting of this vital constitutional provision.

VIII. INTO THE SUNSET

Ronald Reagan was by far the oldest president to serve. He had survived a serious assassination attempt, colon cancer, and skin cancer. Politically, he had survived the loss of control of Congress and an international arms-for-hostages scandal that threatened to result in his impeachment. The stock market had crashed dizzily in October 1987, sending shock waves through financial markets, but it soon rebounded. The prestige press emphasized every political embarrassment and hyped such issues as homelessness and income disparity as crises that the administration was unwilling or unable to handle.

Still, the economy continued to boom, generating millions of new jobs. Tax revenues doubled on Reagan's watch—a tribute to the success of supply-side economics that his critics once derided as *Reaganomics*.[48]

When Mikhail Gorbachev came to Washington, D.C., in December 1987, the press delighted in showing him wading into lunchtime crowds on the capital's fashionable Connecticut Avenue. His obvious boyish delight in mixing with Americans on the streets reminded some of the popular movie of the day—*Ferris Bueller's Day Off.* It would have seemed churlish to point out that half a billion people held at bayonet point under Soviet rule had no similar freedom of movement.

So, too, was Reagan determined to break through the "bubble" that protected him and get a real sense of the Russian people. Unexpectedly, during a 1988 trip to the Soviet Union, the president and Mrs. Reagan got out of their limousine to walk around Moscow's famed Arbat district. The Russian crowd responded with delight. The Arbat is a district known for its greater commercial and artistic freedom. Very quickly, however, the KGB muscled its way into the friendly crowd, pushing, punching, manhandling the Reagans' admirers.[49] They kicked and shoved everyone, including American reporters. "Leave them alone, these are Americans," cried Reagan White House staffer Mark Weinberg. Reagan recorded in his diary that night his reaction to the

Soviets' brutalizing their own people: "Perestroika or not, some things have not changed."[50]

Reagan, politically weakened and consigned by the political pundits to lame-duck status, signed an Intermediate Nuclear Forces (INF) agreement with Gorbachev. Under the terms of the agreement, the United States would remove the Pershing II missiles Carter had promised NATO as a counterweight to the placement of Soviet SS-19 and SS-20 missiles in Eastern Europe. INF was the Zero Option that Reagan had proposed in 1983. The mere suggestion of this Zero Option had caused the Soviets to react with outrage. In protest, the Soviet Delegation had walked out of the arms control talks at Geneva. For that portion of the Western intelligentsia that sees arms control as an indicator of East-West relations, this Soviet move had spread panic. Nuclear war—with its attendant horrors of megadeaths and nuclear winter—loomed before them. Terrified, Western anti-war demonstrators had rallied in their millions to demand a nuclear freeze. Reagan had held firm.

Now, Gorbachev was coming to him *and on his terms*. As Churchill might have said: "Some lameness! Some duck!" All previous arms control agreements had merely sought to slow the rate of growth of weapons systems. This was the first agreement that actually *reduced* the number of offensive nuclear weapons.

Reagan was being Reagan. He had always had a horror of nuclear warfare. He had always said that the United States must negotiate out of strength. He was now putting into practice those eloquent words from John F. Kennedy's Inaugural address: "Let us never negotiate out of fear. But let us never fear to negotiate."

Reagan's skillful negotiating strategy paid off. Following the Soviets' withdrawal from Afghanistan, Reagan visited Moscow in late May 1988.*

---

* After the fall of Communism, this author informally polled top Reagan defense officials. Asked what single thing led to the collapse of the Soviet system, they answered most frequently: Stingers—those mobile, shoulder-fired missiles the Afghan *Mujahaddin* used to deadly effect against the Soviet invaders.

While press attention at home was focused overwhelmingly on the upcoming presidential campaign, Reagan pressed on, carrying his appeal for freedom to the heart of the Soviet Empire.

The pressures unleashed by Gorbachev's perestroika continued to build. The 1986 meltdown of a nuclear power plant at Chernobyl, in the Ukraine, had caused thousands of deaths. The Soviet state was shown to be corrupt, inefficient, and heedless of human life. The environmental impact of Communist rule was seen to be nothing less than catastrophic.

Now, Reagan stood in the resplendent St. George's Hall in the Kremlin. He responded to a formal welcoming speech from Gorbachev. There, amid the gold and crystal and rich tapestries of the Tsars—and among the paintings of saints—Reagan looked steadily at the General Secretary of the Communist Party of the Soviet Union and said, "God *bless* you." It was the first time the name of God had been uttered aloud in that place in seventy years. And it was heard by every citizen across the twelve time zones of the Soviet Union.

Some of the Communist leaders who heard these words "visibly blanched." A Soviet diplomat later recalled the moment: "The . . . impregnable edifice of Communist atheism was being assaulted *before* [our] *very eyes*."[51]

Reagan insisted on meeting with Jewish refuseniks. When one of them was denied permission to visit the U.S. Embassy, Reagan told his Soviet hosts he would go to the man's apartment. Embarrassed, the KGB backed down. Reagan invited hundreds of religious believers to a reception at Spaso House.[52] He stressed the need for religious freedom to be part of any meaningful perestroika.

Invited to address students at Moscow State University, Reagan leaped at the chance to talk to the sons and daughters of the Soviet ruling class— the *nomenklatura*. He praised "the first breath of freedom" they had seen in this "Moscow Spring." These knowledgeable young students could not miss his reference. Many of their parents had had their hopes for a relaxation of tyranny in the Eastern bloc dashed when Soviet tanks rolled into Czechoslovakia in 1968. That was the brutal end of the "Prague Spring."

Now, standing under a huge, scowling bust of Lenin, Reagan patiently laid out the case for freedom in the information age. Marx was wrong to see materialism at the center of human existence, he said. The new computer revolution was powered by the silicon chip—whose material basis was the same as the most plentiful substance on earth—sand. In order for a state to compete in the modern world, though, the computer revolution demanded free minds. No state could enjoy progress when every fax machine, every photocopier, every computer hard drive had to be controlled by the secret police.

He returned again and again to the spiritual basis of freedom. To these young people who had been schooled in atheist materialism from kindergarten, he boldly proclaimed:

> Even as we explore the most advanced reaches of science, we are return-
> ing to the age-old wisdom of our culture, a wisdom contained in the
> Book of Genesis in the Bible. In the beginning was the spirit, and it
> was from this spirit that the material abundance of creation issued
> forth. But progress is not foreordained. The key is freedom—freedom
> of thought, freedom of information, freedom of communication.

He ended his address with an appeal to these future leaders of Russia:

> We do not know what the conclusion of this journey will be, but we're
> hopeful that the promise of reform will be fulfilled. In this Moscow
> spring, this May 1988, we may be allowed that hope—that freedom,
> like the fresh green sapling planted over Tolstoi's grave, will blossom
> forth at last in the rich, fertile soil of your people and culture. We may
> be allowed to hope that the marvelous sound of a new openness will
> keep rising through, ringing through, leading to a new world of recon-
> ciliation, friendship, and peace.
>
> Thank you all very much and *da blagoslovit vas gospod!* God
> bless you.[53]

As Reagan departed the Soviet Union, he gave the first nationally televised address to the Soviet people. He had been prepped by America's leading Russian scholar, James Billington. Reagan reached out to the *babushkas* (grandmothers). These aged women were the true spiritual leaders of Mother Russia, Billington said. Reagan praised them—and blessed them.

There would be no Appomattox (1865) or Surrender Ceremony on board the USS *Missouri* (1945) to mark the end of the Cold War. If we search for the defining moment when the USSR ceased to threaten the life and liberty of the world, it might be seen at Reykjavik. Secretary of State George Schultz thought this was the turning point. So did Mikhail Gorbachev.* Although the press in 1986 lamented the "failure" to sign an arms control agreement, Gorbachev noted that it was the first time they had engaged in deep discussions on the future of nuclear weapons and the future of the superpower relationship.[54]

But even without tens of thousands of nuclear-tipped missiles, the Soviet Union could still be a deadly menace. The massive preponderance of Soviet troops and tanks was the reason the Western democracies had sought protection under their "nuclear umbrella" from the earliest days of the Cold War. Margaret Thatcher knew this. She worried that Reagan and Gorbachev would be carried away by their nuclear-arms-cutting enthusiasms and forget the threat of Soviet conventional armed strength.[55] With her keen sense of history, with her passion for freedom in Europe, she was a true heir of Winston Churchill. There could be no secure peace in which the United States abandoned its truest ally.

If, therefore, we seek that defining moment when the Cold War ended, we might look to New York harbor on 7 December 1988. Mikhail Gorbachev had just delivered his speech to the UN General Assembly. In it, the Soviet ruler announced massive cuts in *conventional armed forces in Europe*. He would cut his troop strength by 500,000 men, his tanks

---

* Reagan's friend Charles Z. Wich congratulated him on the plane ride home. "You just won the Cold War," Wich said (O'Sullivan, John, *The President, the Pope, and the Prime Minister: Three Who Changed the World*, Washington, D.C.: Regnery Publishing, 2006, p. 284).

divisions by a quarter, and his combat aircraft by 500. Now, Mrs. Thatcher could affirm the course of human events.[56]

President Reagan and Vice President George H. W. Bush, who had just been elected to become the nation's 41st president, awaited their Soviet guest on Governors Island, just south of Manhattan Island. Reagan strongly approved of Gorbachev's speech to the UN that morning. Reagan had always said there was not distrust in the world because there are arms; there are arms because there is distrust. Now, Reagan and his designated successor welcomed the Soviet initiative. To be sure, the *need* to cut his conventional forces was forced on Gorbachev in no small measure by the internal failings of Communism and by the economic pressure that Reagan had been applying since the day he came to office. Ronald Reagan had planted his flag and now Gorbachev was coming to him.

The worldwide Communist system had made a charnel house of the twentieth century. Fully 100 million people had been killed by Communism.[57] The red flag never brought any of its chained peoples closer to peace, justice, or equality. Gorbachev seemed to understand this—at least at some level. While claiming all along to be a loyal Communist, Gorbachev reveled in the greater freedom he saw in the West. The Soviet rulers had come in their grim succession—Lenin, Stalin, Khrushchev, Brezhnev, Andropov, Chernenko. But Gorbachev was different. He was the first Soviet ruler with whom we could speak about peace with freedom, peace with safety, peace with justice. He was the Soviet ruler who had not waded through blood in his path to power.

As Mikhail Sergeivich Gorbachev left the United Nations headquarters at Turtle Bay, he proceeded south along FDR Drive to South Ferry. His limo swept him past Wall Street, the dynamo of America's powerful free market economy. There, George Washington had taken the oath of office as the first elected president nearly two centuries before Gorbachev's arrival. There George Washington had kissed the Bible.

The Communist Party's general secretary would embark for Governors Island at the ferry terminal, in the shadow of the World Trade

Center. As it plowed its way ponderously across the narrow divide that separates Governors Island from Manhattan, the ferry would take just five or six minutes to carry the distinguished Soviet visitor to his meeting with two American presidents. During the short trip, Gorbachev would have a commanding view of New York harbor. He would have time to think about that Lady in the Harbor—Lady Liberty. He would see Ellis Island, where millions had come, yearning to breathe free. Here they found America, the last best hope of earth.

That white, squat, lumbering Coast Guard ferry was the furthest thing we might imagine from the power and pomp of that 1945 surrender ceremony aboard the USS *Missouri*. There would be no surrender in the Cold War. But there would be something better. On that chilly day in New York harbor, peace glided into that ferry slip, quietly, almost unannounced, almost unperceived. Not bad, as Reagan would say—not bad at all.

EPILOGUE

(After 1989)

It's possible that the right words cannot yet be found to describe the nation's history since Ronald Reagan's presidency ended in 1989. Historical objectivity requires more time to pass for us to digest those decades. This history is not yet complete and clear, and objects in the rearview mirror are much closer than they appear. Many of the actors who have been on the national stage for the last thirty years are still alive. I wish to be fair to the times and root out any prejudice occasioned by my association with them.

Nevertheless, a lot has happened since the Reagan era. History keeps moving with great speed and momentous events. And sometimes it moves with barely noticed incidents that, in the end, turn out to be milestones.

In many ways, 1989 was a long time ago. If you asked someone to "e-mail me," or said "check out my website (or blog)," or began a phrase with "www," or asked if an article was "available online," or tried to tell someone what was on your "Twitter feed," you would get a blank stare. "Amazon" was simply a river in South America.

Thirty years ago, a young man named Barack Obama—a second-year law student—had just been elected the first black president of the *Harvard*

Law Review. At the same time, a charismatic developer well known in New York named Donald Trump had just published his first bestseller and appeared for the first time on the cover of *Time* magazine.

I write this epilogue as someone who has tried to observe the last thirty years of our nation's history with care. I had a close-up view of some events, and even took part in a few. The following pages involve some on-the-scene reporting and reflection. I have tried to cover some episodes that, while not yet digested by history, will assuredly prove markers for the years to come.

I. THE CHOPPY SEAS OF THE 1988 ELECTION

Vice President George H. W. Bush had a distinguished career in public life. The son of a well-respected U.S. senator, he had enlisted in 1943, becoming the youngest pilot in the navy at that time. He flew more than fifty combat missions in World War II, including one in which he had to bail out of his plane after it was struck by enemy antiaircraft fire during a raid against the Japanese in the Bonin Islands.[1] Later, after a career in the oil business in Texas, he become a member of the House of Representatives from Texas, a U.S. ambassador to the United Nations, the chairman of the Republican National Committee, an envoy to the People's Republic of China, and the director of the Central Intelligence Agency.

Vice President Bush had faithfully supported Ronald Reagan through both terms of his dramatic and course-altering presidency. Bush remained the consummate gentleman and clean-government professional—no Spiro Agnew or Richard Nixon. When he declared his intention to run for the Republican nomination for president, however, he found he had plenty of opponents.

There was the Kansan, Senate Republican Leader Bob Dole. And there was Congressman Jack Kemp, Republican from New York, who represented the charismatic, young Supply-Siders (those who believed in economic growth through marginal tax rate cuts). Kemp was also a social conservative and foreign policy hawk. His base was tied to a philosophy of economic growth through tax cuts, social renewal, and tough rhetoric for the Soviet Union and its satellites. He was also the principal author and spokesman on Capitol Hill for the tax cuts that helped define the Reagan presidency.

Dole and Kemp weren't the only opponents. The carefully laid plans of many Republican hopefuls (including Delaware Governor Pete du Pont and former Secretary of State Alexander Haig) were thrown into disarray by the entrance of Rev. Pat Robertson, president of the Christian Broadcasting Network, into the race. Robertson's appeal to evangelicals was said to be equivalent in the GOP to Rev. Jesse Jackson's appeal to black Americans in the Democratic ranks.

Bush's nomination would typically have been a near coronation because he was the sitting vice president loyally serving a beloved president. Richard Nixon, for example, had had little trouble wrapping up the Republican nomination following eight years' service with the popular Eisenhower in 1960. As party machines began to fade over the years, however, it was becoming necessary to show real strength at the grassroots and to actually earn the votes of primary voters and activists. Thus, in a split field, Bush's nomination was far from assured.

In January 1988, with polls showing him in second place in the February Iowa caucuses, Vice President Bush went on the *CBS Evening News with Dan Rather* for a wide-ranging interview. Dan Rather was, even then, considered a biased anchor, eager to embarrass Republicans. When Rather tried to badger Bush with questions about his alleged involvement in Iran-Contra, Bush pushed back—strongly. After a series of unremitting questions, the dialogue on national television went this way:

Rather: I don't want to be argumentative, Mr. Vice President.
Bush: You do, Dan.
Rather: No . . . no, sir, I don't.

Bush: This is not a great night, because I want to talk about why I want to be president, why those 41 percent of the people are supporting me. And I don't think it's fair . . .

Rather: And Mr. Vice President, if these questions are . . .

Bush: . . . to judge my whole career by a rehash on Iran. How would you like it if I judged your career by those seven minutes when you walked off the set in New York?

Rather: Well, Mister . . .

Bush: Would you like that?

Rather: Mr. Vice President . . .

Bush: I have respect for you, but I don't have respect for what you're doing here tonight.[2]

For many years, George H. W. Bush had been seen as somewhat disconnected from the conservative grassroots of the Republican Party, too genteel to stand up for conservative principles, too close to the establishment, too Northeast preppy and not enough Midwest, Southwest, or just plain West as Barry Goldwater, Richard Nixon, and Ronald Reagan had been. Many observers thought that in this interview, by taking on CBS and Dan Rather, George H. W. Bush showed a new, fighting spirit. Throughout the primaries, he slugged hard and ultimately won the nomination.

For the Democrats, Senator Gary Hart of Colorado had been regarded as the leading candidate. But he made the mistake of inviting a young woman, not his wife, to spend the night in his Washington townhome—after challenging the press to tail him. Hart denied all impropriety and denounced the reporters who "hid in the bushes" to trap him. Then a tabloid newspaper published a picture of him with the woman on his lap. They were shown aboard a pleasure boat eponymously named *Monkey Business*. Hart was quickly forced out of the race in 1987, leaving no obvious candidate, and a national conversation ensued. People debated the proper role of the media in its intrusion into the private lives of public figures (as they saw it) and the people's right to know (as the media defined it). This unresolved theme would loom large for the next three decades and unfold at higher and higher levels with increasing dissonance and effect at every strain.

The Democrats' choices came down to, among others, Tennessee Senator Al Gore, Arizona Governor Bruce Babbitt, Illinois Senator Paul Simon, civil rights leader Rev. Jesse Jackson, and Massachusetts Governor Michael Dukakis. Delaware Senator Joe Biden had dropped out of the race the year before, after the press had reported allegations of his plagiarism of a British politician's speeches and his fibbing about his college and law school records.

For the Democrats, Massachusetts Governor Michael Dukakis outlasted his opponents and cruised to a fairly easy nomination. For vice president, he selected an established, more conservative Texan, Senator Lloyd Bentsen, just as George H. W. Bush had selected a running mate known for his conservative credentials, U.S. Senator Dan Quayle from Indiana.

While the presidential race of 1988 sounded out a lot of cultural themes, including fights over crime, drugs, and patriotism, in the end it proved to be not much of a contest. Bush carried forty states for a near landslide total of 426 electoral votes.

The year 1988 almost ended with the major news story being Bush's election. But, just before Christmas, on 21 December, Pan Am Flight 103 exploded over Lockerbie, Scotland, killing all 259 people on board and another 11 on the ground.[3] It was no extraordinary aviation accident or tragedy due to mechanical or pilot error. The plane was blown up. The cause: a bomb in the luggage compartment planted by Libyan terrorists. This was the deadliest terrorist attack on American civilians in our history up to that point—more than 180 Americans were on board, including dozens of college students coming home from their studies abroad. An inquiry was begun.

The nation, its eyes still stained with tears, looked forward to a new year coming. Ronald Reagan bade farewell to the nation in a televised address on 11 January 1989. He warned the country not to neglect the teaching of American history. He said if we forget what we have done, we will cease to be who we are. It was a warning about forgetting that achieved a special poignancy in view of his later diagnosis with Alzheimer's disease. He spoke of high American ideals, especially freedom:

> And the image that comes to mind like a refrain is a nautical one—a small story about a big ship, and a refugee, and a sailor. It was back in the early eighties, at the height of the boat people. And the sailor was hard at work on the carrier *Midway*, which was patrolling the South China Sea. The sailor, like most American servicemen, was young, smart, and fiercely observant. The crew spied on the horizon a leaky little boat. And crammed inside were refugees from Indochina hoping to get to America. The *Midway* sent a small launch to bring them to the ship and safety. As the refugees made their way through the choppy seas, one spied the sailor on deck, and stood up, and called out to him. He yelled, "Hello, American sailor. Hello, freedom man."

Like that American sailor, Americans and many others throughout the world saw Ronald Reagan as their freedom man.

II. AN UPSURGE OF FREEDOM ABROAD

Few presidents had come to office with greater preparation than George Herbert Walker Bush, and that preparation was key to the years ahead. What issues the forty-first president would have on his plate in January 1989 would not—as with almost every president—be the same for which history, even recent history, would remember his presidency.

While President Bush was busy trying to implement his domestic agenda, issues around the world were seemingly taking even greater precedence and attention. On the domestic front, few issues animated the country, and President Bush, as much as the scourge of and destruction from illegal drugs. With serious attention put on this issue by both Presidents Reagan and Bush, and with tremendous efforts and focus from the American people and several coalitions, this country succeeded in reducing drug use in America by nearly 60 percent between 1979 and 1992.[4]*

Abroad, the powerful movements for freedom that Ronald Reagan helped unleash throughout the world were felt even as far away as China. In April 1989, thousands of students demanding liberalization from the Communist Party's stringent rule began gathering in Beijing's vast, historic Tiananmen Square following the death of the popular former Chinese Communist Party general secretary, Hu Yaobang.[5]

Meanwhile, the aging leader of China, Deng Xiaoping, had been responsible for helping end the madness of Mao's Great Proletarian Cultural Revolution. He pledged to put China on the path to modernization and permitted much greater economic opportunity for the 1.2 billion Chinese.[6] And as is so often the case when reforms toward liberalization and more freedom are instituted in autocratic or tyrannical regimes, the improved living conditions in China created what many in similar situations have called "a revolution of rising expectations."

Deng would, however, move only so far. He had been responsible for ousting Hu from power a few years earlier after Hu allowed other student demonstrations to take place without cracking down on them. Those demonstrations—in 1985 and 1986—had already shown a youth interested in less repression and more freedom, as the students carried posters with slogans such as "Law, Not Authoritarianism" and "Long Live Democracy."[7]

---

* As of this writing, the issue has risen again and increased to just a little below the high-water mark of rates in 1979 ("Results from the 2017 National Survey on Drug Use and Health," https://www.samhsa.gov/data/sites/default/files/cbhsq-reports/NSDUHDetailed Tabs2017/NSDUHDetailedTabs2017.htm#tab1–1B).

In Tiananmen Square, the "Gate of Heavenly Peace" near the center of Beijing, thousands upon thousands of students gathered over the days and weeks; they read long lists of confusing, sometimes even contradictory, demands. But they also read Chinese translations of America's Declaration of Independence and Lincoln's Gettysburg Address, and they erected a papier-mâché statue that was a Chinese version of the Statue of Liberty.[8]

In short order, tanks ran over hundreds of these Chinese, killing them, and PLA soldiers fired their rifles into the crowd. Within hours, fleeing students were hunted down and killed. Quickly, the Communist regime's forces cleared away hundreds of bodies, burned them, and hosed down the square, the ceremonial heart of ancient China.[9] Two days later, Deng went on Chinese national television to report to the people and congratulate the soldiers, saying, "They are truly the people's army, China's Great Wall of Steel." Of the dead, Deng said only this: "Their aim was to topple the Communist Party, socialism, and the entire People's Republic of China and set up a capitalist republic."[10]

Americans were outraged, as were people throughout the civilized world. President Bush had counseled calm and had urged the Chinese rulers to act with restraint. All through the crisis, Bush had tried to maintain a close relationship with the Chinese leaders while pressing for lenient treatment for the students.

On another front of the Cold War, Bush still faced a dangerously unstable Soviet Union. He was trying to nudge, cajole, and persuade Mikhail Gorbachev to make greater reforms, to show more regard for human rights.

The changes were not long in coming. The summer of 1989 saw Poland's first free elections. With the victory of Solidarity, a freedom revolution began to spread in Eastern Europe. Hungary and Czechoslovakia bubbled with excitement. The restive peoples of the Soviet Union's captive nations could no longer be contained.[11]

East Germany, that rump state held under stern Stalinist rule for forty-five years, soon felt the upsurge of freedom. Defying the menacing gaze of the secret police—the Stasi—East Germans flocked to their once-empty Lutheran churches to hear passionate appeals for democracy and human rights. Czechoslovakia's and Hungary's new, more relaxed regimes opened their borders with East Germany. The East German regime was supposedly their ally in the Warsaw Pact. Thousands of young East Germans bundled into their rickety Trabant automobiles and made their roundabout way to freedom in West Germany. The trickle soon became a flood.[12]

In short order, Chairman Gorbachev made it clear that he would not send in Soviet tanks to prop up the unpopular Communist regime in East Germany; this would not be Beijing all over again. Gorbachev knew that there were too many cameras. The whole world was, indeed, watching.

And then the Berlin Wall fell.

Two years prior, President Reagan had gone to Berlin and described it as "a gash of barbed wire, concrete, dog runs, and guard towers." Perhaps the most famous words of Reagan's presidency were those he uttered that summer day in 1987: "General Secretary Gorbachev, if you seek peace, if you seek prosperity for the Soviet Union and Eastern Europe, if you seek liberalization: Come here to this gate! Mr. Gorbachev, open this gate! Mr. Gorbachev, tear down this wall!" And now, within hours of the granting of travel by the East German government, the German citizens were, themselves, taking pickaxes to the scar.

Bush would be widely criticized for failing to catch the mood of exhilaration, for being out of touch with the spirit of the times. But to be fair, there were several things to explain Bush's seemingly calm attitude amid the elation over what was happening a continent away. First, he knew that we were not out of the woods yet. And there was a bear in those woods. Who knew what the Soviet reaction would be?

Others knew full well the United States' contribution to this great and new moment. West German Chancellor Helmut Kohl, for instance, after returning from Berlin, told Bush, "Without the U.S., this day would not have been possible. Tell your people that."[13]

As the new decade dawned, attention in Europe focused on two questions: What would become of East and West Germany, and what would happen to the Inner Empire of the Soviet Union? In 1990, the first of those questions would be answered. Bush quietly decided that the United States would stand for German reunification, provided that it occurred peacefully and by consent of the German people themselves. In making this decision, he was guided by the United States of America's bound word. We had promised the Germans this for forty-five years. Bush would keep that promise.

Others doubted the wisdom of such a stand. Prime Minister Margaret Thatcher, for example, was not so sure. Britain had spent much of the twentieth century preventing the rise of a Germany powerful enough to dominate all of Europe. France's Francois Mitterrand, similarly, hesitated.[14] Helmut Kohl felt isolated. Is this not why the Germans had joined NATO? Wasn't German reunification at the heart of the Western Alliance?

German reunification came in 1990 because Bush firmly believed that America's word, once given, must be honored. He had refused to "dance on the Berlin Wall" so that he might usher in a new era in international life. Germany had been the flashpoint of the Cold War for almost half a century. The conflicts between the USSR and the Western Allies began almost as soon as Hitler shot himself in 1945. German issues dominated the headlines: the Soviet blockade of West Berlin of 1948, Soviet tanks crushing a revolt in East Berlin in 1953, the extended crisis of 1959–61 as Khrushchev threatened to drive the Western Allies out of West Berlin, and finally the monstrous Berlin Wall itself. If at any point during those years a serious analyst had said that East and West Germany would be reunited without bloodshed, that a unified Germany would remain within NATO, and that the Soviet Union would agree to all of this, people would have thought the analyst had gone mad. No thoughtful person believed it could happen. Without Bush's patience and persistence—without his conception of "duty, honor, country"—the United States could not have played the peacemaker role that it did.

III. STORMS IN THE DESERT

The world's attention soon shifted from celebration in Europe to crisis in the Middle East. On 2 August 1990, Iraq's dictator, Saddam Hussein, invaded neighboring Kuwait. Not only was Saddam's invasion a naked act of aggression but it also threatened a major realignment of the balance of power in the Middle East, especially as Hussein had threatened to turn Kuwait "into a graveyard" if any other country tried to stand in his way. If Saddam's aggression went unanswered, though, he would likely have seized Saudi Arabia as well—and Iraq, Saudi Arabia, and Kuwait were basically known for one export: oil.

But it was not just "all about oil." Saddam Hussein used his oil revenues to finance his republic of terror. He maintained power by the sword—torturing his citizens, even gassing people to death as he had done to thousands of Iraqi Kurds two years before. Had his invasion of Kuwait been allowed to stand, had he followed up by overrunning Saudi Arabia, Saddam would have become the new Saladin; he would have claimed leadership of the Arab world. And he would have had the resources to make his claim stick.

Bush wasn't having it. "This aggression will not stand," he said. He overcame advice from the commentariat not to get involved and began building Operation Desert Shield to defend the Saudi kingdom from a Saddam attack.[*] He also immediately began building an international coalition to force Saddam out of Kuwait; the effort became known as Desert Storm. When Prime Minister Thatcher visited Bush at Camp David, she was widely quoted as saying, "This is no time to go wobbly, George."

---

[*] It was at this time that a radicalized Saudi millionaire named Osama bin Laden, who had helped organize and fund Arab freedom fighters battling the Soviets in Afghanistan, offered to help the Saudi government defend itself and its oil fields from an Iraqi incursion. The Saudi government decided to put its trust in the American government instead. Angered by the U.S. presence on what was considered holy land, bin Laden felt betrayed and moved to the Sudan.

Thatcher could be forgiven for worrying about U.S. resolve, especially considering the U.S. Congress. Even then, former president Jimmy Carter was lobbying furiously to stop a U.S.-led military effort against Saddam's invasion.[15] It is worth recalling that Carter was president when Iran took American hostages, and he allowed those hostages to remain in captivity for 444 days.

Fortunately for Bush, the Soviets were preoccupied at home. The Inner Empire was unraveling. The Baltic states of Lithuania, Estonia, and Latvia strained for their independence. And there were rumblings in the Ukraine as well. This meant that the Soviets' support for their Mideast client, Saddam Hussein, would not be forthcoming. Bush asked Congress for a resolution authorizing the use of force. It passed by a wide margin in the House, but only narrowly in the Senate.

Bush had developed a trusting relationship with Margaret Thatcher, King Fahd, Hosni Mubarak, and Mikhail Gorbachev over many years. He observed to one friend that now it all came together—his experience at the UN, the CIA, and his stint as envoy to China. He overcame Carter's efforts and went on to gain the UN's approval for the use of force to liberate Kuwait.

Contrary to much popular wisdom at the time, Saddam Hussein was not exclusively a secular Arab leader, or at least he was willing to use his religion as it suited his political purposes. In attempts to unite other Islamic states around him, he played up his theocratic tendencies. For example, Hussein ensured pictures of him praying to Allah were disseminated across the world. He had personally funded the building of Sunni mosques in Iraq and in other countries, and he changed the Iraqi national flag to add the words *Allahu Akbar* (God is great) in his own handwriting.[16]

Hussein's desired allies did not come, and the war did not last long. Following his strategic aerial bombardment plan, General H. Norman Schwarzkopf led a combined ground force of almost thirty nations. Americans, of course, made up the bulk of the half million that overwhelmed the dispirited Iraqis in Kuwait and southern Iraq. Schwarzkopf's brilliant success cut off the Iraqis in Kuwait. Thousands fled from Kuwait along the main road to Baghdad. It soon became "the Highway of Death" as U.S. warplanes decimated Saddam's vaunted Republican Guards.

This is not to say Hussein did not wreak certain havoc. He did try to make good on one promise: attempting to turn Kuwait and one other nation "into a graveyard." He launched Scud missiles at Israel's capital city, Tel Aviv, as well as into Haifa, in an effort to do as much damage to Israel as possible and unite other Arab nations around him.[17] (Israel was a nonparty to Desert Storm, at President Bush's pleading.) And he lit Kuwait's oil fields on fire, "creating a large scale environmental disaster" so immense it could be seen from outer space. CNN described it this way: "Day vanished into night, black rain fell from the sky, and a vast network of lakes was born . . . lakes of oil as deep as six feet. Saddam also poured 10 million barrels of oil into the sea. Thousands of birds perished, and the people of the Persian Gulf became familiar with new diseases."[18]

With the military liberation of Kuwait achieved, Bush stopped the war one hundred hours into the major ground combat. General Schwarzkopf met Saddam's generals to negotiate a ceasefire. Incredibly, Saddam had survived the complete rout of his army and country in what he had called "the mother of all battles," as Americans quickly withdrew their forces but maintained northern and southern "no fly" zones in Iraq in an attempt to contain Saddam from further aggression. America erred, however, in urging Iraqi citizens to rise up and overthrow Saddam Hussein—we did not back them up, and he unleashed a new, postwar slaughter on the thousands who tried.[19]

Bush and his advisors were criticized by many on the right (including me) for not liberating Iraq from Saddam, but we would later see the wisdom in the administration's decision—several years later with the Iraq war of 2003. America's impressive victory in the Gulf War was achieved by February 1991, and many argued our Vietnam Syndrome was over. For years, many Americans had been hesitant or gun-shy to deploy massive military force because the memory of Vietnam still rang too clearly in their heads. Desert Storm put an end to that for the time being, and a brief moment of patriotic fervor and success permeated the country.

As a personal aside, I would like to note that George H. W. Bush was the kindest boss I ever had. A man of great decency, concerned for others' personal well-being and their families, he said yes to any meeting I requested and returned every phone call I ever placed to him. His hand-written and typed notes were models of decorum and goodwill, always with an inquiry or wish for a family member or family event he knew about. He was also tremendously athletic—an avid jogger and tennis player, a fine line-drive-hitter, to say nothing of his skydiving in his retirement.

In spending time with President Bush, one could not help picking up one overarching sense and theme of the man: a deep, abiding love of country—a quiet patriotism that stirred constantly within. Nowhere did I see this more pronounced than on a 1990 trip with him to Portland, Oregon. We were looking out a hotel window at the predawn. I had agreed to go jogging with him, and then he saw protestors burning garbage, protesting any number of things. One thing they were burning was the American flag. Bush turned to me and said, "I understand these young people and their protests—but what really gets to me is when they burn the American flag. Nothing gets me like that. Can anything be more dis-respectful? Do they have any idea of what people have done to keep that flag held high?" I remember thinking, *If only the rest of the world could hear this man and the weight he puts in his deeply reflective moments like that—if only they could witness his sense of America. He would be loved with the greatest.*

But that was not the public Bush; he was always more comfortable keeping his deepest feelings private. To my mind, however, he was a very empathetic man who cared about more people and things than the public record would ever show.

IV. "IT'S THE ECONOMY, STUPID!": THE ELECTION OF 1992

By the end of 1991, the bloom was off the rose for President Bush. His stratospheric approval ratings were at a record high of more than 90 percent after the miraculous victory of Operation Desert Storm and his mobilization of so many other countries to join the American effort—a high place to be, and a high place from which to fall.

The lightning-quick victory in the Middle East became a distant memory for many as the economy went south and took the president's approval ratings along with it. By November 1991 (one year ahead of the presidential election), his approval hovered just above 50 percent.[20] The low numbers were an invitation for opposition. The president soon faced an insurgency within his own party and a bevy of Democrats eager to take him on.

Then there was H. Ross Perot. The Texas billionaire and entrepreneur was angered by the partisan bickering over the budget in Washington. In 1992 he began to send out hints during several appearances on the Larry King television show on CNN that he would consider running for president as an independent. Perot was something of a hero, if not an iconoclast, in the national mind. A Texarkana-born graduate of Annapolis, he had long supported the navy and other veteran causes and had earned a good deal of publicity for personally funding efforts to help deliver food and gifts to our soldiers in Vietnam. In 1983 he had become the subject of a famous novel (*On Wings of Eagles* by Ken Follett) for his successful, privately funded and planned rescue of two of his employees who were held in Iran against their will in 1979.[21]

To many, Perot was the living embodiment of the American dream and American patriotism. His was a rags-to-riches story, but he was also known for his old-school ways. He was not a glamorous cocktail-circuit billionaire; he dressed and lived fairly modestly, and he required his employees to remain clean-cut (they could not have beards or mustaches, and they had to follow a strict dress code). While most would have assumed that he was a Republican, he was not a fan of President Bush and had even opposed the Gulf War.[22]

Perot, like conservative columnist Pat Buchanan, who was also challenging President Bush, was tapping into an increasingly sour national mood. It might have been exhaustion. In addition to the Gulf War, the nation had won an incredible victory in ending the Cold War. That existential clash had threatened Americans with annihilation for four decades. Relieved of that burden, people focused on the economy. Heavy industry in the Rust Belt states—Pennsylvania, Ohio, Michigan, and Illinois—had been hit hard by the shift to an information- and service-based economy. American heavy manufacturers suffered from the effects of global competition. The recession had ended by April 1991, but as with any recession, it takes time to recover, including from job losses. The unemployment rate had gone from just over 5 percent when President Bush was inaugurated in 1989 to over 7 percent by the end of 1991.[23]

Meanwhile, the Democrats had not occupied the White House since 1979 and were determined to regain it after more than a decade of Republican control. But there was one major problem: no nationally recognized Democratic leader was able to take the spotlight and run for president. Many had thought the charismatic and articulate Democratic governor of New York, Mario Cuomo, would run, but he inexplicably decided not to do so.

Nonetheless, on the Democratic side, candidates lined up. Former Massachusetts Senator Paul Tsongas had a compelling personal story of triumph over adversity. He had left the Senate to spend more time with his family in 1984 when he was diagnosed with cancer. Through grit and determination, aided by the best medical care system on earth, Tsongas had pulled through. By 1992, he was in remission. Senator Bob Kerrey of Nebraska was the first Medal of Honor winner ever to run for president; he was a straight talker and war hero, having lost part of one leg in Vietnam. Former California governor Jerry Brown (better known in the 1970s) threw his hat in the ring. And then there was the governor of Arkansas, William Jefferson Clinton.

Bill Clinton was a political *wunderkind*. He had been elected five times in solidly Democratic Arkansas but was still only forty-five years old. A Rhodes Scholar with a law degree from Yale, he was articulate and tall and had the capacity to light up a room. His gift of gab was noticeable.

Unfortunately for Clinton, the "buzz" among Democrats was that he was unelectable because of what was politely called "the character issue." Rumors of his womanizing were legend far beyond Arkansas. He also had a tangled story to tell about his failure to report for the Vietnam-era draft. Noting Clinton's penchant to try to satisfy almost any audience, Paul Tsongas dubbed him "pander bear."

Clinton had proclaimed himself a "New Democrat." He had been a force in the Democratic Leadership Council—a group that struggled to make the party more competitive and centrist following disastrous defeats suffered by the party's dominant McGovern liberal wing. To this end, Clinton would stress his support for capital punishment—a sharp distinction from the politics of Michael Dukakis four years before. He pledged "to end welfare as we know it." He pitched his campaign to the forgotten middle class: "people who pay their taxes, obey the laws and play by the rules of the game." Abortion, he said, should be "safe, legal . . . and rare." And as a white southerner, Clinton was like Jimmy Carter in that he had established a strong, empathetic relationship with black Americans. This tie would prove critical and saving to him throughout his political life.

Bill Clinton was also a very effective public speaker and even better debater, and given his young age, he represented a generational shift in electoral politics. Clinton could ham it up like few other candidates in recent memory.

Clinton was elected with almost 45 million popular votes (43 percent) and a comfortable 370 electoral votes. President Bush received just over 39 million popular votes (37 percent) and 168 electoral votes. Perot won close to 20 million popular votes (19 percent).

V. 1993: A PROPHETIC YEAR

If Bill Clinton was known for a major effort in his first term, it was his attempt to reform the nation's healthcare system. First Lady Hillary Clinton spearheaded the initiative. Despite the uniqueness of such a high-profile position for an unelected and unconfirmed official, Mrs. Clinton was known as a serious policy professional. Highly educated and constantly probing public issues, she was qualified for the task as a matter of public policy, less so politically. The difficulty was that, since she was the president's wife, none of his advisors could credibly criticize her work. She had never run for an office or learned the great political arts her husband had honed. Ultimately, her plan would fail to launch, saving healthcare reform for another day and another administration.

The year 1993 would prove prophetic on even bigger fronts. On Friday, 26 February, a little past noon, an explosion rocked the World Trade Center in New York City. It was no ordinary explosion. The physical plant of the building hummed along just fine; nobody fumbled a candle or cigarette in one of the offices; no car overheated; no exhaust system backfired. No, this was a 1,400-pound urea nitrate bomb stashed inside a Ryder van and driven into the World Trade Center parking garage.[24] And when it detonated,

> the hyper-intensive shockwave bored a six-story canyon into the bowels of the complex. Seven people were killed (one of the six officially listed murder victims having been well along in her pregnancy), over a thousand were injured, and the structural damage—from a device that had cost only a few thousand dollars to build—would cost nearly a billion dollars to repair.[25]

Why had Middle Eastern–style terrorism come to us in 1993? Had we not been a net help to so many Muslims from Kuwait to Afghanistan? It has been said that, while America goes to war after all other options fail, and that the U.S. fights its wars more nobly than any other country, we do not always end our wars as decisively as we enter or wage them. Perhaps this is due to a hatred of war and a desire to end wars as quickly as possible—to get out, to move on to more peaceable actions and carry forward in the actions of a country that wants to live in peace. And while we were rightfully credited with helping save Afghanistan from its Soviet occupiers, just as we were rightfully credited with saving Kuwait and Saudi Arabia from their Iraqi neighbors, many—especially restive Islamic radicals—remained dedicated to their continued radicalism, unhappy with the failures in their own societies. Psychologists can study to the end of time why adherents to a radical theology become angered with others, especially those who have helped them. At the end of the day, though, the philosopher Hannah Arendt probably had it right: nothing can be so blinding to reality as the power of ideology. Or hardened, unreformed theocracy.

The Middle East had long been a hotbed of terror, ideology, and theocracy, sometimes fueled by Arab nationalism, sometimes by Islamism, and sometimes by the very toxic confluence of both. Israel, as a Jewish state, had known this terror for decades, before and since its founding. Other Western countries had as well. Not so much the United States, the most powerful Western nation in the world. The United States had neither adopted Islam as its religion (it did not neighbor a Muslim country) nor did it support radical Islamist states, such as Iran. Instead, the United States sponsored democracies such as Israel and helped support the more stable Middle Eastern states that wanted to be our allies (troublesome as many of them were).

Aside from the failed attempt to reform healthcare, President Clinton did successfully initiate a tax hike and pass temporary gun control legislation—after highly partisan fights. But if there seemed to be little bipartisanship in Washington, D.C., there was one success the White House achieved with the help of Republicans, or most Republicans anyway: the North American Free Trade Agreement (NAFTA), which broke down trade barriers among the United States, Canada, and Mexico.

NAFTA had become—as with any international trade debate—a contentious issue pitting various interests against each other. Free Trade Democrats had to fend off opposition from the labor unions, which were worried about job losses due to manufactured goods exported from countries without labor protections. Free Trade Republicans had to fend off opposition from the more isolationist wing of the party (recall that the Smoot-Hawley tariff of the Great Depression was sponsored by Republicans) and many in their grassroots who were distrustful of international agreements. Vice President Al Gore would debate the leading opponent of NAFTA, Ross Perot, in a highly watched debate on CNN. Perot, as during the campaign, deployed a lot of great slogans, but Gore proved the superior debater with a better command of the facts.

The Congress passed NAFTA with 132 Republicans and 102 Democrats voting for it in the House and 27 Democrats and 34 Republicans voting for it in the Senate.[26] It was a rare moment of bipartisanship in an otherwise highly rancorous year. But as is often the case with a new president's first year, it set the course for the next three years a template of the debate and first term of the Clinton presidency. That template would be— depending on your party—an admixture of the economy and/or taxes, the Middle East peace process and/or terrorism, and domestic extremism and/or personal responsibility and ethics.

As for the failed healthcare reform effort, labeled "Hillarycare," some would say the left had overreached by trying to push a bill that was too big and too expensive. Some would say Clinton's other pieces of domestic legislation distracted enough of Congress's attention working out a satisfactory bill that could pass muster with the natural give-and-take compromises that accompany any piece of major legislation. Some would say the legislation was too hard to explain in a simple manner.

In the first year of the Clinton presidency, few journalists sensed the political earthquake that was rumbling below the surface. For better or worse, more and more people were beginning to distrust the administration. This, despite the fact that not since FDR and Eleanor had the White

House seen the president and First Lady so thoroughly involved in the day-to-day workings of the government. But the First Lady and her husband had fared horribly on their signature issue.

VI. A REPUBLICAN "REVOLUTION" AND A SECOND TERM FOR BILL CLINTON

As the 1994 Congressional elections approached, Republicans on Capitol Hill got busy crafting a strategy. Georgia Republican Congressman Newt Gingrich came up with a plan for November with Ross Perot's former pollster, Frank Luntz. They called it the Contract with America. Gingrich thought of this Contract as an unprecedented and abbreviated party platform for a midterm election.

That election, called by many the Republican Revolution, was an elephant stampede. The GOP gained fifty-two seats in the House of Representatives, and the party won a majority of the House for the first time since 1954. The Senate, too, became Republican. Gingrich, the mastermind of so much of this, became the Speaker of the House of Representatives.

Stung by the voters' rejection, Bill Clinton had to scramble to face the new, assertive GOP opposition in Congress. He was nothing if not agile. Gingrich and his allies succeeded in passing many meaningful reforms, but they soon overreached. During 1995, the House Republicans demanded that Clinton commit to balancing the federal budget in seven years "using CBO numbers." This meant the nonpartisan Congressional Budget Office (CBO) had to "score" the final budget agreement. Americans outside the Washington Beltway thought the battle—as important as it was—was a tempest in a teapot. Few average citizens had any idea what "using CBO numbers" meant. And when Republicans allowed the federal government to be shut down for lack of funding, there was a predictable backlash against Speaker Gingrich.

EPILOGUE

The worst case of domestic terrorism in America occurred in April 1995. Although many initially thought it might be another attack by Islamic extremists, it turned out otherwise. Two homegrown American boys who were angry at the federal government for any number of reasons set off a bomb at the Alfred P. Murrah Federal Building in Oklahoma City. The blast destroyed the building, incinerated dozens of cars, and damaged scores of nearby structures. Worse, it took the lives of 168 Americans, including 19 children.[27]

The cowardly bombing shook the nation, but it was not the only violence in the air that year. Another domestic terrorist known as the Unabomber had sporadically mailed letter bombs to American citizens, such as university professors and corporate leaders, since 1978. He had severely injured dozens of people and by 1995 had killed three.* Five days after the Oklahoma City bombing, the Unabomber struck again, killing a forestry executive in California. The terrorist outlined his motives in a 35,000-word manifesto in which he decried the effects of industrialization. Federal authorities eventually tracked him down and arrested him in a primitive cabin near Lincoln, Montana.[28]

In 1995, another story spawned endless hours of cable news and radio chatter, speculation, and commentary: O. J. Simpson. In October, a jury found Simpson not guilty for the murder of his ex-wife, Nicole Brown Simpson, and her friend Ronald Goldman. To say this verdict rocked the nation would be a great understatement. The televised trial and outcome were dominating cultural and entertainment events. And they caused more than a little disgust and disquietude.

Cultural issues aside for the moment, Senator Bob Dole seemed the consensus Republican presidential candidate going into 1996—he had been around a long time, and people felt he deserved his shot. He faced Pat Buchanan and others, such as former Tennessee governor Lamar

---

* One of his targets was my good friend Professor David Gelernter of Yale University; his book on the Unabomber, *Drawing Life*, is one of the best pieces of nonfiction to be published in the 1990s.

Alexander and businessman Steve Forbes, in the New Hampshire primary in a race nobody could predict. Buchanan won a narrow victory there with Dole finishing second.[29] It was to be Buchanan's high-water mark, just as he had made New Hampshire his best showing in early 1992. But Buchanan didn't leave New Hampshire without a lot of enthusiasm. Even though his support was more deep than wide, he could still energize his very loyal base, and he had a way with words. He instructed his followers on the eve of New Hampshire's results with typical Buchanan rhetorical gusto: "They're going to come after this campaign with everything they've got. Do not wait for orders from headquarters, mount up everybody and ride to the sound of the guns."[30] Those guns didn't roar, and Dole won the Republican nomination.

On Election Day, Bill Clinton triumphed, buoyed by a good economy and masterful campaign skills. Just two years after the voters had punished Clinton and his party, they now returned him to office. He was the first Democrat since Franklin D. Roosevelt to be elected to a second four-year term.

The election was not the only thing going on in 1996. The nation's intelligence agencies had opened up a dossier on Osama bin Laden, a little-known terrorist financier and agitator hailing from Saudi Arabia, finding him to be of increasing danger to the United States. The year before, he had written an open letter to the king of Saudi Arabia (a U.S. ally), urging him to wage a campaign against the U.S. forces stationed there. In that rambling letter, bin Laden wrote: "It is not reasonable to keep one's silence about transforming the [Saudi] nation to an American protectorate to be defiled by the soldiers of the Cross with their soiled feet in order to protect your crumbling throne and the preservation of the oilfields in the kingdom."[31]

In June 1996, another terrorist attack struck at America and Americans abroad, when a truck bomb blew up the Khobar Towers in Saudi Arabia where U.S. troops were housed. It killed 19 American soldiers and wounded 372.[32] In August 1996, bin Laden openly declared war on America in a *fatwa* (a religious ruling) he issued: "Declaration of War

Against the Americans Who Occupy the Land of the Two Holy Mosques: "There is no more important duty than pushing the American enemy out of the holy land," he wrote.[33]

By this time, bin Laden was expelled from the Sudan and had moved his headquarters and his team of associates to Afghanistan.[34]

VII. IMPEACHMENT

The year 1997 was a slow news year for the United States—with two exceptions. That was the year two non-Americans with very close followings in the United States (and much of the rest of the world) died: the elegant and charitable Princess Diana of Great Britain and the saintly and even more charitable Mother Teresa of Calcutta. Diana was killed at the young age of thirty-seven in an automobile accident in Paris. She had been loved—as so many Americans had loved Great Britain's royal family—but she was respected even more for her charitable work for AIDS and her campaign against landmines. Mother Teresa died five days later at the age of eighty-seven. Few people in the world were as respected for their humility and work on behalf of the underprivileged and diseased as Mother Teresa and her Missionaries of Charity. She was also known as a strong proponent of the seamless web of life and could deliver a powerful message about life in the most touching way.

If 1997 was a slow news year, 1998 would surely make up for it.

On 21 January 1998, readers of the *Washington Post* saw a page-one story alleging that President Clinton had asked an aide to lie.[35] Two days prior, the *Drudge Report* had alleged that *Newsweek* was holding a story about an affair the president had with a White House intern named Monica Lewinsky. The *Post*'s 21 January headline read "Clinton Accused of Urging Aide to Lie." It was not just any lie, but a lie under oath. This allegation, if true, was the serious crime of suborning perjury. If it involved others, it was obstruction of justice.

Even to a country used to winking or making some peace with the allegations of their chief executive's past skirt chasing, the story that quickly came out was one of stunning recklessness and tawdriness. Lewinsky was only six years older than the president's eighteen-year-old daughter at the time. The *Wall Street Journal* on 22 January quoted former Clinton communications director George Stephanopoulos that sex with a twenty-four-year-old intern in the White House Oval Office could lead to Clinton's impeachment.[36] High-level Clinton administration officials were shocked at the allegation's recklessness. They wondered whether he should resign.

Clinton immediately responded to the crisis by denying everything. Wagging his finger at the cameras, he angrily said, "I did *not* have sexual relations with that woman, Miss Lewinsky." Soon the country would learn that Monica Lewinsky had made dozens of visits to the White House, including after her internship was over, had received gifts from Bill Clinton, had gotten help finding a job from top White House legal advisor Vernon Jordan, and had received a post-internship job offer from UN Ambassador Bill Richardson.

People were of a mixed opinion about all of this. While many were upset that the president could be so reckless and suborn perjury, he was defended by a Democratic party that kept bragging on how well the country was doing economically. An effort to impeach President Clinton did not bode well for Republicans in November of 1998.

The 1998 midterm elections produced not an increase of forty Republican seats, as Speaker Gingrich had confidently predicted, but a *loss* of five. And that wasn't all. In short order, a Republican House revolt forced Gingrich to resign not only from the speakership but also from Congress.

As 1999 dawned, Americans gave Clinton high approval ratings and strongly opposed his conviction and removal from office. Republicans in the House labored hard to show that impeachment was not about sexual misconduct, but instead about lying under oath and obstructing justice. The argument was being won neither with the American public at large nor in the Senate. The economy was strong, the budget was balanced, and people seemed to have had enough of scandal.

Both sides exhausted themselves in the struggle over impeachment. The nation faced another two years with a president who had been politically neutered. Although he continued to be personally popular, he was wounded and considered a "lame duck," perhaps a year earlier than most presidents finishing their second term.

On the culture front, the nation was shocked in April 1999 when two students at Columbine High School in Colorado went on a shooting rampage, killing twelve fellow students, a teacher, and themselves. Thankfully, a bomb they planted in the school cafeteria never detonated, or the death count would have been in the hundreds.[37] Trying to determine the motivation of the two killers became an endless round of speculation and allegation based on their clothing (trench coats and combat boots), their activities in their spare time (playing violent video games), and their behavior at school in the weeks leading up to the massacre (fellow students reported seeing the two assassins giving Nazi salutes to each other and noted a fascination with Nazi principles by at least one of the killers).[38]

The debate about guns, teens, school safety, ideology, and video game imagery surfaced again. Beyond a greater awareness by teachers, administrators, and parents about teen violent expression, imagery, and writing, little could be resolved or concluded about how to prevent the triggers in the minds of seriously disturbed youths who could or would kill like this. As one psychologist looking into the Columbine massacre put it, "These are not ordinary kids who played too many video games. These are not ordinary kids who just wanted to be famous. These are simply *not ordinary kids*. These are kids with serious psychological problems."[39] Tragically, Columbine was not the last school shooting in America.

VIII. THE WORLD PIVOTS
ON A GRAIN OF SAND

If the mid- to late 1990s were dominated by presidential scandal and national lectures about constitutional law out of Washington, something else was going on in the rest of the country—a technological and business revolution that would change not only this country but also the rest of the world. Thank the grain of sand (from which silicon comes) as the flint stone that sparked this bloodless revolution. When asked what he would put in a time capsule that best represents America in the twenty-first century, business magazine mogul and former presidential candidate Steve Forbes answered: "In addition to the Declaration and the Constitution, I'd have a grain of sand, because that's the basis of silicon—the whole information age. It shows what a free people can achieve and only a free people can achieve writing whole worlds on grains of sand. A true symbol of American inventiveness."[40]

Today, we take for granted communication and research devices such as smartphones, Internet connections, e-mail, personal computers, laptops, and Wi-Fi. Roughly 90 percent of Americans now have computers in their homes and use the Internet. Percentages are even higher for cell phone ownership.[41] But this was not always so; not long ago there was a much different world of communication, research, and business.

Cell phones are now the size of a deck of cards or smaller, but thirty years ago they were the size of a brick, for those who had cell phones unattached to a case or automobile. Home computers thirty years ago were the size of a medium suitcase and attached to a hard drive that was equally large. They were used primarily for word processing, games, and number crunching. Going "online" or "e-mailing a document" was scarcely available, and most Americans (never mind anyone anywhere else) would not know what was meant by those terms back then. Just twenty years ago, e-mail was hardly something that could be done away from the home or office.

While once we thought of mobile phones on the shoe of Maxwell Smart or the watch of Dick Tracy as fantasies, while once we used modified typewriters with a ruler-sized screen that held 5k of memory to process word documents, this all changed as the decade of the 1990s began.

All kinds of revolutionary inventions and innovators were becoming known. For instance, Michael Dell, who built customized computers, had the idea to sell directly to customers rather than through third parties, which kept prices down and allowed clients to more finely tailor their orders to their individual specifications.[42] All along the way, two college dropouts, Steve Jobs and Steve Wozniak, were perfecting their concept of easy-to-use home computers bearing the name Apple. By the late 1980s and early 1990s, Apple computers were preferred by graphic design artists and college students, and in short order Apple created ever more modern-looking computers known as iMacs that would expand into yet more and more home and small business use.

Then there were the Internet gurus who saw e-commerce possibilities, taking the World Wide Web from a research tool to a global shopping market. The Internet started as a Department of Defense project that then became a tool linking university research communication systems. As it gradually opened to public use in the early 1990s, innovators like Bill Gates of Microsoft soon dominated the race by bundling their browser into personal computer operating systems that individuals purchased from other computer companies.

There was America Online, founded by Steve Case. AOL brought the Internet and e-mail to a general audience with rudimentary understandings of the new World Wide Web and e-mail systems. Amazon, founded by Jeff Bezos in 1994, started an online book-selling venture that expanded into selling everything from vacuum cleaners to computers. Amazon ultimately created its own electronic book, the Kindle, ironically challenging the need or desire for the very product it began selling in the mid-1990s.[43] Bezos's and Amazon's accomplishments were enough to land him as the *Time* magazine Person of the Year in 1999. By the end of the twentieth century, consumers were buying some $15 billion of consumer goods over the Internet.[44] Today online consumer spending is in the hundreds of billions.[45]

There was also eBay, under the leadership of Meg Whitman, which further democratized the American and international marketplace with an online auction house where anyone could sell anything and buyers could bid for the price. The company ultimately boasted millions of users and created its own industry of people who made their living selling through the site.[46]

And there were the search engines, from Yahoo to Google, that made searching for information possible to those not subscribed to fee-based services such as Nexis and Westlaw. There were news sites like Drudgereport.com, begun by Matt Drudge in 1995, breaking stories that mainstream newspapers missed or were late in scooping. So pervasive would the Internet, i-commerce, and personal computing become that today we can laugh at this 1995 report from the Pew organization: "Few see online activities as essential to them, and no single online feature, with the exception of E-Mail, is used with any regularity. Consumers have yet to begin purchasing goods and services online, and there is little indication that online news features are changing traditional news consumption patterns."[47]

As e-mail and telecommuting became more popular, business could be conducted without a telephone or in-person conference. Knowing the value of a stock in Japan was a five-second search away for the American investor via the Internet. A draft essay could be sent to a publication or editor instantaneously, with edits going back to the author just as fast. No longer would one have to go to a government office to file certain forms; one could do that online. Want to know what was written by a favorite author in a newspaper across the country? Look it up online as you read the whole newspaper or any part of it. Want to know how many members of a given party sit in the Australian Parliament? Three clicks away at most. Want to know the biography of a certain prospective hire or employer? As recently as Bill Clinton's reelection, this was all brand new.

The late 1990s saw explosive technological and related economic growth from all this, creating what would later become known as the *dot-com boom*. Many new companies were started, and many new millionaires were made. The computer, the microchip, the Internet, e-mail, and e-commerce literally changed America and the world—and fast.

How much wealth, how many jobs, and how much freedom (political and personal) were created by all this is difficult to quantify. Some comments of economic historian John Steele Gordon lead to certain conclusions, though:

> In 1954 the gross domestic product of the United States—the sum of all the goods and services produced in the country that year—was about $380 billion. In 2003 it was $10.9 trillion. . . .
>
> The reason is plain enough: the computer. It is the most profound technological development since the steam engine ignited the Industrial Revolution two centuries ago, perhaps since the agricultural revolution ignited civilization itself 10 millennia ago. None of the biggest changes in business in the last 50 years would have been possible—or would have evolved as they did—had it not been for the computer.[48]

While the future was happening at home, the medieval was still stalking us abroad. On 12 October 2000, the USS *Cole* was docked in the Aden port of Yemen on a refueling stop. The *Cole*, a naval destroyer, was in the Middle East to help enforce UN sanctions against Saddam Hussein's Iraq. On the morning of 12 October, while the *Cole* was refueling, two men in a small inflatable boat loaded with high explosives approached the destroyer and detonated a blast, blowing a hole the size of a house into the *Cole*'s side.[49] The blast was so strong, it shook the buildings near the port. Seventeen U.S. sailors were killed—as were the suicide bombers. For days, to anyone paying attention, one could see the images of the *Cole* listing with the scarred blast hole in its side. As the national press had broadcast in the aftermath of the bombing, Osama bin Laden and his network were immediate prime suspects. Bin Laden and his number two, Ayman al-Zawahiri, had spent a good deal of time in Yemen, preaching and recruiting, and both Yemeni and American investigators were focusing on a bin Laden associate (Tawfiq bin-Attash) as one of the *Cole* operation's masterminds.[50]

But that was not the extent of the *Cole* bombing, at least not for Osama bin Laden. In short order, bin Laden's terrorist camps would soon fill with new recruits and money, and bin Laden had ordered the head of his media operation—one Khalid Sheikh Mohammed—to create a video reenactment of the *Cole* bombing to use for propaganda and further recruiting.[51] At the same time, bin Laden began dispersing his leadership in Afghanistan, wagering his camps would be targeted by an American military retaliation.[52] Bin Laden's camps were never bombed, however.

IX. A DISPUTED ELECTION

Meanwhile, 2000 was an election year. Vice President Al Gore had supported his beleaguered chief loyally through the yearlong struggle of impeachment. Among Republicans, the race included two heavyweights—Texas Governor George W. Bush and Arizona Senator John McCain. The others, magazine publisher Steve Forbes, conservative grassroots activist Gary Bauer, former Ambassador Alan Keyes, and columnist Pat Buchanan, were fairly quickly dispatched.

John McCain was a navy aviator who spent five years in North Vietnam's "Hanoi Hilton" as a prisoner of war. Though beaten and tortured, he did not make much of his service and would dismiss his suffering, like most war heroes, leaving it to others to speak of. But for all of his humility, McCain had attained almost mythic status for millions of veterans and admirers.

George W. Bush, son of the former president, Yale and Harvard graduate, had grown up in West Texas. Whenever he was asked what the difference was between him and the father he loved and respected, he answered: *Midland.*

Bush sensed the public's distaste for Clinton bashing. He would not replay the ugly partisan battles of the two previous years. Instead, he pledged to restore "dignity and honor" to the White House. Americans were smart, he figured. They would get it. Bush made no secret of the fact that he had lived a youthful life of too much partying and drinking. But he had changed his ways after a religious conversion and with the help of personal counseling from Billy Graham. Bush was a repentant man who had, as they say, been there and done that—and was long ago finished with all that.

Throughout the campaign, Al Gore kept his distance from Bill Clinton. To suggest a distance without openly breaking with Clinton's philandering, Gore selected Connecticut's Senator Joe Lieberman as his running mate. Lieberman, a practicing Orthodox Jew, had spoken the most critical words about Bill Clinton's conduct of any Democrat (even though he would not vote to convict him on impeachment charges) and was known for nothing so much as his upstanding personal character. Within the Democratic Party, he created excitement as the first Jewish candidate on a national ticket.

Bush was slightly ahead in most polls leading up to Election Day. Few could have predicted the monthlong nightmare to come.

When the closest election in U.S. history appeared to give Florida and the majority of the electoral college votes to George W. Bush, Al Gore telephoned his rival to concede. As he was on his way to Nashville's War Memorial Auditorium to make the announcement public, however, his campaign aides called and begged him to wait.[53] By then, the difference in Florida was down to two thousand votes *and dropping.* It was too soon to concede, they pleaded. Gore decided to cancel his announcement and call Governor Bush again.

It will forever be amazing that the 2000 election came down to 537 disputed votes in the one state out of fifty where the brother of the

Republican presidential nominee was the governor. Dramatists could not plot something so improbable. The fact that the two Bush brothers were in their precise positions at that precise moment will forever appear to some as a conspiracy. It matters little that alleged charges of systematic disenfranchisement of Democratic voters were found false. It matters little that to believe such charges, one must believe that these voters were systematically defrauded by Democratic election officials in overwhelmingly Democratic counties.

Al Gore lost his home state of Tennessee along with its eleven electoral votes. Had Gore won his home state, he would have won not only the popular vote but also the electoral college vote and become president. One has to go back to George McGovern's 1972 campaign to find a candidate who lost his home state.

Still, amazingly enough in the new century that had brought us satellite news and the Internet, for several weeks after the election of 2000, due to the alleged irregularities on the ballots and the legal fighting over them in Florida, there was still no definitive answer about who won Florida and, thus, who won the presidency.

During these weeks, known as the "Florida recount," teams of election officials—and lawyers from both campaigns who had swept into Florida—tried to assess voters' intentions in ballots that had been discarded for error because they were not fully punched or read as fully punched. (The term *hanging chad* would describe a dangling piece of paper from the ballot that did not completely separate after punching; other terms included *dimpled chads* and *pregnant chads* for ballots that seemed marked but did not separate from the ballot at all.) Then there was the claim of mistake from older voters about the *butterfly ballot* that had the names of the candidate on one side but a corresponding number to select that name on the other side. Numerous recounts and rules for recounts came from various election boards and Florida courts in what seemed to be an interminable legal and election process confusion.

The U.S. Supreme Court finally had to step in to resolve the situation.

On 12 December 2000, it put an end to the endless recounts of disputed ballots. In *Bush v. Gore*, the Court ruled 5–4 that using different recount methods in different counties was unconstitutional, and that there was not enough time to conduct a constitutionally acceptable recount before the electoral college met. Four weeks of hanging chads and pregnant chads had brought the country perilously close to a constitutional breakdown. Al Gore conceded the election the day following the Supreme Court's ruling.

After the election, *USA Today*, the *Miami Herald*, and the Knight-Ridder newspaper chain conducted a canvass of some 64,000 disputed ballots. Under *three of four scenarios*, Bush won. Under the rules demanded by the Gore-Lieberman ticket, Bush won.[54]

The year 2000 ended, as would soon the presidency of Bill Clinton. There was no substantial action against Osama bin Laden. Saddam Hussein was still running Iraq—and thwarting international inspections.

X. SEPTEMBER 11

When George W. Bush took the oath on 20 January 2001, he became the first man since John Quincy Adams to occupy the same high office his father had held. As was the case with the younger Adams, his father was in good health to savor the honor. After eight years of conflict, controversy, and scandal, Americans once again longed for domestic tranquility. The prospects seemed bright.

The economy had done rather well in the late 1990s, especially with the boom in the high-tech and Internet industries. Names like Yahoo and Intel had become commonplace. Java suddenly meant more than a cup of coffee or an exotic locale. And online "day traders" became the Wild West gunslingers of the "new economy." Federal Reserve Chairman Alan Greenspan, along with President Clinton's secretaries of the Treasury, had borne testimony to all kinds of new and creative financial instruments that would help in the home loan and housing markets.

Yet by the beginning of 2001, the boom was showing a bust, and famous Internet companies known as *dot-coms* were becoming known as *dot-bombs*. Jack Kemp wrote a syndicated op-ed in January of 2001, the opening line of which was, "Virtually everyone agrees that George W. Bush confronts a rapidly weakening economy as he assumes the presidency."[55] One headline in the *New York Times* in early 2001 read, "Economy Grew at Slowest Rate in 5 Years in 4th Quarter," and the article went on to cite experts debating whether the United States was heading toward a recession.[56]

The president wanted to take on two big issues on the domestic front: taxes and education. And the Left was still angry over the Supreme Court decision vindicating the Bush election in the first place.

Then came 9/11.

September 11, 2001 is one of those dates—like December 7, 1941—that changes the landscape, that tilts the earth. On the East Coast, it was a beautiful morning. I had walked a few blocks in downtown Washington to a recording studio to tape some statements on education; my staff was meeting (as it had every Tuesday morning at the offices of Empower America) for a regular Bible study, overlooking the White House and the Old Executive Office Building on Seventeenth and Pennsylvania Avenue.

For those who were tuned in to the *Today Show* that morning, here was how the news unfolded before the nation's eyes:

> **Matt Lauer:** We're back at 9:00 Eastern time on this Tuesday morning. And we're back with dramatic pictures of an accident that has happened just a short time ago. You're looking at the World Trade Center in lower Manhattan where just a few minutes ago, we're told, that a plane—some reports are that it was a small commuter plane—crashed into the upper floors of one of the Twin Towers. You can see fire and flames, or smoke, billowing from that tower. There is a gaping hole on the north side of the building. That's the side you're seeing to the left-hand

side of your screen right now. And other damage to the west side of that building, which is to the right side of your screen. This, of course, happened just before the morning commute, before people were heading into their offices, and while I'm sure some people were already at work. Immediately, there is speculation or cause for concern. This is the World Trade Center that was the center of a terrorist bombing some years ago. So the questions have to be asked, was this purely an accident or could this have been an intentional act. But either way, extensive damage has been done to this building.

Katie Couric: Obviously, horrified commuters were—were absolutely devastated when they heard this explosion. We talked with somebody a moment ago about that, Jennifer Oberstein, and also another eyewitness, Elliott Walker, who is actually a producer here on the Today Show. . . . Elliott, can you hear me?

Ms. Elliott Walker: Yes. Hi, Katie.

Couric: Hi, Elliott. Tell me where you are and what you saw.

Ms. Walker: Well, I live in this area. I returned to my apartment. But I was walking down the sidewalk delivering my young daughter to school. And we heard a very loud sound, the kind of sound you hear when a plane is, you know, going fast past you "Nnnnnn," followed by an enormous crash and an immediate explosion. I don't think we could feel shock waves, but we—we sort of felt like we did. And we were in a position where we could see the Trade Center almost immediately between the other buildings, and an enormous fireball that must have been 300 feet across was visible immediately, a secondary explosion, I think, and then plumes of smoke. I must be—there must have been a three-block cloud of—of white smoke. Now, from where I was on the street a moment ago, you can, in fact, see smoke leaving the building on three sides. It seems to be coming out on at least four or five floors. The area is filled with hundreds of dozens of pieces of paper that are just sort of floating like confetti. The area is swarmed with emergency vehicles and sirens. Obviously . . .

Couric: Elliott . . . you seen any—any evidence, Elliott, of—of people being taken out of the building? You say that emergency vehicles are there. Understandably so. But, of course, the major concern is human loss.

Ms. Walker: Oh, my goodness. Oh, another one just hit. Something else just hit, a very large plane just flew directly over my building . . .

Al Roker: Oh, my . . .

Ms. Walker: . . . and there's been another collision. Can you see it?

Couric: Yes.

Lauer: Yes.

Couric: Oh, my . . .

Lauer: You know what . . .

Ms. Walker: . . . and that looked more like a 747.

Lauer: . . . we just saw a plane circling the building. We just saw a plane circling the building, a second ago on the shot right before that.

Ms. Walker: I think there may have been another impact. Can you tell? I just heard another very loud bang and a very large plane that might have been a DC-9 or a 747 just flew past my window, and I think it may have hit the Trade Center again. . . . I wonder if there are air traffic control problems.[57]

Indeed, there were no air traffic control problems. Four civilian airliners had been hijacked and turned into enormous human-and-fuel-carrying missiles aimed at targets in New York City and Washington, D.C. One of those planes, headed for D.C., crashed over Shanksville, Pennsylvania. Nineteen young men—fifteen of them from Saudi Arabia—took over the jetliners using box cutters as weapons, and they used these airplanes as weapons of mass destruction. And mass destruction and slaughter were what America got.

The two jets that crashed minutes apart into the World Trade Center caused hundreds of deaths on impact, including all the people on board, who died instantly. The fires the planes started resulted in both skyscrapers collapsing in less than two hours. Their structural steel skeletons first buckled from the heat, and then the upper floors pancaked downward, killing thousands. The death toll of nearly three thousand (2,975 to be exact) from the attacks in New York, at the Pentagon, and at the hijacked plane crash in Shanksville, Pennsylvania, exceeded the total numbers of dead from the last major attack on America at Pearl Harbor (2,388 killed). But unlike the attack at Pearl Harbor, the 9/11 attacks were specifically directed against civilians.

The stories of death and tragedy, the stories of heroism and survival from this horrific day are far too numerous to recount. There were the stories of the police officers and firefighters who ran up the towers to save as many people as possible—as those people were running down the stairs for their lives—and were killed. There's the story of Father Mychal Judge, the chaplain for the New York City Fire Department, who was killed after giving last rites to another fireman. Before he went into the towers, New York City Mayor Rudolph Giuliani saw him and shouted, "Mychal, please pray for us," to which the priest shouted back, "I always do."[58] In his pocket was a prayer he had composed and would often hand out:

> Lord, take me where You want me to go;
> Let me meet who You want me to meet;
> Tell me what You want me to say,
> and keep me out of Your way.[59]

Defense Secretary Donald Rumsfeld was in his office in the Pentagon when he heard the crash. American Airlines Flight 77 had plowed into the building. "The 69-year-old former Navy pilot was jolted and rushed to the scene," the *New York Times* reported. "'He went outside the building and was helpful in getting several people that were injured onto stretchers,' said a Pentagon spokesman, Rear Adm. Craig Quigley. 'He was out there 15 minutes or so helping the injured.'"[60]

Back in New York City, there were the two hundred people who jumped from the Twin Towers to their deaths; they chose to jump rather than be burned to death. And as they jumped, with makeshift parachutes, "the force generated by their fall ripped the drapes, the tablecloths, the desperately gathered fabric, from their hands" as they lived out their final ten seconds of life in free fall.[61]

There was Rick Rescorla, the security chief of Morgan Stanley, who had spent the last part of his professional career practicing evacuation strategies and died while helping others escape from Ground Zero; his last recorded words were, "As soon as I make sure everyone else gets out." He said those words in response to Morgan Stanley Regional Manager John Olson, who was yelling at him: "Rick, you've got to get out, too!"[62] There was the former assistant director of the FBI, John O'Neil, who was on bin Laden's case in the 1990s and after the USS *Cole* attack; he had left the agency to become the head of security at the World Trade Center. There were so many.

So many untold stories of tragedy and heroism on and after 9/11, but perhaps none grabbed the attention as that which took place over Shanksville, Pennsylvania. On US Air Flight 93, businessman Todd Beamer picked up an airplane telephone and transmitted information to the GTE operator, who filled him in on the other flights. Beamer told the operator that he and a few others were planning to try and take the plane back from the terrorists. Beamer prayed the Lord's Prayer with the operator, and then "after the prayer was finished . . . Beamer dropped the phone, leaving the line open. It was then that the operator heard Beamer's words:

'Let's roll.' They were the last words she heard. The phone went silent, and the plane crashed, killing all 44 people aboard." Flight 93 went down in an open field in Pennsylvania (and the terrorists did not complete their mission of attacking the White House), thanks to the efforts of a handful of everyday, hardworking Americans. "Let's roll" became a popular bumper sticker and a watchword in post-9/11 America.[63]

XI. CONFRONTING TERRORISM

The next day, 12 September 2001, the *San Francisco Examiner*'s single-word headline in bold said what much of the nation was thinking: *"Bastards!"*[64]

On Friday, the president told the nation and the world what America was thinking. At the National Cathedral he led the country in a memorial service but said, "The conflict was begun on the timing and terms of others. It will end in a way and at an hour of our choosing." That was the American way in war: first Americans prayed, and then they prepared to fight. Later that day, standing on a pile of rubble in New York City, President Bush was thanking rescue workers via a handheld megaphone as the crowds were shouting, "USA! USA!" When some yelled they couldn't hear the president, the crowd quieted, and he shouted: "I can hear you. The rest of the world hears you. And the people who knocked these buildings down will hear all of us soon!" At that point, there was no doubt—the president was resolved, the nation was resolved, and the war that was declared and inflicted upon the United States would be joined.

By that time, it was becoming ever clearer that the attacks were the work of Osama bin Laden and his terrorist organization, Al Qaeda. Americans all over the country started delving into who Osama bin Laden was and just what kinds of things were going on in Afghanistan and in the rest of the Arab world—a world many had not focused on for many years. Bush threatened the Taliban government in Afghanistan with war if it did not turn over the leaders of Al Qaeda. They did not and would not, and the war came.

Bush soon knew he was the last thing that he expected to be when he ran for president—a wartime president. Shortly after sending troops into Afghanistan, he would speak of an "axis of evil" in the world—countries that both abused human rights at home and threatened civilized nations abroad. Those countries Bush identified were Iran, Iraq, and North Korea.

As for Saddam Hussein and Iraq, Saddam had used chemical weapons on his own people and started two wars in the Middle East: one against Kuwait, one against Iran. By most accounts, he had actually killed more Muslims than any other person in modern history. Saddam had also violated more than a dozen United Nations resolutions relating to weapons of mass destruction, and the UN Security Council had found Iraq "in flagrant violation" of prior demands that it destroy such weapons.

President Bush was not the first to point all this out. Clinton had signed the 1998 Iraq Liberation Act and had said, "Some day, some way, I guarantee you he'll use [his] arsenal." The chief of the German Intelligence Service had recently said, "It is our estimate that Iraq will have an atomic bomb in three years." And Richard Butler, who headed the UN team investigating Iraq's WMD program, had said, "Saddam Hussein is a homicidal dictator who is addicted to weapons of mass destruction."[65]

Inside his own country, Saddam's record of terror and repression was as abominable as it could possibly be. In the words of Kenneth Pollack, the former director of Gulf Affairs at the National Security Council under Clinton:

This is a regime that will gouge out the eyes of children to force confessions from their parents and grandparents. This is a regime that will crush all of the bones in the feet of a two-year-old girl to force her mother to divulge her father's whereabouts. This is a regime that will hold a nursing baby at arm's length from its mother and allow the child to starve to death to force the mother to confess. This is a regime that will burn a person's limbs off to force him to confess or comply. This is

a regime that will slowly lower its victims into huge vats of acid. . . . This
is a regime that applies electric shocks to the bodies of its victims. . . .
This is a regime that in 2000 decreed that the crime of criticizing the
regime would be punished by cutting out of the offender's tongue.[66]

The day after the anniversary of 11 September in 2002, Bush made his
case against Iraq to the United Nations General Assembly. The tenor of
his speech was that ousting Saddam from power, if he would not comply
with UN disarmament resolutions and inspection orders, was an effort
to vindicate the UN as much as it was an effort to protect the free world.
He opened by stating, "After generations of deceitful dictators and broken
treaties and squandered lives, we've dedicated ourselves to standards of
human dignity shared by all and to a system of security defended by all.
Today, these standards and this security are challenged."[67]

The authorization to use force in Iraq passed the House of
Representatives in mid-October, 296–133; voting yes were 81 Democrats
and 215 Republicans.[68] In the Democratic-controlled Senate, the vote was
77 to 23.[69] Among the prominent Democrats voting for the resolution
were House Minority Leader Dick Gephardt; Pennsylvania Congressman
Jack Murtha; Maryland Congressman Steny Hoyer; U.S. Senators Hillary
Clinton, Joe Biden, Dianne Feinstein, John Kerry, Harry Reid, John
Edwards, and Senate Majority Leader Tom Daschle.[70]

Among the Democrats who had voted for the resolution, there was
fairly unanimous agreement about the danger that Saddam Hussein
posed. On the eve of his vote, John Kerry had stated, "I will be voting to
give the President of the United States the authority to use force—if necessary—to disarm Saddam Hussein because I believe that a deadly arsenal
of weapons of mass destruction in his hands is a real and grave threat to
our security."[71] On the eve of her vote, Senator Clinton said,

In the four years since the inspectors left, intelligence reports show that
Saddam Hussein has worked to rebuild his chemical and biological

weapons stock, his missile delivery capability, and his nuclear program. He has also given aid, comfort, and sanctuary to terrorists, including al Qaeda members. . . . It is clear, however, that if left unchecked, Saddam Hussein will continue to increase his capacity to wage biological and chemical warfare, and will keep trying to develop nuclear weapons.[72]

Of course, not all of the Democrats believed in ousting Saddam; several thought he could still be contained, even though he was not coming clean on his weapons of mass destruction. In Chicago, a then little-known Illinois state senator named Barack Obama gave a speech at an antiwar rally. The crowd of about one thousand people was led by Rev. Jesse Jackson as the audience sang songs like "Give Peace a Chance" and held rally signs such as "War Is Not an Option."[73]

Just days before the president's State of the Union address in 2003, Chief UN Weapons Inspector Hans Blix testified to the UN that Iraq simply would not come clean: "Iraq appears not to have come to genuine acceptance—not even today—of the disarmament which was demanded of it and which it needs to carry out to win the confidence of the world and live in peace."[74] And Secretary Powell had said, "Time is running out. We've made it very clear from the very beginning that we would not allow the process of inspections to string out forever."[75]

XII. WAR IN IRAQ

As the lead-up to the confrontation with Iraq was taking place, the hunt for other Al Qaeda operatives was on. The U.S. was fighting a multi-front war already, and in the first week of March 2003, Americans were reminded of that with the biggest capture of an Al Qaeda terrorist yet: Khalid Sheikh Mohammed in Pakistan. Mohammed, the uncle of Ramzi Yousef (who was responsible for the 1993 World Trade Center bombing), was the mastermind of the 11 September attacks and the most senior Al

Qaeda leader after bin Laden and Ayman al-Zawahiri. Mohammed would prove a touchstone of several controversial anti-terrorism policies, from being detained initially in a foreign—or black—site in another country before being transferred to Guantanamo Bay, to being interrogated with the use of water-boarding. The US government had waterboarded three Al-Qaeda terrorists, and while there was a dispute as to whether Democrats signed off on such enhanced interrogation or not, by 2015 the use of this technique to elicit information from detainees was banned in US law. Whatever the debate and subsequent ban, this method yielded results and valuable information.[76]

The initial incursion into Iraq went much more smoothly than many had predicted, and by April 2003 Baghdad was in coalition hands. Many Iraqis, as well as many coalition partners watching from abroad, were further buoyed when television crews showed Iraqis tearing down posters of Saddam Hussein, throwing shoes at his images, and with the help of the U.S. Marines, toppling a huge statue of him in one of Baghdad's central squares.[77]

At the beginning of May, President Bush famously copiloted a navy jet onto the USS *Abraham Lincoln* off the coast of California to deliver a nationwide address to cheering crowds, declaring, "Major combat operations in Iraq have ended."[78] It was the first time a U.S. president had landed on an aircraft carrier by plane. Bush, who was a fighter pilot in the National Guard, could not have been happier about the perfect landing or the announcement he was making. In the backdrop of his statement to the troops (and the world) was hanging a huge banner that read, "Mission Accomplished."

But there was much more ahead.

Massachusetts Democratic Senator John Kerry, who was gearing up for a run for the presidency in 2004, started voicing his opposition to the president and trying to change the conversation about what constituted a military victory: "The president's going out to an aircraft carrier to give a speech far out at sea ... while countless numbers of Americans are frightened stiff about the economy at home."[79] Soon others were raising questions, such as where was Saddam? And where were his stockpiles of WMDs?

Bob Schieffer of CBS News spoke for many when he said, "It's now clear the job is bigger and more complicated than officials expected."[80] Even though two world-famous Palestinian terrorists were found in Iraq— Abu Nidal (one of the most famous terrorists of the 1970s and 1980s) and Mohammed Abbas (a longtime associate of Yasser Arafat who masterminded the *Achille Lauro* hijacking)—and American troops had killed Saddam's two sons (known for their barbarism among the Iraqi populace as well as their rape chambers), several problems were beginning to make people nervous.

If reminders of terrorism in Iraq were needed beyond the violence inflicted on the coalition's military, Americans were shocked to see a video released of a Pennsylvania communications expert and civilian, Nick Berg, who had traveled to Iraq on his own to do what he could to help the cause there and perhaps even start a business. The video showed Iraqi terrorists beheading the twenty-five-year-old Berg. Terrorists had also blown up the UN offices in Baghdad, killing the UN envoy and others there. And the military coalition, as well as Iraqi allies it was training, was facing shootings and car bombings in other areas of Iraq.

Meanwhile, coalition forces in Iraq were not finding evidence of Saddam's vaunted weapons of mass destruction—at least not anywhere near the levels Americans thought there would be. The absence of WMDs led to accusations at home, especially from Bush's political foes, that the administration had "lied" about the weapons to start a war. The calls to withdraw from Iraq began to grow.

It has been said that in modern history, second terms are a mixed blessing at best. Richard Nixon scandalized himself out of office in his second term. Ronald Reagan had a time of it overcoming the Iran-Contra affair. And Bill Clinton was impeached. The next four years for Bush and the country were met with great promise but also great peril.

In his 2004 victory, Bush decisively, and without any nagging question, won reelection. He beat Kerry by more than three million votes. Bush stated that he had "earned capital in the campaign, political capital, and now I intend to spend it." He identified his proposed second-term agenda: "Social Security and tax reform, moving this economy forward, education, fighting and winning the war on terror."[81] Any one of those issues would be hard enough to take on—especially what had long been considered "the third rail" of politics, Social Security reform. Many had viewed Bush as a wartime president and wished to see the war on terror prosecuted vigorously and brought to an end so that then the other issues could be addressed.

In his 2005 Inaugural Address, the president spoke to what was increasingly becoming his view of the mission abroad: to help build democratic institutions throughout the Middle East and to foster democracy throughout the world. To Bush, it was clear that in not finding WMDs in Iraq, this would now be the ancillary benefit of what America had begun to seriously accomplish in Afghanistan and Iraq: the building of two democracies, including (in the case of Iraq) the first Arab democracy in history.

Bush's view was that the U.S. had gone to war with Iraq for the purpose of protecting our national security, but he had also spoken of Saddam's human rights abuses and the sponsoring and coddling of terrorists. In the entire indictment, WMDs were a preeminent but not exclusive part. And as others had pointed out, had not other wars changed emphases *in medias res*?

On economic matters, the administration had placed tariffs on steel imports, upsetting the notions and doctrines of free trade. And the administration had been slow to act on the growing concern of illegal immigration. Estimates put the number of illegal immigrants living in the country as high as ten million. Critics warned that such levels were causing budgetary and social problems. On foreign policy, most conservatives were foursquare with the president in fighting terrorism and maintaining the course in Iraq, but many had thought the U.S. was too appeasing of countries like China, where religion was anathema, and Saudi Arabia, from where more poisonous indoctrination was flowing than from perhaps any other country.

Many of Bush's critics, especially Democrats, declared that the military mission in Iraq had gone as far as it could go. It was time to get out. Yet too many had forgotten what Iraq was before we went in. It was a place led by a ruthless barbarian who, thanks to our work, was in jail and by the end of 2006 would be hanged after an Iraqi court found him guilty of crimes against humanity. In three years, Iraq had gone from an entrenched tyranny to a fledgling democracy, but it could not yet stand alone.

Bin Laden had called on the U.S. to leave Iraq and called for Muslim fighters to join the struggle to push the Americans out. The administration was determined not to give him a victory. In its view, no country could be expected to go from barbarism to democracy on a theoretical deadline. Terrorists who behead civilians were not to be left alone to destroy our new ally, the first democracy in the Arab world.

Meanwhile, little good was being reported out of Iraq—also deemed "the Republicans' war." Terrorists flocked there to fill the vacuum left by an ousted Saddam Hussein. For the midterm elections of 2006, most pollsters were showing November 2006 to be a loss for Republicans—and it was.

The Republicans lost thirty seats in the House and six seats in the Senate.[82] The most interesting race of the year was Democrat Joe Lieberman's Senate reelection in Connecticut. The left of the Democratic Party wanted to punish him for his staunch support of the Iraq War—in truth, few were as articulate and supportive as he was—and they defeated him in the primary. Lieberman ran in the general election as an independent and held off his Democratic and Republican challengers.

Democratic Congresswoman Nancy Pelosi from California would become the new Speaker of the House—the first female to ever hold that position—and a new year would soon begin, with Democrats in control on Capitol Hill. And charged by their supporters to get the U.S. out of Iraq.

The Bush administration had other ideas. A new plan was in the works. In January of 2007, the president announced a new commander in Iraq and a new strategy: the commander, General David Petraeus; the strategy, "a surge." The administration was going to ramp up and send more troops into Iraq with a counterinsurgency plan developed by General Petraeus and General Jack Keane. If previous generals heading the multinational forces in Iraq had become symbols of the problems and the violence there, David Petraeus and the surge would, in short order, be given one last chance to turn it all around—or fail once and for all.

The most extreme thing said about Iraq in April of 2007 belonged to Majority Leader Harry Reid. At a news conference discussing why timelines for withdrawal should be imposed and why the surge of troops to Iraq was the opposite direction he thought we should take, he said, "I believe myself that the secretary of state, secretary of defense and—you have to make your own decisions as to what the president knows—that this war is lost and the surge is not accomplishing anything as indicated by the extreme violence in Iraq."[83]

"This war is lost" was the statement that would shoot across the world. America was in the midst of a war and a new plan for winning, with increased troops on the field of battle, and the leader of the U.S. Senate pronounced the war "lost." He was criticized far and wide both within the country and by the troops, who did not want to hear that and did not believe they were fighting for a lost cause or for a war that had ended. As perhaps the leading Republican in the Senate arguing for the surge and for sticking it out in Iraq, John McCain had said, "If the war is lost, who won?" But such was the state of heated rhetoric in 2007.

XIII. THE 2008 ELECTION

The 2008 presidential contest featured several Democrats vying for their party's nomination. Senator Barack Obama—the one who had given an antiwar speech as a state senator in 2002, who had dazzled the

Democratic Convention with a keynote speech in 2004, and who had served less than one term in the U.S. Senate—emerged as a serious candidate. Senator Obama and his advisors read the mood of the country and thought it needed something different, something substantially different: a change. Obama was young (forty-six years old in 2007), a newcomer to Washington, against the Iraq War from the beginning, articulate, and a black American. His middle name was Hussein. He was different; he was change. And in February of 2007, on a frigid day in Springfield, Illinois, he announced to a crowd of thousands that he was running for president.

Senator Hillary Rodham Clinton had already announced her candidacy in January. Hers was just as interesting a story. Never elected to office until she ran for Senate from New York in 2000, she had been a divisive figure in politics during her husband's tenure in office and was much watched as a senator. By 2007, she knew something about the name "Clinton." There was no bigger name or draw in Democratic Party politics. She was a hero to many Democratic women, her husband was still a great party fund-raiser and political mind, and together they could gin up their political machine of advisors and friends for whom they had done favors over their long years in public service.

On the Democratic side were the first truly plausible candidates for president who were female and black. Others entered the Democratic ring as well, but none as interesting as these two.

The Republicans nominated the strongest and most ardent supporter of the surge and the campaign in Iraq, Senator John McCain of Arizona. Never one to revel in the conventional wisdom of his party or a poll, McCain had justifiably earned the nickname of "Maverick." He had announced he would run for president for 2008, and his announcement was marked with not a few raised eyebrows. He was a war hero like few others, having had bones and teeth crushed in a Vietnam prison camp after his plane was shot down, and he took that beating for more than five years. But he was also a Republican like few others. He had opposed President Bush's initial tax cuts and had disappointed much of the Republican base on other initiatives he had taken on over the years—from campaign finance reform legislation to antitorture legislation, which many had deemed was too vague and would hamstring intelligence and military efforts. He had a solid voting record on most right-to-life issues but was in favor of federal funding of embryonic stem cell research (which the right-to-life community strenuously opposed), and he was separated from much of the conservative base on his liberal immigration views. And he was not a frequent speaker on or to social issues. Still, he thought his long service in the party and his dedication to the troops and military put him in the right place and right time to run for president in 2008—even if much of the country was opposed to his position on the Iraq War. About that, he would say, "I'd rather lose an election than lose a war."

The opening of President Bush's final year in office seemed to secure him in his place as a lame duck. His approval ratings had not improved, and he began the year at a record low—with 32 percent of Americans approving of the job he was doing and 66 percent disapproving. He was, simply put, "beset by growing economic concerns on top of the long unpopular war in Iraq." If Clinton was morally compromised in his last year in office, Bush was politically compromised in his. Yes, Iraq was turning around, but the war was very unpopular in most of the country (some 64 percent were saying it was not worth fighting) and so was much else about the administration (with 77 percent saying the country was heading in the wrong direction).[84] With those numbers, it was difficult to get out any kind of positive message. The country was ready for a big change and was listening to the candidates for president.

Obama, who had served only two years in the Senate, was taking on the strongest Democratic political machine recent history had known: the Clintons—a former president and a powerful senator. He was the opposite of their establishment machine and had attracted the youth like few others, reminding people perhaps of Eugene McCarthy or even Bobby Kennedy. He was a gifted speaker and seemingly never broke a sweat. He was "cool," young, and athletic. For the antiwar activists, he was on the right side from the beginning, and for the liberals on other issues, he was that and more (some ratings had him the most liberal member of the Senate).

This was the chance of so many to fulfill the lifelong dream of putting a black man into the White House. If change was what the Democrats or country wanted, this man was it. This dream was given purchase when Obama won the Iowa caucuses in early January. It was a remarkable feat and an explicit response to those who would worry that the country was not ready to elect a black man to the presidency; Iowa's population, after all, was overwhelmingly white—a good test for the proposition. Obama proved to be a remarkably able campaigner and managed to clinch the nomination.

As 2008 moved on, the violence in Iraq continued to abate; "victory" seemed not so far off. What General Petraeus and the military had done in Iraq was nothing short of miraculous. They were the true turnaround experts of the year.

This fact did not make the war much more popular. Most in America had tuned out the good news. Obama insisted that Iraq was the "wrong war" that took our focus off the "right war" in Afghanistan. If elected, he said, he would get us out. In contrast, McCain would not back down from Iraq and made every effort to show his credibility and experience on foreign and defense affairs as compared to Obama's experience, which was little to none.

The polling going into the election showed a tight race. It was neck and neck through September, with McCain ahead of or behind Obama by only a few points.[85]

When it was time to pick running mates, Obama went for experience and confidence building, someone who would show the country that, though he was young and not very experienced on the international scene, his vice president would be. He chose Senate Foreign Relations Committee Chairman Joe Biden of Delaware. Biden was nothing if not experienced; he'd been in the Senate since 1973.

McCain, ever the maverick, knew he needed to go the other way. Experience he had; exuberance and an electrification of the base he needed. He chose the then-little-known first-term governor of Alaska, Sarah Palin. And did she ever electrify! An attractive young governor with an informal way of speaking, Palin was the mother of five with her youngest (who had Down syndrome) born that year. Her eldest son had enlisted in the army and was off to Iraq. She was pro-life, she was pro-Iraqi victory, she was energetic and unabashed in her conservatism, and she was unknown to most. But for many conservatives, this is what they needed to support McCain (who had an uneasy relationship with the base).

The media went after Palin intensely, and she did not fare well in her nationally televised interviews. Some on the left despised her—and started all forms of false rumors about her and her family on the Internet.

It had been a year of increased job losses, and there were worries of a coming recession. Only a few predicted how bad it would be. The Dow Jones plummeted 2,400 points in the week ending October 10.[86] The month prior, financial services firm Lehman Brothers had declared bankruptcy—the largest bankruptcy in the history of the United States.[87] Triggered by the collapse of a housing bubble and deep problems in the subprime mortgage industry, the worst financial crisis since the Great Depression hit the United States. The administration proposed and the Congress passed a $700 billion bailout that allowed the U.S. Treasury to purchase troubled assets from financial firms to help ease the credit crisis.[88] The country was in a recession, and McCain's polls would show no more leads.[89]

McCain was not the greatest debater, and he was uneasy talking to core Republican issues such as social policy or tax cuts. He was much more comfortable speaking about pork and government waste—not the issues that had typically been known to lead a charge up a hill on domestic policy. Obama did as well or better than McCain in the debates—the man with little experience showed he could stand head-to-head with the man of experience, and he made no grave errors.

One would make a name for himself as an author and liberal activist; the other was never at ease with the status quo in his own party. Come 2008, one would argue and campaign on the themes of hope and change for America; the other focused on the themes of experience and strength.

On 4 November 2008, the United States once again demonstrated its unique gift to the world—peaceful, democratic elections. Americans gave more than sixty-six million votes to Barack Obama to elect him as their forty-fourth president and the first black president of the United States.

There was a deep recession in the land. There were unfinished wars in Afghanistan and Iraq. Osama bin Laden and Ayman al-Zawahiri were still alive. Iran was on track to becoming a nuclearized nation. North Korea was testing missiles. Russia was flexing its muscles. And a new president, with a new approach to the country and the world, would take the reins of power with new hopes and new fears in the country he was charged to lead.

Four years before he delivered the keynote at the Democratic National Convention in Boston, eight years before he was the nominee of the Democratic Party at the convention in Denver, Barack Obama was unable to obtain credentials to even enter the Democratic Convention in Los Angeles. This, too, is testimony to the greatness of America: from practically nothing to leader of the free world in eight years—and a racial minority at that. "It is the experience of men that always returns to the equality of men" in America, G. K. Chesterton once wrote.[90]

The election of President Barack Obama achieved that one great dream of Martin Luther King Jr.: this man was judged not by anything more or less than the content of his character. To many, his election was a giant step forward in erasing our original stain of slavery. To others, it was a culmination of all this country had done to erase that stain, from the Civil War to the Civil Rights Act. *Boston Globe* columnist Jeff Jacoby recently provided polling numbers that show the growth of Americans' views on race:

In 1958, 48 percent of white Americans polled by Gallup said that "if colored people came to live next door," they would be likely to move. By 1978, only 13 percent still said that; by 1997, the proportion had fallen to 1 percent....

That's only one measure of racism's profound decline. Friendship is another....

In 1964, a mere 18 percent of white Americans claimed to have a friend who was black. Four decades later, Gallup found that the proportion of interracial friendships had more than quadrupled: 82 percent of whites said they had close nonwhite friends (and 88 percent of blacks reported having close friends who were not black).[91]

XIV. LOOKING BACK TO 1776

The two-term Obama presidency is still being debated. In domestic affairs, perhaps its signature legacy will be a government overhaul of healthcare, today still known as Obamacare—legislation that not a single Republican in Congress voted for. In foreign affairs, Obama's most significant legacy may be his decision to engage Iran, first by refusing to support an organic protest movement against the mullahs in 2009, and later by offering the Iranian government billions of dollars to delay developing nuclear weapons. Both legacies are, to this day, hugely controversial. Both, to this day, are marked to be undone by the president who succeeded Barack Obama.

That president is, obviously, Donald J. Trump, who against almost all predictions won the 2016 election, first against fifteen other announced Republicans, then against Hillary Clinton in an electoral college victory of 304 to 227.

All of these events are still too close for much historical analysis, though the markers are there: healthcare and the Middle East. One can easily add China and Russia, illegal immigration, and a growing problem we began to tackle in earnest in the 1980s and early 1990s that has come back again: surging illegal drug use.

In looking back at all these years, I still come back to years further back, to 1776. How we help make real the promises and principles of the Declaration of Independence in this country, and other countries, will vary. But it is those promises and principles we mean whenever we speak of such things as "American exceptionalism." Today there is great conflict and division in America. It is not clear if our vast family still thinks of our country as exceptional, that is to say, rare and unique in its greatness and accomplishments. To be clear, for those of us standing with the view that we still are the last best hope of earth, we do not think there is anything better about any given race in America. We do not think there is anything better about any given first, middle, or last name in America. We do not think there is anything better about any particular bloodline in America. What we do think are better than anything else in the world are the promises and principles of America. When we stand up for them, when we fight for them, when we defend them, we are standing and fighting and defending a cause greater than any self-interest. And when we decline to stand, fight, and defend those promises and principles, we become aliens to our very founding, our very nation, our very best history.

ACKNOWLEDGMENTS

This book has been a labor of love, as were the three volumes from which it was distilled. My love for our country has been deepened and made more intense by this project. I could not have completed this task without the help and encouragement of friends and colleagues.

The task of reducing three volumes to one was large and the work involved was mighty. I am indebted to John Cribb for shouldering much of the task and its intricacies, and of course to Seth Leibsohn who has helped shepherd this book all its way through and worked hard on the epilogue.

Bob Morrison, my former colleague at the Department of Education, has been with the project from the beginning. He has been of immense help. His effort has been exemplary, and his love of the project has been contagious. With William Faulkner, Bob believes "the past isn't dead—it isn't even past."

Vin Cannato, Al Felzenberg, Michael Forastiere, Steve Ochs, Bill Schultz, Max Schultz, Tevi Troy, and Ken Watson provided many solid recommendations. I thank each for his friendship and valuable help.

Brian Kennedy, the Claremont Institute, Lawrence and Susan Kadish, and Noreen Burns encouraged and supported me and this project. They all think and encourage "big." I thank them.

ACKNOWLEDGMENTS

Bob Barnett—as usual—counseled, advised, and made the deal that made the book possible.

Webster Younce, my editor, is wise, patient, and always ready to help. I am grateful for his guidance, as I am for the expert skill of the entire Thomas Nelson team. Joel Miller, my editor on the original three books that went into making this one, is likewise a wonderful colleague and friend.

My wife, Elayne, encouraged, read, and offered her always probing commentary and judgment. I am grateful to her and to my sons, John and Joseph, for their love and support.

NOTES

Introduction

1. Abraham Lincoln, "The Perpetuation of Our Political Institutions," address before the Young Men's Lyceum of Springfield, Illinois, January 27, 1838, https://quod.lib.umich.edu/l/lincoln/lincoln1/1:130?rgn=div1;view=fulltext.

2. Abraham Lincoln, "The Perpetuation of Our Political Institutions."

3. Said in a conversation with the author.

4. Abraham Lincoln, "Annual Message to Congress," December 1, 1862, https://quod.lib.umich.edu/l/lincoln/lincoln5/1:1126?rgn=div1;view=fulltext.

5. Donald, David Herbert, *Lincoln*, Simon & Schuster, New York: 1995, p. 222.

6. Louis D. Brandeis, "What Publicity Can Do," *Other People's Money*, chapter 5, p. 92 (1932). First published in *Harper's Weekly*, December 20, 1913.

7. William J. Bennett, "History—Key to Political Responsibility," in William Bennett and Jean Kirkpatrick, *History, Geography, and Citizenship: The Teacher's Role*, Ethics and Public Policy Essay No. 63, April 1986, p. 6.

8. Ronald Reagan, "Farewell Address to the Nation," January 11, 1989, https://www.reaganfoundation.org/media/128652/farewell.pdf.

9. Catherine Drinker Bowen wrote this in an essay called "Bernard DeVoto: Historian, Critic, and Fighter." The essay was included on pages vii-xix of the book *The Year of Decision: 1846* by Bernard Augustine DeVoto, Boston: Houghton Mifflin Co., 1943, xix.

Chapter 1: The Greatest Revolution

1. Isaacson, Walter, *Benjamin Franklin: An American Life*, Simon & Schuster, New York: 2003, p. 224.

2. Isaacson, *Benjamin Franklin*, p. 224.

3. Bobrick, Benson, *Angel in the Whirlwind: The Triumph of the American Revolution*, Penguin Books, New York: 1997, p. 72.

4. Morgan, Edmund S., *Benjamin Franklin*, Yale Nota Bene, New Haven, Conn.: 2003, pp. 152–153.

5. Morgan, Edmund S., and Helen M. Morgan, *The Stamp Act Crisis*, Collier, New York: 1967, p. 311.

6. Morison, Samuel Eliot, Henry Commager Steele, and William E. Leuchtenburg, *A Concise History of the American Republic*, Oxford University Press, New York: 1977, p. 68.

7. Morgan, Edmund S., *The Birth of the Republic: 1763–1789*, University of Chicago Press, Chicago: 1956, p. 19. Ferling, John, *A Leap in the Dark: The Struggle to Create the American Republic*, Oxford University Press, New York: 2003, p. 31.

8. Mayer, Henry, *A Son of Thunder: Patrick Henry and the American Republic*, University Press of Virginia, Charlottesville: 1991, p. 93.

9. Freeman, Douglas Southall, *George Washington: A Biography, Vol. III*, Charles Scribner's Sons, New York: 1951, p. 129.

10. Bobrick, *Angel*, p. 72.

11. Freeman, *George Washington*, p. 136.

12. Freeman, *George Washington*, p. 136.

13. Ferling, *Leap*, p. 35.

14. Morison, Commager, and Leuchtenburg, *Concise History*, p. 69.

15. Ferling, *Leap*, p. 35.

16. Ferling, *Leap*, p. 35.

17. Robson, Eric, *The American Revolution in Its Political and Military Aspects, 1763–1783*, Norton Library, W. W. Norton & Company, New York: 1966.

18. Resolutions of the Continental Congress, October 19, 1765, http://avalon .law.yale.edu/18th_century/resolu65.asp.

19. Ferling, *Leap*, p. 40.

20. Ferling, *Leap*, p. 40.

21. Ferling, *Leap*, p. 38.

22. Maier, Pauline, *From Resistance to Revolution: Colonial Radicals and the Development of Opposition to Britain, 1765–1776*, W. W. Norton & Company, New York: 1991, p. 81.

23. McCullough, David, *John Adams*, Simon & Schuster, New York: 2001, p. 62.

24. Catton, Bruce, and William B. Catton, *The Bold and Magnificent Dream: America's Founding Years: 1492–1815*, Gramercy Books, New York: 1978, p. 255.

25. Robson, *American Revolution*, p. 45.

26. Ferling, *Leap*, p. 40.

27. Catton and Catton, *Bold*, p. 264.

28. Robson, *American Revolution*, p. 63.

29. Robson, *American Revolution*, p. 64.

30. Robson, *American Revolution*, p. 65.

31. Robson, *American Revolution*, p. 64.

32. Maier, *Resistance*, pp. 114–115.

33. Maier, *Resistance*, p. 114.

34. Robson, *American Revolution*, p. 65.

35. Ferling, *Leap*, p. 84.

36. Ferling, *Leap*, p. 71.

37. Clark, Ronald W., *Benjamin Franklin: A Biography*, Random House, New York: 1983, p. 58.

38. Bobrick, *Angel*, p. 86.

39. Bobrick, *Angel*, p. 86.

40. Robson, *American Revolution*, p. 66.

41. Catton and Catton, *Bold*, p. 267.

42. Robson, *American Revolution*, p. 67.

43. Catton and Catton, *Bold*, p. 268.

44. Ferling, *Leap*, p. 86.

45. Churchill, Winston S., *The Great Republic: A History of America*, Random House, New York: 1999, p. 62.

46. Ferling, *Leap*, p. 106.

47. Ferling, *Leap*, p. 106.

48. Bobrick, *Angel*, p. 90.

49. Churchill, *Great Republic*, p. 62.

50. Bobrick, *Angel*, p. 91.

51. Catton and Catton, *Bold*, p. 269.

52. Flexner, James Thomas, *Washington: The Indispensable Man*, Little, Brown and Company, Boston: 1969, p. 58.

53. Ferling, *Leap*, p. 108.

54. Catton and Catton, *Bold*, p. 272.

55. Fischer, David Hackett, *Paul Revere's Ride*, Oxford University Press, New York: 1994, p. 96

56. Fischer, *Revere's Ride*, p. 104.

57. Fischer, *Revere's Ride*, p. 109.

58. Leckie, Robert, *George Washington's War: The Saga of the American Revolution*, HarperCollins, New York: 1993, p. 110.

59. Leckie, *Washington's War*, p. 110.

60. Leckie, *Washington's War*, p. 110.

61. Leckie, *Washington's War*, p. 115.

62. Catton and Catton, *Bold*, p. 279.

63. Churchill, *Great Republic*, p. 65.

64. Brands, H. W., *The First American: The Life and Times of Benjamin Franklin*, Doubleday, New York: 2000, p. 502.

65. Catton and Catton, *Bold*, p. 276.

66. Catton and Catton, *Bold*, p. 277.

67. Maier, Pauline, *American Scripture: Making the Declaration of Independence*, Alfred A. Knopf, New York: 1997, p. 33.

68. Maier, *American Scripture*, p. 33.

69. Maier, *American Scripture*, p. 33.

70. Paine, Thomas, *Common Sense*, Barnes & Noble Books, New York: 1995, pp. 19–20.

71. Paine, *Common Sense*, p. 42.

72. Morison, Commager, and Leuchtenburg, *Concise History*, p. 80.

73. Morison, Commager, and Leuchtenburg, *Concise History*, p. 80.

74. Green, Ashbel, *The Life of the Revd. John Witherspoon*, edited by Henry Lyttleton Savage, Princeton University Press, Princeton, N.J.: 1973, pp. 159–160.

75. Maier, *American Scripture*, p. 98.

76. Maier, *American Scripture*, p. 135.

77. Spalding, Matthew, ed., *The Founders' Almanac*, The Heritage Foundation, Washington, D.C.: 2001.

78. Brands, *The First American*, p. 512.

79. Spalding, *Founders' Almanac*, p. 230.

80. Leckie, *Washington's War*, p. 265.

81. McCullough, David, *1776*, Simon & Schuster, New York: 2005, p. 170.

82. McCullough, *1776*, p. 175.

83. McCullough, *1776*, p. 190.

84. McCullough, *1776*, p. 191.

85. Flexner, *Washington*, p. 84.

86. Fischer, David Hackett, *Washington's Crossing*, Oxford University Press, New York: 2004, p. 108

87. Brands, *The First American*, p. 527.

88. Churchill, *Great Republic*, p. 67.

89. Leckie, *Washington's War*, p. 329.

90. Leckie, *Washington's War*, p. 343.

91. Leckie, *Washington's War*, p. 401.

92. Catton and Catton, *Bold*, p. 307.

93. Leckie, *Washington's War*, p. 417.

94. Leckie, *Washington's War*, p. 419.

95. Letter from George Washington to John Banister, delegate in Congress, Valley Forge, April 21, 1778, https://oll.libertyfund.org/titles/washington-the-writings-of-george-washington-vol-vi-1777–1778.

96. Leckie, *Washington's War*, p. 492.

97. Leckie, *Washington's War*, p. 499.

98. Bobrick, *Angel*, p. 378.

99. Leckie, *Washington's War*, p. 546.

100. Leckie, *Washington's War*, p. 565.

101. Churchill, *Great Republic*, p. 74.

102. Bobrick, *Angel*, p. 416.

103. Bobrick, *Angel*, p. 419.

104. Churchill, *Great Republic*, p. 82.

105. Churchill, *Great Republic*, p. 82.

106. Bobrick, *Angel*, p. 402.

107. Bobrick, *Angel*, p. 402.

108. Bass, Robert D., *Swamp Fox: The Life and Campaigns of General Francis Marion*, Sandlapper Publishing, Orangeburg, S.C.: 1974, p. 175.

109. Bass, *Swamp Fox*, p. 175.

110. Bobrick, *Angel*, p. 426.

111. "The Battle of the Waxhaws," South Carolina Encyclopedia, http://www
.scencyclopedia.org/sce/entries/waxhaws-battle-of-the/.

112. "The Battle of the Waxhaws," South Carolina Encyclopedia.

113. Keegan, John, *Fields of Battle: The Wars for North America*, Vintage
Books, New York: 1997, p. 178.

114. Keegan, *Fields of Battle*, p. 178.

115. Catton and Catton, *Bold*, p. 319.

116. Bobrick, *Angel*, p. 448.

117. Bobrick, *Angel*, p. 452.

118. Keegan, *Fields of Battle*, p. 184.

119. Bobrick, *Angel*, p. 453.

120. Bobrick, *Angel*, p. 459.

121. Bobrick, *Angel*, p. 462.

122. Bobrick, *Angel*, p. 464.

123. Bobrick, *Angel*, p. 464.

124. Leckie, *George Washington's War*, p. 110.

125. Flexner, *Washington*, p. 170.

126. Flexner, *Washington*, p. 174.

127. Flexner, *Washington*, p. 174.

128. Clark, Harrison, *All Cloudless Glory: Vol. II*, Regnery Publishing,
Washington, D.C.: 1996, p. 62.

129. Bobrick, *Angel*, p. 479.

130. Bobrick, *Angel*, p. 480.

Chapter 2: Reflection and Choice: Framing the Constitution

1. Bailyn, Bernard, David Brian Davis, David Herbert Donald, John L.
Thomas, Robert H. Wiebe, and Gordon S. Wood, *The Great Republic: A
History of the American People*, Little, Brown and Company, Boston: 1977,
p. 302.

2. Morison, Samuel Eliot, Henry Steele Commager, and William S.
Leuchtenburg, *A Concise History of the American Republic*, Oxford
University Press, New York: 1977, p. 108.

3. Morison, Commager, and Leuchtenburg, *Concise History*, p. 109.

4. Hitchens, Christopher, *Thomas Jefferson: Author of America*,
HarperCollins, New York: 2005, p. 51.

5. Morris, Richard B., *Witnesses at the Creation: Hamilton, Madison, Jay and the Constitution*, Holt, Rinehart and Winston, New York: 1985, p. 219.

6. Morison, Commager, and Leuchtenburg, *Concise History*, p. 113.

7. Morison, Commager, and Leuchtenburg, *Concise History*, p. 113.

8. Rossiter, Clinton, *1787: The Grand Convention*, The Macmillan Company, New York: 1966, p. 56.

9. Mayer, Henry, *A Son of Thunder: Patrick Henry and the American Republic*, University Press of Virginia, New York: 1991, p. 375.

10. Peterson, Merrill D., ed., *Thomas Jefferson: Writings*, The Library of America, New York: 1984, p. 882.

11. Ketcham, Ralph, *James Madison: A Biography*, University Press of Virginia, New York: 1990, p. 186.

12. Van Doren, Carl, *The Great Rehearsal*, Viking, New York: 1948, p. 7.

13. Mayer, *Son of Thunder*, p. 375.

14. Van Doren, *Great Rehearsal*, p. 6.

15. Rossiter, *1787*, p. 41.

16. Ketcham, *James Madison*, p. 183.

17. Van Doren, *Great Rehearsal*, p. 5.

18. Bowen, Catherine Drinker, *Miracle at Philadelphia: The Story of the Constitutional Convention, May to September, 1787*, American Past/Book-of-the-Month Club, New York: 1986, p. 20.

19. Van Doren, *Great Rehearsal*, p. 5.

20. Bowen, *Miracle*, p. 20.

21. Ketcham, *James Madison*, p. 195.

22. Bowen, *Miracle*, p. 24.

23. Bowen, *Miracle*, p. 106.

24. Bowen, *Miracle*, p. 131.

25. Morison, Commager, and Leuchtenburg, *Concise History*, p. 114.

26. Koch, Adrienne, *Jefferson & Madison: The Great Collaboration*, Oxford University Press, New York: 1976, p. 53.

27. Koch, *Jefferson & Madison*, p. 53.

28. Brands, H. W., *The First American: The Life and Times of Benjamin Franklin*, Doubleday, New York: 2000, p. 678.

29. Bowen, *Miracle*, p. 83.

30. Bowen, *Miracle*, p. 32.

31. Bowen, *Miracle*, p. 187.

32. West, Thomas G., *Vindicating the Founders: Race, Sex, Class, and Justice in the Origin of America*, Rowman & Littlefield, Lanham, Md.: 1997, p. 17.

33. Rossiter, *1787*, pp. 32–33.

34. Rossiter, *1787*, p. 32.

35. Bowen, *Miracle*, p. 201.

36. Bowen, *Miracle*, p. 201.

37. Morris, *Witnesses*, p. 215.

38. Bowen, *Miracle*, p. 201.

39. Bowen, *Miracle*, p. 202.

40. Morris, *Witnesses*, p. 216.

41. Morris, *Witnesses*, p. 216.

42. Brands, *First American*, p. 690.

43. Brands, *First American*, p. 689.

44. Ketcham, *James Madison*, p. 202.

45. Bowen, *Miracle*, pp. 98–99.

46. Morgan, Edmund S., *The Meaning of Independence: John Adams, George Washington and Thomas Jefferson*, W. W. Norton & Company, New York: 1976, p. 29.

47. Van Doren, *Great Rehearsal*, p. 15.

48. Brands, *First American*, p. 691.

49. Bowen, *Miracle*, p. 29.

50. Brookhiser, Richard, *Alexander Hamilton, American*, The Free Press, New York: 1999, p. 72.

51. Brookhiser, *Alexander Hamilton*, p. 72.

52. Brookhiser, *Alexander Hamilton*, p. 162.

53. Morison, Commager, and Leuchtenburg, *Concise History*, p. 121.

54. Morison, Commager, and Leuchtenburg, *Concise History*, p. 121.

55. Ketcham, *James Madison*, p. 266.

56. Morison, Commager, and Leuchtenburg, *Concise History*, p. 121.

57. Mayer, *Son of Thunder*, pp. 436–437.

58. Morison, Commager, and Leuchtenburg, *Concise History*, p. 121.

59. Brookhiser, *Alexander Hamilton*, p. 74.

Chapter 3: The New Republic

1. Flexner, James Thomas, *Washington: The Indispensable Man*, Little, Brown and Company, Boston: 1974, p. 215.

2. Flexner, *Washington*, p. 215.

3. Hunt, John Gabriel, ed., *The Inaugural Addresses of the Presidents*, Gramercy Books, New York: 1995, p. 6.

4. Jaffa, Harry V., *A New Birth of Freedom: Abraham Lincoln and the Coming of the Civil War*, Rowman & Littlefield, Lanham, Md.: 2000, p. 491.

5. Rhodehamel, John, ed., *George Washington: Writings*, The Library of America, New York: 1997, p. 767.

6. Ketcham, Ralph, *James Madison: A Biography*, University Press of Virginia, New York: 1990, p. 290.

7. Ketcham, *James Madison*, p. 290.

8. Koch, Adrienne, *Jefferson & Madison: The Great Collaboration*, Oxford University Press, New York: 1976, p. 41.

9. "Letter from Alexander Hamilton to James Duane," 3 September 1780, Founders Online, National Archives, https://founders.archives.gov /documents/Hamilton/01-02-02-0838.

10. Flexner, *Washington*, p. 258.

11. Flexner, *Washington*, p. 258.

12. Flexner, *Washington*, p. 259.

13. Ferling, John, *A Leap in the Dark: The Struggle to Create the American Republic*, Oxford University Press, New York: 2003, p. 346.

14. Flexner, *Washington*, p. 268.

15. McDonald, Forrest, *The American Presidency: An Intellectual History*, University Press of Kansas, Lawrence, Kan.: 1994, p. 230.

16. McDonald, *American Presidency*, p. 230.

17. McDonald, *American Presidency*, p. 230.

18. Brookhiser, Richard, *Alexander Hamilton: American*, The Free Press, New York: 1999, p. 104.

19. Brookhiser, *Alexander Hamilton*, p. 104.

20. Elkins, Stanley, and Eric McKitrick, *The Age of Federalism: The Early American Republic, 1788–1800*, Oxford University Press, New York: 1993, p. 356.

21. Elkins and McKitrick, *Age of Federalism*, p. 358.

22. Catton, Bruce, and William B. Catton, *The Bold and Magnificent Dream: America's Founding Years, 1492–1815*, Gramercy Books, New York: 1978, p. 426.

23. Elkins and McKitrick, *Age of Federalism*, p. 481.

24. Morison, Samuel Eliot, Henry Steele Commager, and William S. Leuchtenburg, *A Concise History of the American Republic*, Oxford University Press, New York: 1977, p. 139.

25. McDonald, *American Presidency*, p. 241.

26. Catton and Catton, *Bold*, p. 427.

27. Bailey, Thomas A., *A Diplomatic History of the American People*, Prentice-Hall, Inc., Englewood Cliffs, N.J.: 1980, p. 79.

28. Elkins and McKitrick, *Age of Federalism*, p. 483.

29. Rhodehamel, *George Washington*, p. 971.

30. McCullough, David, *John Adams*, Simon & Schuster, New York: 2001, p. 469.

31. McCullough, *John Adams*, p. 469.

32. Furet, Francois, and Mona Ozouf, eds., trans. by Arthur Goldhammer, *A Critical Dictionary of the French Revolution*, The Belknap Press of Harvard University Press, Cambridge, Mass.: 1989, p. 143.

33. Furet and Ozouf, *French Revolution*, p. 145.

34. Morison, Commager, and Leuchtenburg, *Concise History*, p. 143.

35. Zvesper, John, *From Bullets to Ballots: The Election of 1800 and the First Peaceful Transfer of Political Power*, The Claremont Institute, Claremont, Calif.: 2003, p. 100.

36. Elkins and McKitrick, *Age of Federalism*, p. 694.

37. Churchill, Winston S., *The Great Republic: A History of America*, Random House, New York: 1999, p. 103.

38. Ferling, *Leap*, p. 422.

39. Elkins and McKitrick, *Age of Federalism*, p. 729.

40. Peterson, Merrill D., ed., *Thomas Jefferson: Writings*, The Library of America, New York: 1984, p. 455.

41. Elkins and McKitrick, *Age of Federalism*, p. 721.

42. Elkins and McKitrick, *Age of Federalism*, p. 723.

43. Jaffa, *New Birth*, p. 59.

44. Bailey, *Diplomatic History*, p. 95.

45. Bailey, *Diplomatic History*, p. 98.

46. Bailey, *Diplomatic History*, p. 98.

47. McCullough, *John Adams*, p. 586.

48. McCullough, *John Adams*, p. 567.

49. Koch, *Jefferson & Madison*, p. 212.

50. Elkins and McKitrick, *Age of Federalism*, p. 736.

51. McCullough, *John Adams*, p. 549.

52. McCullough, *John Adams*, p. 550.

53. McCullough, *John Adams*, p. 548.

54. Catton and Catton, *Bold*, p. 443.

55. Elkins and McKitrick, *Age of Federalism*, p. 747.

56. Elkins and McKitrick, *Age of Federalism*, p. 744.

57. McCullough, *John Adams*, p. 562.

58. Hunt, *The Inaugural Addresses of the Presidents*, p. 25.

59. Koch, *Jefferson & Madison*, p. 217.

60. Jaffa, *New Birth*, p. 61.

Chapter 4: The Jeffersonians

1. Parton, James, *Life of Thomas Jefferson* (Boston: James R. Osgood and Company, 1874), pp. iii, 165.

2. Roosevelt, Theodore, *The Naval War of 1812*, Naval Institute Press, Annapolis, Md.: 1987, p. 405.

3. Dreisbach, Daniel, L., *Thomas Jefferson and the Wall of Separation*, New York University Press, New York: 2002, p. 48.

4. Dreisbach, *Wall of Separation*, p. 19.

5. Dreisbach, *Wall of Separation*, p. 19.

6. Dreisbach, *Wall of Separation*, p. 18.

7. Peterson, Merrill D., ed., *Thomas Jefferson: Writings*, The Library of America, New York: 1984, p. 1082.

8. Peterson, *Writings*, p. 1082.

9. Peterson, Merrill D., *Thomas Jefferson and the New Nation*, Oxford University Press, London: 1987, p. 704.

10. Peterson, *New Nation*, p. 704.

11. McCullough, David, *John Adams*, Simon & Schuster, New York: 2001, p. 583.

12. Peterson, *New Nation*, p. 708.

13. Whipple, A. B. C., *To the Shores of Tripoli: The Birth of the U.S. Navy and Marines*, William Morrow and Company, New York: 1991, p. 20.

14. Hitchens, Christopher, *Thomas Jefferson: Author of America*, HarperCollins Publishers, New York: 2005, p. 126.

15. Hitchens, *Author of America*, p. 128.

16. Hitchens, *Author of America*, p. 129.

17. Whipple, *Shores of Tripoli*, p. 27.

18. Morison, Samuel Eliot, *The Oxford History of the American People, Volume 2: 1789–Reconstruction*, Penguin Books, New York: 1994, p. 89.

19. McDonald, Forrest, *The Presidency of Thomas Jefferson*, University of Kansas Press, Lawrence, Kan.: 1976, p. 77.

20. Peterson, *New Nation*, p. 799.

21. Morison, *Oxford History*, vol. 2, p. 89.

22. Whipple, *Shores of Tripoli*, p. 282.

23. Wheelan, Joseph, *Jefferson's War: America's First War on Terror, 1801–1805*, Carroll & Graf Publishers, New York: 2003, p. 363.

24. Wheelan, *Jefferson's War*, p. 368.

25. Ambrose, Stephen E., and Sam Abell, *Lewis & Clark: Voyage of Discovery*, National Geographic Society, Washington, D.C.: 1998, p. 28.

26. Morison, *Oxford History*, vol. 2, p. 90.

27. Fleming, Thomas, *The Louisiana Purchase*, John Wiley & Sons, Inc., Hoboken, N.J.: 2003, p. 110.

28. Fleming, *Louisiana Purchase*, p. 117.

29. Fleming, *Louisiana Purchase*, p. 117.

30. Fleming, *Louisiana Purchase*, p. 80.

31. Fleming, *Louisiana Purchase*, p. 86.

32. Ketcham, Ralph, *James Madison: A Biography*, University of Virginia Press, Charlottesville, Va.: 1990, p. 417.

33. Fleming, *Louisiana Purchase*, p. 120.

34. Fleming, *Louisiana Purchase*, p. 134.

35. Kukla, Jon, *A Wilderness So Immense: The Louisiana Purchase and the Destiny of America*, Alfred A. Knopf, New York: 2003, p. 286.

36. Kukla, *Wilderness*, p. 286.

37. Morison, *Oxford History*, vol. 2, p. 92.

38. Kukla, *Wilderness*, p. 296.

39. Cerami, Charles A., *Jefferson's Great Gamble*, Sourcebooks, Naperville, Ill.: 2003, p. 205.

40. Ambrose and Abell, *Lewis & Clark*, p. 28.

41. Ambrose and Abell, *Lewis & Clark*, p. 37.

42. Ambrose and Abell, *Lewis & Clark*, p. 37.

43. Ambrose, Stephen E., *Undaunted Courage: Meriwether Lewis, Thomas Jefferson, and the Opening of the American West*, Simon & Schuster, New York: 1996, p. 99.

44. Ambrose and Abell, *Lewis & Clark*, p. 36.

45. Morison, *Oxford History*, vol. 2, p. 92.

46. Ambrose and Abell, *Lewis & Clark*, p. 143.

47. Ambrose, *Undaunted*, p. 154.

48. Ambrose, *Undaunted*, p. 171.

49. Morison, *Oxford History*, vol. 2, p. 93.

50. Ambrose, *Undaunted*, p. 89.

51. Morison, *Oxford History*, vol. 2, p. 94.

52. Brookhiser, Richard, *Alexander Hamilton, American*, The Free Press, New York: 1999, p. 211.

53. Holland, Barbara, *Gentlemen's Blood*, Bloomsbury, New York: 2003, pp. 113–115.

54. Brookhiser, *Alexander Hamilton*, p. 211.

55. Brookhiser, *Alexander Hamilton*, p. 213.

56. Brookhiser, *Alexander Hamilton*, p. 213.

57. Brookhiser, *Alexander Hamilton*, p. 214.

58. McDonald, *Presidency of Thomas Jefferson*, p. 87.

59. Koch, Adrienne, *Jefferson & Madison: The Great Collaboration*, Oxford University Press, New York: 1976, p. 228.

60. Morison, *Oxford History*, vol. 2, p. 95.

61. Fleming, Thomas, *Duel: Alexander Hamilton, Aaron Burr, and the Future of America*, Basic Books, New York: 1999, p. 383.

62. Morison, *Oxford History*, vol. 2, p. 95.

63. Morison, *Oxford History*, vol. 2, p. 96.

64. Morison, *Oxford History*, vol. 2, p. 96.

65. Fleming, *Duel*, p. 392.

66. Morison, *Oxford History*, vol. 2, p. 99.

67. Morison, *Oxford History*, vol. 2, p. 98.

68. McDonald, *Presidency of Thomas Jefferson*, p. 106.

69. McDonald, *Presidency of Thomas Jefferson*, p. 106.

70. Peterson, *Writings*, p. 528.

71. Peterson, *New Nation*, p. 920.

72. Morison, *Oxford History*, vol. 2, p. 105.

73. Morison, *Oxford History*, vol. 2, p. 105.

74. Utley, Robert M., and Wilcomb E. Washburn, *Indian Wars*, Houghton Mifflin Company, Boston: 1977, p. 117.

75. Morison, *Oxford History*, vol. 2, p. 109.

76. Utley and Washburn, *Indian Wars*, p. 121.

77. Leckie, Robert, *The Wars of America*, Harper & Row, New York: 1981, p. 233.

78. Leckie, *Wars of America*, p. 232.

79. Morison, *Oxford History*, vol. 2, p. 109.

80. Morison, *Oxford History*, vol. 2, p. 111.

81. Morison, *Oxford History*, vol. 2, p. 113.

82. Berton, Pierre, *The Invasion of Canada: 1812–1813*, Penguin Books Canada, Toronto: 1980, p. 254.

83. Berton, *Invasion of Canada*, p. 256.

84. Berton, *Invasion of Canada*, pp. 257–259.

85. Morison, *Oxford History*, vol. 2, p. 121.

86. Morison, *Oxford History*, vol. 2, p. 121.

87. Leckie, *Wars of America*, p. 288.

88. Lord, Walter, *The Dawn's Early Light*, Johns Hopkins University Press, Baltimore, Md.: 1972, pp. 72–73.

89. Lord, *Dawn's Early Light*, p. 176.

90. Leckie, *Wars of America*, p. 296.

91. Leckie, *Wars of America*, p. 296.

92. Leckie, *Wars of America*, p. 298.

93. Remini, Robert V., *The Life of Andrew Jackson*, Penguin Books, New York: 1988, p. 72.

94. Morison, *Oxford History*, vol. 2, p. 124.

95. Remini, *Life*, p. 84.

96. Morison, *Oxford History*, vol. 2, p. 129.

97. Morison, *Oxford History*, vol. 2, p. 125.

98. Remini, Robert V., *The Battle of New Orleans: Andrew Jackson and America's First Military Victory*, Penguin Books, New York: 1999, pp. 66–68.

99. Remini, *Battle*, p. 189.

100. Leckie, *Wars of America*, p. 310.

101. Remini, *Battle*, p. 88.

102. Remini, *Life*, p. 99.

103. Morison, *Oxford History*, vol. 2, p. 126.

104. Remini, *Life*, p. 104.

105. Remini, *Battle*, p. 152.

106. Remini, *Battle*, p. 142.

107. Remini, *Life*, p. 105.

108. Remini, *Battle*, p. 192.

109. Remini, *Battle*, p. 199.

110. Morison, *Oxford History*, vol. 2, p. 139.

111. Peterson, *Writings*, p. 1434.

112. Peterson, *Writings*, p. 1434.

113. Bailey, Thomas A., *A Diplomatic History of the American People*, Prentice-Hall, Inc., Englewood Cliffs, N.J.: 1980, p. 181.

114. Bailey, *Diplomatic History*, p. 182.

115. Bailey, *Diplomatic History*, p. 185.

116. Bennett, William J., ed., *Our Sacred Honor*, Simon & Schuster, New York: 1997, p. 413.

117. Young, Daniel, "Marquis and Me: Jefferson and Lafayette," *The Cavalier Daily*, April 13, 2005, http://www.cavalierdaily.com/article/2005/04/marquis-and-me-jefferson-and-lafayette.

118. Young, "Marquis and Me."

119. Koch, *Jefferson and Madison*, p. 260.

120. McCullough, *John Adams*, p. 603.

121. Peterson, *Writings*, p. 1517.

122. McCullough, *John Adams*, p. 646.

Chapter 5: Jackson and Democracy

1. Morison, Samuel Eliot, *The Oxford History of the American People, Volume 2: 1789–Reconstruction*, Penguin Books, New York: 1994, p. 159.

2. Remini, Robert V., *John Quincy Adams*, Henry Holt and Company, New York: 2002, p. 123.

3. Remini, Robert V., *The Life of Andrew Jackson*, Penguin Books, New York: 1988, p. 44.

4. Remini, Robert V., *The Jacksonian Era*, Harlan Davidson, Arlington Heights, Ill.: 1989, p. 13.

5. Holland, Barbara, *Gentlemen's Blood*, Bloomsbury, New York: 2003, p. 51.

6. Remini, *Era*, pp. 53–54.

7. Remini, *John Quincy Adams*, p. 127.

8. McDonald, Forrest, *The American Presidency: An Intellectual History*, University Press of Kansas, Lawrence, Kan.: 1994, p. 317.

9. Remini, *Era*, p. 20.

10. Morison, *Oxford History*, vol. 2, p. 163.

11. Remini, *Life*, p. 190.

12. Remini, *Life*, p. 191.

13. Remini, *Life*, p. 11.

14. Morison, *Oxford History*, vol. 2, p. 167.

15. Burstein, Andrew, *The Passions of Andrew Jackson*, Alfred A. Knopf, New York: 2003, p. 175.

16. Remini, Robert V., *Andrew Jackson*, Vol. 2, University Press (1950), p. 326.

17. Coit, Margaret L., *John C. Calhoun: American Portrait*, Houghton Mifflin Company, Boston, 1950, p.24.

18. Coit, *Calhoun*, p. 44.

19. Coit, *Calhoun*, p. 45.

20. Peterson, Merrill D., *The Great Triumvirate: Webster, Clay, and Calhoun*, Oxford University Press, New York: 1987, p. 18.

21. Hofstadter, Richard, *The American Political Tradition: And the Men Who Made It*, Vintage Books, New York: 1948, p. 74.

22. Hofstadter, *Political Tradition*, p. 74.

23. Hofstadter, *Political Tradition*, p. 75.

24. Hofstadter, *Political Tradition*, p. 78.

25. Remini, *Life*, p. 195.

26. "The Second Reply to Hayne," January 26–27, 1830, www.dartmouth .edu/~dwebster/speeches/hayne-speech.html.

27. Ketcham, Ralph, *James Madison: A Biography*, University Press of Virginia, Charlottesville, Va.: 1990, p. 641.

28. Freehling, William W., *Prelude to Civil War: The Nullification Controversy in South Carolina, 1816–1836*, Harper & Row, New York: 1966, p. 192.

29. Ketcham, *James Madison*, pp. 640–641.

30. Farber, Daniel, *Lincoln's Constitution*, University of Chicago Press, Chicago: 2003, p. 67.

31. Freehling, *Prelude*, p. 193.

32. Remini, *Era*, p. 66.

33. Remini, *Life*, p. 239.

34. Remini, *Life*, p. 239.

35. Remini, *Era*, p. 66.

36. Morison, *Oxford History*, vol. 2, p. 177.

37. Remini, *Era*, p. 68.

38. Freehling, *Prelude*, p. 53.

39. Freehling, *Prelude*, p. 11.

40. Freehling, *Prelude*, p. 53.

41. Remini, *Life*, p. 235.

42. Remini, *Life*, p. 236.

43. Freehling, *Prelude*, p. 157.

44. Remini, *Era*, p. 68.

45. Remini, *Era*, p. 69.

46. Morison, *Oxford History*, vol. 2, p. 254.

47. Remini, *Era*, p. 41.

48. Morison, *Oxford History*, vol. 2, p. 188.

49. Remini, *Life*, p. 219.

50. Morison, *Oxford History*, vol. 2, p. 192.

51. Remini, *Era*, p. 45.

52. Bailyn, Bernard, David Brian Davis, David Herbert Donald, John L. Thomas, Robert H. Wiebe, and Gordon S. Wood, *The Great Republic: A History of the American People*, Little, Brown and Company, Boston: 1977, p. 439.

53. Utley, Robert M., and Wilcomb E. Washburn, *Indian Wars*, Houghton Mifflin Company, Boston: 1977, p. 137.

54. Utley and Washburn, *Indian Wars*, p. 138.

55. Morison, *Oxford History*, vol. 2, p. 189.

56. Remini, *Era*, p. 51.

57. Utley and Washburn, *Indian Wars*, p. 139.

58. Morison, *Oxford History*, vol. 2, p. 192.

59. Morison, *Oxford History*, vol. 2, p. 193.

60. Remini, *Life*, p. 218.

61. Morison, *Oxford History*, vol. 2, p. 193.

62. de Tocqueville, Alexis, *Democracy in America*, trans., ed., Harvey Mansfield, University of Chicago Press, Chicago: 2000, p. 309.

63. de Tocqueville, *Democracy*, pp. 310–311.

64. Morison, *Oxford History*, vol. 2, p. 209.

65. Morison, *Oxford History*, vol. 2, p. 211.

66. Bailyn et al., *Great Republic*, p. 598.

67. Morison, *Oxford History*, vol. 2, p. 318.

68. Bailyn et al., *Great Republic*, p. 599.

69. Morison, *Oxford History*, vol. 2, p. 319.

70. Morison, *Oxford History*, vol. 2, p. 303.

71. DeVoto, Bernard, *The Year of Decision: 1846*, Houghton Mifflin Company, Boston: 1942, p. 55.

72. DeVoto, *Year of Decision*, p. 65.

73. Morison, *Oxford History*, vol. 2, p. 308.

74. Leckie, Robert, *The Wars of America*, Harper & Row, New York: 1981, p. 325.

75. Bailey, Thomas A., *A Diplomatic History of the American People*, Prentice-Hall, Inc., Englewood Cliffs, N.J.: 1980, p. 228.

76. Bailey, *Diplomatic History*, p. 229.

77. Bailey, *Diplomatic History*, p. 235.

78. Leckie, *Wars of America*, p. 325.

79. Bailey, *Diplomatic History*, p. 254.

80. Leckie, *Wars of America*, p. 326.

81. Morison, *Oxford History*, vol. 2, p. 323.

82. Morison, *Oxford History*, vol. 2, p. 321.

83. Leckie, *Wars of America*, p. 326.

84. Leckie, *Wars of America*, p. 327.

85. Bailey, *Diplomatic History*, p. 259.

86. Morison, *Oxford History*, vol. 2, p. 325.

87. Morison, *Oxford History*, vol. 2, p. 325.

88. Morison, *Oxford History*, vol. 2, p. 325.

89. Cain, William E., ed., *William Lloyd Garrison and the Fight Against Slavery*, Bedford Books of St. Martin's Press, Boston: 1995, p. 115.

90. Morison, *Oxford History*, vol. 2, p. 327.

91. Leckie, *Wars of America*, p. 374.

92. Leckie, *Wars of America*, p. 375.

93. "America's Wars: U.S. Casualties and Veterans," InfoPlease, http://www.infoplease.com/ipa/A0004615.html.

94. DeVoto, *Year of Decision*, pp. 472–476.

95. Morison, *Oxford History*, vol. 2, p. 325.

96. Morison, *Oxford History*, vol. 2, p. 330.

97. Remini, *John Quincy Adams*, p. 155.

98. Cain, *William Lloyd Garrison*, p. 121.

Chapter 6: The Rising Storm

1. Graebner, Norman A., *Empire on the Pacific: A Study in Continental Expansion*, Regina Books, Claremont, Calif.: 1983, pp. 224–225.

2. Morison, Samuel Eliot, *The Oxford History of the American People: Volume 2: 1789–Reconstruction*, Penguin Books, New York: 1994, p. 334.

3. Brands, H. W., *The Age of Gold: The California Gold Rush and the New American Dream*, Doubleday, New York: 2002, p. 63.

4. Brands, *Age of Gold*, p. 48.

5. Brands, *Age of Gold*, p. 46.

6. Peterson, Merrill D., *The Great Triumvirate: Webster, Clay, and Calhoun*, Oxford University Press, New York: 1987, p. 452.

7. McPherson, James M., *The Illustrated Battle Cry of Freedom: The Civil War Era*, Oxford University Press, New York: 2003, p. 60.

8. McPherson, *Battle Cry*, p. 53.

9. Peterson, *Great Triumvirate*, p. 456.

10. Peterson, *Great Triumvirate*, p. 455.

11. Peterson, *Great Triumvirate*, p. 456.

12. Bartlett, John, *Bartlett's Familiar Quotations*, 10th ed. (1919), s.v. "5393: Henry Clay," http://www.bartleby.com/100/348.4.html.

13. Daniel Webster, "The Seventh of March Speech," Dartmouth, www .dartmouth.edu/~dwebster/speeches/seventh-march.html.

14. Peterson, *Great Triumvirate*, p. 463.

15. Morison, *Oxford History*, vol. 2, pp. 338–339.

16. Peterson, *Great Triumvirate*, p. 467.

17. Peterson, *Great Triumvirate*, p. 496.

18. Vance, James E. Jr., *The North American Railroad: Its Origin, Evolution, and Geography*, Johns Hopkins University Press, Baltimore, Md.: 1995, p. 32.

19. Vance, *Railroad*, p. 95.

20. Vance, *Railroad*, p. 107.

21. Morison, *Oxford History*, vol. 2, p. 342.

22. Carnes, Mark C., ed., *A History of American Life*, revised and abridged, Simon & Schuster, New York: 1996, p. 530.

23. Carnes, *American Life*, p. 532.

24. Carnes, *American Life*, pp. 530–532.

25. McFeely, William S., *Frederick Douglass*, Simon & Schuster, New York: 1991, p. 93.

26. Stampp, Kenneth M., *America in 1857: A Nation on the Brink*, Oxford University Press, New York: 1990, p. 215.

27. Faust, Patricia L., ed., *Historical Times Illustrated Encyclopedia of the Civil War*, Harper & Row, New York: 1986, p. 609.

28. Carnes, *American Life*, p. 537.

29. Carnes, *American Life*, p. 537.

30. Morison, *Oxford History*, vol. 2, p. 217.

31. Morison, *Oxford History*, vol. 2, p. 340.

32. Morison, *Oxford History*, vol. 2, p. 340.

33. Carnes, *American Life*, p. 536.

34. Morison, *Oxford History*, vol. 2, p. 272.

35. Carnes, *American Life*, p. 646.

36. Morison, *Oxford History*, vol. 2, p. 359.

37. Morison, *Oxford History*, vol. 2, p. 341.

38. "Harriet Beecher Stowe 1811–1896," AmericanCivilWar.com, https://americancivilwar.com/women/hbs.html.

39. Andrews, William L., *The Oxford Frederick Douglass Reader*, Oxford University Press, New York: 1996, p. 113.

40. Andrews, *Douglass Reader*, p. 129.

41. Frederickson, George M., *William Lloyd Garrison: Great Lives Observed*, Prentice-Hall, Inc., Englewood Cliffs, N.J.: 1968, p. 92.

42. Andrews, *Douglass Reader*, p. 93.

43. Stampp, *America in 1857*, p. 54.

44. Basler, Roy P., ed., *The Collected Works of Abraham Lincoln*, vol. 2, Rutgers University Press, New Brunswick, N.J.: 1953, p. 323.

45. McPherson, *Battle Cry*, p. 117.

46. Oates, Stephen B., *The Approaching Fury: Voices of the Storm, 1820–1861*, HarperCollins, New York: 1997, p. 300.

47. McPherson, *Battle Cry*, p. 124.

48. Stampp, *America in 1857*, p. 92.

49. Hunt, John Gabriel, ed., *The Inaugural Addresses of the Presidents*, Gramercy Books, New York: 1995, p. 177.

50. Stampp, *America in 1857*, p. 93.

51. Stampp, *America in 1857*, p. 95.

52. Jaffa, Harry V., *Crisis of the House Divided*, University of Chicago Press, Chicago: 1982, p. 310.

53. Morison, *Oxford History*, vol. 2, p. 363.

54. Stampp, *America in 1857*, p. 105.

55. McPherson, *Battle Cry*, p. 84.

56. Stampp, *America in 1857*, p. 104.

57. Basler, *Works*, vol. 2, p. 466.

58. Jaffa, *Crisis*, p. 311.

59. McPherson, *Battle Cry*, p. 63.

60. Donald, David Herbert, *Lincoln*, Simon & Schuster, New York: 1995, p. 204.

61. Morison, *Oxford History*, vol. 2, p. 365.

62. Oates, *Approaching Fury*, p. 262.

63. Jaffa, *Crisis*, p. 337.

64. Oates, *Approaching Fury*, p. 256.

65. Jaffa, *Crisis*, pp. 332–333.

66. Donald, *Lincoln*, p. 229.

67. Oates, Stephen B., *To Purge This Land with Blood: A Biography of John Brown*, University of Massachusetts Press, Amherst, Mass.: 1984, p. 282.

68. Freeman, Douglas Southall, *R. E. Lee: A Biography*, Charles Scribner's Sons, New York: 1936, p. 395.

69. Freeman, *R. E. Lee*, p. 399.

70. McPherson, *Battle Cry*, p. 162.

71. Oates, *Purge*, p. 337.

72. Oates, *Purge*, p. 318.

73. Oates, *Purge*, p. 318.

74. Oates, *Purge*, p. 345.

75. Oates, *Purge*, p. 351.

76. Oates, *Purge*, pp. 351–352.

77. Donald, *Lincoln*, p. 239.

78. Basler, *Works*, vol. 3, p. 550.

79. Catton, Bruce, *The Coming Fury*, Doubleday, Garden City, N.Y.: 1961, p. 61.

80. Catton, *Fury*, p. 61.

81. Catton, *Fury*, p. 161.

82. Donald, *Lincoln*, p. 277.

83. Catton, *Fury*, p. 224.

84. Catton, *Fury*, p. 264.

85. Catton, *Fury*, p. 264.

86. Hunt, *The Inaugural Addresses of the Presidents*, pp. 187–197.

Chapter 7: Freedom's Fiery Trial

1. "1969. Anne M. Buford," *Respectfully Quoted: A Dictionary of Quotations* (1989), http://www.bartleby.com/73/1969.html.

2. Catton, Bruce, *The Coming Fury,* Doubleday, Garden City, N.Y.: 1961, p. 138.

3. Catton, *Fury,* p. 137.

4. Catton, *Fury,* p. 106.

5. Basler, Roy P., ed., *The Collected Works of Abraham Lincoln*, Volume 4, Rutgers University Press, New Brunswick, N.J.: 1953, p. 154.

6. Donald, David Herbert, *Lincoln*, Simon & Schuster, New York: 1995, p. 137.

7. Davis, William C., *Look Away! A History of the Confederate States of America*, The Free Press, New York: 2002, pp. 97–98.

8. Davis, *Look Away!*, p. 66.

9. Davis, *Look Away!*, p. 66.

10. Jaffa, Harry V., *A New Birth of Freedom: Abraham Lincoln and the Coming of the Civil War*, Rowman & Littlefield, Lanham, Md.: 2000, p. 222.

11. "The Papers of Jefferson Davis," Jefferson Davis' First Inaugural Address, Alabama Capitol, Montgomery, February 18, 1861, https://jeffersondavis .rice.edu/archives/documents/jefferson-davis-first-inaugural-address.

12. Freeman, Douglas Southall, *R. E. Lee: A Biography*, Charles Scribner's Sons, New York: 1934, p. 433.

13. Freeman, *R. E. Lee*, p. 435.

14. Freeman, *R. E. Lee*, p. 436.

15. Freeman, *R. E. Lee*, p. 437.

16. Catton, *Fury,* p. 253.

17. Catton, *Fury,* p. 252.

18. Catton, *Fury,* p. 278.

19. Catton, *Fury,* p. 286.

20. Catton, *Fury,* p. 297.

21. Catton, *Fury,* p. 302.

22. Catton, *Fury,* p. 311.

23. McPherson, James M., *The Illustrated Battle Cry of Freedom: The Civil War Era*, Oxford University Press, New York: 2003, p. 215.

24. Farber, Daniel, *Lincoln's Constitution*, University of Chicago Press, Chicago: 2003, p. 16.

25. Blight, David W., *Frederick Douglass' Civil War,* Louisiana State University Press, Baton Rouge, La.: 1989, p. 64.

26. McDonald, Forrest, *The American Presidency: An Intellectual History*, University Press of Kansas, Lawrence, Kan.: 1994, pp. 400–401.

27. Basler, Roy P., ed., *The Collected Works of Abraham Lincoln*, vol. 4, Rutgers University Press, New Brunswick, N.J.: 1953, pp. 438–439.

28. McPherson, *Battle Cry*, p. 244.

29. Morison, Samuel Eliot, *The Oxford History of the American People, Volume 2: 1789–Reconstruction*, Penguin Books, New York: 1972, p. 394.

30. Donald, David Herbert, *We Are Lincoln Men*, Simon & Schuster, New York: 2003, p. 197.

31. Borritt, Gabor S., ed., *Lincoln's Generals*, Oxford University Press, New York: 1994, p. 22.

32. Borritt, *Lincoln's Generals*, p. 25.

33. Morison, *Oxford History*, vol. 2, p. 414.

34. McPherson, *Battle Cry*, p. 358.

35. Morison, *Oxford History*, vol. 2, p. 425.

36. Borritt, *Lincoln's Generals*, p. 15.

37. Morison, *Oxford History*, vol. 2, p. 414.

38. Williams, T. Harry, *Lincoln and His Generals*, Vintage Books, New York: 1952, p. 114.

39. Borritt, *Lincoln's Generals*, p. 46.

40. Morison, *Oxford History*, vol. 2, p. 430.

41. Tucker, Spencer C., *A Short History of the Civil War at Sea*, SR Books, Wilmington, Del.: 2002, p. 40.

42. Tucker, *Civil War at Sea*, p. 40.

43. McPherson, *Battle Cry*, p. 311.

44. Morison, *Oxford History*, vol. 2, p. 421.

45. McPherson, *Battle Cry*, p. 313.

46. McPherson, *Battle Cry*, p. 353.

47. Blight, *Douglass' Civil War*, p. 154.

48. Donald, *Lincoln*, p. 367.

49. Blight, *Douglass' Civil War*, p. 139.

50. Blight, *Douglass' Civil War*, p. 125.

51. Blight, *Douglass' Civil War*, p. 145.

52. Blight, *Douglass' Civil War*, p. 145.

53. Donald, *Lincoln*, p. 368.

54. Donald, *Lincoln*, p. 369.

55. Sears, Stephen W., *Landscape Turned Red: The Battle of Antietam*, Ticknor & Fields, New York: 1983, p. 225.

56. Moe, Richard, *The Last Full Measure: The Life and Death of the First Minnesota Volunteers*, Henry Holt and Company, New York: 1993, p. 187.

57. Sears, *Landscape*, p. 316.

58. McPherson, *Battle Cry*, p. 466.

59. Sears, *Landscape*, pp. 294, 296.

60. Sears, *Landscape*, p. 296.

61. Williams, *Lincoln and His Generals*, p. 176.

62. Williams, *Lincoln and His Generals*, p. 177.

63. Waugh, John C., *The Class of 1846*, Warner Books, New York: 1994, p. 365. The reference in Lincoln's statement is to Exodus 6:5.

64. Morison, *Oxford History*, vol. 2, p. 435.

65. Charnwood, Lord, *Lincoln: A Biography*, Madison Books, Lanham, Md.: 1996, p. 236.

66. Morison, *Oxford History*, vol. 2, p. 438.

67. Guelzo, Allen C., *Lincoln's Emancipation Proclamation: The End of Slavery in America*, Simon & Schuster, New York: 2004, p. 354.

68. Guelzo, *Emancipation*, p. 354.

69. Guelzo, *Emancipation*, p. 181.

70. Guelzo, *Emancipation*, p. 182.

71. Klingaman, William K., *Abraham Lincoln and the Road to Emancipation: 1861–1865*, Viking, New York: 2001, p. 227.

72. Guelzo, *Emancipation*, p. 182.

73. Guelzo, *Emancipation*, p. 183.

74. Klingaman, *Road to Emancipation*, p. 228.

75. Guelzo, *Emancipation*, p. 2.

76. "Emancipation Proclamation," National Archives, https://www.archives .gov/exhibits/featured-documents/emancipation-proclamation/transcript .html.

77. McPherson, James M., ed., *We Cannot Escape History: Lincoln and the Last Best Hope of Earth*, University of Illinois Press, Chicago: 1995, p. 9.

78. Blight, *Douglass' Civil War*, p. 96.

79. Cornish, Dudley Taylor, *The Sable Arm*, University Press of Kansas, Lawrence, Kan.: 1987, p. 132.

80. Morison, *Oxford History*, vol. 2, p. 419.

81. McPherson, *Escape*, p. 507.

Chapter 8: A New Birth of Freedom

1. Borritt, Gabor S., ed., *Lincoln's Generals*, Oxford University Press, New York: 1994, p. 85.

2. McPherson, James M., *Hallowed Ground: A Walk at Gettysburg*, Crown Publishers, New York: 2003, p. 80.

3. McPherson, *Hallowed*, p. 81.

4. McPherson, *Hallowed*, pp. 81–82.

5. McPherson, *Hallowed*, p. 85.

6. Sears, Stephen W., *Gettysburg*, Houghton Mifflin Company, Boston: 2003, p. 294.

7. McPherson, James M., *The Illustrated Battle Cry of Freedom: The Civil War Era*, Oxford University Press, New York: 2003, p. 222.

8. McPherson, *Battle Cry*, p. 222.

9. McPherson, James M., *For Cause and Comrades: Why Men Fought in the Civil War*, Oxford University Press, New York: 1997, p. 21.

10. Borritt, *Lincoln's Generals*, p. 89.

11. Bunting, Josiah, III, *Ulysses S. Grant*, Henry Holt and Company, New York: 2004, p. 39.

12. Borritt, *Lincoln's Generals*, p. 98.

13. Basler, Roy, ed., *The Collected Works of Abraham Lincoln*, vol. 6, Rutgers University Press, New Brunswick, N.J.: 1953, p. 328.

14. Basler, *Works*, vol. 6, p. 329.

15. Sears, *Gettysburg*, p. 495.

16. Foote, Shelby, *Stars in Their Courses: The Gettysburg Campaign*, The Modern Library, New York: 1994, pp. 258–259.

17. Foote, *Stars*, p. 259.

18. Carhart, Tom, *Lost Triumph: Lee's Real Plan at Gettysburg—And Why It Failed*, Penguin Books, New York: 2005, p. xiii.

19. McPherson, *Cause and Comrades*, pp. 526–527.

20. Morison, Samuel Eliot, *Oxford History of the American People, Volume 2: 1789–Reconstruction*, Penguin Books, New York: 1972, p. 451.

21. Wills, Garry, *Lincoln at Gettysburg*, Simon & Schuster, New York: 1992, p. 21.

22. Wills, *Lincoln at Gettysburg*, p. 25.

23. Basler, *Works*, vol. 7, p. 25.

24. Anastaplo, George, *Abraham Lincoln: A Constitutional Biography*, Rowman & Littlefield, Lanham, Md.: 1999, p. 226.

25. Goodwin, Doris Kearns, *Team of Rivals: The Political Genius of Abraham Lincoln*, Simon & Schuster, New York: 2005.

26. Bunting, *Ulysses S. Grant*, p. 51.

27. Bunting, *Ulysses S. Grant*, p. 53.

28. McFeely, William S., *Grant: A Biography*, W. W. Norton & Company, New York: 1981, p. 153.

29. Bunting, *Ulysses S. Grant*, p. 58.

30. Bunting, *Ulysses S. Grant*, p. 58.

31. Bunting, *Ulysses S. Grant*, pp. 58–59.

32. McFeely, *Grant*, p. 152.

33. Turner, Justin G., and Linda Levitt Turner, *Mary Todd Lincoln: Her Life and Letters*, Alfred A. Knopf, New York: 1972, p. 155.

34. Turner, *Mary Todd Lincoln*, p. 156.

35. Goodwin, *Rivals*, p. 549.

36. Goodwin, *Rivals*, p. 550.

37. Basler, *Works*, vol. 6, pp. 406–410.

38. Waugh, John C., *Re-Electing Lincoln*, Crown Publishing, New York: 1997, p. 295.

39. "Major General William T. Sherman," American Civil War (website), http://www.mycivilwar.com/leaders/sherman_william.htm.

40. Borritt, *Lincoln's Generals*, p. 152.

41. Waugh, *Re-Electing*, p. 297.

42. Basler, *Works*, vol. 7, p. 282.

43. McPherson, *Cause and Comrades*, p. 734.

44. Nevins, Allan, *The War for the Union, Volume 3: The Organized War*, Charles Scribner's Sons, New York: 1971, p. 293.

45. McPherson, *Battle Cry*, p. 264.

46. "The Meigs Family," Arlington National Cemetery, http://www.arlington cemetery.net/meigs.htm.

47. Ward, Geoffrey C., *The Civil War: An Illustrated History*, Alfred A. Knopf, New York: 1990, p. 316.

48. Donald, David Herbert, *Lincoln*, Simon & Schuster, New York: 1995, p. 567.

49. Grant, U. S., *Personal Memoirs of U. S. Grant*, vol. 2, Charles L. Webster & Company, New York: 1885, p. 485.

50. Grant, *Memoirs*, pp. 489–490.

51. Winik, Jay, *April 1865: The Month That Saved America*, HarperCollins, New York: 2001, p. 197.

52. Winik, *April 1865*, pp. 197–198.

53. Morison, *Oxford History*, vol. 2, p. 499.

54. Peterson, Merrill D., *Lincoln in American Memory*, Oxford University Press, New York: 1994, p. 4.

55. Peterson, *Lincoln*, p. 4.

56. Peterson, *Lincoln*, p. 7.

57. Crocker, H. W., III, *Robert E. Lee on Leadership*, Prima Publishing, Roseville, Calif.: 2000, p. 164.

58. Flood, Charles Bracelyn, *Grant and Sherman: The Friendship That Won the Civil War*, Farrar, Stauss and Giroux, New York: 2005, pp. 332–333.

59. Morison, *Oxford History*, vol. 2, p. 286.

Chapter 9: To Bind Up the Nation's Wounds

1. Bailey, Thomas A., *A Diplomatic History of the American People*, Prentice-Hall, Inc., Englewood Cliffs, N.J.: 1980, p. 353.

2. Catton, Bruce, *This Hallowed Ground: The Story of the Union Side of the Civil War*, Castle Books, Edison, N.J.: 2002, p. 398.

3. Catton, *Hallowed*, p. 399.

4. Catton, *Hallowed*, p. 400.

5. "Oliver Wendell Holmes Jr.: 1884 Memorial Day," http://www.people.virginia.edu/~mmd5f/memorial.htm.

6. "1884 Memorial Day."

7. "The Martyr" was originally published in *Battle Pieces and Aspects of the War*, Herman Melville, Harper & Brothers, New York: 1866.

8. Bunting, Josiah, III, *Ulysses S. Grant*, Henry Holt and Company, New York: 2004, p. 71.

9. Bunting, *Ulysses S. Grant*, p. 71, emphasis added.

10. Bunting, *Ulysses S. Grant*, p. 71.

11. Bunting, *Ulysses S. Grant*, p. 72.

12. Trefousse, Hans L., *Andrew Johnson: A Biography*, W. W. Norton & Company, New York: 1989, p. 198.

13. Trefousse, *Andrew Johnson*, p. 198.

14. Smith, Jean Edward, *Grant*, Simon & Schuster, New York: 2001, p. 417.

15. Smith, *Grant*, p. 418.

16. Smith, *Grant*, p. 418.

17. Smith, *Grant*, p. 418.

18. Smith, *Grant*, p. 422.

19. Smith, *Grant*, p. 422.

20. Donald, David Herbert, Jean H. Baker, and Michael F. Holt, *The Civil War and Reconstruction*, W. W. Norton & Company, New York: 2001, p. 479.

21. Morison, Samuel Eliot, *Oxford History of the American People, Volume Two: 1789–Reconstruction*, Penguin Books, New York: 1972, p. 515.

22. Trefousse, *Andrew Johnson*, p. 243.

23. Morison, *Oxford History*, vol. 2, p. 514.

24. Foner, Eric, and Olivia Mahoney, *America's Reconstruction: People and Politics After the Civil War*, HarperCollins, New York: 1995, p. 82.

25. Smith, *Grant*, p. 424.

26. Smith, *Grant*, p. 425.

27. Foner and Mahoney, *Reconstruction*, p. 82.

28. Trefousse, *Andrew Johnson*, p. 233.

29. Morison, *Oxford History*, vol. 2, p. 510.

30. Donald, Baker, and Holt, *Civil War*, p. 481.

31. Morison, *Oxford History*, vol. 2, p. 511.

32. Smith, *Grant*, p. 426.

33. Bunting, *Ulysses S. Grant*, p. 78.

34. Smith, *Grant*, p. 427.

35. Bunting, *Ulysses S. Grant*, p. 78.

36. Smith, *Grant*, p. 426.

37. Morison, *Oxford History*, vol. 2, p. 512.

38. Morison, *Oxford History*, vol. 2, p. 513.

39. Trefousse, *Andrew Johnson*, p. 341.

40. Morison, *Oxford History*, vol. 2, p. 516.

41. Smith, *Grant*, p. 444.

42. Foner and Mahoney, *Reconstruction*, p. 91.

43. Rehnquist, William H., *Grand Inquests: The Historic Impeachments of Justice Samuel Chase and President Andrew Johnson*, William Morrow and Company, New York: 1992, pp. 240–241.

44. Morison, *Oxford History*, vol. 2, p. 519.

45. Donald, Baker, and Holt, *Civil War*, p. 490.

46. Donald, Baker, and Holt, *Civil War*, p. 490.

47. Morison, *Oxford History*, vol. 2, p. 517.

48. Bunting, *Ulysses S. Grant*, p. 20.

49. Smith, *Grant*, p. 489.

50. Donald, Baker, and Holt, *Civil War*, p. 479.

51. Donald, Baker, and Holt, *Civil War*, p. 500.

52. Gates, Henry Louis Jr., ed., *Douglass*, Library of America, New York: 1994, p. 885.

53. Bunting, *Ulysses S. Grant*, p. 141.

54. Bunting, *Ulysses S. Grant*, p. 141.

55. Bunting, *Ulysses S. Grant*, p. 141.

56. Bunting, *Ulysses S. Grant*, p. 142.

57. McFeely, William S., *Frederick Douglass*, Simon & Schuster, New York: 1991, p. 266.

58. McFeely, *Frederick Douglass*, p. 267.

59. McFeely, *Frederick Douglass*, p. 269.

60. Bailyn, Bernard, David Brian Davis, David Herbert Donald, John L. Thomas, Robert H. Wiebe, and Gordon S. Wood, *The Great Republic: A History of the American People*, Little, Brown and Company, Boston: 1977, p. 769.

61. *Time Almanac 2004*, Pearson Education, Needham, Mass.: 2003, pp. 175, 179.

62. Grosvenor, Edwin S., and Morgan Wesson, *Alexander Graham Bell*, Harry N. Abrams, New York: 1997, p. 69.

63. Grosvenor and Wesson, *Alexander Graham Bell*, p. 73.

64. Rehnquist, William H., *Centennial Crisis: The Disputed Election of 1876*, Vintage, New York; 2005, p. 8.

65. Morison, *Oxford History*, vol. 2, p. 59.

66. Trefousse, Hans L., *Rutherford B. Hayes*, Times Books, New York: 2002, p. 79.

67. Rehnquist, *Crisis*, p. 101.

68. Bunting, *Ulysses S. Grant*, p. 116.

Chapter 10: An Age More Golden Than Gilded?

1. Gordon, John Steele, *An Empire of Wealth: The Epic History of American Economic Power*, HarperCollins, New York: 2004, p. 211.

2. Gordon, *Empire*, p. 235.

3. Gordon, *Empire*, p. 248.

4. Gordon, *Empire*, p. 244.

5. Trefousse, Hans L., *Rutherford B. Hayes*, Times Books, New York: 2002, p. 89.

6. Morison, Samuel Eliot, *Oxford History of the American People, Volume 3:*

1869 Through the Death of John F. Kennedy, 1963, Penguin Books, New York: 1972, p. 40.

7. Trefousse, *Rutherford B. Hayes*, p. 96.

8. Trefousse, *Rutherford B. Hayes*, p. 113.

9. Trefousse, *Rutherford B. Hayes*, p. 125.

10. Grosvenor, Edwin, and Morgan Wesson, *Alexander Graham Bell*, Harry N. Abrams, New York: 1997, p. 105.

11. Grosvenor and Wesson, *Alexander Graham Bell*, p. 107.

12. Morison, *Oxford History of the American People*, vol. 3, p. 40.

13. Jeffers, H. Paul, *An Honest President*, HarperCollins, New York: 2000, p. 192.

14. Freidel, Frank, and Hugh Sidey, "Chester A. Arthur," The White House (website), https://www.whitehouse.gov/about-the-white-house/presidents/chester-a-arthur/.

15. Jeffers, *Honest President*, p. 117.

16. Bailyn, Bernard, David Brian Davis, David Herbert Donald, John L. Thomas, Robert H. Wiebe, and Gordon S. Wood, *The Great Republic: A History of the American People*, Little, Brown and Company, Boston: 1977, p. 850.

17. Morison, *Oxford History*, vol. 3, p. 69.

18. Morison, *Oxford History*, vol. 3, p. 105.

19. Morison, *Oxford History*, vol. 3, p. 69.

20. Israel, Paul, *Edison: A Life of Invention*, John Wiley & Sons, Hoboken, N.J.: 1998, p. 174.

21. Morison, *Oxford History*, vol. 3, p. 72.

22. Morison, *Oxford History*, vol. 3, p. 46.

23. Morison, *Oxford History*, vol. 3, p. 45.

24. Jeffers, *Honest President*, p. 186.

25. Schlesinger, Arthur, M., Jr., ed., *The Almanac of American History*, G. P. Putnam's Sons, New York: 1983, pp. 357–358.

26. Smith, Jean Edward, *Grant*, Simon & Schuster, New York: 2001, p. 626.

27. Smith, *Grant*, p. 609.

28. Smith, *Grant*, p. 627.

29. Smith, *Grant*, p. 627.

30. Levine, Benjamin, and Isabelle F. Story, "Statue of Liberty: Joseph Pulitzer," Liberty State Park, http://www.libertystatepark.org/statueof liberty/sol3.shtml.

31. Jeffers, *Honest President*, p. 187.

32. *Time Almanac 2004*, Pearson Education, Needham, Mass.: 2003, pp. 175, 179.

33. Smith, *Grant*, p. 516.

34. Donald, David Herbert, *Lincoln*, Simon & Schuster, New York: 1995, pp. 393–395.

35. Morison, *Oxford History*, vol. 3, p. 60.

36. Utley, Robert M., and Wilcomb E. Washburn, *Indian Wars*, Houghton Mifflin Company, Boston: 1977, p. 227.

37. Utley and Washburn, *Indian Wars*, p. 227.

38. Morison, *Oxford History*, vol. 3, p. 61

39. Morison, *Oxford History*, vol. 3, p. 61

40. Utley and Washburn, *Indian Wars*, p. 294.

41. Morison, *Oxford History*, vol. 3, p. 63.

42. Utley and Washburn, *Indian Wars*, pp. 299–300.

43. Jeffers, *Honest President*, p. 207.

44. Brands, H. W., *TR: The Last Romantic*, Basic Books, New York: 1997, p. 184.

45. Elshstain, Jean Bethke, *Jane Addams and the Dream of American Democracy*, Basic Books, New York: 2002, p. 95.

46. Elshtain, *Jane Addams*, p. 83

47. Elshtain, *Jane Addams*, p. 97.

48. Elshtain, *Jane Addams*, p. 94.

49. Jeffers, *Honest President*, p. 220.

50. Jeffers, *Honest President*, p. 222.

51. Bailyn et al., *Great Republic*, p. 790.

52. Schlesinger, *Almanac*, p. 370.

53. Schlesinger, *Almanac*, p. 370.

54. Morison, *Oxford History*, vol. 3, p. 48.

55. Bailyn et al., *Great Republic*, p. 878.

56. Bailyn et al., *Great Republic*, p. 786.

57. "John Deere," https://www.deere.com/en/our-company/about-john-deere/.

58. Bailyn et al., *Great Republic*, p. 778.

59. McFeely, William S., *Frederick Douglass*, Simon & Schuster, New York: 1991, p. 300.

60. Bailyn et al., *Great Republic*, p. 796.

61. Harvey, Rowland Hill, *Samuel Gompers: Champion of the Toiling Masses*, Stanford University Press, New York: 1935, p. 101.

62. Harvey, *Samuel Gompers*, p. 101.

63. Bailyn et al., *Great Republic*, p. 881.

64. Krass, Peter, *Carnegie*, John Wiley & Sons, Hoboken, N.J.: 2002, p. 285.

65. Morison, *Oxford History*, vol. 3, p. 85.

66. Krass, *Carnegie*, p. 294.

67. Krass, *Carnegie*, p. 272.

68. Carnegie, Andrew, "Wealth," *North American Review*, 148, no. 391, June 1889: 653, 657–62.

69. Krass, *Carnegie*, p. 295.

70. Krass, *Carnegie*, p. 277.

71. Krass, *Carnegie*, p. 268.

72. Krass, *Carnegie*, p. 295.

73. Krass, *Carnegie*, p. 295.

74. Krass, *Carnegie*, p. 288.

75. Krass, *Carnegie*, p. 288.

76. Jeffers, *Honest President*, p. 248.

77. Jeffers, *Honest President*, pp. 227–228.

78. Krass, *Carnegie*, p. 296.

79. Morison, *Oxford History*, vol. 3, p. 111.

80. Meacham, Jon, *Franklin and Winston: An Intimate Portrait of an Epic Friendship*, Random House, New York: 2003, p. 150.

81. Jeffers, *Honest President*, p. 272.

82. Brands, H. W., *The Reckless Decade: America in the 1890s*, St. Martin's Press, New York: 1995, p. 147.

83. Brands, *Reckless*, p. 147.

84. Morison, *Oxford History*, vol. 3, p. 112.

85. Morison, *Oxford History*, vol. 3, p. 113.

86. Graff, Henry F., *Grover Cleveland*, Times Books, New York: 2002, p. 119.

87. Harvey, *Samuel Gompers*, p. 78.

88. Bailyn et al. *Great Republic*, p. 883.

89. McFeely, *Frederick Douglass*, p. 377.

90. McFeely, *Frederick Douglass*, p. 380.

91. McFeely, *Frederick Douglass*, p. 380.

92. McFeely, *Frederick Douglass*, p. 383.

93. Morison, *Oxford History*, vol. 3, p. 116.

94. O'Toole, Patricia, *When Trumpets Call: Theodore Roosevelt After the White House*, Simon & Schuster, New York: 2005, p. 15.

95. Morison, *Oxford History*, vol. 3, p. 116.

96. Brands, *Reckless*, p. 299.

97. Gutmann, Peter, "Antonin Dvorak," Classical Notes, http://www.classical notes.net/classics/newworld.html.

98. Gutmann, "Dvorak."

99. Gutmann, "Dvorak."

100. Gutmann, "Dvorak."

Chapter 11: The American Dynamo—Shadowed by War

1. Morris, Edmund, *The Rise of Theodore Roosevelt*, Ballantine Books, New York: 1979, p. 493.

2. Brands, H. W., *TR: The Last Romantic*, Basic Books, New York: 1997, p. 280.

3. Zimmermann, Warren, *First Great Triumph*, Farrar, Strauss and Giroux, New York: 2002, p. 229.

4. Roosevelt, Theodore, with additional text by Richard Bak, *The Rough Riders*, Taylor Publishing, Dallas, Tex.: 1997, p. 113.

5. Bailey, Thomas A., *A Diplomatic History of the American People*, Prentice-Hall, Inc., Englewood Cliffs, N.J.: 1980, p. 454.

6. Bailey, *Diplomatic History*, p. 456.

7. Bailey, *Diplomatic History*, p. 461.

8. Morris, *Rise*, p. 610.

9. Morris, *Rise*, p. 608.

10. Morris, *Rise*, p. 608.

11. Morris, *Rise*, p. 607.

12. Traxel, David, *1898: The Birth of the American Century*, Alfred A. Knopf, New York: 1998, pp. 143–144.

13. Morris, *Rise*, p. 647.

14. Traxel, *Birth*, p. 135.

15. Traxel, *Birth*, p. 137.

16. Traxel, *Birth*, p. 179.

17. Traxel, *Birth*, p. 181.

18. Roosevelt, *Rough Riders*, p. 121.

19. Morris, *Rise*, p. 634.

20. Morris, *Rise*, p. 646.

21. Traxel, *Birth*, p. 193.

22. Gilbert, Martin, *Churchill: A Life*, Henry Holt and Company, New York: 1991, p. 80.

23. Morison, Samuel Eliot, *The Oxford History of the American People, Volume 3: 1869 Through the Death of John F. Kennedy, 1963*, Penguin Books, New York: 1972, p. 118.

24. Zimmermann, *Triumph*, p. 250.

25. Morison, *Oxford History*, vol. 3, pp. 123–124.

26. Traxel, *Birth*, p. 215.

27. Morris, *Rise*, pp. 673–674.

28. Morris, *Rise*, p. 673.

29. Brands, *Last Romantic*, p. 363.

30. Morris, *Rise*, p. 685.

31. Brands, *Last Romantic*, p. 368.

32. Morison, *Oxford History*, vol. 3, p. 127.

33. Beisner, Robert L., *Twelve Against Empire: The Anti-Imperialists, 1898–1900*, McGraw-Hill Book Company, New York: 1968, p. 125.

34. Morris, *Rise*, p. 741.

35. Morison, Samuel Eliot, Henry Steele Commager, and William E. Leuchtenburg, *A Concise History of the American Republic*, Oxford University Press, New York: 1977, p. 514.

36. "Theodore Roosevelt Inaugural" pamphlet, National Historic Site, New York, National Park Service, U.S. Department of the Interior.

37. Morris, Edmund, *Theodore Rex*, Random House, New York: 2001, p. 54.

38. Bailey, *Diplomatic History*, p. 488.

39. Brands, *Last Romantic*, p. 455.

40. Brands, *Last Romantic*, p. 457.

41. Harbaugh, William Henry, *Power and Responsibility: The Life and Times of Theodore Roosevelt*, Farrar, Straus and Giroux, New York: 1961, p. 169.

42. Harbaugh, *Power*, p. 169.

43. Morris, *Theodore Rex*, p. 174.

44. Harbaugh, *Power*, p. 158.

45. Harbaugh, *Power*, p. 160.

46. Harbaugh, *Power*, p. 307.

47. Morison, *Concise History*, p. 136.

48. Harbaugh, *Power*, p. 164.

49. Morison, Commager, and Leuchtenburg, *Concise History*, p. 518.

50. Morison, Commager, and Leuchtenburg, *Concise History*, p. 518.

51. Harbaugh, *Power*, p. 215.

52. Brands, *Last Romantic*, p. 509.

53. Morris, *Rex*, p. 114.

54. Morison, Commager, and Leuchtenburg, *Concise History*, p. 520.

55. Carlson, Allan, *The "American Way": Family, and Community in the Shaping of the American Identity*, ISI Books, Wilmington, Del.: 2003, pp. 1–2.

56. Bailey, *Diplomatic History*, p. 499.

57. Morris, *Rex*, p. 104.

58. Morris, *Rex*, p. 102.

59. Bailey, *Diplomatic History*, p. 493.

60. Bailey, *Diplomatic History*, p. 495.

61. Bailey, *Diplomatic History*, p. 497.

62. Bailey, *Diplomatic History*, p. 497.

63. Brands, *Last Romantic*, p. 469.

64. Morison, Commager, and Leuchtenburg, *Concise History*, p. 498.

65. Brands, *Last Romantic*, p. 634.

66. Morison, Commager, and Leuchtenburg, *Concise History*, p. 522.

67. Morison, *Concise History*, p. 155.

68. Morison, *Concise History*, p. 157.

69. Bailyn, Bernard, David Brian Davis, David Herbert Donald, John L. Thomas, Robert H. Wiebe, and Gordon S. Wood, *The Great Republic: A History of the American People*, Little, Brown and Company, Boston: 1977, p. 840.

70. Gilbert, Martin, *A History of the Twentieth Century, Volume 1: 1900–1933*, William Morrow and Company, New York: 1997, p. 243.

71. Bailyn et al., *Great Republic*, p. 943.

72. Brands, *Last Romantic*, p. 670.

73. "Estimated Wealth of 12 Men Lost in Titanic Disaster is $191 Million," *Truro Daily News*, St. John, New Brunswick, 27 April 1912, p. 3.

74. Lynch, Don, and Ken Marschall, *Titanic: An Illustrated History*, Madison Press Limited, New York: 1992, p. 19.

75. Lynch and Marschall, *Titanic*, p. 192.

76. Gilbert, *History of the Twentieth Century*, vol. 1, p. 265.

77. Lynch and Marschall, *Titanic*, pp. 184–185.

78. Morison, *Concise History*, p. 162.

79. Gould, Lewis L., *Grand Old Party: A History of the Republicans*, Random House, New York: 2003, p. 181.

80. Brands, *Last Romantic*, p. 679.

81. Brands, *Last Romantic*, p. 707.

82. Brands, *Last Romantic*, p. 708.

83. Gould, *Grand Old Party*, p. 188.

84. Brands, *Last Romantic*, p. 712.

85. Morison, *Concise History*, p. 164.

86. Bailyn et al., *Great Republic*, p. 963.

87. Brands, *Last Romantic*, p. 719.

88. Bailyn et al., *Great Republic*, p. 924.

89. Brands, *Last Romantic*, p. 717.

90. Brands, *Last Romantic*, p. 721.

91. Morison, *Concise History*, p. 166.

92. Bailyn et al., *Great Republic*, p. 942.

93. Morison, *Concise History*, p. 168.

94. Heckscher, August, *Woodrow Wilson: A Biography*, Charles Scribner's Sons, New York: 1991, p. 306.

95. Morison, *Concise History*, p. 169.

96. Bailyn et al, *Great Republic*, p. 974.

97. Morison, *Concise History*, p. 169.

98. Heckscher, *Woodrow Wilson*, p. 396.

99. Heckscher, *Woodrow Wilson*, p. 290.

100. Morison, *Concise History*, p. 173.

101. Heckscher, *Woodrow Wilson*, p. 292.

102. Heckscher, *Woodrow Wilson*, p. 309.

103. Peterson, Merrill D., *Lincoln in American Memory*, Oxford University Press, New York: 1994, p. 170.

104. Bailyn et al., *Great Republic*, p. 958.

105. Morison, *Concise History*, p. 167.

106. Bailyn et al., *Great Republic*, p. 946.

107. Morison, *Concise History*, p. 167.

108. Fromkin, David, *Europe's Last Summer: Who Started the Great War in 1914?*, Alfred A. Knopf, New York: 2004, pp. 134–135.

109. Fromkin, *Europe's Last Summer*, pp. 135–136.

110. Fromkin, *Europe's Last Summer*, p. 157.

Chapter 12: America and the Great War

1. Pollard, Albert Frederick, "The Breach of the Peace," in *A Short History of the Great War*, http://www.ibiblio.org/HTMLTexts/Albert_Frederick _Pollard/A_Short_History_Of_The_Great_War/chapter01.html.

2. Bailey, Thomas Andrew, *A Diplomatic History of the American People*, Prentice-Hall, Inc., Englewood Cliffs, N.J.: 1980, p. 501.

3. Gilbert, Martin, *A History of the Twentieth Century, Volume One: 1900–1933*, William Morrow and Company, New York: 1997, p. 25.

4. Martel, Gordon, *The Origins of the First World War*, Longman, New York: 1996, p. 85.

5. Remak, Joachim, *The Origins of World War I: 1871–1914*, Harcourt Brace College Publishers, San Diego, Calif.: 1995, p. 138.

6. Gilbert, *History of the Twentieth Century*, vol. 1, p. 19.

7. Gilbert, *History of the Twentieth Century*, vol. 1, p. 26.

8. Gilbert, *History of the Twentieth Century*, vol. 1, p. 23.

9. Gilbert, *History of the Twentieth Century*, vol. 1, p. 25.

10. Keegan, John, *An Illustrated History of the First World War*, Hutchinson, London: 2001, p. 65.

11. Keegan, *Illustrated History*, p. 71.

12. Keegan, *Illustrated History*, p. 74.

13. Keegan, *Illustrated History*, p. 103.

14. Keegan, *Illustrated History*, pp. 100–101.

15. Keegan, *Illustrated History*, p. 119.

16. Leckie, Robert, *The Wars of America*, Harper & Row, New York: 1981, p. 599.

17. Massie, Robert K., *Castles of Steel: Britain, Germany and the Winning of the Great War at Sea*, Random House, New York: 2003, p. 530.

18. Massie, *Castles*, pp. 532–534.

19. Morison, Samuel Eliot, *The Oxford History of the American People, Volume 3, 1869 Through the Death of John F. Kennedy, 1963*, Penguin Books, New York: 1972, p. 179.

20. Massie, *Castles*, p. 535.

21. Black, Conrad, *Franklin D. Roosevelt: Champion of Freedom*, Public Affairs, New York: 2003, p. 73.

22. Bailey, *Diplomatic History*, p. 579.

23. Keegan, *Illustrated History*, p. 176.

24. Gilbert, *History of the Twentieth Century*, vol. 1, p. 457.

25. Tuchman, Barbara W., *The Zimmermann Telegram*, The Macmillan Company, New York: 1966, p. 172.

26. Black, *Champion of Freedom*, p. 77.

27. Morison, *Oxford History*, vol. 3, p. 183.

28. Black, *Champion of Freedom*, p. 77.

29. Bailey, *Diplomatic History*, p. 588.

30. Tuchman, *Zimmermann Telegram*, p. 4.

31. Tuchman, *Zimmermann Telegram*, p. 23.

32. Keegan, *Illustrated History*, p. 351.

33. Tuchman, *Zimmermann Telegram*, p. 40.

34. Morison, *Oxford History*, vol. 3, p. 217.

35. Renehan, Edward J., *The Lion's Pride: Theodore Roosevelt and His Family in Peace and War*, Oxford University Press, New York: 1998, p. 125.

36. Tuchman, *Zimmermann Telegram*, pp. 181, 185.

37. Tuchman, *Zimmermann Telegram*, p. 14.

38. Tuchman, *Zimmermann Telegram*, p. 183.

39. Tuchman, *Zimmermann Telegram*, pp. 184–186.

40. Tuchman, *Zimmermann Telegram*, p. 187.

41. Heckscher, August, *Woodrow Wilson: A Biography*, Charles Scribner's Sons, New York: 1991, p. 440.

42. Heckscher, *Woodrow Wilson*, p. 441.

43. O'Toole, Patricia, *When Trumpets Call: Theodore Roosevelt After the White House*, Simon & Schuster, New York: 2005, p. 310.

44. Black, *Champion of Freedom*, p. 82.

45. Millard, Candice, *River of Doubt: Theodore Roosevelt's Darkest Journey*, Random House, New York: 2005, p. 480.

46. Millard, *River of Doubt*, p. 481.

47. Millard, *River of Doubt*, p. 1.

48. Brands, H. W., *TR: The Last Romantic*, Basic Books, New York: 1997, p. 743.

49. Brands, H. W., *Woodrow Wilson*, Times Books, New York: 2003, p. 6.

50. Brands, *Woodrow Wilson*, p. 7.

51. Brands, *Last Romantic*, p. 784.

52. Brands, *Last Romantic*, p. 783.

53. Brands, *Last Romantic*, p. 783.

54. O'Toole, *Trumpets Call*, p. 311.

55. Gilbert, *History of the Twentieth Century*, vol. 1, p. 461.

56. Gilbert, *History of the Twentieth Century*, vol. 1, p. 455.

57. Bailey, *Diplomatic History*, p. 561.

58. Leckie, *Wars of America*, p. 625.

59. Morison, *Oxford History*, vol. 3, p. 199.

60. Leckie, *Wars of America*, p. 635.

61. Keegan, *Illustrated History*, p. 375.

62. Renehan, *Lion's Pride*, p. 160.

63. Leckie, *Wars of America*, p. 632.

64. "Churchill and the Great Republic," Library of Congress, http://www.loc.gov/exhibits/churchill/wc-affairs.html.

65. Heckscher, *Woodrow Wilson*, p. 466.

66. Morison, *Oxford History*, vol. 3, p. 205.

67. Leckie, *Wars of America*, p. 641.

68. Leckie, *Wars of America*, p. 641.

69. Morison, *Oxford History*, vol. 3, p. 206.

70. Heckscher, *Woodrow Wilson*, pp. 471–472.

71. Bailyn, Bernard, David Brian Davis, David Herbert Donald, John L. Thomas, Robert H. Wiebe, and Gordon S. Wood, *The Great Republic: A History of the American People*, Little & Brown: 1977, p. 1039.

72. Heckscher, *Woodrow Wilson*, pp. 470–471.

73. Morison, *Oxford History*, vol. 3, p. 204.

74. Leckie, *Wars of America*, p. 653.

75. Renehan, *Lion's Pride*, p. 197.

76. Renehan, *Lion's Pride*, p. 200.

77. Heckscher, *Woodrow Wilson*, p. 482.

78. Leckie, *Wars of America*, p. 654.

79. Bailey, *Diplomatic History*, p. 599.

80. Gilbert, *History of the Twentieth Century*, vol. 1, p. 520.

81. Keegan, *Illustrated History*, p. 395.

82. Gilbert, Martin, *The First World War: A Complete History*, Henry Holt and Company, New York: 1994, p. 501.

83. Gilbert, *First World War*, p. 503.

84. Gilbert, *First World War*, p. 447.

85. Gilbert, *First World War*, p. 494.

86. Gilbert, *History of the Twentieth Century*, vol. 1, p. 534.

87. Brands, *Woodrow Wilson*, p. 103.

88. Gilbert, *First World War*, p. 507.

89. Barry, John M., *The Great Influenza*, Viking, New York: 2004, flyleaf.

90. Barry, *Great Influenza*, p. 387.

91. Renehan, *Lion's Pride*, p. 218.

92. Brands, *Last Romantic*, p. 811.

93. O'Toole, *When Trumpets Cal*, p. 404.

94. Heckscher, *Woodrow Wilson*, p. 512.

95. Gilbert, Martin, *Churchill: A Life*, Henry Holt and Company, New York: 1991, p. 403.

96. Gilbert, *Churchill: A Life*, p. 403.

97. Brands, *Woodrow Wilson*, p. 104.

98. Gould, Lewis L., *Grand Old Party: A History of the Republicans*, Random House, New York: 2003, p. 217.

99. Gould, *Grand Old Party*, pp. 217–218.

100. Heckscher, *Woodrow Wilson*, pp. 545–546.

101. Will, George, "Can We Make Iraq Democratic?" *City Journal*, Winter 2004.

102. Kissinger, Henry, *Diplomacy*, Simon & Schuster, New York: 1994, p. 237.

103. Lentin, Antony, *Lloyd George and the Lost Peace: From Versailles to Hitler, 1919-1940*, St. Martin's Press, New York: 2001, p. 48.

104. Brands, *Last Romantic*, p. 804.

105. Miller, Nathan, *Theodore Roosevelt: A Life*, William Morrow and Company, New York: 1972, p. 563.

106. Brands, *Last Romantic*, p. 805.

107. O'Toole, *Trumpets Call*, p. 403.

108. Gilbert, *First World War*, p. 517.

109. Macmillan, Margaret, *Paris 1919: Six Months That Changed the World*, Random House, New York: 2001, p. 476.

110. Mee, Charles L., Jr., *The End of Order: Versailles 1919*, E. P. Dutton, New York: 1948, pp. 215–216.

111. Mee, *End of Order*, p. 216.

112. Macmillan, *Paris 1919*, p. 469.

113. Churchill, Winston S., *The World Crisis,* Volume IV, Charles Scribner's Sons, New York: 1927, pp. 275–276.

114. Bailey, *Diplomatic History*, p. 609.

115. Macmillan, *Paris 1919*, p. 467.

116. Black, *Champion of Freedom*, p. 114.

117. Knock, Thomas J., *To End All Wars: Woodrow Wilson and the Quest for a New World Order*, Oxford University Press, New York: 1992, p. 251.

118. Ambrosius, Lloyd E., *Woodrow Wilson and the American Diplomatic Tradition: The Treaty Fight in Perspective*, Cambridge University Press, Cambridge, UK: 1987, p. 48.

119. Ambrosius, *Diplomatic Tradition*, 109; Stone, Ralph, *The Irreconcilables*, University Press of Kentucky, Lexington, Ky.: 1970, p. 180.

120. Macmillan, *Paris 1919*, p. 492.

121. Kissinger, *Diplomacy*, p. 234.

122. Ambrosius, *Diplomatic Tradition*, p. 83.

123. Ambrosius, *Diplomatic Tradition*, p. 181.

124. Heckscher, *Woodrow Wilson*, p. 598.

125. Heckscher, *Woodrow Wilson*, pp. 609–610.

126. Brands, *Woodrow Wilson*, p. 125.

127. Hoover, Herbert, *The Ordeal of Woodrow Wilson*, McGraw-Hill Book Company, New York: 1958, p. 276.

128. Witcover, Jules, *Party of the People: A History of the Democrats*, Random House, New York: 2003, p. 330.

129. Brands, *Woodrow Wilson*, pp. 126–127.

130. Stone, *Irreconcilables*, p. 162.

131. Mee, *The End of Order*, p. 263.

132. Heckscher, *Woodrow Wilson*, p. 632.

133. Bailey, Thomas A., *Woodrow Wilson and the Great Betrayal*, The Macmillan Company, New York: 1945, p. 344.

134. Mee, *The End of Order*, p. 263.

Chapter 13: The Boom and the Bust

1. "Commentary," Losing the Peace, July 1992, by Joshua Muravchik, https://www.commentarymagazine.com/articles/losing-the-peace/.

2. http://www.archives.gov/digital_classroom/lessons/woman_suffrage/woman_suffrage.html.

3. Kramer, Hilton, "Who Reads Mencken Now?" *New Criterion*, January 2003, https://www.newcriterion.com/issues/2003/1/who-reads-mencken-now.

4. Black, Conrad, *Franklin D. Roosevelt: Champion of Freedom*, Public Affairs, New York: 2003, p. 137.

5. Black, *Champion of Freedom*, p. 138–139.

6. Alter, Jonathan, *The Defining Moment: FDR's Hundred Days and the Triumph of Hope*, Simon & Schuster, New York: 2006, p. 83.

7. Black, *Champion of Freedom*, p. 141.

8. Black, *Champion of Freedom*, p. 141.

9. Black, *Champion of Freedom*, p. 161.

10. Black, *Champion of Freedom*, p. 146.

11. Black, *Champion of Freedom*, pp. 170–171.

12. Black, *Champion of Freedom*, p. 143.

13. Marks, Carole, and Diana Edkins, *The Power of Pride: Stylemakers and Rulebreakers of the Harlem Renaissance*, Crown Publishers, Inc., New York: 1999, p. 83.

14. Marks and Edkins, *Power of Pride*, p. 100.

15. Marks and Edkins, *Power of Pride*, p. 63.

16. Gates, Henry Louis, Jr., and Cornel West, *The African-American Century: How Black Americans Have Shaped Our Country*, The Free Press, New York: 2000, pp. 131–132.

17. Gates and West, *African-American Century*, p. 100.

18. Perret, Geoffrey, *Eisenhower*, Random House, New York: 1999, pp. 244–245.

19. Perret, *Eisenhower*, p. 244.

20. Morison, Samuel Eliot, *The Oxford History of the American People, Volume 3: 1869 Through the Death of John F. Kennedy, 1963*, Penguin Books, New York: 1994, p. 263.

21. Gilbert, Martin, *A History of the Twentieth Century, Volume 1: 1900–1933*, William Morrow and Company, New York: 1997, p. 625.

22. Morison, *Oxford History*, vol. 3, p. 263.

23. Morison, *Oxford History*, vol. 3, p. 262.

24. Black, *Champion of Freedom*, p. 162.

25. Morison, *Oxford History*, vol. 3, p. 262.

26. Morison, *Oxford History*, vol. 3, p. 277.

27. Morison, *Oxford History*, vol. 3, p. 261.

28. Witcover, Jules, *Party of the People: A History of the Democrats*, Random House, New York: 2003, p. 338.

29. Noonan, Peggy, "Why the Speech Will Live in Infamy," *Time* magazine, 31 August 1998.

30. Perret, *Eisenhower*, p. 179.

31. Smith, Richard Norton, "The Price of the Presidency," *Yankee Magazine*, January 1996.

32. Perret, *Eisenhower*, p. 193.

33. Perret, *Eisenhower*, p. 186.

34. Wallace, Max, *The American Axis: Henry Ford, Charles Lindbergh, and the Rise of the Third Reich*, St. Martin's Press, New York: 2003, p. 95.

35. Wallace, *American Axis*, p. 95.

36. Wallace, *American Axis*, p. 96.

37. Perret, *Eisenhower*, p. 256.

38. Perret, *Eisenhower*, p. 260.

39. Wallace, *American Axis*, pp. 244–245.

40. Perret, *Eisenhower*, p. 258.

41. Wallace, *American Axis*, p. 97.

42. Linder, Douglas O., "The Leopold and Loeb Trial: A Brief Account," 1997, https://papers.ssrn.com/sol3/papers.cfm?abstract_id=1024295.

43. Linder, "Leopold and Loeb Trial."

44. Linder, "Leopold and Loeb Trial."

45. Witcover, *Party of the People*, p. 337.

46. Smith, "The Price of the Presidency."

47. Smith, "Price of the Presidency."

48. Perret, *Eisenhower*, p. 190.

49. Larson, Edward J., *Summer for the Gods: The Scopes Trial and America's Continuing Debate Over Science and Religion*, Basic Books, New York: 1997, p. 97.

50. Larson, *Summer for the Gods*, p. 181.

51. Larson, *Summer for the Gods*, p. 181.

52. Mencken, H. L., "Sahara of the Bozart," *New York Evening Mail*, 13 November 1917.

53. Larson, *Summer for the Gods*, p. 182.

54. Larson, *Summer for the Gods*, p. 190.

55. Larson, *Summer for the Gods*, pp. 199–200.

56. Larson, *Summer for the Gods*, p. 241.

57. Perret, *Eisenhower*, p. 280.

58. Perret, *Eisenhower*, pp. 281–282.

59. Perret, *Eisenhower*, p. 282.

60. Berg, A. Scott, *Lindbergh*, G. P. Putnam's Sons, New York: 1998, p. 114.

61. Berg, *Lindbergh*, p. 115.

62. Berg, *Lindbergh*, p. 121.

63. Berg, *Lindbergh*, p. 122.

64. Morison, *Oxford History*, vol. 3, p. 232.

65. Berg, *Lindbergh*, p. 118.

66. Berg, *Lindbergh*, p. 172.

67. Berg, *Lindbergh*, p. 173.

68. "Gertrude Stein Quotes," BrainyQuote, http://www.brainyquote.com /quotes/authors/g/gertrude_stein.html.

69. Morison, *Oxford History*, vol. 3, pp. 263–264.

70. Bailey, Thomas A., *A Diplomatic History of the American People*, Prentice-Hall, Inc., Englewood Cliffs, N.J.: 1980, p. 650.

71. Morison, *Oxford History*, vol. 3, p. 263.

72. Bailey, *Diplomatic History*, p. 650.

73. Gilbert, *History of the Twentieth Century*, vol. 1, p. 702.

74. Perret, *Eisenhower*, p. 298.

75. Perret, *Eisenhower*, p. 297.

76. Gould, Lewis L., *Grand Old Party: A History of the Republicans*, Random House, New York: 2003, p. 246.

77. Gould, *Grand Old Party*, p. 245.

78. White, William Allen, *A Puritan in Babylon: The Story of Calvin Coolidge*, The Macmillan Company, New York: 1938, p. 437.

79. Lambert, Craig, "Bobby Jones' Brief Life of a Gold Legend: 1902–1971," March-April 2002, Harvard magazine, https://harvardmagazine.com /2002/03/bobby-jones.html.

80. Gould, *Grand Old Party*, p. 248.

81. Perret, *Eisenhower*, p. 312.

82. Perret, *Eisenhower*, p. 310.

83. Perret, *Eisenhower*, p. 313.

84. Gilbert, *History of the Twentieth Century*, vol. 1, p. 770.

85. Gilbert, *History of the Twentieth Century*, vol. 1, p. 771.

86. Perret, *Eisenhower*, p. 404.

87. Morison, *Oxford History*, vol. 3, p. 285.

88. Gilbert, *History of the Twentieth Century*, vol. 1, p. 768.

89. Gilbert, *History of the Twentieth Century*, vol. 1, p. 768.

90. Gilbert, *History of the Twentieth Century*, vol. 1, p. 768.

91. Watkins, T. H., *The Hungry Years: A Narrative History of the Great Depression in America*, Henry Holt and Company, New York: 1999.

92. Barone, Michael, *Our Country: The Shaping of America from Roosevelt to Reagan*, The Free Press, New York: 1990, p. 43.

93. Morison, *Oxford History*, vol. 3, p. 291.

94. Leuchtenburg, William E., *Herbert Hoover*, Times Books, New York: 2009, p. 140.

95. Gilbert, *History of the Twentieth Century*, vol. 1, p. 753.

96. Morison, *Oxford History*, vol. 3, p. 275.

97. Gould, *Grand Old Party*, p. 256.

98. Ketcham, Richard M., *The Borrowed Years: 1938–1941, America on the Way to War*, Random House, New York: 1989, p. 19.

99. Perret, *Eisenhower*, p. 480.

100. Perret, *Eisenhower*, p. 480.

101. Perret, *Eisenhower*, p. 481.

102. Witcover, *Party of the People*, p. 355.

103. Alter, *Defining Moment*, p. 82.

104. Fausold, Martin L., ed., *The Hoover Presidency: A Reappraisal*, State University of New York Press, New York: 1974, pp. 90–91.

105. Jenkins, Roy, *Franklin Delano Roosevelt*, Times Books, New York: 2003, p. 61.

106. Alter, *Defining Moment*, p. 119.

107. Gould, *Grand Old Party*, p. 261.

108. Morison, *Oxford History*, vol. 3, p. 296.

109. Black, *Champion of Freedom*, p. 270.

110. Witcover, *Party of the People*, p. 361.

111. Alter, *Defining Moment*, p. 218.

112. Alter, *Defining Moment*, p. 218.

Chapter 14: FDR and the New Deal

1. Witcover, Jules, *Party of the People: A History of the Democrats*, Random House, New York: 2003, p. 362.

2. Morison, Samuel Eliot, *The Oxford History of the American People, Volume 3: 1869 Through the Death of John F. Kennedy, 1963*, Penguin Books, New York: 1994, p. 303.

3. Allen, Frederick Lewis, *Since Yesterday: The Nineteen Thirties in America*, Harper & Brothers, New York: 1940, pp. 139–140.

4. Johns, Bud, *The Ombibulous Mr. Mencken*, Synergistic Press, Santa Fe, N.M.: 1968, p. 36.

5. Kobler, John, *Ardent Spirits*, Putnam, New York: 1973, p. 340.

6. Morison, *Oxford History*, vol. 3, p. 306.

7. Klehr, Harvey, John Earl Haynes, and Fridrikh Igorevich Firsov, *The Secret World of American Communism*, Yale University Press, New Haven, Conn.: 1995, p. 8.

8. Hamby, Alonzo, *For the Survival of Democracy: Franklin Roosevelt and the World Crisis of the 1930s*, The Free Press, New York: 2004, pp. 240–241.

9. Hamby, *Survival*, pp. 240–241.

10. Barone, Michael, *Our Country: The Shaping of America from Roosevelt to Reagan*, The Free Press, New York: 1990, p. 67.

11. Churchill, Winston S., *The Second World War, Volume 1: The Gathering Storm*, Houghton Mifflin Company, Boston: 1948, p. 192.

12. Churchill, *Second World War*, vol. 1, p. 194.

13. Hart-Davis, Duff, *Hitler's Games: The 1936 Olympics*, Harper & Row, New York: 1986, p. 68.

14. Hart-Davis, *Hitler's Games*, p. 75.

15. Levy, Carol, "The Olympic Pause," *The Jewish Magazine*, October 2000, http://www.jewishmag.com/36MAG/olympic/olympic.htm.

16. Hart-Davis, *Hitler's Games*, p. 79.

17. Levy, "Olympic Pause."

18. Levy, "Olympic Pause."

19. Levy, "Olympic Pause."

20. Hart-Davis, *Hitler's Games*, p. 188.

21. Author interview with Guy Walters, author, *Berlin Games: How the Nazis Stole the Olympic Dream*, William Morrow and Company, New York: 2006.

22. Hart-Davis, *Hitler's Games*, p. 177.

23. Burgan, Michael, "Great Moments in the Olympics," *World Almanac Library*, 2002, p. 13.

24. Wallace, Max, *The American Axis: Henry Ford, Charles Lindbergh, and the Rise of the Third Reich*, St. Martin's Press, New York: 2003, pp. 114–115.

25. Hart-Davis, *Hitler's Games*, p. 128.

26. Hart-Davis, *Hitler's Games*, p. 128.

27. Gilbert, Martin, *A History of the Twentieth Century, Volume 2: 1933–1951*, William Morrow and Company, New York: 1998, p. 15.

28. Black, Conrad, *Franklin D. Roosevelt: Champion of Freedom*, Public Affairs, New York: 2003, p. 381.

29. Witcover, *Party of the People*, p. 375.

30. Witcover, *Party of the People*, p. 374.

31. Getlin, Josh, "The Past Master: Historian Doris Kearns Goodwin believes an awareness of then helps us understand now. So she examines the lives of Presidents, mostly recently FDR—and his wife, Eleanor," *Los Angeles Times*, 19 September 1994, https://www.latimes.com/archives/la-xpm-1994 -09-19-ls-40577-story.html.

32. Gould, Lewis L., *Grand Old Party: A History of the Republicans*, Random House, New York: 2003, p. 272.

33. Gould, *Grand Old Party*, p. 272.

34. Barone, *Our Country*, p. 96.

35. Barone, *Our Country*, p. 101.

36. Gould, *Grand Old Party*, p. 273.

37. Barone, *Our Country*, p. 113.

38. Black, *Champion of Freedom*, p. 411.

39. Barone, *Our Country*, p. 113.

40. Witcover, *Party of the People*, p. 378.

41. Mooney, Michael Macdonald, *Hindenburg*, Dodd, Mead and Company, New York: 1972, p. 234.

42. Mooney, *Hindenburg*, p. 239.

43. Rich, Doris L., *Amelia Earhart: A Biography*, Smithsonian Institution, Washington D.C.: 1989, pp. 161, 212, 229.

44. Rich, *Amelia Earhart*, p. 162.

45. Rich, *Amelia Earhart*, p. 259.

46. Rich, *Amelia Earhart*, pp. 270–271.

47. Beschloss, Michael R., *Kennedy and Roosevelt: The Uneasy Alliance*, W. W. Norton & Company, New York: 1980, p. 157.

48. Beschloss, *Kennedy and Roosevelt*, p. 153.

49. Beschloss, *Kennedy and Roosevelt*, p. 154.

50. Beschloss, *Kennedy and Roosevelt*, p. 113.

51. Gilbert, *History of the Twentieth Century*, vol. 2, p. 177.

52. Gilbert, *History of the Twentieth Century*, vol. 2, p. 199.

53. Gilbert, *History of the Twentieth Century*, vol. 2, p. 201.

54. Gilbert, Martin, *Churchill: A Life*, Henry Holt and Company, New York: 1991, p. 601.

55. Beschloss, *Kennedy and Roosevelt*, pp. 178–179.

56. Beschloss, *Kennedy and Roosevelt*, pp. 171, 176.

57. Beschloss, *Kennedy and Roosevelt*, p. 177.

58. Beschloss, *Kennedy and Roosevelt*, p. 174.

59. Beschloss, *Kennedy and Roosevelt*, p. 180.

60. Beschloss, *Kennedy and Roosevelt*, p. 178.

61. "Writer Comes 'Face to Face' with History," *Daily Republic*, November 1, 2008, https://www.mitchellrepublic.com/news/1515590-writer-comes -face-face-history.

62. "Building Big: Empire State Building," PBS, http://www.pbs.org/wgbh /buildingbig/wonder/structure/empire_state.html.

63. http://goldengatebridge.org/research/SafetyFirst.php.

64. Evans, Richard J., *The Third Reich in Power*, Penguin Press, New York: 2005, p. 302 (illus).

65. LaPointe, Joe, "The Championship Fight That Went Beyond Boxing," *New York Times*, June 19, 1988, https://www.nytimes.com/1988/06/19/sports /the-championship-fight-that-went-beyond-boxing.html.

Chapter 15: America's Rendezvous with Destiny

1. Lily Rothman, "Here's the History of *Time*'s Person of the Year Franchise," *New York Times*, December 11, 2018, http://time.com/5047813/person-of -the-year-history/.

2. Gilbert, Martin, *A History of the Twentieth Century, Volume 2: 1933–1951*, William Morrow and Company, New York: 1998, p. 205.

3. Beschloss, Michael R., *Kennedy and Roosevelt: The Uneasy Alliance*, W. W. Norton & Company, New York: 1980, p. 189.

4. Public Papers of the Presidents of the United States: F.D. Roosevelt, 1939, Volume 8, p. 300.

5. Ketchum, Richard M., *The Borrowed Years: 1938–1941, America on the Way to War*, Random House, New York: 1989, p. 161.

6. Black, Conrad, *Franklin D. Roosevelt: Champion of Freedom*, Public Affairs, New York: 2003, p. 522.

7. Black, *Champion of Freedom*, p. 523.

8. Ketchum, *Borrowed Years*, pp. 156–157.

9. Black, *Champion of Freedom*, p. 523.

10. Diane Bernard, "The Night Thousands of Nazis Packed Madison Square Garden for a Rally—and Violence Erupted," Washington Post, December 9, 2018, https://www.washingtonpost.com/history/2018/12/09/night-thousands-nazis-packed-madison-square-garden-rally-violence-erupted/?utm_term=5bc13985e399.

11. Berg, A. Scott, *Lindbergh*, G.P. Putnam's Sons, New York: 1998, p. 370.

12. Berg, *Lindbergh*, p. 372.

13. Ketchum, *Borrowed Years*, pp. 280–283.

14. Ketchum, *Borrowed Years*, p. 283.

15. Ketchum, *Borrowed Years*, p. 283.

16. Ketchum, *Borrowed Years*, p. 284.

17. Ketchum, *Borrowed Years*, p. 285.

18. Meacham, Jon, *Franklin and Winston: An Intimate Portrait of an Epic Friendship*, Random House, New York: 2003, p. 42.

19. Gilbert, Martin, *Churchill: A Life*, Henry Holt and Company, New York: 1991, p. 624.

20. Weigel, George, *Witness to Hope: The Biography of Pope John Paul II*, Cliff Street Books, New York: 1999, pp. 50–51.

21. Courtois, Stéphane, Nicolas Werth, and Jean-Louis Panné, *The Black Book of Communism: Crimes, Terror, Repression*, Harvard University Press, Cambridge, Mass.: 1999, p. 6.

22. Kagan, Donald, *On the Origins of War*, Doubleday, New York: 1995, p. 414.

23. Krauthammer, Charles, "Short-Term Gain, Long-Term Pain," *Washington Post*, 11 August 2006, A19.

24. Worthy, Larry, "Atlanta Premiere of *Gone with the Wind*," About North Georgia, http://ngeorgia.com/feature/gwtwpremiere.html.

25. Gilbert, *Churchill: A Life*, p. 645.

26. Gilbert, *Churchill: A Life*, p. 646.

27. Meacham, *Franklin and Winston*, p. 51.

28. Black, *Champion of Freedom*, p. 554.

29. Jackson, Julian, *The Fall of France: The Nazi Invasion of 1940*, Oxford University Press, New York: 2003, p. 181

30. Jackson, *The Fall of France*, p. 210.

31. International Churchill Society, Their Finest Hour, June 18, 1940, House

of Commons, https://winstonchurchill.org/resources/speeches/1940-the
-finest-hour/their-finest-hour/.

32. Harrisson, Tom, *Living Through the Blitz*, Schocken Books, New York: 1976, p. 101.

33. Overy, Richard, *The Battle of Britain: The Myth and the Reality*, W. W. Norton & Company, New York: 2000, p. 162.

34. Murrow, Edward R., *This Is London*, Simon & Schuster, New York: 1941, p. 135.

35. Ketchum, *Borrowed Years*, pp. 342–343.

36. Barone, Michael, *Our Country: The Shaping of America from Roosevelt to Reagan*, The Free Press, New York: 1990, p. 140.

37. Barone, *Our Country*, p. 146.

38. Barone, *Our Country*, p. 143.

39. Peters, Charles, *Five Days in Philadelphia*, Public Affairs, New York: 2005, p. 182.

40. Barone, *Our Country*, p. 147.

41. Meacham, *Franklin and Winston*, p. 95.

42. Wallace, Max, *The American Axis: Henry Ford, Charles Lindbergh, and the Rise of the Third Reich*, St. Martin's Press, New York: 2003, p. 249.

43. Wallace, *American Axis*, p. 275.

44. Wallace, *American Axis*, p. 277.

45. Wallace, *American Axis*, p. 257.

46. Wallace, *American Axis*, p. 260.

47. Wallace, *American Axis*, p. 277.

48. Wallace, *American Axis*, p. 285.

49. Jenkins, Roy, *Churchill: A Biography*, Farrar, Straus and Giroux, New York: 2001, p. 659.

50. Gilbert, Martin, *Churchill and America*, The Free Press, New York: 2005, p. 701.

51. Gilbert, *Churchill and America*, p. 702.

52. Gilbert, *A History of the Twentieth Century*, vol. 2, p. 380.

53. Gilbert, *Churchill and America*, p. 705.

54. Meacham, *Franklin and Winston*, p. 107.

55. Meacham, *Franklin and Winston*, p. 105.

56. Meacham, *Franklin and Winston*, p. 108.

57. Meacham, *Franklin and Winston*, p. 108.

Chapter 16: Leading the Grand Alliance

1. Ferguson, Niall, *Empire: The Rise and Demise of the British World Order and the Lessons for Global Power*, Basic Books, New York: 2002, p. 332.

2. Barone, Michael, *Our Country: The Shaping of America from Roosevelt to Reagan*, The Free Press, New York: 1990, p. 147.

3. McDougall, Walter A., *Promised Land, Crusader State: The American Encounter with the World Since 1776*, Houghton Mifflin, Boston: 1997, p. 151.

4. Beschloss, Michael, *Kennedy and Roosevelt: The Uneasy Alliance*, W. W. Norton & Company, New York: 1980, p. 238.

5. Barone, *Our Country*, 147.

6. *The World at War*, film documentary produced by Thames Television, Ltd., London: 1974, vol. 2, Barbarossa.

7. Wilson, Theodore A., *The First Summit: Roosevelt and Churchill at Placentia Bay, 1941*, University Press of Kansas, Lawrence, Kan.: 1991, p. 91.

8. Acheson, Dean, *Present at the Creation: My Years in the State Department*, W. W. Norton, New York: 1987, Books-on-Tape, Cassette 1, Side 1.

9. Morison, Samuel Eliot, *The Oxford History of the American People, Volume 3: 1869 Through the Death of President Kennedy, 1963*, Penguin Books, New York: 1965, p. 357.

10. Lord, Walter, *Day of Infamy*, Henry Holt and Company, New York: 2001, p. 212.

11. Lord, *Day of Infamy*, p. 212.

12. Lord, *Day of Infamy*, p. 158.

13. Lord, *Day of Infamy*, p. 217.

14. Lord, *Day of Infamy*, p. 218.

15. Black, Conrad, *Franklin Delano Roosevelt: Champion of Freedom*, Public Affairs, New York: 2003, p. 692.

16. Black, *Franklin Delano Roosevelt*, p. 692.

17. Leckie, Robert, *The Wars of America*, Harper & Row, New York: 1981, p. 735.

18. van der Vat, Dan, *Pearl Harbor: Day of Infamy—An Illustrated History*, Basic Books, New York: 2001, p. 158.

19. "Statistics of World War II," The History Place, http://www.historyplace.com/worldwar2/timeline/statistics.htm.

20. Gilbert, Martin, *The Second World War: A Complete History*, Henry Holt and Company, New York: 1989, p. 275.

21. Gilbert, *Second World War*, p. 274.

22. Gilbert, *Second World War*, pp. 274–275.

23. Roberts, Andrew, *Churchill: Walking with Destiny*, Viking, New York: 2018, p. 693.

24. Gilbert, Martin, *Churchill: A Life*, Henry Holt and Company, New York: 1991, p. 714.

25. Bercuson, David, and Holger Herwig, *One Christmas in Washington: Churchill and Roosevelt Forge the Grand Alliance*, Overlook Press, New York: 2005, p. 129.

26. Bercuson and Herwig, *One Christmas*, p. 130.

27. Bercuson and Herwig, *One Christmas*, p. 143.

28. Leckie, *Wars of America*, p. 741.

29. Dear, I. C. B, gen. ed., and M. R. D. Foot, consulting ed., *The Oxford Companion to World War II*, Oxford University Press, New York: 1995, p. 115.

30. Dear and Foot, *Oxford Companion*, p. 115.

31. Dear and Foot, *Oxford Companion*, p. 309.

32. Dear and Foot, *Oxford Companion*, pp. 632–633.

33. Remembering Daniel K. Inouye, Remarks by Senator McConnell, Congressional Record Volume 158, Number 163 (Tuesday, December 18, 2012), pages S8115-S8116.

34. Williams, Nathan, "What Happened to the 8 Germans Tried by a Military Court in World War II?" History News Network, July 8, 2002, http://hnn .us/articles/431.html.

35. Berg, Scott A., *Lindbergh*, G. P. Putnam's Sons, New York: 1998, p. 437.

36. Gates, Henry Louis, Jr., and Cornel West, *The African-American Century: How Black Americans Have Shaped Our Country*, The Free Press, New York: 2000, p. 53.

37. Quoted in Sowell, Thomas, "Enemies Within," *Jewish World Review*, 9 January 2002, http://www.jewishworldreview.com/cols/sowell010902.asp.

38. Barone, *Our Country*, pp. 159–160.

39. Gates and West, *African-American Century*, p. 183.

40. Gilbert, Martin, *Auschwitz and the Allies: A Devastating Account of How the Allies Responded to the News of Hitler's Mass Murder*, Henry Holt and Company, New York: 1981, pp. 72–73.

41. Frantzman, Seth J., Strange Bedfellows, *Jerusalem Post*, May 7, 2008, https://www.jpost.com/Magazine/Features/Strange-bedfellows.

42. Gilbert, Martin, *Jerusalem in the Twentieth Century*, John Wiley & Sons, Hoboken, N.J.: 1996, p. 162.

43. Meacham, Jon, *Franklin and Winston: An Intimate Portrait of an Epic Friendship*, Random House, New York: 2003, p. 192.

44. Ferguson, *Empire*, p. 346.

45. Ambrose, Stephen E., *American Heritage New History of World War II*, Viking, New York: 1997, p. 365.

46. Ambrose, *World War II*, p. 365.

47. Brinkley, David, *Washington Goes to War*, Ballantine Books, New York: 1988, p. 131.

48. Greene, Bob, *Once Upon a Town: The Miracle of the North Platte Canteen*, HarperCollins, New York: 2002, p. 13.

49. Greene, *Once Upon a Town*, pp. 14–15.

50. Greene, *Once Upon a Town*, back jacket.

51. Barone, *Our Country*, p. 162.

52. Ambrose, *World War II*, p. 419.

53. Dear and Foot, *Oxford Companion*, p. 689.

54. White, David Fairbank, *Bitter Ocean: The Battle of the Atlantic, 1939–1945*, Simon & Schuster, New York: 2006, front jacket.

55. Hickam, Homer H., Jr., *Torpedo Junction*, Naval Institute Press, Annapolis, Md.: 1989, p. xi.

56. White, *Bitter Ocean*, p. 247.

57. Hickam, *Torpedo Junction*, p. vii.

58. Dear and Foot, *Oxford Companion*, p. 271.

59. Dear and Foot, *Oxford Companion*, pp. 748–749.

60. Donovan, Charles A., "At War with God," *Citizen Magazine*, Focus on the Family, 2002.

61. Soames, Mary, *Clementine Churchill: The Biography of a Marriage*, Houghton Mifflin, Boston: 1979, p. 420.

62. Soames, *Clementine Churchill*, pp. 420–421.

63. Costello, Matthew, "The Wings of Franklin Roosevelt: The Dixie Clipper and the Sacred Cow," The White House Historical Association, September 27, 2017, https://www.whitehousehistory.org/the-wings-of-franklin-roosevelt-1.

64. Dear and Foot, *Oxford Companion*, p. 515.

65. Dear and Foot, *Oxford Companion*, p. 1174.

66. Fleming, *Duel*, 183, p. 188.

67. Gilbert, *Churchill: A Life*, p. 815.
68. Soames, *Clementine Churchill*, p. 420.
69. Soames, *Clementine Churchill*, p. 461.
70. Dear and Foot, *Oxford Companion*, p. 1059.
71. Ambrose, *World War II*, p. 254.

Chapter 17: America Victorious

1. Offner, Larry, "The Butch O'Hare Story," *St. Louis*, July 29, 2006, https://www.stlmag.com/The-Butch-OHare-Story/.
2. From a speech by Rep. Ralph Hall (Texas), 30 May 1996, The Congressional Record.
3. John Basilone, "U.S. Postal Service to Dedicate Distinguished Marines Stamps," Gunnery Sergeant, November 3, 2005, http://www.leatherneck.com/forums/archive/index.php/t-23130.html.
4. Bennett, William J., and Cribb, John T. E., *The American Patriot's Almanac*, Nashville: Thomas Nelson, 2010, p. 40.
5. Nisbet, Robert, *Roosevelt and Stalin: The Failed Courtship*, Regnery Gateway, Washington, D.C.: 1988, p. 45.
6. Meacham, Jon, *Franklin and Winston: An Intimate Portrait of an Epic Friendship*, Random House, New York: 2003, p. 250.
7. Meacham, *Franklin and Winston*, p. 251.
8. Barone, Michael, *Our Country: The Shaping of America from Roosevelt to Reagan*, The Free Press, New York: 1990, p. 168.
9. Ambrose, Stephen E., *American Heritage New History of World War II*, Viking, New York: 1997, p. 282.
10. Pogue, Forrest C., *George C. Marshall: Interviews and Reminiscences for Forrest C. Pogue*, George C. Marshall Research Foundation, Lexington, Va.: 1991, pp. 108–109.
11. Larrabee, Eric, *Commander in Chief: Franklin D. Roosevelt, His Lieutenants, and Their War*, U.S. Naval Institute Press, Annapolis, Md.: 1987, pp. 98–99.
12. Eisenhower, John S. D., *General Ike: A Personal Reminiscence*, The Free Press, New York: 2003, p. 99.
13. Gilbert, Martin, *Churchill: A Life*, Henry Holt and Company, New York: 1991, p. 756.
14. Eisenhower, Dwight D., *Crusade in Europe*, Johns Hopkins University Press, Baltimore, Md.: 1948, p. 194.

15. Eisenhower, Dwight D., *At Ease: Stories I Tell to Friends*, Doubleday, New York: 1967, p. 270.

16. Beschloss, Michael R., *Eisenhower: A Centennial Life*, HarperCollins, New York: 1990, p. 66.

17. Leckie, Robert, *The Wars of America*, Harper & Row, New York: 1981, p. 796.

18. Leckie, *Wars of America*, p. 796.

19. "A 'Mighty Endeavor': D-Day," Franklin D. Roosevelt Library and Museum, https://fdrlibrary.org/d-day.

20. Ambrose, *World War II*, p. 487.

21. Netting, Conrad J., IV, "Delayed Legacy," *USAA Magazine*, no. 2, 2004, p. 24.

22. Overy, Richard, *Why the Allies Won*, W. W. Norton & Company, New York: 1995, p. 319.

23. Soames, Mary, *Clementine Churchill: The Biography of a Marriage*, Houghton Mifflin, Boston: 1979, p. 479.

24. Eisenhower, *Crusade in Europe*, pp. 296–297.

25. Perret, Geoffrey, *Eisenhower*, Random House, New York: 1999, p. 308.

26. De Gaulle, Charles, *The Complete Memoirs*, Carroll & Graf Publishers, New York: 1998, p. 647.

27. Eisenhower, *Crusade in Europe*, p. 298.

28. Meacham, *Franklin and Winston*, p. 295.

29. Dear, I. C. B, gen. ed., and M. R. D. Foot, consulting ed., *The Oxford Companion to World War II*, Oxford University Press, New York: 1995, p. 1252.

30. Gilbert, Martin, *Auschwitz and the Allies*, Henry Holt and Company, New York: 1981, p. 341.

31. Beschloss, Michael, *The Conquerors: Roosevelt, Truman and the Destruction of Hitler's Germany, 1941–1945*, Simon & Schuster, New York: 2002, p. 59.

32. Beschloss, *Conquerors*, p. 41.

33. Black, Conrad, *Franklin D. Roosevelt: Champion of Freedom*, Public Affairs, New York: 2003, p. 974.

34. McCullough, David, *Truman*, Simon & Schuster, New York: 1992, p. 314.

35. McCullough, *Truman*, p. 314.

36. Goodwin, Doris Kearns, *No Ordinary Time: Franklin and Eleanor Roosevelt, The Home Front in World War II*, Simon & Schuster, New York: 1994, p. 532.

37. Goodwin, *No Ordinary Time*, p. 532.

38. Barone, *Our Country*, p. 176.

39. Barone, *Our Country*, p. 178.

40. Beschloss, Michael R., *Kennedy and Roosevelt: The Uneasy Alliance*, W. W. Norton & Company, New York: 1980, p. 257.

41. Beschloss, *Kennedy and Roosevelt*, p. 259.

42. "Stalin, Man of the Year: 1939," *Time* magazine, 1 January 1940, https://first100years.org.uk/nancy-astor-viscountess-astor/. .

43. Ambrose, Stephen E., *The Victors: Eisenhower and His Boys: The Men of World War II*, Simon & Schuster, New York: 1998, pp. 299–300.

44. Ambrose, *World War II*, pp. 300–301.

45. Leckie, *Wars of America*, p. 816.

46. Dear and Foot, *Oxford Companion*, p. 52.

47. Eisenhower, John S. D., *The Bitter Woods*, G. P. Putnam's Sons, New York: 1969, p. 462.

48. Black, *Champion of Freedom*, p. 1043.

49. Black, *Champion of Freedom*, p. 1062.

50. McDougall, Walter A., *Promised Land, Crusader State: The American Encounter with the World Since 1776*, Houghton Mifflin, Boston: 1997, p. 156.

51. McDougall, *Promised Land*, p. 155.

52. Black, *Champion of Freedom*, p. 1066.

53. Black, *Champion of Freedom*, p. 1058.

54. Black, *Champion of Freedom*, p. 1070.

55. Churchill, Winston S., *The Second World War, Volume 1: The Gathering Storm*, Houghton Mifflin, Boston: 1948.

56. Meacham, *Franklin and Winston*, p. 317.

57. Black, *Champion of Freedom*, p. 1074.

58. Nisbet, *Roosevelt and Stalin*.

59. Gaddis, John Lewis, *The Cold War: A New History*, Penguin Press, New York: 2005, p. 22.

60. Weinstein, Allen, and Alexander Vassiliev, *The Haunted Wood: Soviet Espionage in America—the Stalin Era*, Random House, New York: 1999, p. 269.

61. Weinstein and Vassiliev, *Haunted Wood*, p. 196–197.

62. Beschloss, *The Conquerors*, p. 190.

63. Roosevelt, "Yalta Address."

64. Dear and Foot, *Oxford Companion*, p. 642.

65. Bush, George H. W., "Forrestal Lecture," U.S. Naval Academy, Annapolis, Md., 4 March 2004.

66. Collier, Peter, and David Horowitz, *The Roosevelts: An American Saga*, Simon & Schuster, New York: 1994, p. 430.

67. Collier and Horowitz, *Roosevelts*, p. 430.

68. Collier and Horowitz, *Roosevelts*, p. 432.

69. Cutler, Stanley, "Review of Robert H. Jackson's 'That Man: An Insider's Portrait of Franklin D. Roosevelt,'" History News Network, http://hnn.us/articles/1834.html.

70. Goldstein, Richard, "George L. Street, 86, Commander of the Submarine Tirante in World War II," *New York Times*, March 5, 2000, https://www.nytimes.com/2000/03/05/us/george-l-street-86-commander-of-the-submarine-tirante-in-world-war-ii.html.

71. Black, *Champion of Freedom*, p. 1112.

72. McCullough, *Truman*, p. 353.

73. Black, *Champion of Freedom*, p. 1119.

74. Ambrose, *World War II*, p. 457.

75. Ambrose, *World War II*, p. 80.

76. Neal, Steve, *Harry and Ike: The Partnership That Remade the Postwar World*, Charles Scribner's Sons, New York: 2001, p. 48.

77. Speech at London, England, June 12, 1945 (Guildhall Address), Dwight D. Eisenhower Presidential Library, Museum and Boyhood Home, Pre-Presidential Speeches, https://www.eisenhower.archives.gov/all_about_ike/speeches/pre_presidential_speeches.pdf.

78. McCullough, *Truman*, pp. 375–376.

79. Cooke, Alistair, *The American Home Front: 1941–1942*, Atlantic Monthly Press, New York: 2006, p. xi.

80. Summers, Chris, "Red Army Rapists Exposed," BBC News, April 29, 2002, http://news.bbc.co.uk/1/hi/world/europe/1939174.stm.

81. Mee, Charles L., Jr., *Meeting at Potsdam*, M. Evans & Company, New York: 1975, p. 224.

82. Gilbert, *Churchill*, p. 855.

83. McCullough, *Truman*, p. 442.

84. McCullough, *Truman*, p. 443.

85. Harmon, Christopher, "Are We Beasts? Churchill and the Moral Question of World War II 'Area Bombing,'" https://apps.dtic.mil/dtic/tr/fulltext/u2/a529814.pdf.

86. Dear and Foot, *Oxford Companion*, p. 604.

87. Dear and Foot, *Oxford Companion*, p. 836.

88. Frank, Richard B., "Why Truman Dropped the Bomb," *Weekly Standard*, 8 August 2005.

89. Dear and Foot, *Oxford Companion*, p. 773.

90. Ambrose, *World War II*, p. 597.

91. "Order of the Boot," International Churchill Society, https://winston churchill.org/resources/quotes/order-of-the-boot/.

Chapter 18: Truman Defends the Free World

1. Muller, James W., ed., *Churchill's Iron Curtain Speech Fifty Years Later*, University of Missouri Press, Columbia, Mo.: 1999, p. 6.

2. Muller, *Iron Curtain Speech*, p. 96.

3. Muller, *Iron Curtain Speech*, p. 66.

4. Barone, Michael, *Our Country: The Shaping of America from Roosevelt to Reagan*, The Free Press, New York: 1990, p. 187.

5. Muller, *Iron Curtain Speech*, p. 79.

6. Muller, *Iron Curtain Speech*, p. 102.

7. Graebner, Norman A., *Cold War Diplomacy, 1945–1960*, D. Van Norstrand, New York: 1962, p. 28.

8. Beschloss, Michael, *The Conquerors: Roosevelt, Truman and the Destruction of Hitler's Germany, 1941–1945*, Simon & Schuster, New York: 2002, p. 275.

9. King, Henry T., Jr., "Robert Jackson's Place in History: Nuremberg Revisited, Chautauqua Institution," *The Paragraph*, June 13, 2003, https://theparagraph .com/documents/robert-jackson's-place-in-history-nuremberg-revisited/.

10. Barone, *Our Country*, p. 187.

11. Ferrell, Robert H., *Harry S. Truman: A Life*, University of Missouri Press, Columbia, MO: 1994, pp. 194–195.

12. Ferrell, *Harry S. Truman*, p. 181.

13. Beschloss, *Conquerors*, p. 276.

14. Gaddis, John Lewis, *We Now Know: Rethinking Cold War History*, Oxford University Press, New York: 1997, pp. 14–15.

15. Ferrell, *Harry S. Truman*, p. 253.

16. Barone, *Our Country*, p. 192.

17. Morison, Samuel Eliot, Henry Steele Commager, and William E. Leuchtenberg, *A Concise History of the American Republic*, Oxford University Press, New York: 1977, p. 676.

18. Barone, *Our Country*, p. 193.

19. Radosh, Ronald, and Allis Radosh, *Red Star Over Hollywood: The Film Colony's Long Romance with the Left*, Encounter Books, New York: 2005, p. 48.

20. Radosh and Radosh, *Red Star*, p. 112.

21. Radosh and Radosh, *Red Star*, p. 114.

22. Radosh and Radosh, *Red Star*, p. 115.

23. Billingsley, Kenneth Lloyd, *Hollywood Party: How Communism Seduced the American Film Industry in the 1930s and 1940s*, Forum, Roseville, Calif.: 2000, p. 157.

24. Billingsley, *Hollywood Party*, p. 125.

25. Billingsley, *Hollywood Party*, p. 125.

26. Gilbert, Martin, *Israel: A History*, William Morrow and Company, New York: 1997, p. 187.

27. Ferrell, *Harry S. Truman*, p. 311.

28. Spalding, Elizabeth Edwards, *The First Cold Warrior: Harry Truman, Containment, and the Remaking of Liberal Internationalism*, University Press of Kentucky, Lexington, Ky.: 2006, p. 98.

29. Spalding, *First Cold Warrior*, p. 96.

30. Spalding, *First Cold Warrior*, pp. 96–97.

31. Ferrell, *Harry S. Truman*, p. 311.

32. Gilbert, *Israel*, p. 191.

33. Clay, Lucius D., *Decision in Germany*, Doubleday, New York: 1950, p. 365.

34. Ferrell, *Harry S. Truman*, p. 259.

35. Barone, *Our Country*, p. 208.

36. Ferrell, *Harry S. Truman*, p. 314.

37. Humphrey, Hubert H., *The Education of a Public Man: My Life and Politics*, Doubleday, New York: 1976, p. 111.

38. Ferrell, *Harry S. Truman*, pp. 295, 297.

39. Gould, Louis L., *Grand Old Party: A History of the Republicans*, Random House, New York: 2003, p. 316.

40. Beschloss, Michael, *Eisenhower: A Centennial Life*, Edward Burlingame Book, New York: 1990, p. 94.

41. Ferrell, *Harry S. Truman*, pp. 268–269.

42. Humphrey, *Education*, p. 111.

43. Humphrey, *Education*, p. 110.

44. McCullough, David, *Truman*, Simon & Schuster, New York: 1992, p. 467.

45. McCullough, *Truman*, p. 467.

46. McCullough, *Truman*, p. 652.

47. McCullough, *Truman*, p. 652.

48. McCullough, *Truman*, p. 652.

49. Barone, *Our Country*, p. 214.

50. McCullough, *Truman*, p. 654.

51. Barone, *Our Country*, p. 220.

52. Haynes, John Earl and Harvey Klehr, *Venona: Decoding Soviet Espionage in America*, Yale University Press, New Haven, Conn.: 1999, p. 156.

53. Brands, H. W., *Cold Warriors: Eisenhower's Generation and American Foreign Policy*, Columbia University Press, New York: 1988, p. 7.

54. Ferrell, *Harry S. Truman*, p. 253.

55. "President Truman's Statement Announcing the First Soviet A-Bomb," Atomic Archive, 23 September 1949, http://www.atomicarchive.com /Docs/Hydrogen/SovietAB.shtml.

56. Weinstein, Allen, *Perjury: The Hiss-Chambers Case*, Alfred A. Knopf, New York: 1978, p. 67.

57. Haynes and Klehr, *Venona*, p. 156.

58. Schweizer, Peter, *Reagan's War: The Epic Story of His Forty-Year Struggle and Final Triumph Over Communism*, Random House, New York: 2002, p. 16.

59. Schweizer, *Reagan's War*, p. 16.

60. Janken, Kenneth Robert, *White: The Biography of Walter White, Mr. NAACP*, New Press, New York: 2003, p. 320.

61. Janken, *White*, pp. 320–322.

62. Barone, *Our Country*, p. 237.

63. Leckie, Robert, *The Wars of America*, Harper & Row, New York: 1981, p. 849.

64. Gaddis, John Lewis, *The End of the Cold War*, Penguin Press, New York: 2005, p. 74.

65. Leckie, *Wars of America*, p. 877.

66. Leckie, *Wars of America*, p. 878.

67. Leckie, *Wars of America*, p. 881.

68. Leckie, *Wars of America*, p. 856.

69. Morison, Samuel Eliot, *The Oxford History of the American People, Volume 3, 1869 Through the Death of President Kennedy*, 1963, Penguin Books, New York: 1965, p 436.

70. Gaddis, *End of the Cold War*, p. 47.

71. Gaddis, *End of the Cold War*, p. 47.

72. Morison, *Oxford History*, vol. 3, p. 438.

73. Gaddis, *End of the Cold War*, p. 55.

74. Morison, *Oxford History*, vol. 3, p. 436.

75. Gould, *Grand Old Party*, p. 322.

76. Spalding, *First Cold Warrior*, p. 217.

77. McCullough, *Truman*, p. 829.

78. Spalding, *First Cold Warrior*, p. 228.

79. Spalding, *First Cold Warrior*, p. 228.

Chapter 19: Eisenhower and Happy Days

1. Beschloss, Michael R., *Eisenhower: A Centennial Life*, HarperCollins, New York: 1990, p. 106.

2. Beschloss, *Eisenhower*, p. 106.

3. Beschloss, *Eisenhower*, p. 111.

4. Brands, H. W., *Cold Warriors: Eisenhower's Generation and American Foreign Policy*, Columbia University Press, New York: 1988, p. 185.

5. Hunt, John Gabriel, ed., *The Inaugural Addresses of the Presidents*, Gramercy Books, New York: 1995, p. 412.

6. "Judge Kaufman's Statement Upon Sentencing the Rosenbergs for Atomic Espionage," Digital History, 1951, http://www.digitalhistory.uh.edu/disp _textbook.cfm?smtID=3&psid=1118.

7. Radosh, Ronald, *Commies*, Encounter Books, New York: 2001, p. 46.

8. Barone, Michael, *Our Country: The Shaping of America from Roosevelt to Reagan*, The Free Press, New York: 1990, p. 267.

9. Gaddis, John Lewis, *The End of the Cold War*, Penguin Press, New York: 2005, p. 50.

10. Morison, Samuel Eliot, *The Oxford History of the American People, Volume 3: 1869 through the Death of John F. Kennedy, 1963*, Penguin Books, New York: 1994, p. 439.

11. Powers, Richard Gid, *Not Without Honor: The History of American Anticommunism*, The Free Press, New York: 1995, p. 268.

12. Pullum, Geoffrey K., "At Long Last," Language Log, June 9, 2004, http://itre .cis.upenn.edu/~myl/languagelog/archives/001036.html.

13. Ambrose, Stephen E., *Eisenhower: The President*, Simon & Schuster, New York: 1984, p. 81.

14. Powers, *Not Without Honor*, p. 268.

15. Barone, *Our Country*, p. 270.

16. Beschloss, *Eisenhower*, p. 128.

17. Barone, *Our Country*, p. 269.

18. Barone, *Our Country*, p. 271.

19. Eisenhower, Dwight D., *Crusade in Europe*, Johns Hopkins University Press, Baltimore, Md.: 1997, p. 468.

20. Eisenhower, *Crusade in Europe*, p. 476.

21. Wicker, Tom, *Dwight D. Eisenhower*, Times Books, New York: 2002, p. 47.

22. Wicker, *Dwight D. Eisenhower*, p. 53.

23. Wicker, *Dwight D. Eisenhower*, p. 50.

24. Frady, Marshall, *Martin Luther King, Jr.*, The Penguin Group, New York: 2002, p. 35.

25. Frady, *Martin Luther King, Jr.*, pp. 49–50.

26. Frady, *Martin Luther King, Jr.*, p. 48.

27. Frady, *Martin Luther King, Jr.*, p. 52.

28. Beschloss, *Eisenhower*, p. 137.

29. Beschloss, *Eisenhower*, p. 140.

30. Beschloss, *Eisenhower*, p. 138.

31. Beschloss, *Eisenhower*, p. 122.

32. Beschloss, *Eisenhower*, p. 126.

33. Ambrose, *Eisenhower: The President*, p. 80.

34. Parrett, Geoffrey, *Eisenhower*, Random House, New York: 1999, pp. 74–75.

35. Beschloss, *Eisenhower*, p. 126.

36. Barone, *Our Country*, p. 299.

37. Wicker, *Dwight D. Eisenhower*, p. 99.

38. McDougall, Walter A., *The Heavens and the Earth: A Political History of the Space Age*, Basic Books, New York: 1985, p. 221.

39. Beschloss, *Eisenhower*, p. 153.

40. Duncan, Francis, *Rickover: The Struggle for Excellence*, Naval Institute Press, Annapolis, Md.: 2001.

41. Duncan, *Rickover*, p. 5.

42. Duncan, *Rickover*, p. 14.

43. Author interview with Captain John Gallis (USN Ret.), interview recorded 17 July 2006.

44. Gilbert, Martin, *A History of the Twentieth Century, Volume 3: 1952–1999*, William Morrow and Company, New York: 1999, p. 222.

45. Bischof, Gunther, and Stephen E. Ambrose, eds., *Eisenhower: A Centenary Assessment*, Louisiana State University Press, Baton Rouge, La.: 1995, p. 100.

46. Taranto, James, and Leonard Leo, *Presidential Leadership: Rating the Best and the Worst in the White House*, The Free Press, New York: 2004, p. 164.

47. Ambrose, *Eisenhower: The President*, p. 393.

48. Bischof and Ambrose, *Centenary Assessment*, p. 251.

Chapter 20: Passing the Torch

1. Barone, Michael, *Our Country: The Shaping of America from Roosevelt to Reagan*, The Free Press, New York: 1990, p. 331.

2. Barone, *Our Country*, p. 332.

3. Hunt, John Gabriel, ed., *The Inaugural Addresses of the Presidents*, Gramercy Books, New York: 1995, pp. 428, 431.

4. Gaddis, John Lewis, *The End of the Cold War*, Penguin Press, New York: 2005, p. 71.

5. Reeves, Richard, *President Kennedy: Profile of Power*, Simon & Schuster, New York: 1993, p. 171.

6. Reeves, *Profile of Power*, p. 224.

7. Beschloss, Michael R., *The Crisis Years: Kennedy and Khrushchev, 1960–1963*, HarperCollins, New York: 1991, p. 211.

8. Reeves, *Profile of Power*, p. 172.

9. Schefter, James, *The Race: The Uncensored Story of How America Beat Russia to the Moon*, Doubleday, New York: 1999, p. 81.

10. McDougall, Walter A., *The Heavens and the Earth: A Political History of the Space Age*, Basic Books, New York: 1985, p. 318.

11. Glenn, John, and Nick Taylor, *John Glenn: A Memoir*, Bantam Books, New York: 1999, p. 253.

12. Glenn and Taylor, *John Glenn*, p. 255.

13. Glenn and Taylor, *John Glenn*, p. 255.

14. Glenn and Taylor, *John Glenn*, p. 255.

15. Reeves, *Profile of Power*, p. 345.

16. Gilbert, Martin, *A History of the Twentieth Century, Volume 3: 1952–1999*, William Morrow and Company, New York: 1999, p. 280.

17. LaCouture, Jean, *De Gaulle: The Ruler, 1945–1970*, W. W. Norton & Company, New York: 1991, p. 375.

18. Reeves, *Profile of Power*, p. 406.

19. Gilbert, *History of the Twentieth Century*, vol. 3, p. 282.

20. Gilbert, *History of the Twentieth Century*, vol. 3, p. 282.

21. Beschloss, *Crisis Years*, p. 543.

22. Barone, *Our Country*, p. 346.

23. Beschloss, *Crisis Years*, p. 547.

24. Gilbert, *History of the Twentieth Century*, vol. 3, p. 275.

25. Reeves, *Profile of Power*, p. 327.

26. Transcript of PBS documentary series *Eyes on the Prize: America's Civil Rights Experience* (originally aired in 1987), https://www-tc.pbs.org/wgbh /americanexperience/media/filer_public/b9/02/b902b327-70e0-4a4c-80d4 -db9ca54941ab/eyes_on_the_prize_transcript.pdf.

27. Gilbert, *History of the Twentieth Century*, vol. 3, p. 301.

28. Gilbert, *History of the Twentieth Century*, vol. 3, p. 301.

29. "Inaugural address of Governor George Wallace, which was delivered at the Capitol in Montgomery, Alabama," 14 January 1963, Alabama Department of Archives and History, Alabama, http://www.archives.state .al.us/govs_list/inauguralspeech.html.

30. Gilbert, *History of the Twentieth Century*, vol. 3, p. 301.

31. Frady, Marshall, *Martin Luther King, Jr.*, Penguin Group, New York: 2002, p. 51.

32. Reeves, *Profile of Power*, p. 522.

33. Reeves, *Profile of Power*, p. 523.

34. "Letter from a Birmingham Jail [King, Jr.]," 16 April 1963, African Studies Center, University of Pennsylvania, https://www.africa.upenn.edu/Articles _Gen/Letter_Birmingham.html.

35. Humphrey, Hubert H., *The Education of a Public Man: My Life and Politics*, Doubleday, Garden City, N.Y.: 1976, p. 269.

36. Reeves, *Profile of Power*, p. 581.

37. Reeves, *Profile of Power*, p. 583.

38. Frady, *Martin Luther King, Jr.*, p. 124.

39. Reeves, *Profile of Power*, pp. 320–321.

40. Badger, T. A., "Nellie Connally Recalls JFK Slaying in New Book," Middletown Press, November 7, 2003, https://www.middletownpress.com /news/article/Nellie-Connally-recalls-JFK-slaying-in-new-book-11916485 .php.

41. Humphrey, *Education of a Public Man*, p. p. 273.

42. Humphrey, *Education of a Public Man*, p. 278.

43. Johnson, Scott, "Misremembering Hubert," Power Line Blog, May 28, 2011, https://www.powerlineblog.com/archives/2011/05/029116.php.

44. Humphrey, *Education of a Public Man*, p. 285.

45. Edwards, Lee, *Goldwater: The Man Who Made a Revolution*, Regnery Publishing, Washington, D.C.: 1995, p. 115.

46. Edwards, *Goldwater*, p. 150.

47. Edwards, *Goldwater*, pp. 116, 122–123.

48. Edwards, *Goldwater*, p. 274.

49. Dallek, Matthew, "Turning Right in the Sixties," *The Atlantic*, December 1995, http://www.theatlantic.com/issues/95dec/conbook/conbook.htm.

50. Edwards, *Goldwater*, p. 275.

51. Edwards, *Goldwater*, p. 317.

52. Barone, *Our Country*, p. 376.

53. Edwards, *Goldwater*, p. 300.

54. Edwards, *Goldwater*, pp. 242, 330.

55. Edwards, *Goldwater*, p. 279.

56. Edwards, *Goldwater*, p. 318.

57. Edwards, *Goldwater*, p. 319.

58. Edwards, *Goldwater*, p. 332.

59. Beschloss, *Crisis Years*, p. 513.

60. Reeves, Richard, *Profile of Power*, pp. 475, 476.

61. Frady, *Martin Luther King, Jr.*, p. 163.

62. Frady, *Martin Luther King, Jr.*, pp. 163–164.

63. Frady, *Martin Luther King, Jr.*, p. 165.

64. Podhoretz, Norman, *Why We Were in Vietnam*, Simon & Schuster, New York: 1982, pp. 31–32.

65. Podhoretz, *Vietnam*, p. 57.

66. Gilbert, *History of the Twentieth Century*, vol. 3, p. 354.

67. Gould, Lewis L., *Grand Old Party: A History of the Republicans*, Random House, New York: 2003, pp. 370–371.

68. Gould, *Grand Old Party*, p. 372.

69. Podhoretz, *Vietnam*, p. 67.

70. Podhoretz, *Vietnam*, p. 84.

71. Podhoretz, *Vietnam*, p. 88.

72. Gilbert, *History of the Twentieth Century*, vol. 3, p. 366.

73. Gilbert, *History of the Twentieth Century*, vol. 3, p. 366.

74. Leckie, Robert, *The Wars of America*, Harper & Row, New York: 1981, p. 1010.

75. Leckie, *Wars of America*, p. 1009.

76. Leckie, *Wars of America*, p. 1007.

77. Radosh, Ronald, and Allis Radosh, *Red Star Over Hollywood: The Film Colony's Long Romance with the Left*, Encounter Books, New York: 2005, p. 90.

78. Podhoretz, *Vietnam*, p. 90.

79. Podhoretz, *Vietnam*, p. 91.

80. Frady, *Martin Luther King, Jr.*, pp. 202–204.

81. Humphrey, *Education of a Public Man*, p. 384.

82. Humphrey, *Education of a Public Man*, p. 385.

83. Gilbert, *History of the Twentieth Century*, vol. 3, p. 387.

84. Gould, *Grand Old Party*, p. 374.

85. Gould, *Grand Old Party*, p. 379.

86. *The Race for the Moon: The American Experience*, PBS, 26 February 2007.

87. Chaikin, Andrew, *A Man on the Moon: The Voyage of the Apollo Astronauts*, Penguin Books, New York: 1994, p. 121.

88. Chaikin, *Man on the Moon*, p. 121. Quotation from Genesis 1:1–4 (KJV).

89. Chaikin, *Man on the Moon*, p. 134.

Chapter 21: Nixon's the One

1. Hansen, James R., *First Man: The Life of Neil A. Armstrong*, Simon & Schuster, New York: 2005, p. 1.

2. Hansen, *First Man*, p. 3.

3. Hansen, *First Man*, pp. 2–3.

4. Chaikin, Andrew, *A Man on the Moon: The Voyages of the Apollo Astronauts*, Penguin Books, New York: 1994, p. 189.

5. Chaikin, *Man on the Moon*, p. 199.

6. Hansen, *First Man*, p. 470.

7. Chaikin, *Man on the Moon*, p. 200.

8. Hansen, *First Man*, p. 474.

9. Chaikin, *Man on the Moon*, p. 200.

10. Chaikin, *Man on the Moon*, p. 213.

11. Kennedy, John F., "Remarks at the Dedication of the Aerospace Medical Health Center, San Antonio, Texas, November 21, 1963," John F. Kennedy

Presidential Library and Museum, https://www.jfklibrary.org/archives
/other-resources/john-f-kennedy-speeches/san-antonio-tx-19631121.

12. McDougall, Walter A., *The Heavens and the Earth: A Political History of the Space Age*, The Johns Hopkins University Press, Baltimore, Md.: 1985, p. 411.

13. Chaikin, *Man on the Moon*, p. 24.

14. McDougall, *Heavens and the Earth*, pp. 411, 432.

15. McDougall, *Heavens and the Earth*, p. 455.

16. Chaikin, *Man on the Moon*, p. 208.

17. Chaikin, *Man on the Moon*, p. 204.

18. Chaikin, *Man on the Moon*, p. 205.

19. McDougall, *Heavens and the Earth*, p. 454.

20. McDougall, *Heavens and the Earth*, p. 412.

21. Magnet, Myron, *The Dream and the Nightmare: The Sixties' Legacy to the Underclass*, Encounter Books, New York: 2000, p. 169.

22. Magnet, *Dream and the Nightmare*, p. 169.

23. Barone, Michael, *Our Country: The Shaping of American from Roosevelt to Reagan*, The Free Press, New York: 1990, p. 468.

24. "The Real Woodstock Story," http://www.woodstockstory.com/bands performerssetsplaylists1969.html.

25. Barone, *Our Country*, p. 468.

26. Leckie, Robert, *The Wars of America*, Harper & Row, New York: 1981, p. 1017.

27. Goldstein, Richard, "Hugh Thompson, 62, Who Saved Civilians at My Lai, Dies," *New York Times*, January 7, 2006, https://www.nytimes.com /2006/01/07/us/hugh-thompson-62-who-saved-civilians-at-my-lai-dies .html.

28. Associated Press, "Another Vineyard Calamity for Kennedys," *USA Today*, July 21, 1999, http://www.usatoday.com/news/index/jfk/jfk038.htm.

29. Barone, *Our Country*, pp. 470, 472.

30. Barone, *Our Country*, p. 476.

31. Podhoretz, Norman, *Why We Were in Vietnam*, Simon & Schuster, New York: 1982, p. 147.

32. Barone, *Our Country*, p. 477.

33. Podhoretz, *Vietnam*, pp. 147, 149.

34. Barone, *Our Country*, p. 476.

35. Kissinger, Henry, *White House Years*, Little, Brown, and Company, Boston: 1979, p. 733.

36. Hayward, Steven F., *The Age of Reagan: The Fall of the Old Liberal Order, 1964–1980*, Random House, New York: 2001, p. 278.

37. Hayward, *Reagan*, p. 258; Barone, *Our Country*, p. 487.

38. Barone, *Our Country*, p. 487.

39. Frum, David, *How We Got Here: The 70s—The Decade That Brought You Modern Life (For Better or Worse)*, Basic Books, New York: 2000, p. 298.

40. Barone, *Our Country*, p. 473.

41. Barone, *Our Country*, p. 478.

42. Blake, Judith, "Abortion and Public Opinion: The 1960–1970 Decade," *Science* 171, 12 February 1971, pp. 540–549.

43. Frum, *How We Got Here*, p. 249.

44. Thompson, Kenneth W., ed., *The Nixon Presidency: Twenty-Two Intimate Portraits of Richard M. Nixon*, University Press of America, Lanham, Md.: 1987, pp. 9, 32.

45. Ambrose, Stephen E., *Wild Blue: The Men and Boys Who Flew the B-24s Over Germany*, Simon & Schuster, New York: 2001, p. 102.

46. Ambrose, *Wild Blue*, p. 214.

47. "Acceptance Speech of Senator George McGovern," Presidential Campaigns and Candidates, Miami Beach, FL, 14 July 1972, http://www.4president.org/speeches/mcgovern1972acceptance.htm.

48. Thompson, *Nixon Presidency*, p. 54.

49. Chaikin, *Man on the Moon*, p. 546.

50. Chaikin, *Man on the Moon*, p. 546.

51. Kissinger, Henry, *Ending the Vietnam War: A History of America's Involvement In and Extrication From the Vietnam War*, Simon & Schuster, New York: 2003, p. 414.

52. Kissinger, *Ending the Vietnam War*, p. 415.

53. Frum, *How We Got Here*, p. 18.

54. Thompson, *Nixon Presidency*, p. 11.

55. Lader, Lawrence, *Abortion II: Making the Revolution*, Beacon Press, Boston: 1973, p. 223.

56. Thompson, *Nixon Presidency*, p. 196.

57. Hayward, *Reagan*, p. 418.

58. Barone, *Our Country*, p. 520.

59. Barone, *Our Country*, p. 517.
60. Germond, Jack W., *Fat Man in a Middle Seat: Forty Years of Covering Politics*, Random House, New York: 1999, p. 119.
61. Frum, *How We Got Here*, p. 26.
62. Germond, *Fat Man*, p. 114.
63. Edwards, Lee, *Goldwater: The Man Who Made a Revolution*, Regnery Publishing, Washington, D.C.: 1995, p. 398.

Chapter 22: The Year the Locusts Ate

1. Thompson, Kenneth W., ed., *The Nixon Presidency: Twenty-Two Intimate Portraits of Richard M. Nixon*, University Press of America, Lanham, Md.: 1987, p. 64.
2. Barone, *Our Country: The Shaping of American from Roosevelt to Reagan*, The Free Press, New York: 1990, p. 532.
3. Frum, David, *How We Got Here: The 70s—The Decade That Brought You Modern Life (For Better or Worse)*, Basic Books, New York: 2000, p. 305.
4. Barone, *Our Country*, p. 539.
5. Frum, *How We Got Here*, p. 305.
6. Frum, *How We Got Here*, p. 307.
7. Frum, *How We Got Here*, p. 307.
8. Courtois, Stéphane, Nicolas Werth, Jean-Louis Panné, and Andrezej Paszkowski, *The Black Book of Communism: Crimes, Terror, Repression*, Harvard University Press, Cambridge, Mass.: 1999, pp. 590–591.
9. Barone, *Our Country*, p. 550.
10. Germond, Jack W., *Fat Man in a Middle Seat: Forty Years of Covering Politics*, Random House, New York: 1999, p. 125.
11. Germond, *Fat Man*, p. 127.
12. Shirley, Craig, *Reagan's Revolution: The Untold Story of the Campaign That Started It All*, Nelson Current, Nashville: 2005, p. 37.
13. Shirley, *Reagan's Revolution*, pp. 163–164.
14. Cannon, Lou, *Ronald Reagan: The Role of a Lifetime*, Public Affairs, New York: 2000, pp. 457–458.
15. Shirley, *Reagan's Revolution*, p. 161.
16. Shirley, *Reagan's Revolution*, p. 161.
17. Shirley, *Reagan's Revolution*, p. 162.
18. Shirley, *Reagan's Revolution*, p. 162.

19. "Remarks of Gerald R. Ford in Philadelphia, Pennsylvania (Bicentennial Celebration)," Gerald R. Ford Presidential Library and Museum, 4 July 1976, https://www.fordlibrarymuseum.gov/library/speeches/760645.asp.

20. D'Souza, Dinesh, *Ronald Reagan: How an Ordinary Man Became an Extraordinary Leader*, The Free Press, New York: 1997, p. 78.

21. Reagan, Ronald, "Reagan Writes," *New York Times*, 31 December 2000, https://archive.nytimes.com/www.nytimes.com/library/magazine/home /20001231mag-reagan.html.

22. Barnes, Fred, "Comments on the Passing of President Ford," FOX *News*, 30 December 2006.

23. D'Souza, *Ronald Reagan*, p. 79.

24. Hayward, Steven F., *The Age of Reagan: The Fall of the Old Liberal Order, 1964–1980*, Random House, New York: 2001, p. 482.

25. http://www.nationalcenter.org/ReaganConvention1976.html.

26. Hayward, *Reagan*, p. 480.

27. Kengor, Paul, "A Pair for History: Presidents Ford and Reagan," *National Review*, 27 December 2006, https://www.nationalreview.com/2006/12 /pair-history-paul-kengor/.

28. D'Souza, *Ronald Reagan*, p. 79.

29. Barone, *Our Country*, p. 543.

30. Barone, *Our Country*, p. 555.

31. Barone, *Our Country*, p. 557.

32. Hunt, John Gabriel, ed., *The Inaugural Addresses of the Presidents*, Gramercy Books, New York: 1995, pp. 466, 465.

33. Carter, Jimmy, "1976 Democratic National Convention Acceptance Address," American Rhetoric, 15 July 1976, http://americanrhetoric.com /speeches/jimmycarter1976dnc.htm.

34. Hayward, Steven F., *The Real Jimmy Carter*, Regnery Gateway, Washington, D.C.: 2004, p. 91.

35. Hayward, *Carter*, p. 91.

36. Frum, *How We Got Here*, pp. 312–313.

37. Frum, *How We Got Here*, p. 327.

38. Churchill, Winston, "Vice of Capitalism," International Churchill Society, 22 October 1945, https://winstonchurchill.org/resources/quotes /vice-of-capitalism/.

39. Frum, *How We Got Here*, p. 334.

40. Hayward, *Carter*, p. 111.

41. Hayward, *Carter*, p. 114.

42. Taranto, James, and Leonard Leo, eds., *Presidential Leadership: Rating the Best and the Worst in the White House*, The Free Press, New York: 2004, p. 191.

43. Hayward, *Carter*, p. 114.

44. Hayward, *Carter*, p. 110.

45. Barone, *Our Country*, p. 571.

46. Barone, *Our Country*, p. 574.

47. Pearce, Joseph, *Solzhenitsyn: A Soul in Exile*, Baker Books, Grand Rapids, Mich.: 2001, p. 234.

48. Pearce, *Solzhenitsyn*, p. 236.

49. Barone, *Our Country*, p. 583.

50. Germond, *Fat Man*, p. 137.

51. Barone, *Our Country*, p. 580.

52. Hayward, *Carter*, pp. 162–163.

53. Barone, *Our Country*, p. 587.

54. Author interview with William B. Weide, University of Washington alumnus, who attended the Toon lecture in 1982. Interview recorded 7 January 2007.

55. Hayward, *Carter*, p. 141.

56. Frum, *How We Got Here*, p. 343.

57. Barone, *Our Country*, p. 592.

58. Hayward, *Carter*, p. 161.

59. Hayward, *Carter*, p. 182.

60. Haynes, John Earl, and Harvey Klehr, *Venona: Decoding Soviet Espionage in America*, Yale University Press, New Haven, Conn.: 1999, p. 246.

61. Hayward, *Carter*, pp. 186–187.

62. Hayward, *Reagan*, p. 712.

Chapter 23: Reagan and Revival

1. Hunt, John Gabriel, ed., *Inaugural Addresses of the Presidents*, Gramercy Books, New York: 1995, p. 476.

2. D'Souza, Dinesh, *Ronald Reagan: How an Ordinary Man Became an Extraordinary Leader,* The Free Press, New York: 1997, p. 89.

3. Mitchell, Daniel, "Cutting Taxes Faster Would Help Everyone," *New York*

Times, February 5, 2002, https://www.nytimes.com/2002/02/05/opinion /cutting-taxes-faster-would-help-everyone.html.

4. Deaver, Michael K., *A Different Drummer: My Thirty Years with Ronald Reagan*, HarperCollins, New York: 2001, p. 146.

5. *Reagan: The American Experience*, PBS, 23 February 1998.

6. Deaver, *Different Drummer*, p. 111.

7. Barone, Michael, *Our Country: The Shaping of America from Roosevelt to Reagan*, The Free Press, New York: 1990, p. 617.

8. Barone, *Our Country*, p. 617.

9. Schweizer, Peter, *Reagan's War: The Epic Story of His Forty-Year Struggle and Final Triumph Over Communism*, Doubleday, New York: 2002, p. 215.

10. Barone, *Our Country*, p. 620.

11. Reeves, Richard, *President Reagan: The Triumph of Imagination*, Simon & Schuster, New York: 2005, p. 88.

12. Spector, Ronald H., *At War at Sea: Sailors and Naval Combat in the Twentieth Century*, Recorded Books, Prince Frederick, Md.: 2002, disc 17.

13. Reeves, *Triumph of Imagination*, p. 108.

14. Reeves, *Triumph of Imagination*, pp. 108–109.

15. Reeves, *Triumph of Imagination*, p. 110.

16. Baker, James A., III, *Personal Reminiscence*, FOX News Channel, "Special Report," 6 October 2006.

17. Barone, *Our Country*, p. 614.

18. Reagan, Ronald, "Remarks at the Annual Convention of the National Association of Evangelicals in Orlando, Florida," Ronald Reagan Presidential Library and Museum, 8 March 1983, https://www.reagan library.gov/research/speeches/30883b.

19. Deaver, *Different Drummer*, p. 95.

20. Schweizer, *Reagan's War*, p. 196.

21. Reagan, Ronald, "Remarks at a Ceremony Commemorating the 40th Anniversary of the Normandy Invasion, D-day," Ronald Reagan Presidential Library and Museum, 6 June 1984, https://www.reagan library.gov/research/speeches/60684a.

22. Germond, Jack W., *Fat Man in a Middle Seat: Forty Years of Covering Politics*, Random House, New York: 1999, p. 163.

23. *Reagan: The American Experience*.

24. Carynnyk, Marco, "The Killing Fields of Kiev," *Commentary* 90, no. 4, October 1990.

25. *Reagan: The American Experience.*

26. *Reagan: The American Experience.*

27. Morris, Edmund, *Dutch: A Memoir of Ronald Reagan*, Random House, New York: 1999, p. 586.

28. D'Souza, *Ronald Reagan*, p. 9.

29. Barone, *Our Country*, p. 661.

30. Schweizer, *Reagan's War*, p. 106.

31. Morris, *Dutch*, p. 600.

32. *Reagan: The American Experience.*

33. Reagan, Ronald, *An American Life: The Autobiography*, Simon & Schuster, New York: 1990, pp. 675–679.

34. *Reagan: The American Experience.*

35. *Reagan: The American Experience.*

36. *Reagan: The American Experience.*

37. *Reagan: The American Experience.*

38. *Reagan: The American Experience.*

39. Ochs, Stephen J., "Mr. Gorbachev, Tear Down This Wall!" *Georgetown Prep AlumNews*, Summer 2004, pp. 13–15.

40. Ochs, "Mr. Gorbachev."

41. Ochs, "Mr. Gorbachev."

42. Ochs, "Mr. Gorbachev."

43. Robinson, Peter, "Tear Down This Wall," *Reader's Digest*, February 2004.

44. Ochs, "Mr. Gorbachev."

45. Robinson, "Tear Down This Wall."

46. Barone, *Our Country*, p. 660.

47. Fund, John, "The Borking Begins," *Wall Street Journal*, January 8, 2001, https://www.wsj.com/articles/SB122417070632840737.

48. *Reagan: The American Experience.*

49. Reeves, *The Triumph of Imagination*, p. 469.

50. Reeves, *Triumph of Imagination*, p. 469.

51. Schweizer, *Reagan's War*, p. 272.

52. *Reagan: The American Experience.*

53. Schweizer, *Reagan's War*, p. 275.

54. *Reagan: The American Experience.*

55. O'Sullivan, John, *The President, the Pope, and the Prime Minister: Three Who Changed the World*, Regnery Publishing, Washington, D.C.: 2006, p. 303.

56. O'Sullivan, *President, Pope, Prime Minister*, p. 303.

57. Gaddis, John Lewis, *The End of the Cold War*, Penguin Press, New York: 2005, p. 117.

Epilogue

1. "George Herbert Walker Bush, 12 June 1924–30 November 2018," Naval History and Heritage Command, https://www.history.navy.mil/content /history/nhhc/research/histories/biographies-list/bios-b/bush-george -h-w.html.

2. "George H. W. Bush," *American Experience*, 4 December 2018, PBS.

3. "Timeline: The Bombing of Pan-Am Flight 103," *Washington Post*, 1999, http://www.washingtonpost.com/wp-srv/inatl/longterm/panam103 /timeline.htm.

4. "Drug Use Trends Since 1979," PBS, https://www.pbs.org/wgbh/pages /frontline/shows/drugs/charts/chart1.html.

5. Richelson, Jeffrey T., and Michael L. Evans, eds., "Tiananmen Square, 1989: The Declassified History," National Security Archive, *Electronic Briefing Book,* no. 16, June 1, 1999, http://www.gwu.edu/~nsarchiv /NSAEBB/NSAEBB16/documents/index.html#1–6.

6. Kahn, Joseph, "China to Give Memorial Rite to Hu Yaobang, Purged Reformer," *New York Times,* November 15, 2005, http://www.nytimes.com /2005/11/15/international/asia/15china.html.

7. Richelson and Evans, "Tiananmen Square."

8. Kristof, Nicholas D., "Chinese Students, in About-Face, Will Continue Occupying Square," *New York Times*, 30 May 1989, https://www.nytimes .com/1989/05/30/world/chinese-students-in-about-face-will-continue -occupying-square.html.

9. Wright, David C., *The History of China*, Greenwood Press, Westport, Conn.: 2001, p. 180.

10. Wright, *History of China,* p. 180.

11. Domber, Gregory F., ed., "Solidarity's Coming Victory: Big or Too Big? Poland's Revolution as Seen from the U.S. Embassy," *Electronic Briefing Book*, no. 42, The National Security Archive, George Washington University, 5 April 2001, http://www.gwu.edu/~nsarchiv/NSAEBB/NSAEBB42/.

12. McCartney, Robert J., "Reform in East Germany: How Much, How Soon?" *Washington Post*, 13 October 1989, https://www.washingtonpost.com

/archive/politics/1989/10/13/reform-in-east-germany-how-much-how-soon
/60fa7cad-c363-427d-9e58-42ed6f1618b3/?utm_term=.40d16104d5b5.

13. Kohl, Helmut, quoted in Schlesinger, Robert, *White House Ghosts: Presidents and Their Speechwriters,* Simon & Schuster, New York: 2008, p. 376.

14. Bush, George, and Brent Scowcroft, *A World Restored,* Alfred A. Knopf, New York: 1998, p. 187.

15. Hayward, Steven F., *The Real Jimmy Carter,* Regnery Publishing, Washington, D.C.: 2004, p. 10.

16. Qassim, Abdul-Zahara, "Iraqi Lawmakers Vote to Change Flag," *Fox News,* 22 January 2008, https://www.foxnews.com/wires/2008Jan22 /0,4670,IraqFlagDispute,00.html.

17. British Broadcasting Corporation, "1991: Iraqi Scud Missiles Hit Israel," *On This Day: 18 January,* http://news.bbc.co.uk/onthisday/hi/dates /stories/january/18/newsid_4588000/4588486.stm.

18. Chilcote, Ryan, "Kuwait Still Recovering from Gulf War Fires," CNN, 3 January 2003, http://www.cnn.com/2003/WORLD/meast/01/03/sproject .irq.kuwait.oil.fires/index.html.

19. Bauder, David, "America's Fighting Spirit Fills Airwaves on Home Front," *Deseret News,* 17 February 1991, https://www.deseretnews.com/article /147570/americas-fighting-spirit-fills-airwaves-on-home-front.html.

20. Toner, Robin, "Casting Doubts: Economy Stinging Bush," *New York Times,* 26 November 1991, http://www.nytimes.com/1991/11/26/us /casting-doubts-economy-stinging-bush.html.

21. "Ross Perot: The Billionaire Boy Scout," *Entrepreneur,* 10 October 2008, http://www.entrepreneur.com/growyourbusiness/radicalsandvisionaries /article197682.html.

22. "The Political Fray," All Politics: CNN, n.d., http://www.cnn.com/ALL POLITICS/1996/conventions/long.beach/perot/political.fray.shtml.

23. U.S. Department of Labor, Bureau of Labor Statistics, "Civilian Unemployment Rate: 1948–2009," 6 November 2009, http://research .stlouisfed.org/fred2/data/UNRATE.txt.

24. McCarthy, Andrew C., *Willful Blindness,* Encounter Books, New York: 2008, p. 8.

25. McCarthy, *Willful Blindness,* p. 8.

26. Clymer, Adam, "Senate Approves Brady Legislation and Trade Accord," *New York Times,* 21 November 1993, http://www.nytimes.com/1993/11/21 /us/senate-approves-brady-legislation-and-trade-accord.html.

27. "Oklahoma City Bombing," Federal Bureau of Investigations web site, Famous Cases and Criminals, https://www.fbi.gov/history/famous-cases /oklahoma-city-bombing.

28. "Unabomber," Federal Bureau of Investigations, Famous Cases and Criminals, https://www.fbi.gov/history/famous-cases/unabomber.

29. Richard L. Berke, "Politics: The Overview; Buchanan a Narrow Victor Over Dole in New Hampshire," *New York Times,* 21 February 1996, http://www.nytimes.com/1996/02/21/us/politics-the-overview-buchanan -a-narrow-victor-over-dole-in-new-hampshire.html.

30. Buchanan, Patrick J., speech, Manchester, N.H., 20 February 1996, quoted in "1996 Victory Speech," *Patrick J. Buchanan, Right from the Beginning,* http://buchanan.org/blog/1996-victory-speech-manchester-nh-183.

31. bin Laden, Osama, "An Open Letter to King Fahd on the Occasion of the Recent Cabinet Reshuffle," 3 August 1995, https://en.wikisource.org/wiki /An_Open_Letter_to_King_Fahd_on_the_Occasion_of_the_Recent _Cabinet_Reshuffle.

32. National Commission on Terrorist Attacks Upon the United States, "The Foundation of New Terrorism," *9/11 Commission Report,* 17 October 2004, http://govinfo.library.unt.edu/911/report/911Report_Ch2.htm.

33. bin Laden, Osama, "Declaration of War Against the Americans Who Occupy the Land of the Two Holy Mosques," 23 August 1996, https://www .pbs.org/wgbh/pages/frontline/shows/binladen/who/edicts.html.

34. Brinkley, Douglas, quoted in Hayward, *Real Jimmy Carter,* p. 221.

35. Schmidt, Susan, Peter Baker, and Toni Locy, "Clinton Accused of Urging Aide to Lie," *Washington Post,* 21 January 1998, A1, http://www.washington post.com/wp-srv/politics/special/clinton/stories/clinton012198.htm.

36. Kalb, Marvin, *One Scandalous Story: Clinton, Lewinsky, and Thirteen Days That Tarnished American Journalism,* Free Press, New York: 2001, p. 161.

37. Senior, Jennifer, "The End of the Trench Coat Mafia," *New York Times,* 16 April 2009, review of *Columbine,* by Dave Cullen, Hachette, New York: 2009, http://www.nytimes.com/2009/04/19/books/review/Senior-t.html.

38. Toppo, Greg, "10 Years Later, the Real Story Behind Columbine," *USA Today,* 14 April 2009, http://www.usatoday.com/news/nation/2009-04 -13-columbine-myths_N.htm.

39. Toppo, "10 Years Later."

40. Forbes, Steve, quoted in Associated Press, "Candidates Ruminate on a

Time Capsule," *Boston Globe,* 11 January 2000, http://graphics.boston
.com/news/politics/campaign2000/news/Candidates_ruminate_on_a
_time_capsule+.shtml.

41. "Networked Families," Pew Research Center, 19 October 2008,
http://www.pewinternet.org/Reports/2008/Networked-Families.aspx?r=1.

42. Dell, Michael, "The Origins of Dell, Inc.," eCorner, 1 May 2007,
https://ecorner.stanford.edu/video/the-origins-of-dell-inc/.

43. DePillis, Lydia, and Ivory Sherman, "Amazon's Extraordinary Evolution:
A Timeline," CNN Business, 4 October 2018, https://www.cnn.com
/interactive/2018/10/business/amazon-history-timeline/index.html.

44. Ramo, Joshua Cooper, "Jeffery Preston Bezos: 1999 Person of the Year,"
Time, 1999, http://content.time.com/time/specials/packages/article
/0,28804,2023311_2023309,00.html.

45. Leggatt, Helen, "U.S. Online Retail Sales May Break $200 Billion Barrier,"
BizReport, 1 August 2007, http://www.bizreport.com/2007/08/us_online
_retail_sales_may_break_200_billion_barrier.html.

46. See "The eBay Community," https://www.ebayinc.com/our-company/our
-history/.

47. "Americans Going Online . . . Explosive Growth, Uncertain Destination,"
Pew Research Center, 16 October 1995, http://people-press.org/report/136/.

48. Gordon, John Steele, "The 50 Biggest Changes of the Last 50 Years,"
American Heritage 55, no. 3, June/July 2004, https://www.americanheritage
.com/50-biggest-changes-last-50-years.

49. British Broadcasting Corporation, "2000: Suicide Bombers Attack USS
Cole," *On This Day: 12 October,* http://news.bbc.co.uk/onthisday/hi/dates
/stories/october/12/newsid_4252000/4252400.stm.

50. Novak, Jane, "Yemen's Truce with Al Qaeda: Who Will Be the Next
Victims?" *Weekly Standard,* 31 October 2007.

51. National Commission on Terrorist Attacks Upon the United States,
"From Threat to Threat," *9/11 Commission Report,* 17 October 2004,
http://govinfo.library.unt.edu/911/report/911Report_Ch6.htm.

52. Wright, Lawrence, *The Looming Tower,* Vintage Books, New York: 2007,
p. 374.

53. Toobin, Jeffrey, *Too Close to Call: The Thirty-Six Day Battle to Decide the
2000 Election*, Random House, New York: 2001, p. 24.

54. Toobin, *Too Close to Call*, p. 278.

55. Kemp, Jack, "The Bush Tax Agenda," *Townhall*, 24 January 2001, http://townhall.com/columnists/JackKemp/2001/01/24/the_bush_tax_agenda.

56. Leonhardt, David, "Economy Grew at the Slowest Rate in 5 Years in 4th Quarter," *New York Times*, 1 February 2001, http://www.nytimes.com/2001/02/01/business/economy-grew-at-slowest-rate-in-5-years-in-4th-quarter.html.

57. "Breaking News on September 11th," NBC News, New York, NBC Universal, 11 September 2001, https://archives.nbclearn.com/portal/site/k-12/browse/?cuecard=1419.

58. Wapshott, Nicholas, "Firemen Seeking Sainthood for 9/11 Priest," *London Times*, 22 February 2003, https://www.thetimes.co.uk/article/firemen-seeking-sainthood-for-911-priest-ck79gzlff62.

59. "President Bush Attends National Prayer Breakfast," Hilton Washington Hotel, Washington, D.C., February 1, 2007, https://georgewbush-whitehouse.archives.gov/news/releases/2007/02/20070201.html.

60. Don Van Natta and Lizette Alvarez, "A Day of Terror: Attack on Military," *New York Times*, September 12, 2001, https://www.nytimes.com/2001/09/12/us/day-terror-attack-military-hijacked-boeing-757-slams-into-pentagon-halting.html.

61. Junod, Tom, "The Falling Man," *Esquire*, September 1, 2003, https://classics.esquire.com/the-falling-man.

62. Greyhawk, "911 Remember: Rick Rescorla Was a Soldier," *Mudville Gazette*, September 2003.

63. The Avalon Project, "September 11, 2001: Attack on America, Congressional Record, House of Representatives, On Terrorist Attack of September 11, 2001; September 17, 2001," Lillian Goldman Law Library, Yale Law School, http://avalon.law.yale.edu/sept11/cr_016.asp.

64. Johnson, Steve, and Doug George, "San Francisco Paper Puts Visceral Reaction on Page 1," *Chicago Tribune*, 13 September 2001, https://www.chicagotribune.com/chi-0109130346sep13-story.html.

65. Bennett, William J., *Why We Fight: Moral Clarity and the War on Terrorism*, Doubleday, New York: 2002, p. 192.

66. Bennett, *Why We Fight*, pp. 192–193.

67. "President's Remarks at the United Nations General Assembly," United Nations, New York, 12 September 2002, https://georgewbush-whitehouse.archives.gov/news/releases/2002/09/20020912-1.html.

68. "Threats and Responses: House Vote on Iraq Resolution," *New York Times*, 12 October 2002, http://www.nytimes.com/2002/10/12/us/threats -and-responses-house-vote-on-iraq-resolution.html.

69. Mitchell, Alison, and Carl Hulse, "Threats and Responses: The Vote; Congress Authorizes Bush to Use Force Against Iraq, Creating a Broad Mandate," *New York Times*, 11 October 2002, http://www.nytimes.com /2002/10/11/us/threats-responses-vote-congress-authorizes-bush-use -force-against-iraq-creating.html.

70. "Senate Vote on Passage: H. J. Res. 114: Authorization for Use of Military Force Against Iraq Resolution of 2002," Govtrack, 11 October 2002, http://www.govtrack.us/congress/vote.xpd?vote=s2002–237.

71. Kerry, John, quoted in Scott Johnson's "The Democrats' Greatest Hits: The WMD Collections," PowerLine, 22 December 2003, http://www .powerlineblog.com/archives/2003/12/005426.php.

72. Clinton, Hilary, quoted in Johnson's, "Democrats' Greatest Hits."

73. Frank James, "Obama's 'Big' 2002 Anti-War Speech Wasn't Big Then," *Chicago Tribune*, March 25, 2008, https://www.chicagotribune.com /chinews-mtblog-2008–03-obamas_big_2002_antiwar_speech-story.html.

74. Blix, Hans, quoted in Julia Preston, "Threats and Responses: Report to Council; U.N. Inspector Says Iraq Falls Short on Cooperation," *New York Times*, 28 January 2003, http://www.nytimes.com/2003/01/28/world /threats-responses-report-council-un-inspector-says-iraq-falls-short -cooperation.html.

75. Colin Powell, quoted in Preston, "Threats and Responses."

76. Thiessen, Marc, "On Waterboarding: Let's Stick to the Facts," *Washington Post*, 15 November 2011, https://www.washingtonpost.com/blogs/post -partisan/post/on-waterboarding-lets-stick-to-the-facts/2011/11/15 /gIQAHHiiON_blog.html?utm_term=.d48b33ab31f0.

77. "Saddam Statue Toppled in Central Baghdad," CNN, 9 April 2003, http:// www.cnn.com/2003/WORLD/meast/04/09/sprj.irq.statue/.

78. "Commander in Chief Lands on USS Lincoln," CNN, 2 May 2003, http:// www.cnn.com/2003/ALLPOLITICS/05/01/bush.carrier.landing/.

79. "Commander in Chief," CNN.

80. Schieffer, Bob, quoted in Bootie Cosgrove-Mather, "Are More Troops Needed in Iraq?" CBS News, 4 August 2003, http://www.cbsnews.com /stories/2003/08/04/opinion/schieffer/main566537.shtml.

81. Froomkin, Dan, "Bush Agenda: Bold but Blurry," *Washington Post,* 5 November 2004, http://www.washingtonpost.com/wp-dyn/articles/A27833 –2004Nov5.html.

82. America Votes 2006, "U.S. Senate," CNN, http://www.cnn.com/ELECTION /2006/pages/results/senate/.

83. Reid, Harry, quoted in Jeff Zeleny, "Leading Democrat in Senate Tells Reporters, 'This War Is Lost,'" *New York Times,* 20 April 2007, http://www .nytimes.com/2007/04/20/washington/20cong.html.

84. Langer, Gary, "Poll: A New Low in Approval Starts Bush's Year," ABC News, 15 January 2008, http://abcnews.go.com/PollingUnit/Vote2008 /story?id=4133095&page=1.

85. "White House 2008: General Election Trial Heats Up," Polling Report, http://www.pollingreport.com/wh08gen.htm.

86. Smith, Aaron, "Wall Street's Red October," CNNMoney.com, October 31, 2008, https://money.cnn.com/2008/10/31/markets/october_stocks_tough _month/index.htm?postversion=2008103116.

87. Mamudi, Sam, "Lehman Folds with Record $613 Billion Debt," *Wall Street Journal,* 15 September 2008, http://www.marketwatch.com/story /lehman-folds-with-record-613-billion-debt?siteid=rss.

88. "Bailout Plan Wins Approval; Democrats Vow Tighter Rules," *New York Times,* 4 October 2008, http://www.nytimes.com/2008/10/04/business /economy/04bailout.html?pagewanted=2.

89. "White House 2008," Polling Report, http://www.pollingreport.com /wh08gen.htm.

90. Chesterton, Gilbert Kieth, *What I Saw in America,* New York: Dodd, Mead & Co., p. 17.

91. Jacoby, Jeff, "As MLK Foresaw, Racism in America Has Been Largely Overcome," *The Boston Globe,* 18 January 2019, https://www.bostonglobe .com/opinion/2019/01/18/mlk-foresaw-racism-america-has-been-largely -overcome/XbmWARnPaYQInZGFSHyugO/story.html.

INDEX

Note: *n* after page number refers to footnotes.

INDEX

disunion risk, 45
purpose, 38
Aryans, 413
Ashbrook, John, 656
Asia. *See also specific countries*
assassination
of Franz Ferdinand, 308–309
of J. F. Kennedy, 611–613
of R. F. Kennedy, 634
of M. L. King, 633
of McKinley, 331–332
assassination attempt
on John Paul II, 698
on Reagan, 695–696
assembly line production, 407
Astor, John Jacob, 349
Astor, Lady, 444
atheistic philosophies, 411
Marxism-Leninism and, 596
and Russian space exploration, 641
Atlanta, Sherman in, 248
Atlantic Charter, 478
Atlantic Ocean, war casualties from U-boats, 495
Atlee, Clement, 533, 534
atomic bomb
atmospheric test ban, 604
development, 531–532, 534
Goldwater views on use, 618
race to build, 459
Truman orders, 535–536
Attucks, Crispus, 8
Atzerodt, George, 258
Augusta (USS), 473, 478
Auschwitz, 489, 513, 529
photographs, 515
Austria-Hungary, 387
assassination of heir to throne, 358–359
Austria, Nazi control, 447
automobiles, 407, 418
gasoline shortages, 665
aviation industry, 348. *See also* aircraft
"axis of evil," 772

Baader-Meinhof Gang, 686
Babbitt, Bruce, 736
"backbencher," 541*n*
Baer, George, 335, 336
Baker, Howard, 664, 683, 720
Baker, Newton D., 370, 377
balancing federal budget, 752
Balfour, Arthur James, 389
Balfour Declaration of the British Government, 550
ballistic missile defense, 701
Baltimore & Ohio Railroad (B&O), 167
Baltimore, in War of 1812, 111–112
Baltimore Sun, 396–397
bank failures, 313, 423
"bank holiday," 430
Banks, Nathaniel, 218
Baratarian pirates, 114
Barbary coast, 90–92
Barbé-Marbois, Francois, 93
"barn burner," 175*n*
Barney, Joshua, 111

Barnwell, Robert, 193–194
Barone, Michael, 576
Barry, John M., 384
Bartholdi, Frédéric-Auguste, 282, 296
Bartlett, Josiah, 17
baseball, 419
Basilone, John, 504–505
Bastogne, 520
Bataan, 484
Bataan Death March, 485
Battle. *See specific battle name*
Baucus, Max, 670*n*
Bauer, Gary, 762
Bay of Pigs, 594
Bayard, James A., 85
Beamer, Todd, 770–771
Beanes, Dr., 112
"Bear Flag Republic," 158
Beauregard, Pierre Gustave Toutant, 203, 225
Beckwith, Byron de la, 608
Bedford, Gunning, 45, 46
Bee, Bernard, 208
Beecher, Henry Ward, 176
"Beecher's Bibles," 176
Begin, Menachem, 683
Beirut, Lebanon, suicide bombing of Marine barracks, 703, 718
Belgium, invasion, 364, 365
Bell, Alexander Graham, 282, 290, 292
Bell, John C., 192
Bell Telephone Company, 292
Belleau Wood, 380
Belomor Canal, in Soviet Union, 452
Ben-Gurion, David, 549
Benedict XVI (pope), 450*n*
Benes, Eduard, 448
Benton, Jesse, 112
Benton, Thomas Hart, 112, 154, 158, 165
Bentsen, Lloyd, 736
Berg, Nick, 776
Beria, Lavrentii, 521
Berlin, Irving, 380, 492
Berlin
divided, 551
Khrushchev and, 595
Berlin Airlift of 1948, 550–552
Berlin Wall, 597–598, 721–722
fall of, 740
Bernstein, Leonard, 319
Berry, Charles A., 638
Bethune, Mary McLeod, 439, 561
Beyond Good and Evil (Nietzsche), 408
Bezos, Jeff, 759
Bible
Douay version, 171
on manned moon flight, 637
Paine's use of, 17
Bicentennial Celebration, xi, 675–676
Biddle, Francis, 487
Biden, Joseph, 724, 736, 782
"Big Bertha," 368
Big Business, opposition to FDR, 440–441
Big Foot, 302
Big Three

INDEX

INDEX

INDEX

Herold, Davey, 259
Hess, Rudolph, 543
Hessian troops, 17–18, 21
    Washington treatment of, 24
highway fatalities, 1911, 348
"Highway of Death," 744
Hill, James J., 337
Himmler, Heinrich, 529
Hinckley, John, Jr., 695
Hindenburg, 443–444
"hippies," 626
Hirohito, Japanese surrender, 536
Hiroshima, Japan, 535
Hiss, Alger, 324, 556, 559
historic documents, preservation in War of 1812, 111
history textbooks, xiii–xiv
Hitler, Adolf, 429
    assassination attempt, 512
    books of, 408
    Chamberlain meeting with, 448
    Churchill and, 462
    "commissar order," 488
    counteroffensive against Allies, 519–520
    deception on invasion, 511
    declaration of war on U.S., 482
    "Final Solution of Jewish Problem in Europe,"
        489, 513
    Mein Kampf, 383, 413
    and J. Owens, 437
    in Paris, 463
    reaction to FDR death, 528
    Reich Chancellory, 452
    Stalin agreement with, 459
    suicide, 528
    as *Time* "Man of the Year," 454–455
    and United States, 482
    WWI and, 382
Ho Chi Minh City, 671
Höfdi House, 716
Hohnzollern (yacht), 363
Holland
    German invasion, 461
    support in War for Independence, 27
Hollywood film community. *See also* movies
    Communist support in, 547–548
Hollywood Independent Citizens Committee of the
    Arts, Sciences, and Professions (HICCASP), 548
Holmes, Oliver Wendell, 262–263, 426
Holocaust, 472, 483
    concentration camps, 438–439, 513, 529
    deniers, 529*n*
    Eisenhower record collection on, 529
    FDR speaking against, 515–516
    "Final Solution of the Jewish Problem in Europe,"
        489, 513
home computers, 758
Home Owner's Loan Corporation, 431
Homestead Act, 273, 309
Homestead Strike, 311
Homma, General, 484, 485
homosexuality, 593*n*, 711
Hooker, "Fighting Joe," 226, 242
    resignation, 228
Hoover, Herbert, 404, 544

    as Commerce secretary, 402
    Depression and, 424
    on economy, 423
    as Food Administration head, 379
    message on economy, 422
    presidential campaign in 1932, 427
    presidential election, 419–420
    veto of early bonus for WWI veterans, 425
    views on poverty, 420
hope, xiii, 786
Hopkins, Harry, 490, 506
Hornet (USS), 485
Horseshoe Bend, Battle of, 113
hostages in Middle East, 719
    from U.S. Iran embassy, 687, 689, 695, 743
"House Divided" speech of Lincoln, 184
House, Edward M., 358, 380
House of Representatives. *See also* U.S. Congress
    Constitutional Convention compromise on, 46, 51
    Un-American Activities Committee, 555, 559–560
Houseman, John, 432*n*
Housing and Urban Development Department, 624
Houston, Sam, 148
How the Other Half Lives, 339
Howard, Jacob M., 268
Howard, Leslie, 461
Howard, Oliver O., 266
Howe, Louis, 398
Howe, William, 15, 22, 25
Hu Yaobang, 738
Hudson, Rock, 711
Hudson's Bay Company (Britain), 151, 153
Hué, South Vietnam, 629
Hughes, Charles Evans, 369, 403
Hughes, Emmett John, 571
Hughes, John, 2, 236
Hughes, Langston, 402
Hughes, Sarah T., 612
Hugo, Victor, 615
Hull, Cordell, 479
Hull, William, 107
Hull House, 305
Humphrey, Hubert H., 593, 626
    and 1948 Senate race, 554
    1968 candidacy, 634–635
    and Civil Rights bill, 609, 615
    on Goldwater voting record, 619
    and Taft-Hartley Bill, 546
Hungary, 739
    dictatorship in, 429
    Paris Peace Conference and, 387
    soviet government in, 383
Hurley, Patrick J., 559
Hurston, Zora Neale, *Their Eyes Were Watching God*, 401
Hussein, Saddam, 742, 743, 772–773, 778
    human rights abuses, 777
Hutchinson, Thomas, 8
hydroelectric power, 452

Iacocca, Lee, 714
Iceland, U.S. naval vessels and, 475
Ickes, Harold, 492
idealism, vs. realism, 395–396
Illinois, Northwest Ordinance and, 39

INDEX

immigrants
  in 1830s, 144
  in Chicago slums, 305
  in city slums, 287
  illegal, 777
  Jewish, 299
  prevention of voting by, 171
  railroads and, 167, 280
  restrictions in 1920s, 406
impeachment
  of A. Johnson, 271–273
  of Clinton, 755–757
  of Nixon, 663, 666
  risk to Reagan, 719–720
import duties, 355
impressment, 103
"In God We Trust," 579
Inchon landing, 563–564
inclusion, Jackson statement for, 131
income tax, 355
Independence Hall (Philadelphia), 43
Indian agents, Grant appointment of, 300–301
Indiana, Northwest Ordinance and, 39
Indians, 106
  Grant and, 283
  hostility against, 109
  Jackson and removal, 141–146
  Lewis and Clark gifts for, 97
  treatment of, 300
  uprising in Alabama, 112
  and western settlement, 106
  in Wyoming Valley, Pa, 27
industrial paternalism, Pullman and, 314
industrial revolution, 293
industrial workers, 305
inflation
  in 1971, 652
  Ford response to, 669
  gold standard and, 316
  post-WWII, 543
inflation bill, Grant veto of, 276–277
The Influence of Sea Power Upon History, 362
influenza pandemic of 1918–1919, 384
informed patriotism, xvi
Ingersoll, Ralph, 520
Inherit the Wind, 413
inheritance tax, 355
Inland Waterways Commission, 342
Inouye, Daniel K., 486–487
Inskip, Thomas, 668n
L'Insurgente (French frigate), 77
Intercontinental Ballistic Missiles (ICBMs), 584
Intermediate Nuclear Forces (INF) agreement, 726
Intermediate Range Ballistic Missiles, in Cuba, 600
International Centennial Exhibition (Philadelphia), 281
The International Jew, 408
International Military Tribunal, 542
Internet, 758, 759
interregnum, 428
Interstate Commerce Commission (ICC), 606
Interstate Highway System, 583, 590
"Intolerable Acts," 11
Iran-Contra Affair, 718–720
Iraq, 778

and 2008 election campaign, 782
congressional authorization to use force, 773–774
counterinsurgency plan, 779
Iraq Liberation Act (1998), 772
Irish Americans, 310
  and Alien and Sedition Acts, 78
  and Jackson, 131
Irish Brigade, 230
Iron Curtain, 541–542
Iron Moulders' Union, 169
Islamic radicals, 750
Ismay, Bruce, 350
isolationists in U.S., 461, 469, 475–476
Israel, 549–550, 750
  Egypt invasion of, 664
  Nasser's goal of destroying, 627
  Scud missiles launched at, 744
Italy, 501–502, 519
  dictatorship in, 429
  as German ally, 475
Iwo Jima, 535

Jackson, Andrew, 124–125, 130
  accusation of adultery, 125
  and the bank, 146–150
  diversity of troops, 114–115
  duels, 125–126
  inauguration, 128–129
  military leadership against Creeks, 112–113
  and New Orleans victory, 116
  opposition to nullification, 137
  Proclamation on Union, 138
  sympathy for South Carolina, 140
  toast by, 137
  veto on bank charter, 147
Jackson, C.D., 571
Jackson (Fort), 113
Jackson, Henry M. "Scoop," 666, 683
Jackson, Jesse, 736
Jackson, Mahalia, 609–610
Jackson, Rachel, 127
Jackson, Robert H., 542
Jackson, Thomas J. (Stonewall), 189, 208, 218, 226–227
Jackson-Vanik Amendment, 666
Jacobite, 4
Jacobson, Eddie, 550
Jacoby, Jeff, 784
Jaffa, Harry, 63, 617
Japan, 445
  assault on China, 479
  Hitler's treaty with
  MacArthur and, 552–553
  oil embargo by U.S., 479
  Soviets in war against, 523
  surrender, 536
  torture of POWs in Philippines, 526
  U.S. declaration of war, 481
Japan-Russian war, 346
Japanese Americans, internment, 486
Japanese Imperial Navy, 496
Jay, John, 34
  as chief justice, 61
  and Constitution ratification, 53
Jay's treaty, 73

884

INDEX

INDEX

INDEX

INDEX

INDEX

Tumulty, Joseph, 358, 373
Turkey
    Cuban missile crisis and, 603*n*
    U.S. support for, 544
Turner, Benjamin S., 279
Tuskegee Airmen, 488, 656
Twain, Mark
    and Arthur, 291
    on crime, 293–294
    "Gilded Age," 287
    and Grant's Memoirs, 296
    on Wagner, 281*n*
two-party system, 70–71
Tyler, John, 149
    assumption of presidency, 149–150

U-2 jets
    downed in Russia, 588
    for spying, 586
U-boat (*unterseeboot*) attacks, 494–496
    and blackout need, 493
    convoy system to overcome, 376
    on *Sussex*, 368
Ukraine, Stalin control of, 418
Unabomber, 753
Uncle Tom's Cabin (Stowe), 172
unconditional surrender, by Germans, 529
Undeclared Naval War with France (1798–1800), 79–80
Underground Railroad, 165
Underwood Tariff, 355
unemployment
    1929 to 1932, 422
    in 1930s, 439
    in 1980s, 698
    in 1989 and 1991, 747
Union
    Webster on dissolution, 164
    Webster's defense of, 135–136
Union armies
    demobilization, 269
    Grant command over, 242–243
Union Pacific railroad, 337
United Hatters, 169
United Mine Workers union
    strike, 335
    strike threat, 494
United Nations, 484
    in Korean conflict, 564
    Roosevelt and, 525
    Security Council, 522–523, 562–563, 772
    "We Charge Genocide" petition, 561
United Nations General Assembly, China or Taiwan, 651
United States
    centennial celebration, 279
    economic conditions, 552, 652–653
    financial conditions in 1780s, 39
    German disregard in WWI, 370
    and German militarism, 362
    industry conversion to wartime economy, 377
    international perception of weaknesses, 155
    political creed, 19–20
    warfare in Middle East, 749–750
    as world leader, 538–539

WWI declaration of war, 372
U.S. armed forces. *See also* U.S. Navy
    all-Nisei 100th Battalion, 486
    ban on flogging, 171
    deaths in WWI, 395
    Department of Defense, 56, 561–562
    Executive Order on desegregation, 556
    first amphibious landing by Navy, 156
    Marines in Mexico, 157
    Marines in WWI, 375
    military conscription, 236–237, 468, 491
    peacetime buildup, 698
    troop withdraw from Europe, 539–540
U.S. Capitol, completion, 252
U.S. Coast Guard, 350, 421, 495
U.S. Congress. *See also* U.S. House of Representatives
    Constitutional Convention compromise on, 46
    declaration of war on Britain in 1812, 107
    elections. *See* congressional elections
    and executive, 47
    FDR before joint session, 481
    first, 61
    military appropriations in 1810, 105–106
    post-Civil War Republicans in, 279
    reason for Philadelphia meeting in 1787, 43–44
    Senate Rule XXII, 608–609
    Washington resignation of military command, 36
U.S. Constitution. *See also* Constitutional Convention
    First Amendment, 63, 88
    Second Amendment, 64
    Third Amendment, 64
    Fourth Amendment, 64
    Fifth Amendment, 64
    Sixth Amendment, 64
    Seventh Amendment, 64
    Eighth Amendment, 64
    Ninth Amendment, 64
    Tenth Amendment, 64
    Thirteenth Amendment, 267, 275
    Fourteenth Amendment, 268, 275
    Fifteenth Amendment, 270, 275, 277, 279, 605
    Eighteenth Amendment, 393
    Nineteenth Amendment, 393, 396
    Twenty-first Amendment, 431
    Twenty-second Amendment, 567–568
    Twenty-fifth Amendment, 150*n*, 392*n*, 665
    Twenty-seventh Amendment, 63*n*
    Article VI on religious liberty, 47
    Bill of Rights, 55, 56, 63–65
    census as requirement, 49
    Commerce clause, 163
    Equal Rights Amendment (ERA), 654, 680–681, 704
    framers' education, 43
    Garrison and, 173
    Preamble, 56
    ratification, 52–57
    signing ceremony, 53
    slave trade compromise, 50, 104
U.S. Department of Education, 711
U.S. Department of Energy, 684
U.S. Department of Housing and Urban Development, 624
U.S. House of Representatives
    Constitutional Convention and, 47

901

INDEX

ABOUT THE AUTHOR

Dr. William J. Bennett is one of America's most influential and respected voices on cultural, political, and educational issues. Host of *The Bill Bennett Show* podcast, he is also the Washington Fellow of the American Strategy Group. He is the author and editor of more than twenty-five books, and lives in North Carolina.